CONTEMPORARY
Jewish-American
Dramatists and Poets

CONTEMPORARY
Jewish-American
Dramatists and Poets

A Bio-Critical Sourcebook

Edited by
JOEL SHATZKY AND MICHAEL TAUB

Emmanuel S. Nelson, Advisory Editor

Greenwood Press
Westport, Connecticut
London

Library of Congress Cataloging-in-Publication Data

Contemporary Jewish-American dramatists and poets : a bio-critical
   sourcebook / edited by Joel Shatzky and Michael Taub.
      p.   cm.
   Includes bibliographical references and index.
   ISBN 0–313–29461–5 (alk. paper)
   1. American drama—Jewish authors—Dictionaries.   2. American
drama—Jewish authors—Bio-bibliography—Dictionaries.   3. American
drama—20th century—Bio-bibliography—Dictionaries.   4. American
drama—20th century—Dictionaries.   5. Jews in literature—
Dictionaries.   I. Shatzky, Joel.   II. Taub, Michael.
PS153.J4C68   1999
810.9'8924'0904—dc21   98–46811
   [B]

British Library Cataloguing in Publication Data is available.

Library of Congress Catalog Card Number: 98–46811
ISBN: 0–313–29461–5

First published in 1999

Greenwood Press, 88 Post Road West, Westport, CT 06881
An imprint of Greenwood Publishing Group, Inc.
www.greenwood.com

Printed in the United States of America

The paper used in this book complies with the
Permanent Paper Standard issued by the National
Information Standards Organization (Z39.48–1984).

10 9 8 7 6 5 4 3 2 1

In memory of my mother, Bess Shatzky (1908–1997), who taught me to love my secular Jewish heritage.

—Joel Shatzky

I am deeply grateful to Joseph C. Landis and Ellen Schiff, leaders in the field of Jewish drama and theater, for their enormous help, encouragement, and friendship. This volume's drama section is an example of what can happen when good seeds are planted.

—Michael Taub

Contents

Preface   xvii

Drama Section

Introduction   3
  by *Ellen Schiff*

Woody Allen   10
  by *Richard Moody*

Jon Robin Baitz   18
  by *Michael Taub*

Paddy Chayefsky   25
  by *Edward Isser*

Sarah Blacher Cohen   33
  by *Catharine Gabriel Carey*

Jules Feiffer   38
  by *Herbert Liebman*

Harvey Fierstein   44
  by *Ben Furnish*

Herb Gardner   53
  by *Andrea Most*

Israel Horovitz   59
  by *Leslie Kane*

Arthur L. Kopit   68
   by *Michael C. O'Neill*

Tony Kushner   79
   by *Dennis A. Klein*

James Lapine   90
   by *Joshua Berg*

Arthur Laurents   95
   by *Bette H. Kirschstein*

Barbara Lebow   102
   by *Eric Sterling*

Norman Lessing   109
   by *Norman J. Fedder*

David Mamet   113
   by *Leslie Kane*

Emily Mann   127
   by *Ben Furnish*

Donald Margulies   136
   by *Oren Safdie*

Arthur Miller   141
   by *Benjamin Nelson*

Ronald Ribman   159
   by *Darrell B. Lockhart*

Murray Schisgal   166
   by *Darrell B. Lockhart*

Martin Sherman   173
   by *Eric Sterling*

Elizabeth Swados   180
   by *Elizabeth Lloyd-Kimbrel and Joel Shatzky*

Alfred Uhry   186
   by *Michael Taub*

Wendy Wasserstein   191
   by *Michael Taub*

Poetry Section

Introduction   201
   by *John Hollander*

Marvin Bell   209
  by *Michael Taub and Joel Shatzky*

Charles Bernstein   212
  by *Loss Pequeño Glazier*

Chana Bloch   220
  by *Merle Bachman*

Stanley Burnshaw   226
  by *Michael Taub and Joel Shatzky*

Richard J. Fein   229
  by *Sheva Zucker*

Irving Feldman   233
  by *Jennifer Lewin*

Edward Field   240
  by *Diane Stevenson*

Charles Fishman   245
  by *William James Austin*

Allen Ginsberg   251
  by *Maria Damon*

Louise Glück   267
  by *Linda Rodriguez*

Jorie Graham   275
  by *Karen Bender*

Allen Grossman   279
  by *Daniel Tobin*

Anthony Hecht   288
  by *Joel Shatzky and Michael Taub*

Michael Heller   291
  by *Norman Finkelstein*

Edward Hirsch   298
  by *Joel Shatzky and Michael Taub*

John Hollander   301
  by *Mark Rudman*

Richard Howard   306
  by *Daniel Kane*

David Ignatow   312
  by *Barry Fruchter*

Milton Kessler
by *Adam Schonbrunn*   320

Abraham Moses Klein
by *Rachel Feldhay Brenner*   324

Kenneth Koch
by *Joseph Lease*   330

Richard Cory Kostelanetz
by *Chris Semansky*   335

Aaron Kramer
by *Tamra Plotnick*   343

Stanley Kunitz
by *David Caplan*   349

Irving Layton
by *Caren Irr*   355

Denise Levertov
by *Karla Alwes*   362

Philip Levine
by *Steven Schreiner*   369

Lyn Lifshin
by *Hugh Fox and Joel Shatzky*   375

Allen Mandelbaum
by *Henry Weinfield*   382

Robert Mezey
by *Joel Shatzky and Michael Taub*   390

Stephen Mitchell
by *Stephen Monte*   395

Howard Moss
by *Burt Kimmelman*   402

Howard Nemerov
by *Miriam Marty Clark*   411

George Oppen
by *Kenneth Sherwood*   420

Joel Oppenheimer
by *Lyman Gilmore*   431

Robert Pinsky
by *Charles S. Berger*   443

Carl Rakosi   448
    by *Steve Shoemaker*

Charles Reznikoff   460
    by *Genevieve Cohen-Cheminet*

Adrienne Rich   476
    by *Jonathan Gill*

David Rosenberg   483
    by *Joel Shatzky and Michael Taub*

M. L. Rosenthal   487
    by *William Harmon*

Jerome Rothenberg   491
    by *Pierre Joris*

Mark Rudman   501
    by *Theodore Blanchard*

Muriel Rukeyser   507
    by *Michele S. Ware*

Delmore Schwartz   515
    by *Jennifer Lewin*

Howard Schwartz   521
    by *Michael Castro*

Armand Schwerner   528
    by *Norman Finkelstein*

Alan Shapiro   536
    by *Richard Chess*

David Shapiro   542
    by *Thomas Fink*

Harvey Shapiro   549
    by *Robert S. Friedman*

Karl (Jay) Shapiro   554
    by *David R. Slavitt*

Louis Simpson   560
    by *Blossom Steinberg Kirschenbaum*

Myra Sklarew   575
    by *Joshua Saul Beckman*

Gerald Stern   579
    by *Harriet L. Parmet*

Mark Strand   587
    by *Neil Arditi*

Nathaniel Tarn   594
    by *Joel Shatzky and Michael Taub*

Louis Zukofsky   597
    by *Dror Abend-David*

Appendix   605

Selected Bibliography   607

Drama Index   611

Poetry Index   623

About the Editors and Contributors   649

Preface

Like fiction, Jewish-American poetry and drama play an important role in contemporary American culture. The recent death of Allen Ginsberg recalls in his public persona, particularly in the 1960s, what "a poet" can mean to our culture: a prophet crying out against society's injustices.

As this reference book demonstrates, there are also many fine Jewish-American dramatists active in today's theatre. They include David Mamet, Wendy Wasserstein, Tony Kushner, Donald Margulies, and Israel Horovitz of the younger generation and Arthur Miller and Herb Gardner of a slightly earlier period. The variety of Jews who are depicted is rather overwhelming: the gay Jews who come out of the closet in Harvey Fierstein's plays and serve to complement the more complex visions of Kushner's *Angels in America*; the liberated Jewish women of Wasserstein and Emily Mann who must still deal with a patriarchal society; the satires of Arthur Kopit and Woody Allen that create fantasies of the archetypal Jewish mother and the archetypal nebbish.

The care with which Jews were portrayed, shorn of the characteristics of the shtetl, as evidenced by Arthur Miller's generalized characterizations in *Death of a Salesman* and *After the Fall*, is largely ignored today in the wide and wild variety of figures that both mock and embrace stereotype. To consider only a few of the most notable of these contemporary figures, we contrast the work of the prewar-born Arthur Miller and Herb Gardner with the younger Tony Kushner, Wendy Wasserstein, David Mamet, Jon Robin Baitz, and Donald Margulies. In discussing their work, we also touch on the drama of other playwrights in this sourcebook, such as Barbara Lebow and Alfred Uhry.

Significantly, only a few of Gardner's plays—*I'm Not Rappoport* and *Conversations with My Father*—show thematic links with some of the earlier Jewish-American greats like Clifford Odets and Elmer Rice as they explore ethnic identity in America. While his one-act play *Goldberg Street* does touch on the sensitive issue of anti-Semitism in America, David Mamet has yet to write a full-length ''Jewish'' play. In terms of treatment of the Holocaust, however, Jewish-American playwrights have been more forthcoming.

Lola and Max in Margulies' *The Model Apartment* are Holocaust survivors; so are Baitz's Isaac Geldhart in *The Substance of Fire* and Lusia Weiss in Lebow's *A Shayne Maidel*. While Margulies treats the subject through his unique brand of comedy, Baitz and Lebow paint a serious picture of characters possessed by guilt, constantly hounded by demons from their past. Miller and Uhry, on the other hand, have strategically placed their latest works, *Broken Glass* and *The Last Night of Ballyhoo*, respectively, in pre-Holocaust Jewish America of the late 1930s. Though very different in tone and style, these dramas are an attempt to come to grips with a painful, often controversial question, what David Wyman called ''The Abandonment of the Jews,'' abandonment, sadly, even by Jews.

Wasserstein's highly entertaining satires of American Jewry—*Isn't It Romantic?* and *The Sisters Rosensweig*—focus primarily on such traditionally Jewish themes as marriage and family, all in the context of the dramatist's preoccupation with society's treatment of women in general and, specifically, career women like Sara Rosensweig.

Tony Kushner's work deals with the problem of AIDS in a unique and engaging way, as well as with the political implications of the disease as embodied in the death of Roy Cohen, the closet homosexual homophobe and notorious McCarthy-era power broker. We can see here the socially concerned Jew turning to a highly controversial subject unabashed. Thus, these figures of American drama have enriched the scope and provided the needed moral and cultural complexity to the contemporary theatre in ways that we will more fully appreciate in the future.

Jewish-American poets are also a diverse group of artists. As with all artists, their poetics reflect personal temperaments (conflicted spirits versus reconciled spirits), geography (''New York poets,'' ''midwestern poets''), and affiliation (conservative/academics like Nemerov, experimental like Koch, prophetic like Ginsberg). Likewise, the degree to which Jewishness informs their work depends on a multitude of factors, the most crucial of which would be geography (a poet growing up in Brooklyn is more likely to absorb ethnic influences than one growing up in a rural area) and parentage (children of survivors or of earlier immigrants from Eastern Europe, many from Russia, would, generally, be more sensitive to issues of anti-Semitism, persecution, and social injustice than others).

One senses, perhaps, in the different generations of Jewish-American poets a struggle to include the burden of the Jewish experience and its joys in a situation that was defined by the larger culture often in terms of strategies of representation. For some poets the most excellent maneuver was a Jewishness announced in a kind of self-conscious naturalism, as in the case of certain of the ''objectivists'' and a disciple, Harvey Shapiro, where a humble ordinariness is raised to the level of mythical rhetoric of the city. The "language school" has some of the political and prophetically Jewish qualities that one might find in Charles Bernstein's notions of the liberation in representational strategies. But there is no evidence that the Jewish element, theme, or topic is dominant. One may find "Jewish humor" in Koch, for example, but that is not necessarily a defining aspect. In fact, those most defined by Jewish "content" are not necessarily the outstanding poets of the period. As with all verbal arts, to succeed, one must find the right style, the right aesthetic through which one may annunciate an agenda, an ideology, without sounding too propagandistic, preaching, or parochial.

But notwithstanding all these caveats, poets as diverse as Nemerov, David Shapiro, and Allen Ginsberg cannot be truly or fully understood without some knowledge of their relationship to their own Jewishness. All of these poets, in their tone, their topics, and the very grain of the music, derive their work, at least in part, from a shared response to the Jewish fate, the Jewish conscience, the Jewish story. At the least, as Arthur A. Cohen once put it in conversation, Judaism has given its artists the highest sense of standards.

The first part of this reference book includes alphabetically arranged entries for dramatists, while the second provides entries for poets. Each entry contains a brief biography, a discussion of major works and themes, a review of the critical response to the author's writings, and a bibliography of primary and secondary sources. The volume also includes selected, general bibliographies on the drama and poetry of contemporary Jewish-American writers.

We give special thanks to the staff at the Poetry and Books Collection of SUNY, Buffalo. We would also like to thank the library staff at SUNY, College at Cortland.

DRAMA SECTION

Introduction

Ellen Schiff

The phenomenon of Jewish-American theatre—plays, playwrights, and productions—occupies a curious position in Jewish-American literature. Jewish dramatists have been writing popular works about Jews for the American theatre since that institution came into its own following World War I. A well-received play about the Berger family in the 1930s was hardly regarded as more extraordinary than one about the sisters Rosensweig sixty years later. Paradoxically, because Jewish plays are so well established in the American theatre, their status as a discrete canon often escapes recognition. (As one who has long been studying the subject, I frequently have to correct the impression that my field is Yiddish theatre.) Hence, it is appropriate to welcome the present collection as a major contribution to the growing mass of critical material that is finally giving theatrical achievement its scholarly due.

Since this chapter focuses on the fundamental components of Jewish-American theatre—the scripts and their authors—a definition is in order: the Jewish-American repertoire consists of a rapidly expanding body of plays—there are already several hundred—that bring to the stage some aspect of the Jewish experience and that are written in English, usually by Jews, for the general theatregoing public.

Playwriting is, of course, only one dimension of the enormous Jewish contribution to American theatre. Jewish producers and impresarios as well as writers and performers animated this country's vaudeville circuits, burlesque houses, music halls, and experimental little theatres. They worked shoulder to shoulder with their fellow Americans to create a national theatre.

The integration of Jews into the general population is interestingly reflected in the work of Jewish-American dramatists. From the first they have written both explicitly Jewish and distinctly non-Jewish scripts. In fact, this alternating focus emerges as one of the most enduring traditions of Jewish-American play-wrights.

Consider, for example, Elmer Rice, a pioneer of modern American theatre. His Pulitzer-winning *Street Scene* (1925) and his antifascist *Flight to the West* (1940) include Jews in featured roles; by contrast many of Rice's other works—among them his expressionistic *The Adding Machine* (1923)—have no Jewish content at all. Then there is *Counsellor-at-Law* (1931). This classic play tells the story of a brilliantly accomplished New York attorney whose Jewish values and immigrant origins foil his ambitions for full acceptance into the social aristocracy.

The Arthur Miller oeuvre is similarly checkered by alternating Jewish and non-Jewish scripts. Miller's very first play, *They Too Arise* (1936, unpublished), deals with a garment manufacturer who refuses to join his bigger colleagues in strikebreaking activities because "Maybe it's honest for the steel companies to work this way, but it ain't the way for Jewish men to act." Miller did not again write a Jewish play until *Incident at Vichy* (1965). Following that have come the screenplay adaptation of Fania Fenelon's Auschwitz memoirs, *Playing for Time* (1981), and *Broken Glass* (1994). Whether *Death of a Salesman* (1949) is a crypto-Jewish family play continues to spark debate. Miller inadvertently encourages the discussion when he remarks, as he did in accepting a 1995 Jewish Cultural Achievement Award, "I don't write the characters that have a sign on them saying 'Jew.'" Still, as the fabulous Gregory Solomon of *The Price* (1968) demonstrates, when it suits Miller's purposes, he knows how to fashion a character who incarnates major chapters of Jewish history.

With or without explicitly Jewish content, Arthur Miller's plays are distinguished by their emphasis on individual integrity and social responsibility. The playwright's autobiography, *Timebends*, makes clear that these concerns grow directly from his Jewish roots. In this regard, the Miller oeuvre carries forward a theme that dominates the stage of the 1920s and 1930s. Jewish playwrights during those decades used the theatre to present the case for the vulnerable and the beset. Like Rice's *The Adding Machine*, Paul Sifton's *The Belt* (1927) dramatizes the depersonalization of humanity in a world run by machines. John Wexley's *They Shall Not Die* (1934) responds vigorously to the Scottsboro case, in which nine black men were wrongly convicted of rape. Following its electrifying premiere in 1935, Clifford Odets' one-act about a taxi driver's strike, *Waiting for Lefty*, took off across the nation and around the world, arguably the most famous agitprop play ever written.

While drama like this was clearly inspired by left-wing politics and cases du jour, the works rest solidly on traditional Jewish regard for human worth and social responsibility. Those values illuminate many non-Jewish scripts by Jewish playwrights, among them two of Arthur Miller's greatest, *All My Sons* (1947) and *The Crucible* (1953). The moral tone of these early plays continues to distinguish the Jewish-American repertoire, just as the concept of theatre as a forum for intellectual as well as emotional activity characterizes the orientation of its authors.

Those qualities can be seen in a variegated, but representative, sampling. In Herman Wouk's *The Caine Mutiny Court Martial* (1954), a Jewish attorney's respect for the career military men who ensured the safety of America's Jews during World War II causes him bitter regrets for his courtroom defeat of a naval commander whose erratic behavior had provoked a shipboard rebellion. Howard Sackler's Pulitzer-winning *The Great White Hope* (1968) exposes the egregious bias suffered by a black prize-fighter despite the desperate efforts of his Jewish manager to shield him. In Emily Mann's *Annulla: An Autobiography* (1977), a Jewish-American woman records with deference the intrepid title character's accounts of outwitting her tormentors in occupied Europe. In Allan Havis' *Haut Gout* (1986), an American doctor who has invented an infant formula intended for Third World countries puts his thriving practice on hold to follow his humanitarian goals, only to be betrayed by both his host country and his own.

Moral tone and intellectualism are certainly not the only signatures of Jewish-American drama. The repertoire has always been leavened by the comic spirit. Typically, self-mocking humor is a legacy of the Yiddish theatre. It is humor that first proved its enormous popular appeal in English on the vaudeville stage. As an example, Aaron Hoofman's ironically entitled *Welcome Stranger* (1920) incorporates healthy dollops of comic relief into one of the earliest scripts to deal forthrightly with American anti-Semitism. Its Jewish newcomer to a New England village immediately meets the enmity of the town fathers, who lose no time in trying to make him uncomfortable. He sunnily remarks, "The way you treat me, already I feel at home." From arch humor (in any of George S. Kaufman's dozens of collaborations), to situation comedy (Sylvia Regan's 1953 *The Fifth Season*, where Yiddish comedian Menasha Skulnik made his English-language debut), to pure slapstick, Jewish dramatists had audiences rolling in the aisles while Neil Simon's funny bones were still growing.

As the plays of the last-named pair remind us—think, for instance, of *Brighton Beach Memoirs* (1984) and *The Goodbye People* (1974)—family is a pre-eminent theme of the Jewish-American repertoire. (Of course Jews have no monopoly on a subject that dominates American drama from Eugene O'Neill and Tennessee Williams to Lorraine Hansberry and August Wilson.) Whole chapters of the Jewish-American experience are mirrored in the evolution of the Jewish families depicted onstage.

For example, the struggle of immigrants to "make it" in America and the inevitable conflicts between first- and subsequently born generations of Americans are often set in the framework of family situations. There is a direct line from Clifford Odets' *Awake and Sing!* (1935) to Mark Harelik's *The Immigrant* (1985) and Herb Gardner's *Conversations with My Father* (1991). Works like these celebrate the fundamental role of family even as they expose the failures, frustrations, and rages of individual members.

In the last few decades, however, Jewish family plays have undergone radical revision. Everything has changed: the kinds of problems families have, the frankness with which they are portrayed, and, most significantly, even the definition of the Jewish family. James Lapine's delightful parody *Table Settings* (1980) reminds us that not all members of Jewish families are Jews. Gentle, bewildered, or thwarted immigrant fathers have been superseded by family heads who are tyrannical (Dick Goldberg's *Family Business* [1976]), unfaithful (Neil Simon's *Broadway Bound* [1987]), and disdainful (Jon Robin Baitz's *The Substance of Fire* [1991]). The latest permutations of the conventional Jewish mother include the alcoholic go-getter (Woody Allen's *The Floating Light Bulb* [1982]) and the mod mom who cuts up her wedding gown to go trick-or-treating with her sons (Donald Margulies' *The Loman Family Picnic* [1988]).

The foregoing, unprecedented family members represent a large population of fresh, often outré dramatis personae whom Jewish-American playwrights have introduced into the repertoire. They constitute one of Jewish-American dramatists' most significant contributions to the American theatre: a throng of fully dimensional, more authentic Jewish characters who supplant the little band of stock types that trod international stages for centuries.

One of the earliest champions of this estimable pursuit was Clifford Odets. The scrupulous care and sensitivity with which he describes the dramatis personae in his introduction to *Awake and Sing!* remain unrivaled six decades later. It is thrilling to read of Alfred Kazan's shock of recognition at *Awake and Sing!* at hearing ''blunt Jewish speech'' and seeing ''my mother and father and uncles and aunts occupying the stage.'' (That said, one must in fairness note that Jewish dramatists have also introduced or perpetuated new stereotypes. Odets himself is guilty of doing exactly that, by representing scriptural figures as stock types in his Noah play, *The Flowering Peach* [1954].)

It is not just in verisimilitude that the dramatis personae who have recently made their debut in the repertoire differ most from their forebears. However imperishable the criterion ''Is it good for the Jews?'' by and large, Jewish-American playwrights have not shied away from depicting their coreligionists in all their human dimensions—including, as the previous examples illustrate, the less than exemplary. What has altered strikingly since the 1980s is the confidence with which the Jewish characters declare from the stage their convictions about contemporary Jewish lifestyles or attitudes. In doing so, they keep pace with Jews on the other side of the footlights.

Two scenes written about a half century apart illustrate the point. At the height of a family argument in *Awake and Sing!*, the twenty-something, discontented Ralph Berger is challenged by his beleaguered mother, Bessie, to ''go out and change the world if you don't like it.'' Then Bessie adds, ''But I'll tell you a big secret: My whole life I wanted to go away too, but with children a woman stays home. A fire burned in my heart too, but now it's too late.'' In an emotional scene in Wendy Wasserstein's *Isn't It Romantic?* (1983) Janie, with a brand-new graduate degree, tries to explain to her parents that their conventional expectations, however well meant, are wrong for her. Stung to the core, Janie's mother, no *Yiddishe momma* in her tie-dyed leotards, lashes out in a speech that would make Bessie Berger holler for smelling salts:

I'm a modern woman too, you know. I have my dancing, I have your father, and I have my beautiful grandchild and Ben [Janie's brother]. I don't need you to fill up my life. I'm an independent woman—a person in my own right.

Nor is it just new-style parents who assert themselves in ways that echo scenes played out offstage. In Harvey Fierstein's *Widows and Children First* (1979), Arnold Becker, a self-assured, gay man, has already offended his Jewish mother by likening his loss of a lover, the victim of gay bashers, to her more conventional widowhood. The last straw falls when Mrs. Becker learns that Arnold is adopting the gay teenager whom he has been raising by the very values she had taught him. To Mrs. Becker's explosion, Arnold responds:

There is nothing I need from anyone except love and respect. And anyone who can't give me those two things has no place in my life. . . . You are my mother, and I love you. I do. But if you can't respect me. . . . Then you've got no business being here.

The self-confidence with which Jews represent themselves in the public forum of end-of-the-century theatre is one of the many consequences of the iconoclastic turbulence of the 1960s. Hardly a corner of American life passes untouched by the Vietnam War, the civil rights movement, the cultural revolution, the first settings of the women's movement, cultural pluralism, and newfound pride in ethnic heritage. Having discussed in my Introduction to *Fruitful and Multiplying* the ways the 1960s redirected and reshaped the theatre, ethnic creativity, and Jewish presence and self-image, I offer here a summary of the consequences of those years.

1. The proliferation of noncommercial and experimental theatres—off- and off-off-Broadway—together with the increase in the number and sophistication of regional producing companies across the nation greatly expanded the opportunities for dramatists to develop and mount new work.

2. The establishment in 1965 of the National Endowments for the Arts and Humanities, along with the enhanced efforts of private foundations to fund the arts, translated into financial support for the nation's invigorated appreciation of the value of the arts and those who create them.

3. The flourishing of Jewish pride in a climate favoring the cultivation of ethnic roots. Concern about preserving tradition and fostering continuity led the Council of Jewish Federations in 1960 to establish the National Foundation for Jewish Culture (NFJC). The foundation serves as an influential advocate of Jewish theatre. In 1980, the NFJC convened the First Jewish Theatre Conference/festival, which astounded even its sponsors with the evidence it revealed of the depth and breadth of Jewish theatrical activity in America.

4. The establishment in New York in 1974 of two professional theatres, Stanley Brechner's American Jewish Theatre and Ran Avni's Jewish Repertory Theatre. These producing companies continue to foster the repertoire and help authenticate Jewish

theatre by enhancing its profile in the city still central to Jewish and theatrical life in America.

5. The founding in 1985 of the Council of Jewish Theatres, recently reorganized as the Association for Jewish Theatre (AJT), an affiliate of the Jewish Community Centers Association. The AJT brings together a variety of theatre personnel and a network of producing companies throughout North America. An important dimension of its member theatres' mission is the development of new Jewish plays. Works like Barbara Lebow's *A Shayna Maidel*, Donald Margulies' *The Model Apartment*, and Shelley Berman's *First Is Supper* were nurtured by AJT houses.

Such influential developments as these occurred within the frame of two historic events of colossal importance that altered both public perceptions of Jews and Jewish self-image. The first was the understanding and appreciation on these shores of the full significance of the Holocaust. The second was the creation of the state of Israel and its brilliant success as military strategist. The Six-Day War in 1967 is widely regarded as a defining moment that forever transformed the Jewish identification of countless once-indifferent or disaffected Americans.

Abundant evidence of the impact of these forces on the Jewish-American theatre lies in the explosion in the number of playwrights and the heightened popularity across the country of explicitly Jewish plays, which, of course, display the assertiveness earlier noted.

It is worthwhile to signal one area in which social change has caught up with the Jewish-American theatre, rather than the other way round. Although there are certainly more women writing for the stage today than ever, that seems a function of the general increase in numbers of dramatists. The careers of Fannie Hurst, Bella Spewack, Edna Ferber, Sylvia Regan, Rose Franken, and Lillian Hellman demonstrate that Jewish women playwrights did not have to stand outside locked stage doors until the 1960s.

The story of the Jewish-American repertoire is the story of an institution that has matured steadily across the twentieth century. It thrives in postwar America, which accepts unquestioningly the onstage presence of a broad variety of Jews in a vast spectrum of situations. However up-to-the-minute its topics and dramatis personae, the Jewish-American repertoire continues to reflect certain traits that have characterized it from its beginnings.

To illustrate the point, one might venture an ostensibly outlandish comparison between Odets' classic *Awake and Sing!* and the contemporary vanguard masterwork Tony Kushner's *Angels in America*. The sixty years between them are manifest in the cast of characters, the situation, the dialogue, and structure of the plot, their use of stage, and even the demands they make of their audiences. Yet beyond those disparities the similarities accumulate: each script in its own way is vitally concerned with the disintegration of family structure, with political and economic circumstances and their effects on the vulnerable. Each explores the consequences of misguided ethics and questionable morality. Each searches for answers in tradition, which is only partially responsive, and, its earnest quests not withstanding, each finds ways to make audiences smile.

Perhaps most important, since the theatre's primary mission has always been to please the audience, each has proven impressively successful at the box office. Doubtless, the single most significant achievement of the Jewish-American repertoire is remaining true to its traditions as it earns ever-expanding popularity throughout an increasingly multicultural America.

BIBLIOGRAPHY

Brenman-Gibson, Margaret. *Clifford Odets: American Playwright*. New York: Atheneum, 1982.

Fierstein, Harvey. *Widows and Children First*. In *Torch Song Trilogy*. New York: Gay Presses, 1978.

Odets, Clifford. *Awake and Sing!* In *Six Plays of Clifford Odets*. New York: Grove Weidenfeld.

Schiff, Ellen. *Fruitful and Multiplying: Nine Contemporary Plays from the American Jewish Repertoire*. New York: Penguin/Mentor, 1996.

Wasserstein, Wendy. *Isn't It Romantic?* in *The Heidi Chronicles and Other Plays*. New York: Vintage, 1991.

WOODY ALLEN   (1935–   )

Richard Moody

BIOGRAPHY

As Allen's biographer, Eric Lax, succinctly states, "Woody Allen was born in Brooklyn, New York in the spring of 1952, when Allen Stewart Konigsberg, who was born in the Bronx on December 1, 1935, settled on the name as a suitable cover" (9). Lax asserts that when the teenage Konigsberg was about to start his comedy career by sending in one-liners to newspaper columnists, he chose the name because it was funnier than his own, and, as he was shy, it would divert attention from his peers who might read them. Thus, "Woody Allen" became the public face of Allen Konigsberg.

From the anonymity of his newspaper one-liners as a teenager, Allen progressed professionally to gag-writing for television celebrities like Sid Caesar, Buddy Hackett, and Jack Parr. However, dissatisfied with having his skits altered in interpretation and performance by others, Allen gave up this lucrative career and struck out on his own as a stand-up comic in the early 1960s. This evolution allowed for both an expansion of his artistic range (from anonymous one-line jokes to skits) and an increase of control (performing his own material). This refusal to compromise and desire for total, godlike control of his life became a characteristic manifestation of Allen's alter ego characters as well.

On the basis of the appeal of his stand-up routines, Allen was offered the chance to write and star in the films *What's New, Pussycat?* (1965), *What's Up Tiger Lily?* (1966), and *Casino Royale* (1967), and his directorial debut followed in 1969 with *Take the Money and Run*, which he also wrote and starred in. This endeavor initiated the artistic direction he would follow for the next twenty-five years, with the exception of those few films in which he has starred for other directors. Throughout this period Allen has also written prose pieces—primarily

l" death—as Allan "fools" a
he fearful "beyond."

nother Bergman obsession, De-
ontact with humans. Kleinman,
in the middle of the night by a
prehending a maniacal strangler
e his deference to the project (he
hman is coerced into involvement
nstruction until he himself is mur-
g, "Cooperate. . . . God is the only
ial statement about life itself. We
m Deity, either diverting ourselves
s "churches" of belief about Deity.
of the "plan" to appease, avoid, or
ls there is no plan. Deity is simply
indiscriminately with no motive. In
llen's play points out the futility of

e stage for Allen's one-act *God* (1975),
l actor struggle to find a suitable ending
he writer a prize in the Athenian Drama
g career. Their efforts are thwarted by
cters with the actions they are contriving
llian turn as the actor points out the idea
a stage, leading them to break the fourth
rding the issue of the ending. Ultimately,
ty of the various playwrights involved—
Lorenzo Miller (who claims to have "writ-
ppears in the play—the godlike characters
tably, this leads to questioning Deity's con-
at there is no God, they then struggle with
ion of free will (as evidenced by problems
vior), but when they concede the possibility
question why Deity seems to refuse contact
veryone, then Man is not responsible for his
o usurp Deity's power and remove from his
ts in matters of life and, more crucially, death.
lead to existential discussion over God's ex-
for the actors telling them, "God is dead. . . .
y return to their original concerns regarding an

uggle to free themselves from control by others,
ascistic control over their peers, the progress of

for the *New Yorker*—that have since been published in book form *(Without Feathers, Getting Even*, and *Side Effects)*, as well as plays.

While volumes have been written about his films, and much attention has been given his prose, little acknowledgment has been paid to Allen's work as a playwright. The reason could be that his output in this field has been inconsistent. While Allen has directed twenty-seven films (with the release of *Deconstructing Harry* in 1998), he has published only three full-length plays and a handful of one-acts.

His first Broadway play, *Don't Drink the Water*, was written after *Pussycat* in 1966, which had become the highest-grossing film comedy to that date. The subsequent success of *Water* (eighteen months on Broadway) led to Allen's writing a stage vehicle for himself, *Play It Again, Sam*, in 1969. Both plays were later turned into films. *Water* starred Jackie Gleason in 1968 and was remade for television in 1993, directed by and starring Allen himself in the leading role. *Sam* made Allen a success as a playwright and star and was made into a film in 1971, with Allen again in the lead. This, however, was the end of Allen's career on the stage.

Allen then became obsessed with perfecting his skills as a screenwriter and director, only occasionally penning experimental one-acts such as *Death Knocks* (published in 1971), then *Death* in 1975, both existential, expressionistic variations on a theme concerning the inevitability of death. *God* in 1975, was a Pirandellian farce concerning a Greek writer and actor trying to end their play with the help of the audience. Then, in 1981, Allen mounted a Broadway production of his *The Floating Light Bulb*, a childhood memoir à la Tennessee Williams that starred Beatrice Arthur. As recently as July 1995, *Theatre Today* published Allen's one-act, *Central Park West*, a searing study of adultery.

MAJOR WORKS AND THEMES

Essentially, Allen's works tend to follow one basic pattern of life experience, which is repeated in various shadings in his films, plays, and prose. Allen's alter ego characters are usually implied to be the victims of parents who are constantly battling or have become blissfully oblivious to each other. In either event, the child is rejected by the parents for not conforming sufficiently to their way of life. This rejection leads to a desire to be accepted by others—ironically, both to prove the parents wrong for the rejection and to reject others in imitation of this parental behavior. As the child matures, this leads to conflict with society as a whole but often specifically with the Jewish culture, leading to the contention—held by many critics—that Allen's works are metaphors for Jewish assimilation into Gentile society. However, the most pointed conflicts concern the characters' relations with Gentile romantic partners and with Deity—whom they attempt to dominate.

The societal ambivalence toward Jews and Jewish tradition is manifest in Allen's portraying Jews as either animalistic and crude in comparison to more refined Gentiles or vibrant and life-affirming in comparison to comparatively sterile and repressed Gentiles. The latter treatment is graphically portrayed in Allen's Cold War comedy *Don't Drink the Water* (1968), which concerns a Jewish family of caterers from New Jersey who are accused of spying while on tour in Russia and find themselves seeking sanctuary for weeks in the American embassy. Patriarch Walter Hollander is the prototypical "ugly" American who mocks the Gentile embassy officials and makes constant demands regarding the food to be served and actions to be taken, all the while asserting that his tax dollars entitle him to such rights. Such behavior is contrasted with the polished decorum of the efficient Gentile officials, who present an image of calm and efficiency and secretly desire power over others, leading to fascism.

Allen seems to find that the Jewish family is ultimately preferred over the Gentiles, for in the context of the *Water* pivotal character, Axel Magee, the son of the American ambassador, is characterized as a bumbling failure as a politician who is implied to find release from Gentile repression via his marriage to Hollander's daughter, Susan. The implication is that her consenting to marry him will function as an adoption into the family and culture in which he more rightfully belongs.

Marriage is also treated with ambivalence. While the excitement and freedom of promiscuity promised by the sexual revolution of the 1960s result in a life of constant upheaval and insecurity, for Allen's characters the institution of marriage simultaneously provides security (acceptance) but also entraps individuals in a lifelong commitment (necessitating compromise and so sublimation of their individual will). Thus, while in *Water*, Walter and Marian Hollander are simply oblivious to each other, there is implied hope for more in the marriage of Axel and Susan. However, in *Play It Again, Sam* (1969), the comedy turns bittersweet. While central character Allan Felix tells us that he had "begged" his own parents to divorce, he himself suffers when wife, Nancy, leaves him because he drops his more active facade and turns from a "doer" into a "watcher," which causes her to become bored and restless.

In Allen's oeuvre, it is customary for the Jewish male characters to seek entrance into the Gentile world via striving to attain the image of suave, macho media images of Gentile masculinity (James Bond, Humphrey Bogart's characters)—or "doers"—then use the facade to initiate a relationship with a blond, sexy, Gentile female, or "shiksa." This wrong-headed approach is soon rendered disastrous by the male characters' ensuing efforts to "prove" the commitment of the romantic partner via subtle, but insistent, sexual and intellectual demands. Thus, after Nancy leaves in *Sam*, Allan's renewed efforts at a nervous brand of aggressive masculinity—spurred on by the sexist advice from the ghost of Humphrey Bogart in Allan's mind—may be subconsciously to avenge himself for Nancy's abandonment rather than an effort to forge a loving relationship. Allan finally finds acceptance in his relationship with shiksa Linda Christie— explaining to her that she is "the only platonic friend" he's ever had—but he nevertheless chooses to endanger this through sexual intimacy with her. What

Allen's career indicates he is caught up in the same struggle, since Allen has been accused of ''borrowing'' extensively from the thematic concerns and plot-lines of other artists. While his films are often compared to those of Fellini (*Stardust Memories*) and Bergman (*Hannah and Her Sisters, Another Woman*), Allen's plays also seem reworkings of the work of other playwrights. According to Lax, for example, Allen admits a kinship between *Water* and Kaufman's *You Can't Take It with You*, and I have suggested the influence of Tennessee Williams on *Bulb* and Edward Albee on *West*. While some have criticized this tendency in Allen's work, critic Sam Girgus suggests the idea that Allen does not ''crib'' the work of others but does take on their subject matter.

CRITICAL RECEPTION

Allen's most popular plays have been *Don't Drink the Water* and *Play It Again, Sam*, though both received mixed reviews in their initial runs. Many felt, as did Harold Clurman in *The Nation*, who described *Water*—Allen's self-confessed ''joke machine''—as having ''funny lines and situations which spring from the reality of odd-ball, carefree, boozy conviviality. Let us tell jokes, helter-skelter. If one of them flops—and a number of them do—we tell another to compensate for the brief lull'' (652).

Reviews of *Sam* were slightly more favorable due to Allen's casting himself in the lead role of Allen Felix, which brought associations with his popular stand-up comedy. Clurman commented, ''Allen appeals because he is perpetually hesitant, baffled, desperately inadequate and altogether honest about the constant failure at almost everything that is meaningful to him. Some of his jokes are cheap, but many are penetrating in their equivalency'' (282–83). However, Gerald Weales in *Commonweal* observed, ''There is . . . no environment at all. Although the best friend, monomaniacal about where he can be reached, is a one-gag creation and the women are conventional types (the sex-talker, the despairing intellectual), they have neither setting nor substance. 'Sam' is a one-character play, a Woody Allen monologue and as such it is characteristic of current Broadway practice in which stand-up comedians with TV reputations— Alan King, Jackie Mason—are asked to do their usual thing in what passes for a dramatic context'' (438).

Critics such as T. Kalem in *Time* referred to *The Floating Light Bulb* as ''no more than a shucked oyster shell of a play,'' and, according to director Ulu Grosbard, Allen himself was disappointed with it. Allen critic Annette Wernblad feels the problem with the play is that ''Allen's first noncomic drama, like his first noncomic films, is highly derivative, and its characters, as well as its dramatic tensions, are so well-known that ultimately they become facile and uninteresting'' (92).

Critics have found the one-act plays regarding ''Death'' and ''God'' to be more intellectually stimulating and daring. Foster Hirsch asserts that *God* reads like an intro to the writer's unconscious, Woody Allen raving in public. Self-indulgent and reckless, the play nonetheless has terrific energy and real intellectual daring, containing Allen's deepest treatment yet of the abstract, ultimate questions that have cast their enchantment over him'' (43).

BIBLIOGRAPHY

Works by Woody Allen

"Central Park West." *American Theatre*, July 1995, 12.6: 35–46.
Death: A Comedy in One Act. New York: Samuel French, 1975.
"Death Knocks." In *The Complete Prose of Woody Allen*, pp. 183–95.
Don't Drink the Water. New York: Random House, 1967.
The Floating Light Bulb. New York: Random House, 1982.
God: A Comedy in One Act. New York: Samuel French, 1975.
Play It Again, Sam. New York: Random House, 1969.

Works about Woody Allen

Brode, Douglas. *The Films of Woody Allen*. New York: Citadel Press, 1991.
Erens, Patricia. *The Jew in American Cinema*. Bloomington: Indiana University Press, 1984.
Friedman, Lester D. *Hollywood's Image of the Jew*. New York: Frederick Ungar, 1982.
Girgus, Sam. "Philip Roth & Woody Allen: Freud & the Humor of the Repressed." In *Semites and Stereotypes: Characteristics of Jewish Humor*. Ed. Avner Ziv and Anat Zajdman. Westport, CT: Greenwood Press, 1993.
Grosbard, Ulu. Interview. *New York Times*, Jan. 28, 1981, 1.
Hirsch, Foster. *Love, Sex, and Death, and the Meaning of Life: The Films of Woody Allen*. New York: Limelight Editions, 1990.
Jacobs, Diane. *But We Need the Eggs: The Magic of Woody Allen*. New York: St. Martin's Press, 1982.
Lax, Eric. *Woody Allen: A Biography*. New York: Alfred A. Knopf, 1991.
McCann, Graham. *Woody Allen, New Yorker*. Cambridge: Polity Press, 1991.
Pogel, Nancy. *Woody Allen*. Boston: Twayne, 1987.
Wernblad, Annette. *Brooklyn Is Not Expanding: Woody Allen's Comic Universe*. Madison, NJ: Fairleigh Dickinson University Press, 1992.
Yacowar, Maurice. *Loser Take All: The Comic Art of Woody Allen*. New York: Ungar, 1990.

Reviews

Don't Drink the Water

Clurman, Harold. "Theatre." *The Nation*, Dec. 12, 1966, 203: 652.
"Diasporadic Fun." *Time*, Nov. 25, 1966, 88: 88.
Gill, Brendan. "Assorted Approaches." *The New Yorker*, Dec. 3, 1966, 42: 155.

Play It Again, Sam

Clurman, Harold. "Theatre." *The Nation*. Mar. 3, 1969, 208: 282–83.
"New Plays." *Time*, Feb. 21, 1969, 93: 42.
Weales, Gerald. "The Stage." *Commonweal*, July 11, 1969, 90: 438.

The Floating Light Bulb

Gill, Brendan. "Sometimes the Moon. *The New Yorker*, May 4, 1981, 57: 101–2.
Kalem, T. E. "Home Rule." *Time*, May 11, 1981, 117: 83.
Kroll, Jack. "The Heartbreak Kid." *Newsweek*, May 11, 1981, 97: 93.
Weales, Gerald. "Flawed and Fascinating." *Commonweal*, Sept. 11, 1981, 108: 501.

JON ROBIN BAITZ (1961–)

Michael Taub

BIOGRAPHY

Jon Robin Baitz is only in his mid-thirties, but *Substance of Fire, Three Hotels*, and *A Fair Country* have already secured him a solid place in the forefront of contemporary American drama.

Baitz was born in 1961 in Los Angeles, the son of an international company executive who took his family with him to places like Brazil and South Africa. He spent his senior year at Beverly Hills High School, and instead of going to college he traveled to Europe and Israel. At twenty and back in Los Angeles, he started going to plays; the play that changed his life forever was Chekov's *The Cherry Orchard*. He now lives in New York with celebrated director Joe Mantello.

MAJOR WORKS AND THEMES

Baitz's first produced play was *The Film Society*, first shown by the *Los Angeles Actors' Theatre* in 1988. Like his subsequent works, *The Film Society* deals with a moral dilemma. The setting is South Africa, a private school struggling to stay on course amid financial difficulties and ideological disputes among the faculty.

The year is 1970. Apartheid is firmly in place. Terry Sinclair, a former teacher at Blenheim, has made the mistake of socializing with blacks and once inviting a black priest to speak at commencement ceremonies, for which he was promptly fired. In his fight to regain his position and reputation, Terry tries to recruit Jonathon Balton, a teacher at the school, who it turns out, is only interested in his "film society," an ongoing series of soft, noncontroversial movies. Jonathon's mother is a rich old lady and generous benefactor of the school. When

Hamish Fox, the principal, dies, Mrs. Balton pressures the school board to appoint her son Jonathon as principal. As headmaster, Jonathon can effect change—and it should be said to his credit that he does have a conscience. However, in the end, he opts for the safety of preserving the status quo over change. This is evident in his handling of Terry's wife, Nan Sinclair, a teacher who makes the mistake of asking her class to write on what the administration considers sensitive political issues. Faced with the choice of keeping his job or firing her, he lets her go.

Written from firsthand experience in South Africa, Baitz's play is, naturally, an antiapartheid statement, but, like all good works of art, *The Film Society* reaches well beyond its prescribed boundaries. In the final analysis, the play depicts the impotence of generally well meaning people to oppose a political system they know full well is immoral but for purely selfish reasons needs to be preserved. The play makes no allusions to Jewishness or anything Jewish until well into the second act, where an old teacher, Neville Sutter, is found arguing with Mrs. Balton over contract terms for Jonathon. The old lady insists on her conditions, prompting Sutter to say: "Must we negotiate like Jews?" (*The Film Society*, 56).

In his second produced play, *The Substance of Fire*, Baitz is very careful about explicit comments on anything Jewish, quite a feat considering that his protagonist, Isaac Geldhart, is a Holocaust survivor. This drama was first shown at the *Long Wharf Theatre* in New Haven, Connecticut, in 1990. In some respects this play features another Jonathon, another morally conflicted hero.

Isaac is a New York publisher of scholarly books. His company is in danger of bankruptcy unless it allows publication of widely read, trashy novels. His two sons and daughter, who are minority shareholders, eventually prevail over his objections and rescue the firm from financial disaster.

Following fierce debates over the morality of such a decision, the second act focuses almost entirely on Isaac, an aging, retired businessman living alone in a Manhattan apartment. Afraid that their father suffers from mental instability, the children arrange for psychiatric observation by Marge Hackett, a trained social worker who visits him regularly. These professional sessions end up becoming personal exchanges between two wounded souls. It turns out that Marge is the widow of a key city official who committed suicide several years back, following a highly publicized financial scandal. Her reputation ruined, penniless and bitter, Marge is in as much need of psychological support as is her patient, Isaac. Once beyond sarcasm and cynicism, the two manage to develop genuine concern for each other. The play ends with Isaac's asking her to dinner. She replies, "It would be nice, Isaac" (*Substance of Fire*, p. 66).

Adopting an optimistic view, Isaac manages to survive the battle against insanity and isolation. Earlier, he had to survive the loss of a business he had built from scratch. To him, yielding to cheap, popular tastes means compromising principles and, in effect, the end of the business as he had envisioned it. Of course, before that, he survived the horror of living through the war while hiding in a dark basement. The guilt of living while so many died, however, stays with him. Then, some years later, came the death of his wife. All this suffering has left him with emotional scars that manifest themselves in his cynical, bitter, fatalistic attitude. To some extent he, too, like many Jewish emigrants from Eastern Europe, is somewhat ambivalent toward America. On one hand, America is the land of opportunity and freedom, "di goldene land," as it was known across the ocean, but it is also a place where greed and the irresistible need to succeed squash old, traditional values.

Generally, Isaac is successful in concealing his past and repressing his feelings. But whenever he loses control, especially when fighting with his children, deep-seated memories do surface. In those painful moments he is overcome by anger and remorse. While surviving rather remarkably, Isaac is also acutely aware that "trying to pick up where you leave off" is futile, as he once tells his daughter Sara (*Substance*, p. 34). With Marge, Isaac might get another chance at life; at least he might attempt to pick up where he left off.

In making Isaac Geldhart a Holocaust survivor, Baitz elevates his protagonist to tragic proportions. He is a modern-day Job, a man who suffers unjustly, emerges from the ruins, raises a family, and builds a successful business, only to find his world collapse again. In this context, the Holocaust symbolizes, above all, the destruction of prewar Europe, the "Old World," with its appreciation of traditions and cultural values. Thus, in Baitz's drama the Holocaust is basically a universal manifestation of evil, only vaguely a Jewish calamity.

Obviously, Isaac is an assimilated Jewish intellectual. Not surprisingly, his children are alienated from Judaism since they associate Jewishness with their father's problems and his troubling past "over there" in Europe. They move almost exclusively in WASPish circles, and any trace of Jewishness would only hinder their chances of being fully accepted. The repression of Jewish identity is partly due to Isaac's disinterest in ethnic or religious matters and perhaps an unconscious attempt to shield his children from evil (anti-Semitism) by erasing their Jewishness, a common phenomenon among Holocaust survivors suffering from persecution complex.

Though worlds apart, it is interesting to compare the Geldharts in *The Substance of Fire* with Charlie and Josh, father and son in Herb Gardner's classic immigrant drama *Conversations with My Father*. To American-born Josh, the past evokes feelings of love and connectedness; his grandmother's books and photographs are not something to be ashamed of but "extraordinary things, full of people looking like us—some great old books in Russian and Yiddish." (Gardner, p. 13).

Echoing the dark dramas of Tom Stoppard and Simon Gray, *The End of the Day*, which premiered at New York's Playwrights Horizons in 1992, is a black comedy about Graydon Massey, an Englishman and clinical psychologist who marries Helen Lasker, daughter of a wealthy, Jewish-American family. For ten years they live harmoniously in Malibu, but when the action starts, they are divorced. Hilton Lasker, Helen's father, arrives at Massey's house and demands an "accounting" of the money he had spent on the ex-son-in-law.

Hilton feels that Massey has used his money and daughter to get American citizenship and to set up a clinic. He warns him against thinking of his in-laws as "schmucks and patsies" and pressures him to pay him back right away (15). Massey explains that his aristocratic British family had disowned him when, against their wishes, he came to America and married a Jew, not, as would have been proper and expected, a blue-blooded Englishwoman.

The scene shifts to the clinic, where Massey treats, among others, gay men whose friends are dying of AIDS. Marton, an old school friend, appears at Massey's clinic. He has reached "bottom" but hopes that through the sale of drugs and other criminal activity he will recover and make money. He wants Massey as a partner. Massey refuses the offer. Finally, Massey is confronted by his ex-wife, who reproaches him for divorcing her. She repeats some of Hilton's charges, adding a few colorful, personal elements to the exchange: "We know I'm a dumb JAP blond, but how do you sleep with someone for ten years? . . . And you fell in love with my father, my family, big, larger than life, broad-hipped robust American ethnics, as you'd put it. Kikes as your friend would say" (39). The outcome of this rather farcical meeting is Helen's insistence on a rare painting in Massey's home in London as part of the settlement.

Back in London, Massey realizes that it would be very difficult to return to the old ways, especially to his parents' choice of a wife for him—Lady Stoat, a cynical, practical, masculine version of Helen. While Stoat derides his American episode, he informs her that no future is possible between them: "I'll never give you what you want. I'll be reduced to affairs, flare-ups, booze-ups, affairs" (60). His rapid-fire sarcastic outburst does not in the least rattle Lady Stoat. She suspects that a change of mind is not out of the question. With check and painting in hand, Massey leaves her wondering and returns to Malibu and his clinic.

There, he is again hounded by Marton, clearly a Mephisto-type character who tempts Massey into more shady deals, but, most shockingly, he prods Massey into admitting that he is a homosexual like himself. As Marton explains, Massey is the victim of "dreadful relationships with women, you dress too well to be straight, your mother was domineering, and your dad remote" (71). Marton is rejected. In a sudden, but by no means surprising, turn of events, Massey accepts Lady Stoat's hand, meaning that he is now owner of several large corporations, founder of an art gallery in Los Angeles bearing his family's name, and financier of a new, improved psychiatric clinic. Ironically, Hilton and Helen work for him. In short, Massey is finally a true American success story. All is forgiven and forgotten—Hilton, who earlier threatened to spread his "kishkes all over the Negev," now loves him. (73). His daughter Helen is so proud of him that she thinks if he were born in America, he could run for president.

Like the plays of Simon Gray and Alan Ayckbourn, Baitz's *The End of the*

Day is a satire of British mores, especially the pretentious nature of the upper classes. The play also lambastes the low-class Jewish businessman, his crassness, hypocrisy, and pushy mannerisms. It is unclear whether Massey's solution to wed Lady Stoat so he could become an American millionaire signals victory or defeat. In effect he has turned himself into a magnified version of Hilton. Perhaps Massey has been too deeply infected by Hilton's materialism to resist Lady Stoat's hand. True, he is probably losing some self-respect and compromising on love, but in return he is capable of promoting art and building medical facilities.

While *The End of the Day* treats moral dilemmas in a comical way, *Three Hotels* is a serious play about the compromises undermining the lives of powerful men like Hilton and Massey. It was first shown in 1992 by New York Stage and Film Company in association with the Powerhouse Theater at Vassar College and in 1993 by New York's Circle Repertory Company, starring Ron Rifkin, who also played Isaac in *Substance of Fire*, and Christine Lahti. The play consists of three monologues—the first and last by Ken Hoyle and the one in the middle by his wife, Barbara.

Ken Hoyle is an executive working for an international baby formula company. He is in charge of opening new markets in Third World countries. Ken is the son of Jewish parents. His mother lives in a Jewish old-age home in Baltimore. She is from Odessa, and her first languages are Yiddish and Russian. Occasionally, he misses her cooking, especially her chicken soup. His father was once a "commie," most likely American-born, and he would send Ken to left-wing summer camps in Peekskill. This explains the reason Ken served in the Peace Corps. When he joined the high-powered corporate world, Ken changed his name from Hirschkovitz to Hoyle. Though successful and generally respected, Ken knows that he is called a "Hebe" by some. He suspects that Kroener, his superior, is an anti-Semite.

But anti-Semitism is not Ken's main problem. He is increasingly concerned about the morality of introducing dangerous products for testing and eventual distribution to poor countries in Africa and Central and South America. Appropriately, Ken's monologues take place in hotel rooms in Tangier, Morocco, and Oaxaca, Mexico. Since he is up for a major promotion, he is naturally anxious and tense. Will they accept him or reject him purely on merit, or will his Jewishness be a factor? Precisely because he is Jewish, he feels he must excel beyond their expectations. He cannot give them any excuse to deny him his proper due. But this former Peace Corps volunteer cannot escape the gnawing feeling that, in a sense, he is the "Kissinger and Nixon of baby formula," a monster to all those millions of innocent creatures (46).

His fate is sealed by a speech delivered by Barbara to other Mulcahey and Kroener wives at a company retreat in the Virgin Islands. In her presentation, Barbara warns them against complacency and callous disregard for the welfare of the natives. She cautions them against allowing their husbands to become "monsters" by compromising their morals and losing their sense of social responsibility. Naturally, the company chiefs find her speech too ''inflammatory'' and decide to fire Ken.

In the play's final scene—a hotel room in Oaxaca, Mexico—Ken has time to reflect on his life. Outside, the natives are celebrating the ''Day of the Dead,'' an annual ritual honoring their departed loved ones, a Mexican version of the Jewish ''Yizkor.'' As he prepares to bury his corporate career with Mulcahey and Kroener, Ken ponders his relationships, his family, and friends. This is a proper time to mourn the loss of his son, who was killed senselessly on a beach in Brazil when he struggled with thieves who were stealing his watch. Though a random crime, can this murder be viewed as retribution for the company's killing of children with their unsafe baby formulas?

On an unconscious level Ken feels guilty for his son's death, a 1990s version of the binding of Isaac. In the Bible Abraham blindly obeys God's command to sacrifice Isaac as proof of his unwavering faith in him. Here, Ken sacrifices his son on the altar of his corporate career by bringing him to Brazil and exposing him to danger. While the cruel God of the Bible does ultimately reward his faithful servant, Mulcahey and Kroener turn out to be woefully ungrateful ''Gods.'' Of course, on a realistic level this analogy does not work (the crime could have happened anywhere). Any way we look at it, the play is a chilling warning against blind obedience, against a corporate world that empties its employees of ethical conscience and basic humanity.

Harry Burgess, the protagonist of *A Fair Country*, Baitz's 1996 play, is also crushed by insidious corporate machines; this time, however, it is the mighty Central Intelligence Agency (CIA). Harry is a U.S. information officer stationed in South Africa. He is an idealist who believes he can use his position to fight apartheid (the play is set in the late 1970s) while performing official duties of spreading American culture and goodwill to this deeply divided and troubled society. His tour of duty, however, is cut short by an offer to work in Western Europe for the *Voice of America* radio broadcast. For decades this government-funded station filled Eastern European airwaves with a combination of suppressed home-front news and capitalist propaganda. The problem is that this job is actually a front for some questionable CIA activities. In short, Harry agrees to become a CIA agent, putting his family's financial concerns before conscience and principles. Like Ken Hoyle in *The End of the Day*, he, too, must pay the price for selling out: while here no life is taken, the events severely shatter the emotional life of his wife and sons. In the end, when it is too late, Harry laments his decision: ''We should have stayed home. . . . To think that we could do anything decent with the world'' (quote from *New York Times*, February 20, 1996).

CRITICAL RECEPTION

Most critics praise Baitz's courage in tackling difficult moral issues. They point out that in America he is among only a handful of playwrights capable of dealing seriously with such problems as racial injustice and political oppression. His plays usually generate a great deal of discussion and analysis. Vincent Canby writes that Baitz is "occupying theatrical territory that once was the turn of Arthur Miller and Lillian Hellman" (1). While some of his early plays have been found to be a bit ponderous and dark, his latest efforts are marked by lively dialogue and dramatic suspense. Shown in America's most prestigious theatres, his works attract some of the country's best actors.

BIBLIOGRAPHY

Works by Jon Robin Baitz

Dates in parentheses refer to stage productions if different from dates of publication.
The Film Society. (1988). New York: Samuel French, 1989.
The Substance of Fire. (1990). New York: Samuel French, 1991.
The End of the Day. (1992). New York: Samuel French, 1991.
Three Hotels. New York: Samuel French, 1992.
Three Hotels—Plays and Monologues. New York: Theatre Communications Group, 1994.
A Fair Country. (1996). Not as yet published.

Works about Jon Robin Baitz

Canby, Vincent. Rev. of *A Fair Country*. *New York Times*, February 20, 1996, 1, 17.
Holden, Stephen. Rev. of *Substance of Fire* (film). *New York Times*, December 6, 1996, 5.
Interview with Robin Baitz. *New York Times*, February 24, 1996, 1, 4.
Jefferson, Margo. Rev. of *A Fair Country*. *New York Times*, March 3, 1996, 1, 18.
Weber, Bruce. Rev. of *Substance of Fire* (Play). *New York Times*, October 30, 1994, 1, 32.

PADDY CHAYEFSKY   (1923–1981)

Edward Isser

BIOGRAPHY

Sidney (Paddy) Chayefsky, the son of Russian immigrants, was born on January 29, 1923, in New York City. Chayefsky's father, after losing a fortune in the depression, moved the family into a lower-middle-class, ethnic neighborhood in the Bronx. The Chayefsky family was religious, and Sidney was forced to study Hebrew and attend synagogue regularly. Between 1940 and 1943, Chayefsky enrolled at the City College of New York. After graduating, he enlisted in the army and one year later was wounded by a land mine in Germany. While recuperating from his injury in England, Chayefsky wrote a musical comedy about the armed services that was entitled *No T.O. for Love*. This cabaret piece was performed for troops at various installations with Chayefsky in the leading role.

At the end of the war, Chayefsky returned to New York and found work at his uncle's print shop. His writing career resumed when he used a $500 grant from Garson Kanin to write an autobiographical play about an aspiring Jewish writer from the Bronx. Unable to get this piece produced, Chayefsky went to Hollywood in 1946 to study acting at the Actor's Lab and break into films. One year later he was awarded a Junior Writer's contract with Universal Pictures, but Chayefsky quickly grew disenchanted and left Hollywood. After returning to New York, he spent two years struggling to survive as a writer by selling gags and skits to television comedians and even doing his own stand-up routines. Chayefsky's first breakthrough occurred in 1948–1949, when a story he wrote for *Good Housekeeping* magazine—"A Few Kind Words from Newark"—was optioned for $25,000 to Twentieth Century-Fox. Although the movie was never produced, the advance money allowed Chayefsky to pursue a career as a writer.

In 1952, after a stint writing weekly half-hour episodes, Chayefsky began writing hour-length plays for radio and television. His first television play—"Holiday Song"—about a cantor who loses his faith in the midst of the High Holy Days established Chayefsky as a major figure in the new medium. In the next three years, Chayefsky wrote ten more television plays that were critical and popular successes. Some of these plays were reworked into Broadway productions and major motion pictures. In 1955, *Marty* was produced as a movie and garnered Chayefsky an Academy Award for Best Screenplay. *Middle of the Night* was produced on Broadway in 1956, starring Edward G. Robinson, and ran for almost two years before it was also made into a movie. Other television plays adapted to film were *The Catered Affair* and *The Bachelor Party*. In 1959, Chayefsky's first play written specifically for the stage, *The Tenth Man*, began an extended run on Broadway.

The 1960s were not kind to Chayefsky, and his fortunes faltered. Plays such as *Gideon, The Passion of Josef D.*, and *The Latent Heterosexual* received mixed reviews and were commercial failures. He wrote two screenplays for Hollywood during this period—*The Americanization of Emily* and *Paint Your Wagon*, both of which proved to be commercial and critical failures. In the 1970s Chayefsky's career enjoyed a remarkable rebound when two of his screenplays—*The Hospital* and *Network*—won the Academy Award for Best Screenplay. In 1981, shortly after the release of his last movie—*Altered States*—Chayefsky succumbed to cancer and died.

MAJOR WORKS AND THEMES

Throughout his career, Chayefsky was a political activist for liberal causes. As he grew older, he became more interested—almost obsessed—about issues dealing with Judaism and Israel. In 1971, he was a founding member and a driving force in a pro-Israeli group called Writers and Artists for Peace in the Middle East. That same year he became a delegate to the International Conference on Soviet Jewry. In 1978, during the telecast of the Academy Awards, Chayefsky received a standing ovation when he criticized Vanessa Redgrave for using her acceptance speech to make anti-Israeli statements.

Paddy Chayefsky was not a particularly original writer. With no formal training in the art of playwriting and minimal theatrical experience, his stage work tended to be derivative. He learned to write by analyzing and dissecting the work of Ibsen and Hellman, borrowing themes and dialogue from Odets, Miller, and O'Neill, and later stealing ideas from artists such as Robert Altman, Szymon Ansky, Bertolt Brecht, and Archibald MacLeish. Chayefsky, however, was a master craftsman who perfected and popularized the esoteric ideas of more original artists. Although he never achieved the stage successes of Miller, Odets, or O'Neill, he nevertheless managed to win three Academy Awards for screenwriting. Movies such as *Marty, The Hospital*, and *Network* gave Chayefsky the respect and stature in Hollywood that had eluded him in the legitimate theatre.

Jewish characters and Jewish themes are prevalent in many of Chayefsky's plays. The television dramas "Holiday Song" and "The Reluctant Citizen" are specifically about Jewish concerns. Broadway plays such as *The Tenth Man* and *Gideon* examine the philosophical underpinnings of the Jewish faith, and other plays such as *Middle of the Night, The Passion of Josef D.*, and *The Latent Heterosexual* feature Jewish characters.

Chayefsky's first full-length television play—"Holiday Song"—examines the post-Holocaust existential crisis of Jewish faith. The story is about a cantor on Long Island who—on the day before Rosh Hashanah—decides that he cannot sing in the synagogue service because he has lost his belief in God. The rabbi of the congregation is shocked and desperate. The cantor is dispatched to see a famous rebbe in Manhattan who will cure him of his skepticism. On the subway platform, however, a conductor puts him on the wrong train. The only other passenger is a despondent woman who is about to commit suicide. The woman, from the same Dutch town as the cantor, is a survivor of Auschwitz who has lost her husband and children. The cantor stops her from committing suicide and sees her safely home. He then returns to the same subway platform and tries once more to find the correct train to Manhattan. Again, he is misled by the same conductor onto another deserted train going the wrong way. The only other passenger on this train is a sad Jewish fellow who has lost his wife and children at Auschwitz. The cantor realizes that the man is the husband of the woman he just saved. He unites the couple and returns to the platform a third time looking for the mysterious conductor who facilitated this miracle. The cantor learns from another conductor that no such man works at the station. The cantor—who had lost his faith in God—realizes that he has come face-to-face with a messenger of the Lord. With renewed faith, the cantor returns to Long Island, and the play concludes with his singing at the Rosh Hashanah service.

Chayefsky's second television play—"The Reluctant Citizen"—is about a Holocaust survivor who arrives in America in 1946. The survivor—Kimmer—distrusts authority and bureaucrats and is terrified of anything new or different. The play chronicles how a young social worker at the Educational Alliance on the Lower East Side of New York is able to remove the barriers that Kimmer has erected. The play, based on incidents involving an elderly cousin of Chayefsky who had come to New York after the war, ends with Kimmer's taking the oath of allegiance and becoming an American citizen.

Chayefsky's next two television plays—"Printer's Measure" and "Marty"— feature Irish and Italian characters, respectively. The language, scenarios, and interaction of both pieces have a strong ethnic/urban flavor that feels very Jewish. As with the crypto-Jews in the plays of Odets and Miller, one senses strongly that Chayefsky is hiding the Jewishness of his characters for the sake of audience appeal. After "Holiday Song" and "The Reluctant Citizen," Chayefsky evidently felt the need to reach out to a larger constituency.

Chayefsky utilizes crypto-Jewish characters in a number of his later television plays. In these works no mention of ethnic identity is made whatsoever. In plays like "The Big Deal," "The Bachelor Party," "Catch My Boy on Sunday," and "The Mother," the characters speak in Jewish cadences, live in urban settings, and have middle-class concerns. The influence of Miller and Odets is felt most sharply in these plays, particularly in "The Big Deal," which is derivative of *Death of a Salesman*.

Chayefsky's first Broadway drama, *Middle of the Night*, features a number of Jewish characters. This play—a May–December romance—sets forth the proposition that love is a redemptive element that must be pursued regardless of social consequences. The protagonist of the play is a widowed, middle-aged clothing manufacturer named Jerry Kingsley, who falls in love with Betty Preiss—a young clerical worker in his office. Judaism plays a minor role in the play and becomes an issue only because Jerry is Jewish, and Betty is not. The anti-Semitism of Betty's mother and Jerry's sister's disapproval of a non-Jewish girl serve as an impediment to the romance. The extent of Kingsley's Jewishness is demonstrated only by his speech pattern and his concern with social issues.

Chayefsky embraced a Jewish theme in the first play he wrote specifically for the stage. His adaptation of Ansky's *The Dybbuk* proved to be Chayefsky's greatest critical and commercial theatre success. *The Tenth Man*, directed by Tyrone Guthrie, premiered on November 5, 1959, at the Booth Theatre in New York City. At a rundown synagogue in Mineola, Long Island, a group of Jews meet to hold a morning minyan service. It is a strange collection, consisting of a cynical former revolutionary, a retired, dissolute businessman, a mystical cabalist who was an apostate in his youth, a young rabbi more concerned with gimmicks to increase his flock than in spiritual matters, and a few grumpy old Jewish men. Unfortunately, due to a snowstorm and a dwindling congregation, the group is hard-pressed to find the requisite ten men that Jewish law requires to hold a service. One elderly member of the congregation, Foreman, arrives with his mentally disturbed granddaughter. The girl, Evelyn, is about to be institutionalized because she is a violent schizophrenic, but Foreman believes that her suffering is caused by an evil dybbuk that has seized her body. Foreman seeks to arrange a ceremony that will exorcise the spirit. Meanwhile, the sexton of the congregation has found a lawyer named Arthur Landau wandering the streets and has brought him to the synagogue to be the tenth man for the minyan. Landau is a successful lawyer whose marriage has fallen apart. He is coming off a two-day drunken binge and is feeling suicidal. On his way to his therapist, he happened to be passing by the synagogue when the sexton cornered him.

Landau and Evelyn meet in the rabbi's office, and a mystical connection emerges between the two. Evelyn sees in Landau her savior and clings to him for emotional and psychological support. Landau, however, is loath to get involved with this clearly disturbed girl. In the interim, the old cabalist Hirschmann experiences a religious epiphany and believes that God has cleansed his soul. Hirschmann agrees to conduct the exorcism of the dybbuk that supposedly haunts the girl. A dybbuk is excised, but from Landau, not Evelyn. Landau loses all suicidal desires and his selfish orientation. He proclaims his intention to sacrifice himself for Evelyn: "I will cherish this girl, and give her a home. I will tend to her needs and hold her in my arms when she screams out. . . . Her soul is mine now—her soul, her charm, her beauty—even you, her insanity, are mine" (p. 153). The play ends with Landau and Evelyn's exiting together to be married.

The Tenth Man is one of the most Jewish plays ever produced on Broadway. No other play has been set entirely in a synagogue, used the Torah as a prop, and dramatized a minyan service. Yet for all its outward Jewishness, *The Tenth Man* is strangely devoid of religion. This is because, in part, Hebrew is never spoken onstage (all prayers are in English) and because the playwright's treatment of the material is shallow. Jewish customs, philosophy, and mysticism are all referred to but are never fully explicated. The conclusion of the play is so abrupt and so poorly delineated that we are left adrift with an aphorism instead of an explanation.

In 1961, as *The Tenth Man* concluded its Broadway run, Chayefsky created another play that addressed the imperative of faith in Judaism. This work—*Gideon*—dramatized a tale from the Old Testament contained in Chapter 6 of the Book of Judges. *Gideon* was a summation and reiteration of themes that Chayefsky first enunciated in "Holiday Song." The title character in the play repeatedly tests and challenges God to prove his divinity. God has chosen Gideon to be his messenger on Earth because the shepherd is a rather shallow, uninspiring fellow. The Lord wants an Everyman like Gideon to lead the Israelites into battle against the Midianites so that there will be no doubt that the miracle of victory against a superior force is God's doing and not that of a man. Gideon, however, is a recalcitrant hero. At first he is reluctant to participate, and after the enemy is defeated, he demands some degree of credit and recognition. Gideon and God clash over the Israelite's lack of humility and his insistence on free will. God demands love and discipline from Gideon, but the Israelite refuses. The play concludes with God and Gideon's parting ways. Chayefsky's point is that the Jews will not be subservient creatures to God. Rather, they will strive to create and accomplish according to their own will. The price for this freedom, however, is alienation from the Lord. God still exists, but he is now separate and apart from his chosen people.

Gideon opened in New York on November 9, 1961, at the Plymouth Theatre. The play was a critical and popular failure. Chayefsky—the master of the Jewish/urban/ethnic vernacular—"the Clifford Odets of the 1950s"—had sought to create a poetic drama akin to Archibald MacLeish's *J. B.* Chayefsky, however, was not a poet, and the result was a strained and hackneyed piece of work that failed miserably.

After *Gideon*, Chayefsky never attempted to write a play on a Jewish theme again. His next two dramas—*The Passion of Josef D.* and *The Latent Heterosexual*—featured Jewish characters but had nothing to do with Judaism. *The Passion of Josef D.* is a post-Brechtian examination of the rise of Stalin. It is one of the most interesting and original plays that Chayefsky wrote. Unfortunately, directed by Chayefsky on Broadway in 1964, it lasted exactly one week before closing. *The Latent Heterosexual* played in Dallas, London, and Los Angeles but never made it to New York. Written and produced in 1968 as a star vehicle for Zero Mostel, the play is a tasteless exercise in homophobia that will probably never be revived without major textual alterations.

CRITICAL RECEPTION

Chayefsky, who was considered by one critic to be the "Clifford Odets of the 1950s" (Shub 527), was arguably more successful in film and television than on the stage. He made a far greater impression on the American public in such brilliant screenplays as *Marty, The Hospital,* and *Network* than in such works as *The Tenth Man, Gideon,* and *The Passion of Josef D.*

Of his plays, *The Tenth Man* received the most favorable responses as it enjoyed a run of a year and a half on Broadway. Kenneth Tynan stated: "Mr. Chayevsky is a wonderfully creative listener. The best of his dialogue is as meaty as any I have heard since the heyday of Clifford Odets" (qtd. in Clum 69), while Gore Vidal dubbed Chayevsky "a writer with a first-rate imagination . . . and a master of the theatre" (qtd. in Clum 70). But *Gideon* did not fare as well, as Robert Brustein's attack on the play considered it flawed with "religious pieties, vaudeville effects with Herman Wouk metaphysics" (Brustein 21).

In contrast, *Marty, The Hospital,* and *Network* all won Oscars for Best Screenplay, and *Marty* also won the New York Film Critics Award. It seems that these screenplays enjoyed their success in their appeal to a more general audience than his stage plays, but Chayevsky was very much a product of the "Golden Age" of television in his earliest efforts, and his dialogue seems more effective on the screen than onstage. Howard Beale's "I'm mad as hell and I'm not going to take it anymore" from *Network* has become a part of the general culture as an expression of the rage and frustration with the injustices of American society. Perhaps that element of social concern, ironic as it was meant to be in this film, best expressed Chayevsky's search for a more socially aware and just America.

BIBLIOGRAPHY

Works by Paddy Chayefsky

Dates in parentheses refer to stage productions if different from dates of publication.

Plays

Middle of the Night. (1956). New York: Random House, 1957.
The Tenth Man. (1959). New York: Random House, 1960.
Gideon. New York: Random House, 1961.
The Passion of Josef D. New York: Random House, 1964.
The Latent Heterosexual. (1968). New York: Random House, 1967.

ERRATA

Page 95: Arthur Laurents was born on July 14, 1917. He remains alive and active at the time of this book's publication. This error is not the fault of the author of the entry, Bette H. Kirschstein.

Teleplays

"Holiday Song." NBC, September 14, 1952.
"Printer's Measure." NBC, April 26, 1953.
"Marty." NBC, May 24, 1953.
"The Big Deal." NBC, July 19, 1953.
"The Bachelor Party." NBC, October 11, 1953.
"The Sixth Year." NBC, November 20, 1953.
"Middle of the Night." NBC, September 19, 1954.
"The Catered Affair." NBC, May 22, 1955.
"The Great American Hoax." CBS, May 15, 1957.

Screenplays

"Marty." United Artists, 1955.
The Bachelor Party. United Artists, 1957. New York: New American Library, 1957.
The Goddess. Columbia, 1958. New York: Simon and Schuster, 1958.
"Middle of the Night." Columbia, 1959.
"The Americanization of Emily." Metro-Goldwyn-Mayer, 1964.
"Paint Your Wagon." Paramount, 1968.
"The Hospital." United Artists, 1971.
"Network." United Artists, 1976.
"Altered States" (under the pseudonym Sidney Aaron). Warner Bros., 1980. Published
    as a novel, New York: Harper, 1978.

Works about Paddy Chayefsky

Books

Clum, John. *Paddy Chayevsky*. Boston: Twayne, 1976.
The Collected Works of Paddy Chayevsky. 4 vol. New York: Applause Books, 1995.
Considine, Shaun. *Mad as Hell: The Life and Work of Paddy Chayevsky*. New York:
    Random House, 1994.

Articles

Brustein, Robert. "All Hail, Mahomet of Middle Seriousness." Review of *Gideon*. *The
    New Republic*, November 27, 1961, 21.
Chayefsky, Paddy. "In Praise of Reappraised Picture-Makers." *New York Times*, January
    8, 1956.
———. "Art Films—Dedicated Insanity." *The Saturday Review*, December 21, 1957.
———. "From the Notebooks of Josef D." *New York Herald Tribune*, February 2, 1964.
Gussow, Mel. "Chayefsky: Writer with Love of Words." *New York Times*, August 3,
    1981.
Horowitz, Susan. "Paddy Chayefsky Speaks Out." *The Saturday Review*, November 13,
    1976.
Mitgang, Herbert. "Chayefsky: A Man of Passion." *New York Times*, August 5, 1981.
Moss, Robert F. "The Agonies of a Screenwriter." *The Saturday Review*, May 1981.
Phillips, McCandlish. "Focusing on Chayefsky." *New York Times*, January 3, 1972.

Sayre, Nora, and Robert B. Silvers. ''An Interview with Paddy Chayefsky.'' *Horizon*, September 1960.

Shatzky, Joel. ''Paddy Chayefsky: Americanizing *The Dybbuk*.'' *Jewish Currents*, January 1983, 24–27, 31.

Shub, Anatole. ''Paddy Chayefsky's Minyan: *The Tenth Man* on Broadway.'' *Commentary* 28, December 1959, 523–27.

Zolorow, Sam. ''Chayefsky Plan to Be a Director.'' *New York Times*, June 26, 1963.

SARAH BLACHER COHEN (1936–)

Catharine Gabriel Carey

BIOGRAPHY

"What would I do if I couldn't perform?" Totie laments in Sarah Blacher Cohen's play *Sophie & Totie & Belle*. Born on June 13, 1936, to Russian-Jewish immigrant parents in Appleton, Wisconsin, Cohen constructs dramatic characters who enact her various performative *selves* in reaction to the presence of Yiddish culture, language, and humor in her home; the inherited and progressively disabling condition she shared with her mother and siblings; and the necessarily creative definition of her own female identity, given the narrow, Old World gender stereotype to be, above all else, "a Yiddishe Mame."

In childhood Cohen confronted her own physical disability (a condition that affected her limbs) with a decision to be comic. Her particular brand of "wry/rye" humor is linked to her pleasure-loving father, who fled to the American Midwest to escape becoming *cannon fodder* for the czar. Mr. Blacher peddled junk in a horse and wagon, ready to entertain with stories of his narrow escape or shorten his working day to play cards with the goyim, who knew him as "Louie, the White Jew"; later, this gregariousness paid off when he bought and sold junk to World War II factories, thus financing Sarah's college education. Awkward in the domestic sphere, young Sarah recalls her "chief early pleasures" as singing heartily with her father and male friends at Orthodox services and joining afterward in their Yiddish songs and jokes. Despite her mother's attempts to "tone her down" and prevent her from "being a burden," this alliance with male voices greatly increased her determination to be heard in public ("Interview" 7, 27: 96).

As a high school student in Appleton, Cohen's humor was the "social lubricant" that helped ease her way into a restrictive Gentile community. Valedictorian and "president of everything," she wrote, directed, and acted in plays; however, unlike the subject of her play, *Molly Picon's Return Engagement*, the *spritna* Molly Picon, whom Cohen envied as a combination of physical dexterity and mental ability, Cohen realized early that she lacked the physical skills required for theatrical roles and chose to "perform" her mental agility in the academic arena, first in high school, then in college, teaching. In her academic ventures, Cohen's performative *script* was to prove the unusual possible. She jokes that the authors she writes about then go on to win the Nobel Prize ("Interview" 7, 27: 96): Saul Bellow, the topic of her dissertation at Northwestern; first book published as an assistant professor at SUNY Albany (1974) and short story author of her first independent play adaptation (1993); Isaac Bashevis Singer, with whom she collaborated on an adaptation of *Schlemiel the First* (1984); and Cynthia Ozick, about whom Cohen wrote numerous articles and lectures, culminating in a book on Ozick's humor (1994).

Cohen's academic work contributed greatly to the vigor of new ethnic studies programs across the country. During this time of intense public attention to the Holocaust, Cohen undertook a particular project—what he called "Preserving Yiddish and Jewish-American Culture Virtually Destroyed by the War"—first through literary-historical studies of Jewish-American performers (1987, 1991) and then by the dramatic restoration of notable "unkosher" Jewish comediennes in a series of plays on Sophie Tucker, Belle Barth, Totie Fields, and Molly Picon. *Sophie & Totie & Belle*, cowritten with Joanne Koch, was first produced in Philadelphia in 1992. Cohen's *Molly Picon's Return Engagement* was performed in such places as Syracuse University, the Empire Center in Albany, and the Philadelphia Academy (1994, 1995). *Sophie Tucker Red Hot Yiddish Mama* was mounted at Mt. Holyoke College and the Miami Jewish Museum (1995) and at Hartford and Albany (1997).

The Ladies Locker Room (1989) was collected in her anthology *Making a Scene: The Contemporary Drama of Jewish-American Women* (1997). Cohen's impetus for undertaking a strenuous double career as scholar/playwright is explored in this autobiographical play, which features Jewish-American prototypes—a young professor, an octogenarian shtetl refugee, a Hadassah socialite, and a non-Jewish expectant mother—coming "to accept their flawed beings." She sees herself using the integrative implement of humor to weave the "bits and pieces" of her life into the comic fabric of the play, no longer a "sheltered critic, set in her ways, [but] a vulnerable playwright, ready to revise and please . . . that Jewish tailor willing to make the pants longer or shorter to please the customers" ("Living and Writing" 206). The death of Cohen's brother, recognition of her need for a structure to combat discouragement and depression, a challenge from Ozick to put aside her "sober prose [to] permit herself a descent . . . into the region of the trivial" (Ozick, *Art* ix), and the encouragement of her husband, Gary, were all factors that precipitated Cohen's first play. *The Ladies Locker Room* was first staged as a benefit for Disability Services at the University of Albany and the Albany Jewish Community Center; from the proceeds, scooters for the mobility-impaired were purchased for the university, and a driveway for the handicapped was built and dedicated at the Albany Jewish Community Center in 1992.

MAJOR WORKS AND THEMES

Themes emerge in Cohen's plays around motifs of excess and lack that typify the problematics of the assimilative immigrant personality. In Cohen's adaptation of Bellow's short story "The Old System," obese Tina is the injured child who, because of maternal degradation and familial slight, is entitled to receive redress from her family. Cohen's adaptation literally "rounds out" Tina's rotundity: how it feels to carry and manage excess, *too much* appetite, sexual exuberance, verbosity, family feeling. While Tina might initially be seen as a figure of the female *vilde chaye* (wild beast), her out-of-control grabbing for denied affection and demands for proof of love exact its "pound of flesh," not from her envied brother's *blood money* as intended but from her own psychic self in the form of ravaging cancer. Cohen increases Tina's dimensionality as a forgivable Shylockian figure when the tragic effects of her negative assignment in the family system are understood retrospectively by her adult brother and cousin, who as males and favored sons must embrace their individual contributions to Tina's neediness, which shows up in her personality as megalomania.

Lack in the midst of plenitude is an emergent theme in *The Ladies Locker Room* as Cohen details Professor Susan's struggle with depression over physical clumsiness, her protective shield of being overly busy with professional endeavors, and the prospect of aborted romance and barrenness. Susan discovers in the course of the play, set in a Jewish community center where the women disrobe and reassemble themselves for the street, that the lack she perceives in herself exists in the *black hole* memories of the other women as well. This play also challenges the absoluteness of the term *childless*; each of the females in the communal spirit of the locker room finds the chutzpah to assist the character facing an obstetrical emergency in giving birth, thereby rebirthing her own feelings of self-worth by the play's end.

The "performer plays" that follow illustrate the restorative power of the performative through a humor that derives from overstatement. The theme of too much exuberance continues in the larger-than-Hartford, Connecticut, larger-than-the-stage character of Sophie Tucker, whose public role precluded child care of her son. Despite stage jokes about being a "runaway mother," Tucker's name did become synonymous with her theme song, "The Yiddishe Mama," exemplifying what Cohen calls "the art of verbal retrieval" (*Jewish Wry* 5), the discrepancy at the heart of Jewish humor that allows one, at least for the moment, to conquer, enjoy, and exploit the state of simultaneously having both everything and nothing at all.

The eloquence of lack is apparent in the monologue Cohen supplies Totie Fields in a tour de force audition in heaven with Tucker and Belle Barth. In the

style of Cyrano's monologue, Fields digresses on the advantages of her prosthetic leg (the leg and a breast were lost as her health declined following cosmetic surgery). Beyond this bravado, however, she discovers real plenitude in
the prospect of female solidarity, where lack and excess get balanced by the
mutual contributions of the women. Totie announces this communal route to
wholeness: "There's just one act here. We go as a group, or not at all" (*Sophie
and Totie and Belle* 62).

The plays underscore the communal solidarity that is the gift of Yiddish
culture, with its rich lore of contentious striving but ultimately loyal family love.
Molly Picon's career illustrates the gift's ironic twists and unexpected turns but
at the same time assures that it offers a narrative for full and broad human
development. The husband–wife team eventually enters a less evenly matched,
but profoundly fertile, period for the development and sharing of their independent talents. Picon moves beyond her typecasting as the Yiddish ingenue,
playing the stage roles denied to her in her earlier married and stage life. As
female adapter of plays by males (Singer and Bellow), collaborator with her
partner Joanne Koch, and independent playwright, Cohen's career movement,
like Picon's, slopes toward the flexible give-and-take of interdependence. Furthermore, this narrative push toward fuller personal development and sounding
of individual talent through multiple modes of expression, in Cohen's hands as
she works out the Molly Picon retrospective, manages to be quite highly culturally specific to the coming-of-age experiences of the Jewish-American female.
In terms of general audience reception, however, the appeal of her plays is
consummately cross-cultural as well.

CRITICAL RECEPTION

Cohen's dramatic efforts have received praise from local reviewers, the Jewish
press, and colleagues in the field of Jewish-American literature. Critics have
noted the vibrancy of Cohen's dramatic situations. Clearly, the "old system"
is "a world Cohen found personally palpable, and so she injected the play with
the kinds of humorous dialogue she knew from experience would fit just right"
(Reda 1). She has been singled out for her ability to milk the humor and richness
of the *mamaloshen*, a matter of "hearing the voices" (Ozick letter) and sensing
the comedic possibility in her primary materials. "Cohen, a scholar of comedy,
dwelled on those scenes, those funny juxtapositions" (K. Cohen 4).

Cohen's negotiation of her role as adapter for the stage is another area of
comment, including self-comment. "Animating" interiority (Kennedy letter) is
the challenge that Cohen sets for herself, and she repeatedly meets this dramatic
requirement by utilizing a self-reflective narrator as a character. Despite taking
liberties with the text to creatively supply what she imagines to be her characters' dark or comic aspects, she has consistently received praise for her veracity
to the original text.

BIBLIOGRAPHY

Works by Sarah Blacher Cohen

Drama

Dates in parentheses refer to dates of performance.
Schlemiel the First. (1984).
The Ladies Locker Room. (1989).
Cowritten with Joanne Koch. *Sophie Tucker Red Hot Yiddish Mama.* (1991).
Cowritten with Joanne Koch. *Sophie & Totie & Belle.* (1992).
The Old System (adaptation). (1993).
Cowritten with Joanne Koch. *Belle.* (1994).
Molly Picon's Return Engagement. (1994).
Cowritten with Joanne Koch. *Soul Sisters* (1998).

Books

Saul Bellow's Enigmatic Laughter. Urbana: University of Illinois Press, 1974.
Cynthia Ozick's Comic Art: From Levity to Liturgy. Bloomington: Indiana University Press, 1994.

Edited Works

Comic Relief: Humor in Contemporary American Literature. Urbana: University of Illinois Press, 1978.
From Hester Street to Hollywood: The Jewish-American Stage and Screen. Bloomington: Indiana University Press, 1983.
Jewish Wry: Essays on Jewish Humor. Bloomington: Indiana University Press, 1987.
Making a Scene: The Contemporary Drama of Jewish-American Women. Syracuse, NY: Syracuse University Press, 1997.
Essays on Cynthia Ozick. Syracuse, NY: Syracuse University Press, 1998.
The Drama of the Physically Challenged. Syracuse, NY: Syracuse University Press, 1998.

Works about Sarah Blacher Cohen

Capewell, George. "A Musical on Three Funny Ladies." *Miami Herald*, February 18, 1993.
Cohen, Kate. "Saul Bellow on Stage Keys Some Local History." (rev. of *The Old System*). *The Jewish World*, March 18, 1993.
Cohn, Robert. "Humor Triumphs over Despair in *Ladies' Locker Room*." *St. Louis Jewish Light*, May 30, 1990.
Personal interview with Sarah Blacher Cohen. Albany, NY, July 26, 1996 (unpublished).
Kennedy, Bill. "Letter to Sarah Cohen." Averill Park, NY, August 20, 1993.
Ozick, Cynthia. *Art and Ardor.* New York: Alfred A. Knopf, 1983.
———. "Letter to Sarah Cohen." New York, April 1, 1993.
———. "Living and Writing the Jewish-American Play: The Ladies Locker Room." *Studies in American Jewish Literature*, Fall 1992: 204–14.
Reda, Vinny. "Sarah and Saul." *Update, the University at Albany.* 1993.
Sklarew, Myra. "Letter to Sarah Cohen." Washington, DC, Spring 1993.

JULES FEIFFER   (1929–   )

Herbert Liebman

BIOGRAPHY

Jules Ralph Feiffer was born in New York City on January 26, 1929. Educated at James Monroe High School, the Art Students League, and the Pratt Institute, he served as a graphics artist in the U.S. Army from 1951 to 1953. In 1956 he joined the *Village Voice* as a cartoonist, his work eventually becoming syndicated to enormous popularity, both in the United States and abroad. He married Judith Sheftel in 1961 and was divorced in 1983, when he married Jennifer Allen. He is the father of two daughters, one from each marriage.

Feiffer is primarily known as a cartoonist of superb satirical insights, wickedly dissecting our concerns with psychoanalysis, sexual politics, race relations, political chicanery, and the general, absurd events that emerge in the day-to-day effort to simply survive. What is less known, however, is that Feiffer is also a novelist, having published three works of fiction, and a screenwriter with four feature film credits. In addition, Feiffer is a prolific playwright and stated in an interview in 1991 (Holden) that he prefers playwriting to "almost anything," anything, that is, except his desire to become a "novelist," claiming that his principal influences were Dostoyevsky and Freud. Nonetheless, always self-critical, Feiffer admitted that he lacked the prose facility to become a novelist, noting that as a "novelist you have to know what's about you and describe it." With typical Feiffer wit, he then observed that he doesn't "know anything" that is occurring around him and, besides, lacks the literary skills "to describe things very well" (DiGaetani 57).

MAJOR WORKS AND THEMES

Interestingly, there is a direct correspondence between Feiffer's cartoons and the conception and construction of his plays. If one examines Feiffer's cartoons, they are, in effect, minisatiric dramas, brief dialogues or monologues infused with surgical wit that slices deeply into the center of personal, social, and political turmoil. Within the panels, the pacing and ultimate epiphany of the characters produce dramatic effects that Feiffer has readily translated onto the stage. Moreover, as in his cartoons, Feiffer's principal thematic interest in his plays is to dramatically exploit his satiric skills upon the public and private concerns of American society—concerns that stretch from the political deception and criminal behavior of U.S. government officials, including the president, in *The White House Murder Case* (1970), to the analysis of the smothering psychological effects of Jewish family life in *Grown Ups* (1987), to an examination of gender warfare and sexual mores in *Carnal Knowledge* (1988; originally produced as a film in 1971) and *Eliot Loves* (1990).

Feiffer's technique, which is trenchant and compelling as a cartoonist, does not always work successfully as a dramatist, for his interest is often more in exposing the absurdity of the situation than in the development and exploration of theme and character. If one looks at *Feiffer's People*, originally published in 1967, the various, brief dramatic sketches like ''1st Woman—2nd Woman'' or ''Young Man and Older Man Seated at Cafe Table'' or ''Dancer'' that constitute the work can easily be transcribed, almost word for word, to the panels of a cartoon for inclusion in a newspaper. This is, for the most part, central to Feiffer's strength and weakness as a playwright. Like his cartoons, his plays are examinations of bizarre and ludicrous situations that are initially explosively humorous, but the problem is sustaining such humor on the stage without the play's descending into a one-joke situation. Apparently, throughout his career, Feiffer has been aware of this danger and has employed a wide variety of techniques, some successful, some not so successful, in constructing his plays so that the work develops beyond the bounds of its cartoon conception. Indeed, in certain plays, particularly in his charming and hilarious review on loneliness in the city, *Hold Me* (1977), Feiffer has managed to translate directly onto the stage his cartoon structure into a series of witty and tight sketches and vignettes. This form of free and liquid structure, minimalist and almost Brechtian in execution, may very well be the best dramatic medium for Feiffer's particular talent.

In Feiffer's first produced play, *Crawling Arnold* (1961), its central character, Arnold, a thirty-five-year-old sibling, takes to crawling along the floor in jealous reaction to his two-year-old brother. Arnold, fearful of his own sexual inadequacy, is actually reacting to the sexual potency of his seventy-year-old parents, mindless white liberals who are obsessed with obeying the law. In addition, the play aims satirically at a wide variety of targets, including bomb shelters, inept social workers, and unfocused black rage—Millie, the black maid, demonstrates for separate, but equal, bomb shelters. The situation of the play would work very well as a cartoon, but as drama it is difficult to sustain, partly because Arnold's crawling is appropriate for the swift processing of cartoon humor but not the sustained length of a play, even a brief, one-act play. The inclusion of the other targets, now almost all dated, tends to pad the comedy rather than to expand its conception and develop its characters—or even to comment intelligently upon its central significance, if there is a central significance. Arnold, like his parents, Barry and Grace, like Millie the maid, like the social worker, Miss Sympathy, is one-dimensional, and once the joke is understood, the play in its thinness suffers.

In Feiffer's next work, his most celebrated play, *Little Murders* (produced in 1967), there is considerably more effort at dramatic construction and character development, although this play, like *Crawling Arnold*, retains a cartoonlike conception of both character and situation. *Little Murders* is an absurdist and savage attack upon the predatory and pathological structure of the family itself as well as its surrounding urban environment, a loony milieu of random violence. The characters are all Feiffer cartoons, but drawn with considerable wit and scorching savagery: the gay-bashing father, Carol Newquist, who cannot stand to be called by his first name because of its effeminate connotations; the masculine and manipulative daughter, Patsy, who is murdered at the end, apparently to no one's particular distress, certainly not her family's; the equally manipulative and hostile mother, Marjorie, who operates behind a veneer of decorous behavior; the fragile and bookish son, Kenny, who explodes with homicidal glee as he and his father fire rifles into the streets; and Patsy's curious fiancé, a photographer, Alfred Chamberlain, who now takes photographs only of things, particularly excrement, having completely lost his interest in humanity.

Perhaps the funniest creation in the play is the hippie clergyman, Henry Dupas, who arrives to marry Patsy and Alfred and preaches a wild sermon that condones the use of hallucinogenic drugs, divorce, and even infidelity because "any step one takes is useful . . . is positive, because it is a part of life" (*Little Murders* 39). Martin Esslin, who praised the play, nevertheless called it a "three-dimensional Feiffer strip cartoon." Intruding into this family's situation are intermittent, obscene phone calls—heavy breathing—and the ever-present street noise—construction, traffic, the drone of helicopters.

Finally, Patsy is killed by a stray bullet through the window, and the family arms itself and begins firing back onto the street, much to Mrs. Newquist's delight. In fact, only by participating in the carnage does the Newquist family redeem itself as cohesive in this very dark and upside-down world. After the gun battle, at the very end of the play, Marjorie Newquist observes: "It's so nice to have my family laughing again. You know for a while I was really worried" (*Little Murders* 63). Feiffer's not-too-subtle point is hammered home, as his vision of our urban society disintegrates into pathological violence.

Little Murders, incidentally, had an interesting history. In 1967 it failed after one week on Broadway but later that year was produced at the Royal Shakespeare Company to generally favorable reviews and won the London critics' prize for best foreign play. It resurfaced two years later in New York City in a successful off-Broadway production, earning both an Obie and an Outer Circle Drama Critics Award, and was also produced as a feature film.

An excellent example of Feiffer's talent for probing a specific, unfolding political event upon the stage is *The White House Murder Case*. This is clearly the political cartoon transformed into absurdist drama. Produced in 1970, the principal target here is the ongoing Vietnam conflict, as well as the U.S. government's vicious propaganda efforts at justifying the war.

In Feiffer's play, the United States is now fighting an insurrection in Brazil— instead of slaughtering the Vietcong, we're engaged in eliminating Chicos. An accidental use of nerve gas—a weapon that was not even supposed to be in Brazil—has gone awry and kills 750 American troops. The play then situates itself in the White House as the president and his cabinet determine what lie to tell the American people about their butchery of their own soldiers. However, the president's wife, Mrs. Hale, is for peace and denounces the practice of lying. To save the government from what is viewed simply as a potential embarrassment, should Mrs. Hale expose what actually occurred, Stiles, the postmaster general, conveniently kills her with a placard bearing the message "Make Love Not War" (*The White House Murder Case* 51). The murderer, for not confessing to the crime, is rewarded with the post of secretary of state by the president. Thus, one lie covers another in the putrescent matrix of governmental officialdom, and criminal behavior, even murder, is richly rewarded. The very soul of the U.S. government is itself exposed as spiritually and hopelessly venal—an entity that is incapable of ever communicating the simple truth. Moreover, the play, in the timely context of official fabrications like the Gulf of Tonkin incident and the My Lai massacre, must have struck audiences with chilling and macabre relevance.

CRITICAL RECEPTION

The critical reaction to Feiffer's plays has been predictably mixed. Although a considerable number of influential critics have warmly praised his efforts— critics like Frank Rich, Mel Gussow, Stephen Holden, Edith Oliver, and John Lahr—they often include in their praise a caveat underlining the playwright's theatrical weaknesses. For example, Stephen Holden notes that Feiffer's play *Grown Ups*, a play that he admires, is nevertheless not "grandly designed drama, but rather a series of connected sketches that omit much important information." Interestingly, Frank Rich, however, sees the same weakness as "Strindbergian verve," which demands that the audience must follow "kicking and questioning if need be." John Lahr, in commenting on *The White House Murder Case*, notes that "Feiffer's satire is more literary than theatrical. He embraces the grotesque but he does not extend it into a theatrical style"(107). Perhaps the most interesting piece of criticism is Martin Esslin's comments on the London production of *Little Murders* in 1967. Esslin, who admired the play with reservations, muses, nevertheless, on why it failed in New York and succeeded in the U.K. Curiously, his explanation is much more cultural and political than aesthetic. He believes that the English, both "Left wingers and true-blue

Tories,'' delighted in seeing the United States unravel in bloody mayhem. As a result of the recent race riots in Cleveland and Buffalo in 1967—riots that were widely covered on British television—the London audience found the satire ''enjoyable'' because it was ''directed against vices'' that were, they believed, uniquely American. The play, regardless of its lack of theatrical merits, reassured the English audience that the United States was on its way to ''a holocaust of bloodshed.''

Finally, Feiffer is very much a Jewish-American playwright, even though the word ''Jew'' infrequently appears in his plays. Like an earlier generation of Jewish writers like Roth, Malamud, and Bellow, Feiffer examines through his sophisticated and witty lens the same Jewish concerns; unlike the same writers, however, Feiffer often does not identify his characters as Jewish. Cynthia Ozick, in her recent collection of essays, *Fame and Folly* (New York: Alfred A. Knopf, 1996), observed that Jewish writers are those who are in the world and simultaneously judge its worldliness. Feiffer is always there, very much in the center of what is occurring and of what is trendy, very much an inhabitant and simultaneous moral observer of experience. He has, to some extent, submerged his Jewish identity, perhaps in the desire to penetrate more deeply into the larger culture, but his urban Jewish wit and sophistication, whether or not explicitly identified, invariably flash sharply into focus.

For example, in the play *Grown Ups*, a play that explores the dynamics of Jewish family life, particularly in the relationship between the overachiever son Jake, a successful reporter for the *New York Times*, and his curiously insensitive parents, Helen and Jack, the word ''Jew'' never appears. Jake's recent interview of Henry Kissinger fails to impress his parents because Kissinger has not yet interviewed Jake. This is classic Jewish humor in depicting the impossibility of the child, no matter how important his accomplishments, of ever winning full or even partial parental appreciation. Indeed, all the characters in *Grown Ups* are manifestly New York City Jews, but they are never explicitly identified as such. Feiffer himself, in an interview with the playwright Christopher Durang, referred to Helen and Jack in *Grown Ups* as his own ''parents,'' characters who were ''conventional'' Jews (13).

In a sense, this particular focus, the ability to be within and without simultaneously, is Feiffer's greatest achievement as both a cartoonist and a playwright. He holds a mirror up for us to observe ourselves and others in the midst of a wide range of personal and political turmoil. Cushioned by his wit and the clarity of his focus, we see the frequent absurdity and cruelty of human behavior, including our own; and, although we laugh at the humor, we also cry, perhaps quietly, at the ugly truths Feiffer exposes.

BIBLIOGRAPHY

Works by Jules Feiffer

Crawling Arnold. New York: Dramatists Play Service, 1963.
Feiffer's People. New York: Dramatists Play Service, 1967.
The White House Murder Case. New York: Samuel French, 1970.
Knock, Knock. New York: Samuel French, 1976.
Hold Me. New York: Dramatists Play Service, 1977.
Little Murders. New York: Samuel French, 1986.
Grown Ups. New York: Samuel French, 1987.
Carnal Knowledge. New York: Dramatists Play Service, 1988. (Now available only in manuscript from Dramatists Play Service.)
Eliot Loves. New York: Grove, 1990.

Works about Jules Feiffer

DiGaetani, John L. *A Search for a Postmodern Theater: Interviews with Contemporary Playwrights*. Westport, CT: Greenwood, 1991. 56–63.
Durang, Christopher. "Jules Feiffer, Cartoonist-Playwright." *Dramatists Guild Quarterly* 23, Winter 1987. 8–17.
Esslin, Martin. "A Strike for Murders." *New York Times*, July 23, 1967: C5.
Gussow, Mel. "Still Nasty after All These Years." *New York Times*, November 21, 1990: C15.
Holden, Stephen. "Feiffer's Family Cauldron, 10 Years Old But Fresh." *New York Times*, January 24, 1991: C18.
Kerr, Walter. "They Might Have Made It." *New York Times*, June 4, 1967: D23.
Lahr, John. "Jules Feiffer and Sam Shepard: Spectacles of Disintegration." *Astonish Me: Adventures in Contemporary Theater*. New York: Viking, 1973. 103–7.
Oliver, Edith. "The Theatre: Love and Laughter." *The New Yorker*, June, 18, 1990. 67.
Rich, Frank. "Grown Ups by Feiffer." *New York Times*, December 11, 1981: C3.
———. "Little Murders, Jules Feiffer's 60's Satire." *New York Times*, May 7, 1987: C22.
Weales, Gerald. "Jules Ralph Feiffer." *Contemporary Dramatists*. Ed. K. A. Berney. London: St. James Press, 1993. 176–77.
Whitfield, Stephen. "Jules Feiffer and the Comedy of Disenchantment." *Hester Street to Hollywood: The Jewish American Stage and Screen*. Ed. Sarah Blacher Cohen. Bloomington: Indiana University Press, 1983. 167–81.

HARVEY FIERSTEIN   (1954–)

Ben Furnish

BIOGRAPHY

Harvey Forbes Fierstein was born June 6, 1954, in Brooklyn, New York, where he and his brother, Ronald, grew up in the Bensonhurst area. Fierstein's father, Irving, a handkerchief manufacturer, married his mother, Jacqueline (née Gilbert), a public school librarian, when she was nineteen, and he twenty-nine. Their marriage lasted thirty-three years until his death.

Fierstein began performing as a female impersonator at a Lower East Side club as a teenager (at 270 pounds, his specialty was Ethel Merman). He recalls his ''triple life'' at the time, nights at the club, living at home with his parents, and going to school full-time. He won his first theatrical role in a 1971 Andy Warhol production, *Pork*, at La Mama Experimental Theatre Club, playing the lead character: an overweight, asthmatic, lesbian maid.

Fierstein earned a B.F.A. in painting from Pratt Institute in 1973. His mother and father encouraged Harvey toward art education because teachers have some flexibility in their schedules compared to many occupations, but his mother recalled that Fierstein lasted exactly one day as a teacher in the Brooklyn school where she worked.

Torch Song Trilogy, which catapulted Fierstein to fame, is substantially autobiographical. The protagonist, Arnold Beckhoff, is, like Fierstein, a gay, Jewish drag performer who has, as Fierstein did, an on-again, off-again relationship with a schoolteacher who leaves him for a woman. Theatrically, the play grew out of Fierstein's work with La Mama, where it first appeared as three separately written and produced one-acts: *The International Stud* (1978), *Fugue in a Nursery* (1979), and *Widows and Children First!* (1979). *Widows* contains one of Fierstein's other best-remembered characters: Mrs. Beckhoff, Arnold's mother, who is, as Fierstein and others have described her, "the typical Jewish mother." Mrs. Beckhoff, however, appears to be a more fictional character than Arnold. Fierstein's mother said she didn't mind being compared to Mrs. Beckhoff: "She's very funny. . . . But I never thought of myself as that character" (Bernstein 100)—she thought Fierstein's expressive grandmother Bertha Gilbert may have partially inspired Mrs. Beckhoff but that the character is "universal." Neither she nor Fierstein speaks of his experiencing the same vocal disapproval from his family that Mrs. Beckhoff displays toward Arnold. Fierstein told his family he was gay when he was thirteen: "There was no screaming or crying in my presence. I was what I was and it wasn't a family decision" (Clarke). "We were brought up with the feeling that the family unit was everything, and something as minuscule as my being gay was not going to disrupt that," Fierstein recalls (Kakutani).

Despite good reviews, Fierstein was unable to find a producer to fund staging the entire trilogy until the Glines, a gay arts organization, agreed to take on the project in 1981. That successful off-off-Broadway production moved off-Broadway, then to Broadway, where it ran for over two years. His next play, the stage adaptation of *La Cage aux Folles*, ran four years on Broadway.

Fierstein has won the Obie (1982); two Tonys for *Torch Song*, writing and acting (1983) and for *La Cage aux Folles*, best musical and best book for a musical (1984); Oppenheimer Award (1983); Drama Desk Award (1983, for writing and acting); Dramatists Guild Hull-Warriner Award (1983); Los Angeles Drama Critics Circle Award (1984); Fund for Human Dignity Award (1983); and Awards for Cable Excellence (ACE) awards for best writing and best dramatic special for *Tidy Endings* (1988). Other awards include the Association of Comedy Artists; Theater World; Brooklyn Walk of Fame plaque; grants from Rockefeller Foundation, CAPS (Creative Artists Public Service), Ford Foundation, and the Public Broadcasting Service.

Fierstein has not written for the stage since 1988, but his performing career continues to flourish. Notable among his more than seventy stage appearances are his lead performances in a 1991 revival of Robert Patrick's *The Haunted Host* and *Pouf Positive*. Film performances include *Garbo Talks* (1983); *Apology* (1986); his own *Torch Song Trilogy* (1988); *Mrs. Doubtfire* (1993); *The Harvest* (1993); *Bullets over Broadway* (1994); *Dr. Jekyll and Ms. Hyde* (1995); *Independence Day* (1996); *Kull the Conqueror* (1997); narration for the documentary *The Times of Harvey Milk* (1984) and appearance in the documentary *The Celluloid Closet* (1996); such television roles as his own *Tidy Endings* (1988); *In the Shadow of Love: A Teen AIDS Story* (1991); a regular role in the series *Daddy's Girls* and guest appearances on *Cheers* (received Emmy nomination), *The Simpsons*, *Murder She Wrote*, *Miami Vice*, *Loving*, *Politically Incorrect*, "Swellegant Elegance" (a PBS Cole Porter tribute special), and *Sesame Street*. His 1995 album *This Is Not Going to Be Pretty*, a live recording of his one-man act, combines songs and stand-up, autobiographical humor.

Describing himself as "a performer, not an actor," Fierstein credits Red Skelton, Zero Mostel, Ethel Eichelberg, and other "great clowns" as influencing his performing style (Horwitz 19). Fierstein also has said that his humor was shaped by the gay sensibility of growing up learning to understand how he doesn't fit into the dominant society: "It's a humor based on seeing the opposite—which is also very Jewish" (Kakutani).

Fierstein has maintained a high public profile through frequent television talk show and news appearances. Whether in his famous 1992 Bennington College commencement address, which, among other things, affirmed his identity as a gay man, a Jew, and a radical, or at the nationally televised Tony Awards when he shocked many viewers by publicly thanking his lover, Fierstein has refused to apologize for, or conceal, who he is. Meeting controversy with disarming flamboyance, he has recast themes and images familiar to previous Jewish-American dramatists in a way that has won admission of openly, affirmatively gay dramatists, issues, and characters to the mainstream American theatre.

MAJOR WORKS AND THEMES

The most conspicuous central theme common to Fierstein's major plays is the search for love and family commitment. He depicts this theme in all its major aspects: sex, courtship, marriage, parenthood—and mature self-love. His treatment of this highly traditional theme is revolutionary because he explores each aspect from a gay perspective, which, in turn, reflects two other major themes: the Other (usually the gay man, often the Jew) vis-à-vis the dominant society and the Other's use of humor to see the self as normal in the face of what it finds the dominant society's abnormality. *Torch Song Trilogy* is proto-typical in all three themes, and although his search for love and family com-mitment is not explicitly Jewish, Arnold's (and Fierstein's) view of this theme reflects his desire to perpetuate his own family's positive, nurturing qualities.

Torch Song's Arnold Beckhoff opens the play with a monologue reflecting on his as-yet-unsuccessful search for love. While Fierstein shows sex as a nec-essary part of Arnold's search, as it is for the characters in *Safe Sex* and *Forget Him*, sex alone cannot stretch to fill the need for every other aspect of love and family commitment. Arnold learns this when loneliness and sexual need drive him to visit the International Stud bar's back room. The result is a hilariously unsatisfactory, anonymous sexual encounter that leaves Arnold searching for love as before. *Forget Him*'s Michael learns that he doesn't really want to leave Eugene, despite Michael's fear of missing an even more all-perfect sexual part-ner ("Him") out there somewhere. In *Safe Sex*'s first two plays, two couples must look beyond sex for a different reason: the threat of AIDS.

Several Fierstein protagonists search for a mutually committed, loving, lasting relationship; in such courtship, they confront a significant obstacle: fear. *Torch Song*'s Ed, a bisexual teacher, backs away from Arnold precisely because of their compatibility. Scared of who he is, Ed leaves Arnold for Laurel, a woman whom he marries. Arnold then meets Alan, an eighteen-year-old model tired of men who just use him for sex. Alan's fear of Ed's place in Arnold's past causes Alan to seduce Ed. In *Safe Sex*, the fastidious Ghee fears AIDS—and Mead's poor hygiene generally. *Forget Him*'s Michael fears that there may be a more perfect mate for him than Eugene. Characters must learn that their love is what matters, not the fear, before their courtship can lead to marriage.

Commitment, not legal status, defines *marriage* in Fierstein's work, and by that standard, *La Cage aux Folle*'s George and Albin, who in over twenty faithful years together have raised son Jean-Michel, are as married as any couple ever on the stage. By that standard, Arthur (in *On Tidy Endings*, the third play in *Safe Sex*) claims legitimate rights as surviving spouse to Collin, whom he nursed through AIDS. As Arthur reminds Collin's ex-wife Marion: "I paid in full for my place in his life and I will *not* share it with you" (69).

Likewise, commitment, love, and respect determine family and parental relationship, not mere blood. Arnold earns parental status to David in *Torch Song*, and Arnold must tell his own mother, in the face of her disapproval of his gay identity: "You are my mother, and I love you. I do. But if you can't respect me . . . you've got no business being here" (152). Albin earns his "maternal" relationship to Jean-Michel doubly during *La Cage* when he does what Jean-Michel's birth mother refuses to do: show up to meet the parents of Jean-Michel's fiancée, Anne. In *Spookhouse*, Connie must reject her own son Wayne; he nullifies his rights as a family member by seducing his sister and committing other sociopathic acts.

Mature self-love, which empowers honesty, overpowers fear, and demands respect, is Fierstein's sine qua non for an authentic ability to love others. At *Torch Song*'s end, Arnold, Ed, and David can have a future as a family because each has learned to love himself and thus find freedom to care for others. In *La Cage*, Albin personifies mature self-love as he sings Jerry Herman's song, "I Am What I Am." In *Spookhouse*, social worker Sam cannot help his clients because he displays more embarrassment than self-respect. His generosity toward them quickly turns to victimization of them.

In Fierstein's plays, the Other, whether gay man or Jew, must confront the dominant society rather than being segregated from it. Arnold as a gay man finds himself competing with, then consoling, the heterosexual Laurel. Then he must defend himself gamely against his mother's scorn at his open gayness and his adoption of David.

When Ed first meets Arnold, he finds exotic appeal in Arnold's Jewish features and claims surprise (as though complimenting Arnold) that he is Jewish, not Italian or Spanish. When Arnold and Alan visit Ed and Laurel at the latter's country house, Arnold disappoints Laurel's assumption that he will attend church with them. He keeps awkwardly making jokes, to Alan's chagrin, as she presses him on the point. Fortune-teller Connie Janik in *Spookhouse* feigns surprise to learn that Sam Wilbur is gay: "I just thought you were Jewish" (58). She sees how she can make him uncomfortable; then Sam learns how he can make her uncomfortable when he asks why his friendship threatens her. She replies that the dirtiest word in the language is "Yid." She is, as it turns out, a Jew whose non-Jewish husband's family only reluctantly accepted her. Perhaps trusting Sam as a fellow outsider, Connie does not banish him as she did all her other social workers, but he unjustly threatens her with the dominant society's laws until she must flee her own home.

Fierstein spells out the relation between Jewish and gay perspectives most explicitly when David remarks to Ed that he didn't understand why one of the first things Arnold did when David moved in was to show him the spot where Alan was killed by gay bashers until—

About a week later we were watchin' the news on T.V. and there was this protest march; a bunch of Jews marchin' against Nazis. They had these signs that said, "Never Again" and "We Remember." And I looked over at Arnold and he was like cryin' real soft, and just like that I connected. I knew why he showed me this. (153)

In Fierstein's plays, Otherness is not terminal alienation. His gay protagonists use humor to reconfigure normalcy, thereby obliterating misconceptions that the dominant society uses to discredit gay legitimacy. In *La Cage* (as in Fierstein's early, unproduced *Cannibals Just Don't Know Better*), Jean-Michel's gay parents must cope with the tragedy that he is marrying a woman. The play's central source of humor lies in George's and Albin's conventionality as a couple in every respect but their gayness. *Forget Him* is a Jewish folktale with a twist: Michael seeks out a matchmaker to find his ideal man, whom he meets at a synagogue, no less. The third plays in *Torch Song* and *Safe Sex* display the conventional structures of romantic and domestic comedy, which contrast humorously with the plays' departure from convention in depicting gay relationships. But the humor serves not to ridicule but to validate gay (and other) relationships.

CRITICAL RECEPTION

Torch Song Trilogy is Fierstein's greatest achievement onstage. Not only was it a trailblazer as Broadway's first affirmatively gay-theme play, but it was also a leading play of the 1980s. Don Shewey sees *Torch Song*'s appearance as professional theatre's intersection with the hitherto noncommercial gay theatre movement. Almost all commercial reviewers, including Mel Gussow, Clive Barnes, Stanley Kauffmann, and even John Simon, praised the play highly. A conspicuous exception was Walter Kerr, who described Fierstein's humor as self-mockery that blocked any sympathy that Kerr might have had for Arnold. Fierstein has taken exception with some critics' conclusions that *Torch Song* is a universal, rather than a gay, play. That struggle between the particular experience of a group and universal experience of humanity is also a familiar one for Jewish writers. Frances Gray notes Fierstein's place in what she calls the New York Jewish tradition by his self-reflexive humor "whereby you disarm your adversaries by insulting yourself before they can do it'' (320). Gray and almost every other critic noted *Torch Song*'s evocations of the stereotypical Jewish mother, whether through Arnold's mother or Arnold himself. John Simon, in recalling Kenneth Tynan's adage that American theatre's two main types of humor are the Jewish and the homosexual, praised *Torch Song*'s successful crossbreeding of the two.

Some gay critics, such as John Clum, express disappointment in *Torch Song*, particularly its concluding act, because its gay relationships follow traditional heterosexual patterns too closely. When *Torch Song* was filmed in 1988, some critics concluded that AIDS—the play predates the epidemic—had rendered play and film dated, even though the play's affirmation of gay life is otherwise intact.

For William Green, *Torch Song*'s use of comedy as commentary casts Fierstein as an heir to those dramatists (e.g., Neil Simon, Ossie Davis, Sam Shepherd) who have used bittersweet comedy to allow audiences to identify with ''the lonely, isolated, alien, or oppressed individual in American society'' (218).

La Cage aux Folles received wide attention as the first Broadway musical to showcase a gay relationship. But critics were shocked not by the show's daring but by its tameness. Howard Kissel recalled Hugh Southern's theory that the predominantly Jewish creators of the classic Broadway musicals prior to *Fiddler on the Roof* felt compelled to avoid overtly Jewish subjects; Kissel felt that *La Cage aux Folles* was *Fiddler*'s equivalent for the 1980s musical theatre's ''predominantly homosexual'' major figures.

Spookhouse, unfortunately, has yet to attract sustained study or comment, except for a lukewarm reception from Edith Oliver.

Critics have noted *Safe Sex*'s structural similarities with *Torch Song*, another trilogy of one-acts that moved from nonrepresentationalist to realist styles to depict contemporary gay life. Gregory Gross groups *Safe Sex* with two other AIDS plays by Jewish playwrights (William Hoffman's *As Is* and Larry Kramer's *The Normal Heart*). Gross finds in each work reverberations of the Holocaust (e.g., in *Safe Sex*, he notes characters' reluctance to call themselves survivors) and Jewish and other forms of humor used as what Auschwitz survivor Victor Frankl calls the ''soul's weapons . . . for self-preservation'' (Gross 66).

Legs Diamond underwhelmed Broadway critics. Fierstein's decision to render Legs as more aspiring entertainer than gangster was not enough to inspire sympathy for Legs. The show became legendary for its production problems even before officially opening. Fierstein was later quoted expressing regret for becoming involved with the project, which he entered late in production to revise a problematic script.

In assessing the significance of Fierstein's drama, many critics and reviewers have found the aesthetic questions are not always clearly separable from the political ones. Yet he has won admirers, as well as critics, representing a wide spectrum of social views. Fierstein has integrated gay and Jewish experiences and conventions, creating a dramatic perspective that combines humor with renewed ethical ideals of family, honesty, and self-respect.

BIBLIOGRAPHY

Works by Harvey Fierstein

Plays

In Search of the Cobra Jewels: An Archeomystorical Poeseurie (Original title: *Who's Afraid of Ellen Stewart?*). Produced at Playwrights Workshop Club at Bostiano's Studio, NY, October 4, 1972.

Flatbush Tosca: Or Fear the Painted Devil. A Comic Melodrama. Produced New York City, Theatre Ensemble, May 25, 1975.

The International Stud. New York: Samuel French, 1978. Produced La Mama Experimental Theatre, 1976.

Fugue in a Nursery. New York: Samuel French, 1979. Produced La Mama Experimental Theatre, 1979a.

Widows and Children First! New York: Samuel French, 1979. Produced La Mama Experimental Theatre, 1979b.

Torch Song Trilogy. (Includes *The International Stud, Fugue in a Nursery, Widows and Children First!*). Produced Richard Allen Center, NY, 1981. New York: Gay Presses of New York, 1981; New York: Villard Books, 1987; New York: Samuel French, 1982.

La Cage aux Folles. New York: Samuel French, 1987. Music and lyrics by Jerry Herman, from the French play by Jean Poiret. Produced Colonial Theatre, Boston, 1983.

Safe Sex. New York: Atheneum, 1987a. (Includes *Manny and Jake, Safe Sex, On Tidy Endings*). "Safe Sex" in *The Way We Live Now: American Plays and the AIDS Crisis.* Ed. M. Elizabeth Osborne. New York: Theatre Communications Group, 1990. 76–98.

Spookhouse. In *Plays International* 2, No. 12, July 1987b, 56–64. Produced at Playhouse 91, New York, 1984.

Forget Him. In *Out Front: Contemporary Gay and Lesbian Plays.* Ed. Don Shewey. New York: Grove Press, 1988a. 335–53.

Legs Diamond: The Almost Totally Fictitious Musical Hystery of Legs Diamond. With Charles Suppon; songs by Peter Allen. Produced at the Mark Hellinger Theatre, New York, December 26, 1988b.

Screenplays

Tidy Endings. Dir. Gavin Millar. Home Box Office/Sandollar, 1988a.
Torch Song Trilogy. Dir. Paul Bogart, New Line Cinema, 1988b.

Works about Harvey Fierstein

Barnes, Clive. " 'Song' of Love and Laughter" (Rev. of *Torch Song Trilogy*). *The New York Post*, July 15, 1982. Reprinted in *New York Theatre Critics Reviews* 44, No. 9, May 30–June 6, 1983, 245–46.

Bernstein, Fred A. "Wouldn't You Be Proud?" *People Weekly*, May 12, 1986, 95–102. Reprint of "Jackie Fierstein." In *The Jewish Mothers' Hall of Fame*. New York: Doubleday, 1986.

Brustein, Robert. "Musicalized Propaganda" (rev. of *La Cage aux Folles*). In *Who Needs Theatre?: Dramatic Opinions*. New York: Atlantic Monthly Press, 1987. 167–70.

Clarke, Gerald. " 'No One Opened Doors for Me': Harvey Fierstein and Torch Song Win Two Big Tonys." *Time*, June 20, 1983, 80.

Clum, John. *Acting Gay: Male Homosexuality in Modern Drama*. New York: Columbia University Press. 265–70.

Cohen, Jodi R. "Intersecting and Competing Discourses in Harvey Fierstein's *Tidy Endings*." *Quarterly Journal of Speech* 77, 1991, 196–207.

Gray, Frances. "Harvey Fierstein." In *International Dictionary of Theatre: Playwrights*. Ed. Mark Hawkins-Dady. Detroit: St. James Press, 1994. 319–21.

Green, William. *Torch Song Trilogy: A Gay Comedy with a Dying Fall. Maske und Kothurne*, 30, 217–24.

Gross, Gregory D. "Coming Up for Air: Three AIDS Plays." *Journal of American Culture* 15, Summer 1992, 63–67.

Gussow, Mel. "Fierstein's 'Torch Song.' " *New York Times*, November 1, 1981, 81.

Harty, Kevin J. " 'All the Elements of a Good Movie': Cinematic Responses to the AIDS Pandemic." In *AIDS: The Literary Response*. Ed. Emmanuel S. Nelson. New York: Twayne, 1992. 121–22.

"Harvey Fierstein." *America Online's Live Chat Session*. [http://www.plump.com/hfonline.htm].

Henry, William A. "*Legs Diamond* Shoots Blanks." *Time*, January 9, 1989, 67.

Horwitz, Simi. "The Substance of Fierstein." *TheaterWeek* 4, No. 42, May 27–June 2, 1991, 17–23.

Kakutani, Michiko. "Fierstein and 'Torch Song': A Daring Climb from Obscurity." *New York Times*, July 14, 1982, C17.

Kauffmann, Stanley. "Torch Song Trilogy" (rev.). In *Theater Criticisms*. New York: Performing Arts Journal Books, 1983. 150–51. Reprinted from *Saturday Review*, March 1982.

Kerr, Walter. " 'Torch Song Trilogy'—Self-Mockery as a Shield." *New York Times*, Section II, June 27, 1982, H3, H16.

Kissel, Howard. "Flawed 'Diamond' " (rev. of *Legs Diamond*). *New York Daily News*, December 27, 1988. Reprinted in *New York Theatre Critics' Reviews* 49, No. 18, December 31, 1988, 90–91.

———. "Hiding Behind One-Liners" (rev. of *Safe Sex*). *New York Daily News*, April 6, 1987. Reprinted in *New York Theatre Critics' Reviews* 48, No. 7, April 20–27, 1987, 301.

———. "La Cage aux Folles" (rev.). *Women's Wear Daily*, August 22, 1983. Reprinted in *New York Theatre Critics Reviews* 44, No. 11, July 11–17 1983, 190–91.

Lawson, D. S. "Harvey Fierstein." In *The Gay and Lesbian Literary Heritage*. Ed. Claude J. Summers. New York: Henry Holt, 1995, 273–74.

———. "Rage and Remembrance: The AIDS Plays." In *AIDS: The Literary Response*. Ed. Emmanuel S. Nelson. New York: Twayne, 149–51.

Oliver, Edith. "Boo!" (rev. of *Spookhouse*). *The New Yorker* 60, No. 13, May 14, 1984, 131.

Portaniere, Michael. "Carrying the Torch." *TheaterWeek* 48, No. 2, July 10–16, 1989, 33–37.

Powers, Kim. "Fragments of a Trilogy: Harvey Fierstein's 'Torch Song.' " *Theater* 14, No. 2, Spring 1983, 63–67.

Rich, Frank. "The Musical 'Cage aux Folles.' " *New York Times*, August 22, 1983, C13.

Shewey, Don. "Gay Theatre Grows Up." *American Theatre*, May 1988, 10–17, 52–53. Reprinted as "Introduction" in *Out Front: Contemporary Gay and Lesbian Plays*. Ed. Don Shewey. New York: Grove Press, 1988. xi–xxvii.

Simon, John. "Addled Adaptations" (rev. of *Torch Song Trilogy*). *National Review*, March 24, 1989, 46–48.

———. "The Gay Desperado." *New York Magazine* 14, No. 49, 1981, 110–11.

———. "Playing It Safe" (rev. of *Safe Sex*). *New York*, April 20, 1987, 66–67.

Stein, Harry. "Playboy Interview: Harvey Fierstein." *Playboy* 35, No. 8, August 1988, 43–57.

Stone, Peter. "Landmark Symposium: *Torch Song Trilogy.*" *Dramatists Guild Quarterly* 20, No. 4, 1984, 13–25. Reprinted in *Broadway Song and Story: Playwrights/ Lyricists/Composers Discuss Their Hits*. Ed. Otis L. Guernsey. New York: Dodd, Mead, 1985. 151–62.

"Torch Song Trilogy." *Film Review Annual 1989*. New York: Jerome S. Ozer, 1989. 1466–73.

HERB GARDNER   (1934–   )

Andrea Most

BIOGRAPHY

Herb Gardner is best known for his early Broadway comedy *A Thousand Clowns* (1962), later made into a movie starring Jason Robards, and his more recent work *I'm Not Rappaport* (1985) and *Conversations with My Father* (1992). Primarily a comic writer, Gardner in his plays focuses on nonconformist or eccentric New Yorkers whose fantasy worlds serve as a shield against the harsher realities of their lives. Gardner's work has often been compared with Neil Simon's, although a darker strain in his writing distinguishes it from Simon's celebratory sentimentality.

Herb Gardner was born December 28, 1934, in Brooklyn, New York. Gardner's plays have a distinctly New York sensibility, clearly informed by the neighborhoods in which he was raised (primarily the Coney Island area and the Lower East Side) and the diverse spectrum of characters whom he encountered during his childhood. He attended the High School of the Performing Arts in New York, graduating in 1952, and went on to Carnegie Institute of Technology in Pittsburgh and Antioch College in Yellow Springs, Ohio, to study sculpture and drama, but he soon returned to New York to live and work. In 1957, he married the actress Rita Gardner.

Like his character Arthur in *The Goodbye People*, Gardner originally intended to become a sculptor but found himself employed instead designing nativity scenes for the Bliss Display Company. After being fired for "making cross-eyed wise men" (*New York Times*, June 2, 1985, 2: 4), Gardner briefly became a cartoonist, creating the relatively successful "Nebbishes" syndicated strip. Determined to become a playwright, however, he left cartooning for the Broadway stage and enjoyed immediate success with his first play, *A Thousand*

Clowns. This was followed by *The Goodbye People* (1968), starring Milton Berle and directed by Gardner himself; *Thieves* (1974); *I'm Not Rappaport*, which starred Judd Hirsch and Cleavon Little and won the 1986 Tony Award for Best Play, the Outer Critics Circle Award for Outstanding Play, and the John Gassner Playwriting Award; and *Conversations with My Father*, which garnered the Best Actor Tony for Hirsch. His one-act plays include *How I Crossed the Street for the First Time All by Myself*, *The Forever Game*, and *I'm with Ya, Duke*.

For his film adaptation of *A Thousand Clowns*, Gardner won Best Screenplay Award from the Screenwriters Guild as well as Academy Award nominations for Best Screenplay and Best Picture. He also wrote the screenplays for *Thieves*, *The Goodbye People* (which he also directed), and *Who Is Harry Kellerman and Why Is He Saying Those Terrible Things about Me?*, an adaptation of one of his short stories that appeared in *The Best American Short Stories of 1968*. In addition, Gardner has written a novel, *A Piece of the Action* (1958), and a number of plays for television.

MAJOR WORKS AND THEMES

Although only his most recent play, *Conversations with My Father*, deals directly with Jewish issues such as anti-Semitism, Yiddish culture, the Holocaust, and religious observance, all of Gardner's work operates within a distinctly Jewish framework, incorporating Jewish themes and archetypal Jewish characters drawn from Yiddish and American immigrant literature. Many of his plays explore the tension between immigrant parents and American children and the ambivalent feelings of second-generation Jews toward their ethnic and religious identity. Gardner's views on assimilation tend to be refracted through the dialogue of eccentric marginal characters whose tenuous relationship to the mainstream gives them a unique, often comic perspective on the foibles of Jews eagerly angling to become "American."

Gardner's characters are constantly concerned with where they fit—where they have come from, how well they have adapted, how well they play the new roles in which they find themselves. In *A Thousand Clowns*, Gardner pokes fun at Jews from immigrant families who try to hide their identity behind newly acquired accents. The young child Nick instantly identifies Dr. Sandra Markowitz's accent, impressing her by guessing not only her home city but her neighborhood and the influence of her graduate education (East Bronx, with a little bit of Massachusetts). Likewise, Nat in *I'm Not Rappaport* uses various assumed names—Sam Schwartzman, for one—and his lifetime membership in the Young Socialists' Club to demonstrate his resistance to the bland assimilatory impulses of his daughter.

Max in *The Goodbye People* claims not to know his daughter, who has just changed her name from the obviously Jewish Shirley Silverman to the more neutral-sounding Nancy Scott. Nancy herself exposes her ambivalence about her ethnicity when she reveals that she has been "remade" as an American: "This is Dr. Graham's nose! A top nose! This is Mr. Gaston's hair! This is my agent's name and this is Dr. Berman's attitude and this voice I'm talking to you with is from Madame Grenier, the vocal coach!" (30). Her father, Max's, response to his "new" daughter is less than warm: "Whatsa matter, they couldn't leave you with something? They took away a nose and left a message" (47). Max has similar conflicts with his son Michael, who claims that although he was never ashamed of his father's accent, he cannot understand why it seems to get thicker every year.

In *Conversations with My Father*, the conflicts between father and child are no less intense, but the assimilatory impulses are reversed. Eddie's first son, Joey, wants to wear a yarmulke, but his father forbids him to do so on the street. He redecorates his saloon in "Early American," plays patriotic songs on the jukebox, models his American accent on those he hears in the movies, and changes his name from Itzik Goldberg to Eddie Ross in order to take "the Jew lid off his boys." When his son dies fighting in World War II, Eddie renounces God, refuses ever to enter a synagogue again, and, when he discovers he is dying, even gets tattooed to avoid being buried in a Jewish cemetery. While the sons, Joey and Charlie, love to spend time with their boarder the Yiddish actor Zaretsky (he does a twelve-minute version of *The Dybbuk*), Eddie worries that his influence will prevent them from becoming "real" Americans and pushes Joey toward boxing and the army instead.

When Eddie discovers one of his son Charlie's poems, he is deeply impressed and deeply worried. He gives Charlie a lecture on *narrishkeit* (nonsense) created by luftmensch, meaning, as Eddie explains, "guys who live on the air—from which we get the term 'no visible goddamn means of support' " (126). Eddie wants his son to make it as an uptown lawyer, and "poem-writing" seems to him like a foolish waste of time. He encourages Charlie to become a lawyer instead. Gardner, unlike Eddie, is quite sympathetic to the traditional Jewish luftmensch character, a dreamer or artist who can't quite make it in the real world. While in Yiddish literature this character is often portrayed as a pathetic product of the poverty of the shtetl, in Gardner's Jewish-American scene, the luftmensch becomes a hero of the spirit, a nonconformist who resists the constraints of the crass, workaday world.

The luftmenschen and artists in Gardner's plays are often those who resist assimilation—they find "white bread" American culture dull and stultifying. Murray in *A Thousand Clowns* receives job offers to write for major television stations, but he cannot tolerate the notion of wearing a suit and getting up at the same time every day—he cherishes his nonconformity and does not want to compromise himself in any way. As long as he is unemployed, Murray is considered an unfit guardian of his nephew, yet so important to him is his freedom that he is even willing to risk the chance that the child will be taken away in order to protect it. In spite of his irresponsibility, his messy apartment, his unshaven face, and his generally rude treatment of those around him, Murray is the most sympathetic character in the play. Unlike the "suits" around him, he is full of joie de vivre and always good for a laugh.

In *The Goodbye People*, the aging Max, who has dreams of reopening the Coney Island hot dog stand that failed twenty-two years earlier, teaches the young Arthur, who cannot seem to quit his job making elves for Santa's workshop, the joys of being a luftmensch. Max's plan is clearly doomed to failure (he wants to open the beach café in February), yet Arthur eagerly invests in it nonetheless. The lesson he learns, Gardner seems to be saying, is far more important than the money he loses. From Max, Arthur learns the importance of believing in dreams, living life in the present, and ignoring anyone who tries to pin you down to the constraints of "normalcy."

Nat, the theatrical octogenarian in *I'm Not Rappaport*, continues to fight for his type of *narrishkeit*—a socialist utopia—even though, as his daughter Clara (named, of course, for the union leader Clara Lemlich) reminds him, "the battle is over, Comrade . . . Nothing's happened, nothing's changed" (62). Nat's efforts produce little tangible effect, and his inability to really *see* the world around him causes real harm to himself and others. Although Eddie Ross in *Conversations with My Father* seems to be the harshest critic of luftmensch dreams and the most avid assimilationist, he himself also embodies this quality in his various schemes to get "uptown." Each time he redecorates and reopens his bar, he is convinced he has discovered the key to prosperity and never fully understands why others don't respond to his vision as he himself musters. Irascible and angry as he is, Eddie is still a beloved character, his very ability to imagine a different life qualifying him as one of Gardner's unlikely heroes.

Despite the conventional style and commercial sentimentality of most of Gardner's work, this particular focus on the nonconformist and the imaginative artist makes Gardner's plays interesting as artifacts of Jewish-American culture. Gardner's heroes are mythmakers—men who deeply believe in the necessity of theatricality and imagination in everyday life. Murray's and Nick's private vaudeville performances, Max's dream of reopening Hawaiian Ecstasy, Nat's incessant role-playing and storytelling (which his daughter calls "lying"), and Eddie's constant redesigning of the saloon all have in common a belief that one can renew one's life through performance. With the proper set, the right accent, a stage name, colored lights, and music, these men believe they can be whoever they want to be. As ambivalently assimilating Jewish characters faced every day with the question, Who am I?, they take all the latitude this question allows. Seeing the possibility of refashioning themselves, however, they mistakenly assume they can also redesign the world around them. As Max Silverman says, "for ecstasy, people show up." Unfortunately, the "ecstasy" (or socialism or vaudeville or early America) that might have worked once is long gone; Gardner's characters survive in time capsules of their own making, both mourning and celebrating the worlds that exist only in their own heads and, for a brief moment, on Gardner's stage.

CRITICAL RECEPTION

Critical response to Gardner's work has been decidedly mixed. His first Broadway play, *A Thousand Clowns*, received overwhelmingly positive reviews, launching the young Gardner on a professional playwriting career. Critics lauded him as a fresh comic talent with an ability to make his characters come alive onstage. Howard Taubman was particularly impressed, focusing on Gardner's "capacity for looking about him and seeing the world with shrewdness and humorous detachment" (2). Gardner's next two plays, *The Goodbye People* and *Thieves*, did not fare so well. While critics were willing to forgive the episodic nature of *A Thousand Clowns* in the face of its humor and well-developed characters, they deeply criticized the next two plays for their lack of strong narrative structure. Clive Barnes of the *New York Times* also faulted *The Goodbye People* for stereotyped characters and clichéd ideas, and John Simon of *New York Magazine* similarly critiqued the play's "phoniness." Clive Barnes likewise thought *Thieves* lacked "substantive action" and lamented a fatal lack of originality in its ideas and characters.

With *I'm Not Rappaport*, however, Gardner finally recovered some of the public and critical acclaim he had received for *A Thousand Clowns*, although the accolades were definitely qualified. Reviewers praised *Rappaport* for its warmth and entertaining humor but complained again of a weak, episodic plot and seemingly disconnected subplots. Clive Barnes was able to justify the sketchiness of the plot, writing, "It doesn't matter . . . the play triumphantly exists in its concept" (*New York Post*). Edith Oliver found his "jokey ideas . . . frequently amusing," and Frank Rich noted a "pervasive sweetness" in the relationship between the characters (*New York Times*, June 7, 1985). Yet while many critics found the characters of Midge and Nat eminently enjoyable, they felt that any serious message about the plight of senior citizens was ultimately undercut by their seemingly frivolous humor. Rich was not convinced by the moral message and agreed with John Simon that the sentimentality of the play was "contrived for soft-hearted liberals to feel that everyone is winning in the race between the races" (73). With *Conversations with My Father*, Gardner headed into new, more sophisticated territory, and the work received correspondingly serious, largely positive critical attention. Even the hard-to-please Frank Rich, who still criticized the "unfinished" episodic nature of the plot, found the play ultimately satisfying. He praised the author's "most flavorful writing" to date and favorably noted his "passionate affection for the Old World" and the warmth and comedy with which he unsentimentally portrayed a diverse and difficult group of characters. With *Conversations with My Father*, Gardner established himself as a serious Jewish-American playwright from whom critics eagerly await further theatrical reflections on the fate of Jewish-American identity in the late twentieth century.

BIBLIOGRAPHY

Works by Herb Gardner

Plays

Dates in parentheses indicate production if different from date of publication.
The Elevator. New York: French, 1952.
A Thousand Clowns. New York: Random House, 1962.
The Goodbye People. (1968). New York: French, 1974.
Who Is Harry Kellerman and Why Is He Saying Those Terrible Things about Me? (screenplay). New York: New American Library, 1971.
Thieves. (1974). Included in *A Thousand Clowns, Thieves, The Goodbye People*. New York: Doubleday, 1979.
Love and/or Death. Produced New York, 1979.
I'm Not Rappaport. (1985). New York: Grove, 1988.
Conversations with My Father. (1992). New York: Pantheon, 1994.

Novel

A Piece of the Action. New York: Simon and Schuster, 1958.

Works about Herb Gardner

Barnes, Clive. Rev. of *The Goodbye People*. *New York Times*, December 4, 1968:52.
———. Rev. of *I'm Not Rappaport*. *New York Post*, June 7, 1985. Reprinted in *New York Theatre Critics Reviews* 46, No. 11: 224.
———. Rev. of *Thieves*. *New York Times*, April 8, 1974: 44.
Bennetts, Leslie. "Most Funny Stuff Is Born of Pain." *New York Times*, June 2, 1985: 2: 4.
Gussow, Mel. Rev. of *I'm Not Rappaport*. *New York Times*, January 19, 1986: 2A: 2.
Oliver, Edith. Rev. of *I'm Not Rappaport*. *The New Yorker*, June 17, 1985: 118.
Rich, Frank Rev. of *Conversations with My Father*. *New York Times*, March 30, 1992: C11.
———. Rev. of *I'm Not Rappaport*. *New York Times*, June 7, 1985: C3.
Simon, John. "Faking It." *New York Magazine*, June 24, 1985: 72.
Taubman, Howard. "People Can Be Fun." *New York Times*, April 15, 1962: II: 1.
———. Rev. of *A Thousand Clowns*. *New York Times*, April 6, 1962: 31.

ISRAEL HOROVITZ   (1939–)

Leslie Kane

BIOGRAPHY

Born Arthur Israel Horovitz in 1939 to Charles and Hazel Solberg Horovitz in Wakefield, Massachusetts, Israel Horovitz grew up and attended high school in Wakefield, a working-class community north of Boston whose distinctive linguistic patterns and accents have characterized numerous Horovitz plays set in either Wakefield or Gloucester. While still a teenager, Horovitz began a lifelong commitment to running and writing, submitting his first novel, *Steinberg, Sex, and the Saint* at the age of thirteen, a work whose rejection he credits with launching his career in the theatre.

A peripatetic playwright of dazzling productivity, high energy, and tenacious, competitive spirit, Israel Horovitz's introduction to literature came in the form of books he was paid to destroy in his uncle's junk shop and baling room. His first dramatic work, *The Comeback*, a reworking of *Richard II*, written when he was seventeen, had its premiere in 1958 at Emerson College, Boston, as a curtain-raiser for Arthur Miller's *A Memory of Two Mondays*. Honing his craft at the Old Poets Theatre, Cambridge, Massachusetts, and attending Salem State College for one year, during which time he married artist Dorothy Keefe, Horovitz became a fellow at the Royal Academy of Dramatic Art in London, where in 1965 he earned the distinction of being the first American playwright to be appointed playwright-in-residence at the Royal Shakespeare Company and the Aldwich Theatre in London. Upon his return to the United States, the young writer became a charter member of the Eugene O'Neill Memorial Theatre Foundation in Waterford, Connecticut, where a number of his plays, including *It's Called the Sugar Plum*, *The Primary English Class*, and *The Wakefield Plays*, had staged readings or performances.

Horovitz burst upon the New York theatre scene in 1967–1968, when successful productions of four one-act plays, *Line*, *The Indian Wants the Bronx*, *Rats*, and *It's Called the Sugar Plum*, heralded him as a brilliant new, socially committed playwright. *Line*, a grotesque allegory of the American success myth, which opened at La Mama in New York in 1967, also occasioned Horovitz's acting debut when the playwright took the part of the line-eater who left New York on the eve of the play's opening night for Hollywood. Since that time, Horovitz has won acclaim for *Line*, the longest running off-Broadway play in New York history and staged for twenty seasons in Paris; *The Indian Wants the Bronx*, considered a genre classic of violence; *The Wakefield Plays; Park Your Car in Harvard Yard*; and *North Shore Fish*, the latter two being his most accessible and successful Gloucester plays.

The Primary English Class and *An Israel Horovitz Trilogy*, also known as *The Sault Ste. Marie Trilogy*, exemplify Horovitz's investigations of ethnicity, the latter drawing its power and poignancy from memory, a prevalent and powerful trope in Horovitz's late work. *The Widow's Blind Date*, which originally premiered in Gloucester, reopened off-Broadway in 1989 and played to sold-out performances in Paris and Darmstadt, Germany. Horovitz's *Park Your Car in Harvard Yard* enjoyed a successful run on Broadway in 1991 with Jason Robards and Judith Ivey and has drawn a veritable following in Paris, and *Fighting over Beverley*, which premiered in Gloucester in 1993, has been warmly received.

Winner of two Obies for *The Indian Wants the Bronx* and the double-bill *The-Honest-to-God Schnozzola* and *Leader*, the French Critics Prize, the Prix du Plaiser de Théâtre, the Drama Desk Award, Plays and Players Best Foreign Play Award, the Prix Italia, and the Elliot Norton Prize for outstanding contribution to the theatre of Boston, as well as a recipient of a New York State Council of the Arts Fellowship, Fluorite Foundation Award, Guggenheim Fellowship, a National Endowment of the Arts Award, a Rockefeller Fellowship, and an Award in Literature from the American Academy of Arts and Letters, Israel Horovitz has written more than fifty plays, has been translated into nearly twenty-five languages, and continues to be one of the most theatrically innovative playwrights in America. No playwright, with the exception of O'Neill, has had more plays produced in the French language. Indeed, not only does Horovitz maintain a home in Paris, a favorite and frequent venue for his plays, but the playwright has just written two plays of a new cycle set in Paris.

Horovitz is the founder and artistic director of the New York Playwrights Lab (NYPL), a weekly workshop for full-time, professionally produced playwrights originally associated with the Actors Studio in 1975, whose original members included Peter Parnell, Peter Vetere, Bruce Serlin, and Nancy Fales; the NYPL, now a project of the Joseph Papp Public Theatre, not only is still active but counts among its current members Marlena Meyer, Frank Pugliesi, Jonathan Marc Sherman, and Seth Svi Rosenfeld. In 1979 Horovitz founded the Gloucester Stage Company, the only theatre of its kind in the country where the playwright-in-residence is founder, artistic director, and producer. On a more personal note, in 1981 Horovitz married former British marathon champion Gillian Adams, whose twins Hannah and Oliver were born in 1986. Horovitz also has three children from his earlier marriage, Rachael, Matthew, and Adam.

A number of fine actors have made their debuts as Horovitz characters, among them Al Pacino, Richard Dreyfus, Jill Clayburgh, John Cazale, Marsha Norman, and Diane Keaton. In addition to his substantial literary output, the playwright has been a producer, director, stage manager, actor, and screenwriter. Author of the screenplays *The Strawberry Statement* (Cannes Film Festival Prix du Jury), *Author! Author!*, and recently completed *Strong-Men, The Deuce, Letters to Iris, Payofski's Discovery*, and an adaptation of Kipling's *Captains Courageous*, Horovitz has also written a novel, novella, and radio drama, "The Chips Are Down," broadcast February 1996 on BBC. Moreover, he has directed the world-premiere productions of many of his plays in English and French, including *Spared, Hopscotch, Strong-Man's Weak Child, Widow's Blind Date*, and *Line*.

MAJOR WORKS AND THEMES

Horovitz's fascination with self-sustaining fictions, characters as an expression of social dislocation, intimations of menace, seemingly aimless, colloquial speech laced with innuendo, realistic props metamorphosed into instruments of torture, and intrusion of memory and betrayal informs his work and suggests obvious comparisons with Samuel Beckett, with whom Horovitz enjoyed a relationship. He readily acknowledges the influence of Eugène Ionesco and Harold Pinter, whose *Homecoming* was in rehearsal when the young playwright was in residence at the Royal Academy of Dramatic Art. His criticism of wanton violence and moral void, his consideration of the delicate balance between illusion and reality, and the use of trilogies place him firmly in the tradition of American drama and invite comparison to both O'Neill and Albee. But, his refusal to repeat himself, reflected in a body of work composed of realistic plays, absurdist fantasies and parables, and dark chamber plays characterized by "a rich and gorgeous theatrical sense and real breathing, living people" (Barnes, *Line* 20), clearly account for his worldwide appeal, even though some plays, especially prior to the 1980s, lacked the imaginativeness and power of his early success.

Although Horovitz's recent work is largely realistic, psychologically darker, and more personal than earlier plays, his technical virtuosity, superb ear for dialogue, images of alienation, powerful central metaphor, taut balance between the comic and the terrifying, and social consciousness account, in large part, for his staying power and critical respect. Indeed, dramatizing how violence can and does spring from futility and frustration, Horovitz's best theatrical work dramatizes an extraordinary study of the psychology of terrorism. Turning back to the issues of power and fear that occupied him in the 1960s, Horovitz seems to be fulfilling earlier promise by addressing issues of social terror, personal responsibility, and essential vulnerability with a verbal dexterity and control of character and plot that attest to his maturity and have never been more relevant. Although Peter Sagal correctly posits that Horovitz "more recently" is dedicated to "an increasingly gentle portrayal of human frailty," it must be added that his most compelling work balances frailty, family, and the violence and bloodshed that he "resorted to in early works to blow them [audiences] out of their conformist chairs" (247).

Horovitz's monumental *Wakefield Plays*, composed of *The Alfred Trilogy* and its companion quartet, *The Quannapowitt Quartet* (named for Lake Quannapowitt, where the young Horovitz, an amateur marathoner, regularly ran), combining allegory and dark comedy to depict sexual greed, guilt, and impotence, portrays the adventures of Alfred, a celebrated citizen of Wakefield who returns to unravel a confusing narrative of his past. The trilogy and the quartet depict, with great humor and almost perfect dramatic unfolding, human loss, the power of mythology, the poignancy of human failure, and the universality of the quest for present understanding.

Whereas *The Wakefield Plays* are weighty with buried betrayals and mythic importance, Horovitz's Gloucester cycle of plays (fourteen at last count, including *Barking Sharks* [1995]) written during much of the late 1980s to 1990s is set in his adopted hometown, Gloucester, Massachusetts, a declining fishing community of great beauty. They dramatize working-class people confronting social problems, among them a dying trade, a drug problem, and a community at risk. Among the plays are the notable *North Shore Fish*, *Fighting Over Beverley*, and *Henry Lumper*. Its self-appointed local bard staging the staunch pride and vicissitudes of "livin' local" and dedicated to capturing and preserving the speech patterns and idioms of the community, Horovitz has "fashioned himself as the voice and the heart and the conscience" of the picturesque community that has inspired such artists as T. S. Eliot, Winslow Homer, and Edward Hopper (Berkrot 39). In stark contrast to spare, early plays, whose tension derives from the complicity between surrealism and logic, his current work, which may be his best, is largely realistic.

Reflecting the playwright's maturity, sensitivity, social and familial consciousness, and the thematics of his substantive canon, especially the buried betrayals, poignancy of failure, and quest for personal truths that characterize *The Wakefield Plays* (*The Alfred Trilogy* and its companion quartet), Israel Horovitz has written *Unexpected Tenderness* (1993), a searing ethnic drama that exposes deep emotional scars. Playing to sold-out performances at the Gloucester Stage, *Unexpected Tenderness* was heralded as outstanding during its New York production in early fall 1994 as "among Horovitz's very best" (Barnes 1994, p. 26). Yet in the Preface to the published script, the playwright observes that *Unexpected Tenderness* "seems to me to be the sort of play a writer should write as his/her first play. It is a rite of passage . . . extremely personal, dark, funny, and sad. However bizarre, *Unexpected Tenderness* is, more than anything else, a family play . . . [one] I avoided writing for some thirty years. It is a story I never particularly wanted to tell" (*Two New Plays* vii). No wonder. Tropologically and structurally recalling Horovitz's body of work, *Unexpected Tenderness*, one of his most provocative and clearly most revealing work, cuts to the bone, confronts demons of familial abuse, and stands ''sweet,'' ethnic comedy on its head. While this is not the first occasion that one finds allusions to Horovitz's life in his work—the fleet-footed Archie in *Widow's Blind Date*, the ethnic playwright in *Author! Author!*, the returning hero in *The Alfred Trilogy*—the playwright, putting distance between himself and his work, contends that while this play ''contains some of the most dramatic moments of my childhood,'' it is simultaneously filled with ''some of my very best adult lies'' (vii).

Stunningly, *Unexpected Tenderness* recalls *The Sault St. Marie Trilogy—Today, I Am a Fountain Pen*, *A Rosen by Any Other Name*, and *The Chopin Playoffs*, a trilogy of family plays that balance the larger issues of Jewish life with more intimate themes of family relationships, heritage, and heroism, which Robert Skloot wisely characterizes as Horovitz's ''ethnic masterpiece'' (*IH* 33). Adapted from a book of autobiographical stories by Canadian writer Morley Torgov, whose experience growing up among mercantile Jews is light years away from Wakefield, more a hotbed of ''good old Yankee persecution'' than ''a hotbed of Hebraic thought'' or practice, for that matter, Horovitz's strongest identification with Judaism is his name (qtd. in *IH* 196–99). Commissioned by the Community Project of the National Foundation for Jewish Culture, Horovitz's trilogy of Jewish plays, directed by Stephen Zuckerman, who also mounted a highly successful production of *Unexpected Tenderness*, was staged in early 1986 at the American Jewish Theatre, with stirring performances by Barbara eda-Young, Josh Blake, and Sol Frieder, seen frequently in Horovitz's work. Of the three plays, ''*Rosen* presents the strongest expression of the social and familial tension brought about by ethnic struggle. As a result, its emotional subtext is deepest and its resolution most satisfying . . . [by keeping] uppermost in our attention the fact that there is a war raging in Europe (it is 1943) in which the enemy is dedicated to destroying Jews'' and in which Horovitz ''features prominently the terrible results of anti-Semitism'' (Skloot, *IH* 33–34). In *Unexpected Tenderness* both familial tension and war are similarly kept uppermost in our attention, as is the child's sharp condemnation of the flawed morality of patriarchal figures. Like *Rosen*, *Unexpected Tenderness* was inspired by, and dramatizes, a speech made by the thirteen-year-old playwright during a national oratory contest. ''The name of the [extemporaneous] speech, or the topic,'' Horovitz recalled in a recent interview with this author, ''was 'From Kalitsky to Kaye,' and it was about name changing,'' whereas ''everybody's prepared speech was: 'We have nothing to fear but fear itself,' which was, of course, a line spoken and made famous by none other than Jew-hater Franklin Delano Roosevelt'' (qtd. in *IH* 196–97).

The latter topics—fear, Jew-hating, and truth-telling—serve as the basis of *Unexpected Tenderness*. Moreover, while the later play bears strong resonance to *Rosen*, like the majority of Horovitz's work written in the last decade, *Unexpected Tenderness* is lengthier and more realistic, portraying actions centered on the threat or the appearance of violence and the lack of communication (Jacobi, *IH* 167). Its use of historical paradigm progressively revealed, recurring verbal and sexual aggression, intimidation, sexist behavior, and competitiveness specifically betray the darker shaping of two more recent Horovitz plays: *The Widow's Blind Date*, in which memories evoked are discomforting, intense, revelatory, and ultimately shattering, and *Strong Man's Weak Child*, where a trinity of dreams, desire, and deception is colored by the metaphysical reality of a child's death. Unifying what he terms his "Plays of my Mother" and "Plays of my Father" (*Two New Plays* viii), Horovitz fuses gentle and violent rhythms in *Unexpected Tenderness*, bringing the war to the home front, where hatred fueled by jealousy threatens this family with extinction.

Set in a small New England town in the 1950s, not unlike Wakefield, Massachusetts, where the playwright was raised and exposed to no small amount of "anti-Semitic shit" (Horovitz, qtd. in *IH* 198), *Unexpected Tenderness*, paralleling American dramatic tradition, returns to the home, what Matthew Roudané terms the nerve center for his self-disclosing dramas. But lest we forget the centrality of the home and the kitchen, that favorite communal and spectatorial space, to Jewish-American culture and literature, Horovitz's setting is universal *and* site-specific. Told from the dual perspective of fourteen-year-old Roddy Stern, whose English-sounding name reflects a practice of first- and second-generation New England Jews to give their children non-Semitic-sounding names (Horovitz letter, March 19, 1996), and Roddy as an adult, the precise observations of these narrators render this memory play "not your run-of-the-matzoh Jewish comedy" (Barnes 26). The diction of grandparents Haddie and Jacob, a "blend of Eastern European and Western Massachusetts," interrogatories, inverted word order, Yiddish phrases, Holocaust imagery, emphasis on identity, heritage, and tradition, moral focus, and *menschlichkeit* further and firmly establish the ethnicity, pungency, and humor that are of a piece in *Unexpected Tenderness*, rendering it a disturbing dramatization of recollected personal and cultural history.

Inexorably, we are carried along by young Roddy's preparation for the Red Feather Oratory Contest, coupled in memory with a deeply suppressed picture of his mother beaten by his insanely jealous father. Delicately balancing joy and sadness in one of the play's most moving moments, the text of Roddy's Red Feather Oratory speech—its clarified vision, polished prose, explicit condemnation of Roosevelt's indifference to imperiled Jews, and assertion of courage and dignity in the face of brutality and threatening forces—is mirrored in his mother, Molly's bearing, bruises, and emblematic suitcases. Horovitz has fashioned a fitting conclusion to *Unexpected Tenderness* that both replays the slap that Stanley Rosen receives from his father when he asserts his Jewish identity at the end of *Rosen* and recalls the "unexpected tenderness" that Roddy's meddling in parental arguments regularly earned him. The lesson Roddy takes away from Roosevelt's indifference and his father's betrayal of family, then, is a personal definition of morality and kindness; a Jew like Stanley Rosen, he not only rejects victimhood and chooses identity but embraces *menschlichkeit*.

In *Unexpected Tenderness* Horovitz faces his own past, and the experience, which bathes his entire canon in a new light, is heart-wrenching, uplifting, and dramatically cohesive. Robert Skloot got it exactly right when he observed that we are profoundly diminished if we fail to recognize that Horovitz's "pervasive concern with the newcomer-outsider makes his work on the ethnic condition of America one of the salient features" of his impressive body of work (*IH* 28).

CRITICAL RECEPTION

Virtually unchallenged among American playwrights in the range of his writing, Horovitz has, until recently, attracted scant scholarly attention, with the exception of Barry B. Williams' "Images of America" and Martin Jacobi's critical bibliography, his work having been largely overshadowed, in America at least, by Sam Shepard and David Mamet, who came of age in the same generation. *Israel Horovitz: A Collection of Critical Essays* addresses that critical need. Presenting the most current and provocative thinking on Horovitz's prodigious body of work, it commences a dialectic on performance and structure, measurably extending assessment and recognition of his dramatic career. This book also includes the first scholarly interview with the playwright, conducted by Leslie Kane, substantively advancing knowledge of the playwright and his plays. Previous biographical essays include Ross Wetzeson's "Author! Author!—It's Horovitz" and Peter Sagal's "The Mellowing of Israel Horovitz." Horovitz is also listed in *Critical Study of Drama*, *Contemporary Authors*, *Dictionary of Literary Bibliography*, and *Contemporary Dramatists*.

BIBLIOGRAPHY

Works by Israel Horovitz

First Season: The Indian Wants the Bronx, Line, It's Called the Sugar Plum, Rats. New York: Random, 1968a.

The Indian Wants the Bronx. New York: Dramatists Play Service, 1968b; In *Off-Broadway Plays.* Harmondsworth, U.K.: Penguin, 1970.

It's Called the Sugar Plum. New York: Dramatists Play Service, 1968c.

Rats. New York: Dramatists Play Service, 1968d.

Morning. New York: Samuel French, 1969. Reprinted as *Clair-Obscur.* Paris: Gallimard, 1972. In *Morning, Noon and Night.* With Terrence McNally and Leonard Melfi. New York: Random, 1969.

Acrobats and Line. New York: Dramatists Play Service, 1971a.

The Honest-to-God Schnozzola. New York: Breakthrough Press, 1971b.

Leader and Play for Trees. New York: Dramatists Play Service, 1971c.

Dr. Hero. New York: Dramatists Play Service, 1973.

Alfred the Great. New York: Dramatists Play Service, 1974. New York: Harper and
     Row, 1974.
The Primary English Class. New York: Dramatists Play Service, 1976a.
Uncle Snake: An Independence Day Pageant. New York: Dramatists Play Service, 1976b.
Hopskotch and *The 75th* (Parts One and Two: *The Quannapowitt Quartet*). New York:
     Dramatists Play Service, 1977a.
Man with Bags. Adapted from Eugene Ionesco's *L'Homme aux valises.* Trans. Marie-
     France Ionesco. New York: Grove, 1977b.
Stage Directions and Spared (Parts Three and Four: *The Quannapowitt Quartet*). New
     York: Dramatists Play Service, 1977c.
Mackerel. Vancouver, Canada: Talonbooks, 1979a.
*The Wakefield Plays: Alfred the Great, Our Father's Failing, Alfred Dies, Hopskotch,
     The 75th, Stage Directions, Spared.* New York: Bard/Avon, 1979b.
A Christmas Carol: Scrooge and Marley. Adapted from Charles Dickens' *A Christmas
     Carol.* New York: Dramatists Play Service, 1980.
The Widow's Blind Date. New York: Theatre Communications Group, 1981.
The Former One-on-One Basketball Champion and *The Great Labor Day Classic.* New
     York: Dramatists Play Service, 1982.
The Good Parts. New York: Dramatists Play Service, 1983a.
Today I Am a Fountain Pen. New York: Dramatists Play Service, 1983b.
The Chopin Playoffs. New York: Dramatists Play Service, 1987a.
*An Israel Horovitz Trilogy: Today I Am a Fountain Pen, A Rosen by Any Other Name,
     The Chopin Playoffs.* Garden City, NY: Fireside Theatre, 1987b.
A Rosen by Any Other Name. New York: Dramatists Play Service, 1987c.
Faith. New York: Dramatists Play Service, 1989a.
Henry Lumper. New York: Dramatists Play Service, 1989b.
North Shore Fish. New York: Dramatists Play Service, 1990.
*Three Gloucester Plays: Park Your Car in Harvard Yard, Henry Lumper, North Shore
     Fish.* Garden City, NY: Fireside Theatre, 1992.
Israel Horovitz Two New Plays: Unexpected Tenderness and Fighting over Beverley.
     Garden City, NY: Fireside, 1994.

Works about Israel Horovitz

Barnes, Clive. Rev. of *Line. New York Times,* January 18, 1968.
Barnes, Clive. Rev. of *Unexpected Tenderness. New York Post,* October 17, 1994, 26.
Berkrot, Peter. "Israel Horovitz." *American Theatre* (October 1992): 39+.
Bigsby, C. W. E. *A Critical Introduction to Twentieth Century Drama.* Vol. 3. New York:
     Cambridge University Press, 1985, 27.
Clurman, Harold. "Theatre." *The Nation* (February 12, 1986): 221.
Cohn, Ruby. *New American Dramatists 1960–1990.* 2d ed. New York: St. Martin's Press,
     1991, 64–67.
Combs, Robert. "O'Neill and Horovitz: Toward Home," In *IH,* ed. Leslie Kane, 39–49.
Connolly, Thomas F. "The Place, the Thing: Israel Horovitz's Gloucester Milieu." In
     IH, 113–24.
Demastes, William. " 'We Gotta Hang Together': Horovitz and the National Cycles of
     Violence." In *IH,* ed. Leslie Kane, 15–25.

Jacobi, Martin. "Ed Lemon: Prophet of Profit." In *IH*, 167–68.

Jacobi, Martin. "Israel Horovitz." In *American Playwrights Since 1945*: A *Guide to Scholarship, Criticism, and Performance*. Ed. Philip C. Kolin. Westport, CT: Greenwood Press, 1989, 179–89.

Kane, Leslie, ed. *Israel Horovitz: A Collection of Critical Essays*. Westport, CT: Greenwood, 1994. [*IH*]

Kovac, Kim Peter. "Israel Horovitz." *Dictionary of Literary Biography. Twentieth Century American Drama*. Vol. 7. Ed. John MacNicholas. Detroit: Gale Research, 1981, 51–68.

Sagal, Peter. "The Mellowing of Israel Horovitz." *Boston Magazine* 86 (October 1986): 239–48.

Skloot, Robert. "Ins and Out: The Ethnic World of Israel Horovitz." In *IH*, 27–38.

Sogliuzzo, A. Richard. "Israel Horovitz." In *Contemporary Dramatists*. 4th ed. Ed. D. L. Kirkpatrick. Chicago: St. James Press, 1988, 264–67.

Westzeson, Ross. "Author! Author!—It's Horovitz." *New York* (August 2, 1982): 28–35.

Williams, Barry B. "Image of America." *Theatre Journal* 34 (May 1982): 223–32.

ARTHUR L. KOPIT   (1937–   )

Michael C. O'Neill

BIOGRAPHY

Born in Manhattan on May 10, 1937, Arthur Lee Kopit spent most of his child-hood in Lawrence, New York. His father, George, was a jewelry salesman mar-ried to Maxine Dubin; the couple also had a daughter, Susan, eight years younger than her brother. Kopit claims that as a child on suburban Long Island he enjoyed listening to radio serials such as *Superman* and performing puppet shows with hand puppets for his schoolmates. While attending Lawrence High School, Kopit wrote for the school newspaper, worked in a Jewish country club, and nurtured a lifelong interest in basketball (Kopit is 6' 3-¼" tall). After grad-uation in 1955, he attended Harvard University on a scholarship to study elec-trical engineering but soon came under the influence of Robert Chapman and Gaynor Bradish, both of whom stimulated Kopit's interest in the theatre. His first play, a one-act titled *The Questioning of Nick*, won a Harvard playwriting contest in 1957, and Kopit himself directed a televised version of the play for WNHC in New Haven, Connecticut, in 1959. Before he graduated Phi Beta Kappa with a bachelor of arts degree in 1959, six more of Kopit's plays were produced at Harvard: *Gemini*; *Don Juan in Texas*, written in collaboration with Wally Lawrence; *On the Runway of Life, You Never Know What's Coming Off Next*; *Across the River and into the Jungle*, an Ernest Hemingway parody; *Au-bade*, a Samuel Beckett-like piece originally titled *Through a Labyrinth*; and *Sing to Me through Open Windows*, a revised version of which was produced off-Broadway in 1965. The *Harvard Advocate* also published the first act of his proposed three-act play *To Dwell in a Place of Strangers* in 1958.

    While touring Western Europe on a Shaw Travelling Fellowship in 1959, Kopit completed *Oh Dad, Poor Dad, Momma's Hung You in the Closet and*

I'm Feelin' So Sad, which played to enthusiastic audiences at Harvard and trans-ferred to Cambridge's Agassiz Theater in January 1960; directed by Jerome Robbins, the New York production of *Oh Dad* opened at the Phoenix Theater on February 26, 1962. In addition to a Ford Foundation grant to finance the Cambridge production, Kopit won both the Vernon Rice Award and the Outer Circle Award for *Oh Dad*. After playing 454 performances on Broadway, suc-cessfully completing an eleven-week national tour, and being produced to ac-claim in over a dozen countries, *Oh Dad* allowed Kopit the financial security to devote himself full-time to writing for the theatre at age twenty-five.

Kopit directed the Paris production of *Oh Dad* in 1963 but that same year canceled the production of his next play, a double-bill called *Asylum: Or, What the Gentlemen Are Up To, Not to Mention the Ladies* after five previews. He rewrote part of it as *Chamber Music* the following year; in 1964 he also com-pleted two other one-acts, *The Hero* and *The Conquest of Everest*, both of which were produced in New York. He received a Rockefeller Foundation grant to develop two other one-acts, *The Day the Whores Came out to Play Tennis* and *Mhil'daiim*, for the University of Minnesota and the Tyrone Guthrie Theater in Minneapolis, respectively, also in 1964. Kopit withdrew the plays in a disa-greement with the university, but one of them, *The Day the Whores Came Out to Play Tennis*, directed by Gerald Freeman, was billed with *Sing to Me through Open Windows*, directed by Joseph Chaikin, in an off-Broadway production that opened on March 15, 1965, at the Players' Theater.

Kopit's most important play, *Indians*, was written and revised over a three-year period from 1966 to 1969, with financial support from both a Guggenheim Fellowship and a Rockefeller grant. The play premiered in London on July 4, 1968, in a Royal Shakespeare Company production under the direction of Jack Gelber; a substantially revised version of the play followed at the Arena Stage in Washington, D.C., on May 6, 1969, and the Broadway production, under the direction of Gene Frankel, opened on October 13, 1969, at the Brooks Atkinson Theater. Robert Altman's 1976 film *Buffalo Bill and the Indians: Or, Sitting Bull's History Lesson* is loosely based on Kopit's script for *Indians*.

While Kopit's reputation continued to grow through international productions of *Indians*, he met with few other successes. His plays—*What Happened to Thorne's House?* (1972), an outdoor environmental production he directed in East Dorset, Vermont, with a cast of local musicians and townspeople; *Louisiana Territory; or, Lewis and Clark—Lost and Found* (1975), which he directed in Middletown, Connecticut; and *Secrets of the Rich* (1976), which was directed by Lynn Meadow at the O'Neill Center's National Playwrights' Conference—have never been published. He also was playwright-in-residence at Wesleyan University in 1975 and 1976 and a CBS fellow at Yale University from 1976 to 1977. He joined the faculty of the Yale School of Drama as an adjunct professor of playwriting from 1977 to 1980.

Seven months before Kopit was commissioned to write a play for National Public Radio's *Earplay* in 1976, his father suffered a stroke and died within a year. Kopit's experience with his father's affliction led him into the study of aphasia and the writing of *Wings*, which was produced as a radio play in 1977. An expanded version of the play, directed by John Madden, opened at the Yale Repertory Theater on May 3, 1978; productions in New York and London followed. The radio version of *Wings* won the Italia Prize in 1979, and *Wings* was awarded the 1979 Pulitzer Prize in drama. The Public Broadcasting System televised *Wings* on April 23, 1983, and a musical version of the play by Jeffrey Lunden and Arthur Perlman, directed by Michael Maggio, premiered at Chicago's Goodman Studio Theater in 1992, with subsequent productions in 1993 at the New York Shakespeare Festival and in London.

His short play *Good Help Is Hard to Find* was produced in June 1981 as part of New York's Ensemble Studio Theater Marathon, and in 1982 Kopit won the Tony Award for Best Musical for his libretto for *Nine*, an adaptation, with music and lyrics by Maury Yeston, of Frederico Fellini's *8 ½*. Also in 1982, Kopit shaped a new translation of Henrik Ibsen's *Ghosts*, starring Liv Ullmann, for performances in Washington, D.C., and New York. Shortly thereafter, he began work with Yeston on a musical version of Gaston Leroux's *The Phantom of the Opera*, but the team postponed the premiere until January 31, 1991, at the Music Hall in Houston, Texas. Meanwhile, a miniseries of *The Phantom of the Opera*, adapted by Kopit from his play and directed by Tony Richardson, was televised by the National Broadcasting Company in March 1990.

Kopit's exploration of nuclear destruction, *End of the World*, directed by Harold Prince, opened May 6, 1984, in New York at the Music Box Theater; it was produced in England as *The Assignment* in September 1985. Subsequent productions of *End of the World* included the Cleveland Play House production, directed by Thomas Riccio, in March 1985 and the American Repertory Theater's production in Cambridge, directed by Richard Foreman, in December 1986. After *End of the World*, Kopit turned increasingly to regional theatre endeavor, creating a six-hour extravaganza at the Mark Taper Forum in Los Angeles called *Discovery of America*, based on the journals of Cabeza de Vaca, who in 1512 became the first European to cross North America. He also premiered a scathing satire of Hollywood written as a stylistic parody of David Mamet, *Bone-the-Fish*, in 1989 at the Humana Festival of New Plays in Louisville, Kentucky. *Bone-the-Fish*, revised and retitled *Road to Nirvana*, opened at the American Repertory Theater in Cambridge on April 1, 1990, at New York's Circle Repertory Theater on March 7, 1991, and at Chicago's Steppenwolf Theater on March 13, 1993.

In addition to the television work already noted, Kopit has written the following for television: "The Conquest of Television" (1966), "Promontory Point Revisited" (1969), "Starstruck" (1979), "Hands of a Stranger" (1987), and "In a Child's Name." He is the recipient of a National Institute of Arts and Letters Award and was elected to the American Academy of Arts and Letters in 1971. He also received a grant from the National Endowment for the Arts in 1974. Since 1981, Kopit has been an adjunct professor of playwriting at the City College of New York, and since 1982 he has been a council member of the Dramatists Guild.

Kopit is married to Leslie Ann Garis, a writer and former concert pianist. They have three children and reside in Wilton, Connecticut.

MAJOR WORKS AND THEMES

Kopit's apprentice work, including *Oh Dad*, reflects his struggle with established dramatic forms and, more generally, literary history that demonstrates what George Wellwarth has called Kopit's "wry imagination." As his career progressed, he continued to experiment with dramatic form and to use language in outrageous and inventive ways, but Kopit's emphasis shifted to an exploration of the limits of theatricality through which he implicitly began to discuss such complex topics as genocide, American mythology, aphasia, nuclear war, and definitions of masculinity.

The Questioning of Nick, a realistic one-act influenced, in part, by 1950s melodramatic television police shows, follows two policemen's interrogation and psychological manipulation of a high school basketball player until he confesses to throwing games for payoffs. According to Kopit, *The Questioning of Nick*, which draws upon his own experience playing basketball as an adolescent, is "the only realistic play I have written." Although embodied in a realistic form that Kopit quickly abandoned, *The Questioning of Nick* hints at a shaping idea that becomes fairly standard in his later work: an initial premise that action and events determine character and, further, that characters, such as Nick and, much later, Buffalo Bill in *Indians* and Michael Trent in *End of the World*, are helplessly underarmed in the battle against events.

Sing to Me through Open Windows, rewritten many times until the playwright finally settled for the 1964 published version, represents Kopit's attempt to work within dramatic forms, such as expressionism, that are diametrically opposed to the realism of *The Questioning of Nick*. A memory play with music by Victor Ziskin and Thomas Beveridge, *Sing to Me*, through images, obscure language, and a disjointed narrative, treats the development of a boy, Andrew Linden, who escapes the stifling environment of his classroom, gets lost in a surrounding symbolic forest, takes refuge in the strange house of an aging magician named Ottoman, and returns there once a year for five years to watch the magician, with the help of a clown, perform tricks. Much of the odd, idiosyncratic atmosphere of *Sing to Me* is achieved through the use of sound in theatrically striking ways, a technique Kopit refined further in *Oh Dad*, *Chamber Music*, *Indians*, and *Wings*.

Oh Dad, subtitled *A Pseudoclassical Tragifarce in a Bastard French Tradition*, is a highly derivative, often satiric collage of theatrical modes and outrageous comment on mid-twentieth-century culture that, taken collectively, has not aged very well. A widowed world traveler, Madame Rosepettle, settles into a Havana hotel with her emotionally backward, stuttering son, Jonathan, in order to meet and destroy Commodore Roseabove, the richest and most eligible bachelor in the Caribbean. Jonathan falls in love with Rosalie, whom his mother loathes. The body of Jonathan's father, which Madame Rosepettle has had stuffed and carries with her on her travels, falls out of the closet and onto the bed where Jonathan and Rosalie are cuddled. Repulsed by Rosalie's advances and terrified by the paternal interruption, Jonathan smothers the girl to death.

Superimposed upon the ridiculous action of *Oh Dad* are numerous indications of Kopit's rich theatrical satire; for example, Rosalinda the fish is a *reductio ad absurdum* of the Greek chorus; the dialogue abounds in allusions to *Hamlet*; the Rose names and the two Venus's-flytraps poke fun, respectively, at Tennessee Williams' *The Rose Tattoo* (1951) and *Suddenly, Last Summer* (1958); Jonathan, like Clov in Beckett's *Endgame* (1958), looks out at a void through his telescope and stutters in a sly parody of the incoherent musings of the Theater of the Absurd; and Madame Rosepettle, like Claire Zachanassian in Friedrich Durrenmatt's *The Visit* (1956), travels with a huge entourage that includes a coffin.

Oh Dad is also heavily influenced by black comedy, very popular in the late 1950s and early 1960s in America and perhaps best exemplified by Edward Albee's *The American Dream* (1961). Both plays contain lengthy descriptions of the torturous destruction of an individual, for instance, but, unlike Albee's play, the moral outrage of *Oh Dad* is never spoken; instead, Kopit relies completely upon wild theatricality and irreverent parody to indict the society of his time as seen by a precocious Harvard undergraduate.

Kopit continued his penchant for outrageous titles in *The Day the Whores Came Out to Play Tennis*, a comic fable that parodies Anton Chekhov's *The Cherry Orchard* (1903). Set in the former nursery room of a suburban Jewish country club called the Cherry Valley, the play concerns the dilemma posed by a group of prostitutes who come out from the city, take over the tennis courts, and refuse to leave, their tennis balls pounding in the audience's ears, much like the final axes of Chekhov's play, as the lights fade.

The most sustained and widely performed of the plays Kopit wrote between *Oh Dad* and *Indians*, however, is *Chamber Music*, which chronicles a board meeting in a mental hospital ward attended by eight insane women, each of whom believes she is a famous historical figure. The personages of *Chamber Music*—Mrs. Mozart, Osa Johnson, Gertrude Stein, Pearl White, Amelia Earhart, Queen Isabella, Joan of Arc, and Susan B. Anthony—represent different epochs and different movements in arts and politics. By reincarnating them through each inmate's mad delusion, Kopit blends all of history into the single temporal and spatial world of the play while calling into question the relationship of identity to history and myth.

Indians explores this theme further through the device of Buffalo Bill's Wild West Show, which Kopit deconstructs in the play as a violent and racist myth-making machine. The central figure of *Indians*, Buffalo Bill Cody, represents the American character at large—bumbling but well-meaning and ultimately unable to recognize the destruction he has caused by contributing to a myth that sanctioned the genocide of Native Americans. A thrilling theatrical spectacle that ironically captures the spirit of the original Wild West Shows, *Indians* contrasts such historical figures as Sitting Bull and Wild Bill Hickok with their mythologized counterparts, thus questioning the validity of our perceptions of history. Kopit has commented that *Indians* also explores the connection between the American conquest of the West and the U.S. involvement in Vietnam. This dimension gives *Indians* a complexity and immediacy that make it one of the most important American plays of the 1960s.

Using audacious sound and imagery and calling upon the technological resources of the theatre in an indispensable way, *Wings* enters the inner world of a former aviatrix daredevil, Emily Stilson, who suffers a stroke and undergoes rehabilitation. As the aphasiac Mrs. Stilson tries to put the pieces of her shattered world back together, Kopit attempts to explore thought and feeling beyond the infrastructure of linguistic habit and, in the process, creates in Mrs. Stilson his most fully realized, believable, and sympathetic character.

Kopit moved from an examination of inner turmoil to that of outer horror in *End of the World*, in which the playwright's surrogate, Michael Trent, is commissioned to write a play about impending nuclear destruction. As he did in *Indians*, Kopit adopts a metatheatrical device—here a private-eye parody with the playwright as detective—to arrive at the conclusion that Trent shares with those who are involved in nuclear proliferation an attraction to the powerful force of evil.

Of his last play of note, *Road to Nirvana* (1991), Kopit said it was "the wildest thing I've ever written." In trying to secure a movie deal with a Madonna-like pop star, two would-be Hollywood producers push the limits of civilized behavior in a series of obscene and vulgar male rituals that echo the hilarious sophomoric sensibility of *Oh Dad* while simultaneously ridiculing a morally hopeless world with a cynical maturity grounded in profound despair.

Kopit's place in the canon of Jewish-American dramatists is assured, although his work, like Arthur Miller's *All My Sons* and *Death of a Salesman*, for example, is less concerned with ethnic particulars than with more universal themes, reflected in the Jewish experience, of suffering, responsibility, isolation, and familial bonds. Kopit demonstrates in *The Questioning of Nick* and in the character of Ned Buntline in *Indians* a facility for the peculiarities of ethnic language rhythms, yet in the two plays that draw most heavily on his own experience, *Wings* and *End of the World*, he transforms the real-life Jewish sources for the protagonists—his father and himself, respectively—into fully realized characters who, like Joe Keller and Willy Loman, transcend ethnic particulars to comment upon universal problems of suffering and responsibility.

Nonetheless, some of Kopit's other work does reveal a more clearly Jewish sensibility, especially *Oh Dad*, which anticipates the satires of Bruce Jay Friedman and creates in the character of Madame Rosepettle ("Rosenblumenblatt") a monstrous precursor to the stereotypical Jewish mother who appears in the work of Woody Allen, Neil Simon, and Philip Roth. Although written in colloquial American diction, *Oh Dad* is sprinkled with Jewish ethnic expressions. When Madame Rosepettle finds a common dime in her son Jonathan's coin collection, she exclaims, "[W]hat is a dime doing in here? Fegh!" (21). She cross-examines Rosalie, the young woman she rightly regards as a rival for her son's affections in a manner worthy of Sophie Portnoy: "Can you cook?" When the girl says that she can, Madame Rosepettle responds, "Not good enough!" (45). Her final line of dialogue in *Oh Dad* reflects a comic syntax: "As a mother to a son I ask you. What is the meaning of this?" (89).

The members of the besieged country club in *The Day the Whores Came Out to Play Tennis* embody in their speech an urban Jewish idiom, despite their flight to the suburbs, and Kopit's sharp ear for Jewish colloquialisms is perhaps most noteworthy in *Road to Nirvana*, his satire of Hollywood in a style that lampoons his fellow Jewish-American playwright David Mamet.

From his early works, such as *Sing to Me through Open Windows*, through *Indians* and *Phantom*, Kopit demonstrates a fascination with ritual and spiritual quests reflected in Judaism, and the genocide of Native Americans chronicled in *Indians* would have a special resonance for Jewish Americans.

CRITICAL RECEPTION

Bradish, Kopit's tutor at Harvard, wrote in the Introduction to the published version of *Oh Dad* that the young playwright had a promising future, an opinion with which most critics at the time *Oh Dad* was produced concurred. Wellwarth observes that *Oh Dad* is a "brilliant satiric take-off on the conventions of the avant-garde drama," although Martin Esslin claims that Kopit's fun in *Oh Dad* "spoils his opportunity to transmute his material into a grotesque poetic image" (291). Nonetheless, Allen Lewis describes the play's imaginative effects and bold theatricality as "a technician's delight" (198).

In the years following the success of *Oh Dad*, Kopit had some difficulty escaping such labels as "silly" and "undergraduate," although Gerald Weales observed of *The Day the Whores Came Out to Play Tennis* that "it is difficult to escape the suburban Jewish milieu and the suspicion that this play is not making a general social point, but some kind of oblique comment on the Negro middle-class exodus, following the sons and grandsons of immigrants into the safe suburbs."

Critical reaction to *Indians* was mixed, and a revival at the McCarter Theater in October 1991 received an unfavorable review by Alvin Klein, who found the echoes of Vietnam in the play too forced. Morris Freedman has described *Indians* as "an attempt" at an American tragedy because "it is more than an experiment and less than an achievement" (123). Julius Novick called the play "a neo-Brechtian chronicle of events on the Great Plains" (3), yet Lewis condemned *Indians* because the technical devices in the play "divert attention from the central theme" and because "Kopit was unable to achieve the poetry or vision of Brecht's mature historical realism" (199). A more perceptive understanding of Kopit's methodology in *Indians* was demonstrated by Clive Barnes in his review of the original New York production: "A play does not have to have those old linear guidelines of a beginning, a middle and an end. A play does not have to present a consistent mood, or even a consistent viewpoint. A play can be a group of images, some tragic, some even coarse" (57). Perhaps the most thorough critical analysis of *Indians* to be found is a dialogue between John Lahr and Kopit published as an unpaginated insert in the 1971 Bantam paperback edition of the play.

Wings was much more positively received by the critics, and Doris Auerbach has noted that Kopit considers it to be his best play. The musical version of *Wings* that premiered in Chicago in 1992 was enthusiastically reviewed by Joel Henning and David Richards, but when the production opened in New York, both Frank Rich and John Simon were less positive about its merits, preferring the original play.

Critical opinion about *End of the World* was sharply divided. Reviewers such as Rich objected to Kopit's use of show business gossip in a play about the weighty matter of nuclear destruction, but Benedict Nightingale praised the play for balancing its humor with an urgent and serious purpose. Weales lamented a theatre season that embraced Tom Stoppard's *The Real Thing* (1984), another play with a playwright as its protagonist, over *End of the World*, which he considered a much superior work. In reviewing the American Repertory Theater's production of *End of the World* in January 1987, Edwin Wilson cited Luigi Pirandello as one of Kopit's influences, and Dragan Klaic has placed *End of the World* in a dramatic spectrum that includes works by Georg Kaiser, Karel Capek, and Durrenmatt.

Kopit's attempts to satirize Mamet generally and *Speed-the-Plow* (1991) specifically in *Road to Nirvana* were disparaged by such critics as Barnes and Rich, who suggested that Kopit's play was mean-spirited and less an achievement than Mamet's work. Novick and Edith Oliver, however, admired Kopit's bold, albeit repetitive, satire in the play's language. Most reviews of *Road to Nirvana* commented upon the play's scatalogical action and base imagery, affirming Wellwarth's observation made two decades previously:"Kopit has a distinct tendency to view the rotting underside of life from below" (21).

A key to any critical appraisal of Kopit's work, however, might be the playwright's own remarks about his relationship to the theatre. "You can be moved in the theatre in a way that nothing else can move you," Kopit has said (72). "To me, theater should be an experience like a little child going to a circus, a fun-house, not knowing what you're going to see. Really to be turned on. A theater that is written, verbal, not improvised, yet owes something to jazz . . . because it has spontaneity" (20).

BIBLIOGRAPHY

Works by Arthur L. Kopit

Dates in parentheses are of performance when different from date of publication.

Oh Dad, Poor Dad, Mama's Hung You in the Closet and I'm Feelin' So Sad. New York: Hill and Wang, 1960.

The Day the Whores Came Out to Play Tennis and Other Plays. New York: Hill and Wang, 1965.

Chamber Music (1964). London: Methuen, 1969.

Indians. New York: Hill and Wang, 1969.

Wings. New York: Hill and Wang, 1978.

Good Help Is Hard to Find (1981). New York: Samuel French, 1982.

Ghosts: A Drama by Henrik Ibsen. (Translation). New York: Samuel French, 1982.

Nine: The Musical (1982). (Book. Music and lyrics by Maury Yeston. Adapted from the Italian by Mario Fratti). New York: Samuel French, 1983.

End of the World. New York: Hill and Wang, 1984.

Road to Nirvana (1990). New York: Farrar, Straus, and Giroux, 1991.

Phantom, 1991.

Essays

"The Vital Matter of Environment." *Theatre Arts* 45, no. 4 (April 1961): 12–13.

"Thank You, Annette Funicello." *Saturday Evening Post*, July 16, 1966, 75–77.

"An Immovable Feast." *Esquire*, May 1988, 112–13.

Works about Arthur L. Kopit

Adler, Thomas P. "Public Faces, Private Graces: Apocalypse Postponed in Arthur Kopit's *End of the World*." *Studies in the Literary Imagination* 21, no. 2 (Fall 1988): 107–18.

Auerbach, Doris. *Sam Shepard, Arthur Kopit and the Off-Broadway Theater*. Boston: Twayne, 1982.

Barnes, Clive. "Road to Nerve-racking." *New York Post*, March 8, 1991: 42.

———. "Theater: Kopit's 'Indians.' " *New York Times*, October 14, 1969: 57.

Bradish, Gaynor F. "Kopit, Arthur (Lee)." *Contemporary Dramatists*. Ed. James Vinson, 3rd ed. New York: St. Martin's, 1982. 455–58.

Brustein, Robert. "New American Playwrights." *Modern Occasions*. Ed. Philip Rahv. New York: Farrar, Straus and Giroux, 1966. 123–218.

Calta, Louis. "News of the Rialto: A. Kopit's Latest." *New York Times*, January 31, 1965, sec. 2, 1.

Cohn, Ruby. "Camp, Cruelty, Colloquialism." *Comic Relief: Humor in Contemporary American Literature*. Ed. Sarah Blacher Cohen. Urbana: University of Illinois Press, 1978. 281–303.

Dieckman, Suzanne Burgoyne, and Richard Brayshaw. "Wings, Watchers, and Windows: Imprisonment in the Plays of Arthur Kopit." *Theater Journal* 35, no. 2 (May 1983): 195–212.

Edgerton, Gary. "Wings: Radio Play Adapted to Experimental Stage." *Journal of Popular Culture* 16, no. 4 (1983): 152–58.

Esslin, Martin. *The Theater of the Absurd.* Rev. ed. Garden City, New York: Doubleday Anchor Books, 1969.

Freedman, Morris. *American Drama in Social Context.* Carbondale: Southern Illinois University Press, 1971.

Gassner, John. "Broadway in Review." *Educational Theater Journal* 14 (May 1962): 169–71.

Grant, Thomas M. "American History in Drama: The Commemorative Tradition and Some Recent Revisions." *Modern Drama* 19 (December 1976): 327–39.

Hennessy, Brendan. "Arthur Kopit." In *Behind the Scenes: Theater and Film Interviews from the Transatlantic Review.* Ed. Joseph F. McCrindle. New York: Holt, 1971. 70–76.

Henning, Joel. "Theater: A Stroke Victim's Inner Struggle." *Wall Street Journal,* November 23, 1992, sec. A, 12.

Hollander, John. "The Question of American Jewish Poetry." In *What Is Jewish Literature?* Edited with an introduction by Hana Wirth-Nesher. Philadelphia: Jewish Publication Society, 1994.

Hughes, Catherine. *American Playwrights: 1945–75.* London: Pitman, 1976.

Jiji, Vera M. "Indians: A Mosaic of Memories and Methodologies." *Players* 47 (Summer 1972): 230–36.

Jones, John B. "Impersonation and Authenticity: The Theater as Metaphor in Kopit's *Indians.*" *Quarterly Journal of Speech* 59 (December 1973): 443–51.

Kauffmann, Stanley. *Persons of the Drama: Theater Criticism and Comment.* New York: Harper and Row, 1976.

Kelley, Margot Anne. "Order within Fragmentation: Postmodernism and the Stroke Victim's World." *Modern Drama* 34, no. 3 (September 1994): 383–91.

Kelly, Kevin. "Kopit's 'Road to Nirvana'—'Wildest Thing I've Ever Written.' " *Boston Globe,* April 1, 1990, sec. B, 30.

Klaic, Dragan. *The Plot of the Future: Utopia and Dystopia in Modern Drama.* Ann Arbor: University of Michigan Press, 1991.

Klein, Alvin. " 'Indians' an Echo of Vietnam." *New York Times,* October 20, 1991, New Jersey ed., 13.

Kopit, Arthur, "Interview." *Behind the Scenes: Theater and Film Interviews from the 'Transatlantic Review.'* Ed. Joseph F. McCrindle. New York: Holt, Rinehart and Winston, 1971.

Lahr, John. "Arthur Kopit's *Indians*: Dramatizing National Amnesia." *Evergreen Review* 13 (October 1969): 19–21, 63, 67.

———. "*Indians*: A Dialogue Between Arthur Kopit and John Lahr." Ed. Anthea Lahr. Insert in Bantam edition of *Indians.* New York: Bantam, 1971.

Lewis, Alan. *American Plays and Playwrights of the Contemporary Theater.* New York: Crown Publishers, 1970.

McCrindle, Joseph F. (ed.). *Behind the Scenes: Theater and Film Interviews from the 'Transatlantic Review.'* " New York: Holt, Rinehart, and Winston, 1971.

Murch, Anne C. "Genet-Triana-Kopit: Ritual as 'Danse Macabre.' " *Modern Drama* 15 (March 1973): 369–81.

Myers, Norman J. "Two Kinds of Alaska: Pinter and Kopit Journey through 'Another Realm.' " *The Pinter Review* (1992–1993): 11–19.

Nightingale, Benedict. "Kopit's 'End of the World' Is Serious, Urgent Drama." *New York Times*, May 20, 1984, sec. 2, 7–8.

Novick, Julius. "Kopit's 'Nirvana': Meat Ax Satire." *New York Observer*, March 18, 1991, 21.

———. " 'Liberty and Justice'—for Indians?" *New York Times*, May 18, 1969, sec. D, 3.

Oliver, Edith. "House of Mamet." *New Yorker*, March 18, 1991, 82.

O'Neill, Michael C. "History As Dramatic Present: Arthur L. Kopit's *Indians.*" *Theater Journal* 34 (December 1982): 493–504.

Przemcka, Irma. "European Influence on the Theater of Edward Albee, Arthur Kopit, and Sam Shepard." *Cross-Cultural Studies: American and European Literatures: 1945–1985.* Ed. Mirko Jurak. Ljubljana, Yugoslavia: English Department, Filozofska Fakilteta, 1988. 491–95.

Rich, Frank. "A Musical Made of the Story of a Stroke." *New York Times*, March 10, 1993, sec. 3, 13.

———. "Art Imitates Art (and Artists) and the Cost Sounds Excruciating." *New York Times*, March 8, 1991, sec. C, 1.

———. "Stage: New Kopit Play." *New York Times*, May 7, 1984, sec. C, 15.

Richards, David. "A Haunting New Musical Illuminates a Gallant Soul." *New York Times*, November 22, 1992, sec. 2, 5.

Rinear, D. L. "*The Day the Whores Came Out to Play Tennis*: Kopit's Debt to Chekhov." *Today's Speech* 22 (Spring 1974): 19–23.

Simon, John. "Two From the Heart, Two From Hunger." *New York*, March 18, 1991, 76–77.

Szilassy, Zoltan. *American Theater of the 1960s.* Carbondale: Southern Illinois University Press, 1986.

Taylor, John Russell. "Kopit Goes West." *Plays and Players* 15 (September 1968): 16–19.

Weales, Gerald. *The Jumping Off Place: American Drama in the 1960's.* London: Macmillan, 1969.

———. "Playwright's Dilemma: Stoppard and Kopit." *Commonweal* 111 (1984): 404–405.

Wellwarth, George. *The Theater of Protest and Paradox.* New York: New York University Press, 1964.

Westarp, Karl Heinz. "Myth in Peter Shaffer's *The Royal Hunt of the Sun* and in Arthur Kopit's *Indians. English Studies* 65, no. 2 (April 1984): 120–28.

Wilson, Edwin. "Art vs. Life: Grappling with Pirandello." *Wall Street Journal*, January 7, 1987, 19.

Zins, Daniel L. "Waging Nuclear War Rationally: Strategic 'Thought' in Arthur Kopit's *End of the World.*" *The Nightmare Considered: Critical Essays on Nuclear War Literature.* Ed. Nancy Anisfield. Bowling Green, OH: Popular, 1991. 123–39.

TONY KUSHNER (1956–)

Dennis A. Klein

BIOGRAPHY

Tony Kushner is the product of an upbringing in New York City and Lake Charles, Louisiana, in a home alive with Judaism, leftist politics, and the arts. His parents met when they played side by side at the New Orleans Philharmonic, then moved to Manhattan, where Tony was born on July 16, 1956. When Tony was two years old, they moved again, this time to Lake Charles, Louisiana, on the fringe of Cajun country. The spontaneity of the dialogue among the characters in his plays seems a reflection of his childhood in a home filled with conversation about politics, ethics, and music. His family observed Passover seder in Reform style; and the grandmother of this family, which saw the birth of Roosevelt's New Deal, lived with an active fear of the dreaded Joseph McCarthy. The political, ethical, and religious attitudes with which Kushner grew up permeate the speech of the dramatic characters he went on to create.

Kushner's formal education took place in New York City, first at Columbia University as an undergraduate student majoring in medieval studies, an interest that emerges in *Angels in America*, and then as a graduate student in theatre at New York University (NYU). During these years Kushner saw as many plays as he could and made acquaintances and professional decisions that determined the course of his life. At Columbia, he met Kimberly Flynn, with whom he shared mutual interests in Freudian psychology and Marxist politics, as well as literary and social theory and criticism. It was not only with Flynn that Kushner was discussing Freud; he was seeing an analyst at the time in an attempt to reverse his orientation from homosexual to heterosexual. At NYU, not another straight woman but rather a gay man became a driving force in his life. There he met his then-lover Mark Bronnenberg, and they along with Flynn started a theatrical company, for which Tony wrote and directed plays. One of those plays, *La Fin de la Baleine: An Opera for the Apocalypse* incorporated Flynn's ideas on sadomasochism with a concern about environmental destruction, which is a theme in the play *Slavs! Baleine* featured Stephen Spinella, who went on to play the role of Baz in *A Bright Room Called Day* and later won the Tony Award for the featured actor in the role of Prior Walter in *Angels in America.* Kushner's interest in history emerges in his next play, *The Heavenly Theatre,* about a peasant uprising in France during the sixteenth century.

In 1985, Kushner won a seven-year fellowship in directing from the National Endowment for the Arts to work with the St. Louis Repertory Theatre. Kimberly Flynn had recently been in an auto accident that left her brain-damaged, and Kushner had to make his plans and decisions around her condition. Her misfortune and the need for Kushner to care for her had a dramatic redemptive quality, if one that filled Tony with pangs of guilt. It became the basis for AIDS-infected Prior in *Angels.* During that same period, in 1990, his mother, with whom he was very close, died of lung cancer. He then started work on *Perestroika,* a play replete with the negative feelings of absence, abandonment, and loss. Kushner, an activist for gay rights and AIDS research, currently resides in Manhattan.

MAJOR WORKS AND THEMES

Kushner's plays fall into two categories: adaptations from other languages and original works. Four plays fit into the first category: *The Illusion,* adapted from Pierre Corneille's 1636 French comedy *L'Illusion*; *The Good Person of Sezuan,* an adaptation of Bertolt Brecht's twentieth-century German play *Der gute Mensch von Sezuan* (whose title is often inaccurately translated as *The Good Woman of Setzuan*); Goethe's *Stella*; and *A Dybbuk,* an English version of S. Ansky's Yiddish play. While the latter play, which was produced at the Hartford Stage before moving to New York, demonstrates Kushner's knowledge of Jewish traditions and an interest in Jewish themes and in supernatural phenomena, his adaptation of Corneille's play is the most dramatically interesting, since it blends the situation in the French play with characters from Fernando de Rojas's *La Celestina,* a 1499 Spanish work. Kushner wrote the play on a $700 commission from the New York Theater Workshop, where it was performed in October 1988, with Stephen Spinella in the role of the magician's servant. It went to the Hartford Stage Company in January 1990 and then to the Los Angeles Theater Center in April 1990 and won the Los Angeles Critics' Circle Award for the best production of the year. The plurality of roles and overlapping situations would be a prominent feature of *Angels in America.*

In his keynote address at the Fifth Annual OutWrite Conference, held in Boston on March 3, 1995, Kushner gave his recipe for lasagna and then went on to make the comparison between a good lasagna and a good play: "[I]t should be overstuffed: It has a pomposity, and an overreach: Its ambitions extend in the direction of not-missing-a-trick . . . [p]retentiousness, overstatement, rhetoric and histrionics, grandiosity and portentousness'' (*Thinking* 61–62). If this description applies to good theatre in general, it applies to *Angels in America* in spades.

The entity collectively referred to as *Angels in America* is composed of two separate plays that share the same characters, plot, and sets. Kushner started writing *Millennium Approaches*, the first part of the pair, in 1988, and its theatrical history is rather involved. It was first produced by the Center Theater Group in workshop format at the Mark Taper in Los Angeles in May 1990. It went on to have its world premiere performance with the Eureka Theatre Company in San Francisco in May 1991. From there it moved to the National Theatre in London in January 1992 and finally opened on Broadway in March 1993. In the process, it won every possible award: Bay Area Drama Critics' Award, Los Angeles Drama Critics' Circle Award, London Evening Standard Award, London Drama Critics' Circle Award, the Tony Award, New York Drama Critics' Circle Award, Drama Desk Award, and the Pulitzer Prize.

What is it about this play that has earned it such universal acclaim? Each individual play, as well as the unit, is a masterpiece, a seamless tapestry of seemingly unrelated characters and themes, all of which come to form a coherent whole. The best place to start a journey into *Angels in America* is with its subtitle, *A Gay Fantasia on National Themes*. That subtitle identifies its aesthetics, its structure, and its subject matter. Kushner revealed in an interview that he wrote *Angels* with the intention of preaching to the converted: ''[W]hen I started writing *Angels in America*, the one thing I took as an absolute given is that we [homosexuals] all agreed that it is okay to be gay. . . . I thought the most boring thing I could conceivably do is to write a play trying to convince people that it was good to be gay, because we got past that, I mean that was what Mark [*sic*] Crowley did in *Boys in the Band* '' (Arons 55). But *Angels'* appeal extends way beyond the gay community, a fact to which its list of mainstream awards serves testimony. But, of course, the plays *are* gay in their ambience and sensibility; they take the gay milieu for granted and deal with subjects such as AIDS, self-loathing homosexuals, and ''coming out,'' all of which are of interest to the gay, theatregoing public.

Next Kushner states that his work is a ''fantasia,'' a work of free-flowing form and with liberal departures from reality. The subject matter of ''national themes'' extends from McCarthy-era politics and the execution of the Rosenbergs to the political power structure of the 1980s, with Roy Cohn right near the top. *Angels* covers the American demographic landscape from Old World Jewish to American-founded Mormon, from Salt Lake City to New York City, black and white, gay and straight, rich and poor, the empowered and the disfranchised. It is so all-encompassing that the present writer finds it to be not only the most important American play of our age but perhaps the most important play ever written in or about the United States. Its spirit of patriotism derives from the freedom with which it criticizes who and what we Americans

are. In the same address that contains the recipe for lasagna, Kushner went on
to say that "this selfsame pretentiousness and grandiosity was my birthright as
an American" (63). On that premise and in that belief Kushner's characters
exist and behave. It is at once the quintessential gay, Jewish-American, and New
York play.

Angels is a sweeping panorama, a modern-day epic of personal tragedies with
national, religious, and otherworldly implications. There are three major plot-
lines and any number of minor, small subplots. The three main plots involve
Louis Ironson, a secular, Jewish word processor given to lofty declamations on
political, philosophical, and ethical issues who is leaving his lover, Prior Walter,
who is infected with AIDS. In the second, which strongly parallels the first,
Joseph Pitt, a Mormon and chief clerk at the Federal Court of Appeals, is leaving
his Valium-addicted wife, Harper, for Louis. Then there is Roy Cohn, Joe's
mentor and the powerful attorney and right-hand man of Senator Joseph Mc-
Carthy; like Prior, Cohn has AIDS. Add to this group Belize, a campy black
ex-drag queen, now nurse to Roy Cohn; and Hannah, Joe's mother, who moves
from Salt Lake City to Brooklyn when Joe leaves his wife, and one is ready to
delve into the drama of personal and interrelated problems. Hannah reveals the
method behind what may seem to be the madness of this work; she utters the
word "interconnectedness," and suddenly the whole work becomes clear. In
fact, the interconnections are the brilliance of the work, which is constructed on
the basis of interlocking triangles. There is the Prior-Louis-Joe amorous triangle,
which connects with the Hannah-Joe-Louis marital triangle, which intersects the
Harper-Hannah-Prior fantasy triangle. In addition, there is the Roy-Belize-Prior
health triangle. Besides the triangles, there are parallel lines, which equate the
gay relationship between Louis and Prior with the heterosexual marriage between Harper and Joe.

Roy Cohn provides the strongest contrast in the work with the other characters. In a play that takes homosexuality for granted, that even flaunts and
glorifies it, Roy is the lone holdout as "closet queen." Not only is he self-
loathing, but he is in complete denial and has written his own definitions about
who and what homosexuals are and are not: they are about timidity, not about
political clout. Witness his tirade to the doctor who breaks the news to him that
he has AIDS:

Not ideology, or sexual taste, but something much simpler: clout . . . who will pick up
the phone when I call, who owes me favors. Homosexuals are not men who sleep with
other men. Homosexuals are men who in fifteen years of trying cannot get a pissant
antidiscrimination bill through City Council. (*MA* 45)

He goes on to distinguish between himself and all other gay men in that he
brings his male lovers to the White House, and President Reagan smiles at them
and shakes their hands. Cohn would no doubt make good on his threat to his
physician that he would ruin him if word got out that he has AIDS rather than

liver cancer, as Cohn claims. Cohn may be able to fool everyone else in New York, but not Belize. In a New York insider joke, Kushner, through Belize, makes reference to "[t]he Killer Queen Herself. New York's number-one closet queer" (*P* 26), and Prior thinks that Belize is talking about former mayor Ed Koch, the bachelor about whom there were persistent speculations of homosexuality.

What drives the other characters and makes them tick? Any such discussion must start with Louis, the modern-day, secular, leftist, intellectual Jew who is conflicted between the feelings of love and devotion for Prior and his wish to be rid of the obligation of caring for a lover with AIDS and with the guilt that that desire spawns in him. One insight in this play is how little young, secular, American Jews know about their religion. That message comes through from the first act of *Millennium* to the final act of *Perestroika*. In the first instance, Louis is plagued by feelings of guilt because he knows that he is going to move out on Prior. By chance he comes across a rabbi to whom he tries to pour out his soul. In essence, he wants to know "what does the Holy Writ say about someone who abandons someone he loves at a time of great need?" The rabbi suggests that Louis find himself a priest: "Catholics believe in forgiveness. Jews believe in Guilt" (25). The line may have dramatic value in the development of Louis' character and may get a laugh in the theatre, but at the cost of betraying the Jewish belief behind Yom Kippur (the Day of Atonement) and the whole ten-day period of the High Holy Days, the time during which human remorse is rewarded with Divine forgiveness. In the second instance, Kushner evokes a laugh from the knowing segment of the audience when Louis, in an attempt to recite the Kaddish over the dead body of Roy Cohn, instead recites the Kiddush, the prayer over wine: a prayer's a prayer.

The third Jewish character in the play is the ghost of Ethel Rosenberg, who Roy Cohn made sure was executed rather than imprisoned for life for her crime of espionage. She embodies the spirit of Jewish forgiveness, recites the Kaddish over Cohn's body, and is one of the angels of the play's title. The second angel is Hannah Pitt. She is also the bridge between Salt Lake City, where she begins, and New York, where she ends up. She is a person who is able to rise above her personal feelings and demonstrate true compassion. She accompanies Prior to the hospital and stays with him through his crisis. She not only defines metaphorically what an angel is but also does so verbally: "An angel is just a belief, with wings and arms that can carry you" (*P* 105).

The "national themes" include the AIDS epidemic, the politics behind treatment of the disease, and homosexuality as a political as well as a personal issue; American Judaism and the immigration that brought Jews to the United States; racism; poverty; abuse of drugs; and New York City as the mecca of national migration. In the real world, every patient infected with AIDS dies. The treatment that each one receives depends on where one ranks in the political hierarchy. Roy Cohn was the most powerful man to die of AIDS and therefore had at his disposal the best treatment available, AZT at the time *Angels* takes place.

The stash that Cohn is able to acquire leads to a racist and homophobic confrontation between him and Belize. Roy feels entitled to the best treatment because he worked for it, unlike Belize and his kind, who think that everything is coming to them. Cohn calls Belize a "nigger cunt spade faggot and lackey" and "Mongrel. Dirge. Slave. Ape," to which Belize lashes back with terms like "Shit-for-brains filthy-mouthed selfish motherfucking cowardly cocksucking cloven-hoofed pig" and finally "Greedy kike" (P 61). The point is that racism and anti-Semitism are always just below the surface of any political or social confrontation.

Even Louis and Belize cannot have a civil discussion without prejudice's rearing its ugly head. They accuse each other of hating Jews or blacks, depending on which one is talking. It is important to keep in mind the two characters involved: one is a liberal Jew, in whom a feeling of social guilt is a given; and the other person is a black who has Louis as his closest friend. To Louis, "race here is a political question . . . there are no angels in America, no spiritual past, no racial past, there's only the political, and the decoys and the ploys to maneuver around the inescapable battle of politics" (MA 92). But there are angels in America, at least in this play. There are Ethel and Hannah, not to count the two nurses, Prior's nurses and Belize, who are by definition "angels of mercy." Two more appear later in the play.

The epic that begins with *Millennium* has as its first scene something of a prologue. It is a monologue by a rabbi at a funeral, and it foreshadows the death of Roy Cohn in *Perestroika*. The rabbi gives, in brief, a history of Jews in America, tracing them from their villages in Russia and Lithuania to the Grand Concourse in the Bronx and Flatbush in Brooklyn. He reminds the attendees at the funeral (i.e., the audience), "You do not live in America. No such place exists. Your clay is the clay of some Litvak shetl, you are the air of the steppes. . . . But every day of your lives the miles that voyage between that place and this one you cross. Every day. You understand me? In you that journey is." (MA 10–11). Jews, he is saying, will never know a permanent home and will always be outsiders. Kushner draws parallels in the plays between Jews and homosexuals and, by extension, blacks and the homeless, the outsiders to mainstream American society. That's why Louis goes through life feeling like "Sid the Yid," as if he were wearing earlocks and a long black coat, just as Woody Allen felt at a Gentile dinner in *Annie Hall*.

There is a second journey that takes place, in *Perestroika*. It is the journey of a nineteenth-century Mormon family making the trek in a covered wagon from Missouri to Salt Lake City. The scene takes place in a diorama at the Mormon Visitor's Center, across from Lincoln Center in New York City and just one block west of Central Park. The diorama is a part of the games that Kushner plays between reality and fantasy: the diorama comes to life, and sure enough Louis appears in it questioning how a fundamentally theocratic religion can exist in a pluralist democracy. He is addressing Joe, and Prior is watching the scene. Here Prior meets Harper, who is a volunteer at the center. Harper thinks that she has met Prior before, and she is both correct and incorrect. They never met in any *physical* way, but they appeared in each other's fantasies in *Millennium*, Prior's brought on by fever and hers by Valium. In another one of his fantasies, Prior is visited by two Priors past, Prior 1, who died of the plague, "the spotty monster" (*MA* 86), and Prior 2, who died of bad water in seventeenth-century London.

Finally, there are two "real" angels in the play. One is a character who appears for the first time in the final scene of *Millennium*. She crashes through a frightened Prior's ceiling—"*[v]ery* Steven Spielberg" (*MA* 118), he says— and announces that Prior is a Prophet, that she is the messenger, and that the Great Work is about to begin. She appears throughout *Perestroika*, and Prior can tell when she is going to make an appearance by his sexual response. This is also the Angel with whom, like the biblical Jacob, Prior wrestles and against whom he prevails.

New York City is as fundamental to *Angels in America* as it is to a film by Woody Allen. Kushner shows a love for the city and treats everything from the Promenade in Brooklyn Heights to the Bethesda Fountain in Central Park as sacred icons. Central Park has the same dualistic angelic-demonic qualities as does the holy-sinful city of Salt Lake, where good Mormons are willing to smoke as long as no one can see them. Central Park is the place where Louis can go for an anonymous homosexual encounter and where Prior can go to enjoy his favorite angel, the one atop the Bethesda Fountain: "I like them best when they're statuary. They commemorate death but they suggest a world without dying" (*P* 147). On an optimistic note Kushner ends his play, suggesting that its message is not death but life and that there is a hopeful future for sufferers of AIDS and outsiders one and all: "We won't die secret deaths anymore. The world only spins forward. We will be citizens. The time has come. . . . *more life.*/The Great Work begins" (*P* 148).

New York and Salt Lake are hardly the only locations in the plays. One scene—in one of Harper's fantasies—takes place as far south as Antarctica, where she wishes to spend a vacation; and another scene is as far north as Heaven, which Prior visits during a fever-induced attack and which looks like San Francisco after the earthquake of 1906. The announcement in Heaven of the nuclear disaster at Chernobyl serves as an introduction to *Slavs!*

A Bright Room Called Day ran at Theatre 22 in New York in April 1985, then at the Eureka Theatre in San Francisco in October 1987, and again in New York at the Public Theatre in January 1991. *Bright Room* is, in part, a historical play, which makes parallels between the period of the Weimar Republic of the 1930s in Germany, just as the Nazis were about to come to power, and the Reagan-Bush era of the 1980s and 1990s in the United States. As in *Angels*, there is an interrelationship of subjects: here the treatment of Jews by the Nazis; and Jews in American politics, as it affects their lives. The play takes place in Agnes Eggling's low-rent apartment in Berlin in 1932 with slides depicting the events and the times and the "Interruptions" in Zillah's apartment in 1990.

Zillah left Great Neck, Long Island, to move to Berlin during "the Triumph of the Brain-Dead," the period of "National Senility" (41), that is, the Reagan-Bush era. She wanted to get away from the party that brought America Iran-Contra. The comparison between AIDS and the Holocaust—*the* standard for Evil with a capital E—and between the American and German leaders is explicit: "It's 1942; the Goerings are having an intimate soiree; if he got an invitation, would Pat Buchanan feel out of place? Out of place? Are you kidding? Pig heaven, dust off the old tuxedo, kisses to Eva and Adolf" (50). He continues with comparisons to Presidents Reagan and Bush and concludes that "as long as they look like they're playing in Mr. Hitler's Neighborhood we got no reason to relax" (51). Zillah states that the purpose of the play is "to remember, to recall: dismantle the memorial, disinter the dead" (15) and to see history as she conjures it up. In Berlin, it is January 1, 1932, and an angel has passed over to begin the new year. Through the character of Baz, who works for the Berlin Institute for Human Sexuality, Kushner makes an implicit connection between leftist politics and homosexuality: Baz believes that his sexual orientation keeps him informed about the proletarians because he has sex with them.

In addition to its themes and structure, *Bright Room* shares common ground with *Angels* in its use of fantasy. Baz surrenders "reason to the angelic hosts of the irrational" (44) when he relates how he saw that "[t]he dead man was sitting up in the snow . . . as I passed by I gave him one of my oranges. He took it" (45). Baz may not be the spokesperson for the playwright, at least not the only one. Annabella Gotchling, a communist artist in her mid-forties, voices the line "The dreams of the Left/are always beautiful" (67), Agnes elucidates the play's title in the epilogue:

> I fear the end
> I fear the way
> I fear the wind
> Will make me stray
> Much farther than
> I want to stray
> Far from my home
> Bright room called day;
> Past where deliverance or hope
> Can find me. (89)

Kushner's latest play is *Slavs! (Thinking about the Longstanding Problems of Virtue and Happiness)*. Its first production was by the Actors Theatre of Louisville, Kentucky, at the Humana Festival of New American Plays on March 8, 1994. There was a staged reading with Olympia Dukakis, Tracey Ullman, and Madeline Kahn on June 6, 1994, at the Walter Kerr Theatre in New York for the benefit of the Lesbian Avengers' Civil Rights Organizing Project. That same month, the Steppenwolf Theatre Company produced it in Chicago; and in November it opened at the New York Theatre Workshop with Marisa Tomei. It played, too, at the Hampstead Theatre in London, Center Stage in Baltimore, the Yale Repertory Theatre, and the Mark Taper Forum in Los Angeles.

If *Angels* is about sexual politics and *Room* about fascist politics, then *Slavs!* is about environmental politics and the end of Marxism. The play shares a common character with *Angels* in Aleksii Antedilluvianovich Prelapsarianov, the world's oldest living Bolshevik. Once again there is a gay character, this time a lesbian, and once again an exaltation of communism, but an equally important issue this time is environmental safety. Exposure to nuclear energy is producing, at the lowest level, blind fish and chronic fatigue and at its worst, an epidemic of thyroid cancer and leukemia. In addition, Russia is falling apart and has reduced its commitment to its people in order to support foreign interests. "The United States is becoming our landlord" (17). Racism and anti-Semitism are concerns again in this play: "Dark-skinned people from the Caucasus regions, Muslims, Asiatics, swarthy inferior races have flooded Moscow, and white Christian Russians such as you and I are expected to support them. . . . the Great Pan-Slavic Empire has been stolen from us by the International Jew" (172). By the end of the play, the faithful communists are forced to recognize that the socialist experiment has failed. Unlike *Angels*, which Kushner ends with a hopeful note, he ends *Slavs!* on a questioning one about dim prospects for the future: "What is to be done?" (10). The published edition of *Slavs!* appears in a book that also contains seven essays (one the text of the speech to OutWrite), two poems, and a prayer. The subjects throughout are America, homosexuality, socialism (including the relationship between homosexual liberation and socialism), racism, and anti-Semitism. The prayer is for a cure for AIDS.

CRITICAL RECEPTION

Reviewers fell over each other to give *Angels* the grandest accolades, and the award in that category must go to Frank Rich, writing for the *New York Times*. Even this reviewer, who has earned the nickname "the Butcher of Broadway," recognized the work's extraordinary achievement. He praised the writing of "unspeakable beauty" and "mind-exploding" imagery. He saw in Kushner an artist with the commitment to change the world and the talent to revolutionize the theatre (15). Arthur Lubow got past the subject of AIDS to the play's larger issue, the horrors of American life during the 1980s: "the triumph of heartlessness and the withering of community" (59). John Lahr, also writing in *The New Yorker*, quotes Kushner as saying,

The oppression and suppression of homosexuality is part of a larger political agenda. The struggle for a cure for AIDS and for governmental recognition of the seriousness of the epidemic connects directly to universal health care, which is connected to a larger issue, which is a social net. (127)

The character who has inspired the most commentary is Roy Cohn, with whose portrayal, Kushner acknowledges in a preliminary note to the play, he took liberties. Ross Posnock sees him as a satanic figure who threatens what he calls the play's "central Christian of millenarian redemption" (65). He goes on to question the coherence in what he sees as Kushner's "cross purposes" in *Millennium*: the assimilation of Nietzschean Cohn to the play's redemptive and "Christian project" (70). Daniel Kiefer sees Cohn as a heroically reckless character whose love for the game of life the viewers must admire. William A. Henry III gives the most succinct evaluation of Cohn's character and the one that probably comes the closest of all to the playwright's intention: Cohn's greatest evil characteristic is that he is able to promote discrimination against homosexuals while he himself enjoyed sex with men.

Angels in America is flanked chronologically by *A Bright Room Called Day*, which preceded it, and *Slavs!*, which followed it. Neither one gives even a hint of the artistic level that Kushner reached in *Angels*. To date, no play of Kushner's before or after *Angels* has earned—or deserved—the accolades that that play did.

BIBLIOGRAPHY

Works by Tony Kushner

Angels in America: A Gay Fantasia on National Themes Part I: Millennium Approaches. New York: Theatre Communications Group, 1993. [*MA*]
Angels in America: A Gay Fantasia on National Themes. Part II: Perestroika. New York: Theatre Communications Group, 1994. [P]
"A Dybbuk." Unpublished manuscript.
"The Good Person of Sezuan." Unpublished manuscript.
Plays. New York: Broadway Play, 1992. Contains *A Bright Room Called Day* and *The Illusion.*
"Stella." Unpublished manuscript.
"Guest Speaker." *Architectural Digest*, November 1995: 28, 32. Photograph in his apartment and some autobiographical information.
Thinking about the Longstanding Problems of Virtue and Happiness. New York: Theatre Communications Group, 1995. Contains *Slavs!*; previously published essays "American Things," "Fick oder Kaputt!" "A Socialism of the Skin (Liberation, Honey!)," "With a Little Help from My Friends," "Some Questions about Tolerance," "Copious Gigantic, and Sane"; "On Pretentiousness," the text of Kushner's keynote address at 5th Annual OutWrite Conference, Boston, March 3, 1995; two poems: "An Epithalamion" and "The Second Month of Mourning"; and a prayer.

Works about Tony Kushner

Arons, Wendy. " 'Preaching to the Converted?'—'You Couldn't Possibly Do Any Better!': An Interview with Tony Kushner on September 19, 1994." *Communications from the International Brecht Society* 23, 2 (November 1994): 51–59. On his adaptions; some comments on background of writing *Angels*.

Cheever, Susan. ''An Angel Sat Down at His Table.'' *New York Times*, September 13, 1992: II, 7. Review of *Angels*.

Disch, Thomas M. ''Theater: A Bright Room Called Day/Dead Mother/Unchanging Love.'' *Nation*, March 18, 1991: 352–56. Review of *Bright Room*.

Henry, William A., III. ''Celebrating Gay Anger.'' *Time*, November 23, 1992: 72–74. Review of *Angels*.

Kiefer, Daniel. ''*Angels in America* and the Failure of Revelation.'' *American Drama* 4, 1 (Fall 1994): 21–38. Article on *Angels*.

Lahr, John. ''Beyond Nelly.'' *The New Yorker*, November 23, 1992: 126–30. *Review of Angels* and related comments on Kushner.

Lubow, Arthur. ''Tony Kushner's Paradise Lost.'' *The New Yorker*, November 30, 1992: 59–64. Biographical information on Kushner.

Posnock, Ross. ''Roy Cohen in America.'' *Raritan* 13, 3 (Winter 1993): 64–77.

Rich, Frank. ''Marching Out of the Closet, into History.'' *New York Times*, November 10, 1992: C15–22. Laudatory review of *Angels*.

Simon, John. ''From Broadway to Berlin.'' *New York Magazine*, January 21, 1991: 55–56. Unfavorable review of *Bright Room* that acknowledges Kushner's contributions to the theatre: big topics, free play of ideas, cosmopolitan approach, sophisticated language.

Solomon, Alisa. ''Dialectical Spiritualism.'' *Village Voice*, March 7, 1995: 82. Review of *Dybbuk* at Hartford Stage.

Winer, Laurie. ''Questions Unanswered in Kushner's *Slavs!*'' *Los Angeles Times*, October 27, 1995. Review of *Slavs!* in Los Angeles.

JAMES LAPINE   (1949–   )

Joshua Berg

BIOGRAPHY

James Lapine has led a life of which any aspiring dramatist could only dream, having spent years between the States and France building a career and a tremendous reputation in the theatre. His efforts have earned him the respect and admiration of his peers and his audiences. He presently lives high above New York City in a Central Park West apartment with his wife, the screenwriter Sarah Kernochan, and their daughter.

James Lapine was born in Mansfield, Ohio, in 1949. He did his undergraduate work at Franklin and Marshall, receiving a B.A. in history in 1971. From there he went on to earn an M.F.A. in graphic design from the California Institute of the Arts. He moved to New York City and in 1975 began work as a graphic designer for Yale Drama School's magazine, *Yale Theater*. Lapine has since written and directed numerous productions for the stage and screen and in 1993 began working with Broadway play and musical developer the Schubert Organization.

Critics unanimously laud his work as a director, and his plays earn consistently favorable receptions. His unique talents as a visual design artist, along with his personal experience and heritage as a Jew, help him to create work that is unequivocally the theatre's finest. An intriguing aspect of Lapine's written works is from what they take their inspiration. He has extracted his ideas from unlikely and unique places, including a psychological case study, a poem, and a painting, transmuting them into successful stage plays. He has proven himself equally deft at drawing from conventional inspiration, such as family and the dynamics of love.

MAJOR WORKS AND THEMES

James Lapine's first play was a dramatization of the short, abstract poem/play *Photograph* by Gertrude Stein. It was reworked for the stage and directed by Lapine in New Haven, Connecticut during his tenure at *Yale Theater* magazine. In 1978, under the direction of Lapine, it won an Obie for its production off-off Broadway at the Open Space in Soho.

James Lapine's second major effort as a playwright was *Twelve Dreams*, a drama that takes its mark from a case study of Carl Jung's wherein, according to Jung's theory of "collective unconscious," a little girl predicts her own death through a series of twelve dreams. The foundation of Lapine's story, that a girl presents a book of Twelve Dreams to her father as a gift, reflects Jung's accounts in his book *Man and His Symbols*. The controversial theories of the play's Professor character, who interprets the dreams, emulate Jung's. Other characters fit snugly into Jung's definitions of psychological types, and symbols and references throughout the play delineate typical Jung "archetypes." The play was first produced in 1978 by Lynn Austin's Music-Theater Performing Group/ Lenox Arts Center under Lapine's direction. Its second staging, also directed by Lapine, opened on December 1, 1981, with the New York Shakespeare Festival at the Public Theatre/Martinson Hall in New York City.

What is regarded as James Lapine's professional stage debut as a playwright and director came with his play *Table Settings*. The play was presented first as a workshop piece at Playwright's Horizons of New York in March 1979. Its commercial release came in January 1980, also at Playwright's Horizons. The characters are the members of a middle-class, Jewish-American family. The incidents of the play arise from intergenerational, gender, moral, and other conflicts within and between the characters. The fulcrum about which the action revolves is the dining room table. Referred to by their position within the family, that is, Mother, Older Son, Wife, Granddaughter, and so on, rather than by proper nouns, all of the characters are roundly representative of members of the typical Jewish-American family of the period. The play is made up of numerous titled incidents whose affiliation comes from the characters and their exchanges. Lapine was successful in taking a slice of life within a Jewish-American family, hoisting it onto the stage, and letting the quirky constitution and exchanges of the family hold the audience in its grasp and drive the play forward. Although the play is about a Jewish family, almost everyone can relate to the characters and conflicts in this play, and this gives it wide appeal. *Table Settings* received off-Broadway Best Play commendations, including the George Oppenheimer-Newsday Award for the best new play produced in New York or on Long Island in 1980–1981.

Lapine began, in the early 1980s, what proved to be a very successful collaborative relationship with one of Broadway's best musical composers, Stephen Sondheim. Lapine and Sondheim's first collaborative effort was inspired by another work of art: a painting. Their musical, *Sunday in the Park with George*, is about the life and character of the French painter Georges Seurat and his late nineteenth-century painting *A Sunday Afternoon on the Island of La Grande Jatte*. In his time, Saurat was considered controversial for developing a new type of brush stroke that could be used to fool the eye into seeing colors that were not really there. In taking a work of art seemingly unrelated to live theatre, such as a painting, and giving it life on a stage, Lapine and Sondheim display their own innovation and invention. The piece was commissioned for Lapine by Playwright's Horizons and was created through what Andre Bishop, the director of Playwright's Horizons, called a "hectic, exhilarating" workshop and production process before it opened there in July 1983. *Sunday in the Park with George* began its run on Broadway in April 1984 and went on to win the New York Drama Critics Circle Award for Best Musical. Lapine and Sondheim shared a Pulitzer Prize for drama, and the production won two Tony Awards and eight Tony nominations, including two for Lapine himself for best book of a musical and best direction of a musical.

Lapine and Sondheim's second collaboration, the musical *Into the Woods*, proved also to be immensely successful. The musical showcases the abilities of its creators to artfully illustrate real life's complexities. The music and lyrics are the woof and the warp of this flawlessly woven piece. With *Into the Woods*, Lapine and Sondheim staged a fairy tale, incorporating familiar fairy tale characters and story lines. It entertains with conflict and politics that adults can relate to and with just plain fun that anyone and everyone can enjoy. The show had its debut at the Old Globe Theatre in San Diego, California, in December 1986 and moved to Broadway in November 1987.

Lapine cowrote the book for William Finn's successful Broadway song-play *Falsettos*. It was a fusion of two earlier one-act musicals, *March of the Falsettos*, an Outer Critics Circle Award winner for best off-Broadway play in the 1980–1981 season, and *Falsettoland*, produced off-Broadway ten years after its predecessor. The collective works are about the life of Marvin, a man who leaves his wife and son for a gay lover. The characters in this play are also members of a Jewish family unit, although a much more atypical one than those of Lapine's earlier *Table Settings*. He even incorporates a bar mitzvah as the focus of action of the second act. In the closing scene, the characters recite gibberish rather than Hebrew and play around props that are generic symbols of Judaism to create a bar mitzvah of some verisimilitude but more of just a general atmosphere of Jewish celebration of life, meaningfully, in the hospital room of the character who is dying of AIDS. Once again, the problems that these characters deal with can be just as universal as they are decisively Jewish. The musical explores relationships, family, sexuality, and AIDS, the "mysterious disease" that began its reign of terror in 1981, when the play is set. Both *March of the Falsettos* and *Falsettoland* and the comprehensive *Falsettos* were staged under the direction of James Lapine. Besides winning much critical acclaim for his direction, Lapine received a Tony Award in 1992 for his work on the book for *Falsettos*.

Lapine's most recent straight stage play is the satire *Luck, Pluck, and Virtue*. The play is an adaptation of Nathanael West's novel *A Cool Million*, which parodies the Horatio Alger "rags to riches" narrative. In the play, Lester Price is the forthright, truthful, and gullible lead character whose virtue makes him everybody's easy dupe. Lapine divides this play into a series of vaudeville acts, reminiscent of the way in which he constructed his earlier *Table Settings* from a series of titled incidents. In 1993 *Luck, Pluck and Virtue* played at the La Jolla Playhouse in California and in 1995 at the Atlantic Theater Company in Chelsea.

CRITICAL RECEPTION

Theatre critics have called Lapine "Broadway's best-kept secret," due to his outstanding work in the shadows of Stephen Sondheim. Lapine's most recent collaboration with Stephen Sondheim produced *Passion*, a musical about what happens when the diaphanous membrane separating love, lust, and obsession ruptures. The production is set in 1863 in Italy and is based on the film *Passione d'Amore* and I. U. Tarchetti's novel *Fosca*. *Passion*, developed and produced through Lapine's association with the Schubert Organization, opened on Broadway in 1994 and has won four Tony Awards, including Best Musical.

Lapine's directorial film credits include *Life with Mikey*, a Michael J. Fox vehicle, and *Impromptu*, written by Kernochan about George Sand's infatuation with Frederic Chopin and their ensuing love affair.

James Lapine, playwright, director, and intellectual, is a true dramatist, an agent of drama. He has the rare ability to help his audiences look more closely and intimately at themselves and their world. Whether it is a painting, a homosexual relationship, or an immigrant Jewish grandmother, James Lapine presents them to us, and we are moved to say, "I've seen these things before, but I must not have looked hard enough."

BIBLIOGRAPHY

Works by James Lapine

Dates in parentheses are of performance when different from date of publication.
Photograph (adapted from Gertrude Stein). New York: Open Space, 1978.
Table Settings. New York: Samuel French, 1980.
Twelve Dreams. (1978). New York: Dramatists Play Service, 1982.
With Stephen Sondheim. *Into the Woods*. New York: Theatre Communications Group, 1987.

With Stephen Sondheim. *Sunday in the Park with George*. (1983). New York: Applause
    Theatre Book, 1991.
Passion. New York: Theatre Communications Group, 1994.
With William Finn. *Falsettos*. (1991). New York: Samuel French, 1995.
Luck, Pluck and Virtue (adapted from Nathanael West's *A Cool Million*). New York:
    Atlantic Theater Company, 1995.

Works about James Lapine

Canby, Vincent. "A Morality Tale about Everybody's Fall Guy." *New York Times*, April
    15, 1995, C19.
Gerard, Jeremy. "Lapine Signs on as New Schubert Ally." *Variety*, August 30, 1993.
———. " 'Passion' Performance Not a Passing Fancy." *Variety*, August 22, 1994, 59,
    61.
Hagrefe, Jeffrey. "On the Park with James Lapine, New York Perspectives for the Di-
    rector of *Passion*." *Architectural Digest*, November 1995, 244–49.
Kerr, Walter. "Theater: Lapine's 'Table Settings' at *Playwright's Horizons*." *New York
    Times*, January 15, 1980, C7.
Rich, Frank. "Broadway Boundary Falls amid Reunions." *New York Times*, April 30,
    1992, C17, 20.

ARTHUR LAURENTS   (1918–1998)

Bette H. Kirschstein

BIOGRAPHY

Arthur Laurents was a prolific and versatile man of the theatre. He wrote over twenty plays, ranging from drama, to comedy to musical, and he directed several plays and musicals. Until his death at the age of eighty, he was still an active playwright, writing four plays in the preceding years.

Laurents was born on July 14, 1918, in Brooklyn, New York, to Irving, an attorney, and Ada Robbins Laurents, a grade school teacher. Both Irving and Ada were born in this country of Jewish parents, but their backgrounds were quite different. Irving's family was Orthodox; Ada's family was composed of socialist atheists, many of whom married non-Jews. Irving and Ada made no effort to provide their son with a formal Jewish education. Indeed, Laurents recalled attending only one Passover seder while growing up and undergoing a "phonetic bar mitzvah" for which he memorized Hebrew words without understanding their meaning. As a result of his scant religious upbringing, Laurents was never a practicing Jew. Nonetheless, he asserted that he had "always been very Jewish-conscious," believing that "what you are as a Jew . . . informs you" as a person (interview with author, March 25, 1996).

After Laurents graduated from Erasmus Hall High School in Brooklyn at the age of sixteen, he went to Cornell University, where he majored in English. There, he felt like an outsider because he was younger than many of the other students and because he was Jewish. Although he grew up in an ethnically mixed neighborhood, Laurents asserts that he had very little experience with anti-Semitism as a child. His best friend was Irish Catholic, and his own family had assimilated members of other faiths through intermarriage. At Cornell, however, he suddenly found himself dealing with an undercurrent of prejudice toward Jews.

Upon graduation from Cornell in 1937, Laurents returned to New York City but was unable to find a job because of the depression. As a result, he enrolled in a New York University radio writing course. When one of his original scripts was accepted by the experimental CBS radio program *The Columbia Workshop*, Laurents quit the class, and his radio career began.

In 1941, Laurents was drafted into the army. He spent much of the war in Astoria, Queens, making training films. However, in 1943 he joined a three-person army unit created especially for him to write civilian propaganda radio programs. In the series *Army Service Presents* and *Assignment Home*, Laurents realistically dramatized soldiers' lives on and off the battlefield. In April 1945, the Writers' War Board named his drama *The Face* best radio script of the month. Later that year, Laurents won a Variety Radio Award for the *Assignment Home* series.

At the same time as Laurents worked on the army's radio programs, he wrote episodes for commercial radio series such as *The Man Behind the Gun, The Hollywood Playhouse*, and *The Thin Man*. The exposure he received from his radio career led to his first Broadway production, *Home of the Brave* (1945), which received the Sidney Howard Memorial Award.

Between 1946 and 1957, Laurents had three more dramas produced on Broadway, including *The Time of the Cuckoo*, which provided the basis for the 1955 Katharine Hepburn movie *Summertime*. Then, in 1958, Laurents' career took a new turn. Teaming up with Leonard Bernstein, Jerome Robbins, and Stephen Sondheim, Laurents wrote the book for the musical *West Side Story*. Thus began a fruitful collaboration with Sondheim, who worked with Laurents on three more musicals: *Gypsy* (1960), *Anyone Can Whistle* (1965), and *Do I Hear a Waltz?* (1966). Other renowned musical theatre artists with whom Laurents collaborated include Richard Rodgers, Jule Styne, Betty Comden, and Adolph Green.

In addition to plays and librettos, Laurents wrote eight screenplays. He also directed many plays, some his own and some by others; his production of Jerry Herman and Harvey Fierstein's *La Cage aux Folles* won the 1988 Tony Award for Best Musical.

Among the other honors that Laurents received were a Tony for his 1967 musical *Hallelujah, Baby!*; a Drama Desk Award for the 1974 revival of *Gypsy*; and a Writers Guild of America Award, Golden Globe Award, and National Board of Review Best Picture Award for his screenplay of *The Turning Point* (1978).

MAJOR WORKS AND THEMES

One finds several recurrent themes in Laurents' plays, including sexual freedom versus puritanism; conventional behavior versus individualism; social hypocrisy versus honesty; the fragility of the human psyche; and the importance of self-esteem. However, Laurents' identity as a Jew and a homosexual led him to take social injustice as his major theme. He was always sensitive to the pain of those who endure discrimination, for, in his own words, "As one minority, you can put yourself in another minority's place" (interview with author, March 25, 1996).

Laurents' 1945 radio drama *The Face* contains a speech that sums up the message underlying so many of his plays: "Every single day, people get slapped because of ignorance. They get slapped for religion, for color, for how they talk or what they look like. . . . A man's face doesn't matter any more than his religion, his color, his clothes. It's what he is that counts" (100). Whether the specific injustice addressed is hatred of "cripples" in *The Face*; anti-Semitism in *Home of the Brave*, *The Way We Were*, and *My Good Name*; ethnic or racial prejudice in *West Side Story* and *Hallelujah, Baby!*; or homophobia in *The Enclave* and *Loss of Memory*, Laurents' plays plead for humans to be more tolerant of one another.

Laurents did not consciously set out to write about anti-Semitism when he began his first play, *Home of the Brave*. "I didn't realize how deeply I felt about it [anti-Semitism]," he commented recently (interview with author, March 25, 1996). Unleashing his pent-up emotions resulted in a powerful drama illustrating the harmful effects of prejudice on a sensitive psyche.

As the play opens, Private Peter Coen (Coney) is undergoing treatment by an army psychiatrist at a South Pacific military base during World War II. Coney is unable to walk, but the reason is unclear. In an effort to discover the cause of Coney's psychosomatic paralysis, he is hypnotized and reenacts the traumatic incidents that led to his condition.

Coney reveals that T. J., an angry corporal who feels he deserves a higher rank, has been taking out his resentment on Coney, calling him a "lousy yellow Jew bastard," among other epithets (I.iii). Although Coney has been the butt of anti-Semitism from the time he was a child, it still upsets him. His best friend, Finch, defends him from T. J. However, when under enemy attack, Finch almost calls him a "lousy yellow Jew bastard" (I.iii). Coney is stung. Finch, who has never known a Jew before meeting Coney, has seemed indifferent to his friend's religion. Yet, under pressure, Finch resorts to an ethnic slur. Feeling that Finch "hated me because I was a Jew," Coney comes to believe that he is fated to be different from other men because of his religion (II.iii).

When Finch dies soon after their altercation, Coney feels "glad" (II.ii). Immediately afterward, however, he rebukes himself for what seems to be a monstrous emotion. Is he different from other men, just as anti-Semites have been insinuating for so long, he wonders? What he learns through therapy is that he is not unique. Other soldiers feel relieved when a buddy is killed, and they survive; it is only human. When he no longer views himself as an outsider, Coney can walk again. He says triumphantly at the end, "I was crazy . . . yelling

I was different. I am different. Hell, you're different! Everybody's different—
But so what? It's O.K. because underneath, we're—hell, we're all guys!''
(III.ii).

Laurents remarked once, ''Writing *Home of the Brave* cleansed me about
anti-Semitism and made me feel better equipped to deal with it'' (interview with
author, March 25, 1996). Perhaps that is why after this first play, Laurents turned
away from Jewish characters and focused on other types of outsiders and social
injustice in American society. *West Side Story* depicts the hatred that existed
between whites and Puerto Ricans in the 1950s, as well as the problem of
juvenile delinquency; *Hallelujah, Baby!* traces the painful history of blacks in
America; and *The Enclave* exposes the difficulties one gay man faces when he
comes out of the closet. Then, almost thirty years after writing *Home of the
Brave*, Laurents returned to a Jewish character and situation in his 1973 screenplay and novel *The Way We Were*.

While Coney's speech at the end of *Home of the Brave* affirms the underlying
similarities of all human beings, *The Way We Were* suggests that certain basic
differences can make romantic relationships between Jews and Gentiles difficult.
As in his first play, Laurents once again portrays the debilitating effects of
alienation on a Jewish character. This time, however, he examines the psychological difficulties a Jew experiences when she attempts to fit into the WASP
world, and denies her cultural background.

Katie Morosky is a first-generation American, the daughter of a ''Trotskyite
mother and . . . anarchist father'' who are Jewish by birth but who do not practice their religion. At the upstate New York college Katie attends in the 1930s,
she feels alienated, for her frizzy hair, frumpy clothes, lack of money, and
communist leanings set her apart from the mostly Gentile student population.
Another student, Hubbell Gardiner, is a quintessential WASP whose good looks
and privileged background both anger and attract her. When they meet again
during the 1940s in New York City, they fall in love. But their innate ethnic
and class differences doom the relationship from the start. As Hubbell says at
one point, ''You don't have the right style for [me]'' (122). Moreover, he recognizes that ''[y]our friends are as wrong for me as mine are for you'' (115).

Katie refuses to break off with Hubbell and convinces him his doubts are
unfounded. After they marry and move to Hollywood, where Hubbell works as
a screenwriter, Katie changes her ''style,'' camouflaging her Judaism so well
that their new friends in Hollywood do not realize she is Jewish. Nonetheless,
Hubbell's fears turn out to be justified: acting the role of Kate Gardiner, WASP
wife, is a strain on Katie, who must deny her essential self in order to fit into
Hubbell's Gentile world. Moreover, Hubbell's tendency to avoid politics and
his insistence that she do the same are lethal for this former member of the
Young Communist League. When he asks her to name names in order to save
his job during the Hollywood blacklist era, she refuses. Katie cannot betray her
principles and herself any longer. She sees through his argument that there aren't

"any names left for you to give them that they don't already have," and she leaves him (256).

Laurents' view that Katie's effort to become a WASP is futile and self-denying is underscored in the brief coda. Katie now lives in New York City with her second husband, David Cohen. She has returned to her roots—political activism—and seems happily married to a man who not only shares her cultural heritage but is a nonconformist as well. His listing in the telephone directory as David X. Cohen suggests his individualism: when asked what the X stands for, Katie responds, "The only David X. Cohen in the book" (262). Katie may never completely get over her love for Hubbell. But whereas Kate Gardiner was an illusion, Katie Cohen is a real, psychologically integrated person.

Between *The Way We Were* and the musical *Nick and Nora*, which Laurents wrote and directed in 1991, he turned his attention to theatre directing and wrote less than he had before. One notable work from this period is the one-act *Loss of Memory* (1983), which treats the theme of anti-Semitism, but with a twist: Laurents suggests that even persecuted groups can be intolerant.

At first, *Loss of Memory* seems to be another exposé of anti-Semitism. Set in Tel Aviv in the mid-1960s, the play presents an encounter between an American Jew and an Israeli who describes his flight from his native Ukraine in 1949 after his family was killed by the Nazis. Hearing this, the American feels "the anger that is always deep within him because of the casual bigotry encountered at home" (490). But the target of Laurents' criticism is not the average American anti-Semite; it is Jewish Israelis. The play reveals that the Israeli, who originally found refuge from anti-Semitism in Israel, now feels "unwanted" there because of homophobia (493). Ironically, he is about to move to Germany in order "to be with my own kind": homosexuals (492). Even Israeli Jews, who should be tolerant because of their experiences during the Nazi era, are capable of discrimination. That the Israeli views Germany as a haven is a strong indictment of Israeli homophobia.

Laurents tended not to focus on Jewish characters and themes in the bulk of the works he wrote in his long career. His most recent plays, however, all present Jewish characters, and *My Good Name* (1996) concentrates exclusively on Jewish themes. Revisiting several of the issues raised in *The Way We Were*—the conflicts inherent in marriages between Jews and Gentiles, Jews as outsiders, Jewish envy of WASPs, Jewish efforts to "pass," and anti-Semitism—*My Good Name* adds a new element: the self-hating Jew. This play, which has not yet been published, promises to spark controversy both within and without the Jewish community. It suggests that in his last years Laurents was producing some of his most interesting work.

CRITICAL RECEPTION

Scholars have paid little attention to Laurents. The most extensive academic discussion of his work is by Gerald Weales, who devotes about ten pages to him in *American Drama since World War II*. Since Weales' book was published in 1962, however, it covers only Laurents' plays up to *Invitation to a March* (1961). In *Freud on Broadway* (1970), David Sievers examines the psychological aspects of three early plays, including *Home of the Brave*. The bulk of the criticism of Laurents' work is reviews.

Home of the Brave had an interesting critical reception. While Laurents pointedly concentrated on prejudice against Jews, contemporary reviewers interpreted the work as a protest against bigotry in general. When the play became a film in 1949 (Laurents did not write the screenplay and did not approve it), the main character, Peter Coen, became the black soldier Mossie.

Amazingly, a 1949 reviewer of the film version praised it for changing the character's identity because "the original thesis has perhaps been overworked in the movies" (qtd. in Schiff 376). It is true that *Gentleman's Agreement*, which addressed the theme of anti-Semitism, had appeared two years earlier. But as Laurents comments, *Gentleman's Agreement* was "the movie that said you better be nice to a Jew because he might turn out to be a gentile" (interview with author, March 25, 1996). Neither Hollywood nor Broadway had "overworked" the anti-Semitism theme. Rather, it seems that people were uncomfortable with the subject and preferred to ignore it.

The two critical high points of Laurents' career were *West Side Story* and *Gypsy*. Brooks Atkinson of the *New York Times* called the former "incandescent" and the latter a work of "art." But, in general, while reviewers have tended to deem Laurents' work ambitious and interesting, they have also had reservations. Most commonly, Laurents has been faulted for trying to pack too many themes into one play, for failing to develop his characters fully enough, and for allowing his characters to become weighed down by the social issues with which they grapple.

Although theatre critics gave Arthur Laurents more mixed reviews than raves over the course of his long career, they appreciated and applauded his efforts to keep serious drama alive. At a time when, in his words, "Broadway is devoid of excitement and dying from under-nourishment," he continued to write "theater of substance" ("Entertainment" 4). For that, critics and audiences can be grateful.

BIBLIOGRAPHY

Works by Arthur Laurents

The Face. The Best One-Act Plays of 1945. New York: Dodd & Mead, 1945.
Home of the Brave. New York: Random House, 1946.
The Way We Were. New York: Harper, 1972.
Loss of Memory. The Best Short Plays of 1982–1983. New York: Doubleday, 1983.
"Entertainment Is Killing Broadway." *New York Times*, December 17, 1995: Section 2, 4+.

The Radical Mystique. New York: Samuel French, 1996.
My Good Name. (unpublished)

Works about Arthur Laurents

Adler, Thomas. "Arthur Laurents." *Critical Survey of Drama.* Ed. Frank Magill. Vol.
    4. Pasadena, CA: Salem Press, 1994.
"An Ad Lib for Four Playwrights." *Playwrights/Lyricists/ Composers on Theater.* New
    York: Dodd, 1974.
Interview with Jean W. Ross. *Contemporary Authors.* Vol. 8. Detroit, MI: Gale, Re-
    search, 1983.
Atkinson, Brooks. Rev. of *West Side Story. New York Times,* September 22, 1957, 1.
———. Rev. of *Gypsy. New York Times,* May 22, 1959.
Schiff, Ellen. Introduction to *Home of the Brave. Awake and Singing: 7 Classic Plays
    from the American Jewish Repertoire.* New York: Mentor, 1995.
Sievers, David. *Freud on Broadway.* New York: Cooper Square, 1970.
Weales, Gerald. *American Drama since World War II.* New York: Harcourt, 1962.

BARBARA LEBOW

(1936–)

Eric Sterling

BIOGRAPHY

Barbara Lebow, born in Brooklyn, New York, began creating plays at the age of seven and performed them in her driveway to audiences sitting on the front stoop (http://www.eyeonwomen.com/lebow.htm). She earned her B.A. degree in 1958 from Vassar College in Poughkeepsie, New York, and has lived in Atlanta, Georgia, since 1962, when she arrived with her two children (she subsequently had a third). Wanting to expose her children to the theatre, just as her mother had done for her, Lebow inquired about the best children's theatre in Atlanta. She chose the Academy Theatre, joining in 1964. She began by painting sets and later showed to the theatre's artistic director (Frank Wittow) a play she had written for her children. Impressed, Wittow asked her to partake in a workshop, which led to her first play produced on the theatre's main stage, *I Can't Help It* (http://www.eyeonwomen.com/lebow.htm). Lebow now works there as a playwright-in-residence. The dramatist employed "the theatre's community outreach exercises to write plays with special populations, such as women in prison, people who are homeless, and people in drug and alcohol rehabilitation programs" (http://www.eyeonwomen.com/lebow.htm); Lebow is pleased with the successes of these cooperative writing efforts, calling these plays "effectively poetic, to-the-point, dramatic and truthful" (Lebow, "Theater"). The playwright received Georgia Art Council and Bureau of Cultural Affairs Grants for *Tiny Tim Is Dead, A Shayna Maidel, Cyparis,* and *Little Joe Monaghan*; a Mayor's Fellowship in the Arts (1986); a Governor's Award in the Arts (1988); and a TCG/Pew Charitable Trusts National Theatre Artist Residency Program Grant at Theatre in the Square (1994–1996). *The Keepers, A Shayna Maidel,* and *The Empress of Eden* were finalists for the Susan Smith Blackburn Prize. *A Shayna*

Maidel was selected for "Plays-in-Process"; that play and *Little Joe Monaghan* are listed in Burns Mantle *Best Play* yearbooks. Although known for her adult dramas, Lebow has written several children's plays and has also directed.

MAJOR WORKS AND THEMES

Barbara Lebow assails stereotypes and prejudice throughout her drama; several works concern anti-Semitism. Even *Little Joe Monaghan* (1981), which does not concentrate on prejudice, attacks the stereotyping of women's roles in America. Lebow and Wittow coauthored *Night Witch* 1967, which deals with anti-Semitism in the South and is based on a historical incident in which an angry mob in 1915 lynched a Jewish businessman, Leo Frank, after his conviction for murdering a Christian, teenage girl. In the drama, an African-American night watchman (Tom Johnson) finds himself in jail for the murder of a Caucasian girl (Mary Fuller). Because of racial prejudice, Captain Stubbs refuses to believe anything Johnson says—until the accused man implicates his Jewish boss (Aaron Gold). Lebow and Wittow's play attacks racial prejudice as well as anti-Semitism but focuses primarily on the latter. *Night Witch* dramatizes the playwrights' concerns about the fear of outsiders—"the other" (Gold is convicted because he is a Jewish, transplanted northerner living in the South)—and about mob mentality. The play manifests the dangers of mob intimidation as people lose their individuality; those who lynch Gold, taking justice into their own hands, are nameless, faceless characters. Lebow and Wittow dramatize this through the blackout in the last scene. The playwrights implicate Johnson as Mary Fuller's murderer, for the night watchman describes the killing to his lawyer, although blaming it on the mystical Night Witch. The play shows that the angry mob, purportedly seeking justice, is perhaps as evil as the man who slays Fuller.

Lebow's dramas manifest her concern for disfranchised groups—the homeless, the incarcerated, and drug and alcohol users. Her empathy for people who suffer, require help, or need a second chance permeates her works, which have effectively brought the plights of unfortunates to public attention. *Little Joe Monaghan* is about a young woman who bears a child out of wedlock and must leave her family. *A Shayna Maidel* (1985) and *Night Witch* involve the persecution of Jews. Furthermore, *Tiny Tim Is Dead* (1991) and *Trains* (1990) concern the homeless. Lebow bases *Little Joe Monaghan* on the life of an actual person. Josephine Monaghan, a female cowboy in the late nineteenth century, ventured to Idaho from New York after bearing an illegitimate child, Laddie. She lived out west for four decades, disguised as a man (Joe), with no one discovering her true gender until her death. The drama deals with feminism, for Little Joe Monaghan served on juries and voted well before woman suffrage; Lebow contrasts Monaghan, who possesses the physical and mental strength to face the rigorous life of a cowboy, with Helen (Joe's sister), who sews clothes and stays at home to be Laddie's surrogate mother. Joe decides to become a man because the gender switch provides her with freedom and the ability to earn a decent living. Lebow demonstrates the dangers of gender stereotyping when Helen, claiming that Laddie would be hurt if he knew that his mother was a cowboy, informs the boy that his mother is dead; the sister believes that the boy would prefer that his mother be dead than that she comport herself as a man. Helen's lie prevents Joe from returning to New York to reclaim her son. A poignant aspect of the drama involves Joe's frustrated efforts to be close to her son; Lebow employs a metaphor of branding, of the cow and her calf being separated, to dramatize Joe's pain after Helen comes between her and Laddie. The play also focuses on Joe's relationship with her best friend, Fred, who becomes more important to her than Helen or Laddie. Family becomes a significant theme in the drama; Fred claims that "[k]in is plain and simple who you find" (46).

Little Joe Monaghan shares similarities with *A Shayna Maidel*; both dramas, memory plays, manifest Lebow's excellent ear for dialogue. Both works contain dream sequences in the minds of major characters (Joe and Lusia, respectively), people who relive past events. These plays blend reality and fantasy; characters saddened by unfortunate events in their lives (Joe's pregnancy and separation from Laddie and Lusia's inability to travel to New York when trapped in Europe) construct fantasies in which they alter the past to render it more pleasant.

A Shayna Maidel, Lebow's most popular and critically acclaimed play, concerns two sisters, Rose (Rayzel) and Lusia, who become separated before the Holocaust. The Weiss family planned to leave Poland, but Lusia contracted scarlet fever before the trip, causing Lusia and her mother to remain while Rose and her father traveled to New York. The play explores a controversial Holocaust topic—whether those fortunate to escape the Holocaust may comprehend the suffering of the victims and survivors. Jealous of her younger sister, who has lived a comfortable life without knowing hardship, Lusia simultaneously feels guilt because her illness resulted indirectly in her mother's death. Rose does not even miss her mother because she has no memories of her (she left her mother at the age of four). Rose has escaped unpleasant memories, even changing her name from Rayzel Weiss to Rose White in her attempt to assimilate completely into American society. Recognizing the awkwardness that will ensue upon meeting her sister, she attempts to avoid Lusia. Her excuse to her father, that her apartment is not spacious enough for her sister to move in temporarily, exemplifies her initial lack of empathy and understanding. She finds it inconvenient to share an apartment; while she has lived there, Lusia suffered in a concentration camp, without privacy and private property. Rose also callously asks Lusia about the number tattooed on her arm. As the play progresses, the audience watches the development of Rose's understanding: the protagonist awakens with the ritualistic reading of the list of family members who have died and the letter her father kept from her. Subsequently, Rose inscribes a number on her arm to match her sister's. The suffering caused by the Holocaust, which initially separated the two sisters emotionally, ultimately unites them.

Lebow penned, directed, and wrote original songs for *The Adventures of Homer McGundy* (1985). Dr. Emil Proctor exhibits the body of the deceased outlaw McGundy in his traveling medicine show. The play demonstrates "how real-life outlaws on the lone prairie became Hollywood's singing cowboys in the movies" (Sherbert).

Cyparis (1987) involves the 1902 volcanic explosion on Martinique that killed 30,000 people but miraculously spared Auguste Cyparis, who dwelt in a dungeon. The dramatist includes scenes regarding parent–child relationships in which Cyparis talks with his father about fishing and his future and interacts with his son, a product of his relationship with Loulouze, who works for the wealthy Marcellin. In *Cyparis*, Lebow skillfully employs memory and fantasy—techniques that evolved from her writing of *Little Joe Monaghan*; her use of memory and fantasy in *Little Joe Monaghan* helped her as she wrote *A Shayna Maidel*, and the creation of this drama, in turn, aided her as she penned *Cyparis*.

A Maine lighthouse serves as the setting for *The Keepers* (1988), a play about Angeline, a black woman living with her white adoptive parents: a lighthouse keeper/sea captain (Nathaniel) and his sexually repressed wife, Octavia. After a black male is found dead, Angeline learns about her mother and her familial background.

Lebow's *Trains* concerns the short-lived, but intense, moments that occur during conversations on trains. The dramatist mentions that "[o]ne of the things about riding on trains is hearing people's stories . . . , getting close to people because you know you'll never see them again" (Dollar). While riding an Amtrak train through New Jersey, Lebow noticed two men sitting by the tracks; in the play, Lebow creates lives for the two. The drama concerns racial issues; in the first half of the drama, which occurs around the time of the Civil War, the southern white man empathizes with his black mentor but is nonetheless a product and victim of his own history and culture. The second half of the play deals with two contemporary, homeless people who "grapple with the tensions of mutual dependence and the price of personal freedom" (Dollar).

Tiny Tim Is Dead concerns the fantasies and disappointments of six homeless people living on a dead-end street. The characters formerly lived in mainstream society but have become homeless for various reasons. Charlie and Filo are drug addicts, but Azalee has recovered because she has hope for the future and intends to leave this homeless area. Pope, a disabled war veteran, becomes angered by the false hope that the characters experience. Pessimistic, sardonic, and sarcastic, he attempts to deflate the optimism and cheerfulness of others. Lebow employs Charles Dickens' *Christmas Carol* (Tiny Tim in particular) as a metaphor for false hope and despair. The audience realizes, and the characters discover, that the homeless cannot experience a rapid amelioration in their lives as Tiny Tim does. Lebow shows the futility of escapism as Verna disappears and abandons Boy while Charlie suffers withdrawal symptoms. Pope's conception of Tiny Tim's death manifests his belief that fairy tales cannot come true, that people should face, rather than escape from, reality.

Lebow's *Homunculus of Córdoba* (1993) differs from her other dramas in that the playwright's other works are grounded more in reality. This drama is a mystical play set in A.D. 973 in Córdoba, Spain, where Muslims, Christians, and Jews lived in relative harmony. Jewish physician Isaac ibn Ibrahim, who possesses mystical powers, foresees the destruction of Córdoba and tries to prevent it. When the eunuch Yakut threatens him (Yakut dislikes Jews because he had requested death but instead was rendered a eunuch by Jewish doctors), Isaac poisons himself so that he may return to life as a newborn baby whom his own daughter, Judith, will nurse. Isaac possesses much skill as a mystic and is ubiquitous, appearing in reflections and in other characters; his transformation, however, into an infant renders him powerless and at the mercy of Yakut and other characters, both Muslim and Christian. Isaac hopes that his alteration into a baby will allow him to be immortal and thus alter the course of history, preventing bloodshed in places like Córdoba and achieving world peace.

Lebow's most recent play, *The Empress of Eden* (1995), concerns a group of Germans attempting to create an Edenic society in the Galapagos Islands prior to World War II. The work, based on fact, "grew into a fictionalized account of idealists unable to leave behind the decadence of Hitler's Reich" (Hulbert, "Playwright"). The drama opened as a workshop production in which the author solicited audience feedback.

Two themes prevalent in Lebow's dramas are the emphasis on survival and on familial bonds, especially that of mother and child. Furthermore, in her plays Lebow juxtaposes her protagonists, exploring human nature through characters who are polar opposites: Joe (a woman who shatters gender stereotypes) and Helen (who adheres to such stereotypes) in *Little Joe Monaghan*; Rose (an Americanized woman who escaped the Holocaust) and Lusia (a European female who suffered tremendously during the Holocaust) in *A Shayna Maidel*; and Verna (a homeless woman who lives in a world of fantasy and hope) and Pope (a bitter, pessimistic man with bleak expectations for the future) in *Tiny Tim Is Dead*. In *The Homunculus of Córdoba*, Lebow contrasts the impetuous, scientific-minded Hisham with the fearful, devoutly religious monk Julian. Hisham views the rebirth of Isaac as the coming of the Messiah, while Julian fears that the birth will incur the presence of the Antichrist.

CRITICAL RECEPTION

Although critics have praised many of her dramas highly, Barbara Lebow's popularity derives predominantly from *A Shayna Maidel*. Mel Gussow lauds the playwright, for she "has, with tenderness, personalized the tragedy" and has written a powerful, moving play without "overstep[ping] into sentimentality." Joe Brown calls it a "gentle but emotionally potent play." Virtually all reviews of *A Shayna Maidel* praise Lebow for the work's poignant moments, powerful and insightful meanings, excellent dialogue, and complex character portrayals. Reviewers cite several scenes in particular, such as those involving Rose's character development and Lusia's and Mordechai's reading of their lists of relatives. E. R. Isser comments that unlike most Holocaust writers (who dramatize women as objects), Lebow "creat[ed] female protagonists who are fully developed characters . . . [and wrote one of the first plays] that offers a feminist perspective on the destruction of Europe's Jews" (139).

Although renowned for *A Shayna Maidel*, Lebow has written several excellent plays upon which her reputation rests. Linda Sherbert calls *The Adventures of Homer McGundy* "a masterfully conceived Western . . . [,] a fascinating and entertaining exploration of American myth-making about the Old West and the effects of technology on frontiersmen who spoke most meaningfully with their six-shooters."

Paula Crouch remarks that *Cyparis* entices the audience with "rhythmic language and rich, erotic and mysterious images . . . [and is] a richly textured play that not only entertains with an irresistible tale of survival but evokes the sights, sounds and magical lore of the Caribbean isle" of Martinique.

James Flannery says that the dramatist possesses "a vivid sense of characterization, an ease in handling vernacular dialogue, a poetic fluidity of structure and an unabashed willingness to tackle in a direct and open manner themes of profound moral seriousness" (H 3). Lebow is well respected for her dialogue, meaningful ideas, and social conscience. Reviewers admire her for expressing tenderness and emotions without preaching, moralizing, and excessive sentimentalizing.

BIBLIOGRAPHY

Works by Barbara Lebow

With Frank Wittow. *Night Witch*. (1967). Unpublished.
Little Joe Monaghan. (1981, revised 1994). New York: Dramatists Play Service, 1995.
A Shayna Maidel. (1985). New York: Dramatists Play Service, 1988.
The Adventures of Homer McGundy. (1985). Unpublished.
Cyparis. (1987). Unpublished.
The Keepers. (1988). New York: Dramatists Play Service, 1995.
"Theater Can Build Bridge between Arts, Social Welfare Issues." *Atlanta Journal and Constitution*. March 6, 1990, C, 1: 4.
Trains. (1990). Unpublished.
Tiny Tim Is Dead. (1991). New York: Dramatists Play Service, 1993.
The Homunculus of Córdoba. (1993). Unpublished.
The Empress of Eden. (1995). Unpublished.

Works about Barbara Lebow

Brantley, Ben. Rev. *The Keepers*. *New York Times*. September 2, 1994, C, 2: 5.
Brown, Joe. Rev. *A Shayna Maidel*. *Washington Post*. September 26, 1989, D, 3: 1.
Crouch, Paula. Rev. *Cyparis*. *Atlanta Journal and Constitution*. April 17, 1987, P, 2: 1.

Dollar, Steve. Rev. *Trains. Atlanta Journal and Constitution.* October 14, 1990, N, 1: 1.

Flannery, James. "Down-Home Drama Thrives in Atlanta." *New York Times.* July 13, 1986, H 3, 26.

Gussow, Mel. Rev. *A Shayna Maidel. New York Times.* November 29, 1985, C, 3: 1. http://shwww.eyeonwomen.com/lebow.htm

Hulbert, Dan. "Atlantan's Play Gets Polite Reception in London." *Atlanta Journal and Constitution.* May 9, 1990, E, 5: 1.

———. "Playwright Lebow Developing Works on the Galapagos, Cobb." *Atlanta Journal and Constitution.* September 17, 1995, L, 6: 1.

Isser, E. R. "Toward a Feminist Perspective in American Holocaust Drama." *Studies in the Humanities* 17 (1990): 139–48.

Kloer, Phil. "Atlantan's Play Makes It to TV Mostly Intact." *Atlanta Journal and Constitution.* April 24, 1992, G, 6: 1.

Mandl, Bette. " 'Alive Still, in You': Memory and Silence in *A Shayna Maidel.*" In *Staging Difference: Cultural Pluralism in American Theatre and Drama.* Ed. Marc Maufort. New York: Peter Lang, 1995. 259–65.

Murray, Steve. Rev. of Roberto Athayde's *Miss Margarida's Way.* [Directed by Barbara Lebow]. *Atlanta Journal and Constitution.* May 31, 1989, D, 3: 3.

Robinson, Roderick. Rev. *Tiny Tim Is Dead. Atlanta Journal and Constitution.* November 8, 1991, D, 5: 1.

———. Rev. *Trains. Atlanta Journal and Constitution.* October 19, 1990, D, 8: 1.

Sherbert, Linda. Rev. *The Adventures of Homer McGundy. Atlanta Journal and Constitution.* October 25, 1985, P, 8: 1.

NORMAN LESSING   (1911–)

Norman J. Fedder

BIOGRAPHY

Norman Lessing was born June 24, 1911. Although theatre was his initial interest, he makes his living writing for television and film, having authored over 300 teleplays and a number of film scripts. He lives in Santa Monica, California, with his wife, Betty, and they have five daughters. His hobbies are tennis and chess. He coauthored *The World of Chess* and won the Senior Championship of the National Open Tournaments six times (Cohen 68). The dramatic work that has brought him prominence is his play, *36*.

MAJOR WORK AND THEMES

In *36* (1985), Lessing explores Jewish faith from a comic perspective—pitting a reform rabbi's skepticism against the beliefs of a trio of religious zealots. The title refers to the thirty-six saintly men (Lamedvovniks) of Jewish legend for the sake of whose existence God preserves the world. The play dramatizes the quest of three Brooklyn Hasidim—Mendel, Nachman, and Pitzik—to locate and sustain one of these thirty-six. It begins in a Reform temple in Cincinnati where Nachman has been called by "a Voice" to find said Lamedvovnik. The devout Hasidim are as uncomfortable praying in the temple as is the agnostic rabbi in allowing them to do so. But they strike an uneasy alliance. The Hasidim find their saint in the unlikely person of an electrician named Joe Walski, who is engaged in repairing the circuitry of the sanctuary's "window of Heaven" cyclorama, which provides the weekly worshipers with a liturgical light show. Joe protests that it is impossible for him to be this Lamedvovnik since he isn't Jewish, is married to an Irish Catholic, and spent his early years in Poland—

raised by his stepfather, who made him "go to church every other Sunday." But his admission that he was adopted and his eloquent responses to their Talmudic discourse strengthen the Hasidim's resolve to persist in their efforts.

They discover that Joe is circumcised—which would have been unlikely for a Gentile born in Poland. Then they call their archivists in Brooklyn and learn that Joe is, in fact, the son of the Lamedvovnik Yitzhok Halevy, who died in Auschwitz. His pregnant wife was saved by Polish priests. She died shortly after Joe was born, and they cared for him until they had to escape from Poland— at which point they had him adopted by the peasant Walski.

Furthermore, it seems that Joe's wife, Mary—unable to conceive up to this point—has now miraculously become pregnant. She comes in now to confront the Hasidim and tell them to stop bothering her husband. But, however reluctantly, she comes to accept their conviction that Joe is indeed one of the thirty-six.

As Joe becomes absorbed in learning about Judaism, so does Mary—to the point that she determines to forsake her Catholic faith to become a Jew and enlists the rabbi in converting her. We see him giving her a lesson in her kitchen—only to be taken aback by her statement, prompted by her husband, that she wants an Orthodox conversion. In anticipation of this, she's even shaved her head (somewhat) to make way for a sheitel. But she'll settle for what he has to offer now—so she can "get to be Jewish first." He guesses that "it's okay to enlist now and choose your branch of the service later." However, he refuses to proceed until she reveals why she wants to do this. Despite the fact that she has sworn to the Hasidim that she wouldn't tell the rabbi, he forces the truth out of her—that the Hasidim have convinced Joe that he is a Lamedvovnik, and she must become Jewish in order to bear his successor. Railing against these "nuts" who "have no place in this century," the rabbi tears up the conversion certificate and storms out of the house.

At the temple, the rabbi demands that the Hasidim leave immediately because they have gotten this "ignorant laborer" to embrace the "insane superstition" that there really are Lamedvovniks and that Joe is one of them. This leads to a debate between the rabbi and the Hasidim about the literal truth of the Bible, the existence of God, and the possibility of miracles. The Hasidim score highly in this encounter when Nachman seemingly manages to get Pitzik to rise in the air and "fly to Heaven," to the rabbi's amazement. At this point, Joe rushes in with Mary, now possessed by a dybbuk, who it turns out is none other than Nachman's personal demon, Essig. Essig, Nachman reasons, has possessed Mary because Nachman had concealed the "whole truth" that Joe is, in fact, the last Lamedvovnik on Earth—that if he should die without an heir, the world would perish with him. Before Nachman has strength enough to exorcise the dybbuk, he feels he must prove beyond any doubt that Joe is the real thing—"to prevent other and more terrible demons from entering" his and Mary's offspring. So he puts Joe's faith to the test of a debate. Joe must "give God one good reason" to spare the world by defending it against the arguments for its destruction of

Samael, "God's Prosecuting Angel," played by Mendel. Samael's condemnation of the horrors of earthly existence is eloquently refuted by Joe in his closing affirmation: "And with all that, we still love you, God." Joe's winning the debate empowers Nachman to exorcise Essig from Mary in a brief ceremony climaxed by the threat to let loose his shrewish ex-wife, Layamalka, on the demon. Pitzik then enters and admits that the "miracle" of his ascent to Heaven was accomplished by his utilization of the flying harness employed in the temple's production of *Peter Pan*!

But this doesn't diminish the rabbi's return to the faith. The debate and the exorcism have re*Jew*venated him. As he so willingly clapped his hands to acknowledge his belief in fairies when he watched *Peter Pan*, he does likewise for God—expressing his new state of soul by flooding the "Window of Heaven" with light and joining the others in joyous song and dance in praise of the Deity, while the latter, not to be upstaged, has the Divine last word. A "stern powerful Voice" emanates from the window: "Rabbi, Rabbi! . . . Stop trying to flood the joint with light, something's gotta blow!"

CRITICAL RECEPTION

36 provided New York City's Jewish Repertory Theatre with "its first big popular success," according to its associate director, Ed Cohen (68). Artistic director Ran Avni called the comedy "a charming, lovely piece of theatre." Their production opened in June 1980 and was extended beyond the standard sixteen-night run for an added thirty performances (Backalenick 67). It was also given a reading that June at the first national Jewish Theatre Festival at Marymount Manhattan College (Margolis and Weinacht 98) and, following the New York production, was staged at the Jewish Community Center of Cleveland (Cohen 69). While Avni acknowledged that director Marc Daniels "had trouble with the ending" (Backalenick 67), *New York Times* critic Richard F. Shepherd concluded: "It is a breezy, funny play with crisp dialogue and good humorous performances by its cast of six. . . . The theatre is air conditioned and, as one of the characters might say, believe me there are worse ways to spend time on a hot night."

BIBLIOGRAPHY

Work by Norman Lessing

36. In *New Jewish Voices: Plays Produced by the Jewish Repertory Theatre*. Ed. Edward M. Cohen. Albany: State University of New York Press, 1985.

Works about Norman Lessing

Backalenick, Irene. *East Side Story: Ten Years with the Jewish Repertory Theatre*. Lanham, MD: University Press of America, 1988.

Cohen, Edward. "Norman Lessing." In *New Jewish Voices: Plays Produced by the Jewish Repertory Theatre*. Ed. Edward M. Cohen. Albany: State University of New York Press, 1985.

Margolis, Tina, and Susan Weinacht. "Introduction, Jewish Theatre Festival, 1980." *The Drama Review: Jewish Theatre Issue* 24, No. 3 (September 1980). 93–99.

Shepherd, Richard F. "Theater: Jewish Repertory Stages '36.'" *New York Times*, March 23, 1980, III, 11.

DAVID MAMET (1947–)

Leslie Kane

BIOGRAPHY

David Alan Mamet was born November 30, 1947 in Chicago, "the city of broad shoulders" closely associated with the playwright's early career and the setting of numerous plays and films. Mamet's father, Bernard Morris Mamet, a labor lawyer and an amateur semanticist, and his mother, Lenore June (neé Silver), eschewed the Jewish practice of their Ashkenazi parents in what the playwright has characterized as their "rabid pursuit of success" and their desire to be accepted as Americans. As a young man Mamet was especially close to Bernard's mother, Clara Palast Mamet, the daughter of moderately wealthy Jews who owned a candy store in Hrubestow, a small town near the Russian-Polish border, through whom he was exposed to Yiddish, in which he is fluent, and Yiddishkeit. To her and his youngest daughter, named for Clara, the playwright dedicated his novella about Jewish survival, *Passover* (1995). In his childhood Judaism was "defined negatively," recalls Mamet in a recent essay entitled "A Plain Brown Wrapper," in which he recollects the lessons of Chicago's Temple Sinai, whose Reform Judaism the writer has likened to "American Good Citizenship" (*Some Freaks*, 15). Beginning in the mid-1980s, Mamet affirmed his Jewish identity, most obviously in numerous essays in *Some Freaks, The Cabin*, and *Make-Believe Town*, his screenplay, *Russia-Poland*, based on a Hasidic story, *Homicide*, a film that traces a Jewish policeman's search for his Jewish identity, and three plays, *The Disappearance of the Jews, Goldberg Street*, and *The Luftmensch*, which foreground issues of loss, identity, and anti-Semitism. In the late 1980s Mamet's Hollywood hucksters, Bobby Gould and Joey Fox in *Speed-the-Plow*, reveal his overt and continuing examination of issues of legacy, learning, and loyalty. Coupled with the loss of tradition and connection, a dash of chutzpah and moral lapse, Yiddish expressions, and humor, this play typifies the body of his work in which memory, pedagogy, performance, betrayal, and linguistic brilliance play principal roles.

When the playwright was ten years old, his parents were divorced, a traumatic event in the life of the young writer, which he has revisited in *Dark Pony, Reunion*, and *The Cryptogram*. Mamet lived with his mother, her second husband, and his sister Lynn (also a writer), four years his junior, in Flossmor, a model suburb south of Chicago that the playwright detested. Recently recounting his childhood memories in a story of familial abuse entitled ''The Rake,'' the playwright also evokes memories of this period of his life in *The Cryptogram*, set in Chicago in 1957. In 1963 Mamet went to live with his father in the predominantly Jewish Lincoln Park area of Chicago, transferring to the prestigious Francis Parker School, where he met Alaric Jans, who subsequently scored his films. A voracious reader, the playwright claims that he was a disinterested student, learning about literature, the theatre, and society in the bookstore, principally from Beckett, Pinter, and Veblen and the novels of Bellow, Cather, and Dreiser.

As a teenager, Mamet worked as a busboy at Second City, the famed improvisational comedy troupe, and at Hull House, where he gained practical theatrical experience. He made his acting debut as the announcer of *The Golden Door*, a weekly television program of Jewish cultural content produced by his uncle, and had a role in Harold Pinter's *The Homecoming*; however, by the playwright's own account he was ''a terrible actor.'' He also worked as a dancer in Maurice Chevalier's company in Montreal, one of the various jobs the young playwright took to support his work in the theatre, many of which provide the events and realistic dialogue that characterize his writing: he drove a cab, worked at a truck factory, was a short-order cook, wrote copy for *Oui Magazine*, served in the merchant marine for a summer during college, an experience from which he would draw *Lakeboat*, and was employed as an office manager for a real estate office in Chicago, a temporary position between acting jobs that evolved into a year's employment. It served as the catalyst for his Pulitzer Prize-winning *Glengarry Glen Ross*.

Although his father wanted him to pursue a career in law, Mamet enrolled in Goddard College, an alternative liberal arts college in Plainfield, Vermont, spending his junior year ''abroad'' at New York's Neighborhood Playhouse studying under Sanford Meisner, whose influence on Mamet has been enormous. After graduating from Goddard with a B.A. in literature and aspiring to a career in the theater, he taught drama at Marlboro College in Vermont, where his first play, *Camel*, his senior thesis, was presented, and early versions of *Lakeboat* were staged. Returning to Goddard in 1971–1973 as artist-in-residence, Mamet taught acting, formed an acting company, the St. Nicholas Players, comprising students William H. Macy and Steven Schacter, and staged early productions of *Duck Variations, Litko*, and *Sexual Perversity in Chicago*. Shortly thereafter, the playwright returned to Chicago intent on a career in the theatre despite the need to work two or three jobs to support his art.

Although Chicago has been characterized as "one of the most racist and divided cities in America . . . its arts community," notes Todd London, "has a unique history of cooperation": the young playwright became an integral and influential part of Chicago's artistic community (20), bringing to it his example of professionalism and perfection. Mamet's theatre group, renamed the St. Nicholas Theatre Company, joined Mamet in Chicago, but his plays would be staged at the Organic Theatre, the St. Nicholas Theatre, and the Goodman Theatre. By the time Mamet left the St. Nicholas Theatre Company in 1976 to move to New York, because he desired greater artistic challenges and differed with its decision to produce Julian Barry's *Sitcom*, a work whose anti-Semitism was offensive, he had established a close personal and professional relationship with Gregory Mosher, artistic director of the Goodman. Mosher, who directed the premiere of *American Buffalo*, has continued to direct most of the premieres of Mamet's plays.

Successful productions of *Duck Variations* and *Sexual Perversity* garnered praise for the young playwright in 1974, winning him the Joseph Jefferson Award and a substantial commission from the Bernard Horwich Jewish Community Center, for which he would write *Mackinac* (1974) about a Jewish trader, Eziekiel Solomon, and *Marranos* (1975) about an imperiled group of Portuguese Jews trying to reach Amsterdam (both remain unpublished). However, his landmark work, *American Buffalo*, staged at the Goodman Theatre on October 23, 1975, directed by Mosher and starring J. J. Johnston and William H. Macy, brought him national attention. *American Buffalo* was reprised off-off-Broadway in a showcase production at the St. Clement's Theatre directed by Mosher with J. T. Walsh, then a Mamet regular, in the role of Bobby, and on Broadway in 1977, where it received a fine production directed by Ulu Grosbard with Robert Duvall in the role of Teach. A 1980 revival by Arvin Brown resulted in *Buffalo*'s lengthy run in 1981–1982 off-Broadway, moving to Broadway in 1983; a stunning performance by Al Pacino in the role of Teach won the actor accolades both here and abroad. The production, with cast changes, opened in London in 1984, having premiered there in 1978 under the direction of Bill Bryden, who would win fame as the director of the playwright's *Glengarry Glen Ross* London premiere in 1983.

MAJOR WORKS AND THEMES

Given its iambic pentameter, its profanity, its male cast of characters planning a petty heist, and its barely repressed violence, *American Buffalo* was profoundly misunderstood and misjudged by innumerable critics in Chicago and New York who failed to recognize what Richard Christiansen lauded as a work so important that it would change American theatre. Now a classic of the American theatre where the young playwright staked out territory that he has mined for twenty years, *American Buffalo*, "[b]orn of the great Chicago muckraking tradition," has been characterized by Gregory Mosher, whom Mamet bet would win the Pulitzer Prize, as "the funniest most vicious attack ever mounted on the ethos of Big Business and the price it exacts upon the human soul." "Mamet's audacious stylistic breakthrough," continues Mosher, the producer of an exceptional filmed version of the play with Dennis Franz and Dustin Hoffman as Teach, directed by Michael Corrente (1996), "was famously to craft iambic pentameter out of the obscenity-laced vernacular of the underclass. As if that weren't enough, he made the poetry *sound* exactly the way people (well, some people, anyway) talk."

A prolific playwright of dazzling artistry, David Mamet brings to the American theatre a particular sensitivity to the ways in which language is employed as camouflage, apart from its communicative function. The nuances and rhythms of Mamet's language have intrigued and baffled critics for twenty years, but Ruby Cohn, in particular, elucidates the innumerable linguistic devices by which Mamet "quickens [and energizes] speech," employs sound strategically, and conveys "the frenzied pace of contemporary life" (109). Nowhere, asserts Cohn, is this rapid rhythm more obvious or effective than in *American Buffalo, Glengarry Glen Ross*, and *Speed-the-Plow*, in which "grammatical chaos reinforces lexical poverty to convey a general impression of illiteracy" (113). Together with solecisms, digressions and tautologies of everyday speech, and the profanity he "gather[s] . . . in bouquets," Mamet's idiosyncratic use of rhetorical questions, recurrent queries, rising interrogative rhythms, monosyllabic words—the most striking of which are obscenities—elisions, inverted syntax, contradictions, and repetitions convincingly provide testimony of a "fecund creativity," to borrow Anne Dean's phrase, and ethnic sensibility to language to which he alludes in a recent interview on his Ashkenazi heritage. Essentially, Mamet has, to quote Don in *American Buffalo*, the "skill and talent and balls" (4) to craft a dramatic language by whittling words (or what Cohn terms "his whittling way with words" [120]): his is the mastery of rhetorical excess and minimalism.

"I have always felt like an outsider," writes David Mamet in "On Paul Ickovic's Photographs," "and I am sure that the suspicion that I perceive is the suspicion that I provoke by my great longing to *belong*" (*WR* 73). Indicative of what is missing in the lives that he dramatizes, the bonds of friendship, trust, and memory are absolutely central to his aesthetic vision. This essential need and desire to belong, to forge communal relationships, to participate in communal endeavors, to stand alone and act together, to establish a relationship to God and an ethical relationship with one another are a remarkably consistent theme in a body of work distinguished by its diversity. Mamet unifies the secular with the spiritual, the past with the present, the individual with the community, the teacher with the student, the tale-teller and the listener, the actor and the audience. He is aware that despite our need for communication and connection, unions are tenuous, transitory, even exploitative, a point he reiterates in recurring images of disappointing reunions, dissolving marriages, and disintegrating values. Although Mamet encourages us "to change the habit of coercive and frightened action and substitute it for the habit of trust, self-reliance and cooperation" (WR 27), he dramatizes characters who want to be good men but, faced with impossible choices, abandon "a sense of community and collective social goals" in their "obsessive search for success and individuality" (qtd. in Ranvaud 232). Artistically, Mamet bridges European and American traditions of Chekhov, Beckett, Pinter, and Kleist, combines social satire with metaphysics, unites scatological language with lyricism, and connects the frenzied pace of urban life with scrupulous attention to form. For Mamet even the presentation of the play "from its inception in the unconscious of the playwright to its presentation before the public as a whole" must be viewed as a "*community endeavor*" by the artistic community (WR 10). Thus, loyalty not only is a principal trope of his work but informs his working relationship with a group of artists and theatre professionals who have collaborated on Mamet's plays and films, some for nearly twenty years, among them Joe Mantegna, William H. Macy, J. J. Johnston, Felicity Huffman, Patti Lupone, Gregory Mosher, Ricky Jay, Nan Cibula, Mike Nussbaum, John Lee Beatty, J. T. Walsh (deceased), and Michael Merritt (deceased).

The richness and complexity of Mamet's work afford the critic wide opportunity to explore such recurring paradigms as the gambling ritual, reunion, and implied community of teacher and student and storyteller and listener. Additionally, the centrality of the city—whether Chicago or New York—as urban hell or cultural landscape, the exploitation of the individual by the institution, the use of theatrical metaphors, homelessness, home-building, estrangement, and a preoccupation with recollected national and ethnic history typify his canon, linked by familiar themes and structures: the comradeship of men coupled with apparent contempt for the outsider (which has led some to read Mamet's work as misogynist and homosocial—a charge he adamantly refutes), and performance as construct and con-artistry. Probably the most distinctive aspects of Mamet's work are his language and ethical vision. Whether in his moral fables or biting satires, the criminality and corrupting power plays that we observe, as Christopher Bigsby argues in "David Mamet: All True Stories," repeatedly stage betrayals whose social, psychic, and spiritual costs are immense.

David Mamet has written more than thirty plays, among them *A Life in the Theatre* (1977), *The Woods* (1977), *Lakeboat* (1980), *Edmond* (1982), *Glengarry Glen Ross* (1984), *The Shawl* (1985), *Speed-the-Plow* (1988), *Oleanna* (1992), *The Cryptogram* (1995), and an ethnic trilogy entitled *Old Neighborhood*, comprising *The Disappearance of the Jews, Jolly, and Deeny,* which had its world premiere in Cambridge, Massachusetts, in 1997. Of particular interest is this playwright's attack on the business ethos, which alternates with a mythic, redemptive rhythm in such works as *The Woods, Dark Pony*, and *Prairie du Chien,* all of which elicit the critical power of fiction to console and connect.

For example, his imaginative and moving one-acters, *No One Will Be Immune* and *Joseph Dintenfass* (written in 1974 but staged in 1996 at the Ensemble Theatre in New York) attest to Mamet's continual experimentation with form and recurring themes. He has also written numerous sketches, the most notable collected in *Goldberg Street*, three children's plays, four books for children, a collection of poetry, five collections of essays, reminiscences encompassing a broad range of subjects—everything from fairy tales, ethical first principles, radio drama, poker players' wisdom, working in Hollywood, Jewish self-hatred, and anti-Semitism—a book on film directing and another on acting, a novella, two novels, half a dozen television plays, and more than fifteen screenplays.

Invited to write the screenplay for *The Postman Always Rings Twice* and the screenplay for his *Sexual Perversity in Chicago* filmed as *About Last Night* (which he has disavowed), Mamet launched a second career as a screenwriter in 1981, taking as his principal point of departure Eisenstein's theory of montage, namely, that the story is told between the cuts through "a succession of images juxtaposed so that the story moves forward in the mind of the audience" (*Directing* 2). He has since written screenplays for *The Verdict, The Untouchables, Hoffa, We're No Angels, Glengarry Glen Ross*, and *American Buffalo* and *The Spanish Prisoner*, among others, in which the confidence game frequently serves as topic and structural device. This is especially true in Mamet's critically acclaimed film noir *House of Games* (1987), with Ricky Jay, Lindsay Crouse, and Joe Mantegna, where characters and audience are lured by the con game. An original screenplay based on a story idea by longtime friend Jonathan Katz, *House of Games* was the first the playwright directed. He has subsequently directed *Things Change*, a charming fable of quiet personal revelations and bizarre twists of fortune that he cowrote with cartoonist and children's writer Shel Silverstein, and *Homicide*, which portrays an assimilated Jew in search of his Jewish identity. His most recent original screenplay, *The Spanish Prisoner*, (1998), is a film not unlike *House of Games*, and his stage plays in which moral, ethical and emotional betrayals prevail, which he directed, featuring Ricky Jay, Steve Martin, Rebecca Pidgeon, and Felicity Huffman. *The Edge*, an adventure thriller directed by Lee Tamahori, starring Alec Baldwin and Anthony Hopkins, opened in 1997. Writing a screenplay on the life of Fatty Arbuckle and an original screenplay for Barry Levinson, *Wag the Dog*, Mamet, a Renaissance man, has also cowritten the book for *Randy Newman's Faust* and has cowritten lyrics with his second wife, Rebecca Pidgeon, a Scottish actress/singer, for her most recent record albums. He divorced from actress Lindsay Crouse, the mother of Mamet's older daughters, to whom he was married for nearly a decade and who appeared in numerous stage and screenplays, including *The Shawl* and *House of Games*; Pidgeon, whom he married in the early 1990s, has appeared in the London production of *Speed-the-Plow, Homicide*, and *Oleanna* and in his adaptation of J. B. Priestly's *A Dangerous Corner*, which he directed at the Atlantic Theater Company in 1995.

Additionally, Mamet has adapted Anton Chekhov's *Three Sisters, Uncle Vanya* (his screenplay was used for the recent film *Vanya on 42nd Street*), *The Cherry Orchard*, and "Vint," and translated and adapted Pierre Laville's play *Le Fleuve rouge*. In 1986 he cofounded the Atlantic Theater Company with Gregory Mosher and William H. Macy, comprising of New York University students who had studied with Mamet and Macy at the acting school they run in Vermont.

Winner of four Obies for *Sexual Perversity in Chicago, American Buffalo, Edmond*, and *The Cryptogram*, a Joseph Jefferson Award, a New York Drama Critics Award for *American Buffalo*, and the Pulitzer Prize and the Olivier Award for *Glengarry Glen Ross*, and a recipient of a Rockefeller Grant and an award from the American Academy of Arts and Letters, as well as a grant from the New York State Council for the Arts, Mamet is widely considered to be one of the most prolific and powerful voices in contemporary American theatre. A visiting lecturer at the University of Chicago, Yale University, and New York University, Mamet has held the positions of faculty representative to the Illinois Arts Council, a doctor of letters from Dartmouth College (1996), and associate artistic director and writer-in-residence at the Goodman Theatre. He was nominated for an Academy Award for Best Adaptation for *The Verdict*, starring Paul Newman.

CRITICAL RECEPTION

The "not-home" setting that characterizes Mamet's drama and film situates cultural and spiritual relationships in the workplace, where they are devalued, exchanged, and compromised. Although Mamet tempers his mimetics with "mythic *traces* of an authentic past," concludes Matthew Roudané his characters "map out a predatory world" in which only "the fittest (and surely the greediest) might survive" ("Mamet's Mimetics" 25, 27). That the quest for community informs his drama is evidenced by the fact that repeatedly his characters care more about loneliness and intimacy than sexual conquest and business. In fact, Mamet's "nostalgia for family ties, the importance of the father–son relationship, the brooding loneliness of the midwestern landscape, a fascination with men whose lives are dedicated to dollars, suspense, and dark journeys, and the mysterious intimacy of the human voice" (Hinden 33) collectively combine, in Michael Hinden's view, to form Mamet's "continuing quest to establish a vision of community that could create the closeness of family life" (38), the subject of such plays as *Reunion*. The "idealized nexus of human relationships," he correctly observes, is an emotional locale not to be confused with specific geographic locations—Chicago, for example—or cultural places. *Lakeboat*, Mamet's first full-length play, is prototypical, providing the playwright's fully articulated attitude toward community conveyed through a substitute family sharing comradeship in close quarters "at the *margins* of the city."

Whether through mythmaking or intimate confessions, Mamet not only glamorizes their shared fate but "illustrates the crew's potential to cohere through the shared medium of language" (41).

An understanding of Mamet's comedic philosophy and techniques, which find their best model in *Speed-the-Plow*, is crucial to an understanding of his work. Christopher Hudgins provides a compelling argument that Mamet's complex use of irony and comedy is essentially celebratory: that is, it celebrates one's capacity and tenacity to survive, even if that survival is "venal." The sources and mechanisms of Mamet's humor are broad, he suggests, but the most basic definition of Mamet's humor is "deeply ironic": Mamet encourages us "to laugh at and identify with his central characters, to know ourselves, forgive ourselves and to change," with the expectation that ironic identification with these characters should lead to criticism of the system and of the culture and a recognition of how to act morally (225). Mamet attributes his comedy to the influence of the Jewish comedians, whom he watched on television and observed at Second City, and to Lenny Bruce, whose shticks find form throughout his canon.

The playwright's indebtedness to the metadramatic tradition is evident in his con-artistry, the use of such metadramatic "tricks" as choral figures, soliloquy, storytelling, stock characters, and manipulation of the audience. "Like other postmodern dramatists such as John Guare, David Rabe and Maria Irene Fornes," argues Deborah Geis, "Mamet problematizes and even stigmatizes the devices of the metadramatic tradition" while challenging us to rethink these strategies (50). In other words, Mamet plays with and against metadramatic tradition, often employing an entire work to "con" or persuade the audience. Mamet's innovative, postmodern use, what Geis terms his "tricking" of metadramatic tradition, results in theatre—and cinema—as a "house of games." Foregrounded in Mamet's plays, both early and late, is the pedagogical relationship. In addition to its crucial ethical and moral function, the teacher–student paradigm serves as a forum for revising questions of competence and pretense, fairness and injustice, and as a format for the imposition of the teacher's prerogatives of questioning, testing, and punishing. The hierarchy of power that characterizes the teacher–student paradigm in such Mamet works as *Lakeboat, A Life in the Theatre, Squirrels, Sexual Perversity in Chicago, American Buffalo*, and *Oleanna*, typically situates older characters in a pedagogical role emphasizing their the real or imagined empowerment, while other "teachers" view the exercise of authority as a variant of the father–son relationship mitigated and/ or driven by feelings of solicitude and love. Such relationships cut both ways, because the student typically derives knowledge from, and gives sanction to, the teacher.

Mamet's work from *Duck Variations*, to *Glengarry Glen Ross*, *The Shawl*, and even *Oleanna* has been viewed as an attack on the materialistic values of American society. *Edmond*, written just two years before *Glengarry Glen Ross*, is a work "of manifest darkness and depravity" (99), observes Henry Schvey, that may be read as a companion piece to *Glengarry*, given that both examine the wages of hustling and exploitation and the enormous price of personal and institutional moral lapse. A morality play that explicitly reveals Mamet's "apocalyptic vision of a society bent upon self-destruction" (99), *Edmond* is a dark portrayal of the underbelly of New York City in which Mamet merges the grifters of *American Buffalo* with the hustlers of *Edmond*. Although it received a stunning production in Chicago under the direction of Gregory Mosher and earned an Obie, it ran for only seventy-seven performances in New York. Notably, a recent revival by the Atlantic Theater Company has garnered rave reviews: society has caught up with either the artist's vision and/or the protagonist's spiritual quest.

American Buffalo and *Glengarry Glen Ross* are generally considered Mamet's masterpieces and have evoked the most commentary about what the playwright terms "comporting oneself in a capitalist society." Whereas Mosher has described *Buffalo* as a play "about American politics, about ethical choices, about capitalism, about fascism" (qtd. in Jones and Dykes 23–24), New York critics were largely hostile in 1977. Brendan Gill called it "a curiously offensive piece of writing," and John Simon, who is still no fan of Mamet's, believed that it merely "mark[ed] time through its inaction and failure to move the audience" (50). In Britain, where the playwright has a huge following, the play fared better in the British press.

Biting, harrowing, and "stripped of idealistic pretenses," *Glengarry Glen Ross* is a Mamet masterpiece so precise in its realism that Robert Brustein has observed that it takes on "reverberant ethical meanings" (71). Drawing upon the myth of the American dream as its ideological backdrop and evoking a robbery on a grander scale than envisioned by the petty crooks in *American Buffalo*, this play suggests obvious comparisons with *Death of a Salesman*, whose confrontation of beleaguered salesman and indifferent boss the playwright admits provided the catalyst for his play. In *Glengarry Glen Ross*, his purest examination of a society built on merciless exploitation, Mamet has struck a nerve and sparked controversy, exposing mendacity and moral bankruptcy in the marketplace. He has also generated sympathy in his unsentimental, parabolic tale of real estate salesmen—"jacketed jackals" (Kroll 337) and "fast-talking bottom-feeders" (Kemply)—who peddle scorched earth in Arizona and swampland in Florida to gullible Chicagoans, tempered by his admiration for the virtuosity, imaginativeness, and temerity of men who "live on their *wits*" (Mamet, *Glengarry* 96). Much of the success of this award-winning play issues from its distinctively robust and electrifyingly vital language, at once rhythmic and ribald, elliptical and illusory, comic and corrosive. In an impeccably constructed two-act structure comprising three tightly framed duologues in act 1—a form that Mamet has perfected—and the inspired, freewheeling Roma-Levene-Lingk skit, an improvisation between two salesman and a mark set against the devastation of act 2, Mamet stages the exploitation of the injudicious, arouses suspicion, and solves the mystery of criminal actions perpetrated on and by the desperate. One of the finest postwar American plays, it has been characterized as a "sardonic, scabrous and really rather brilliant study of a human piranha pool where the grimly Darwinian law is swallow or be swallowed" (Nightingale), "the Tocquevillian connection between the public self—the hurlyburly of those caught within a business-as-sacrament world—and the private self— the anguished characters' inner self" (Roudané, *Glengarry* 39), and "one of the most exciting verbal concoctions of the modern theatre" (Coveney). Premiering in London at the National Theatre and in Chicago at the Goodman, *Glengarry* not only won the play and production awards but has enjoyed broad popular and critical support. Notable productions of *Glengarry* have been staged worldwide, both in English in Canada, South Africa, and Australia and in translation in Holland, Japan, Finland, Turkey, and Israel. In 1992 James Foley's film, based on a screenplay by the playwright with a new scene added, garnered enormous praise, featuring Al Pacino in the role of Ricky Roma—for which Joe Mantegna won a Tony in Mosher's New York production—Alec Baldwin, Jack Lemmon, and Ed Harris.

Hersh Zeifman observes that Mamet's "closed moral universe" in *American Buffalo* and *Glengarry Glen Ross* is "closed even more tightly by being portrayed as exclusively male" (126, 124). Probably no contemporary playwright has written a body of work that is largely men in the company of men and largely to the exclusion and frequent disparagement of women. In *Speed-the-Plow, House of Games*, and *Oleanna* Mamet intended to challenge criticism of his female portraits, but despite the fact that the women characters in both screenplay and play resist codification and remain enigmatic, charges of misogyny continue. In 1992 *Oleanna* ignited a storm of controversy both in America and in London, where it received a brilliant production directed by Pinter. In fact, Mamet likened it to staging *Anne Frank* at Auschwitz. Written prior to the Clarence Thomas–Anita Hill Senate hearings on sexual harassment, *Oleanna*, a tragedy on the dystopia of academe, nonetheless premiered six months later in Cambridge, Massachusetts. Mamet's recurring tropes of legacy, learning, and home-building, the marginality of outsiders coupled with enhanced focus on deracination and Jewish self-hatred, did little to quiet audience and critical response to the play, which was galvanized on the issue of sexual harassment, given that audiences were divided as to whether the play supported the views of a male professor against claims of an irate female student who, faced with failing his course, set about destroying his career. The battle of wills and wits evolves into the student's challenging the erudite professor, intent initially on "saving" his student through private tutorials and then driven to save both his imperiled career and the home he has purchased for his family. At play's end the ravages of thought control are revealed, the teacher's own moral lapse having made him an easy target.

Between 1982 and 1988 Mamet wrote the minimalist gems *The Disappearance of the Jews, Goldberg Street*, and *The Luftmensch*, his most overtly ethnic work. Apparently bleak and cryptic, these are breakthrough plays whose paradigms, themes, linguistic rhythms, and unmistakably Jewish characters provide stark evidence of the playwright's growing Jewish self-consciousness and self-confidence in a luminous, symphonic structure that particularizes and humanizes experience. Paralleling the two plays that precede it, *The Luftmensch* is linked thematically to the former by specific, ambiguous reference to persecution, loss, anti-Semitism, impotence, the familiar tropes of legacy and learning. Memory is backlit in a new and deeply personal context. Literally a do-nothing or a person without an occupation, a luftmensch is characteristically an impractical, sensitive, often poetic person lacking job or roots who lives or works at will. "A luckless dreamer, a meek *shlimazel*, fate's perpetual patsy" who "forever searches for yesterday," the *luftmensch*, having "no business, trade, calling, nor income," observes Leo Rosten, was "forced to live by improvisation" and typically "starve[s] by his wits" (216–17). Immortalized in Yiddish literature by Sholem Aleichem's *Menachem Mendel*, luftmenschen gained prominence in the late nineteenth century and the early twentieth when unskilled Jewish immigrants, primarily from shtetl communities, migrated to America between the 1880s and 1914. Presumably, this work is informed by the playwright's own memories, as is certainly the case of *Goldberg Street*, based on the loss of Mamet's mother's family during the Holocaust.

Consistent with the archetypal luftmensch down on his luck, the figure whose dramatic presence is realized in Mamet's *The Luftmensch* by a character known only as "B" is a Jew who "was a bird. He never *thought to turn his hand to any of it. Any of the work*" (39). A peddler, he could earn the staggering commission of "eighty ninety dollars" (39), but "he would *spend* the fees" leaving the family without food. "Nothing he touched," not even a coin collection, was valuable (41). However, accepted and loved by "the very people who had over the course of a thousand years destroyed his race" and "[F]ifty short years before it was over once again," the luftmensch embraced new opportunities while maintaining traditions of his youth. Settling in the American Midwest, "[h]e found it all a transient joke,. . . . that it was his to choose, over so quickly" (43). Implicit in the discussion between "A," presumably his son, and "B" is the wealth of the luftmensch's life—his ethnic pride, his love of life, physical strength, freedom, connection to others, and sense of peace—now no more a reality than memories of communal shtetl life or fantasies of fame or fortune in Hollywood. Poignantly, the playwright leaves the audience with "A's" acknowledgment of loss coupled with the wistful, hopeful dream "that one pocket of it still exists" (40). Although *The Disappearance of the Jews, Goldberg Street*, and *Luftmensch* are self-contained works, Mamet has created a Talmudic (con)text in which the meaning and means are interrelated. Resonant, these enigmatic, elliptical scenes collectively dramatize the Jewish-American experience in the last century, notably, their authentic continuity with Jewish past, their articulation of what Cynthia Ozick has characterized as a "New Yiddish"—American English infused with Jewish specificity, nuances, range of idioms, images, and syntax—and their portrayals of Jewish particularity. Whereas other stage plays written during this period, such as *Edmond, Glengarry Glen Ross*, and *Speed-the-Plow*, share a moral focus and clearly outshine these slight works, they offer scant illumination on the spiritual homecoming that the dramatist was himself experiencing.

Mamet's most recent play is a mythical one that returns us to the home, its photos, attic, old friends, and war mementos evoking familiar Mamet territory where personal betrayals wreak enormous damage on loved ones. A memory play—Mamet's own?—*The Cryptogram* presents the playwright's first onstage child and maternal figure in a heart wrenching play that depicts broken promises and familial betrayal. The role of personal narrative and the family is revisited in *Old Neighborhood*.

Considered America's foremost postwar American playwright, David Mamet has exhibited an extraordinary staying power, largely due to his ethical vision, linguistic virtuosity, daring imagination, enduring characters, fearlessness in the face of criticism, and continuing productivity. His sensitivity to language, precision of social observation, concern for metaphor and its dramatic force, theatrical imagination and inventiveness, images of alienation, striking tone poems of betrayal and loss, and brilliant use of comedy account, in large part, for his critical respect and increasing awareness of his overt dramatization of ethnicity.

BIBLIOGRAPHY

Works by David Mamet

Published Plays

A Life in the Theatre. New York: Grove, 1977a.
American Buffalo. New York: Grove, 1977b.
Sexual Perversity and Duck Variations. New York: French, 1977c; Grove, 1978.
The Water Engine and *Mr. Happiness*. New York: Grove, 1978.
Reunion and Dark Pony. New York: Grove, 1979.
Short Plays and Monologues. New York: Dramatists Play Service, 1981.
(Contains *All Men Are Whores, The Blue Hour, In Old Vermont, Litko, Prairie du Chien, A Sermon*, and *Shoeshine*.)
Squirrels. New York: French, 1982.
Glengarry Glen Ross. New York: Grove, 1984.
Goldberg Street: Short Plays and Monologues. New York: Grove, 1985.
Three Children's Plays. New York: Grove, 1986. (Contains *The Poet and the Rent, The Frog Prince*, and *The Revenge of the Space Pandas*.)
Three Jewish Plays. New York: French, 1987. (Contains *The Disappearance of the Jews, Goldberg Street*, and *The Luftmensch*.)
The Woods, Lakeboat, and *Edmond*. New York: Grove, 1987.
Speed-the-Plow. New York: Grove, 1988; London: Methuen, 1989.
The Shawl and Prairie du Chien. New York: Grove, 1985; London: Methuen, 1989.
Oleanna. New York: Vintage, 1993.
The Cryptogram. New York: Vintage, 1995.

Collected Essays, Reminiscences, Lectures

Writing in Restaurants. [*WR*] New York: Viking Penguin, 1986.
Some Freaks. New York: Viking Penguin, 1989.
On Directing Film. New York: Viking, 1991.
The Cabin. New York: Turtle Bay, 1992.
Make-Believe Town: Essays and Reminiscences. New York: Little, Brown, 1996.
Heresy and Common Sense for the Actor. New York: Pantheon Books, 1997.
Three Uses Of the Knife: On the Nature and Purpose of Drama. New York: Columbia
    University Press, 1998.
True and False. Pantheon Books, 1997.

Poetry/Novel

The Village. New York: Little, Brown, 1994.
The Old Religion. New York: Free Press, 1997.

Books for Children

Passover. New York: St. Martin's Press, 1995.
The Duck and the Goat. New York: St. Martin's Press, 1996.

Works about David Mamet

Bigsby, Christopher. *David Mamet.* London: Methuen, 1985.
———. "David Mamet: All True Stories." *Modern American Drama 1945–1990.* London: Cambridge University Press, 1992. 195–230.
Brewer, Gay. *David Mamet and Film: Illusion and Disillusion in a Wounded Land.* Jefferson, NC: McFarland, 1993.
Brustein, Robert. "Show and Tell." *New Republic*, (May 7, 1984): 27–29.
Carroll, Dennis. *David Mamet.* New York and London: St. Martin's Press, 1987.
Cohn, Ruby. "How Are Things Made Round?" In Kane, ed., *David Mamet: A Casebook.* 109–21.
———. "Phrasal Energies: Harold Pinter and David Mamet." In *Anglo-American Interplay in Recent Drama.* Cambridge: Cambridge University Press, 1995. 58–93.
Coveney, Michael. "Glengarry Glen Ross." *Observer*, June 26, 1994. Rpt. *Theatre Record*, June 18–July 1, 1994, 793.
Dean, Anne. *David Mamet: Language as Dramatic Action.* London and Cranbury, NJ: Fairleigh Dickinson University Press, 1990.
Demastes, William. "David Mamet's Dis-Integrating Drama." In *Beyond Naturalism: A New Realism in American Theatre.* Westport, CT: Greenwood, 1988.
Geis, Deborah R. "David Mamet and the Metadramatic Tradition: Seeing the Trick from the Back." In Kane, ed., *David Mamet: A Casebook.* 49–68.
Gill, Brendan. "The Theater: The Lower Depths." *New Yorker* (April 2, 1984): 114.
Hidden, Michael. "Intimate Voices: *Lakeboat* and Mamet's Quest for Community." Kane, ed., *David Mamet: A Casebook.* 33–48.
Hudgins, Christopher C. "Comedy and Humor in the Plays of David Mamet." Kane, ed., *David Mamet: A Casebook*, 191–228.

Jones, Nesta, and Steven Dykes. *File on Mamet*. London: Methuen, 1991.

Kane, Leslie. "In Blood, in Blood Thou Shalt Remember': David Mamet's Marranos." *The Yearbook of English Studies* 24 (1994): 157–71.

———. *Weasels and Wisemen: Ethics and Ethnicity in the Works of David Mamet*. New York: St. Martin's Press, 1998.

———, ed. *David Mamet: A Casebook*. New York: Garland, 1992.

———. David Mamet's "Glengarry Glen Ross": *Text and Performance*. New York: Garland, 1996.

Kemply, Rita. "Mamet's Moral Swamp." *Washington Post*, October 2, 1992, C1.

Kroll, Jack. "Mamet's Jackals in Jackets." *Newsweek* April 9, 1984). Rpt. *New York Critics' Reviews* March (5–11, 1984): 337–38.

London, Todd. "Chicago Impromptu." *American Theatre* 7, No. 4 (July–August 1990): 20.

Mosher, Gregory. "How to Talk Buffalo." *American Theatre* 13, No. 7 (September 1996): 80.

Nightingale, Benedict. "The Sharks Still Have Bite," *Times* (London), June 24, 1994, 35.

Ranvaud, Don. "Things Change." *Sight and Sound* 57, No. 4 (Fall 1988): 231–34.

Rosten, Leo. *The Joys of Yiddish*. New York: Penguin, 1968.

Roudané, Matthew C. "Mamet's Mimetics." Kane, ed., *David Mamet: A Casebook*. 3–32.

———"Public Issues, Private Tensions: David Mamet's *Glengarry Glen Ross*." *South Carolina Review* 19, No. 1 (1986): 35–47.

Schvey, Henry I. "Power Plays: David Mamet's Theatre of Manipulation." Kane, ed., *David Mamet: A Casebook*. 87–108.

Simon, John. Rev. of *Buffalo*. *New York Times*, February 17, 1977, 50.

Vorlicky, Robert. "The American Masculine Ethos, Male Mythologies, and Absent Women." In *Act like a Man: Challenging Masculinities in American Drama*. Ann Arbor: University of Michigan Press, 1995. 25–85.

Zeifman, Hersh. "Phallus in Wonderland." Kane, ed., *David Mamet: A Casebook*. 123–35.

Interviews with David Mamet

"Playboy Interview: David Mamet." *Playboy* (April 1995): 51+.

Roudané, Matthew. *Studies in American Drama* 1 (1986): 73–81.

Savran, David. In *Their Own Words*. New York: TCG, 1988. 132–44.

Schvey, Henry. "Celebrating the Capacity for Self-Knowledge." *New Theatre Quarterly* (February 1988): 89–96.

Bibliographies

Kane, Leslie and Gay Brewer. In *David Mamet: A Casebook*. Ed. Kane.

Schleuter, June. "David Mamet." In *Contemporary Authors, Bibliography Series: American Dramatists*. Detroit: Gale Research, 1989.

Trigg, Joycelyn. "David Mamet." In Philip Kolin, ed., In *American Playwrights since 1945: A Guide to Scholarship, Criticism and Performance*. Westport, CT: Greenwood, 1989.

EMILY MANN (1952–)

Ben Furnish

BIOGRAPHY

Emily Betsy Mann was born April 12, 1952, in Boston. Her father, Arthur Mann, was a history professor, and her mother, Sylvia (neé Blut), was a reading specialist. In 1966, the family moved to the Hyde Park neighborhood near the University of Chicago, where her father taught, and she attended the university's Laboratory High School. She has often recalled the ferment of those years and its impact on her emerging political and artistic viewpoints. Elijah Muhammed lived three doors from her, most of the 1960s radical movements were active in the area, and she watched the neighborhood's spirit shift away from integration as black separatism took hold. She has credited high school theatre teacher Robert Keil with awakening her interest in theatre, which combined her interest in music, art, and literature (Savran 147). She directed her first show there at sixteen. Two other childhood theatre experiences she has recalled include *Fiorello!* on Broadway (her father had written a biography of Fiorello LaGuardia) (Savran 148) and a Second Avenue production of *The Dybbuk* (Schiff 1994, 218).

Prior to graduating Phi Beta Kappa in English from Radcliffe College in 1974, she studied playwriting with William Alfred, completed summer apprenticeships with Tony Richardson and R. David McDonald, and acted and directed with the Harvard-Radcliffe Drama Club. She received a Bush fellowship to attend the University of Minnesota's M.F.A. program in directing, which was affiliated with the Guthrie Theatre, but deliberated between a career in theatre and one in journalism until she found the material for her first play. She and a friend received a grant to study her friend's family history in Europe. In London, Mann met Annulla Allen, her friend's relative and a Holocaust survivor. The transcriptions of her conversations with Allen became the source for *Annulla Allen: Autobiography of a Survivor*, later revised to *Annulla: An Autobiography* (1985).

Mann already had found compelling Holocaust testimonies through the results of her father's direction of an American Jewish Committee oral history project with survivors. She was hampered in learning more about her own family's story because her grandmother could not communicate well, she could not gain access to Russia, from which her father's family had come, and in Poland all traces of her mother's family and their Jewish community had been erased. As the Young Woman's Voice (Mann's counterpart in *Annulla*) says, "There is a wonderful fairy tale about a young girl who loans her relatives to another young girl who doesn't have any" (Schiff, 1996, 212).

As a graduate student at the Guthrie, Mann worked under Michael Langham for two shows. She asked actress Barbara Bryne there to play Annulla, and the play opened at the Guthrie 2 in 1977, went on to Chicago's Goodman Theatre, and was recorded for National Public Radio's *Earplay*. The project led Mann unwittingly to the subject for her second play, *Still Life*: a friend of a friend who saw *Annulla* introduced Mann to a Vietnam veteran so that Mann could hear his story. Despite her initial reluctance, she interviewed the man, his wife, and his mistress. The result was some 800 pages of transcript, which Mann distilled into ninety minutes of performance. She directed the play when it opened at the Goodman Theatre. The play went on to New York's American Place Theatre, winning five Obie Awards in 1981. In 1983, Mann received the New Drama Forum's Rosamond Gilder Award. In 1984, the play won the Fringe First Award at the Edinburgh Festival.

After completing her M.F.A., Mann remained at the Guthrie for five years, becoming the first woman to direct on its main stage (*The Glass Menagerie*, 1979). Her other Guthrie credits include *Ashes* and *Reunion*. From 1977 to 1979, she was artistic director of Guthrie 2. She then became artistic director at the Brooklyn Academy of Music, 1981–1982, where she directed *Oedipus* and *He and She*.

Mann spent the next eight years in a variety of pursuits. She directed shows at some of the nation's finest regional theatres, including *The Value of Names* and *A Weekend Near Madison* at Actors Theatre of Louisville, *A Doll's House* and *The Value of Names* at Hartford Stage Company, *Hedda Gabler* at LaJolla Playhouse, and many others. At times, she worked in film and television in order to fund her work in the theatre. Her screenplays include *Naked: One Couple's Journey through Infertility*, based on Jo Giese Brown's book (1985); *Fanny Kelly*, about a woman captured by a group of Sioux, all of whom are then pursued by U.S. cavalry (1985); *You Strike a Woman, You Strike a Rock: The Story of Winnie Mandela*, for which she traveled to South Africa (1990); and a script about the Greensboro massacre that she later adapted to the stage. Mann married actor Gerry Bamman in 1981, and they had a son, Nicholas Isaac (b. 1983), prior to their divorce. She served on the board of Theatre Communications Group (1983–1987).

Perhaps Mann's most significant stage achievement during this time was her play *Execution of Justice*. Commissioned by San Francisco's Eureka Theatre in 1982, the play depicts the trial of Dan White, who assassinated Mayor George Moscone and fellow city supervisor Harvey Milk, the nation's first openly gay elected official. In 1983, Mann received a Guggenheim Fellowship to support her work on the play. It opened at the Actors Theatre of Louisville in 1984 (the Eureka was in repairs from an arsonist's bomb) and was a winner of its Great American Play Contest. In 1986, Mann became the first woman to direct her own play on Broadway when *Execution* opened at the Virginia Theatre. The play received the Helen Hayes, Playwrights USA, Bay Area Critics, HBO/USA, and Dramatists Guild Women's Committee Awards and a Drama Desk Award nomination. Mann also won National Endowment for the Arts (1984, 1986), McKnight (1985), Creative Artists Public Service (1985), and Bush (1986) fellowships/grants. In 1988, Mann directed a revised *Annulla* at the New Theatre of Brooklyn with Linda Hunt in the title role.

When Mann became artistic director of the McCarter Theatre, Princeton, New Jersey, she voiced commitment to main stage productions of new works from emerging writers, women, and people of color, as well as works that might be too ambitious for the commercial stage. One of her first directing projects was *Betsey Brown: A Rhythm and Blues Musical*, coauthored with Ntozake Shange (adapted from Shange's novel) with music by Baikida Carroll, about a young black girl in 1950s St. Louis.

Mann has directed frequently at the McCarter and been a lecturer at Princeton University. In 1993 at Mark Taper Forum, Mann directed Anna Deavere Smith's *Twilight: Los Angeles, 1992*, a one-woman show inspired by the city's riots of that year. In 1995, she directed her own well-received adaptation of Sarah L. and A. Elizabeth Delany's book *Having Our Say*, which opened at the McCarter and moved to New York's Booth Theater. After the 1995 Oklahoma City bombing and while facing a multiple sclerosis diagnosis (Istel 45), Mann revised one of her screenplays into *Greensboro (A Requiem)* for the stage. It opened in 1996 at the McCarter, with Mark Wing-Davy directing.

MAJOR WORKS AND THEMES

Mann describes her distinctive playwriting method as theatre of testimony. She creates dramatic texts by painstakingly editing transcribed interviews and other sources so that her characters and the words they speak emerge directly from their real-life counterparts. Mann's own selection and arrangement create powerful juxtapositions and emotionally pace the plays in an almost musiclike manner that departs from conventional linear narrative.

Thematically, Mann's plays bring to life social and political issues in all their complexity by depicting their impact on the psyches of individual characters. In this way, her plays avoid the kind of didacticism that subordinates character and art to promoting simplistic conclusions. She is particularly interested in the roots of violence and how it reshapes the personalities of those who survive it. Her characters' experiences include the Holocaust, the Vietnam War, spousal abuse, the gay and black civil rights movements, radical labor organizing, and Ku Klux Klan hatred. But rather than perform actual scenes from these experiences, Mann's characters "testify" as witnesses to what they remember. Audiences figuratively, or at times almost literally, serve as jury members who must interpret the evidence Mann's characters bring before them, less to render clear verdicts of guilt or innocence than to comprehend the motivations of all involved.

As Mann writes about her first play, *Annulla: An Autobiography*, "It has been said, 'A writer always writes the same play.' True or not, I started here, and every play since owes its life to this source" (Schiff, 1996, 191). Despite her far-ranging content and subjects, *Annulla* embodies the key distinguishing quality that recurs in all of Mann's plays. Following her conviction that playwrights have a responsibility to inform and enlighten society, Mann offers a documentary perspective about violence without ever physically reenacting that violence onstage. Tightly blending form and content, she chooses characters who are survivors, witnesses who testify through performance.

Annulla is a one-act conversation between seventy-four-year-old Annulla Allen, who tells much of her life story to a heard-but-not-seen young woman, simultaneously the playwright's persona (a device Mann repeats in *Greensboro*) and interlocutor with the audience. Among her recollections as she sips tea and makes soup in her London flat is how she secured her husband's release from Dachau, passed as an Aryan, and eventually escaped from Nazi Germany. She has been writing a play, *The Matriarchs*; in discussing Hitler and Stalin, she says, "It is common knowledge to us the barbarism of these men. If there were a global matriarchy, you know, there would be no more of this evil" (9).

Two of Mann's plays, *Annulla* and *Greensboro*, deal with overtly Jewish characters and issues. (While some characters in *Execution* are Jewish, this is not discussed in the play.) The Young Woman's Voice in *Annulla* says, "I have a sense from my—both my father and mother—a sense of responsibility, history . . . I think most Jewish children do have this" (25). The Young Woman's conversation with Annulla, her temporarily adopted relative, brings the Young Woman closer to understanding her own family's history and that of Central European Jewry's twentieth-century upheaval and devastation.

In *Greensboro*, doctor-turned-labor-organizer Paul Bermanzohn explains that as a child of Holocaust survivors (his mother escaped from a train bound for Treblinka), he could not dismiss the Klan/Nazi threat. Paul said his mother asked him, " 'Is this why we escaped from Germany? So you could get yourself killed?' But of course what happened to them was *exactly* why I was doing what I was doing" (286–287). Paul alternates his recollections of his parents' horrific memories of the Holocaust with black characters Big George and Ronnie, who, in turn, recall Klan violence and racism when they were growing up. Later in the play, a young skinhead propounds his notions of race by saying, among other things, that a Jew is not white but "just a nigger in disguise" (304). In court, Roland Wayne Wood, one of the Klan/Nazi group, sings an anti-Semitic ditty to the tune of "Jingle Bells" as he testifies. The voice of another character, Jewish defense organization operative Mordechai Levy, appears briefly to warn Greensboro police of the possible Klan ambush; when he asks to speak to a Jewish officer, he is transferred to an Officer Goldberg, who turns out not to be Jewish and who later claims not to recall the conversation.

What Annulla and Paul Bermanzohn's parents witnessed under Hitler was an ultimate miscarriage of Justice in which the innocent were ruthlessly imprisoned and killed. Both *Execution of Justice* (the very title's double meaning implies miscarriage of justice) and *Greensboro* deal with questionable courtroom verdicts. *Execution* shows how Dan White served only five years and one month out of a seven-years-and-eight-months' sentence for remorselessly killing Mayor George Moscone and supervisor Harvey Milk. White, who, as a politician, had, ironically, supported the death penalty, invokes his famous "Twinkie defense," claiming that he was under the influence of junk food at the time he committed the crime and therefore not entirely responsible for his actions. When in real life Dan White committed suicide while on parole in 1985, Mann updated the play's ending.

Greensboro (A Requiem) recalls the Greensboro massacre, when Klan members ambushed a racially integrated group of communist-leaning labor organizers in 1979 (whose parade permit guaranteed them police protection), shooting thirteen people, killing five. This often-forgotten incident (overshadowed in the news media by the Iranian hostage crisis, which broke the next day) resulted in chilling verdicts. Despite television camera footage of the shootings, all-white juries acquitted those charged as acting in self-defense. But, as the play's last lines state, a later, civil trial ruled: "For the first time in American legal history, local police and the Ku Klux Klan were found jointly liable in a wrongful death. The City of Greensboro paid the judgment for the police. No Klan or Nazi member has paid the judgment" (330).

The relation between victim and victimizer leaves neither party unscathed, and justice fails not on one level but on many levels. Perhaps Mann illustrates this moral ambiguity nowhere better than in her second play, *Still Life*. Mark says, "Once you're out there, you know there is no justice" (126). "There" may refer to Vietnam or to the state of mind that engulfed Mark when he decided to shoot three Vietnamese children and their mother and father. "It's no different than what the Nazis did" (124), he says about his killing these five people. Cheryl, Mark's pregnant wife, fears for her life when she is with him. She is disgusted by his lust for battle, recalling, "He said it was the best sex he ever had" (62), and disappointed in her inability to leave him. Nadine, his mistress, describes him as the greatest man she's ever met, professes no shock at his acts, and even says at one point, "I only hope I would have done exactly what Mark did" (104).

Just as *Still Life* compelled Mann to revisit her antiwar activism, *Betsey Brown* and *Having Our Say* were nourished by her civil rights commitments. She traces these to her childhood, learning at Passover that "It is your responsibility . . . because as a Jew you have known slavery—to make sure that you know you cannot rest if anyone is enslaved" (Shteir, "I became an Optimist," 23). Like *Betsey Brown*, *Having Our Say* is a coming-of-age story, even though Betsey is in her teens, and the Delany sisters are over 100. Betsey, a black girl living in racially polarized 1959 St. Louis, has reason to worry if there will be enough love in the world to go around, but her parents give her hope that there is a future for her. *Having Our Say*'s centenarian sisters managed not only to survive the injustice of their times but to thrive, like Betsey Brown, finding hope and love through family but also through refusing to settle for less than what they wanted from life. Bessie Delany became one of two black female dentists in New York, and Sadie became one of the first black female high school teachers there. The sisters realize they have outlived the racist "rebby" boys who used to trouble them. As Sadie says, "That's one way to beat 'em! That's justice!" (60).

CRITICAL RECEPTION

Individually and as a body of work, Mann's plays have established her reputation as one of a relatively small number of today's playwrights who have successfully rendered social and political issues on the stage, swimming against the larger theatrical current of the times that has favored innocuous, relationship-oriented plays. In assessing *Execution*, Schiff numbers Mann among the younger dramatists who are bringing about "the coming of age of American Jewish drama" as they embrace "the tradition of American Jews using the theater to speak out on morality and justice" (1989, 69, 75). Schiff notes that Mann follows Odets in making a jury of her audience, and she praises Mann's overall subtlety and sophistication.

Critics have praised Mann's contribution as a woman to the dramas of the Holocaust and of Vietnam. Richard E. Kramer suggests that Annulla "could stand in for the entire East European Jewish diaspora, shifting as the tide of anti-Semitism moved her family from Vienna, Italy, Germany, and, finally, England" (286). E. R. Isser counts *Annulla* with Barbara Lebow's *A Shayna Maidel* as "the first American dramas that offer a feminist perspective on the destruction of Europe's Jews" (139) and says Annulla offers "a Jewish-Feminist perspective upon the first half of the twentieth century" (141).

Studies by Melanie Smith and Kate Beaird Meyer welcome *Still Life*'s depth of female character exploration; Cheryl and Nadine are subjects of the play in their own right, with their own culpabilities, not mere objects that exist only in relation to Mark. Philip C. Kolin notes that all of Mann's plays "put society itself on trial" (1993, 232) and contain "women who challenge the dominant discourse of subjugation" (1993, 246).

David Savran includes Mann (with David Mamet and Richard Nelson) as "new realists" who explore issues of social conscience as they create "a theatre of questions rather than answers, of confrontation rather than reassurance" (65); in Savran's view, Mann's work deconstructs that of earlier social realists like Arthur Miller by "defamiliarizing" the family. Patricia R. Schroeder, too, juxtaposes Miller's and Mann's work, even calling Mann "heir apparent to Miller as America's foremost social playwright" (250).

Mann's plays have been sustained by top-quality local and regional theatres; she did not have her first Broadway success until *Having Our Say* in 1995 (326 performances), which had premiered at the McCarter. Atypical among Mann's plays, *Having Our Say* received almost unanimous praise from New York-area commercial reviewers. The *New York Times* called it "the most provocative and entertaining family play to reach Broadway in a long time" (Canby 1995, 171).

Mann's other major works, including *Still Life*, *Execution*, and, most recently, *Greensboro*, tended to draw mixed notices from New York reviewers. Despite dismissive ratings from such reviewers as John Simon, *Still Life*'s New York production won five Obie Awards, which resulted in several regional productions. When Mann directed *Execution* on Broadway in 1986, the show (about which Susan Letzler Cole wrote a chapter documenting Mann's rehearsal process) lasted only twelve performances; few reviewers joined Mel Gussow and Ron Cohen in praising the production, although it received numerous awards. Nevertheless, the play has been widely produced and positively reviewed elsewhere across the country (including the Guthrie, DC's Arena, and Seattle's Empty Space). It is too soon to assess the critical impact of *Greensboro*, which has not played beyond the original McCarter production. Vincent Canby generally praised the show, saying Mann's "canny collage of a script . . . discovers a situation that is far more complex and melancholy than that found in agitprop literature" (1996, 113), while others, such as Robert L. Daniels, found the play dull. Given the country's political mood in the late 1990s, Mann is uncertain of the play's future production prospects (Hamlin 100).

Mann has furthered critical discussion of her own work in several significant interviews (e.g., Savran, Betsko and Koenig, Breslauer and Mason). These have special interest because Mann possesses twin creative visions as a major playwright and a major director who often combines these roles in her projects.

BIBLIOGRAPHY

Works by Emily Mann

Dates in parentheses are dates of performance when different from date of publication.
Still Life: A Documentary. (1980). *In Testimonies: Four Plays*. New York: Theatre Communications Group, 1997, 31–132.
Execution of Justice. (1984). *In Testimonies: Four Plays*. New York: Theatre Communications Group, 1997, 133–246.
Annulla: An Autobiography. (1985). *In Testimonies: Four Plays*. New York: Theatre Communications Group, 1997, 1–30.

With Ntozake Shange; adapted from her novel. *Betsey Brown: A Rhythm and Blues Musical*. 1989 (unpublished).
Having Our Say: The Delany Sisters' First 100 Years. (Adapted from the book by Sarah and A. Elizabeth Delany) (1995). New York: Dramatists Play Service, 1996.
Greensboro (A Requiem). (1996). *In Testimonies: Four Plays*. New York: Theatre Communications Group, 1997, 247–330.

Works about Emily Mann

Betsko, Kathleen, and Rachel Koenig. "An Interview with Emily Mann." In *Interviews with Contemporary Women Playwrights*. New York: Morrow, 1987, 274–87.
Breslauer, Jan, and Susan Mason. "Emily Mann" (Interview). *Theatre Magazine* 15, No. 2, Spring 1984, 27–32.
Brustein, Robert. "On Theater" (Rev. of *Still Life*). *New Republic*, March 28, 1981, 24.
Canby, Vincent. "A Visit with Two Indomitable Sisters" (Rev. of *Having Our Say*). *New York Times*, April 7, 1995. Reprinted in *National Theatre Critics' Reviews*, 56, No. 6, 1995, 171.
———. "When Communists Clashed with Nazis and the Klan" (Rev. of *Greensboro: A Requiem*). *New York Times*, February 12, 1996. Reprinted in *National Theatre Critics' Reviews*, 57, No. 4, 1996, 113.
Clendinen, Dudley. "Of Old South Violence Only Yesterday." *New York Times*, February 4, 1996, Section 2, 5–31.
Cline, Ned. "A Provocative Play Brings Back Memories for City; Will It Help Healing? *Greensboro News and Record*, February 15, 1996.
Cohen, Ron. " 'Execution of Justice' " (Rev.) *Women's Wear Daily*. In *New York Theatre Critics' Reviews*, 47. No. 4, March 3–10, 1986, 350.
Cohen, Sonya Freeman. "Emily Mann: The 'Jewish Visionary' behind Princeton's McCarter Theatre." *Jewish Post*, November 28, 1991, 23.
Cole, Susan Letzler. "Emily Mann Directs *Execution of Justice*." In *Directors in Rehearsal: A Hidden World*. New York: Routledge, 1992, 56–72.
Daniels, Robert L. (Rev. of *Greensboro: A Requiem*). *Variety*, February 26, 1996. Reprinted in *National Theatre Critics' Reviews* 57, No. 4, 1996, 114.
Gussow, Mel. "Stage: Emily Mann's 'Execution of Justice.' " *New York Times*, March 14, 1986. In *New York Theatre Critics' Reviews*, 47, No. 4, March 3–10, 1986, 348.
———. "Testimony of a Survivor: Memories and Chicken Soup." (Rev. of *Annulla*). *New York Times*, November 2, 1988, 23C.
Hamlin, Scott. "Out of Danger" (Interview). *Theater* 27, No. 1, Spring 1996, 99–101.
Isser, E. R. "Toward a Feminist Perspective in American Holocaust Drama." *Studies in the Humanities* 17, No. 2, December 1990, 139–48.
Istel, John. "Emily Mann: Searching for Survivors." *American Theatre* 13, No. 2, February 1996, 44–45.
Kilkelly, Ann Gavere. "Emily Mann." In *Notable Women in the American Theatre: A Biographical Dictionary*. Ed. Alice M. Robinson, Vera Mowry Roberts, and Milly S. Barranger. New York: Greenwood Press, 1989, 584–87.
Kissel, Howard. "*Having Our Say* Speaks Volumes about America." *New York Daily News*, April 7, 1995. Reprinted in *National Theatre Critics' Reviews* 56, No. 6, 1995, 170–71.

Kleb, William. "You the Jury: Emily Mann's *Execution of Justice*." *Theater* 16, Fall/Winter 1984, 55–61.

Klein, Alvin. "Now, a Few Words with the Audience." *New York Times*, February 18, 1996, Section 13, 1.

Kolin, Philip C. "Emily Mann: A Classified Bibliography." *Studies in American Drama, 1945–Present*, vol. 4, 1989, 222–66.

———. "Public Facts/Private Fictions in Emily Mann's Plays. In *Public Issues, Private Tensions: Contemporary American Drama*. Ed. Matthew C. Roudané. New York: AMS Press, 1993, 231–48.

Kramer, Richard E. "Annulla: An Autobiography" (Rev.). *Studies in American Drama, 1945–Present*, vol. 4, 1989, 286–89.

Kreizenbeck, Alan. "Emily Mann." In *Theatrical Directors: A Biographical Dictionary*. Ed. John W. Frick and Stephen M. Vallillo. Westport, CT: Greenwood Press, 1994, 259–60.

Meyer, Kate Beaird. "Bottles of Violence: Fragments of Vietnam in Emily Mann's *Still Life*." In *America Rediscovered: Critical Essays on Literature and Film of the Vietnam War*. Ed. Owen E. Gilman and Lorrie Smith. New York: Garland, 1990, 238–55.

Savran, David. *In Their Own Words*. New York: TCG, 1988.

Schiff, Ellen. "Emily Mann." In *Jewish American Women Writers: A Bio-bibliographic and Critical Sourcebook*. Ed. Ann R. Shapiro, Westport, CT: Greenwood Press, 1994, 218–26.

———. "From Black and White to Red and Pink: Political Themes on the American Jewish Stage." *Studies in American Jewish Literature* 8, No. 1, Spring 1989, 66–76.

———. "Introduction." In *Fruitful and Multiplying: Nine Contemporary Plays from the American Jewish Repertoire*. New York: Penguin, 1996, xv–xlvii.

Schroeder, Patricia R. "Hearing Many Voices at Once: The Theatre of Emily Mann." In *Public Issues, Private Tensions: Contemporary American Drama*. Ed. Matthew C. Roudané. New York: AMS Press, 1993, 249–65.

Shteir, Rachel. " 'I Became an Optimist': An Interview with Emily Mann." *Theatre Magazine* 22, No. 1, Fall/Winter 1991, 20–26.

———. "New Artistic Directors Emily Mann." *Theatre Magazine* 21, Winter 1990–1991, 20–26.

Simon, John. "Court and Courtroom" (Rev. of *Execution of Justice*). *New York*, March 24, 1986, 96.

———. "Various Ways to Lose Your Head" (Rev. of *Still Life*). *New York*, March 2, 1981, 52–54.

Smith, Melanie. "Total Denial: Emily Mann's Feminist Techniques in the Context of Popular American Entertainment Culture." *Studies in the Humanities* 17, No. 2, December 1990, 129–138.

DONALD MARGULIES   (1954–)

Oren Safdie

BIOGRAPHY

Donald Margulies was born in Brooklyn, New York, in 1954. He has received drama fellowships from the New York Foundation for the Arts, the National Endowment for the Arts, and the John Simon Guggenheim Memorial Foundation. *Sight Unseen*, a Pulitzer Prize finalist, won the Dramatists Guild/Hull Warriner Award and the Obie Award for Best New American Play. *The Model Apartment* was also a nominee for the Pulitzer Prize in 1996. Margulies is a member of New Dramatists and was elected to the council of the Dramatists Guild in 1993. He lives with his wife, Lynn Street, a physician, and their son, Miles, in New Haven, Connecticut, where he is a visiting lecturer in playwriting at the Yale School of Drama.

MAJOR WORKS AND THEMES

It is interesting to see the progression in Donald Margulies' work as he has explored issues involving childhood, family, religious identity, and the conflicts arising when these elements intersect. While his earlier plays are somewhat abstract and introspective, the later ones tend to be more concrete; they touch on the specific, while transcending the boundaries of the"Jewish Experience." They examine the notion of individual identity as an artist, as son or daughter, or as a person living in exile.

As with many other post–World War II Jewish-American playwrights, the world of Brooklyn and "Old World" characters are present throughout his work, albeit a bit more gentrified. The immigrant experience of fitting into the American melting pot while still holding onto Jewish roots can be seen in some form or another in all of Margulies' works. The duality of wanting to be Jewish while trying to appear as American as possible places Margulies' protagonists in dramatic conflicts. Further complicating these characters' dilemma is the enormous burden of guilt for all that Jews have suffered before them. Margulies' use of nightmares or ghosts from the past enables the playwright to confront their haunted souls much in the way Hamlet was forced to confront the injustice done to his father. In Margulies' case, these ghosts allow his characters a chance to set things straight. We see this in Mort's need to resurrect his wife, Shirley, so as to assure himself that he gave her the best life could offer—*What's Wrong with this Picture?* Or in Lola and Max, who must come to terms with their having survived the Holocaust, by revisiting their life through a dream—*The Model Apartment*. This is more evident in Margulies' later works, culminating in *Sight Unseen*. It is interesting to observe these budding themes in his earlier works, *Found a Peanut* and *Zimmer*. In all his plays the journey of understanding the Jewish-American psyche is a continuous process; this is evident not only in his ability to build from one play to the next but also in his writing process, often rewriting plays that have been already produced. Overall, one senses a preoccupation with trying to reconcile with flaws of human nature and the need for self-forgiveness that drives many of these characters.

Found a Peanut (1984) is a fairly subtle play unless it is taken in the context of the entire Margulies oeuvre. Its bantering dialogue among young children in a mixed Jewish, Irish, and Italian neighborhood in Brooklyn is filled with subtle metaphors regarding Jewish identity in the diaspora and the Holocaust. Margulies demonstrates these points through the cruel nature of child's play and natural hierarchy (pecking order) that exists among these children. The Jewish children in this play often have to fend for themselves against tougher, more established ethnic groups. Undertones of the Holocaust are touched on through the children's fascination with death and their ability to distance themselves from brutality. Margulies leaves much room for directorial interpretation; he permits the use of adult actors dressed in different types of clothing, indicating the author's intention of presenting these children in an adult world.

The Loman Family Picnic (1988) satirizes Arthur Miller's play *Death of a Salesman*, while bringing to light many of the Jewish themes implicit in Miller's script. Margulies concentrates especially on the pressure Jewish parents put on their children to succeed, as well as their obsession with the perfect, wholesome American family. Margulies' characterization of the Loman family demonstrates the discrepancy between Jewish-American families and the polite, well-behaved, Protestant family, such as portrayed on television shows of the late 1950s and early 1960s. But Margulies takes an extra step—he highlights a Jewish family's motivation while explaining the driving force behind the characters in *Death of a Salesman*.

In *What's Wrong with This Picture?* (1985) Margulies deals with the loss of a mother and wife in a middle-class Jewish family and literally resurrects her ghost—she just walks in from the cemetery—in order for her son and husband to make peace with her before she rests in peace. Margulies treats this ghost comedically, and the characters quickly accept the premise of her ghost and continue on with the play as if she had, indeed, come back. Whether this might be too much for an audience to accept is open for debate. *What's Wrong with This Picture?* was revised several times, finally opening on Broadway for a very brief run. It is ironic that this play would be Margulies' Broadway debut, since it is not his strongest work. The reason is not quality but audience appeal. Marketed (and titled) more like a Neil Simon comedy, the play has a more serious edge to it, which might have escaped a Broadway audience that expected quick one-liners and the usual Jewish humor. This is not what his plays are about.

An interesting feature of Margulies' work is his ability to reveal a little bit at a time, peeling back layers until the truth is fully exposed. Nowhere is this more evident than in *The Model Apartment* (1988). The curtain rises on a retired Jewish couple arriving at a condominium in Florida. Yet, things start off on the wrong foot, since their apartment isn't ready, and they have to temporarily occupy the "model apartment" with nailed-down furniture and ashtrays stuck to tabletops. This, no doubt, parallels the Jewish experience of trying to make America one's homeland. As the play progresses, there is mention of a troubled daughter left behind in New York, almost as if the parents were running away from her. But nothing can prepare the audience for her sudden arrival with a retarded, black boyfriend from the ghetto. Suddenly, everything from the couple's haunted past is turned upside-down. We witness a verbal attack of profanity by their daughter, whose obesity can be connected to the fact that she was brought up with a mother who constantly told her how in the concentration camps there was never anything to eat and whose father constantly mourned the death of a previous family. So punishing and vulgar is the attack from Debby about Hitler and Germany that it forces her parents to confront their past in a series of dreams that reveal the horrors of the past. The mother's insistence at having known the legendary Anne Frank and her assertion that Anne was somewhat of a snob are an attempt to humanize the Holocaust and elevate it from an untouchable tragedy into something the audience can identify with.

As the title might suggest, the ghosts in *Sight Unseen* (1992) are lodged in the character's subconscious. Here, all of Margulies' elements from previous plays come together in what could be his most complex and insightful work. He explores different themes in this play. Margulies uses a staggered time structure to unravel several stories from the past. Sometimes, answers are revealed before the questions, thereby turning questions into answers. Jonathan's reunion with a Gentile ex-lover in England is contrasted with a flashback to Jonathan as a young man under pressure from his mother to marry a Jew. Jonathan's success as a painter who expresses his Jewish heritage is contrasted with a German reporter's accusation that he is using the Holocaust for commercial success. Jonathan's urgent need to retrieve an early painting from his ex-girlfriend is an attempt to retrieve the magic that first inspired him to paint. By the end of the play, the past, future, and present all come together to reveal a character who questions not only his commitment to Judaism but also his true intentions behind artistic expression. The parallels between Margulies the playwright and his character as artist dealing with the Holocaust lead one to speculate that this play is autobiographical. Although there are no right answers, the desperate search for the truth makes *Sight Unseen* so powerful.

CRITICAL RECEPTION

For the most part, critics of Margulies' work have been very favorably inclined, often pointing out his ability to present issues like the Holocaust in an original and indirect way that resonates more strongly than many ''issue-oriented'' plays. Ben Brantley of the *New York Times* wrote about *The Model Apartment*: ''[T]he effect of the Holocaust on its survivors and their descendants ... has, of course, been addressed ad infinitum, but Mr. Margulies brings his own singular take, peppered with dark and gentle lyricism, to the phenomenon'' (16).

Critics are impressed by Margulies' ability to surprise. Thus, just when you think you know where the play is going, suddenly, another layer is peeled off, revealing deeper issues. *Sight Unseen* brought Margulies international acclaim and established him as one of America's leading Jewish dramatists. Though *The Loman Family Picnic* and *What's Wrong with This Picture?* were fine works, many critics recognized that with *Sight Unseen*, Margulies has truly come into his own. In the Introduction to his second collection of plays, Michael Feingold wrote of Margulies: ''His gift for raising troublesome issues subtly ... comes with a concomitant gift for ironizing his way around them, for seeing them from all sides'' (xi).

BIBLIOGRAPHY

Works by Donald Margulies

Plays

Found a Peanut. New York Shakespeare Festival, 1984.
What's Wrong with This Picture? Manhattan Theatre Club, 1985.
The Model Apartment. Los Angeles Theatre Center, 1988.
The Loman Family Picnic. Manhattan Theatre Club, 1988.
Pitching to the Star and Other Short Plays. New York: Dramatists Play Service, 1991.
Sight Unseen. Manhattan Theatre Club, 1992.
Sight Unseen and Other Plays. New York: Theatre Communications Group, 1995.
Sholem Asch's God of Vengeance. Long Wharf Theatre, 1996.
Collected Stories. Manhattan Theatre Club, 1997.

Works about Donald Margulies

Brantley, Ben. *New York Times*, October 26, 1995, 16.
Feingold, Michael. ''Introduction'' to *Sight Unseen and Other Plays*. New York: Theatre
    Communications Group, 1995.

ARTHUR MILLER   (1915–   )

Benjamin Nelson

BIOGRAPHY

Arthur Miller was born October 17, 1915, on East 112th Street in New York City to a Jewish family of Germanic stock. He was the second of three children, preceded by a brother, Kermit, and followed by a sister, Joan. His father, Isadore, was a manufacturer of women's coats, and his mother, Augusta, had been a teacher.

After his family had been hit hard by the depression, they moved to Brooklyn. Because of the family's straitened circumstances and because he was not a very distinguished student, Miller had difficulty getting into college. After two years of working at various jobs, he finally was able to enroll at the University of Michigan. There, he began to write plays, mainly for the monetary assistance Michigan offered students through its prestigious Avery Hopwood Awards.

Winning two Hopwood Awards, Miller graduated from Michigan in 1938 and began a career as a writer. But if success came easily at the university, it was a lot more fickle in the outside world, and Miller struggled along for a few years, writing mainly for radio. His first Broadway offering, *The Man Who Had All the Luck*, proved to have an ironic title. It opened November 23, 1944; it closed four days later. Overnight success was still three years around the corner, but when it came, it came loudly.

The production of *All My Sons* in 1947 gained him both popular and critical acclaim, winning the New York Drama Critics Circle Award over Eugene O'Neill's *The Iceman Cometh*. His reputation was further and spectacularly enhanced with the production of *Death of a Salesman* in 1949. The play earned Miller a Pulitzer Prize and became one of the most admired and enduring dramas of the past half century.

In the 1950s, along with Tennessee Williams, Miller dominated the American stage with plays such as *An Enemy of the People* (adapted from Henrik Ibsen, 1950), *The Crucible* (1953), and *A View from the Bridge* and *A Memory of Two Mondays* (1955). During this decade, the author of *The Crucible* was himself victimized by a witch-hunt: the anticommunist hysteria known as McCarthyism. He challenged the House Un-American Activities Committee by refusing to inform on friends and acquaintances and was convicted of contempt. Although the contempt citation was later reversed, and he was never imprisoned, Miller was blacklisted for a time.

In the 1960s, however, he returned to the stage with three powerful dramas: *After the Fall* (1964), *Incident at Vichy* (1965), and *The Price* (1968). The past three decades have witnessed more Miller plays: *The Creation of the World and Other Business* (1973), *The American Clock* (1980), *Danger: Memory: Two Plays* (1987), *The Last Yankee* (1991), *The Ride Down Mt. Morgan* (1992), *Broken Glass* (1994), and *Mr. Peters' Connections* (1998).

Miller is also the author of a book of reportage, *Situation Normal* (1944); a novel, *Focus* (1945); a film script, *The Misfits* (1961); a television script, *Playing for Time* (1980); two autobiographical memoirs, *Salesman in Beijing* (1984) and *Timebends* (1987); and numerous short stories and essays.

Married three times, to Mary Slattery, Marilyn Monroe, and Inge Morath, Miller has three children, Robert, Jane, and Rebecca.

With plays being staged and taught throughout the world, Arthur Miller, like Eugene O'Neill, Tennessee Williams, and Edward Albee, has proven himself one of the driving forces in modern drama.

MAJOR WORKS AND THEMES

Bernard Malamud steadfastly refused to characterize himself as a Jewish-American writer. In numerous interviews he asserted that he was an American writer who happened to be Jewish. Undoubtedly, Arthur Miller would make a similar claim. Nevertheless, viewing the complete body of his writing, one can validly mark the pervasive influence of Miller's Jewishness on his work, those dramas with, as well as those without, a specific Jewish context. From his earliest efforts to his most recent, Miller exhibits what can arguably be called a Jewish sensibility in his overall outlook on the individual and his or her society.

Like his initial dramas of the 1930s, *They Too Arise* is one of Miller's "trunk plays." He refers to them this way because they belong to his youth, and he has never intended to resurrect them for production. The essential value of *They Too Arise* does not lie in its inherent worth as a drama but in its seminal characters and situations and in the thematic directions in which it pointed the aspiring young playwright.

An expansion of a play called *No Villain, They Too Arise* was written by Miller when he attended Michigan University in 1937–1938. It was the first play he wrote not to win a coveted Avery Hopwood Award, but it did manage to

garner the young dramatist financial and critical recognition from the Bureau of
New Plays in 1939.

They Too Arise dramatizes the story of the Simon family: Abe, a manufacturer
of women's coats, his wife, Esther, and their three children, Ben, Arnie, and
Maxine. Family tensions are being exacerbated by a strike of shipping clerks
that could bankrupt the Simon business. During the course of the drama, brother
is pitted against brother, husband against wife, and father against sons as the
economic conflict elicits intensely personal responses from all the members of
the beleaguered family. After facing a number of painful truths about their relationships to each other, the Simons manage to effect a tentative truce by making sacrifices that bring them closer together.

They Too Arise is clearly the work of an idealistic young author living through
the depression of the 1930s. It is didactic, melodramatic, and bulging with social
consciousness and youthful optimism. It is also, however, a prototypical Miller
drama.

To a great extent the Simon family is based on Miller's own, and some of
the sequences are specifically autobiographical. However, while the play reflects
the life and milieu of its author, it also points toward characters and situations
Miller would develop in many succeeding dramas. Intimations of *All My Sons*,
Death of a Salesman, and *The Price* abound in *They Too Arise*, in both characterization and theme. Out of the arena of family conflict—especially father
versus sons and brother versus brother—spiral basic Miller motifs of the individual's relationship to the world and the clash between pragmatism and idealism. They do so in a specific Jewish context, not only in terms of the literal
Simon environment but through what could be termed the Simon outlook.

In a crucial scene in the middle of *They Too Arise*, Abe Simon learns that
his fellow manufacturers are intent on hiring thugs to disperse the strikers who
are threatening their livelihoods. In full awareness that he faces ruination if the
crippling strike continues, the elder Simon addresses his colleagues:

I want you to know . . . that I will not vote to hire gangsters . . . because I feel—I don't
know why—but someway it seems to me that this ain't the way an honest man or honest
men do business. *I can't see that it's the way for Jewish men to act*—that's all I got to
say. But I hope so that I can keep my respect for all of you—hope you will not act like
this—like—like—beasts. (38; emphasis added)

What Abe Simon gropingly tries to express to his fellow manufacturers is
very similar to what subsequent Miller protagonists like Lawrence Newman of
Focus, John Proctor of *The Crucible*, Count Von Berg of *Incident at Vichy*, and
Victor Franz of *The Price* also attempt to convey—to themselves as well as to
others. It is the cry of individual conscience for self-respect, for the need to
hold fervently to one's name and to what the concept of name signifies. Equally
important, in *They Too Arise* Abe Simon's personal integrity is linked to his

Jewishness, not merely in terms of ethnicity but in the humanism inherent in that ethnicity.

Abe's comment that he "can't see that it's the way for Jewish men to act" is a simple, forthright statement. In its simplicity, however, it is firmly entrenched in a 3,000-year foundation of Jewish history and morality. It abounds with echoes of persecution and suffering, law and ethics, hope and possibility, and it reverberates with the voice of a people who never coveted the hero's laurels, who were continually forced into concessions to survive, but who always drew the line at wholly surrendering conscience and identity.

In future works, whether or not the characters and contexts are Jewish, the implication in that single line of dialogue gives substance and definition to the dramatic intent of Arthur Miller. It resonates impressively in *Focus*, Miller's only novel to date and his sole work until *Incident at Vichy* to deal specifically with anti-Semitism.

Lawrence Newman, the protagonist of *Focus*, is a curious, even somewhat bizarre figure. A Gentile, he is employed as a personnel executive by a politely anti-Semitic corporation in New York. One of his responsibilities, which he carries out with singular pride, is screening out undesirable applicants. Although he would not view himself as prejudiced, he nonetheless lives in a restricted area of Brooklyn whose only Jew is a storekeeper whom Newman barely acknowledges. It is not that Newman is particularly friendly with the rest of his neighbors. He doesn't even necessarily like them; but he finds a certain tentative security in accepting their prejudices, and he tries not to analyze his situation very deeply.

Because of failing sight, however, Newman is forced to wear glasses (contact lenses are too uncomfortable), which to his chagrin make him appear decidedly Semitic. This embarrassing new look rapidly leads to a macabre disorientation, and in a series of shameful sequences he actually finds himself in the position of a persecuted Jew. At work and in his neighborhood Newman increasingly becomes a pariah, increasingly undergoes humiliation, and increasingly feels trapped and degraded. But the more he is denigrated, the more he begins to resent those who are responsible. He starts to fight back, at first reluctantly and then with increasing anger that he finds cleansing. After fighting off assailants with the help of Finkelstein, the Jewish storekeeper, Newman feels a kind of pride he has never previously experienced. When the police arrive and assume Newman to be Jewish, he affirms the assumption and in so doing feels "as though he were setting down a weight which for some reason he had been carrying and carrying" (217).

In *Focus*, despite some plot devices that tend to give a new meaning to the term "poetic license"—most obviously, the glasses—Miller still tells a powerful story of racial prejudice, of which anti-Semitism is one salient manifestation. In a painful exchange between Newman and Finkelstein before they become allies, Miller illuminates one basic aspect of this insidious phenomenon: the generalization of individuals into types. Newman can barely comprehend the Jewish merchant as anything more than a stereotypic representative of an alien group.

"You don't understand," he exclaims to Finkelstein in obtuse sincerity, "it's not what *you've* done, it's what others of your people have done."

Finkelstein's reply slashes to the core of Newman's delusion: "In other words," he counters with sardonic anger, "when you look at me you don't see me." (165).

Newman's denial of Finkelstein's particularity is an indication of his moral myopia; it is also a mark of his reluctance to accept himself. Newman must focus inward before he can focus clearly and cogently on others. The action of the novel is precisely this process of focusing. At the end of the book Lawrence Newman does not literally evolve into a Jew, but he does become what the Yiddish word "mensch" signifies: a person of moral and ethical dimension. His odyssey is a redemptive one, and as such it prefigures similar journeys undertaken by subsequent Miller protagonists. It involves the acceptance of commitment to others, not solely as an act of altruism but as the basic consequence of commitment to self. Resonating in this moral and spiritual rebirth is the implication in the words of Ben Simon that there are inherent standards of Jewish behavior and action. In applying these standards to himself, Newman metaphorically becomes the Jew that he so adamantly struggled against in a literal sense.

After the publication of *Focus* Miller returned to his first love, the theatre, and achieved stunning recognition with the two plays that propelled him to the forefront of American drama: *All My Sons* and *Death of a Salesman*. They were followed by a less-than-successful production of Miller's adaptation of Henrik Ibsen's *An Enemy of the People*. Then came *The Crucible*.

In terms of situation and characters *The Crucible* is one of Arthur Miller's least Jewish dramas. As readers and theatregoers have come to know, *The Crucible* dramatizes one of the most tragic and shameful events in American history—the Salem, Massachusetts, witch trials at the end of the seventeenth century. When the play first appeared in 1953, it was also clear that Miller had written not only a historical drama but a white-hot phillipic against the shameful events of his own time, the phenomenon of corporate national hysteria that came to be known as McCarthyism.

The Crucible, however, cannot be limited to either the Salem witch-hunts or the red-baiting of the 1950s. As we are well aware more than forty years after its initial production, Miller's play is a dramatic exploration of mass hysteria in whatever manifestation that terrible phenomenon takes place. It is a drama that has gripped the imagination and held the attention of audiences and readers throughout the world. Indeed, it is hardly coincidental that in terms of productions and copies published, *The Crucible* leads even *Death of a Salesman* in popularity.

But Jewish?

Apparently not. Nary a Jew in sight. Well, maybe not in sight, but not out of mind. Miller's Jewish sensibility is palpably evident in his tragedy of colonial Salem, particularly in the character of the play's protagonist, John Proctor. There are some intriguing similarities between the New England farmer who attains tragic stature and Lawrence Newman, the fastidious, neurotic personnel executive whose development is the central action of *Focus*.

Both men eventually become heroes, although each seems an unlikely candidate for heroism. Both men are initially reluctant. Both hope to gain security and safety by means of accommodation and compromise. Both begin their dramas as uncommitted, even morally neutral and, in Newman's case, something even less than that. Both then find themselves caught up in situations initially beyond their control, in crucibles that threaten to melt them down entirely. However, caught in their respective maelstroms, they begin the lacerating process that will burn away their former identities and, as Newman's name symbolically suggests, enable them to re-create themselves as moral entities.

In Proctor's case rebirth also means death. When he begs his fanatic prosecutor, Deputy Governor Danforth, not to force him to choose between saving his life and betraying his friends who will die in vain if Proctor confesses to witchcraft, he invokes the concept of name. When Danforth asks why Proctor will not give him his signed confession, Proctor responds ''with a cry of his whole soul'':

Because it is my name! Because I cannot have another in my life! Because I lie and sign myself to lies! . . . How may I live without my name! I have given you my soul; leave me my name! (328)

John Proctor is wrong. In refusing to yield his name, he retains his soul, for the two in Miller's thought are synonymous. As the playwright remarked in an interview shortly before the premiere of *The Crucible*:

Nobody wants to be a hero. You go through life giving up parts of yourself—a hope, a dream, an ambition, a belief, a liking, a piece of self-respect. But in every man there is something he cannot give up and still remain himself—a core, an identity, a thing that is summed up for him by the sound of his own name on his own ears. If he gives that up, he becomes a different person, not himself. (Miller, qtd. in *New York Herald Tribune*, June 25, 1953, 22)

In *All My Sons*, Joe Keller kills himself in a desperate effort to atone for losing that core, that identity. In *A View from the Bridge*, the play that followed *The Crucible*, the longshoreman Eddie Carbone also dies in a suicidal effort to restore the identity inherent in name, which, like Joe Keller, he has thrown away through antisocial action. In *The Crucible*, however, Proctor dies to preserve his name, not in atonement for having lost it.

In so doing, the Puritan farmer, like the Gentile personnel executive in *Focus*, adheres to the convictions and values of the Jewish manufacturer in *They Too*

Arise. All of them act upon an awareness that informs so much of Miller's work and thought. Newman and Proctor find, as Proctor states, that they are better than they thought they were—not only because they can stand up for their individual integrity in the midst of great peril but because they have come to realize that this individual integrity is commingled with the lives of others. They do not exist in an existential vacuum. Their worth is measured in terms of their connection to a world, as Joe Keller put it in *All My Sons*, beyond "the building line." While there is nothing exclusively Jewish about this concept, it is certainly inherently Jewish. Perhaps it is most precisely illustrated by a Talmudic commentary that Miller has occasionally cited as relevant to his work: the fish is in the water, and the water is in the fish. Individual integrity and conscience cannot be divorced from the encompassing world in which we live. This is Proctor's ultimate awareness in *The Crucible*. It is palpably Jewish.

Miller returns, at least in part, to specific Jewish subject matter in his play *After the Fall*, which premiered in January 1964. To this day, *After the Fall* is the playwright's most controversial drama, mainly because of its obvious autobiographical content, particularly with respect to its ostensible dramatization of Miller's marriage to Marilyn Monroe. The play was hailed as searingly powerful or damned as tabloid confessional and self-justifying. Interestingly, as the events that caused so much furor more than three decades ago continue to recede in memory, *After the Fall* continues to gain in stature. Obviously, the play has not improved; perhaps its audience has. In terms of appraisal the bottom line is that although *After the Fall* uses autobiographical material, the play is not autobiography. It is about relationships and choices and prices paid and a whole lot more.

Quentin, the protagonist, is a lawyer who, at approximately the middle of his life, reviews the casebook of his existence. In a state of spiritual and psychological crisis, he reviews his life and the people in it in an attempt to move beyond the abyss of despondency into which he has fallen. As he analyzes himself—the drama takes place "in the mind, thought, and memory of Quentin"—he conducts a kind of personal court of inquiry—not seeking absolution or even condemnation but hoping for awareness, for some form of self-realization. With every recollection Quentin clarifies the blurred past, adjusting the lens of his perception and bringing his life slowly and painfully into sharper focus. The process is familiar. Like the thematic development of all Miller dramas, the movement of *After the Fall* is toward deepening awareness and significance.

Leafing through the chapters of his past, Quentin finds losses and betrayals, of him and by him. The more he delves into his life and its relationships, the less judgmental he becomes. He learns to forgive, others as well as himself. He moves from the glib self-assurance of his earlier years to a deeper, more compassionate understanding of human motives and human frailty. He learns, as he states late in the play, that we are all "very dangerous."

The dominant image in *After the Fall* is a blasted stone tower of a concentration camp that Quentin had visited on a trip to Europe. The more Quentin relives events from his past and recalls a life of betrayals, the more the camp tower glows ominously in the dark shadows of his memory, until at the end, when he remembers the agony of his marriage to his second wife, Maggie, and acknowledges that he wanted her to die so that he could be free of her tortured and torturing presence, the camp tower blazes forth implacably. It is the most awesome manifestation of the failure of love and the fact of betrayal.

Until he faces his own complicity with the deceit and cruelty of which he is capable, Quentin is unable to comprehend the monstrous truths embodied in that tower. Now, however, finally confronting the heart of darkness within himself, he dares to speculate on what the tower manifests. Perhaps, he thinks,

this is not bizarre to anyone? And I am not alone, and no man lives who would not rather be the sole survivor of this place than all its finest victims? What is the cure? Who can be innocent again on this mountain of skulls? . . . My brothers died here—but my brothers built this place; our hearts have cut these stones! (113)

Some critics have felt that in applying Holocaust imagery to *After the Fall* and using a Holocaust context to expound upon the angst of a person who had never been in that context, Miller was banalizing and trivializing that most awesome of catastrophes. A careful reading of the play's text, however, lends scant support to this criticism. In *After the Fall* Miller is attempting to comprehend one of many aspects of the Holocaust, namely, the instinct to survive at any cost that enabled so many people to either betray others or turn from them in ambivalent relief. It is hard to deny that this instinct, so prevalent in Holocaust experiences, extends beyond those terrible, bloody parameters.

At the conclusion of his drama, Quentin is aware of the kinship he shares with anyone complicit in evil, because the capability lies in the human heart. Yet, in the full awareness of this dangerous potential, Quentin still dares to hope.

"Is the knowing all?" he wonders.

To know, and even happily, that we meet unblessed, not in that lie of Eden, but after the Fall, after many, many deaths. . . . And the wish to kill is never killed, but with some gift of courage one may look into its face when it appears, and with a stroke of love—as to an idiot in the house—forgive it!—again and again . . . forever? (114)

The deeply Jewish aspect of *After the Fall* does not reside only in its use of the Holocaust, although that use is anything but peripheral. The Jewishness of the play lies in Miller's juxtaposition of despair and hope. The drama balances one individual's agonizing confrontation with the darker forces within himself and humanity, with the tenuous, illogical, yet perdurable, hope that springs not from the evasion of knowledge but from its acceptance.

In this paradoxical union of pain and possibility, Miller again exhibits an age-old, but ongoing, outlook that is inherently part of Jewish experience. A profoundly Jewish sensibility is woven through the complex fabric of *After the Fall*, enriching its meaning and adding dimension to it.

Some of the basic motifs of *After the Fall* can also be found in the play that followed it into the Lincoln Center Repertory Theatre late in 1964. The drama is *Incident at Vichy*, and in characterization, content, and theme it is one of Miller's more obviously Jewish works.

The plot of *Incident at Vichy* is simple, and the action stark and linear. Presented in a single act, the play, which is based on a true story, dramatizes approximately ninety minutes in the lives of a few men in a detention station in Vichy France in the autumn of 1942. The men are awaiting examination to ascertain if they are Jewish. Anyone who is not is free to go; anyone who is will be sent immediately to a concentration camp.

As each man tries to deal with his agonizing dilemma, one after another is plucked away by their inquisitors until only two remain: a Jewish psychiatrist named Leduc and Count Von Berg, a Catholic nobleman. In a stunning denouement the Catholic, allowed to leave, gives the Jew his passport to freedom and offers up his life for the other man's. While the act is startling, it is not wholly surprising. Throughout the hour and a half, in an impassioned and revelatory series of conversations among the detainees, Von Berg has seen his rationalizations and protestations of innocence burn away under the searing examination of Leduc. His final response to the doctor comes in the form of action instead of words.

In *Incident at Vichy*, Arthur Miller applies to a specific moment in Holocaust history a consideration of human nature that he dramatized in *After the Fall*: the individual's potential for evil, coupled with his adamant refusal to acknowledge it in himself. Through the exchanges between Leduc and Von Berg, the playwright considers the basic dilemma of responsibility and commitment—to what extent we may help to perpetuate evil, not by willingly embracing it but by turning our backs on it as long as it does not immediately involve us. As Leduc notes to Von Berg:

Part of knowing who we are is knowing we are not someone else. And Jew is only the name we give to that stranger, that agony we cannot feel, that death we look at like a cold abstraction. Each man has his Jew; it is the other. And the Jews have their Jews. And now, above all, you must see that you have yours—the man whose death leaves you relieved that you are not him, despite your decency. And that is why there is nothing—until you face your own complicity with this . . . your own humanity. (66)

Of course, one can argue validly that the idea of the Jew as the Other falls woefully short of explaining the phenomenon of anti-Semitism, especially as practiced by the Nazis. They did not seek to exterminate Others. They sought to exterminate Jews. With respect to the Jews, Hitler did not deal in metaphysics.

Miller, however, is not attempting to understand the Nazi mentality in *Incident at Vichy*; and in the context of its utterance, Leduc's preceding observation has a painful validity. It focuses not on the virulent hatred of Nazism but on the self-preserving passivity of decent people like the Count. Miller is noting how so many decent human beings aided and abetted the Nazi terror, not overtly, out of conviction, but covertly, out of self-concern. In this context, we may, indeed, all have our Jews.

Von Berg does not discover that he is or ever could be a Nazi. He discovers, in the recognition of his relief at escaping victimization, his relationship to—not equality with—the victimizers. With this discovery, he acts in the only way he feels is left to him in the circumstances.

To debate the utility of the Count's final action in terms of wisdom or waste is useless. Like Proctor's choice in *The Crucible*, Von Berg's decision is far too personal and impassioned to be subjected to dispassionate analysis. It does not even represent an articulate plan of behavior. Simply, the choice he makes is the initial and crucial step a person may take on discovering his or her inherent worth in a world whose values have proven deceptive and inadequate. A protest of the individual soul against inhumanity, it is the final decision of a man who cannot and will not survive at what he considers, wisely or foolishly, to be the price of his integrity.

In *Incident at Vichy* the Gentile becomes the heroic martyr. This is not only understandable but necessary in the context of the play. Only the Gentile has an option; only he is free to go. It is interesting, though, that by forfeiting his freedom and committing himself to moral action, the Catholic nobleman becomes the embodiment of the belief expressed by the Jewish shop owner in *They Too Arise*. There is a way not to act as a Jew as well as a way to act. Von Berg has chosen the latter, and through his choice he has not only acted as a Jew but saved a Jew, and in so doing he has presented the Jew with the same choice. The biblical implications of the brother's keeper resonate in *Incident at Vichy*. Is Count Von Berg his brother's keeper? Obviously. Is he his own, in terms of self-integrity? Definitely.

The Holocaust context and the image of the brother's keeper appear in subsequent Miller dramas. *Playing for Time* (1980), a television script adapted from an autobiographical memoir by Fania Fanelon, is set in a concentration camp and harrowingly depicts the cost to body and soul of the struggle for survival.

In 1994, *Broken Glass* further dramatized the recurring Miller motif of betrayal, guilt, and responsibility in its story of a Jewish-American woman's devastating reaction to the news of Kristallnacht in Nazi Germany. Sylvia Gellburg, a Brooklyn housewife, has lost the use of her legs after seeing pictures of Jews victimized by the Nazis. The broken glass littering the streets of German towns and cities becomes, among other things, a metaphor for her splintered marriage, as macrocosm and microcosm impinge meaningfully upon each other.

Sylvia's paralysis also extends imagistically to her husband Phillip. In the figure of Phillip Gellburg, Miller creates a stunning characterization of a self-hating Jew, destructively trapped between a Jewish identity he is ashamed of, to the point of bitter and irrational hatred, and an impossible and ambivalent desire for acceptance by the Gentile world to which he vainly aspires. He has betrayed himself by repressing his Jewish identity, and he has betrayed his wife by using her as the scapegoat for his feelings of guilt and inadequacy.

In no other Miller play is the phenomenon of a human being denying his most fundamental identity established in so clear and dramatically charged a Jewish context. In *Broken Glass*, each of the major characters, Phillip Gellburg, Sylvia Gellburg, and Harry Hyman, a sympathetic Jewish doctor who treats Sylvia, presents perspectives on the Holocaust.

Hyman, in a naive optimism characteristic of the late 1930s, underestimates the devastating encroachment of the Nazi terror. Sylvia, sensing the gathering horror, is literally paralyzed by her awarenesss. Phillip, most destructively to body and soul, denies all identification with it. Each character is defined, at least in part, by his or her relationship to what is happening in Europe.

As in *After the Fall* and *Incident at Vichy*, Miller in *Broken Glass* is using the Holocaust not only in terrifying literalness but as the baleful context for exploring the complex ramifications of human behavior and relationships.

These relationships, with particular emphasis on the theme of the brother's keeper, are most literally, but imaginatively, dramatized in *The Creation of the World and Other Business* (1972). Here Miller considers the Garden of Eden story in Genesis, with particular emphasis on the fratricidal relationship of Cain and Abel. The play seeks in the act of fratricide, which is the first instance of wholly human conflict in the Bible, some sign of the enigmatic relationship between human beings and God. A character in the play, God is seen not only as permitting this murderous act but as somehow having created humankind with the capacity for perpetuating it. Destructive action is built by God into primal human nature, and brotherhood is fraught with betrayal and violent death. Against this baleful fact of human nature, Adam and Eve feel fear and dismay. As Cain strides off into the world in dark triumph, all his father can do is offer up a plea for mercy. But that cry is characteristic of Miller's outlook. It contains the hope that perseveres in the full awareness of the darkness out of which it emanates. It posits the possibility that Miller insists upon in all of his work.

This insistence upon possibility and viable moral behavior is dramatized humorously and poignantly in a drama that preceded *Broken Glass* and *The Creation of the World and Other Business*. The play is *The Price*, and it is a quintessential Miller creation. In this 1968 drama, Miller returned to the family arena of *Death of a Salesman* and the well-made play structure of *All My Sons*.

The dialogue is basically expository and revelatory, probing into the past and exposing a house built on lies. As Victor and Walter Franz, the brothers who form the drama's nucleus, square off against each other in a long, exhausting, and corrosive verbal fencing match, Miller explores the relationship between actions and consequences, guilt and responsibility, self-preservation and commitment to others. In their parents' old home, Victor, a policeman, and Walter, a physician, begin by discussing how to sell off the furniture and other belongings of their deceased father and mother. Soon, however, the price of furniture becomes a metaphor for other prices paid in their lives. Throughout the harrowing, recrimination-filled afternoon, the echoes of previous family confrontations and conflicts reverberate through the rooms as brother lacerates brother in desperate attempts at self-justification.

Illusions and rationalizations are punctured as the two men, along with Victor's wife, Esther, confront truths they had tried to avoid. Finally, the brothers part, having gained some new knowledge but still essentially powerless to alter roles they have played for the greater portion of their lives. In *The Price* comprehension is not synonymous with change.

Only one of the four characters in the play is admittedly Jewish: the eighty-nine-year-old furniture dealer Gregory Solomon, whom Victor has hired to dispose of the family's belongings. In a story of profoundly serious conflicts, Solomon provides a good deal of what is generally termed comic relief. But this is hardly his main function in the play. He is a quintessential Jewish character—by Arthur Miller out of Sholem Aleichem.

In a drama about survival and the prices it demands, Gregory Solomon, the wandering Jew, is not only the crowning personification of the human will to survive, but of the human's unadulterated zest for living. Marvelously human and humorous, he is a combination of philosopher, sage, and aged imp. Exhibiting the wisdom of Solomon, the canniness of a Yankee trader, and the apparent indestructibility of Jewish tradition itself, Solomon has spent almost a century traveling the world, indulging himself in everything from a stint in the British navy to an acrobatic act in vaudeville, outliving wives and even children, and amassing and losing several fortunes. He has rebounded from at least four economic depressions dating back to 1898, and close upon the age of ninety he still burns with a strong flame that consumes the fear of undertaking a new project in a blaze of anticipation and challenge.

Unlike the brothers Franz, he has lived so fully because he has been able to face life without illusions. Living in an absurd world where, as he puts it, ''it's impossible to know what is important,'' he is convinced that one's existence is dependent on one's perspective, and his is rooted in a wry Jewish sense of paradox and an unflinching belief in his individual worth. His complicated and often hilarious method of bargaining is a manifestation of the ''mental world'' Solomon has fashioned for himself, the tradition to which he owes allegiance, and the conviction there are rules to be followed and standards to be met in the conduct of one's life. For Solomon, as for his Jewish forebears, life must be codified and ritualized, less in terms of religious observance than in terms of ethical standards, and he goes about doing so with solemnity, gusto, and a few perfectly placed and quite mischievous winks.

At times a comic foil to the others, he is also integral to their relationships and to Miller's overall intent in the play. Like Victor, Walter, and Esther, Gregory Solomon has paid his prices for survival. The suicide of his young daughter haunts him with its implications of the failure of love and communication. But he has refused to weave his sorrow into a mourning shroud of guilt and self-recrimination. Nor has he attempted to avert reality by rationalizations and illusions. Like Victor and Walter, he has invented himself, but according to the facts as he knows them, not to erase what he knows but to build upon it.

"Let me give you a piece of advice," Solomon proposes to Victor. "It's not that you can't believe nothing, that's not so hard—it's that you got to believe it. *That's* hard. And if you can't do that, my friend—you're a dead man!" (37).

The juxtaposition of belief and disbelief, commitment and detachment that marks many of Miller's dramas is central to *The Price*. The human embodiment of the need to believe is the ancient furniture dealer, Gregory Solomon. Logically, Solomon should not be undertaking the mammoth job of disposing of the Franz household. But with inherent Jewish chutzpah, Solomon is not about to capitulate to logic. Admitting the implausibility of his task for a person his age, he nevertheless accepts it with a renewed sense of hope and vigor. In his acceptance, in his determination not to be defined by necessity lies his victory.

Although many Jewish characters populate Miller's works, no other figure so lovingly and exuberantly personifies the dramatist's Jewish sensibility than this raffish, modern Solomon with his realistic, yet bouyant, outlook.

Intriguingly, one other Miller character also embodies the playwright's inherently Jewish outlook. He is Willy Loman, the protagonist of *Death of a Salesman* and arguably the most famous figure in American theatre. Certainly, there is nothing overtly Jewish about Willy or about his drama. Still, *Death of a Salesman* has a thematic Jewish subtext.

In its dramatization of two basic themes—the success myth and the yearning motif—*Death of a Salesman* is one of the quintessential American works of the twentieth century. These same motifs, however, are as inherently Jewish as they are American, particularly in their relationship to 2,000 years of diaspora Judaism.

The religious dimension of material success in America had its origin in the Puritan concept of the elect of God, in which tangible, substantive success was viewed as proof of divine favor. Material success was also crucial to diaspora Jewish existence, not as a validation of divine blessing but simply as indispensable to survival. The bottom line was that money and goods might forestall religious persecution.

The phenomenon of yearning, which is a crucial component of the mythic American dream, as embodied in Jay Gatsby, Clyde Griffiths, and numerous literary compatriots, was also a cogent part of the sustaining force that preserved diaspora Judaism. Not the dream of making it in the land of opportunity but the dream of a return to Jerusalem, a reclamation of Jewish destiny—a hope deferred but never extinguished—was diaspora Judaism's variation on the American dream, centuries before that dream ever materialized.

In *Death of a Salesman*, these motifs intertwine and help to define the character and outlook of Willy Loman. An archetypal American figure—the evangelical dreamer as well as the discarded employee—Willy is also, in some respects, the archetypal diaspora Jew, a stranger in a strange land, clutching at his dream with fervent, if illogical, valor, as if the American success myth is his new Jerusalem.

Two final considerations. One involves an episode from Miller's life and the other a short story by him.

On June 21, 1956, in a scene in which life imitated art, namely, the trial sequence of *The Crucible*, Arthur Miller appeared before the House Un-American Activities Committee (HUAC) to testify about his alleged communist affiliations in the 1930s and 1940s. At one point during the hearings, committee counsel Richard Arens sought to embarrass Miller by referring to a statement the playwright had made about the arrest of the expatriate American poet Ezra Pound, who had written and broadcast virulent anti-Semitic diatribes for the fascists and Nazis during World War II. In his statement Miller condemned Pound for what he viewed as clearly treasonous attempts to demoralize American troops fighting in Europe as well as the advocacy of Jewish genocide. Arens used the Miller statement to illustrate the alleged hypocrisy of the dramatist, who, on one hand, advocated freedom of speech and, on the other, scored a fellow artist for using that selfsame freedom.

When Arens pressed Miller on the subject of Pound, Miller grew increasingly outraged. He remembered hearing the Pound broadcasts from Italy on shortwave radio and recalled ''the cold that had flowed into my heart while I was listening to him.'' He saw in Arens' ''pug face . . . the face I had been fighting all my life, and the blood came into my head.'' When he saw Miller's reaction, the committee counsel backed off, and the playwright brought his anger under control. But he realized that the rage coursing through him was twofold. He was sickened by his memory of Ezra Pound's obscene actions: ''Pound had been calling for racial murder and . . . would have happily killed me as a Jew. . . . I had been against men like Pound . . . and I was proud of it'' (Miller, *Timebends* 410). He was sickened, too, by Arens' calculating attempt to use his Jewishness against him. That June day in the hearing room, Arthur Miller's Jewish pride and identity asserted themselves, not only against Pound's genocidal anti-Semitism but against HUAC counsel's insidious and self-righteous attempt to morally coerce him. Miller knew that knuckling under to that kind of pressure was not a way for a Jewish man to act.

Five years before his appearance before HUAC, in 1951, Miller wrote a short story called ''Monte Sant' Angelo.'' Based on a trip the writer took to Italy with a friend of his shortly after World War II, the story tells of two young Americans, Appello and Bernstein, who, on vacation, are seeking members, living and deceased, of Appello's family.

Vaguely uncomfortable with his friend's sentimental journey, Bernstein tags along dutifully but unenthusiastically. One day while they are lunching at a small restaurant near a church whose vaults they have been searching for tombs of the Appello family, a curious incident befalls them. They are drawn to an Italian peasant with whom they have exchanged casual greetings. The longer he watches the stranger, the surer Bernstein becomes that there is some kind of affinity between them. When the man places a loaf of bread into his pack and carefully ties it, Bernstein suddenly smiles his recognition. He turns to Appello and tells his friend that the man is Jewish. When Appello asks him how he knows, Bernstein replies, "The way he works that bundle. It's exactly the way my father used to tie a bundle. And my grandfather. The whole history is packing bundles and getting away. Nobody else can be as tender and delicate with bundles. That's a Jewish man tying a bundle" (Miller, "Monte Sant'Angelo," *I Don't Need You Anymore* (65).

When they question the departing peasant, he expresses bewilderment as to what a Jew is. Nevertheless, his name—a derivation of Moses—and his insistence on returning home before sunset on Friday because it is a family custom, convince the two Americans that unknowingly he does, indeed, have Jewish roots. After the man leaves, Bernstein is strangely excited, and he encourages Appello to continue his search for his family tombs. When his friend finds them, Bernstein, standing before the evidence of Appello's heritage and continuity, feels an overpowering joy. "I feel like . . . at home in this place," he affirms.

He did not move, seeking the root of an ecstasy he had not dreamed was part of his nature. . . . Pride was running through him. Of what he should be proud he had no clear idea; perhaps it was only that beneath the brainless crush of history a Jew had secretly survived, shorn of his consciousness, but forever caught by that final impudence of a Saturday Sabbath in a Catholic country, so that his very unawareness was proof, a proof as mute as stones, that a past lived. A past for me, Bernstein thought, astonished by its importance for him." ("Monte Sant' Angelo," *I Don't Need You Anymore* 69)

Miller's intrinsic Jewishness is poignantly delineated in the story "Monte Sant' Angelo." His insistence in so much of his work on meaningful human connection, on the need for the individual to move beyond the closed ego toward commitment to a world beyond self, on the need to posit meaning in the teeth of absurdity and to affirm identity through moral action is, at the very least, fueled by a strong Jewish sense of history and tradition that is ethically viable.

Stressing the value of personal integrity, Miller does so in a deeply Jewish context. "*The Jew in me*," he has remarked, "shie[s] from private salvation as something close to sin. One's truth must add its push to the evolution of public justice and mercy" (*Timebends* 314; emphasis added).

The Jew in Miller has informed and continues to inform his work with that selfsame insistence. Not through observance and not necessarily through religious belief, but through a deeply felt connection to a people and their basic human values, the Jewishness of Arthur Miller is both palpable and defining.

CRITICAL RECEPTION

In a career that has spanned six decades, Arthur Miller has experienced both critical adulation and reservation. Some of his dramas, particularly those over the past twenty years, have not received strong critical approval. Certainly, *The American Clock, Danger: Memory:, The Last Yankee*, and *Broken Glass* have not garnered the kind of reviews elicited by *All My Sons, Death of a Salesman, The Crucible*, and *The Price*.

One can argue that, like Tennessee Williams, Miller may have been too spectacularly successful too soon and that a blessing became a curse of sorts: his later plays suffer by comparison with his earlier ones. However, even *All My Sons, Death of a Salesman*, and *The Crucible* did not receive unanimous critical approval. A dramatist of strong and controversial opinions, Miller has always elicited the same in his audiences, and not all of them have been flattering.

It is too early to affirm that Miller's work has stood the test of time, but it is noteworthy that no other American dramatist has been respected more than Arthur Miller throughout the world. In England, particularly, he is acclaimed as America's foremost contemporary playwright. From Boise to Beijing, millions of viewers and readers have returned to Miller's dramas repeatedly and found in their specificity a deep quality of universality.

In *Death of a Salesman* Linda Loman demands of her sons that "attention must be paid." This is the demand behind every Miller drama. It is an exhortation that can become strident, but it illuminates the intense desire of one human being to engage in a meaningful dialogue with other human beings. The attention his work has received eloquently validates the ongoing success of that attempt.

BIBLIOGRAPHY

Works by Arthur Miller

Works Consulted

After The Fall. New York: Viking, 1964.
"The Crucible." *Arthur Miller's Collected Plays*. New York: Viking, 1957.
Focus. New York: Reynal and Hitchcock, 1945.
Incident at Vichy. New York: Viking, 1965.
"Monte Sant' Angelo." *I Don't Need You Anymore*. New York: Viking, 1967.
The Price. New York: Viking, 1968.
They Too Arise (typescript). New York: Theatre Collection, New York Public Library, Lincoln Center.
Timebends. New York: Grove Press, 1987.

Plays

Honors at Dawn. (Typescript, 1936). Hopwood Room, University of Michigan, Ann Arbor.
No Villain. (Typescript, 1937). Hopwood Room, University of Michigan, Ann Arbor.
They Too Arise. (Typescript, 1938). Theatre Collection, New York Public Library, Lincoln Center.
"The Man Who Had All the Luck." *Cross-Section: A Collection of New American Writing*. Ed. Edwin Seaver. New York: Fischer, 1944.

All My Sons. New York: Reynal and Hitchcock, 1947.
An Enemy of the People. (Adaptation). New York: Viking, 1951.
The Crucible. New York: Viking, 1953.
A View from the Bridge and A Memory of Two Mondays. New York: Viking, 1955.
A View from the Bridge. Revised. New York: Viking, 1960.
After the Fall. New York: Viking, 1964.
Incident at Vichy. New York: Viking, 1965.
The Price. New York: Viking, 1968.
The Creation of the World And Other Business. New York: Viking, 1973.
Danger: Memory! New York: Grove Press, 1987.
The Archbishop's Ceiling and The American Clock. New York: Grove Press, 1989.
The Ride Down Mt. Morgan. New York: Penguin, 1991.
Broken Glass. New York: Penguin, 1994a.
The Last Yankee. New York: Penguin, 1994b.
Mr. Peters' Connections. New York: Dramatists Play Service, 1998.

Screenplays

The Misfits. (1961).
Playing for Time. (1980).
Everybody Wins. (1990).
The Crucible. (1996).

Reportage

Situation Normal. New York: Reynal and Hitchcock, 1944.

Novel

Focus. New York: Reynal and Hitchcock, 1945.

Stories

I Don't Need You Anymore. New York: Viking, 1967.

Collections

Arthur Miller's Collected Plays. New York: Viking, 1957.
Arthur Miller's Collected Plays. Vol. 2. New York: Viking, 1981.
The Portable Arthur Miller. New York: Viking, 1971.
The Theater Essays of Arthur Miller. Ed. Robert A. Martin. New York: Viking, 1978.

Memoir

Salesman in Beijing. New York: Viking, 1984.

Autobiography

Timebends. New York: Grove Press, 1987.

Works about Arthur Miller

Bibliographies

Ferres, John H. *Arthur Miller: A Reference Guide*. Boston: Hall, 1979.
Hayashi, Tetsumaro. *An Index to Arthur Miller Criticism*. 2d ed. Metuchen, NJ: Scarecrow Press, 1976.

Jensen, George H. *Arthur Miller: A Bibliographical Check-List*. Columbia, SC: Faust, 1976.

Criticism

Bloom, Harold, ed. *Arthur Miller's "Death of a Salesman."* New York: Chelsea, 1988.
Carson, Neil. *Arthur Miller*. London: Macmillan, 1982.
Corrigan, Robert W., ed. *Arthur Miller: A Collection of Critical Essays*. Englewood Cliffs, NJ: Prentice-Hall, 1969.
Freedman, Morris. "The Jewishness of Arthur Miller: His Family Epic." *American Drama in Social Context*. Carbondale: Southern Illinois University Press, 1971, 43–58.
Hayman, Ronald. *Arthur Miller*. New York: Ungar, 1972.
Huftel Sheila. *Arthur Miller: The Burning Glass*. New York: Citadel, 1965.
Martin, Robert A., ed. *Arthur Miller: New Perspectives*. Englewood Cliffs, NJ: Prentice-Hall, 1982.
Moss, Leonard. *Arthur Miller*. New York: Twayne, 1967.
Murray, Edward. *Arthur Miller, Dramatist*. New York: Ungar, 1967.
Nelson, Benjamin. *Arthur Miller, Portrait of a Playwright*. New York: McKay, 1970.
Rahv, Philip. "Arthur Miller and the Fallacy of Profundity." *Literature and the Sixth Sense*. Boston: Houghton Mifflin, 1970, 385–91.
Schlueter, June, and James K. Flanagan. *Arthur Miller*. New York: Ungar, 1987.
Shatzky, Joel. "Arthur Miller's 'Jewish' Salesman." *Studies in American Jewish Literature* 2 (Winter 1976), 1–9.
Welland, Dennis. *Arthur Miller*. New York: Grove Press, 1961.
White, Sidney H. Guide to *Arthur Miller*. Columbus, OH: Merrill, 1970.

Interview

New York Herald Tribune (June 25, 1953), 22.

RONALD RIBMAN   (1932–   )

Darrell B. Lockhart

BIOGRAPHY

Ronald Ribman was born on May 28, 1932, in New York. He served in the U.S. Army from 1954 to 1956. Ribman began his literary career while he was still in graduate school at the University of Pittsburgh, where he earned both his master's degree (1958) and Ph.D. (1962) in English. His doctoral dissertation was titled "John Keats: The Woman and the Vision." While he wrote a significant number of poems, he seemed to find his calling early on as a dramatist. His first play, *Day of the Games*, was published in 1959 but never produced onstage. Nevertheless, Ribman soon gained prominence in the mid-1960s as one of the most promising new American playwrights. On August 27, 1967, he married Alice Rosen, a nurse. They have two children: James and Elana. Ribman is the recipient of numerous prestigious awards, including an Obie (1966, for *Journey of the Fifth Horse*), an Emmy Award nomination (1967, for *The Final War of Olly Winter*), and a Dramatists Guild Award (1977, for *Cold Storage*). He has also been granted fellowships from the Guggenheim Foundation (1970) and the National Endowment for the Arts (1973).

MAJOR WORKS AND THEMES

Harry, Noon and Night opened off-Broadway in 1965 and immediately captured the attention of theatre critics, who both praised and dismissed the work. The play revolves around the antihero protagonist of the title, a failed artist living in Munich in 1955. Thematically, the work operates on at least two levels. Foremost is the presentation of Harry, who struggles with the reality of his failure as an artist and his pride, which impedes him from returning to Ohio

with his older, successful brother who has come in search of him. Both Harry
and his roommate Immanuel, a physically deformed homosexual, represent the
marginalized sector of society. Both men have fallen victim to the dehumanizing
forces of modern, postwar society, and yet both are also victimizers in their
own way. By the end of the second act, Immanuel has successfully driven
Harry's brother away with his strange behavior and psychological manipulation.
Likewise, Harry violently attacks the downstairs neighbors, accusing them of
being Nazis and for being responsible for the German crimes against the Jews.
The play closes with Harry's being taken away by the police. If the nucleus of
the play is the psychological interaction between the protagonists, the secondary
focus derives from the spatial and temporal setting. It is not inconsequential that
Ribman sets his play in postwar Germany. The opposition of Nazi victimizers
and Jewish victims serves not only as an immediate reminder of atrocities of
the war but also as a metaphor for the same type of relationship on an individual
level as enacted through the characters of Harry and Immanuel. Furthermore, in
the first act Ribman carries out an obvious negative critique of the military in
general through the absurd interview that Harry conducts with the young soldier.

Ribman's second play, *The Journey of the Fifth Horse* (produced 1966), won
him an Obie Award. As might be expected from the title, the play continues
Ribman's practice of making marginal figures the center of his works. It takes
place in nineteenth-century Russia, and it is based on the story "Diary of a
Superfluous Man" by Ivan Turgenev (1818–1883). The ingeniousness of the
work lies in Ribman's use of the conventions of metatheatre to create a duality
between his own fifth-horse character, Zoditch, and Chulkaturin, the character
in the Turgenev story. Similarly, *The Ceremony of Innocence* (produced 1967)
is a historical piece set in eleventh-century England. Although the story revolves
around King Ethelred's reluctance to defend England against the invading
Danes, the dialogue resonates with references to contemporary society. While
the play is structurally complex—the use of flashbacks, for example, keeps the
action in a constant state of flux—*Ceremony* lacks the sophistication of the
previous two works in terms of dramatic communication.

Ribman wrote one of his best-known works expressly for television. *The Final
War of Olly Winter* had the distinction of being the first play produced for the
CBS Playhouse project. It aired on January 29, 1967. The war, of course, is the
Vietnam conflict, and the protagonist is a black American soldier who has already seen action in World War II. In spite of often pat exchanges of dialogue,
the play does provide significant commentary on the Vietnam War. Read in
retrospect, *The Final War of Olly Winter* constitutes an important cultural archive of a pivotal time in American history.

Ribman continued his assessment of the far-reaching effects of the Vietnam
War in the one-act play *The Burial of Esposito* (produced 1969), in which a
grieving father strives to come to terms with his son's death at the funeral. He
refuses to believe that it can be true and believes he sees his son rise from the
casket and speak to him. In the end his wife must tear him from the casket

that he has begun to claw at in an attempt to open it. *The Burial of Esposito* was one of a group of three one-act plays that were performed together under the collective title *Passing through from Exotic Places*. The other two plays, *The Son Who Hunted Tigers in Jakarta*, also about a grief-stricken couple who lost their son, and *Sunstroke*, about a Peace Corps volunteer, completed the trilogy. Together, the plays present brief psychological sketches on human behavior and attitudes.

The one-act play *Fingernails Blue as Flowers* (produced 1971) is by far Ribman's most unconventional work. The protagonist, Mr. Naville, is an older millionaire vacationing in Jamaica whose appearance is almost clownish. He wears an old-fashioned, one-piece, striped bathing suit and a straw Panama hat, and his fingernails are painted blue. Naville is overbearing, boorish, arrogant, and he tries to buy and threaten people with his money and power. Critics were seemingly puzzled as to the meaning of the play (Egan, ''Ronald Ribman,'' 1989, 372–73), which received mixed reviews. Whatever the intended message, it is quite apparent that Naville is a caricature of the product of rampant capitalism, rapidly acquired wealth, and emptiness as a human being as he himself describes: ''[W]e can sense within us that untouchable cold spot, that small glacier of chilling ice that year by year pushes deeper against our heart . . . until quite suddenly we have grown much older and find ice crystals forming in the mouth, closing down our speech, paralyzing our tongue, fingernails blue as flowers'' (23).

The full-length play *The Poison Tree* was first performed in 1973, and it was eventually staged on Broadway in 1976. It is considered to be one of Ribman's major works (Weales, ''Ronald Ribman: The Artist of the Failure Clowns'' 80) and certainly one of his most daring. This is because Ribman attempts to realistically re-create not only the ambience of prison life but the realities of that existence from the perspective of black prisoners. Ribman again turns to the dehumanizing of the individual for the dramatic focus of the work. The interaction between the black prisoners and the white guards provides ample space for the voicing of each side's perspective and the portrayal of racial tensions and cultural biases. The prison is the poison tree that slowly destroys the prisoners and the guards. The murder of a guard in the first scene motivates the action that follows throughout the play. *The Poison Tree* is a serious treatment of the societal ills that continue to plague the country more than twenty years after its initial production.

Cold Storage is the play in which the dramatist most closely approximates a specifically Jewish thematic core. It opened in 1977 and went on to enjoy 180 performances on Broadway in 1978, making it Ribman's most commercially successful work (Egan, ''Ronald Ribman'' 1989, 373). There is virtually no action in the play, which consists almost entirely of a conversation between two cancer patients on the rooftop garden of a hospital. Parmigian and Landau find themselves together on the roof, where their conversation ensues. Parmigian is a terminally ill man of Armenian origin, and Landau, a Jewish art dealer, is there for exploratory surgery. Parmigian's belligerent attitude, his rudeness, and his request that Landau push him over the edge make the apparently well-adjusted Landau ill at ease. As the two men talk, argue, and confess to one another, their dialogue reveals a profound statement on the quality of life and the unavoidability of death. As the discussion advances, there is an inversion in the roles the two men play. One discovers that the suicide-prone Parmigian is, in fact, the character who most fervently clings to life, while Landau almost eagerly welcomes death. Landau's "death wish" stems from his guilt as a Holocaust survivor. He tells Parmigian of his family's escape to Portugal, how he is the only one who ultimately survived, and how his survival has haunted him throughout his life. By the end of the play the two men, who in the beginning seemed so opposite, have established a bond based on their newfound respect for both life and death.

In *Buck* (1983) Ribman creates a scathing critique of the television industry and the big-business politics that operate it. The title character is a small-time producer at the bottom of a television empire who is forced to follow the orders of his corrupt superiors. What makes Buck unique is his desire to make the best of a bad situation. His job consists of producing murder reenactments in which he gets personally involved by investigating each case in order to re-create them more realistically. His great fault is his aspiration to lend artistic expression to the filming. The play makes use of numerous character types that represent a wide array of social levels that portray both the good and bad side of human nature.

In *Sweet Table at the Richelieu* (1987), Ribman returns to the same kind of dramatic style used to create *The Journey of the Fifth Horse* and *Ceremony of Innocence* in the sense that the action takes place in an exotic setting at a far remove from the experience of the average American. The action takes place during winter vacation at the Richelieu and pits European old-money people against the nouveau riche American Jeanine. Again, Ribman provides a variety of character types who serve as synedoches for social groups rather than representations of individuals. While the play does provide some interesting and often humorous moments of dialogue, on the whole it is among the dramatist's least accomplished works.

Ribman's most recent work is the comedy *The Rug Merchants of Chaos* (produced 1991). It centers on two bickering couples, the Finkelbergs and the Mottrams, who have hastily hired the broken-down boat of a Japanese sea captain to take them away from a port in South Africa, where they set fire to their own rug-importing business. Through the course of the dialogue it is revealed that this is but the latest in a series of get-rich-quick schemes that have taken them around the globe. These latest characters in Ribman's dramatic corpus join an entire cast of losers who go through life waiting for the right moment to "make it," even though it is readily apparent that they are doomed to failure. One cannot help but be repulsed by, and at the same time sympathetic to, this group of misfits, who constitute a veritable ship of fools not only lost in the Indian Ocean but adrift in the sea of life as well.

In concert, Ribman's plays bring to the fore the frailties of human nature and the nobility of the human spirit by exalting the most common of people who struggle day-to-day to exist in a world that represses and dehumanizes them. His works have been performed by numerous well-known actors, including Dustin Hoffman, Joel Grey, Morgan Freeman, Jimmy Smits, and Fran Drescher, to mention a small sampling.

CRITICAL RECEPTION

In spite of his constant presence in American theater since the 1960s, Ribman has received limited critical attention outside the reviews of theater critics. The most complete study of his early works, including his poetry, remains that of Susan Dietz. Dietz's dissertation continues to be a valuable source of information on Ribman's early work, particularly because it contains texts by the author that have yet to be reproduced elsewhere. Philip J. Egan has been instrumental in providing an amazingly complete and updated bibliography of primary and secondary sources on Ribman's works ("Ronald Ribman: A Classified Bibliography"). Egan has likewise published an informative assessment of Ribman's career in the theatre that includes a production history of his plays ("Ronald Ribman"). Gerald Weales has undertaken the most thorough critical evaluation of Ribman's works. In his book *The Jumping-Off Place*, Weales dedicates several pages to the discussion of Ribman as one of the most promising young American playwrights. Although he briefly examines Ribman's first three plays, his most insightful comments focus on *Harry, Noon and Night*, which he characterizes as "at once funny and gross on the surface, unnecessarily complicated in some of its references, tenuous and sometimes contradictory in its connections, but it is an ambitious and fascinating attempt to use black comedy to transform a potentially conventional character and situation into a statement about human beings that transcends the specific" (231). In an updated appraisal of Ribman's works, Weales expands on his idea of the "failure clown" as a recurrent image and central theme throughout the dramatist's plays inasmuch as the central characters tend to represent underdog-type individuals who attempt to cope with the dismal outlook of their everyday lives ("Ronald Ribman: The Artist of the Failure Clowns"). Rosette C. Lamont has studied the influence of the media in Ribman's *Buck*, a play she characterizes as "not in any sense a didactic piece of theater; it is a poetic fable in which an innocent hero is caught in the web of society's expectations, the social organization from which there is no escape" (149). Egan succinctly summarizes one of the central aspects of Ribman's theater, which relates to Weales' trope of the failure clowns: "Ribman is fascinated with the relationship between the oppressor and the oppressed (who sometimes merge in the same character). The early plays present lonely figures who complain of their isolation and yet, somehow, reinforce it. Characters in other plays—Ethelred in *The Ceremony of Innocence* and the title character in *Buck*—must cope with the horrors of their own power or success. In orchestrating these themes, Ribman consistently concerns himself with language'' (''Ronald Ribman: A Classified Bibliography'' 97).

BIBLIOGRAPHY

Works by Ronald Ribman

The Final War of Olly Winter. New York: CBS Television Network, 1967. Also in *Great Television Plays.* Ed. William I. Kaufman. New York: Dell, 1969. 259–301.

Harry, Noon and Night: A Play in Three Scenes. New York and London: Samuel French, 1967, 1973.

The Journey of the Fifth Horse and Harry, Noon and Night. Boston: Little, Brown, 1967.

The Journey of the Fifth Horse: A Play in Two Acts. New York: Samuel French, 1967. Also, London: Davis-Poynter, 1974.

The Ceremony of Innocence. New York: Dramatists Play Service, 1968.

With Bill Gunn. *The Angel Levine: Screenplay.* N.p.: Belafonte Enterprises (distributed by United Artists), 1970. Based on story by Bernard Malamud.

Passing through from Exotic Places. New York: Dramatists Play Service, 1970. (Contains *The Son Who Hunted Tigers in Jakarta, Sunstroke, The Burial of Esposito*)

The Burial of Esposito. In *The Best Short Plays, 1971.* Ed. with Intro. by Stanley Richards. Philadelphia and New York: Chilton Book, 1971. 155–70.

Fingernails Blue as Flowers. In *The American Place Theatre: Plays.* Ed. and with Intro. by Richard Schotter. Preface by Wynn Handman. New York: Dell, 1973. 1–30.

The Poison Tree: A Drama in Two Acts. New York: Samuel French, 1977.

Cold Storage. Garden City, NY: Doubleday, 1978. Also as *Cold Storage: A New Play in Two Acts.* New York: Samuel French, 1978.

Five Plays by Ronald Ribman. New York: Avon, 1978. (Contains *Harry, Noon and Night, The Journey of the Fifth Horse, The Ceremony of Innocence, The Poison Tree, Cold Storage*)

Buck. New York: Theatre Communications Group, 1983.

Saul Bellow's Seize the Day: Screenplay. New York: Learning in Focus, 1984. Also as *Seize the Day.* New York: Learning in Focus, 1987.

The Rug Merchants of Chaos and Other Plays. New York: Theatre Communications Group, 1992. (Contains *Buck, Sweet Table at the Richelieu, The Rug Merchants of Chaos*)

The Gamblers. In *The Best Men's Monologues of 1993.* Newbury, VT: Smith and Kraus, 1993.

Works about Ronald Ribman

Criticism

Dietz, Susan H. ''The Work of Ronald Ribman: The Poet as Playwright.'' Ph.D. diss., University of Pennsylvania, 1974. Ann Arbor: UMI, 1975.

———. "Ronald Ribman." *American Playwrights since 1945: A Guide to Scholarship, Criticism, and Performance*. Ed. Philip C. Kolin. Westport, CT: Greenwood Press, 1989. 369–78.

Egan, Philip J. "Ronald Ribman: A Classified Bibliography." *Studies in American Drama* 2 (1987): 97–117.

Kelley, Margot A. "Life Near Death: Art of Dying in Recent American Drama." [*Cold Storage*] In *Text and Presentation*. University of Florida Department of Classics Comparative Drama Conference Papers, vol. 8. Ed. Karelisa Hartigan. Lanham, MD: University Press of America, 1988. 117–27.

Lamont, Rosette C. "Murderous Enactments: The Media's Presence in the Drama." [*Buck*] *Modern Drama* 28.1 (1985): 148–61.

Weales, Gerald. *The Jumping-Off Place: American Drama in the 1960's*. New York: Macmillan, 1969. 229–34.

———. "Ronald Ribman." In *Contemporary Dramatists*. 4th ed. Ed. D. L. Kirkpatrick. Chicago: St. James Press, 1988. 449–51.

———. "Ronald Ribman: The Artist of the Failure Clowns." In *Essays on Contemporary American Drama*. Ed. Hedwig Bock and Albert Wertheim. Munich: Max Hueber Verlag, 1981. 75–90.

Interviews

Bennetts, Leslie. "Ronald Ribman Writes of a Violent World." *New York Times* (6 March 1983): B4–5.

Cunningham, Barry. "Ribman Defrosts Own Happy Ending." *New York Post* (January 13, 1978): 41.

DiNovelli, Donna. "Ronald Ribman's Journey to the Sweet Table." *A.R.T. News* (Cambridge) (February 1987): 1, 8.

Leahy, Mimi. "Ron Ribman: A Play about Cable TV." *Other Stages* (New York) (February 24, 1983): 8.

Roiphe, Anne. "I Write about the Human Game." *New York Times* (December 25, 1977): D2, 26.

MURRAY SCHISGAL   (1926–   )

Darrell B. Lockhart

BIOGRAPHY

Murray Schisgal was born November 25, 1926, the son of Eastern European immigrants. He grew up in Brooklyn, where he dropped out of high school to join the navy. He later completed his secondary education and earned a law degree. He married Renee Schapiro in 1958 and has two children, Jane and Zachary. The brief biography in *Contemporary Authors* outlines a series of odd jobs that Schisgal took to work his way through school before he established himself as a playwright in the early 1960s. He received several minor awards for his first works and numerous honors for the screenplay *Tootsie*, which he coauthored with Larry Gelbart, including an Academy Award nomination in 1982 for Best Original Screenplay. Although he is first and foremost a dramatist, Schisgal has written one novel, *Days and Nights of a French Horn Player* (1980).

MAJOR WORKS AND THEMES

Schisgal's first works were produced in London, where he enjoyed relative success prior to making the transition to the New York stage. His three one-act plays, *The Typists, The Postman* (the title of which was later changed to *The Tiger*), and *A Simple Kind of Love Story* opened together in London in December 1960 under the bill *Schrecks* (Weales 98). His first full-length play, *Ducks and Lovers*, was also staged in London a year later, and in 1963 it was followed by *Luv*. These early works share many of the themes that are common to Schisgal's theatre as a whole and that have come to define him as a dramatist. *The Typists* presents a satirical depiction of the drudgery of holding down a typical office job; one sees the characters grow older as the day progresses. In *The Tiger*, a disgruntled postman abducts a young married woman and ties her up in his apartment, where Ben, the abductor, launches into a series of angry speeches on the ills of society. The core of his anger is directed at the system of higher education, which denied his entry into college because he was unable to learn French. Once the threat of immediate danger dissipates, Gloria is then able to dialogue with Ben, and by the end of the play the two establish a romantic relationship. *Ducks and Lovers* is a comical piece about a man who comes back to his family as a duck and ends up in the soup. *Luv*, Schisgal's first hit, presents a bizarre love story between two men and a woman, involving suicide, murder, and relationships. It later inspired a film.

These works set the foundation for subsequent plays, in all of which the middle- to upper-class family unit or the institution of marriage, as a primary social group, provides the sociocultural space for the play. Schisgal's works are commonly formulated around mundane situations involving married couples, families, intimate circles of friends, or the environment of the workplace. Such intimate interpersonal relationships provide the necessary environment for the development and representation of the human experience with profound psychological impact. Schisgal injects a good deal of humor into his works, which conform to both realist and absurdist dramatic practices. However, the characters' speech is often overdetermined by cliché-ridden dialogue and a tendency to overdo a comic situation.

The most prevalent theme in Schisgal's plays is the binary opposition between men and women, played out against the inherently dichotomous backdrop of marriage. Many of his earlier works reveal a decidedly negative outlook and often point to women as the cause of upheaval in the balance of men's lives. It is readily apparent that the emergence of a feminist ethic on the social and cultural scene in the 1960s served to fuel Schisgal's creative imagination and to appeal to a certain sector (middle-class males) of society's paranoia over losing control. For instance, Max in *There Are No Sacher Tortes in Our Society!* (1967) proclaims, "The women are taking over the world. They only want women [for jobs]" (53). Likewise, *All over Town* (1974) can only be read— especially some twenty years later—as an assault against women, who are portrayed as hysterical, hypochondriacal, and simultaneously sexually frustrated and aggressive.

Nevertheless, one should not be too quick to place labels on Schisgal or his works. The farcical, caricaturesque depictions of the overbearing, dominant husband or lover who simply cannot cope with the rapidly changing role of women can be seen as a way to prompt men to realize the absurdity of their behavior. In later works, the female protagonists assertively transform themselves from unhappy housewives into successful career women, ridding themselves of their husbands in pursuit of healthier relationships. The problem is that the majority of Schisgal's men remain stuck in their old habits, unable to change, unwilling to accept women as equals, and many times growing tired of a faithful spouse to seek excitement with a younger woman. The male characters commonly commit stereotypically egregious acts, as does Martin Bloom, a successful New York attorney, in *The Consequences of Goosing* (1988) when he "accidentally" gooses a young woman on the street. When he gets sued, and it turns into a public scandal, he tries to downplay the incident and provide excuses.

In a number of plays Schisgal takes this male angst to an extreme. For example, in *Closet Madness* (1984) two high school buddies, Sam and Billy, are reunited in a hotel room. Sam, who is recently divorced, tries to convince his friend Billy to pursue a homosexual relationship with him, not because he has recently come to terms with his gay identity but because he is frustrated by his failure with women. Billy, who also has relationship problems with his own wife, is almost convinced. They clumsily try to dance together to accustom themselves to same-sex intimacy. Both men "suffer" from the feminism of their wives and feel that they are driven to homosexuality by women who will not conform to their patriarchal ideals. Sam, a playwright, also comments about the professional benefits of being gay. He declares that if he were gay, his play would not have ended so quickly (23). In the end, Billy decides to return to his wife, and the play closes with Sam's dialing up another old friend. As a sideline, Schisgal interjects some playful intertextuality with the film *Tootsie* that ties in neatly with the theme of the play. Similarly, in *The Cowboy, the Indian and the Fervent Feminist* (1993) a woman's husband is driven to insanity by her feminism, as is her male therapist. Even more absurd is the situation presented, in the most realistic manner, in *Summer Romance* (1984), in which Alan leaves his wife for a female gorilla in the Central Park Zoo. When he tires of Gladys, the gorilla, he leaves her for a polar bear.

In *How We Reached an Impasse on Nuclear Energy* (1988) Schisgal provides the setting for a true exercise in gender bending through Dennis and Rosalind, a married couple. Dennis comes home after an extended business trip to find that his wife has grown a full beard and mustache in open acknowledgment and celebration of her masculine characteristics. Although Dennis is repulsed by his wife's appearance, he reluctantly states that he has "consistently acknowledged the intrinsic bisexuality of human beings" (25). He carefully suppresses his anger since he wants to be the liberal husband who does not dictate his wife's actions. She convinces him to explore his femininity by applying makeup, which to his surprise he enjoys. Their outward reversal of gender identity soon leads to a discussion of more deeply rooted feminine/masculine identity traits. Dennis is the commissioner of the Nuclear Power Agency, obviously representative of his patriarchal need to control, dominate, and ultimately destroy nature. In contrast, Rosalind informs him that she has joined the Anti-Nuclear Association for a Cleaner World, symbolic of her feminine closeness with nature, her nurturing instinct, and her harmony with all living things. In the end this is the clash that divides the couple. Dennis refuses to give up his job, feeling that such a request from his wife is an attempt to emasculate him. At the close of the play he repeatedly screams, "I am still a man! I am still the Nuclear Power Commissioner!" (35).

While *How We Reached an Impasse* is a play about gender identities, in other works Schisgal directly takes on human sexuality. The most open of these is also one of his most recent, *Sexaholics* (1994). In the play two sex addicts, both married to other people, engage in a wild affair and tell each other of past sexual escapades. Even though they both attempt to get control of their addiction, in the end they fail. In *Popkins* (1984), one of Schisgal's more complex works, the action progresses through many different scenes and time periods. Chuck Popkins, who works for a small publishing house, undergoes a series of life changes in a brief amount of time. His wife leaves him for another woman who works at his same office, and he is fired from his job. His boss convinces him that the one way to save his job is to go undercover into a prison to convince an inmate that his book should be published. In prison he becomes the author's lover and is successful in obtaining the manuscript for publication, which, in turn, saves the near bankrupt publisher. Because of his success in obtaining numerous popular manuscripts of prison literature, Popkins is able to take control of the company and force his former boss to go undercover into an insane asylum to pursue a manuscript there. Meanwhile, his former wife, Claudia, leaves her lesbian lover, has a relationship with two Costa Rican house painters, and meets a millionaire turned nature guru with whom she hitchhikes to California. He teaches her the real estate business, and she becomes very successful. Ultimately, Chuck and Claudia agree to renew their relationship after deciding that both had changed enough to be together again. Indeed, the necessity of accommodating change in order to maintain a healthy relationship is the basis for the play.

Even though the majority of Schisgal's characters are Jewish, issues of Jewish ethnic and cultural identity surface in relatively few of his plays. *The Pushcart Peddlers* (1979) is his most overtly Jewish-theme work. It addresses the issue of immigration and identity without falling into the trap of the overdone immigrant's tale. The two main characters, Cornelius J. Hollingsworth III (real name, Elias Crapavarnishkes) and Shimmel Shitzman, obvious semiotic signifiers of marginal status, meet on Shitzman's first day off the boat. Cornelius tries to sell Shimmel an "American" name, saying that he will never make it in America with a name like that. At first Shimmel is reluctant, but after having the point proven to him, he buys the name of Samuel P. Stone. Cornelius both swindles and takes Shimmel under his wing to teach him how to make a living on the streets of the new country. They deceive a young flower girl, herself a con artist, into believing that they are soon-to-be theatrical producers. Shitzman/ Stone gets his first free meal and a valuable lesson from the con.

74 Georgia Avenue (1988) is an interesting one-act play about a Jewish man, Marty, who returns to his old neighborhood overcome by nostalgia. He discovers that an elderly black man is living in his family's old apartment and convinces him to let him come in. He learns that Joseph, the present occupant, used to be the janitor at the neighborhood synagogue, and he has in his possession many of Marty's grandfather's clothes, including his skullcap. When Joseph puts on the old clothes, he takes on the persona of Marty's Zada. Although Marty thinks that Joseph must be possessed by a dybbuk, he welcomes the opportunity to communicate with his grandfather and reminisce about times when the entire family was together.

The one-act *The Rabbi and the Toyota Dealer* (1984) is a short comedy as much about sexual exploits as the loss of religious identity. Morton Prince, a wealthy, nonreligious Jew, shows up at his rabbi's house unexpectedly, eager to reclaim his religiosity. He is so out of tune with Jewish religious practice that when he enters the house, he kisses rabbi Guttenberg's ring, and he later calls him Father. Equally outlandish is the fact that Morton wants to donate $75,000 to the temple on the condition that the rabbi place him in a Jewish monastery. Guttenberg patiently explains to him that there is no such thing. Morton also wants to change his surname back to Pipishinsky. The talk eventually turns to the topic of sexual fidelity, and it soon is revealed that Morton has slept with the rabbi's fiancé. Rather than become angered, Guttenberg is suddenly overcome with feelings of inadequacy. The play ends with the two men going to temple to pray together. This short play was later expanded into the two-act *Old Wine in a New Bottle* (1987), with the second act being a reworking of the original *The Rabbi and the Toyota Dealer*.

The Chinese (1968) can be perceived as a Jewish play with no Jewish characters. It is a humorous short piece about a young man and his Chinese immigrant parents. Chester, the son, does not appear to be Chinese. He insists that his parents tell him the truth about his biological progenitors. They explain his appearance by stating that both of them have European ancestors. Growing up, Chester would tell all of his friends that he was Jewish, embarrassed by his immigrant Chinese parents. When he brings a Jewish girl to meet his parents at their home/laundry, she is at first shocked that Chester is able to speak Chinese with his launderers and then appalled to learn that they are his parents. As a result, Chester decides to leave home, and when he does, his parents are free to tell him the truth about his birth. What they reveal is that they were not married when Chester was born, but he is, in fact, Chinese. The play is a clever inversion of the Jewish immigrant story through the eyes of a different immigrant group with a common experience. The fact that Chester wants to assimilate into the dominant culture, in this case the Jewish neighborhood of New York, is a theatrical refraction of Jewish assimilation into mainstream American society at the expense of personal identity. The girlfriend's negative reaction may also be taken as a call for tolerance from the established Jewish population with regard to other immigrant groups.

In other short pieces Schisgal is less overt about Jewish issues. For example, in the dark comedy *The Flatulist* (1980) a young man avenges his father's humiliating job as cheap Borscht-belt clown by killing his agent with fined-tune flatulence. Likewise, in other plays where there is no open treatment of Jewish identity, it is often present in the typology of the characters. Gerald Weales, for example, finds the characters in *Reverberations* (1965, later titled *The Basement*) to be typically Jewish (103).

Murray Schisgal has not attracted a great deal of literary and theatre critics in spite of his relative prominence within the American theatre community. While many of his plays are now quite dated with regard to theme, several of his recent works merit critical appraisal for their unique approach to issues of gender and sexuality.

CRITICAL RECEPTION

While Schisgal's works have been widely staged over the years of his active career as a prominent figure in American theatre, his plays have not been the subject of any significant amount of critical evaluation. The vast majority of the bibliography of Schisgal consists of performance reviews, a sampling of which can be found in the entries on the dramatist in *Contemporary Authors* and *Contemporary Literary Criticism*. Gerald Weales provides a still valuable assessment of his early works in his *The Jumping-Off Place* (1969). The most recent and comprehensive work on Schisgal is that of Kenneth Stuart Blatt, in which he focuses on the playwright's technique of dramatic creation. Blatt characterizes Schisgal's works as experimental and innovative and relates them to the theatre of the absurd. He places Schisgal's works within the tradition of the avant-garde American theatre.

BIBLIOGRAPHY

Dates in parentheses are of performance when different from date of publication.

Works by Murray Schisgal

The Typists and The Tiger. (1963). New York: Dramatists Play Service, 1964.
Luv. (1963). New York: Coward-McCann, 1965.
Fragments, Windows and Other Plays. Introduction by M. J. Arlen. New York: Coward-McCann, 1965. (Contains *Fragments, Windows, Reverberations, Memorial Day, The Old Jew*).
Five One-Act Plays. New York: Dramatists Play Service, 1968.
Jimmy Shine. New York: Dramatists Play Service, 1969.
The Chinese and Dr. Fish. New York: Dramatists Play Service, 1970.
Ducks and Lovers. New York: Dramatists Play Service, 1972.
An American Millionaire. New York: Dramatists Play Service, 1974.
All over Town: A Play in Two Acts. New York: Dramatists Play Service, 1975.
Days and Nights of a French Horn Player (novel). Boston: Little, Brown, 1980a.
The Pushcart Peddlers, The Flatulist and Other Plays. New York: Dramatists Play Service, 1980b. (Contains *The Pushcart Peddlers, The Flatulist, A Simple Kind of Love Story, Little Johnny, Walter*).

Tootsie. (Screenplay with Larry Gelbart). Los Angeles: Script Collectors Service, 1980c.

Twice around the Park. New York: Samuel French, 1983. (Contains two one-act plays: *A Need for Brussel Sprouts* and *A Need for Less Expertise*).

Closet Madness and Other Plays. New York: Samuel French, 1984a. (Contains *Closet Madness, The Rabbi and the Toyota Dealer*, and *Summer Romance*.)

Popkins. (1984b). New York: Dramatists Play Service, 1990.

Jealousy and *There Are No Sacher Tortes in Our Society*! New York: Dramatists Play Service, 1985.

Old Wine in a New Bottle. New York: Dramatists Play Service, 1987a.

Road Show. New York: Dramatists Play Service, 1987b.

Man Dangling: Three Short Plays. New York: Dramatists Play Service, 1988. (Contains *The Consequences of Goosing, How We Reached an Impasse on Nuclear Energy*, and *74 Georgia Avenue*).

Oatmeal and Kisses. New York: Dramatists Play Service, 1990.

The Cowboy, the Indian and the Fervent Feminist. In *The Best American Short Plays, 1991–1992*. Ed. Howard Stein and Glenn Young. New York: Applause Theatre Books, 1992a.

Extensions. In *The Best American Short Plays, 1991–1992*. Ed. Howard Stein and Glenn Young. New York: Applause Theatre Books, 1992b.

Mudtracks. In *EST Marathon 1994: One-Act Plays*. Lyme, NH: Smith and Kraus, 1995a.

Sexaholics and Other Plays. New York: Dramatists Play Service, 1995b (*Contains Sexaholics, The Artists and the Model, The Artists and the Model/2*, and *The Cowboy, the Indian and the Fervent Feminist, Extensions*).

Works about Murray Schisgal

Blatt, Kenneth Stuart. "Murray Schisgal, Playwright." Ph.D. diss., Michigan State University, 1992.

Contemporary Authors. Ed. Pamela S. Dear. New Revision Series 48. New York: Gale Research, 1995, 402–5.

Contemporary Literary Criticism Ed. Carolyn Riley and Phyllis Carmel Mendelson. Detroit: Gale Research, 1976.

Downer, Alan S. "An Interview with MS." In *The American Theater Today*. Ed. Alan S. Downer. New York: Basic Books, 1967, 127–35.

Weales, Gerald. *The Jumping-Off Place: American Drama in the 1960's*. New York: Macmillan, 1969, 97–106.

MARTIN SHERMAN   (1938–)

Eric Sterling

BIOGRAPHY

Martin Sherman was born in Philadelphia on December 22, 1938, the son of Joseph T. (an attorney) and Julia (Shapiro) Sherman. He attended Boston University from 1956 to 1960 and graduated with a bachelors's degree in fine arts from the Division of Theatre Arts in 1960. Although he initially was interested in acting, he decided that he preferred playwriting. His musical *A Solitary Thing* appeared onstage at Mills College in Oakland, California in 1963; Sherman has been a playwright-in-residence at this college and at New York's Playwright's Horizons. He has worked with the Ensemble Studio Theatre in New York and is a member of the Writers Guild of America and the Dramatists Guild. Sherman's dramas have appeared onstage throughout the United States and London. The playwright received a grant from the Wurlitzer Foundation in New Mexico in 1973, a fellowship from the National Foundation for the Arts in 1980, the Dramatists Guild Hull-Warriner Award in 1980 (for *Bent*), and a nomination for the Antoinette Perry Award from the League of New York Theatres and Producers in 1980 (for *Bent*). Sherman currently resides in England.

MAJOR WORKS AND THEMES

The dramas of Martin Sherman differ from those of many contemporary American playwrights in that "he has moved away from an exploration of the myths and debased realities of contemporary U.S. society into more socio-political subjects in historical European settings" (Taylor 888). Sherman's plays contain much satire and humor—even in unfortunate circumstances. Reb Ellis' attempt in *Messiah* to fly via Sabbatai Zvi's inspiration is simultaneously comedic and tragic in its satire of religious zealots. Although Sherman intermingles his wit with human suffering, his humor "frequently leaves audiences with a sense of an affirmation of human strength and resilience. Yet for many Sherman characters, survival is touch and go; often on the very brink of despair, disaster and/or death, most survive, though not all, and none unscathed" (Taylor 888).

The playwright bases his satire *Things Went Badly in Westphalia* (1971) on Voltaire's *Candide*. Joshua, like Candide, searches in vain for the place where everyone is happy. Joshua maintains his optimism despite witnessing multiple assassinations and gang rapes.

Passing By (1974) concerns two homosexuals (Toby and Simon) who meet at the movies in New York and enjoy a one-night stand but subsequently contract hepatitis and recuperate together. Sherman criticizes societal disapproval of homosexuality and manifests how gays in the United States become isolated and lonely because their culture condemns their sexual orientation. Yet Toby and Simon's relationship also ends because both men stress their careers more than their social lives. Sherman canceled production of the play, fearing that audiences might erroneously liken the plot (a gay man contracting a disease from another homosexual) to the AIDS epidemic. He possesses high expectations for later productions "based not only on my fondness for the play but the desire for a healthier atmosphere in which it can be properly perceived" (Introduction 101).

Cracks (1975) parodies mystery dramas and involves the murder of a rock musician (Rick) in California. The characters at the musician's party discover the body and debate what to do next. Sherman focuses on the stereotypes of groupies and Californian lifestyle. The twist in this whodunit is that Sherman leaves the play unresolved, for all nine characters die.

Bent (1979) focuses on Max, an Aryan involved in a homosexual relationship with a nightclub dancer, Rudy. Max encounters trouble from Nazis after engaging in a one-night stand with Ernst Roehm's homosexual lover—just after SA leader Roehm's fall from power. Nazis capture Rudy and Max, but the latter, desperate to save his life, denies knowing his lover and contributes to his death by punching the dancer repeatedly in the presence of soldiers. Max also successfully convinces them (or so he thinks) that he is not gay by engaging in sexual intercourse with a teenage female corpse. Max acts to save his life, yet he destroys his soul by humiliating himself and losing his identity and conscience. Max's self-defacing act allows him to receive a yellow star (for Jews) rather than a pink triangle (for homosexuals). Having heard that Jews receive better treatment than homosexuals in concentration camps (the play concludes in Dachau), Max commits the necrophilic act to obtain a yellow star.

Sherman implies that Nazis treated Jews better than homosexuals. Many Holocaust survivors and historians disagree. Nonetheless, Holocaust scholars focus almost exclusively on Jews and neglect the suffering of other groups, such as homosexuals; *Bent*, therefore, is an important Holocaust literary work partly because of its dramatization of gays during the Holocaust. A major theme is that the sacrifice of identity (in this case, sexual orientation) leads to self-destruction.

When Max denies his lover and his homosexuality, he has nothing left; he is no longer himself. The Nazis attempt to annihilate Max, but in his desperation to survive, he destroys his soul. It is better to die with dignity than to lose one's identity, Sherman implies. Until Max demonstrates his love for Horst by wearing Horst's pink triangle, survival supersedes love and identity. Sherman's play demonstrates how desperate situations, such as the persecution of homosexuals, cause people to act selfishly. James W. Carlsen notes that in regard to "homosexual[ity] in the legitimate theater, it is significant that Richard Gere, a notable and highly acclaimed film actor, accepted the controversial role of Max, and such casting, coupled with his critically praised performance, enhances the credibility of serious and honest presentations of the gay male onstage" (173). Edwin Wilson adds that the play implies that "it is all right for homosexuals to be tender with one another and express their love" (24). Perhaps the most famous scene, which manifests how language plays such a major role in Sherman's work, shows Max and Horst stimulating themselves sexually through verbal communication.

Sherman's *Messiah* (1982) (set in 1665 in Yultishk, a Polish village) concerns the excitement and ultimate disappointment surrounding the false Messiah, Sabbatai Zvi, a Sephardic rabbi. Polish Jews, devastated by Cossacks, prayed for the Messiah to come. Some considered Sabbatai Zvi the Messiah; this false prophet never appears onstage but greatly affects Rachel, the protagonist. This main character, a homely, twenty-eight-year-old woman, reluctantly marries Reb Ellis, an annoyingly talkative, ignorant, but prosperous widower who owns a fruit store. Although she despises the rotund and foolish Ellis, she needs to support her mother (Rebecca), who has not spoken since Cossacks murdered her husband and baby. Rebecca believes that Rachel saw the murders and that the ensuing shock caused the latter's face to turn ugly, disfigured by blotched skin and two enormous front teeth that extend outside her mouth. When Reb Ellis' nephew, Asher, proclaims Sabbatai as the Messiah, the misguided Ellis attempts to cleanse his soul by giving away all his possessions—and those of his new wife. He then proves his faith in Sabbatai by trying to fly to Jerusalem. Ellis climbs to the roof of his house and attempts to fly—only to plunge to his death, leaving Rachel an impoverished widow.

Rachel lusts for Asher, who, in turn, cares only about the Messiah. Asher's acceptance of Sabbatai causes him to break several important Jewish laws, including prohibitions against eating animal fat and against incest (the man sleeps with Rachel—his uncle's wife). He has sex with Rachel because the false Messiah claims that the forbidden is now acceptable, that he (Zvi) will proclaim new laws for Jews to follow. Sherman focuses on Rachel's relationship with God through her monologues; she wavers between faith and doubt, alternately asking for God's blessing and cursing him. She thanks him for saving her from the Cossacks but blames him for her physical ugliness and her terrible husband.

The play concerns the signs from God that people look for, as well as Rachel's struggle with her faith. Faith plays a major role in the characterization of Asher, for he turns away from his zealous love of God to follow a mortal, a false Jewish prophet who eventually becomes a Muslim. Asher commits suicide partly because he feels shameful and sinful after eating nonkosher food and engaging in sexual intercourse with his uncle's wife but also because these actions represent his turning away from God. Sherman implies in this drama that people should place their faith in God, not in human beings. The playwright does not deny the existence of a Messiah but indicates the necessity of patience. As in *Bent*, Sherman stresses in *Messiah* the dangers of desperation. Characters who become despondent or take risks pay a heavy price: just as Max sacrifices his identity by denying his sexual orientation, Asher violates God's laws as he convinces himself and others that Sabbatai Zvi is the Messiah—even when Zvi tells him to ignore the code of ethics by which he has lived his life. Asher, like Max, destroys himself by trying to be someone else, by deviating from the life he has led. Just as Max rejects homosexuality as an escape from the tortures he expects from homophobic Nazi guards, Asher turns from God as an escape from Cossacks; both men die as punishment for their temporary escapes.

When She Danced (1985) studies the life of dancer Isadora Duncan. The play, set in Paris in 1923, consecrates the dancing of Duncan—although the characters cannot verbalize exactly how she danced. Language plays a significant role in this drama; the characters speak different languages and cannot communicate effectively with one another. Sherman preoccupies himself not only with how well Duncan danced but also with how her art affected others.

A Madhouse in Goa (1989) contains two intertwined sections. The first act, set in Corfu in 1966 and involving a southern widow and a homosexual, is comic and purposefully devoid of powerful and provocative sociopolitical importance. The second act, set later in time on the island of Santorini, concerns a dying writer whose only literary success was the plot of the first act. The writer has lost his voice, which "seems almost retributive for his trimming and evasiveness in constructing the earlier story, eschewing all political significance" (Taylor 889). Sherman implies that writers have a responsibility to manifest their feelings about social and political issues—even if these thoughts prove unpleasant and controversial.

CRITICAL RECEPTION

Cracks (a murder mystery, a whodunit) confuses critics, who are unsure what to make of it. Richard Eder believes that the play is sporadically amusing, but he feels cheated by the ending—or lack thereof—which is Sherman's joke at the audience's expense.

Robert Skloot possesses ambivalent feelings about *Bent*, stating that Sherman "skillfully compresses the story of gay oppression in Germany and establishes the sense of real danger and terror that homosexuals endured at the hands of the Nazis'' (118). Skloot feels, however, that the drama ''seems to lapse from its passionate call for justice and freedom for gays, and to decline into a melodramatic love story based on a needless argument about which outlawed group suffered more under the Nazis'' (120). Walter Kerr enjoys *Bent* but considers the first act superior to the second. He does not see a clear relationship between the acts. In his December 3, 1979, review, Kerr states:

> Whether or not author Martin Sherman can carry us all the way to the blistering climax of ''*Bent*,'' he's got a powerful sense of theater going for two-thirds of his bizarre, bloody journey. Along the way he may be willing to use the tricky surprises of suspense melodrama to make sure we're startled to attention, but he never uses them cheaply. (208)

In his review of *Messiah*, Frank Rich states that Sherman ''remains a frustrated playwright''; the reviewer recognizes the play's potential yet considers it a failure. Rich believes that the dramatist's ''writing, the eloquent and shattering pogrom descriptions excepted, rarely proves as sizable and compelling as his ambitions'' (404).

Rich admires Sherman's *When She Danced*, calling the work a ''fascinating play,'' and he lauds Elizabeth Ashley's performance as the protagonist. Rich is especially impressed with the dramatist's comical dinner party scene: ''[a]s written by Mr. Sherman, the scene is an imaginative amalgam of Marx Brothers and Chekhov—a circus of food fights, unrequited lust and ineffectual attempted suicide'' (204).

Rich enjoys Sherman's *Madhouse in Goa*, partly because Vanessa Redgrave performed admirably in a major role. Rich states that ''[h]owever predictable the show business jokes, Mr. Sherman has pertinent points to make about American writers who are 'famous too soon, thrown aside too quickly' '' (85). Rich also likes the playwright's meaning that some authors attempt to take complicated ideas and fit them into tidy, superficial, ''so-called universal truths'' (85). Rich complains that Sherman tries to incorporate too many desultory ideas in the play's last scene.

Bent is doubtlessly Sherman's most famous and most important play; the playwright's fame is based primarily on this drama. Famous actors (such as Bernadette Peters, Ian McKellen, Richard Gere, Elizabeth Ashley, Vanessa Redgrave, Meryl Streep, and Christopher Lloyd) chose to perform in his plays, indicating that they value his work. Theatre reviewers respect Sherman's abilities as a playwright and cite his vast potential and skill with language; they also are impressed with the creative premises of his plays, yet they feel that he does not do justice to these imaginative thoughts. Reviewers believe that he oversimplifies important issues, providing facile answers to complex dilemmas. Theatre critics acknowledge Sherman's talent, but aside from *Bent* (which most consider his masterpiece), they consider his plays to be promising and highly competent but not great aesthetic successes.

BIBLIOGRAPHY

Works by Martin Sherman

Plays

A Solitary Thing. Produced in 1963.
Fat Tuesday. Produced in 1966.
Next Year in Jerusalem. Produced in 1968.
The Night before Paris. Produced in 1969.
Things Went Badly in Westphalia. Produced in 1971. In *The Best Short Plays, 1970.* Ed. Stanley Richards. Philadelphia: Chilton Book, 1970. 371–408.
Passing By. Produced in 1974. *Gay Plays.* Ed. Michael Wilcox. London: Methuen, 1984. 99–120.
Cracks. Produced in 1975. *Gay Plays.* Vol. 2. Ed. Michael Wilcox. London: Methuen, 1986. 103–26.
Soaps. Produced in 1975.
Rio Grande. Produced in 1976.
Blackout. Produced in 1978.
Bent. Produced in 1979. New York: Avon, 1980.
Messiah. Produced in 1982. Oxford: Amber Lane, 1982.
Delta Lady (with Drey Shepperd). Produced in 1984.
When She Danced. Produced in 1985.
A Madhouse in Goa. Produced in 1989.

Play for Television

The Clothes in the Wardrobe (1992).

Works about Martin Sherman

Bommer, Lawrence. Rev. of *Bent. Chicago Tribune*, September 25, 1994, 5, 4:4.
Carlsen, James W. "Images of the Gay Male in Contemporary Drama." In *Gayspeak: Gay Male and Lesbian Communication.* Ed. James W. Chesebro. New York: Pilgrim, 1981: 165–74.
Contemporary Authors: A Bio-Bibliographical Guide to Current Writers in Fiction, General Nonfiction, Poetry, Journalism, Drama, Motion Pictures, Television, and Other Fields. Vol. 123. Ed. Hal May and Susan M. Trosky. Detroit: Gale Research, 1988: 362–363.
Contemporary Literary Criticism: Excerpts from Criticism of the Works of Today's Novelists, Poets, Playwrights, Short Story Writers, Filmmakers, Screenwriters, and Other Creative Writers. Vol. 19. Ed. Sharon R. Gunton. Detroit: Gale Research, 1981. 415–17.
Eder, Richard. Rev. of *Cracks.* June 23, 1977. In *The New York Times Theater Reviews.* New York: *New York Times* and Arno Press, 1979.
International Dictionary of Theatre—Playwrights. Ed. Mark Hawkins-Dady. Vol. 2. Detroit: St. James, 1992: 888–89.
Kerr, Walter. Rev. of *Bent.* December 3, 1979. In *The New York Times Theater Reviews.* New York: *New York Times* and Arno Press, 1981.

————. Rev. of *Bent*. December 16, 1979. In *The New York Times Theater Reviews*. New York: *New York Times* and Arno Press, 1981.

National Playwrights Directory. Ed. Phyllis Johnson Kaye. Waterford, CT: Eugene O'Neill Theater Society, 1981: 386.

Rich, Frank. Rev. of *A Madhouse in Goa*. June 27, 1989. In *The New York Times Theater Reviews*. New York: Times Books and Garland, 1992.

————. Rev. of *Messiah*. December 24, 1984. In *The New York Times Theater Reviews*. New York: Times Books and Garland, 1984.

————. Rev. of *When She Danced*. February 20, 1990. In *The New York Times Theater Reviews*. New York: Times Books and Garland, 1992.

Sherman, Martin. "Introduction." *Passing By*. In *Gay Plays*. London: Methuen, 1984: 101.

Skloot, Robert. *The Darkness We Carry: The Drama of the Holocaust*. Madison: University of Wisconsin Press, 1988: 118–22.

Taylor, Val. "Martin Sherman." *International Dictionary of Theatre*. Vol. 2: *Playwrights*. Ed. Mark Hawkins-Dady. Detroit: St. James, 1992: 888–89.

Wilson, Edwin. Review. "Holocaust and Homosexuality Suffuse New Play." *Wall Street Journal*, December 5, 1979:24.

ELIZABETH SWADOS (1951–)

Elizabeth Lloyd-Kimbrel and Joel Shatzky

BIOGRAPHY

Elizabeth Swados was born in Buffalo, New York, on February 5, 1951, the daughter of Robert Orville Swados, a lawyer, and Sylvia Maisel Swados, an actress and poet. The original family name was Swiadisch, and her father's side of the family came from Vilna, Lithuania, one of the great centers of Jewish culture in prewar Europe. Swados inherited multitalents on both sides of the family: her maternal grandfather was a violinist, her paternal grandmother a concert pianist, and her second cousin was the noted poet and critic Harvey Swados.

Swados' family was not particularly religious, although they attended a Reform synagogue and observed the major Jewish holidays; thus, her education in Jewish traditions and religion was not extensive. Her creative talents, however, were evident at an early age: she learned the guitar and piano and was performing as a folksinger by the time she was twelve. During her summers as a teenager, she became acquainted with Pete Seeger and sang with him.

At the age of sixteen Swados entered college, attending Bennington College, from which she graduated with a B.A. in 1972. Soon after she began her creative partnerships with such noted directors as Andrei Serban (in modern interpretations of Aeschylus and Chekhov), Peter Brook, and, especially, Joseph Papp through the New York Shakespeare Festival. Papp, who was instrumental in introducing many of the greatest talents in drama to the American stage, brought Swados' best-known work, *Runaways*, to Broadway in 1978.

In the 1970s her most successful period, Swados wrote the musical scores to *Medea* (1969), *Agamemnon* (1977), and *The Cherry Orchard* (1978), all directed by Serban; adaptations of the *Ghost Sonata* (1977) and *Alice [or Wonderland] in Concert* (1978), a collaboration with Peter Brook's troupe, which toured Africa with Swados' *Conference of the Birds* in the late 1970s; and the original musical dramas *Nightclub Cantata* (1977), *Runaways* (1978), and *Dispatches: A Rock Musical* (1979), which was based on the Vietnam War memoir of Michael Herr.

This fruitful period was punctuated by personal tragedy when, in 1979, Swados' mother committed suicide. Swados' adored older brother, Lincoln, was diagnosed as schizophrenic and disappeared into a shadow life on New York's streets, sometimes performing as a street musician. He died ten years later under mysterious circumstances. Swados' moving account of life with her family, *The Four of Us: The Story of a Family*, was published in 1991.

In the 1980s Swados began to turn toward her Jewish roots in developing material for her work. She started to do research for her compositions that involved work with rabbis, translators, and scholars. The results have been such pieces as *The Haggadah: A Passover Cantata* with an English text by Elie Weisel (1980); *Esther: A Vaudeville Megillah* (produced 1988); *Jerusalem*, written the same year; *Jonah* (1990); and *Job* (1992). She has not done any major theatrical work since 1992, but she has not stopped working. Her most recent musical score has been for Bill Moyers' *Genesis* series on PBS in 1996. She also wrote introductions for the segments, which were retellings of the Genesis stories under discussion. Swados' numerous awards include Obies for *Medea* (1972), *Runaways* (1976), *Nightclub Cantata* (1977), and *Alice in Concert* (1980) and five Tony nominations for *Runaways* when it appeared on Broadway (1978). She has also been recognized with an Outer Critics Circle Award and a Guggenheim Fellowship. In addition to her theatre career, Swados has taught at Carnegie-Mellon University (1974), Bard College, and Sarah Lawrence College (1976–1977).

MAJOR WORKS AND THEMES

Remarkably precocious, with produced works beginning in her early twenties, Swados has been a pioneer in experimenting with a variety of forms of theatre. She combined vaudeville with religious traditions in *Esther: A Vaudeville Megillah* and has mixed Third World (especially African) materials with jazz, rock, and pop. Swados developed further direction of the American musical *Hair!* (1967) and initiated mixing the most popular elements of contemporary culture with ''serious'' social and political questions in new and refreshing forms. One of a rare breed in the musical theatre—a lyricist, composer, and director— Swados in her early works opened up many possibilities for what had become in the post-Rogers-Hammerstein period a restrictive genre.

In an interview in 1979, Swados described the genesis of her artistic vision:

I grew up in Buffalo, in the city, which is a blue-collar town. But I was also educated in classical music theatre, very intellectual stuff. At the same time I was hanging out

with the kids who listened to the radio all the time. We listened to the newest pop hits
and everything from baseball games to the opera. It seemed to me that that's what made
up the world. It wasn't one thing or the other; it's never been one thing or the other; it
never *should* be one thing or the other. (*CA*, 523)

But beyond the blend of the artistic, intellectual, musical, and everyday, another aspect to Swados' work is of particular interest to readers of this volume:
her Jewish cultural and spiritual sensibilities. In her Introduction to a collection
of contemporary Jewish-American plays, Ellen Schiff notes a number of major
themes that are inherent in Swados' work: "The Family," "Jewish Heritage,"
"What It Means to Be a Jew," "The Quest to Be a Jew," and "Israel" (Schiff
xxxiii, xxxv, xxxviii, xl, xlii). Although Swados did not turn explicitly to Jewish
themes in her earliest work, evident in *Runaways* is a need for family life. The
other themes come to the fore in Swados' "biblical cycle," which includes *The
Haggadah, Song of Songs* (1989), *Esther, Jerusalem, Jonah*, and *Job*.

In her interview Swados says: "I've always thought that the Jewish interpretations of the Old Testament were lively and rich with layers of meaning"
(xxxv). This textual appeal/appreciation is reflected in her attraction to ritual. In
the same interview she further states: "[W]hat I was most influenced by were
the rituals that I saw in Africa, the rituals that I know about in Indonesia, the
religious services that I attended as a Jew in temples, things that were both
functional and dramatic, that contained myth and ancestry and politics and theatre and music" (523).

Although she did not begin her work with strong Jewish roots, like many
assimilated Jews, Swados turned in midcareer to Jewish themes, which have
become dominant in her later work. An example is *The Haggadah: A Passover
Cantata*, which was produced at the New York Shakespeare Festival by Joseph
Papp in 1980. Swados uses her understanding of myth, ritual, and a variety of
theatrical elements to create a public celebration from an intimate Jewish family
tradition. The cantata's narration was adapted from a text by Elie Weisel, but
Swados also included poems by Gabriela Mistral, Kadia Molodowsky, and Weisel in the text, wrote the music, and employed ensemble acting as well as puppets and masks in telling the story of Passover. The variety of instruments used
in the percussion section reveals Swados' eclectic approach in her work (*Haggadah* 7).

Among some of the more notable scenes in *The Haggadah* are those involving
the life of Moses from birth to death. The choral treatment of the narration
recalls Swados' earlier interest in classical Greek drama with its powerful use
of the chorus as a dramatic as well as narrative element. There are also references to the Holocaust, but the contemporary sense of the need for family identification, so powerfully expressed in *Runaways*, appears here, too, when one of
the principal narrators says: "We are told nothing about his [Moses'] adolescence. We are only told that one day he grew up and went out to see his brethren.
. . . The Gerer Rebbe interprets this as meaning: Moses' greatness was that he

went out to join his people'' (15). The cantata ends with lines from the *Song of Songs*: ''Arise, my beloved/My fair one/ and come away/ for lo,/ the winter is past/ . . . and the vines with the tender grape/ give good smell'' (65).

The raucous *Esther* is performed as a vaudeville with a cast of six vaudevillians telling the story of Purim. As one of the narrators declares: ''Everything in this story/Smacks of miracles./ For once it isn't difficult/ To be Jewish'' (7). Such musical and cultural elements as reggae, rock, and ''Motown'' stage directions along with satirical treatment of a beauty contest to determine the successor to the deposed Queen Vashti—''Miss Massapequa Persia'' (21)—demonstrate Swados' irreverent, eclectic, and effective use of contemporary popular culture in giving a new resonance to an old tradition. Esther herself is portrayed as ''Superwoman/spy'' who sings that she is ''off to save the world'' (27). She also insists that the overbearing Mordechai recognize that ''this has to be a female's view of the story'' (33), thus presenting a feminist perspective in a biblical text.

In comments about her reinterpretation of the *Book of Job*, Swados sheds light on her view of the contemporary meaning for her of biblical works: ''Each Biblical story has its own enormously complicated meaning. . . . The Haggadah says that, as long as one man is a slave, no one man can be free. Queen Esther, from my Purim opera . . . was a woman who took over the palace, who gave up love and her family for a larger good.'' Swados views Jonah as a ''stubborn man who refused to take political and moral responsibility and reflects the apathy that has overtaken the younger generation.'' Job she regards as a ''clown,'' the ''only contemporary character who sees things done to him and can't complain about it,'' thus her ''slapstick'' treatment of the biblical tale with professional clowns playing the major roles. However, she also relates Job's suffering to such matters as AIDS, famine, and natural disasters, as well as the personal tragedies of her mother's suicide and brother's early death (Delantier 15). In the *Contemporary Authors* interview, Swados reveals the ethical basis for her approach to Jewish materials, reflecting the core belief in *tikkun*, the moral obligation for those given the gift of life to ''mend the world.'' ''It seems to me that I have a very strong, almost spiritual belief that as a human being I have a responsibility to my fellow human beings on this earth, particularly to the children of this earth, to interpret and work out this world, to understand it better, to fight for a higher quality of living'' (524).

CRITICAL RECEPTION

The reception of Swados' early work was uniformly enthusiastic, especially in response to the refreshing, innovative quality of her material. Of *Nightclub Cantata* Clive Barnes said: ''What is fascinating about 'Nightclub Cantata' is simply its unique mixture of music, drama, and pop entertainment. Miss Swados's own staging is a knockout—the actors are trained like human acrobats—and her choice of source material, much of it written by herself, runs from Sylvia

Plath and Frank O'Hara to Carson McCullers. But in the event it is the music that does it'' (29). Harold Clurman described the work as "gritty, brave, somber, and exhilarating'' (124). Of *Runaways*, Mel Gussow, noting Swados' eclectic approach to "serious" theatre, declared: "With 'Runaways,' [Swados] steps right into the front line of popular American theatrical composers. This is the first musical since 'Hair' to unite successfully, contemporary popular music and the legitimate theatre'' (C3).

Dispatches (1979), however, did not fare as well in the critics' eyes. The musical was an adaptation of Herr's 1977 book about his experiences in Vietnam. Stephen Holden bemoaned how "Swados simply lifted the book's most obvious vignettes and dramatized them for superficial comedy and pathos'' (89); and John Simon is highly critical of the music: "Almost every 'tune' here could be done full justice to by a penny whistle, baby's rattle, and tin drum'' (85).

As has been the pattern with so many creative talents that have enjoyed early success—such as Tennessee Williams, Arthur Miller, and Edward Albee—Swados' later works have been treated unkindly by the critics. Still, though, Alisa Solomon's essay on *Esther* shows an appreciation for Swados' "efforts to represent a key Jewish legend in a fresh, timely way . . . honoring the social purpose that Swados has publicly said she intends in her work'' (cited in Chansky 444). While her efforts at writing fiction have not been exceptional, her nonfiction writing (especially *The Four of Us* and *Listening Out Loud*) captures the best elements of memoir writing, achieving empathy and engagement as well as accessible descriptions of the reasons behind her musical and thematic decisions.

Perhaps her incredible energy and innovative approach in her earliest works created too high a level of expectation for Swados' later theatrical experiments. One of the principal criticisms is that her materials were becoming "derivative." Her collaboration with Garry Trudeau on two satirical revues—*Rap Master Ronnie* (1986) and *Doonesbury* (1984)—made her a target for those who take their political satire too seriously. But Swados is still productive in developing new ways of approaching musical and theatrical expression. Her latest evocative score for Bill Moyers' *Genesis: A Living Conversation*, produced in 1996, indicates that she continues to develop as a creative innovator. Moreover, the Jewish-American theatre is yet to be fully appreciated, for hers is a bold, controversial, and culturally rich view of a people who must continually reinvent themselves in order to remain a vital presence in a frightening and rapidly changing world.

BIBLIOGRAPHY

Works by Elizabeth Swados

Selected Theatre Pieces

Dates in parentheses are dates of performance when different from dates of publication.
Nightclub Cantata. New York: Dramatists Play Service, 1977.

Dispatches, a Rock Musical. Libretto and music, 1979.

The Haggadah: A Passover Cantata. (1980). New York: Samuel French, 1982.

Doonesbury. (1983). Music only; text by Garry Trudeau. New York: Holt, Rinehart, and Winston, 1984.

Rap Master Ronnie. (1984). Music; lyrics cowritten with Garry Trudeau. New York: Broadway Play, 1985.

Alice in Concert (1981). New York: Samuel French, 1987a.

Runaways. New York: Samuel French, 1987b.

Jerusalem. New York: Broadway Play, 1988.

Esther: A Vaudeville Megillah. New York: Broadway Play, 1989a.

The Red Sneaks. 1989b.

Jonah. 1990.

Job: A Circus. 1992.

Genesis: A Living Conversation. Score and introductory text. PBS television series, 1996.

Other Works

The Girl with the Incredible Feeling. New York: Persea Books, 1976. [Juvenile fiction]

Leah and Lazar. New York: Summit Books, 1982. [fiction]

Listening Out Loud: Becoming a Composer. New York: Harper and Row, 1989. [nonfiction]

Inside Out: A Musical Adventure. Boston: Little, Brown, 1990. [juvenile fiction]

The Four of Us: The Story of a Family. New York: Farrar, Straus, and Giroux, 1991. [nonfiction]

The Myth Man. New York: Viking, 1994. [fiction]

Works about Elizabeth Swados

Barnes, Clive. Rev. of *Nightclub Cantata. New York Times,* January 10, 1977, 29.

Chansky, Dorothy. "Elizabeth Swados." In *Jewish American Women Writers.* Ed. Ann R. Shapiro. Westport, CT: Greenwood Press, 1994, 444–51.

Clurman, Harold. Rev. of *Nightclub Cantata. The Nation,* January 29, 1977, 124–25.

Contemporary Authors. Detroit: Gale Research, 1981, 97–100, 522–25. [*CA*]

Delantier, Barabara. "Bible Serves to Inspire Elizabeth Swados." *New York Times,* September 1, 1991, 15.

Gussow, Mel. "Elizabeth Swados—A Runaway Talent." *New York Times Magazine,* March 5, 1978, 19.

———. Rev. of *Runaways. New York Times,* March 10, 1978, C3.

Holden, Stephen. "Hawkish on Swados." Rev. of *Dispatches. Village Voice,* April 29, 1979, 89.

Schiff, Ellen, ed. *Fruitful and Multiplying: Nine Contemporary Plays from the American Jewish Repertoire.* New York: Mentor, 1995.

Simon, John. Rev. of *Dispatches. New York Magazine,* May 7, 1979, 85.

Solomon, Alisa. "Not the Real Megillah." Rev. of *Esther: A Vaudeville Megillah. Village Voice,* March 1, 1988, 94.

ALFRED UHRY   (1936–)

Michael Taub

BIOGRAPHY

Alfred Uhry has earned a respectable place among Jewish-American playwrights on the strength of two plays: *Driving Miss Daisy* (1987) and *The Last Night of Ballyhoo* (1997). Although he has written scripts for movies and musicals, various adaptations and commercials, Uhry was noticed (in fact, became an overnight celebrity) only in 1988, when *Miss Daisy* received the Pulitzer Prize. The movie version with Jessica Tandy and Morgan Freeman won the Oscar for Best Picture, and Uhry won the Oscar for Best Adaptation of a Screenplay.

Uhry was born in 1936 in Atlanta. His parents, Ralph K. and Alene Fox Uhry, were well-to-do German Jews. He was brought up in the Atlanta of the 1940s and 1950s, a typical southern city where gentility and good manners mixed with racial bias and religious prejudice. In an attempt to ''fit in,'' upper-class Jews like the Uhrys had to emulate the Gentile culture around them, often at the expense of Jewish customs and traditions. To some degree, Uhry's plays are a way of reliving his childhood experiences, of understanding his Jewishness and the energy spent on trying to be like everyone else.

Uhry's life changed radically upon entering Brown University, where he studied theatre and writing. Though still conscious of his minority status, he was surrounded by a considerably more liberal society and by many Jews who were not ashamed of their heritage and customs. After graduating, Uhry decided to stay in the Northeast. He went to New York with his writing partner, Bob Waldman, and soon after worked for the composer Frank Loesser, while teaching English and drama at a private high school in Manhattan. Among other works, Uhry wrote lyrics for a musical, *Little Johnny Jones*, at Connecticut's Goodspeed Opera House and for the Broadway musical *The Robber Bride-*

groom. He is married to Joanna Kellogg, and they live in Manhattan. The two have four daughters, all raised Unitarian. For the first time, in 1992, Uhry went to Israel. In a recent interview, he confesses that the trip woke him up, proving that "there was nothing to be ashamed of. . . . It's embarrasing to admit you're ashamed of being Jewish all your life. In the end it was not a prejudice but an ignorance, a hole where the Judaism should be" (Brantley 1).

MAJOR WORKS AND THEMES

Appropriately, *Driving Miss Daisy* takes place in his hometown, Atlanta, a play spanning a period of twenty-five years—1948 to 1973. Daisy Wertham, a Jewish widow portrayed from the age of seventy-two to ninety-seven is the play's main character. The plot revolves around her relationship with Hoke Coleburn, a black man portrayed from the age of sixty to eighty-five, employed by the family as Daisy's chauffeur. The early part of their life together is marked by a great deal of tension, mistrust, and misunderstandings. But as time goes on, the two learn to set aside social, religious, and racial prejudices and build a true and lasting friendship. Their personal struggles unfold against the background of the civil rights movement sweeping the country in the 1960s. Atlanta is a focal point in these political activities since its charismatic leader, the Reverend Dr. Martin Luther King, preached there.

But while the earth is shaking all around them, these two characters are satisfied with the role of passive observers. The closest they ever come to any type of "action" is on a Shabbes morning when their car is stopped near Daisy's temple because of a bomb by white racists who registered their displeasure with the congregation's support for King. But not all Jews are willing to march with the black civil rights leader. Ironically, Daisy's own son, Boolie, is one of them: despite his sympathies, he is afraid that "a lot of the men I do business with wouldn't like it" (41). Daisy, once a hardworking teacher in Atlanta's black ghettoes, is, however, quite enthusiastic about Dr. King's message of social justice and racial equality and is eager to meet him and hear him speak. Hoke, on the other hand, is much more skeptical, as memories of his parents' near-slavery, coupled with a life spent amid deep racial divisions, have left an indelible mark on his soul. As Uhry presents it, it seems that in Atlanta and, by extension, the whole South, support for civil rights depends on social status, not one's religious or ethnic affiliation: Daisy, who comes from modest economic background, is not afraid to speak out, but Boolie, the millionaire, is afraid to do so because it would hurt his business.

Uhry's play is equally interesting in its depiction of the Werthams' relationship with the white Gentile community-business partners, neighbors, and friends in social and civic organizations. Time and again, Daisy chastises Boolie and her daughter-in-law, Florine, for being overly preoccupied with activities involving their Christian friends at the expense of their duties and responsibilities toward their Jewish heritage. One time, around Christmas, while speaking to

Hoke, she says this about Florine: "The Garden Club this and the Junior League that! As if any of them would ever give her the time of day! But she'd die before she'd fix a glass of ice tea for the Temple Sisterhood!" (23). Commenting on Florine's Christmas decorations around the house, she says: "If her grandfather, old man Freitag, saw this, he would jump out of his grave" (23–24).

Clearly, Daisy belongs to a generation of prouder Jews who were more comfortable with their religion and ethnic identity than Boolie and Florine. By comparison, these younger Jews are vastly assimilated, considerably more opportunistic and materialistic than their parents ever were. In an attempt to succeed in a predominantly Christian environment, Boolie and Florine are prepared to do almost anything, even celebrate Christmas if that would buy them membership into the "Episcopalian Club."

The civil rights turmoil of the 1960s is a critical time in American history. In modern Jewish history, one of the most crucial dates is 1939—the start of World War II and the beginning of mass Jewish persecutions resulting in the extermination of 6 million people, and 1939 is the time frame for Uhry's *The Last Night of Ballyhoo*, another work set in Atlanta. Uhry is not the only Jewish-American dramatist interested in the late 1930s: Arthur Miller, in his 1993 *Broken Glass*, focuses on a group of Brooklyn Jews reacting to events in Europe. Like the Werthams of *Miss Daisy*, the Levys and Freitags of *Ballyhoo* are wealthy, assimilated, German Jews. The characters of this drama are two widows and their college-age daughters: Reba and Sunny, Boo and Lala. Once again it is Christmastime, and the Levys and Freitags are busy decorating their Christmas tree. Ballyhoo is a great Atlanta Jewish festival that ends with a big dance. The rather plain-looking Lala has, after many sleepless nights, secured herself a partner in a distant relative from Ohio, while her pretty, Waspish-looking cousin Sunny goes off with Joe, a dashing New York Jew who has recently been employed by the family business.

Having failed to acclimatize herself to college life in the North, Lala lives now with her mother, fantasizing about writing a romantic novel and anxious about attending the premiere of *Gone with the Wind*. Sunny, the bright Wellesley student, on the other hand, is preoccupied with spiritual things and, once attached to Joe, begins to wonder about her identity. Typically, Joe is a real ethnic Jew who uses Yiddish words, questions their goyish customs and habits, and, most importantly, is concerned about the plight of Europe's Jews. As with all plays depicting events occurring on the eve of the Holocaust, the viewer, who knows what is about to happen, shudders at the casual demeanor of the characters onstage. In the end, Joe seems to have awakened the Jewish spirit in his hosts, especially in Sunny, who tries to mimic some of the Yiddish words she has heard from him. Right before curtain fall, the family is, for the first time, having a traditional Shabbes: dinner—candles, Hebrew blessings, and Hebrew songs.

CRITICAL RECEPTION

Uhry's first Broadway work was as lyricist for *The Robber Bridegroom*, for which he received a Drama Desk nomination in 1975 and Tony nomination in 1976. He also achieved some recognition for his adaptation of *Little Johnny Jones* (1982), the George M. Cohan musical that enjoyed a brief Broadway run. With *Driving Miss Daisy*, however, Uhry received his greatest recognition: the 1988 Pulitzer Prize and an Oscar for the best screenplay when he adapted the play in 1990.

In his review of the play in the *New Republic*, Robert Brustein noted: "This odd love story, though it never underestimated the difficulty of intimacy between the races, could easily grow mawkish. . . . It is a tribute to Uhry's discreet understatement that the sentiment does not grow into corn" (29). Mel Gussow adds in his review in the *New York Times* that Uhry "wisely refrains from melodramatic confrontation. The play remains quiet, and it becomes disarming, as it delineates the character with almost offhanded glimpses."

The evaluation of his most recent work, however, *The Last Night of Ballyhoo*, was not nearly so favorable. Upon its opening, Aaron Schloff of *Jewish Week* complained that *Ballyhoo* is too reminiscent of a television *Hallmark Hall of Fame* movie (27), and John Simon, in his review for *New York Magazine*, wrote that "Uhry gets progressively more intramurally Jewish, as various forms of Judaism duke it out, and also more saccharine and, finally, all gooily religious" (52). Ben Brantley in the *New York Times* was hardly less harsh. The play reminded him of "vintage episodes of 'Designing Women' " (1). At this point in his career, Uhry's most successful work, *Driving Miss Daisy*, may well be the one for which he is most noted as a contribution to Jewish-American theatre.

BIBLIOGRAPHY

Works by Alfred Uhry

Dates of production are in parentheses when different from dates of publication.
Here's Where I Belong (lyrics). Unpublished book by Terrance McNally, music by Robert Waldman. New York, 1968.
The Robber Bridegroom. (1975). (lyricist and librettist); music by Robert Waldman. New York: Drama Book Specialists, 1978.
Little Johnny Jones (adapter). New York, 1982.
Driving Miss Daisy. (1987). New York: Communications Group, 1988.
Mystic Pizza (screenplay) with Amy Jones, Peter Howze, and Randy Howze. Metro-Goldwyn-Mayer, 1988.
Driving Miss Daisy (screenplay). Warner Brothers, 1989.
The Last Night of Ballyhoo. New York, 1997.

Works about Alfred Uhry

Brantley, Ben. "Southern Jewish Angst as One-Liners." *New York Times*, February 23, 1997, 1, 29.

Brustein, Robert. Rev. of *Driving Miss Daisy*. *New Republic*, September 28, 1987, 28–30.

Gussow, Mel. Rev. of *Driving Miss Daisy*. *New York Times*, April 16, 1987, 22.

Schloff, Aaron. "Brooklyn Comes to Ballyhoo." *Jewish Week*, March 7, 1997, 27.

Simon, John. "The Last Night of Ballyhoo," *New York Magazine*, March 10, 1997, 52.

Wichtel, Alex. "Remembering Prejudice of a Different Sort." *New York Times*, February 23, 1997, 5, 27.

WENDY WASSERSTEIN (1950–)

Michael Taub

BIOGRAPHY

Wasserstein's plays are about middle- and upper-middle-class northeastern women growing up in the turbulent 1960s. Her characters are likable, endearing, and often amusing. Her drama deals with the conflict of career and motherhood, gender issues, and, to some extent, Jewish questions, rather than with feminism or the women's movement.

Wendy Wasserstein was born in New York in 1950. She attended Calhoun High School on the Upper West Side of Manhattan and graduated from Mount Holyoke College and Yale Drama School. She is the author of *Uncommon Women and Others* (1977), *Isn't it Romantic?* (1979), *The Heidi Chronicles* (1988), *The Sisters Rosensweig* (1992), and *An American Daughter* (1996).

MAJOR WORKS AND THEMES

Uncommon Women and Others is a play about five women graduates of a seven sisters college who decide to hold a reunion in 1978, six years after completing their studies. The action drifts in and out of the play's seventeen episodes. Kate Quinn is a Phi Beta Kappa who loves trashy novels and men. She becomes a busy Washington lawyer. Kate is single. Rita Altabel is outspoken, energetic, a follower of Germaine Greer's feminism; she is married and a struggling writer. Rita is the one who proclaims in their senior year how "amazing" they all will be twenty-five years down the road. Muffet Di Nicola is an attractive, stylish woman who tells her friends that men are very important to her. Six years later she lives alone in Hartford working as an insurance seminar hostess.

Holly Kaplan imagines her future as an unwed mother of two living on Central Park West. Shortly before her senior year at a museum she meets a handsome doctor whom she calls periodically, but he does not remember her. Apparently, Holly is still undecided on her life's direction. In the play's final scene she lists these options: "law, insurance, marry Leonard Woolf, have a baby, birdwatch in Bolivia" (*The Heidi Chronicles and Other Plays* 72). Samantha Stewart is a gentle, attractive woman. Everything about her is understated, the type that made Holyoke the school it was in the 1960s. Sam opts for a traditional marriage by dedicating herself to Robert. She is not ashamed for choosing this role; on the contrary, she is rather comfortable in it.

Written at the height of feminism, *Uncommon Women* explores the choices facing women in America, choices made difficult by conflicting societal expectations of good mothers and devoted wives, on one hand, and professional careers, on the other. While some were able to strike a balance, others took a more radical route, dedicating themselves to feminist causes, resisting marriage, or, like Sam, coming to terms with conventional gender roles. But even those who actually made the choices were beleaguered by uncertainties and confusion. Reflecting the mood of the times, these "uncommon women" will have to wait past 1978 before they eventually become, in Rita's words, "pretty amazing women" (*The Heidi* 72).

Obviously, the Jewish woman here is Holly Kaplan. Soft and vulnerable inside, she is brash and funny on the outside. For example, it takes a great deal of chutzpah to call up someone she met briefly at a museum in Philadelphia, ask him on a date, and discuss marriage. Among others, she asks him if he knew the expression "good ga davened" (*The Heidi* 62), someone whose prayers were answered: a girl who meets a nice Jewish doctor, marries him, and goes to Bermuda on Memorial Day weekends. The lengthy phone conversation is punctuated by jokes about anxious single women and anxious "Jewish mother" types who want their daughters married to nice Jewish doctors. Some might view Holly as pathetic for humiliating herself to this total stranger. Yet Holly is not so desperate as to warrant such criticism. She might be insecure in some regards, but on the whole she is witty and brilliant, the quintessential neurotic, a liberal striving to become an independent woman of the 1970s.

Jewishness is marginal in *Uncommon Women*. It is central in *Isn't it Romantic?* A much more focused play, *Isn't it Romantic?* deals with a "nice Jewish woman," Janie Blumberg, a Harvard M.B.A. living in New York. Like her sisters in *Uncommon Women* she, too, is confronted with the painful choice of career and family. Earlier, women allude to the anxieties they experience from dealing with conflicting parental and societal expectations, mainly their teachers. That is made most explicit by Holly, probably because she is Jewish. But we never meet her parents, or any parents, for that matter.

In *Isn't it Romantic?* parents are actual characters whose values and way of life are shown in detail. By putting them onstage, Wasserstein underscores generation gaps while, at the same time, highlighting the source of the daughters' anxieties. Thus, it is significant that Janie's and Harriet's parents grew up during the war with values that stressed hard, honest work, family, and well-defined gender roles. Typically, Simon, Janie's father, is the sole provider. He is self-employed and doing well. Naturally, he dreams of a son-in-law who will eventually take over the business. He indulges his wife's every whim, from aerobic dancing to expensive clothes. As a good Jewish husband, he spares no expense at pleasing her and Janie. At times, however, his parental concerns become overbearing, forcing Janie to demand privacy.

True to the stereotype, Simon speaks little while Tasha, his wife, talks a great deal. Problems arise when the mother, who expects conformity from Janie, displays rebellious tendencies of her own. One might say that Tasha is an untraditional Jewish mother with traditional values. Among the untraditional things is ordering food and coffee. Sending mixed messages, mainly related to their Jewishness, is the source of stress. While much is made about marrying a "nice Jewish boy," Tasha and Simon are happy to eat sausages; worse, Marty Sterling, the Jewish doctor they want Janie to marry, is helping promote a new, treyf product by a restaurant chain owned by his father. It is not only hypocritical but ironic as well because the same owner, Mr. Sterling, was once Schlimowitz, who, not that long ago, sold only kosher products.

The Jewishness of the Blumbergs and the Sterlings is of the ethnic variety, not religious or Zionist. It mainly takes the form of certain mannerisms, behavioral patterns, and language. Thus, there are irreverence for things considered classy or "goyish"—fashions in furniture, homes, foods—and, of course, extensive use of Yiddish words and sayings. Perhaps more than any other ethnic expression, Yiddish is a signal indicating difference and in a strange way even a comforting feeling of superiority, as if to say that "the goyim are not just different, but are not as good as us." Such ethnic manifestations from a group eager to assimilate might seem strange, but Jews, more than any other minority, feel somewhat guilty for abandoning old traditions and customs, Wasserstein suggests.

Janie's parents use Yiddish extensively. But Marty does, too. He is not ashamed of his Jewishness, having already accomplished his goal of becoming a rich doctor. Thus, we hear such commonly used words as l'chaim, challah, nakhes, alte kakers, mazel tov, and a juicy expression, "Hakn a tchaynik," causing someone a headache, literally, "Banging the kettle" (*Isn't It Romantic?* 121). Janie, for one, tries desperately to free herself from the choking effect of her doting parents and their constant pressures to get married. Because of this, she is extremely uncomfortable with Marty's aggressive approach toward her. His rather hurried plans of marriage, moving to Brooklyn and opening a practice there, are quickly canceled as Janie decides to pursue a career first before committing herself to family life, especially to the kind laid out by Marty.

Interestingly, her Gentile friend, Harriet, is going in the opposite direction— she is prepared to give up her independence and career for a husband who provides for her and the prospects of motherhood. Ironically, but appropriately, her mother, Lillian, is a company executive who, at some point in the marriage, decides to leave her husband to pursue the highly competitive corporate route. While conceding that a solitary life is not perfect, she has no major regrets. She advises Harriet to accept compromises and make the best of life. Unlike Tasha, she does not insist on matrimonial solutions. She leaves it up to Harriet to decide.

To a large degree, Heidi Holland, the protagonist of *The Heidi Chronicles*, is a feminist version of Janie Blumberg. While Janie is basically confused and conflicted about her choices, Heidi devotes an entire life to women's causes. As an art historian she writes and lectures on women artists omitted from the male-dominated canon. The episodic plot, spanning twenty-five years of Heidi's mature life, shows her at consciousness-raising sessions, on- and off-campus rallies, and other forms of feminist activism.

Though Heidi is determined and strong, her choices are, to some degree, determined by the two very different men in her life: Scoop Rosenbaum and Peter Patrone. Scoop is the aggressive stockbroker with a good sense of humor; Peter is the sensitive homosexual who becomes a caring pediatrician in a busy urban hospital. He lives a modest life. Scoop, on the other hand, becomes rich by serving as editor of *Boomer*, an influential yuppie magazine. Not surprisingly, Scoop follows the traditional road by marrying a woman who accepts the role of raising his children; Peter's only family is a small circle of gay friends, some dying of AIDS. However, he and Heidi form a family of sorts through a deep understanding of each other's needs and concerns. He is a guiding force keeping her focused on priorities.

Scoop also cares about Heidi. But he is too cynical, an incurable male chauvinist incapable of fully comprehending Heidi's inner struggles and aspirations. Fifteen years into Scoop's marriage, Heidi realizes that had she married him, she would have left soon after or else accepted a life of unfulfilled dreams. Though Scoop refrains from ethnic references, an occasional "Heidella" toward Heidi gives him away. Also, at one point he tells Heidi he did not marry Lisa not "because she was Jewish" but because she was less perfect than Heidi. He does not want "to come home to an A+ but an A−," a woman who would willingly sacrifice ten years of her life for his success. As we have seen, in *Isn't It Romantic?* the single Jewish woman opts for a career first and family second, while her Gentile counterpart follows a different course; in *The Heidi Chronicles* it is the opposite. We may, therefore, conclude that religious/ethnic considerations are insignificant in arriving at major decisions such as marriage; if anything, it seems parental forces are stronger determinants.

With an adopted baby at her side Heidi seems content. Is this a compromise or cop-out? While some might view her choice as admirably feminist, others could consider it a selfish substitute to conventional motherhood and marriage. Most powerful of all critics, John Simon, declared that her solution to loneliness was "glib" (qtd. by Judith Miller). Heidi, in fact, shows courage; by adopting the child, she is no less of a feminist or in some way dishonest.

Ironically, Wasserstein's next drama, *Sisters Rosensweig*, is the most Jewish while depicting a character who tries very hard to rebel against the Jewish past.

Sara Rosensweig is a fifty-four-year-old banker living in London. She is employed by a Hong Kong firm. The former Brooklyn native is celebrating her birthday with close friends and two younger sisters, Pfeni and Gorgeous. Sara is twice divorced and the mother of Tess. Since leaving New York, she has devoted herself to a successful career and to raising Tess. She makes sure her daughter is totally shielded from any ethnic or religious influences. Occasionally, she sees a certain Nick Pym. It is a convenient arrangement since both are not interested in anything more than an uncommitted, open relationship. Appropriately, he is a blue-blooded Englishman.

Most of the time Sara is a satisfied woman: she has a great job, is financially secure, lives in a nice home, and is the mother of a very smart young woman. Lately, however, Tess has been involved with an eccentric who, for some strange reason, is obsessed with Lithuanian nationalism and wants to take her to Vilnius. Such offbeat activities by Tess make Sara nervous, and she wants her daughter to leave him and think seriously about a career and family. Ironically, she acts toward her daughter as she would hate others acting toward her—like a stereotypical Jewish mother.

While Sara gave marriage two trials, Pfeni is involved with a bisexual theatre director who eventually chooses to leave her for a gay man. She is a forty-year-old reporter and writer for women's causes, traveling to such remote and dangerous places as Kurdistan to cover stories of oppression and sex discrimination. Gorgeous, on the other hand, is happily married to a Jewish lawyer. She is the mother of four and lives in Newton, a suburb of Boston. Like Tasha of *Isn't it Romantic?* she, too, feels the need for something different to spice up her otherwise boring suburban life. So she becomes a radio talk show host, a local version of Dr. Ruth, counseling people on everything from religion to sex. As president of Temple Beth-El Sisterhood, she leads a group of women from Newton on a tour of London's crown jewels and other tourist attractions.

While celebrating her birthday with her sisters and Mervyn Kant—an endearing widower who catches her fancy—Sara gradually realizes that all her wonderful accomplishments do not make up for the fact that she is morally and spiritually adrift. For psychological and professional reasons she felt she had to turn her back on her roots; through her sisters and Mervyn she is reconnected to her childhood, parents, and heritage. Sara realizes that despite its inherent complexities and problems, these roots—her Jewishness—are ultimately her true self. That means welcoming again Shabbat candles, gefilte fish, bagels, Manischewitz wine, and even "Moshe Pupick," a character she knows from an old Jewish song, here reincarnated as Mervyn, the funny Jewish furrier who is falling in love with her.

Mervyn is the quintessential "professional Jew." He is active in B'nai B'rith, speaks some Yiddish, and travels to Israel, where his daughter lives. In short, he never fails to connect everything, in any context, to something Jewish, the

Holocaust, anti-Semitism, or Israel. His personal charm, quick wit, and healthy sense of humor manage to penetrate Sara's outer layer of seriousness and toughness, eventually getting to her softer, feminine side. She surprises everyone, but most of all her own self, when she yields to the temptation of doing something so outrageous, so out of character, as sleeping with him, a man she has just met.

While her sister Pfeni may need more time to find true happiness, by the end of the play Sara is ready to make some meaningful changes, like marrying Mervyn the Jewish furrier. In the touching final scene, mother and daughter are alone onstage. As if trying to purge herself of "Britishness" and "goyishness," Sara exclaims her new mantra: "My name is Sara Rosensweig. I am the daughter of Rita and Maury Rosensweig. I was born in Brooklyn, New York, August 23, 1937. . . . I first sang in the Hanukah Festival in East Midwood Jewish Center. I played a candle" (107).

As one can see, Wasserstein's main characters are high-achieving women at life's crossroads struggling to find a way of balancing family life with a career. In Sara's case, the protagonist, long after making the crucial decisions, is suddenly forced to take another look at her life. Wasserstein presents characters like Marty and Simon Blumberg as comfortable in their role as Jewish stereotypes. On the other hand, she introduces surprises like the deceptive Tasha Blumberg, who looks and sounds like a type but actually is not. On the whole, Jewish women (Holly, Janie, Pfeni, Gorgeous) are socially active, while Jewish men (Marty, Scoop, Mervyn) are driven to selfish pursuits involving power and money. Of course, Peter is an exception.

In *An American Daughter* (1997), Wasserstein returns to some of the issues she explored in *The Heidi Chronicles*: sex discrimination, gender bias, feminism. At the center of this drama is Dr. Lyssa Dent Hughes, the daughter of a famous senator. She is the president's choice for the job of surgeon general. Though highly qualified, she is turned down by the Senate because she once failed to report for jury duty. The year is 1994, and the setting is the Hughes' home in Georgetown, Washington, D.C. The plot is patterned on the Zoe Baird case of the same year, an event that became known as "nannygate." Baird was a successful corporate lawyer who was nominated by Bill Clinton to the position of attorney general. She was rejected by the Senate after it was learned that she had hired an illegal alien as her baby-sitter. In both cases, the common perception was that the extra scrutiny was unjust, that, in fact, it was an indication of deep-seated male prejudice toward women seeking high office. In both cases, the victims are highly successful women trying desperately to juggle a career in politics and motherhood.

As shown here, the many strides made by women in the decades since the sexual revolution of the 1960s have yet to secure them equal treatment at the highest levels of Washington politics. While all legal impediments have been removed, the advancement of women cannot fully take place until male prejudice and bigotry are totally eradicated.

CRITICAL RECEPTION

Wasserstein has received a great deal of attention from both critics in the mass media and drama scholars. *The Heidi Chronicles* won a Tony award, the Pulitzer Prize, and the New York Drama Critics Circle Award among many awards honoring this work. While praise for her craft is universal, especially her lively dialogue, some feel that her handling of serious social issues is somewhat superficial. Reviewing *The Sisters Rosensweig*, David Richards laments that "the play seems to be a watering down of a work that could have been far more intimate and revelatory." (1) Susan Carlson observes that "Wasserstein allows real female relationships to develop, friendships that have been rare in comedy. Freed from the requirement that they bond only with men (and produce the traditional happy ending), Wasserstein's women can choose to bond with each other" (570). Some point out that Wasserstein has written too few works to be considered a major playwright. No matter what the criticism, Wasserstein has a devoted following, especially in the Northeast and among women everywhere who identify with her characters.

In *An American Daughter* Ben Brantley felt that Wasserstein packed a bit too much into one play, producing a work with a weak focus and lack of direction. Furthermore, this critic states that while her characters are lively and entertaining, they seem rather one-dimensional figures spouting funny one-liners.

BIBLIOGRAPHY

Works by Wendy Wasserstein

The Heidi Chronicles and Other Plays. San Diego: Harcourt Brace Jovanovich, 1990.
        (Includes *Uncommon Women* and *Isn't It Romantic?*)
The Sisters Rosensweig. San Diego: Harcourt Brace, 1993.
An American Daughter. New York: Dramatists Play Service, 1998.

Works about Wendy Wasserstein

Berkowitz, Gerald. *American Drama of the Twentieth Century*. New York: Longman, 1992.
Brantley, Ben. Rev. of *An American Daughter*. *New York Times*, April 14, 1997.
Carlson, Susan. "Comic Textures and Female Communities 1937 and 1977: Clare Booth and Wendy Wasserstein." *Modern Drama*, December 1984, 564–73.
Cohen, Esther. "Uncommon Woman: An Interview with Wendy Wasserstein." *Women's Studies* 15, 1988, 257–70.
Keyssar, Helene. "Drama and the Dialogic Imagination: *The Heidi Chronicles* and *Fefu and Her Friends*." *Modern Drama*, March 1991, 88–106.

Mandl, Bette. "Feminism, Post-feminism, and the *Heidi Chronicles*." *Studies in the Humanities*, December 1990, 120–28.

Miller, Judith. *New York Times*, October 19, 1992, 118.

Richards, David. Rev. of *The Sisters Rosensweig*. *New York Times*, November 1, 1992, 1, 6.

POETRY SECTION

Introduction

John Hollander

In introducing this source book of Jewish-American poets and dramatists, I must first observe that a considerable number of poets are not discussed. These are poets largely of the earlier part of the century who, although frequently writing with extreme vividness out of the life of New York in particular, wrote in Yiddish—I think of Moishe-Leib Halpern, Jacob Glatstein, H. Leyvik, Malka Heifetz-Tussman, A. Leyeles, to name a few—who are certainly American poets. But their writing in Yiddish, however secular most of them were, solved certain puzzles of identity that the lives and work of the writers discussed here continue to raise. It is interestingly awkward for a poet to address the question of a double-hyphenated identity right now. It is a time in which, in the United States, an unpleasant phenomenon often called ''identity politics'' has begun to cloud the skies of serious moral and political discourse and to tear away at the social contract that has allowed this peculiar and problematic notion of identity to help fulfill it. The issue of ''Jewish-American poetry'' seems to involve even more problematic questions now than it did in the past.

But it's just the problematic nature of the identity that seems most interesting, rather than the deplorable condition of American public life and private character at the close of the century. One presumably knows what American poetry is (in my case, from having read it and tried to write it and taught its texts in university for what I now realize is two-thirds of my life). Although I am not remotely one, I know what it means to be a Jewish novelist in America, the occupation by which the notion of Jewish writing is almost always gauged. Partially because poetry is deeply oblique, does not truly have the ''subjects'' it might purport—like some illegitimate essay—to have, and will, at its best, be talking in several ways at once, the question of what Jewish-American poetry is gets harder and harder to answer, as more and more American Jews have come in the latter half of the twentieth century to write it. Some years ago I set out to explore this question in an essay, which I would now want to expand upon and emend somewhat. This is partly because it was still not yet clear how the later work of such poets as Allen Grossman, Philip Levine, and—particularly—Irving Feldman, engages Jewish-American experience along a range of complex ways. Feldman's recent work has become more intense, and I might easily have centered these remarks on a consideration of his response to the late Joseph Brodsky in his Nobel Prize acceptance speech. It may be remembered that Brodsky said:

"How can one write poetry after Auschwitz?" inquired Adorno. . . . "And how can one eat lunch?," the American poet Mark Strand once retorted. In any case, the generation to which I belong has proven capable of writing that poetry. (Feldman 48)

Feldman begins one of his two strange, angry poems following on this exchange by seizing on the fatuousness of Brodsky's summation:

In any case (or, as our comedians say "But seriously, folks") has Adorno's question been disposed of, interred beneath the poems written since Auschwitz?—rather than raised again and again like a ghost by each of them? (48)

The range of ironies here is broad: neither Brodsky nor Strand, both Jews, shows awareness of, or concerns for, Jewish tradition in his work, whereas Feldman speaks out of that awareness here. Moreover—and this is the more difficult point—he really means his metaphor of ghostliness, for he does not think—as I do not think—of poetry as being anything more than occasionally explicit. Rather, he implies something else. Poems tell truths about their authors only deeply and by indirection, but only trivially in literal confessional modes. Similarly, a question as deep as Adorno's for any consideration of life, truth, value, history, and, particularly, the poet's constant concern with the relation of work and play can never be shelved.

  I suppose that the three different versions of a Jewish poet that emerge from this anecdote might be adduced as evidence of a complex picture in contemporary America. It cannot be said that there is a great prior tradition of Jewish-American poetry. Only in recent generations have a significant number of significant American poets been Jews—of the forty-one discussed in Richard Howard's important *Alone with America*, eleven are Jewish (as is the editor himself), and two more have one Jewish parent. Given the history of immigration, it is not surprising that in the nineteenth century one can think of only three versifiers, of whom one is almost unknown, who might be adduced. Bret Harte, a California settler, is known for his journalism stories and satirical light verse; Emma Lazarus, a poet of some interest to whom I shall return shortly; and the obscure and amusingly anomalous instance of Penina Moise (1797–1880), born in Charleston, South Carolina. It is hard to resist speaking of her for a few moments. Her *Fancy's Sketch Book* ("By Miss Penina Moise," with a piously modest epigraph from Byron, to the effect that "'Tis but to fill/ A certain portion of uncertain paper;/ Some liken it to climbing up a hill,/ Whose summit, like all hills, is lost in vapour" was published in Charleston in 1833. She also wrote a volume of hymns for Charleston's reformed congregation and remained, even after she lost her sight, a significant literary figure in that city. "To Persecuted Foreigners" from her volume of poetry opens with a general admonition:

> Fly from the soil whose desolating creed
> Outraging faith, makes human victims bleed.
> Welcome! where every Muse has reared a shrine,
> The aspect of wild Freedom to refine. (36)

(The verse, it is true, creaks a bit here and there.) Only in the third stanza does Penina Moise speak of Jewish immigration (which would have been mostly from German territory in those early post-Revolutionary decades):

> If thou art one of that oppressed race,
> Whose pilgrimage from Palestine we trace,
> Brave the Atlantic—Hope's broad anchor weigh,
> A Western Sun will gild your future day. (36)

Here it seems the voice of American enlightenment calling out to Jewish immigrants, among others—the "we" speaks for historical knowledge, rather than Jewish identity. Yet this lady remained as devoted to her congregation and to her salon and reading group for young Jewish ladies as she did to her city of Charleston.

One of our troubles with Penina Moise—whose writing amuses and interests me as historical material—is that one cannot think of her conventional, literary, occasional verse as being real poetry. This brings up another problem. All verse is not poetry—even as, *pace* Molière's M. Jourdain, all talk is not prose—and defining a true poet (as poets in English have always sought to do since Chaucer) can be as interestingly problematic as defining what Jewish literary expression really is.

There are, indeed, cultural and historical moments that enable poetry to play differing roles with great success. For example, there seems to have been something about the cultural-historical construction of the Elizabethan and Jacobean theatre that enabled a great poet to be Shakespeare and something about the American theatre of the nineteenth and twentieth centuries that would prevent all but one or two really fine writers from getting near the stage. Similarly, there was something about a number of times and places in the history of the diaspora that enabled Jewish writers to do remarkable work, with permanent consequences for the vernaculars in which they wrote and, some have even argued, for the notion of Jewish identity itself: Germany and the Double Empire in the later nineteenth and early twentieth centuries yielded much remarkable fiction. For poetry in Hebrew, Spain in the eleventh through fifteenth centuries, Italy in the sixteenth, Israel in the later twentieth, the Pale of Settlement and also New York City for poetry in Yiddish. The Holocaust and its epistemological and moral echoes cradled what may be the only great poetry in German after Rilke, that of Paul Celan. Is it that poetry always struggles with some cultural recalcitrance—even the language itself? Poets use in daily life the talk and the prose of their languages like the natives they are; in poems, though, one becomes at once closer and more estranged from the vernacular of literal discourse.

Emma Lazarus, the only Jewish-American writer of the nineteenth century I could call a real poet (although she died—at the age of thirty-eight in 1887— probably before her work had grown to the stature it might have otherwise reached), put the question of what a diasporic Jewish poetry might be in another, most interesting, but rather problematic, way. Lazarus writes verse in the shadow of American poetry of the first half of the century (although her sequence of prose-poems was more formally adventurous). In a poem on the Venus de Milo her conclusion cannot escape a memory of Heinrich Heine in his last days, a poet with whom she always felt deep affinities:

> Here *Heine* wept! Here still he weeps anew,
> Nor ever shall his shadow lift or move
> While mourns one ardent heart, one poet-brain
> For vanished Hellas and Hebraic pain.

Lazarus is best known for her sonnet "The New Colossus," part of which is engraved at the base of the Statue of Liberty in New York harbor. But in another, more interesting sonnet she marks out what a later romantic, American poet might construe as a Jewish-American agenda. The poem is simply called "1492" and addresses the year itself:

> Thou two-faced year, Mother of Change and Fate
> Didst weep when Spain cast forth with flaming sword,
> The children of the prophets of the Lord,
> Prince, priest and people, spurned by zealot's hate.
> Hounded from sea to sea, from state to state,
> The West refused them and the East abhorred.
> No anchorage the known world could afford,
> Close-locked was every port, barred every gate.

A straightforwardly American poem of the nineteenth century would hail the year as a mother of change only—of Columbus' discovery; but for Lazarus it is symmetrically the year of the expulsion—*galut* (expulsion) being a continuing issue for her—even as she alludes to the *lahat hacherev hatmithapecheth (flaming sword) of bereshith* (Genesis) (the same flaming sword, by the way, that in

Kafka's *Amerika* gets peculiarly substituted for the torch of the Statue of Liberty—Lazarus' "new colossus" as its hero enters New York harbor). The octave of her sonnet is concerned with Fate; but in the last six lines she turns to the other aspect of the year and the matter of America:

> Then smiling, thou unveildst, O two-faced year,
> A virgin world where doors of sunset part,
> Saying, "Ho, all who weary, enter here!
> There falls each ancient barrier that the art
> Of race or creed or rank devised, to rear
> Grim bulwarked hatred between heart and heart!"

We may note the revisionist echo of Dante's "Abandon all hope, you who enter here" inscribed on the gates of hell, as well as what today seem the simple hopes of democracy for the immigrant: it would take a much more grim and sophisticated view of American liberty—seen not from upper-middle-class New York of the 1980s, Jewish or not—to feel that the mechanisms that tumble those bulwarks inevitably enact new, at first invisible ones.

A modern poet might similarly observe that in a simple, schematic way Lazarus looks at an American moment from a Judaic perspective (on the other hand, this is a poem that Longfellow, in the mode of his poem on the Newport cemetery, might conceivably have written?). But the schematic mode—expository even when it is lyrically hortatory—is as characteristic of the poetry as of the sentiment it reflects. In 1882, Lazarus wrote of Jewish identity in the diaspora in a way I now realize has to do as much with poetry as with sociology—even with the peculiar concept of peoplehood that Jewish history has implicitly claimed to be unique. In a strange comparison, she invokes the *pi'el* (intensive voice) form of the Hebrew verb:

Every student of the Hebrew language is aware that we have in the conjugation of our verbs a mode known as the *intensive* voice, which by means of an almost imperceptible modification of vowel points intensifies the meaning of any primitive root. A similar significance seems to attach to the Jews themselves in connection with the people among whom they dwell. They are the intensive form of any nationality whose language and customs they adopt.

This is clearly the voice of German Jewry (although Lazarus was born in New York City), and certainly what we think of as Jewish expression in American literature—with the language and ways of later immigrants from Eastern Europe in its background—might want to say something very different. On the other hand, a modern trope more easily available to those without Hebrew might be identity italicized or, more boldly, in boldface type, which is a very different concept from that of hyphenated identity—and, I should say, on the face of it, more deeply and interestingly American than the usual cliché of hyphenation.

(Or—to push on even further with the kind of heavy pun that only a humorless Derridean would employ—that in every nation of the diaspora the Jews living there are a hyphen-nation.)

So although Lazarus' formulation seems variously right and tragically wrong for certain periods of Jewish history, it remains a powerful one for the ways of writers in diasporic vernaculars. (Given that there was not to be a Third Temple, there is a peculiar sense in which the language of the state of Israel is, like Aramaic, primus inter pares among the tongues of *galut*.) If I were writing as a Jewish-American novelist, the matter of language would play a different role in my discussion. But for a poet, it is crucial. Novelists' worlds have to bear some recognizable relation to the details of ways of life at particular times and places and—crudely put—some such notion as a Jewish-American sensibility, whether or not directed to historically verifiable objects of Jewish-American experience or whatever. But poetry is a somewhat different matter. The language of the King James Bible—for me, a great and fruitful secular text with an immensely complex ironic relation to Torah—has been since childhood a part of my word-hoard (as the acutely non-Semitic Anglo-Saxons called it). Like the French and German songs my mother sang when I was small, its cadences were for me part of nature. A thoughtful kind of American poet can envy poets like Yehuda Amichai and the late Dan Pagis and Carmi their ability to write in the language of the Bible (in my case not because I am particularly observant but perhaps because I am not). The English language itself was conceived and grew up in Christendom, and the language of American literature developed in and out of the Reformation. So, too, did the Reformation shape the peculiar thrust toward the metaphoric and revisionary of what had been institutional and even material of poetry in English since Spenser and Milton. For European Renaissance humanists, Latin and the particular vernacular of each stood in a kind of gendered relation (mother tongue to male authority); for American Jews from Eastern Europe, Yiddish remained *mamaloschen* (the mother tongue), but that did not mean that writing in English was like writing in Latin in the earlier case.

Another question arises, that of the particular kind of Jewish identity that is revealed in the poems of contemporary American writers. There are many modes of affiliation in one's life and many modes of acknowledgment of one's identity and of how one construes it oneself. Among these, Jewish observance may not be an issue so much as Judaic knowledge. Some of this is, indeed, liturgical— the possession of some corpus of texts and songs arising from Sabbath and festival services in childhood, perhaps—but an acquaintance with biblical and postbiblical history generally; with something of the culture of the Jews in periods and places of differing vernaculars (language being of prime importance to poets)—Aramaic, Greek, Arabic, Spanish, Yiddish, German, English; with something of various modes of Judaic culture outside of the stereotyped, twentieth-century American agendas—a few words of Yiddish, Eastern European food, oppressively concerned parents, and so on. Without such knowledge, or something like it, it is hard to cope with a sense of Jewish identity for a poet with enough seriousness and enough knowledge of how true poetry differs from literary verse.

This raises a central—and for me here, final—question. Sentimental, most often not-very-well-turned verses overbrimming with Jewish ''content''—reminiscence, confession, memorial and commemorative—is much more commonly seen today than in the past. But the serious poets whose work is discussed in these pages are all too keenly aware that all writing with an unjustified right margin is not poetry. Nor are literal reports and predictable verbal gestures of expression. Poetry is rather to be located in the profound question of metaphoric writing, of saying one thing and meaning another, of making new sense out of received materials, natural or fabricated, that furnish the lives of our consciousness, of—in short—propounding midrash on the text of What There Is.

At the end of a long, ambitious poem of my own that—difficult as it is— might be said to speak more about many of the issues I've been trying to address than anything else I've written, I recalled something I had read many years before of how the historian Cecil Roth had encountered some ordinary Christian families in Spain and northern Portugal who habitually burned a candle inside a crock or pitcher on Friday evenings; when inquired about this, they replied that they didn't know why but that it had always been done in their families. (The poem in question is a kind of allegorical quest through the colors of the spectrum from red to violet and, at the same time, a sort of romance concerning the recovery of the menorah from the second temple from the bottom of the Tiber and smuggling it back home.) The trope of the candle in the pitcher became central to the conclusion of the poem, and I now realize that it meant as much about an anomalous poetic identity as about a Judaic one.

Poetry itself is, in some ways, like the candle in the pitcher, even though it often misleadingly proclaims itself to be a clear lamp. Indeed, a considerable amount of illumination is essential, and it has also likened itself to a mirror— it is Socrates in Xenophon's, not Plato's, *Symposium* who first points out that a mirror can reflect what is but sheds no light on it, illuminates nothing, while a lamp gives forth light of its own but cannot represent. Poetry is always somehow both mirror and lamp—and I probably mean more by this than both representation and expression. But the candle in the pitcher is what keeps burning, and to that degree, it remains a central metaphor; the straitened and confined light the candle emanates can be perceived only by privileged examination from above—which is what deeply knowledgeable and penetrating criticism can provide. Yet it has to hide itself—in any one of many kinds of pot or pitcher. These might be variously called exposition or relevance or having X or Y as a subject or ''being about'' Z or having W content. But with relation to what will be most admired and accepted at any time in any place, true poetry itself most often remains—in a more institutional domain of *literature*—a strange sort of marrano.

BIBLIOGRAPHY

Feldman, Irving. *Life and Letters*. Chicago: University of Chicago Press, 1994.

Lazarus, Emma. *The Poems of Emma Lazarus*. 2 vols. Boston and New York: Privately Printed, 1888.

Moise, Penina. *Secular and Sacred Works*. Charleston: Privately Printed, 1911.

MARVIN BELL   (1937–   )

Michael Taub and Joel Shatzky

BIOGRAPHY

Marvin Bell was born August 3, 1937, in New York. His father was a Jewish immigrant from the Ukraine, a man who suffered greatly under the Russian czars. His mother was American. Bell studied at Alfred University and Syracuse University and did graduate work at the University of Chicago and University of Iowa. He teaches writing and literature at Iowa. Bell has served as editor or publisher of such journals as *North American Review*, *Iowa Review*, and *American Poetry Review*. He received several poetry prizes and a Guggenheim in 1975.

MAJOR WORKS AND THEMES

Quite often the focus in *Poems for Nathan and Saul* (1966) and *A Probable Volume of Dreams* (1969), Bell's first major publications, is his father's past in anti-Semitic Russia. Thus, "An Afterword to My Father" speaks of loss and displacement, while "The Manipulator" depicts his father's bidding good-bye to the Orthodox rabbis, riding to Poland, and finally, after many months of hardship, arriving in America, where he raises a family. The tone of these poems varies: in "A Poor Jew" Bell shows his comical side, while "The Extermination of the Jews" is serious, even somber. Many of his poems are about love, marriage, divorce, children, politics, and war. Bell's poetics is a mix of structures and styles, ranging from short, compact pieces to longer, complex works.

The Escape into You (1971) is Bell's attempt to cope with the death of his father and a way of breaking free from his preoccupation with his European past. In fact, these poems are written as fifty-four overheard conversations between the divorced self trying to separate himself from the old one. On the whole, these poems are more obscure, considerably more intense than those in the earlier collections. Not surprisingly, there are considerably fewer Jewish references here than before. Finally, *Residue of Song* (1974) can be seen as a coming to terms with personal trauma like the loss of a parent and a divorce. The poet, it seems, has learned to resign himself to accept fate.

Stars Which We See, Stars Which We Do Not See (1977) was unanimously hailed as a great accomplishment. David St. John speaks of Bell's "playful, metaphysical intelligence . . . his verbal intelligence and knotty wit" (314). Seemingly free of the Jewish demons that the "World of Our Fathers" elicits, Bell devotes himself to meditations on a variety of common human concerns. His language is less experimental, and there are less tension and struggle.

CRITICAL RECEPTION

Critics have generally praised Bell's intelligence, the breadth of his poetry, and his unique, aesthetic experiments. His linguistic experimentations do draw an occasional complaint, while some are irritated that his imagery associations are intractably private. David St. John remarks, "Many poets have tried to appropriate into their poems a gritty, tough-talking American character, and to thereby earn for themselves some authenticity. . . . In [*Stars Which . . .*] Bell has found his own voice and the ability to write convincingly about the smallest details of a personal history" (319). The critics all, however, point to the fact that as he matures, the poet is increasingly less explicit in his references to his Jewish background and the Eastern European world of his father.

BIBLIOGRAPHY

Works by Marvin Bell

Poems for Nathan and Saul. Mt. Vernon, IA: Hillside Press, 1966a.
Things We Dreamt We Died For. Iowa City, IA: Stone Wall Press, 1966b.
A Probable Volume of Dreams. New York: Atheneum, 1969.
The Escape into You: A Sequence. New York: Atheneum, 1971.
Residue of Song. New York: Atheneum, 1974.
Stars Which We See, Stars Which We Do Not See. New York: Atheneum, 1977.
These Green-Going-to-Yellow. New York: Atheneum, 1981.
Drawn by Stones. New York: Atheneum, 1984.
New and Selected Poems. New York: Atheneum, 1987.
Iris of Creation. New York: Copper Canyon Press, 1990.
Book of the Dead Man. New York: Copper Canyon Press, 1994a.
A Marvin Bell Reader. Hanover, NH: University Press of New England, 1994b.

Works about Marvin Bell

Baker, David. "Marvin Bell, Essays, Interviews, Poems." *New England Review*, Winter 1983, 332–36.

Dodd, Wayne, and Stanley Plumly. "A Conversation with Marvin Bell." *Ohio Review* 17, Spring–Summer 1976, 41–62.

Howard, Richard. "Residue of Song." *Poetry*, September 1975 35–40.

Lewis, Peter. "The Poetry of Marvin Bell." *Stand* 13, 1972, 34–40.

Murray, G. E. "Stars Which We See, Stars Which We Do Not See." *The Georgia Review* 31, Winter 1977, 967–71.

Oberg, Arthur. "Marvin Bell: Time's Determinant." *The American Poetry Review* 5, May–June 1976, 4–8.

St. John, David. "Oxygen and Small Frictions." *Parnassus: Poetry in Review*, Spring–Summer 1977, 314–20.

CHARLES BERNSTEIN (1950–   )

Loss Pequeño Glazier

BIOGRAPHY

Charles Bernstein was born on April 4, 1950, in New York City to Herman Bernstein and Sherry Kegel, both children of Russian immigrants. Bernstein's father worked in the garment industry, spending a large part of his career as a dress manufacturer. The youngest of three children, Bernstein grew up on Central Park West in Manhattan and attended the Bronx High School of Science. He met Susan Bee (Laufer) in 1968. Bernstein and Bee were married in New Hampshire in 1977; their children, Emma and Felix, were born in 1985 and 1992, respectively. From 1968 to 1972, Bernstein attended Harvard College, where he was active in the antiwar movement. At Harvard, he concentrated in philosophy, studying with Stanley Cavell and Rogers Albritton. His philosophical studies culminated in his senior thesis, "Three Compositions on Philosophy and Literature," a reading of Gertrude Stein's *Making of Americans* through Ludwig Wittgenstein's *Philosophical Investigations*.

In early 1973, Bernstein took a seminar on Emily Dickinson with Robin Blaser at Simon Fraser University, an experience that proved influential for him. Following nine months in Vancouver, Bernstein moved to Santa Barbara, where he worked part-time as a health education coordinator in a community free clinic. Bernstein and Bee moved back to New York in early 1975. Although Bernstein had met poets in Vancouver, Santa Barbara, and San Francisco, it was on his return to New York that he became fully engaged in poetry as public practice. He met Bruce Andrews shortly after his return, spent much time going to St. Mark's Poetry Project and other New York readings, and in 1978 co-founded the acclaimed Ear Inn series with Ted Greenwald. Though Bernstein devoted himself tirelessly to poetry and poetics, his income was not related to literary activity. For nearly twenty years his income came from his work as a medical and health care editor and writer. Bernstein's writing has adapted medical vocabulary for poetic purposes and has continued to explore language's rules and forms as similarly investigated by innovators such as Stein, Wittgenstein, and the objectivists.

In 1978, with Bruce Andrews, Bernstein founded $L=A=N=G=U=A=G=E$ magazine. Bernstein has reflected that the motivation to publish the magazine grew from the exchanges he had in correspondence with Bruce Andrews and Ron Silliman. Produced as xeroxed, coverless, stapled booklets, $L=A=N=G=U=A=G=E$ produced thirteen numbers, three supplements, and an index issue, with a final volume copublished as *Open Letter* 5, no. 1 (1981). Despite its modest format and limited circulation, $L=A=N=G=U=A=G=E$ has proved to be one of the most influential little magazines of the period. $L=A=N=G=U=A=G=E$ also became the namesake for a constellation of literary concerns that has increasingly been mentioned in literary, academic, and poetic discourse. It was never intended, however, to constitute a literary "school" or movement.

Bernstein's poems were published in the important early volumes *Poetic Justice* (1979), *Controlling Interests* (1980), and *Islets/Irritations* (1983). Published in 1984 was *The $L=A=N=G=U=A=G=E$ Book*, a selection of work from $L=A=N=G=U=A=G=E$ magazine. The first collection of Bernstein's essays, *Content's Dream: Essays 1975–1984*, was published in 1986 (reprinted in 1994). Two major works, *Artifice of Absorption* and the substantial collection of poems *The Sophist*, were published in 1987, followed by Bernstein's next large collection of poetry, *Rough Trades*, in 1991. The following year, Bernstein's "How I Painted Certain of My Pictures" was included in *Best American Poetry, 1992*, and his second collection of essays, *A Poetics*, was published by Harvard University Press. Bernstein's most recent collection of poems, *Dark City*, was issued in 1994. This collection presents work by a poet in midcareer and shows Bernstein extending the forms of his craft exquisitely. It includes "The Lives of the Toll Takers," "How I Painted Certain of My Pictures," "Emotions of Normal People," and "The Influence of Kinship Patterns upon Perception of an Ambiguous Stimulus." Much of Bernstein's more recent prose remains uncollected. Of particular importance, however, are two of Bernstein's essays on Jewish writers, "Stein's Identity" and "Reznikoff's Nearness."

A milestone in Bernstein's career was his appointment in 1990 to the position of David Gray Professor of Poetry and Letters, Department of English at the State University of New York at Buffalo, where he is also an associate member of the Department of Comparative Literature. After his appointment, Bernstein cofounded the Poetics Program, a program that now is nationally regarded as at the forefront of the study of poetry. He also directs the Poetics Discussion List, an on-line discussion group that now enjoys international stature, and codirects the Electronic Poetry Center at Buffalo, perhaps the single most extensive site for poetry on the World-Wide Web. Bernstein's work has been published in

Argentina, China, Spain, Australia, New Zealand, France, Switzerland, Germany, Italy, Sweden, Korea, Russia, the Netherlands, Portugal, England, Canada, Mexico, Finland, Yugoslavia, and Japan. Bernstein is a correspondent for *Sulfur* and serves on the editorial boards of numerous literary projects. Of his many readings and public appearances, he has appeared twice in John Zorn's Radical Jewish Culture Festival in New York City.

MAJOR WORKS AND THEMES

The contribution of $L=A=N=G=U=A=G=E$ to poetic thought was to advance a terrain for writing. Though the borders of this terrain were never fixed or limited, language writing foregrounded specific interests that stood in opposition to prevailing academic tastes of the time. "Language writers have used structuralist and poststructuralist theory at times, to furnish ad hoc support for assertions about the problematic status of description, self, and narrative in poetry," Bob Perelman writes. "But these positions have come out of writing practices closely informed by the Modernists, especially Gertrude Stein, and the Objectivists, especially Louis Zukofsky, and to some extent by the New American poets and the New York school. Thus—to be schematic about it—language writing occupies a middle territory bounded on the one side by poetry as currently instituted in the academy and on the other by theory" (307).

Bernstein has objected to the apparatus of the contemporary poetry world he calls "official verse culture":

the poetry publishing and reviewing practices of *The New York Times, The Nation, American Poetry Review, The New York Review of Books, The New Yorker, Poetry* (Chicago), *Antaeus, Parnassus*, Atheneum Press, all the major trade publishers, . . . [and most] major university presses. . . . Add to this the ideologically motivated selection of the vast majority of poets teaching in university writing and literature programs . . . as well as the interlocking accreditation of these selections through prizes and awards judged by these same individuals. ("Academy" 247–48)

Bernstein's objection is to "biased, narrowly focused and frequently shrill and contentious accounts of American poetry, [which claim,] like all disinformation propaganda, to be giving historical or nonpartisan views" ("Academy" 247–48). The struggle with such literary politics is a significant concern of Bernstein's work; writing is not an occupation that exists on its own terms; rather it is a practice of ideology. As McGann has commented, "Bernstein manipulates the visible and audible features of his work because those features give material shape to the writing's social and intellectual commitments. The writing means to declare its ideological goals" (*Black Riders* 109). Indeed, McGann has used the phrase "the poet's office" in describing the concerns of Bernstein's writing; the use of this phrase is not without deeper resonance. The practice of writing is a political act. Thus, Bernstein has edited a volume titled

The Politics of Poetic Form: Poetry and Public Policy. Bob Perelman has written about Bernstein's *A Poetics* (1992), suggesting that "Bernstein frames the book with gestures that make poetry a counter-State or non-State" ("Write" 1994, 309). This view of poetry as a "counterstate" rings true in the title of Bernstein's collection of poems, *Republics of Reality* (1996).

One key enunciation of Bernstein's poetics occurred in his verse essay *Artifice of Absorption.* Called by John Shoptaw (218), "the best introduction to Language poetry likely to be written," this essay in poem format immediately foregrounds the question of genre by its own form. The operative vocabulary of *Artifice* consists of two main terms, "absorption" and "artifice," and effects its argument through an omnibus of brief reviews of who's who in the practice of contemporary poetry. The essay is an excursion, concisely stated, into poetry's terms and gives, through references to other crucial texts in the terrain, specific descriptions of the textual particulars that constitute such writing. The achievement of *Artifice of Absorption* is that it similarly does not simply map a new territory but occupies it through the active engagement of its writing.

Another important theme for Bernstein is the one evoked by the title of *Rough Trades,* that poetry is not only a vocation "business"—and a "rough" one. (See also the poem "Safe Methods of Business," which appears in *The Sophist.*) This theme is more than literary; it is true to Bernstein's generous and activist involvement with poetry. As Jerome McGann has suggested, "The meaning of the work of poets like Lyn Hejinian and Bernstein is partly a function of their involvement with the social and material production of texts" (*Black Riders* 113), and, "like Morris and Pound, both have been actively involved in every aspect of poetry's production—from writing to book design to editing to distribution" (*Black Riders* 187, n. 32). Bernstein's activeness in the "business end" of poetry is not only on principle but out of necessity, given poetry's low status in the publishing industry. It may also reflect the engagement with "commerce" Bernstein saw in his father. Bernstein's poem "Sentences My Father Used" may also provide information about this influence and also stands partly as a meditation, for Bernstein, on growing up Jewish in New York City.

Charles Bernstein is sometimes considered a "difficult" poet. Such a view, however, compromises the difficulty of approaching his written work. The work is, above all, an engagement with its own possibilities. The body of Bernstein's writing is much more than a collection of texts; it is evidence collected in a dynamic investigation not only of language, but inside language. This writing leaves no leaf unturned in exploring textual dimensions, artifices, and apparatuses. It is a record that cannot be collected in a single volume because the disparate nature of each investigation must, of necessity, modify the form it undertakes. As Bernstein has said, "We don't know what Art is or does but we are forever finding out" ("Optimism" 168). Bernstein's work, rather than being difficult, positions the text, its reader, and its meanings into a constellation of activities that open new possibilities made real in writing.

CRITICAL RECEPTION

The most important early event in the reception of Bernstein's work was the 1982 publication of the "Charles Bernstein Issue" of *The Difficulties*, edited by Tom Beckett. Containing critical pieces, homages, and poems, contributors include Ron Silliman, Robert Creeley, Bob Perelman, Jackson Mac Low, Barrett Watten, Alan Davies, and others. This issue of *The Difficulties* is a crucial critical document. There is a variety of responses to Bernstein's work in this collection, such as that of James Sherry: "[Bernstein's] sentences reflect the constant intrusion of the world on the mind and the impossibility of meditation/mediation. . . . Bernstein is not concerned with grammar and sentences as correct . . . [but with] . . . patterns of thought in the patterns of [his] phrases rather than given standards of the shape of the thought as in the grammatically oriented notion of the sentence" (45–46). Craig Watson writes that "the apprehension of meaning is not conditioned by substance or continuity alone, but by the constitution of relations in a network of possibility; the object is mediated and named by our whole experience with it. Cognition is made up of a vast circuitry within which language is gestural and continually subjective. Through these circuits we conduct and create our selves, a reality" (86). Bob Perelman writes that "Bernstein's . . . language-centered writing never fails to be centered around the person, and the pressures of culture and history that thwart language's power" ("A Note" 90).

The recent critical reception of Bernstein's work has commanded the attention of leading national scholars. Particularly important are John Shoptaw's chapter on Bernstein and Ashbery in *The Tribe of John: John Ashbery and Contemporary Poetry*; Hank Lazer's review of *Dark City* in the *American Poetry Review*; Jerome McGann's discussions of Bernstein in *Black Riders, Contemporary Poetry Meets Modern Theory*, and *New Literary History*; Bob Perelman's "Write the Power" in *The Marginalization of Poetry: Language Writing and Literary History*; and Marjorie Perloff's discussions of Bernstein in *Poetic License, Radical Artifice*, and *The Dance of the Intellect*. For example, of Bernstein's poem "Dysraphism," Perloff remarks that it "playfully exploits such rhetorical figures as pun, anaphora, epiphora, metathesis, epigram, anagram, and neologism to create a seamless web of reconstituted words" and that "sensitivity to etymologies and latent meanings is reflected in the poem itself, which is an elaborate 'dysfunctional fusion of embryonic parts,' a 'disturbance of stress, pitch, and rhythm of speech' in the interest of a new kind of urban 'rhapsody' " (Dance 230). Hank Lazer has written of Bernstein's "compositional arsenal," which includes, according to Lazer, "a wide-ranging vocabulary . . . , the recurrence of a peculiarly clotted sound-effect, a kind of line and sound that is deliberately but interestingly difficult to say, [and] a kind of antimellifluousness" (39). McGann writes, "Most of [Bernstein's] poetry does not surrender any of the territory of writing, any of the means to meaning. As a consequence, his writing extends across an unusual semiotic range—from the most minimal

textual units, pre-morphemic, to the most complex rhetorical and semantic structures; and it carries out this 'opening of the field' not as an exercise in, or
display of, imaginative mastery, but as an enactment—literally—of the world
of writing'' (*Black Riders* 111).

Bernstein's critical reception has been most noticeable in the numerous recent
conference panels on his work and in the number of scholarly and poetry gatherings at which he has been a featured or keynote speaker. Bernstein's presence
in the world of contemporary literature is assured; his presence in literary gatherings rarely seems to be less than spectacular. His vision of a multidiscourse
writing is one that has been well received among wide circles of poetry practitioners. Thus, a measure of his success can be seen in his ever-increasing
public—and this is a measure that is not only figural but textual. "It is measure
we have seen," Bernstein writes. "That language is measure. And it is with
this that we make our music—by ourselves, privately (if so that the measure's
heard)—a private act, a revelation of the public. So that writing that had seemed
to distance itself from us by its solitude—opaque, obscure, difficult—now seems
by its distance more public, its distance the measure of its music. A privacy in
which the self itself disappears and leaves us the world'' ("Thought's" 81–82).

BIBLIOGRAPHY

Works by Charles Bernstein

Parsing. New York: Asylum's Press, 1976.

Shade. College Park, MD: Sun and Moon Press, 1978.

L=A=N=G=U=A=G=E. Ed., with Bruce Andrews. New York: 1978–1981; vol. 4
    copublished as *Open Letter* 5, no. 1. Toronto: 1982.

Disfrutes. Needham, MA: Peter Ganick, 1979a; rpt. Needham, MA: Potes and Poets
    Press, 1981; Elmwood, CT: Potes and Poets Press, 1985.

Poetic Justice. Baltimore: Pod Books, 1979b.

Senses of Responsibility. Berkeley, CA: Tuumba Press, 1979c; rpt. Providence, RI: Par-
    adigm Press, 1989.

Controlling Interests. New York: Roof Books, 1980a; rpt. 1986.

Legend, with Bruce Andrews, Steve McCaffery, Ron Silliman, and Ray DiPalma. New
    York: L=A=N=G=U=A=G=E/Segue, 1980b.

The Occurrence of Tune. New York: Segue Books, 1981a; photographs by Susan Bee
    (Laufer).

Stigma. Barrytown, NY: Station Hill Press, 1981b.

Islets/Irritations. New York: Jordan Davies, 1983a; rpt. New York: Roof Books, 1992.

Resistance. Windsor, VT: Awede Press, 1983b.

The L=A=N=G=U=A=G=E Book. Ed., with Bruce Andrews. Carbondale: Southern
    Illinois University Press, 1984.

"The Academy in Peril," "An Interview with Tom Beckett," "Thought's Measure,"
    and "Writing and Method." *Content's Dream: Essays 1975–1984*. Los Angeles:
    Sun and Moon Press, 1986a; rpt. Sun and Moon Classics, 1994.

Content's Dream: Essays 1975–1984. Los Angeles: Sun and Moon Press, 1986b; rpt. Sun and Moon Classics, 1994.

Artifice of Absorption. Philadelphia: Singing Horse Press/Paper Air, 1987a; published as *Paper Air* 4, no. 1.

The Sophist. Los Angeles: Sun and Moon Press, 1987b.

Veil. Madison, WI: Xexoxial Editions, 1987c.

Four Poems. Tucson: Chax Press, 1988.

The Nude Formalism, with Susan Bee. Los Angeles: 20 Pages [Sun and Moon], 1989.

The Absent Father in Dumbo. La Laguna, Islas Canarias, Spain: Zasterle Press, 1990a.

Patterns/Contexts/Time; A Symposium on Contemporary Poetry. Ed., with Phillip Foss. Santa Fe, NM: Recursos de Santa Fe, 1990b (issued as *Tyuonyi* 6/7).

The Politics of Poetic Form: Poetry and Public Policy. Ed. New York: Roof, 1990c.

Fool's Gold, with Susan Bee. Tucson: Chax Press, 1991a.

Rough Trades. Los Angeles: Sun and Moon Press, 1991b.

"In the Middle of Modernism" and "Optimism and Critical Excess." *A Poetics*. Cambridge: Harvard University Press, 1992a.

A Poetics. Cambridge: Harvard University Press, 1992b.

Live at the Ear. Ed. Pittsburgh: Elemenope/Oracular Recordings, 1993a (audio anthology of Ear Inn readings on compact disk).

Dark City. Los Angeles: Sun and Moon Press, 1994.

The Subject. Buffalo, NY: Meow Press, 1995.

Republics of Reality, 1975–1995. Los Angeles: Sun and Moon Press, 1996.

Little Orphan Anagram, with Susan Bee. New York: Granary Books, 1997.

"Reznikoff's Nearness." *Sulfur* 32 (Spring 1993b): 6–38.

"Stein's Identity." *Modern Fiction Studies* 42: 3 (Fall 1996): 485–88.

My Way: Speeches and Poems. Chicago: University of Chicago Press, 1998.

Works about Charles Bernstein

Beckett, Tom, ed. "Charles Bernstein Issue." *The Difficulties* 2, No. 1 (Fall 1982).

Glazier, Loss Pequeño. "Charles Bernstein" entry. *Dictionary of Literary Biography* 169: American Poets since World War II. 5th series. Ed. Joseph Conte. Detroit: Gale, 1996a: 13–28.

———. "Charles Bernstein: An Autobiographical Interview." *Contemporary Authors Autobiography Series*. Detroit: Gale, 1996b: 31–50.

Lazer, Hank. "Charles Bernstein's *Dark City*: Polis, Policy, and the Policing of Poetry." *American Poetry Review* 24, No. 5 (September/October 1995): 35–44.

McGann, Jerome. *Black Riders: The Visible Language of Modernism*. Princeton: Princeton University Press, 1993.

———. "Charles Bernstein's 'The Simply' " in *Contemporary Poetry Meets Modern Theory*. Ed. A. Easthope. UK: Harvester-Wheatsheaf, 1991; Toronto: University of Toronto Press, 1993: 34–39.

[as Mack, Anne; Rome, J. J.; Mannejc, Georg], "Private Enigmas and Critical Functions, with Particular Reference to the Writing of Ch. Bernstein." *New Literary History* 22, No. 2 (Spring 1991): 441–64.

Perelman, Bob. "A Note on Sentences My Father Used." *The Difficulties* 2, No. 1 (Fall 1982): 88–91.

————. "Write the Power." *American Literary History* 6, No. 2 (Summer 1994): 306–24.

————. "Write the Power." *The Marginalization of Poetry: Language Writing and Literary Theory*. Princeton: Princeton University Press, 1996: 79–95.

Perloff, Marjorie. *The Dance of the Intellect: Studies in the Poetry of the Pound Tradition*. Cambridge and New York: Cambridge University Press, 1985.

————. *Poetic License: Essays on Modernist and Postmodernist Lyric*. Evanston, IL: Northwestern University Press, 1990.

————. *Radical Artifice: Writing Poetry in the Age of Media*. Chicago: University of Chicago Press, 1991.

Sherry, James. "Method to the Self." *The Difficulties* 2, No. 1 (Fall 1982): 45–47.

Shoptaw, John. "The Music of Construction: Measure and Polyphony in Ashbery and Bernstein." In *The Tribe of John: John Ashbery and Contemporary Poetry*. Ed. Susan Schultz. Tuscaloosa: University of Alabama Press, 1994: 211–57.

Silliman, Ron. "Controlling Interests." *The New Sentence*. New York: Roof Books, 1985: 171–84.

Watson, Craig. "Fluid Islands." *The Difficulties* 2, No. 1 (Fall 1982): 86–87.

Watten, Barrett. "Controlling Interests." *The Difficulties* 2, No. 1 (Fall 1982): 97.

CHANA BLOCH

(1940–)

Merle Bachman

BIOGRAPHY

Chana Bloch's life as a Jewish poet, translator and scholar has its roots in the Bronx, New York. She was born there on March 15, 1940, to Russian-Jewish parents and grew up in the noise and hubbub of an intensely urban, Jewish environment.

From an early age, Bloch developed a passion for both Judaic studies and English literature. After earning her B.A. at Cornell University (1961), she went on to obtain master's degrees in both Judaic studies and English at Brandeis University (in 1963 and 1965, respectively). Bloch's decision to pursue a Ph.D. in English literature was, ironically, influenced by her attachment to Israel. The degree would enable her to obtain more secure employment at the Hebrew University in Jerusalem, where she had taught English in 1964–1967. Bloch was accepted into the University of California at Berkeley, where she combined her academic interests by focusing on the English metaphysical poet George Herbert and his relationship to biblical literature. By the time she graduated in 1975, Bloch had married an Israeli colleague; however, instead of returning to Jerusalem, she settled down with him in Berkeley. (Ariel Bloch, a scholar of Semitic languages, has provided linguistic support for Chana's translations of Hebrew poetry. Their marriage, which began in 1969, ended in 1994.)

During her years of pursuing an academic career, Bloch began to write and publish both her own poetry and translations of Yiddish and Israeli poets. Since the 1960s, when her translations first began appearing in Jewish periodicals, to the present, Chana Bloch has built an impressive reputation at the intersection of her passions for poetry, translation, and scholarship. She has published seven books in the past two decades, including a major retrospective of Yehuda Amichai's poetry, a critical study of George Herbert, and two volumes of her own poetry. Bloch has won numerous awards for all facets of her work, including the Discovery Award, given by the Poetry Center at the 92d Street Y in New York City, for her poetry (1974); the Columbia University Translation Center's Translation Award for *A Dress of Fire*, a translation of the early work of Israeli poet Dahlia Ravikovitch (1978); a National Endowment for the Humanities Fellowship (1980); the Conference on Christianity and Literature's Book of the Year Award for *Spelling the Word: George Herbert and the Bible* (1986); the Bay Area Book Reviewers Association Translation Award for *Selected Poetry of Yehuda Amichai* (1987); and a National Endowment for the Arts Creative Writing Fellowship (1989–1990). Bloch has also raised two sons, now in their early twenties, and has been a member of the English Department at Mills College in Oakland since 1975, where she also directs the creative writing program.

MAJOR WORKS AND THEMES

Chana Bloch is well known as a translator of Yehuda Amichai, Israel's most beloved contemporary poet. Her translations of the *Selected Poetry* (in partnership with Stephen Mitchell), published in 1986, is the most authoritative edition of Amichai's work available in English. Bloch has said of Amichai's poetry that she is "attracted by a certain astringent quality of mind, a skeptical intelligence that is impatient with camouflage and pathos and self-deceit, that insists on questioning even what it loves" (*Selected Poetry*, Foreword xi). Such a description might well apply to Bloch's own writing. In the domestic space that Bloch's poetry creates, of the immediate family and of the body itself, there are ample intelligence and questioning, coupled with an intensity of perception that lays bare the core of everyday experience.

Despite the interval that separates Bloch's two volumes of poetry—*The Secrets of the Tribe* (1981) and *The Past Keeps Changing* (1992)—the poems they contain form a continuous body of work. Six of the 1981 poems even appear in slightly revised versions in the later book, which adds to the sense of questions that continue to preoccupy her and a vision gradually unfolding. Family is a predominant theme; the poems explore with precision the ambivalent and charged relationships between parent and child, husband and wife, the familial present and past, and (in Amichai's phrase, which Bloch uses at one point as an epigraph) the "hard love" that informs them. *The Secrets of the Tribe*, as an initial journey from the family into a larger world, is permeated with a "tribal," Jewish consciousness. One section of the book, "In the Beginning," contains poems that retell, midrashlike, familiar stories from Genesis. Other poems allude in fresh, provocative ways to the Bible: "Like Adam in his first/ happiness,/ you come out/ and pee in the garden" ("In the Garden" 47). The poet's complex relationship to her Judaism is conveyed in the last stanza of "The Converts": "The converts sway in white silk,/ their necks bent forward in yearning/ like swans,/ and I covet/ what they think we've got'' (32). In *The Past Keeps Changing*, the poet acknowledges, ''The past we started hasn't/ finished with us'' (''Noli Me Tangere'' 26)—yet neither has she finished with the past. ''Fingerprints'' ends: ''Everything happens only once but/I go on asking, and asking is/ the quickest way back'' (18). Yet as Bloch takes up the old questions, the preoccupation with Jewishness recedes into an occasional detail— such as a memory of Jerusalem arising out of the ''green dust'' of a Berkeley street, in the same poem.

In her review of *The Past Keeps Changing*, Frances Mayes writes, ''Chana Bloch's poems could have been written in a circle of lamplight on the kitchen table'' (21). While the poems may not range far outside that domestic ''circle,'' they are stark illuminations of what transpires within it. Mayes adds that although Bloch's poems ''come from the domestic center, they are not mild, not safe, and are never predictable'' (21).

Illustrating this lack of ''safety'' is the ambivalent sense of enclosure and secrecy the poems associate with family, a kind of captivity that flares with both pain and love. In ''The Family,'' the poet describes a set of nesting Russian dolls: ''Every morning we are lifted/ out of each other. . . . At night we drop back/ into each other's darkness. . . . We sleep/ staring at the inside'' (3). Leaving the family of origin and creating one's own family does not mean escaping enclosure but reestablishing it anew. In ''Against Gravity,'' the poet addresses her husband: ''You're secreting a silence around you,/ iridescent, slippery.'' In a later stanza, she continues: ''I carried the child for weeks without telling,/ letting the secret/ feed me. Only you and I knew/ and we closed/ around each other'' (49–50). The powerful desires of mothering are summoned in ''The Ghost Worm Monster'': ''I want him buttoned around me/ against the cold, the way he wants/ to float inside me again, / swaddled in water'' (41). In a series of remarkable poems entitled ''In the Land of the Body,'' the poet confronts a disease that is itself concealed—''a lump of pain/ in a hidden pocket'' (68), a dangerous enclosure within her own body to which ''the hand listens hard'' (71).

The compact, lyric poems in both Bloch's books embody a quality of unusual attentiveness, as if listening for something beyond silence. ''Anniversary'' ends: ''Rosin of sunlight slides up and down/ a string of spiderweb,/ bowing a high note. The eye/ can hear it'' (*The Past* 58). What Chana Bloch's poems ''listen'' for might be what she has called ''the space at the center of everything'' (''Firewood'' 44).

CRITICAL RECEPTION

Chana Bloch's poetry has been critically well received. Her poems have been published in numerous prestigious journals, such as *Ironwood, Ploughshares,* and *Poetry,* and have been included in more than fifteen anthologies, including *The Pushcart Prize, VI: Best of the Small Presses* (1981). *The Secrets of the*

Tribe was a finalist for the Yale Younger Poets Award and won favorable notice in the *San Francisco Review of Books* (January 1981) and *The American Poetry Review* (January 1982). Positive reviews of *The Past Keeps Changing* appeared in the *American Book Review*, the *San Jose Mercury News, Poetry* magazine, and several other periodicals. Her work has been appreciated for its focus on "the haunted domestic landscape . . . what it means to be a woman in the world" (Barresi 42–43).

Frances Mayes detected George Herbert's influence in Bloch's "poetic rigor"—which is not surprising, considering that Bloch spent a period of fifteen years, off and on, engaged in a critical study of Herbert's poetry. The resulting volume, *Spelling the Word: George Herbert and the Bible* (1985), won appreciative reviews in seven critical and academic periodicals, including *Renaissance Quarterly* and *The Times Literary Supplement.*

Bloch's translations, however, have attracted the widest notice, with reviews in the *New York Times Book Review* and *The Nation*. This may be due not only to the quality of her translations but, at least in Yehuda Amichai's case, the stature of the poet she has chosen to translate, who, as reviewer Mark Rudman commented, is "one of the half-dozen leading poets in the world" (32). Rudman also noted that while Amichai's handful of translators "have all ably conveyed the concrete particulars of his world . . . Bloch and Mitchell get inside the text and render a subtler, more complex and formally expert Amichai than we have seen before in English" (33). Bloch is currently at work on a new volume of translations from Amichai's magnum opus "Open Closed Open," in collaboration with University of California, Berkeley-based scholar and critic Chana Krounfeld.

Bloch's efforts to bring the poetry of Dahlia Ravikovitch (lesser known than Amichai outside Israel) to an English-speaking audience have also been praised. About *A Dress of Fire* (1978), Bloch's translation of Ravikovitch's early work, Robert Alter commented in the *New York Times Book Review*: "Miss Ravikovitch's poems . . . have been beautifully refashioned by Chana Bloch, herself an accomplished poet, into English verse strong in diction, nice in idiom, taut in rhythm. I do not think it is an exaggeration to say that many of these poems read almost as well in Mrs. Bloch's versions as they do in the Hebrew." In 1989, *The Window: New and Selected Poems* appeared, an anthology of more than seventy poems spanning Ravikovitch's career (translated in collaboration with Ariel Bloch). They include a selection of outspokenly political and controversial poems that had originally been published in protest of Israel's Lebanon War. Bloch has discussed the decision to translate these poems and make them available to a wider audience in an essay, "The Politics of Translation," originally published in *Tikkun*. As a result of Bloch's bold decision, Ravikovitch's complexity as a poet—and an Israeli woman—is more fully revealed.

Chana Bloch's most recent work of translation was *The Biblical Song of Songs* (1995) (in collaboration with Ariel Bloch). In the volume's Afterword, Robert Alter writes that "the translation . . . brings us closer to the magical freshness of this ancient Hebrew love poetry than has any other English version." (27)

BIBLIOGRAPHY

Works by Chana Bloch

Poetry

The Secrets of the Tribe. New York: Sheep Meadow Press, 1981.
The Past Keeps Changing. New York: Sheep Meadow Press, 1992.
Mrs. Dumpty. Madison: University of Wisconsin Press, 1998.

Translations from Hebrew

Ravikovitch, Dahlia. *A Dress of Fire*. New York: Sheep Meadow Press, 1978.
Ravikovitch, Dahlia. *The Window: New and Selected Poems*. In collaboration with Ariel
    Bloch. New York: Sheep Meadow Press, 1989.
Amichai, Yehuda. *Selected Poetry*. In collaboration with Stephen Mitchell.
New York: Harper and Row, 1986; reissued HarperCollins, 1992; rev. and expanded in
    collaboration with Stephen Mitchell, Berkeley: University of California Press,
    1996.
The Biblical Song of Songs: A New Translation, Introduction and Commentary. In col-
    laboration with Ariel Bloch. New York: Random House, 1995.

Translations from Yiddish

Singer, Isaac Bashevis. "A Wedding in Brownsville." *Commentary* 37 (March 1964);
    reprinted in *Short Friday*. New York: Farrar, Straus, and Giroux, 1964.
Glatstein, Jacob, Abraham Sutzkever, and Aaron Zeitlin. *A Treasury of Yiddish Poetry*.
    Ed. Irving Howe and Eliezer Greenberg. New York: Holt, Rinehart and Winston,
    1969.
Glatstein, Jacob, and Abraham Sutzkever. *The Penguin Book of Modern Yiddish Verse*.
    Ed. Irving Howe et al. New York: Viking, 1987.

Selected Scholarship, Criticism, Essays

Spelling the Word: George Herbert and the Bible. Berkeley: University of California
    Press, 1985.
"Shakespeare's Sister" (review article on Harold Bloom's *The Book of J*). *Iowa Review*
    (Fall 1991): 66–77.
"The Politics of Translation." In *The Writer in the Jewish Community*. Ed. Richard
    Siegel and Tamar Sofer. Rutherford, NJ: Fairleigh Dickinson University Press,
    1993, 67–76.

Works about Chana Bloch

Alter, Robert. Rev. of *A Dress of Fire*, "Hebrew to English." *New York Times Book
    Review*, April 15, 1979, 27.

Barresi, Dorothy. Rev. of *The Past Keeps Changing*, "Spirituality and Memory." *American Book Review*, October/November 1993, 42–43.

Drury, John. Rev. of *Spelling the Word*, "Intuitions of Blessedness." *Times Literary Supplement*, February 28, 1986, 228.

Flamm, Matthew. Rev. of *Selected Poetry* "War—What Is It Good For?" *The Village Voice*, April 14, 1987, 54–55.

Gilbert, Sandra. Rev. of *The Past Keeps Changing*, "How These New Homegirls Sing." *Poetry*, August 1992, 285–304.

Gordin, Jeremy. Rev. of *The Past Keeps Changing*, "An Almost Awful Honesty: The Poetry of Chana Bloch." *Literary Review, Northern California Jewish Bulletin*, July 10, 1992, 10–11.

Hirsch, Edward. Rev. of *Selected Poetry*, "In a Language Torn from Sleep." *The New York Times Book Review*, August 3, 1986, 14–15.

Leider, Emily. Rev. of *The Secrets of the Tribe*, "Literary San Francisco and Points Distant." *San Francisco Review of Books* 6, January/February 1981, 4, 5–6.

Mayes, Frances. Rev. of *The Past Keeps Changing*, "The Department of the Interior." *San Jose Mercury News*, May 24, 1992, 21.

Owens, Rochelle. Rev. of *The Window: New and Selected Poems. American Book Review*, September/October 1989, 69.

Piret, Michael. Rev. of *Spelling the Word. Review of English Studies*, February 1987, 190–96.

Post, Jonathan. Rev. of *Spelling the Word*, "Reforming the Temple: Recent Criticism of George Herbert." *John Donne Journal* 3, 1984, 221–47.

Rudman, Mark. Rev. of *Selected Poetry*, " 'Car, Bomb, God.' " *The Nation*, December 6, 1986, 32–33.

Smith, Dave. Rev. of *The Secrets of the Tribe*, "Some Recent American Poetry: Come All Ye Fair and Tender Ladies." *The American Poetry Review*, January/February 1982, 36–40.

STANLEY BURNSHAW (1906–)

Michael Taub and Joel Shatzky

BIOGRAPHY

Stanley Burnshaw was born in New York on June 20, 1906. He is the son of immigrants who fled Russia to escape the oppression of the Jews that followed the pogroms of the 1880s. Burnshaw tells their story in his trilogy of novels, *The Refusers* (1981). His father received a doctorate in philology from Columbia but rather than become an academic decided to work for a home for Jewish orphans. The home was in Pleasantville, New York, where the Burnshaws lived from 1912 until 1924. For one year, in 1924, Burnshaw studied at Columbia. His studies there were cut short because the family moved to Pittsburgh. He continued, however, at the University of Pittsburgh, from which he graduated in 1925. Determined to become a teacher and writer, he took on a series of jobs involving editing, copywriting, and publishing. He started his own magazine, *Poetry Folio*, where in 1927 he published his first poems.

In 1927 Burnshaw traveled to France, where he met Andre Spire, a powerful influence on his writing career. Their relationship produced Burnshaw's first major publication, *Andre Spire and His Poetry* (1933), a volume of criticism and translations from French into English. After returning to America in 1928, he continued to write while working as an advertising manager for the Hecht Company, as well as a contributing editor for *Modern Quarterly*. In 1933, he received his M.A. from Cornell.

The socioeconomic turmoil of the late 1920s and early 1930s caused him to become involved in leftist causes; he even flirted briefly with communist ideology. In 1939 he started his own firm, the Dryden Press, a company that twenty years later merged with Holt, Rinehart, and Winston. From 1958 until 1962 Burnshaw taught at New York University while editing a variety of books on poetry and criticism. In the 1970s Burnshaw retired to Martha's Vineyard but continued to lecture, write, and give poetry readings.

MAJOR WORKS AND THEMES

In addition to poetry, Burnshaw has written a great deal of fiction, translation, and criticism. By far, the most substantive statements on his Jewishness are found in his prose narratives, *The Refusers: An Epic of the Jews, A Trilogy of Novels Based on Three Heroic Lives* (1981) and *My Friend, My Father* (1985).

Early and Late Testament (1952), the author's first major volume of poems, contains partly reworked political pieces from the 1930s, new, philosophical meditations on the unity of body, mind, and spirit, a lament for a dead child, and speculations on the future of humanity in the age of technology.

Similar concerns are found in his 1972 volume *In the Terrified Radiance*; for our purposes, though, it is his next work, *Mirages: Travel Notes in the Promised Land* (1977), that deserves attention. This is a fifty-page poem about modern Israel, its tragic history, the Arab–Israeli conflict, and what a Jewish state means to an American Jew like Burnshaw.

In the critical arena Burnshaw is best known for his innovative approach to poetry translation. He launched a series of works from European literatures and from Hebrew, titled, *The Modern Poem Itself*, but instead of the usual translation, poems are reprinted in the original and given English phonetic transcriptions and analyses. The coeditors of the Hebrew volume are critic Ezra Spicehandler and Israeli poet and translator T. Carmi. Critics agree, however, that *The Seamless Web: Language–Thinking, Creature–Knowledge* (1970), is Burnshaw's major scholarly work. In it, Burnshaw tries to define the nature of poetry and its function.

CRITICAL RECEPTION

Most of the criticism (for the most part favorable) centers on Burnshaw's contributions to poetry scholarship and literary translation. Some praise him for his direct, simple, narrative style, in sharp contrast with the academic jargon of many scholars. He is hailed as an original, complex poet, a man concerned with humanity and the preservation of the earth's natural resources.

BIBLIOGRAPHY

Works by Stanley Burnshaw

Poetry

Early and Late Testament. New York: Dial Press, 1952.
In the Terrified Radiance. New York: Braziller, 1972.
Mirages: Travel Notes in the Promised Land. Garden City, New York: Doubleday, 1977.

Criticism

The Seamless Web: Language–Thinking, Creature–Knowledge. New York: Braziller, 1970–1972.
Robert Frost Himself. New York: Braziller, 1986.
A Stanley Burnshaw Reader. Athens: University of Georgia Press, 1990.

Novels

The Refusers: An Epic of the Jews, a Trilogy of Novels Based on Three Heroic Lives. New York: Horizon, 1981.
Andre Spire and His Poetry. Philadelphia: Centaur Press, 1933.

Translations

Coedited with Ezra Spicehandler and T. Carmi. *The Modern Hebrew Poem Itself, from the Beginnings to the Present: Sixty-Nine Poems in a New Presentation.* New York: Holt, Rinehart and Winston, 1965, reprinted, Harvard University Press, 1989.

Works about Stanley Burnshaw

Breé, Germaine. "The Poet Is Always Present." *The American Scholar* 39, No. 3, Summer 1970, 522–24.
Dale, Peter. Review of *Seamless Web. Agenda*, Autumn 1974, 32–39.
Dickey, James. *The New York Times Book Review*, September 24, 1972, 4.
Enright, D. J. *Man Is an Onion: Reviews and Essays.* London: Chatto and Windus, 1972, 156–62.
Walsh, Chad. *Book World—The Washington Post*, May 22, 1977, 4.

RICHARD J. FEIN (1929–   )

Sheva Zucker

BIOGRAPHY

Had Richard J. Fein, poet, translator, memoirist, and essayist, been born a generation or two earlier and in Bialystok or Berdichev rather than in Brooklyn, he probably would have been a Yiddish and not an Anglo-Jewish poet. But the focus of his poetry would have been quite different, for his passion for Yiddish, his yearning to reclaim a language that, as he says in his memoir, *The Dance of Leah*, "was my language, a language I had never mastered, but that lurked within me at all times" (16), informs much of his poetry. Indeed, through his multifaceted exploration of his connection to Yiddish he will find his unique place in Jewish-American poetry.

His biography would not lead one to suspect that he, more than other Jewish-American poets of his generation, would be drawn so deeply to Yiddish. Born in Brooklyn, December 5, 1929, to an American-born mother and a father who came to the United States from Poland at age two, he went to New York public schools and had the typical after-school Jewish education. There, as he describes in *The Dance of Leah*, he was introduced to Yiddish only because his Hebrew teachers, despairing of holding his attention, thought he might show more interest in a "living language." At the time, it seemed this exposure had little impact. He attended Brooklyn College and earned both a B.A. and M.A. in English in 1953 and 1955 respectively, and in 1960 a Ph.D. in English from New York University. He considers Walt Whitman and Robert Lowell, about whom he wrote a book (1970), to be his greatest poetic influences and feels particularly connected to Lowell's *Life Studies*. In 1955 he married the former Helen Sherin, a sociologist, and they are the parents of two daughters. From 1963 to 1991 he taught English literature and, in his later years, also Yiddish at the State University of New York at New Paltz. There he served as the coordinator of the Jewish Studies Program from 1977 to 1983. His teaching also took him to the University of Puerto Rico from 1961 to 1963 and the University of Madras in 1972–1973. Only in the mid-1980s did he begin writing poetry seriously, and in 1992 he won the Maurice English Award for a distinguished book of poetry published in an author's sixth decade of life.

MAJOR WORKS AND THEMES

Similarly, only late in his career, in 1975, did Fein return to the Yiddish that he had rejected in his childhood, becoming a fellow at the Max Weinreich Center for Advanced Jewish Studies at the YIVO Institute for Jewish Research in New York. He began studying the language, as he writes in *The Dance of Leah*, because he felt that "[t]he Yiddish language and culture were permanently wounded and I connected my fate to this. American literature did not need me— Yiddish literature did. Then, not long into my work, I realized that I needed Yiddish even more than it needed me" (31).

"I have been vivified by Yiddish," he says in an article in *Midstream* (April 1994), "at the very time it dwindles away. I can say of Yiddish literature and myself: in its end is my beginning" (8). Fein expresses these insights in his poem "Yiddish" in *To Move into the House*, writing, "It's good to know/ you're good for nothing now,/ except for the love I show you./ We could never have come together/ if you were still teeming on the streets,/ re-inventing yourself for textbooks,/ commercials, psychotherapy" (47). He also articulates these themes with characteristic humor and irony in "The Yiddish Poet Yankev Glatshteyn Visits Me in the Coffee Shop," in *At the Turkish Bath*. Here, in a vision, Glatshteyn tells Fein, his translator, "It's all well and good you translate me./ You need it more than I do./ I'm in Yiddish for all time./ . . . But you./ You have to translate yourself into English" (46).

Indeed, Fein likes to fancy himself, as he writes in his article "What Can Yiddish Mean to an American Poet?" *Shofar*, Summer 1996, as "the last Yiddish poet who, however, writes in English" (81). But while the Yiddish poets to whom he feels connected, such as Yankev Glatshteyn, had as their great theme the struggle to define themselves as Jews in a world where belief was no longer possible, Fein searches not for God but for that almost vanished world, both in Europe and in New York, where Jews could reject God but still remain profoundly Jewish. As such, he invokes the very physical place, the sights on the streets of Brooklyn, the hairy, sweating bodies of Jewish men in a *shvitz* (steam bath), or the steamy vapors rising from his European-born grandmother's hot glass of tea. In his vigorous, but delicately nuanced, free verse filled with vivid, highly realistic images, he writes of many things such as nature, old age, other writers and artists, and love, often with a particularly Jewish twist. However, childhood, family, remembrances of Jewish life, and Yiddish itself, the background for all of these, are the frequently recurring themes in his poetry.

The epigram to his first book, *Kafka's Ear* (1990), "When I write, I seem to be in Lithuania," a quotation by the Polish poet Adam Mickiewicz when exiled in Paris, captures the essence of Fein's desire to write "as if," to reinvent that lost world, of both his childhood and, more generally, East European Jewish life on both sides of the Atlantic. The title of his second book, *At the Turkish Bath*, grounds this spiritual yearning in a physical world. In this work, Fein explores his link to *Yiddishkayt* (Yiddish culture) in a variety of possibly real and definitely imagined situations. See, for example, the poems "From the Imagined Life of Ruvn-Yankev Troonk," "Yiddish Lessons in Brighton Beach," and "At the Turkish Bath." In *To Move into the House* Fein reasserts his connection to this world and stresses that he need not, as he says in the title poem, "[w]ait for the dead to leave"; he may, in fact, take possession now. In the poem "Yiddish" he declares this new, strengthened connection: "How long it's taken for us to embrace, for our tongues to find each other." At last, Fein seems to be saying, he has found his voice within the house of poetry and of Yiddish poetry, in particular.

CRITICAL RECEPTION

Of Fein's *At the Turkish Bath*, Thomas Kinsella writes, "Richard J. Fein's is a strong book, written as a whole. There is a formal strength in the individual poems, and in the book as it develops—it grows with its subject. There is a full presentation of a Yiddish writer in an American city, in his setting and in his tradition."

On the jacket cover of *At the Turkish Bath*, M. L. Rosenthal comments on the spirit of Fein's work and the intense connection between him and the Yiddish world that informs much of his poetry: "These are poems of a generous spirit, in love with family memories (whether the buoyant or grievous) and with a fading world of ordinary Jewish life and speech. They are driven by a yearning to hold on to that world, and to the Yiddish of Sholem Aleichem and the moving poets whose artistry Richard Fein has long sought to convey in translation."

Albert Goldbarth, on the back cover of *To Move into the House*, calls Fein, "funky, lusty, glitzily and cynically worldywise; but . . . allied with the voices of Sacred Mystery, and with a deep reverence for the past. What a lively mix!"

Of his Glatshteyn translation, M. L. Rosenthal writes, "We're lucky indeed to have these sensitive, accurate translations by a gifted poet who is also an intelligent, informed reader."

Bloom and Wisse also refer to Fein's *Selected Poems of Yankev Glatshteyn*.

BIBLIOGRAPHY

Works by Richard J. Fein

Poetry

Kafka's Ear. Baltimore: New Poets Series, 1990.
At the Turkish Bath. Baltimore: Chestnut Hills Press, 1994.
To Move into the House. Baltimore: Chestnut Hills Press, 1996.

Translation

Selected Poems of Yankev Glatshteyn. Philadelphia: Jewish Publication Society, 1987.

Prose

Robert Lowell. Boston: G. K. Hall, 1970; Rev. ed., 1979.
The Dance of Leah. Cranbury, NJ: Cornwall Books, 1986.

Works about Richard J. Fein

Bloom, Harold. "Still Haunted by the Covenant." *New York Times Book Review* (January 31, 1988): 3.
Wisse, Ruth. "Found in America." *The New Republic* (September 18, 25, 1995): 52–57.

IRVING FELDMAN   (1928–)

Jennifer Lewin

BIOGRAPHY

Irving Feldman was born on Coney Island and attended City College and Columbia University. He has taught at the University of Puerto Rico, Kenyon College, and the University of Lyon and currently is Distinguished Professor in the Department of English at the State University of New York (SUNY)-Buffalo. He has received fellowship grants from the Guggenheim Foundation and the Academy of American Poets and in 1992 became a MacArthur fellow.

Often a mixture of colloquial diction, brave self-scrutiny, and thick, ethical quandaries, Feldman's poetry has been an original presence in American poetry for more than three decades. Tough-minded and morally serious, his poetry gains didactic power from resisting easy consolations for the pain of so many kinds of loss—loss of utopian illusions about the world, loss of a perfect relationship to language, loss of family members and lovers, and, lastly, loss of nice distinctions between these categories. He notices how words can, but often fail to, maintain our deeper feelings of connection both to individuals and to communities, subjecting his own ability to address these matters to no less attention than to the clearly inadequate answers. In his best poems, many of which take up questions of Jewish-American poetic identity, Feldman daringly tries to make sense of a bleak world in which social experience never quite provides answers we need but leads to unexpected realizations about our conventions for imagining them. Stylistically, his colloquial diction and windy, meaty sentences infuse his work with clarity and strength, making him more of a conversationalist than a formalist.

MAJOR WORKS AND THEMES

Feldman's treatment of Jewish themes is filtered through his emphasis on language. Harold Bloom prophesied: "A Jewry can survive without a Jewish language, but not without language, not without an intense, obsessive concern that far transcends what ordinarily we call literacy" (321). Feldman's poetry displays again and again evidence of his "intense, obsessive concern" (321) with a Jewish literacy and attempts to recover an elusive, often imagined relation to words in which shifting, colloquial rhythms extraordinarily pulse through his readers' minds. In three poetic subgenres that are never wholly disparate—the Holocaust elegy, lyrical reflections on urban Jewish immigrant life, and the retelling of stories from Genesis—Feldman brilliantly establishes his voice among the most powerful, ruminative, and witty contemporary poets.

In Holocaust elegies Feldman relentlessly pursues the metaissue of how contemporary poetry can meaningfully recognize the levels of self-awareness about the construction and ambitions of the growing genre. This distinguishes his work among a host of other poems that attempt to console the reader and survivor. In "The Pripet Marshes," for example, he explores the moral implications of the dramatization of scenes from the Old World, whose vividness simultaneously creates and mourns shtetl, ghetto, city life. Doesn't the poet-narrator, he asks, act as a stage manager, overseeing the creation of believable fictions whose conclusions are horrible, certain death? In "The Pripet Marshes" the narrator chooses "the moment before the Germans will arrive" in setting the scene:

> Often I think of my Jewish friends and seize them as they are
> and transport them in my mind to the shtetlach and ghettos,
>
> And set them walking the streets, visiting, praying in shul,
> feasting and dancing. The men I set to arguing, because I
> love dialectic and song—my ears tingle when I hear their
> voices—and the girls and women I set to promenading or to
> cooking in the kitchens, for the sake of their tiny feet and
> clever hands. (*New and Selected Poetry* 50)

The first word, "often," implies that the creation of such situations is habitual, and verbs like "seize" and "transport" chillingly suggest the poet's moral dubiousness in orchestrating them, "setting" his characters to the music of ordinary life. He catalogs the plot's strangers, friends, lovers, and family (a son, he says, "may stand for me"), brings them to the edge of annihilation, but remains in control of his fantasy: "But there isn't a second to lose, I snatch them all back,/ For when I want to, I can be a God" (*New and Selected Poetry* 51). In the end, however, the narrator joins the people he has brought to life and accepts a mysterious, violent loss of power: "But I can't hold out any longer. My mind clouds over./ I sink down as though drugged or beaten" (*New and Selected Poetry* 52). Alicia Ostriker has judiciously remarked that this poem "enacts the inability of the poetic imagination to defeat the brutality of history, of time, and of human evil" and that it "is a palpable theatricalizing of the scenario of holocaust as a form of pleasure" (110). Although the narrator puts his character in motion to satisfy his aesthetic and erotic pleasure, at times he discovers, poignantly, that they elude his grasp; one sister is "touched with a humanity I cannot exhaust" (110).

Ostriker's analysis can apply to "The Bystander at the Massacre." Additionally, M. L. Rosenthal has commented that George Segal, the sculptor whose work is the main subject of the long title poem of *All of Us Here*—the collection in which "The Bystander at the Massacre" appears—"enabled him to write about the Holocaust without naming it or even preempting it for Jewish experience only or primarily" (*The Poetry of Irving Feldman* 38). In this particular poem, the moral ambiguity belongs not to the narrator as much as to the spectator:

> The bystander at the massacre of innocents
> might have seen his own innocence among the dying
> had not the distance from the spectator of slaughter
> (not all that far off, really) given him the space
> to entertain a doubt—while it wrenched time backward
> and made everything appear unalterable and past
> even as everything kept on racing ahead.
> He might not believe or come in time to what he saw. (*All of Us Here* 14)

By using the line breaks in order to create end-stopped, distinct grammatical clauses, Feldman creates a shape of coherence within a confusing time-space continuum. Yet the illusionistic quality of that shape can be measured in the vagueness of the bystander's "doubt"—does he doubt what he sees, his innocence, his distance? The poem's next section moves to a meditation reminiscent of Auden and Stevens in its characterization of the "ordinariness" of human suffering:

> Is it curiosity? Or a kind of revery?
> or recollections of the city-dweller's pastime,
> watching people busily, simply, living in their lives
> —what can have stopped us here, like angel emissaries
> to a doomed town, to view them while they muse or walk
> about or work at their machines on a sunny day
> torn from the archives or the ordinary? (*All of Us Here* 15)

The narrator's positioning of himself (and other unidentified persons who form the poem's ambiguous "we") as a spectator becomes increasingly problematic as the poem develops, until its final stanza edges toward the unflinching realism that the collective had been trying to banish: "evasion expands to enormous/ complicity, explodes in the spectator's rage/ and demented scream for more bigger quicker death'' (*All of Us Here* 16). The demand for an escalation of violence augments that complicity, and the poem's ending refuses to console even its most naive readers.

"To the Six Million," the third elegy under consideration, is more conventional in tone and address than the previous two. It resembles other Holocaust elegies by Geoffrey Hill, Czeslaw Milosz, and Dan Pagis. Quietly and solemnly, it evokes a landscape saturated with "emptiness" from the perspective of an anonymous person inside a room peering out onto a cold, winter street. By declaring "And many are missing," instead of Hill's "Many have died" (in Feldman's "Of Commerce and Society"), Feldman allows the innumerable "many" greater mystery and emotional resonance and less closure since their status remains questionable, unknowable, something to feel agonized by and helpless toward. Traces of survivor guilt swell within him:

> Should I have been with them
> on other winter days in the snow
> of the camps and ghettos?
> And on the days of their death that was
> the acrid Polish air? (*New and Selected Poetry* 54)

One of the most striking features of Feldman's poems on the Holocaust is his tendency, as in much of his poetry, to resist the sweeping, consolatory gesture. Feldman allows himself the space to let unanswerable questions suspend themselves in air, here as well as in the repetition of "Dear ones, what can I say?" (*New and Selected Poetry* 57) in the second part of the poem. Like Milosz, who asks in "Dedication": "You whom I could not save/ Listen to me," Feldman acknowledges that the survivor's desire to be heard trying to discover the right questions is as integral a part of the work of elegy as finding answers. "Outrage Is Anointed by Levity," a poem whose earlier versions have been provocatively discussed at length by John Hollander (*The Poetry of Irving Feldman* 51–55), addresses these issues, but from the cleverly angered perspective of one who is tired of the smarminess of poets who pretend to be answering Adorno's question, "How can one write poetry after Auschwitz?" with every poetic effort. Among other things, Feldman has the good sense to know when he is and is not doing so.

A second category of Feldman's work is Jewish immigrant life in New York. These poems include "Assimilation" and "The Lost Language," from Feldman's first book of poems, *Works and Days*, "Scene of a Summer Morning" from his second book, *The Pripet Marshes*; "So It Happens" (*Lost Originals*); "Fresh Air: Social Constructions of Reality at Coney Island" (*Teach Me, Dear Sister*); and "The Call" (*All of Us Here*). In "Assimilation" the speaker has dreamed that he died and went to Heaven, where he is surrounded and suffocated by commercialized icons of urban Jewish life of the 1950s and 1960s, written out in Yiddishized English. The rhyme words "Miami Bich/ rich," "Wool-

woits/ skoits,'' and ''Las Vegals/ bagels'' contribute to the comic effect of
spoken languages struggling to accommodate one another. The next poem in
the collection, ''The Lost Language,'' is a much more serious, but rambling and
less focused, meditation on the kind of cultural survival possible for someone
whose connection to Yiddish culture is analogized to a meal that has been eaten
and forgotten. A new kind of survivor guilt emerges in this poem in the following declaration:

> For, after all, it's only disgrace,
> At the very best, to outlive
> (Half-monadnock, half-sieve)
> The saddest thing in the life of the race. (*New and Selected Poetry* 29)

Feldman's ABBA quatrain structure seems effortless in the context of his
casual, humble tone. The sense of shame evoked there is contrasted in a subsequent stanza with a yearning for a prelapsarian relationship to language. The
rhyming of ''reach'' and ''speech'' shows an awareness of the simplicity of
such a utopian vision:

> then there were words in the earth
> That were the things they named
> And lay like manna in easy reach,
> And when you spoke, there was speech. (*New and Selected Poetry* 29)

Language, effortlessly, can be consumed and satisfies; as manna, however, it
still recalls the spatial displacement of the Exodus just as Yiddish exemplifies
a common feature of much of diaspora Jewish culture. Another poem, ''Scene
of a Summer Morning,'' tells of a walk to the butcher shop taken by a young
boy and his mother. The boy, presumably horrified by the scenes of slaughter,
parodies the decalogue as the speaker declares of the ''storeman'' Yankel: ''daringly he takes the live animals/ in vain. Yankel, a life for a life!'' (*New and
Selected Poetry* 49). In ''The Call'' and ''So It Happens'' the subject is, once
again, the difficulty of communicating disappointed and diminishing expectations with life and love. ''So It Happens'' tells the story of a visit from ''a
small forgotten cousin/ from the other side'' trying to match names and faces
from a photograph with the relatives in front of him, believing he has made a
mistake while being assured by them that he has not. The mutual grief, whose
content is never made explicit, arises from his frustration (''Why am I always/
lost and lose my way to/ the appointed heart?'') as well as the relations' equally
moving emptiness; the poem's final two lines reveal that they ''yearn indeed to
become/ those pure incalculable names'' (*Lost Originals* 48). An unarticulated,
irreparable loss has occurred for both parties, as it has in ''The Call,'' where
an estranged relative's attempt to use a discussion of the weather as a pretext
for reestablishing close ties seems pathetic and, somehow, too familiar.

Finally, the third subgenre of poetry Feldman has explored is the reconfiguration of stories from Genesis. Although these poems are more characteristic of his early, rather than his recent, work, they remain powerful examples of contemporary biblical mythology. "Flood" imagines a postdiluvian world in which voices are inflected by immigrant Jewish syntax; after the first day of rain, the grumpy, but patient, speaker confesses, "Everything seemed easier./ In the streets a little mud" (*New and Selected Poetry* 4). "Father and Son" rewrites the Akedah in an exercise in negation, presenting King Lear's world, where the "pitiless son" and father stay fixed in the "daily deadlock, their form of murder":

> Not sacrifice: murder. For it matters
> that no command has brought together
> the proud and loving father, the eager son,
> mercurial and defiant, his image,
> or ordered the day and brushwood for the fire.
> This is no test, but plainly real,
> this Moriah where, unsanctioned, unblessed,
> unpunished, sons and fathers pause and wait,
> and nothing is revealed. (*Leaping Clear* 65)

In many ways, these lines emphasize one of Feldman's characteristic styles, in which the reader is led through a series of bare, seemingly imaginary landscapes, only to discover that he or she is brought to the brink of serious existential despair. The multiple veils of metaphor are thrown aside; the climax awaited by the participants as well as the reader is never achieved. We, too, "pause and wait" for respite from the merciless, atheistic world of the poem. As his ruminations on the Holocaust, urban immigrant life, and biblical tales demonstrate, Feldman consistently points to the ethical dilemmas involved in attending to these themes and exposes truths needing to be wrestled with. We learn not to find happy answers but rather better ways of questioning our sympathies.

CRITICAL RECEPTION

Feldman's critical reception has been sizable and mostly favorable. In the major presses, *All of Us Here* garnered high praise from Katha Pollitt, John Hollander, Calvin Bedient, and J. P. White. In the February 1997 issue of *Poetry* John Taylor reviewed *The Life and Letters*. In April 1989, Harold Schweizer hosted a conference on Feldman's poetry at Bucknell University, at which papers were given by Dennis Donoghue, M. L. Rosenthal, Richard Howard, John Hollander, Charles Altieri, and Schweizer, among others. Many of their assessments of Feldman's work have been noted throughout the previous discussion.

BIBLIOGRAPHY

Works by Irving Feldman

Works and Days. New York: Harper and Row, 1961.
The Pripet Marshes. New York: Harper and Row, 1965.
Magic Papers. New York: Harper and Row, 1970.
Lost Originals. New York: Holt, Rinehart and Winston, 1972.
Leaping Clear. New York: Viking Press, 1976.
New and Selected Poetry. New York: Viking Press, 1979.
Teach Me, Dear Sister. New York: Viking Press, 1983.
All of Us Here. New York: Viking Press, 1986.
The Life and Letters. Chicago: University of Chicago Press, 1994.

Works about Irving Feldman

Bloom, Harold. "The Cultural Prospects of American Jewry." *Agon: Towards a Theory of Revisionism*, 321–30.
Grosholz, Emily. "Marriages and Partings." *The Hudson Review* 40 (1987): 156–65.
Hollander, John. "Human, All Too Human." *New Republic* 197 (1986): 28–30.
Ostriker, Alicia. "My Name Is Laughter: Irving Feldman and the Replaying of the Akedah." In Harold Schweizer, ed. *The Poetry of Irving Feldman: Nine Essays*. Lewisburg, PA: Bucknell University Press, 1992, p. 110.
Rosenthal, M. L. "Some Thoughts on Irving Feldman's Poetry." In Harold Schweizer, ed. *The Poetry of Irving Feldman: Nine Essays*. Lewisburg, PA: Bucknell University Press, 1992, p. 38.
Schweizer, Harold. "Lyric Suffering in Auden and Feldman." *English Language Notes* 31 (1993): 66–75.
———. *The Poetry of Irving Feldman: Nine Essays*. Lewisburg, PA: Bucknell University Press, 1992.
———. " 'Because We Have Been Spared': The Problem of Existence in Feldman's Poetry." *American Studies* 32 (1987): 167–80.

EDWARD FIELD   (1924–)

Diane Stevenson

BIOGRAPHY

Edward Field was born in Brooklyn, but he grew up on Long Island, in a town so hostile to Jews that Jewish families who moved in, once they saw the punishment their children were taking, immediately moved out. Field's mother was Polish; his father Lithuanian. During World War II Field served in the Army Air Force, and as a navigator he flew more than twenty-five missions, surviving a crash into the North Sea. He survived, too, lots of therapy and much spiritual searching, from Gurdjieff to Sufi, almost all of which (not quite all) was intended to cure him by turning him into a nicely functioning heterosexual; but the cures did not take, and Edward Field's status as an outsider was preserved, and the significance this status has carried both in his life and in his poetry was preserved as well.

When I grew up my parents were atheists. That didn't make them any less Jewish. It was the Nazi period. There was a certain assertion of Jewish identity even in a non-believer like my father, who would stay home for Yom Kippur even though it didn't mean anything to him. He was not quite honest about it: [he would say] he didn't eat because he had a stomach ache. When we moved from Brooklyn to Long Island, we moved to a completely Christian community, and they didn't let us forget we were Jews. Actually, it was a center for the German-American Bund. Even if I hadn't been a sissy I would have been beaten up all the time. I think my father didn't expect things to be easy. That's what you got in life.

It was all right, because if you survive something you're stronger. Being a Jew you don't expect it to be easy. Being a Jew is a strength. I don't know exactly how that is; but somehow you know it. In the world I grew up in ''Jew'' was an insult, in my father's world a secret honor; and the inheritance came through. Being gay helped tremendously, and poetry helped a lot.

Poetry was a wonderful discovery when I was eighteen. I was in the army in 1943 getting on a troop train after basic training for a trip across the country to a clerk-typist school in Colorado. A woman was handing out packets with toothbrushes and paperback books. Mine was Louis Untermeyer's *Anthology of Great English Poetry*. By the time I got off the train three days later I knew what I wanted to be. When asked before I could never say: "Do you want to go to college?" I didn't know until too late. Father made me take marketing, a complete mystery to me, in the School of Commerce at New York University. I got out of it by enlisting. During the war I became considerably more sophisticated, but afterwards I was forced to go back to the School of Commerce, because of certain rules concerning the G. I. Bill. I dropped out to go to Paris. I met a poet, Robert Friend, who lives in Israel. He taught me to write poetry; I sounded like myself from the beginning as soon as he released it. Then there was no doubt about poetry. What I couldn't understand was how to make a living.

[When I came back from Europe,] I got little jobs. I'd keep them for two months then quit them. I spent five years studying acting. I was miserable and could hardly write. I was in therapy about three and a half or four years. Brutal. You were there to change; you were supposed to come out heterosexual.

I met Neil Derrick in 1959—a tremendous change in my life. I gave up acting, and I started paying attention to writing again. After twenty-five rejections my book *Stand Up, Friend, with Me* was finally accepted. After that life was different: a Guggenheim, the Lamont Poetry Award, Europe for a year, readings. I could live off my literary life, and I did.

The literary world back then was snobbish. You couldn't write openly as either a homosexual or a Jew. I was never part of the establishment. I was a different kind of person; I came from simple people, shtetl people, whose tradition was still the socialist shtetl tradition. I wanted to write to be understood. Even though ordinary people don't read poems, I still wrote for them. (Unless otherwise indicated, the quoted remarks by Edward Field are from an unpublished interview conducted by the author during the summer of 1996.)

MAJOR WORKS AND THEMES

Edward Field's biography and his poetry are inextricable. The themes of his life are the themes of his poetry: the humiliated and the meek; the meek who are strong, not because they act strong but because they endure: the meek who inherit the earth. When he talks about his life, Edward Field talks about having the qualities of a survivor, of growing up out of sync with the Christian children around him. Being the brunt of other people's contempt made him the opposite of contemptuous; being bullied made him the opposite of a bully; his outsider status, outsider as a Jew and outsider as a homosexual, gave him something quite positive.

Edward Field's poems are strange, secular prayers. They are lamentations, vengeances called down upon enemies, psalms of consolation. They are silly and serious, self-conscious and sincere. *Stand Up, Friend, with Me* received the Lamont Poetry Award in 1962 from the American Academy of Poets and was published in 1963. *Variety Photoplays* followed in 1967, *A Full Heart* in 1978, *Stars in My Eyes* in 1978, *Counting Myself Lucky: Selected Poems, 1963–1992* in 1992. The first book, *Stand Up, Friend, with Me*, is a gentle and radiant book. The second, *Variety Photoplays*, is zanier; it's about the movies. *A Full Heart* returns to the tone and subjects and themes of the first book; and *Stars in My Eyes* returns to the movies of the second. *Eskimo Songs and Stories*, a book of translations, appeared in 1974. He wrote the narration for *To Be Alive*, and in 1965 this documentary film won an Academy Award. With his lifelong companion Neil Derrick, Field has written three novels: *The Potency Clinic* in 1978, *Village* in 1982, and *The Office* in 1987. Two anthologies of poetry complete his work so far: *A Geography of Poets* in 1979 and *A New Geography of Poets* in 1992.

CRITICAL RECEPTION

In the great modernist tradition, Field has given up the comforts of the literary so that his work might be all the more intense and moving. Field believes he is returning to poetry what has been left out, indeed, not even permitted in the other poetry, to erase the distinction between light and serious verse. He also wants his work to contain a level of emotion that critics, in earlier stages of his career, condemned as sentimental. (Bergman, 1991, 95)

Field writes intensely and movingly both about his homosexuality and about his Jewishness. He embraces what others reject:

The porcupine is only one of a series of inappropriate objects of affection that inhabit Field's poetry: Greek goats and donkeys, snow fish, a baby walrus named Ookie, a giant Pacific octopus . . . the most persistent objects of Field's love are the reluctant and unfortunate monsters that are the central features of many horror movies—She, King Kong, The Black Cat, Island of Lost Souls. (Bergman, 1991, 97)

What Field loves he would have us love as well, but the tolerance Field urges on his readers is not always simple. He doesn't want it to be simple. He doesn't want us to feel too comfortable or too complacent with our generosities. We are not to forget that the adorable objects of desire in his poems can also, like homosexuals and Jews, be objects of derision. In real life tolerance requires bravery; it's often hard-earned, and so in Field's poetry, too, we must work for our tolerance. Cockroaches, even when imaginary, are a stretch for most of us when it comes to affection, but in a poem about his New York apartment he pushes us to share his admiration for them, though not without humor. ''His tone is often that of a stand-up comic. . . . He can be very funny, often outrageous, [when] testing our tolerance quotient for shock. Irony abounds. Self-belittlement. Sadness. Love'' (Pomeroy).

Field has critical admirers and critical detractors. For the most part, they divide between those who are sympathetic to the "human context" of his poetry and those who are loyal to an older, stricter sense of what poetry is and should be, between those who approve of his prosaic freedoms and those who disdain his lack of meter and rhyme, between those who embrace his "sincerity" and those who censure his "lack of discipline." All agree, however, that his poetry is a celebration of the meek and the lowly, the outcast and the humiliated.

BIBLIOGRAPHY

Works by Edward Field

Stand Up, Friend, with Me. New York: Grove Press, 1963.
Narration for a documentary film, *To Be Alive*, which won an Academy Award, 1965.
Variety Photoplays. New York: Grove Press, 1967.
Eskimo Songs and Stories. New York: Delacorte Press, 1974 (translations).
Sweet Gwendolyn and the Countess. Gulfport, FL: Konglomerati, 1975.
A Full Heart. New York: Sheep Meadow Press, 1977.
Stars in My Eyes. New York: Sheep Meadow Press, 1978.
New and Selected Poems from the Book of My Life. New York: Sheep Meadow Press, 1987.
Counting Myself Lucky: Selected Poems, 1963–1992. Santa Rosa, CA: Black Sparrow Press, 1992.

Under pseudonym Bruce Elliot, with Neil Derrick

The Potency Clinic. New York: Bleecker Street, 1978.
Village. New York: Avon Books, 1982 (historical saga of Greenwich Village).
The Office. New York: Avon Books, 1987.

Edited Works

A Geography of Poets. New York: Bantam Books, 1979.
Head of a Sad Angel: Stories by Alfred Chester. Santa Rosa, CA: Black Sparrow Press, 1990 (Introduction by Gore Vidal).
Looking for Genet: Essays by Alfred Chester. Santa Rosa, CA: Black Sparrow Press, 1992a (Introduction by Edward Field).
With Charles Stetler and Gerald Locklin. *A New Geography of Poets*. University of Arkansas Press, 1992b.

Works about Edward Field

Bergman, David. "Edward Field." *Dictionary of Literary Biography*, No. 105, 1991, 95–103.
———. "Edward Field: An Interview." *The American Poetry Review*, November/December 1991, 30–34.
Goldstein, Laurence. "The Spectacles of Edward Field." *Parnassus* 15, No. 1, 1989, 240–55.
Howard, Richard. *Preferences*. New York: Viking, 1974, 73–74.

―――――. "Edward Field." In his *Alone with America: Essays in the Art of Poetry in the United States since 1950*. Enlarged ed. New York: Atheneum, 1980, 143–57.

Klein, Michael. "Stay Together, Learn the Flowers, Go Light." *The Kenyon Review* 16, No. 1, Winter 1994, 198.

Pomeroy, Ralph. "Edward Field: Poet as Stand-Up Comic." *Exquisite Corpse*, No. 45, 1994.

CHARLES FISHMAN (1942–)

William James Austin

BIOGRAPHY

The poet Charles Fishman was born July 10, 1942, in Freeport, New York. From there his family moved to the Bronx in New York City, where he lived until he was eight years old. Since that time, he has resided—first as a son and later as a husband and as the father of two daughters—on suburban Long Island. He received his B.A. and M.A. in English literature from Hofstra University (1964–1965) and his D.A. in creative writing from the State University of New York in Albany (1982), where he was given the President's Award for Distinguished Doctoral Dissertation.

Fishman's long career as a poet, scholar, and educator has so far yielded three full-length collections and six chapbooks of his own poetry. He has also published poems, translations, articles, reviews, and fiction in over 300 periodicals, including *Georgia Review*, *New England Review*, *Film Quarterly*, *Beloit Poetry Journal*, the *New York Times*, and *New York Quarterly*. His poetry has appeared in eighteen anthologies with titles and themes as diverse as *Poets for Africa* (1986), *A Measured Response: Poets Respond to Viet Nam and Desert Storm* (1992), and *Images from the Holocaust* (1996).

The poetry of Charles Fishman has won the Gertrude B. Claytor Memorial Award in 1987 from the Poetry Society of America, the New Letters Award for Poetry in 1993, and the Ann Stanford Poetry Prize in 1996.

The most prestigious honors have been reserved for Fishman's most compelling book of poems, *The Death Mazurka*, which was named Outstanding Academic Book of the Year (American Library Association *Choice*, 1989), and received the Gertrude B. Claytor Memorial Award (Poetry Society of America) and in 1990 a Pulitzer Prize nomination.

In the areas of scholarship and education, Fishman has also been the recipient of a number of honors. He was awarded three National Endowment for the Humanities (NEH) Fellowships, in 1974 (Boston University), 1978 (University of California, San Diego), and 1982 (Yale University), and in 1985 served as an NEH reviewer for the *Encyclopedia of the Holocaust*. Additionally, in 1985 he received the State University of New York Chancellor's Award for Excellence in Teaching and in 1990 the New York State/United University Professions Excellence Award. Most recently, Fishman has served as a poetry consultant to the U.S. Holocaust Memorial Museum (1995–) and as an NEH reviewer for the Holocaust translation project (1995).

Fishman is cofounder of the Long Island Poetry Collective, has served on the editorial board of *Esprit*, was a founding editor of *Xanadu*, and continues to serve as poetry editor for various literary journals such as *Gaia*. He is also series editor for *Watermark Poets of North America* (1980–1983). In 1991, *Blood to Remember*, an anthology of American poets edited by Fishman, appeared to critical praise. The collection contains some of the most important and moving Holocaust poetry written in America.

Charles Fishman has read his poetry at universities and other venues across America and Israel. He currently teaches at the State University of New York (SUNY) at Farmingdale, Long Island, where in 1989 he was appointed Distinguished Service Professor. He is the coordinator of the Paumanok Poetry Award International Competition, administered at SUNY Farmingdale, and continues to serve as the director of that university's Visiting Writers Program, which he founded in 1979 and for which he recruits many of the most famous literary voices from America and abroad.

MAJOR WORKS AND THEMES

Fishman's career reflects one of the more prolific poets and scholars of the post-Vietnam era. As a Jew finding his way through a largely Christian-American landscape and deeply appalled by humanity's cauldron of bigotry epitomized by the Holocaust, Fishman has spent much of his creative energy both investigating and celebrating Jewish culture and heritage.

Although the terror of the Holocaust underlies much of Fishman's work, fueling an ongoing search for justice and closure, his poetic vision reaches beyond this singular horror to grapple with the potentially life-affirming qualities of nature and family. Such concerns have energized a poetic landscape in a continuing state of evolution. The early poems are often informed by urban images, no doubt culled, in part, from the poet's childhood in the Bronx. By the time of Fishman's tour de force, *The Death Mazurka*, ''neighborhood'' anti-Semitism had found its most horrific expression in the Holocaust and its consequences. His recent work, however, seems at last to have won an uneasy peace and acceptance of the natural order.

The poems in *Mortal Companions* (1977), Fishman's first full-length collection, represent a survey, often chilling, of the suffering and courage of Jewish immigrants in America. The collection's frontispiece offers a description of the dangers of urban life that nonetheless evokes an image of the pogrom in Eastern Europe. Here is yet another place "where mothers and fathers/ . . . remember their fathers/ who died under streetlamps/ that stood before houses/where gangs shatter streetlamps/ and switchblades leap open" In "Spectrum Elegy," dedicated to the poet's uncle, "The blue of your mechanic's veins/ terrified a battery of fingermen who swore/ to get you . . . / . . . until you dared swing an immigrant Yid fist at America" (24). For Fishman, the stability and security of family have always served as a salve. In "Six-Pointed Star," the birth of his first daughter ensures that the future envisioned by anti-Semites will never happen. "You are the continuance," Fishman says of his child, . . . you make Auschwitz/ less of a mockery (41).

The Death Mazurka, first published in 1987 by Timberline Press, is Fishman's most brilliant achievement. Taken together, the poems serve up a heart-wrenching account of the Holocaust and its consequences. Here the urban landscape of *Mortal Companions* gives way to scenes of ultimate blight and suffering. Yet Fishman is quite capable of commingling images of the Holocaust with his own suburban lifestyle, suggesting that the shelter of suburbia is, in fact, no shelter from memory. In "A Morning at Dachau," two short lines evoke all the horror anyone can stand, wherever one may run: "Outside./ 30 mass graves tidy as patios" (16).

However terrifying much of the imagery may be, the poet is never over-whelmed by despair. In "The Blackness of Jews" he finds redemptive possibilities in family and in his own art. "This is for the children," he writes, "who came to being in darkness/ . . . for those/ who survived to dream again/ of children—children from the fire,/ children from ash and anger" (28). In "Special Report on the Holocaust" Fishman refers to an unnamed survivor, but he may as well be speaking of himself as artist, for "Six million did not/die . . . / one was saved: the one of memory,/ of dream, of continuance, of revenge" (29).

If *The Death Mazurka* is Fishman's revenge, it is an exceptional one. These poems, in no small way, add their cry of "never again" to that of so many graves and of the earth.

The Firewalkers is Fishman's most recent full-length collection. It combines poems from earlier chapbooks with new material. Compared to the poems in previous collections, these are decidedly less violent, both in subject matter and in tone. Fishman, it seems, has at last taken on the task of reconciliation, healing family wounds while surrounding himself with the soothing mysteries of a natural landscape. In "Broich's Boat," Fishman addresses his father directly, reminding him that he was "quick to whip/ Off your belt and threaten my life over practically/ nothing" (13). The image of oppressor and victim, which informs so much of Fishman's work, is here dissolved into the cooling waters of love's rebirth, even in the face of old age and death: "Before you die, father, fish with me again, share/ your secrets: let the tide of our love turn" (14). In

"Cape Hatteras: 1939" Fishman extends the conceit and the desire for understanding: "Have I/ hooked you, father? Will I land/ your heart at last?" (15).
The lines suggest the poet's need to recover love through dominance and control.
They seem, at first glance, the perennial victim's solution. Yet they come in the
form of questions, so the ultimate power to grant or withhold rests with the one
who will answer. In a single metaphor, Fishman manages to locate and contain
the heartbreaking intercourse of love and power.

Much of the poetry in this collection dotes on the quotidian, scenes filled
with goldenrod, dogs chasing after sticks, rainfalls. "There is such pleasure in
weariness!" Fishman writes in "Falling Asleep with Your Children," yet the
old pains are never quite extinguished: "you are safe/ in the ambulance of
Friday" (61). The sense of peace achieved in this collection is, perhaps, tenuous.
Poems that share the poet's love of mother, wife, children nevertheless harbor
some measure of foreboding. Yet what, after the death of so many, remains?
Fishman knows what the answer must be, that "The Death Mazurka" is also
the dance of life, and "Every dance is a protest against our oppressors" (Chaim
Kaplan, headnote, *Death Mazurka*).

CRITICAL RECEPTION

To date there have been no scholarly analyses of Charles Fishman's poetry.
This is astonishing when one considers how often and how well this poetry has
been honored. In order to mount a critical assessment of the work, one must
therefore rely on book reviews and other commentary from some of Fishman's
most celebrated contemporaries.

Of Fishman's earliest work, largely collected in *Mortal Companions*, Cynthia
Ozick writes in a personal note to the poet, "Some of the poems are mysterious
novels-in-little; some are a frightening music. . . . Panic-poems. They express my
spine."

Richard Eberhart, commenting on Fishman's most celebrated collection, *The
Death Mazurka*, pays tribute to the broader implications of the poetry's focus
on the Holocaust: "Charles Fishman's poetry is direct, captivating, philosophical, splendidly evocative of not only the Holocaust but of deep perceptions
about life and death, what it is to be mortal" (*The Death Mazurka*, back cover).
Gerald Stern, equally impressed, calls the poems "terrifying, and pure. . . . one
finger is pointed towards God and one toward that other." In awe of Fishman's
courage and achievement, Stern finally resolves his admiration into the language
of interrogation: "Fishman has done the unthinkable. He has written an entire
book about the murder of the Jews. . . . Had he the right?—Who was he to
speak?—Would it be seen as arrogance?" The answer, for Stern, is clearly won
by the poems: "He has the right. He did it well. . . . He redeems us a little"
(*The Death Mazurka*, Foreword).

Reviews of *The Death Mazurka* have been, quite simply, raves. The April
1988 issue of *Choice* focuses on the salutary qualities of the poet's task, noting

that ''[*The Death Mazurka*] offers a difficult but accessible vision of one man dancing against severest oppression. . . . and their [the poems] strength is that they are redemptive and not forbidding.'' The *Virginia Quarterly Review* is equally impressed by Fishman's aesthetic sense and points out that the poems, ''[u]nrelenting in [their] refusal to compromise with the facts of history, through their sheer integrity, lend new credence to Keats' old formula, Beauty is truth, truth beauty.' ''

Fishman's most recent poetry is collected in *The Firewalkers*. Denise Levertov calls this poetry ''deep, sensuous, musical, and fully alive'' (*The Firewalkers*, back cover). Carolyn Forché celebrates poems of ''recuperative memory and redemption [that] are written out of the wounded landscape of the body and its mortality. . . . the world in its passing.'' She acknowledges Fishman's turn to a broader symbolism: ''The elements become figural here: water, air, fire, the earth, in a language of mystery and desire'' (*The Firewalkers*, back cover).

In sum, the works of Charles Fishman have received the sort of praise reserved only for a century's most compelling voices.

In his review of *Blood to Remember*, S. L. Kremer observes: ''Fishman successfully assembles works that render a historically remote and often painfully resisted subject in a manner that makes the catastrophe real.''

BIBLIOGRAPHY

Works by Charles Fishman

Books

Aurora. Berkeley, CA.: Tree Books, 1974.
Mortal Companions. New York: Pleasure Dome Press, 1977a.
Warm-Blooded Animals. La Crosse, WI: Juniper Press, 1977b.
The Death Mazurka. Lubbock: Texas Tech University Press, 1989.
Zoom. Canton, OH: Singular Speech Press, 1990.
Ed. *Blood to Remember: American Poets on the Holocaust*. Lubbock: Texas Tech University Press, 1991a.
Catlives. Trans. Marina Roscher and Charles Fishman. Lubbock: Texas Tech University Press, 1991b.
As the Sun Goes Down in Fire. Englewood, Cliffs, NJ: Anabiosis Press, 1992.
Nineteenth Century Rain. Winterville, GA: Whistle Press, 1994.
The Firewalkers. Greensboro, NC: Avisson Press, 1996.
An Aztec Memory. North Port, FL.: 1997.

Critical Articles

''In Times of Strangeness.'' foreword to Michael Blumenthal's *Sympathetic Magic*. Huntington, Long Island: Watermark Press, 1980a.
''William Pillin: A Certain Music.'' Critical introduction to Pillin's collected poems *To the End of Time*. Los Angeles: Papa Bach Editions, 1980.

Works about Charles Fishman

"*The Death Mazurka.*" *Choice*, April 1988, 1242.
"*The Death Mazurka.*" *Virginia Quarterly Review*, Winter 1991, 29.
Kremer, S. L. "*Blood to Remember*: American Poets on the Holocaust." *Choice*, July/
      August 1992, 155.

ALLEN GINSBERG (1926–1997)

Maria Damon

BIOGRAPHY

When the subject of Ginsberg as a Jew comes up in most criticism, it is handled as if Judaism, Ginsberg's Judaism in particular, is archaic. Ginsberg's "prophetic, 'Old Testament' voice" is invoked; his raging jeremiads and/or lamentations ("Howl" and "Kaddish") are used as primary evidence. Ginsberg's use of Moloch as a governing trope is mentioned as well ("Howl"), Moloch defined as an "ancient Hebrew deity" (actually, Canaanite) of greed and bloodlust who demanded sacrifice by fire of children by their parents. The prophetic role ascribed to Ginsberg by popular culture and the oratorical bent associated with this prophecying are attributed to Old Testament influences, as if this were an essential Jewish characteristic, rather than to William Blake, one of the poet's greatest heroes and models. Sometimes even Ginsberg's appearance is mentioned, as if he were emulating, again, Old Testament prophets or rabbis instead of his hero Walt Whitman. Indeed, it may be that the famous photographs of Ginsberg with long, wild black hair, long, wavy beard, and Uncle Sam-style top hat parody the radically religious Jews of New York (Lenny Bruce, one of Ginsberg's contemporaries and kindred spirits and the inspiration for the topically comedic poem "America," has a skit in which a hipster mistakes a group of Orthodox rabbis for members of his own social group). However, these Jews are modern American Jews of Eastern European provenance, and so is Ginsberg. His work, like their culture, is marked with the historical circumstances of twentieth-century Jewish America and became increasingly forthcoming about this informing identity.

Irving Allen Ginsberg was born in Newark, New Jersey, in July 1926 to Louis Ginsberg, a high school teacher and minor, formalist, lyric poet with a respectable publishing career, and to Naomi Levy Ginsberg, a Russian-born, communist immigrant of great talent and intelligence who, before her series of mental breakdowns starting when Allen was a child and culminating in her permanent hospitalization in his adulthood, was active in Yiddish branches of the Communist Party and other leftist-oriented activist groups. Ginsberg has credited Naomi and Jewish communist circles with affording him his first contact with poetry; as a child he was taken by his mother to Communist Party meetings, where the Yiddish and English-language party songs constituted his earliest experience with rhythm, language, orality, and community spirit, which were to infuse his sense of poetry—not to mention the fear that to be a poet of the people, one must also be mentally ill, emotionally unstable, a social outsider. The price of this great communitarian exuberance was not only social ostracism but internal torment. At the same time, his father offered another model of poetry and of Jewishness: in poetry, the model of Eliotic and restrained conservatism and in terms of Jewish identity, the earnest, middle-class conformist who hopes through assimilation to stay safe. The price of poetic recognition and social acceptance was self-denial, repression, and a kind of self-diminishing, wounded gratefulness for being allowed to survive—an assimilationist spirit that could be characterized variously as "quiet desperation" or, at the extreme, "Uncle Tomming." What was missing from both of these models was a spirituality that went beyond the material realm, an element that the mature Ginsberg later found in Buddhism rather than Judaism and that he managed to integrate with the vision of an alternative community in which he could both achieve poetic distinction and be himself fully. This has been his major achievement as a poet in the public sphere—beyond the corpus he has produced, he has offered the United States a vision of public poetic activity that embraces alterity, community, a humane engagement with social justice, and a spiritually based, nonjudgmental acceptance of suffering and the human condition.

The transition from the earliest, rhymed, putatively private poetry (published much later as *The Gates of Wrath: Rhymed Poems 1948–1951*), which seems to have been composed in his father's shadow (influenced both by him and in fear of him), to the breakthrough volume *Howl and Other Poems* (1956), which poeticizes a mad, disappointed-utopian outrage (his mother's legacy), was midwifed by the literary aspirations, efforts, and encouragements of a close circle of friends who have subsequently become known as the Beat generation. These friends, whom he met in 1948, included Jack Kerouac, whom he met at Columbia University; Lucien Carr, also a Columbia student, William Burroughs, a Harvard graduate; John Clellon Holmes; and Neal Cassady, a Kerouac "find" who embodied the values of nonacademic, manically verbal and physical spontaneity, and a polymorphously perverse omnisexuality that defied the social, political, familial, and aesthetic repression of the sedated 1950s. Although, with the exception of Carl Solomon, whom Ginsberg met in Rockland State Hospital for the psychiatrically ill, the closest of Ginsberg's friends were not Jewish, they shared with Ginsberg and other American Jews of the period the liminal social position of being inside/outside—as working-class or lumpen-proletariat "white ethnics," sexual minorities, addicts of illegal substances, and dissidents who nonetheless ambiguously and ambivalently profited from the injustices of the capitalist class system and its repressive family values: Jack (né Jean) Kerouac, a working-class French-Canadian whose first language was the vernacular "joual" and who had attended Columbia University on a football scholarship; William Burroughs, heir to the Burroughs Adding Machine fortune, who was a heroin-addicted homosexual: Gregory (né Gregorio Nunzio) Corso, Italian-American foundling and petty criminal who had discovered poetry in prison; Neal Cassady, stunningly handsome, energetic, and intelligent son of an alcoholic drifter, himself an alcoholic drifter and inspirer of much of Ginsberg's erotic longing; Herbert Huncke, gay junkie drifter and raconteur and, eventually, Ginsberg's lover; Peter Orlovsky, a recently discharged navy man of working-class origin whose family was even more haunted by mental and emotional dysfunction than Ginsberg's own.

The demographics of the Beat generation are noteworthy because, as John Arthur Maynard has pointed out, although the stereotype of the Beat artist was the wealthy young man who threw it all away in a puerile gesture of defiance, most Beats were actually from the ranks of the working class or the semiprofessional lower middle classes, often with immigrant parents who had just begun to climb the social ladder open to those groups who were considered white. The issue is relevant to Ginsberg's Jewishness because this was an era in which many top universities were just beginning to abolish quotas regulating the admission of Jews and the Jewish transition from outsider (in Europe) to insider (in America) was in medias res; a Jewish boy from a family of modest aspirations at Columbia was already torn by competing identities and loyalties. Ginsberg's choice to inhabit additionally the marginal and liminal gay/petty criminal/addicts' demimonde could be read as an attempt to hang on to the outsider status that gave Jews a position of social critique; it can also be seen, in the context of his poetics, as an affirmation of the unbounded, unknown, frightening worlds eschewed by the decorousness of the academic, Eliotic tradition—worlds where language is wonderfully distorted, vernacularized, constantly destroyed and reinvented, where it speaks to and from experience not generally acknowledged at the publicly regulated level. In particular, Jack Kerouac's "spontaneous bop prosody" encouraged a free-flowing, improvisatory, long-line prose style (although the technique resonates with European-derived modernist innovations like surrealism, stream-of-consciousness, and the long periodic sentences of Kerouac's idol Marcel Proust, Kerouac's terminology was an attempt to link his literary aspirations to African-American musical genius, an inspiration from the "fellahin" grassroots). Also, William Burroughs' insistence on honesty at the deepest level of fearful, private fantasy led to a series of meetings where the three—Ginsberg, Kerouac, Burroughs—took turns listening to each other as the speaker lay on the floor, à la psychoanalysis, in an atmosphere of complete respect and trust. This exercise helped Ginsberg articulate the parts of his psyche—his fear of madness, his homosexuality, his poetic vulnerability—he had dreaded exposing to the light of rejection; being accepted for who he was played a crucial role in his developing poetics.

According to various biographies, two incidents, one famous and the other not part of mainstream Ginsberg lore, were foundational in shaping Ginsberg's poetics and his sense of personhood. First, the famous incident involves Ginsberg's auditory hallucination of what he was convinced was the voice of William Blake reciting the latter's poem "Ah Sun Flower"; Ginsberg was lying on his bed disconsolate after his affair with Neal Cassady had broken up, and the clairaudient experience provided a pantheistic balm that became, for Ginsberg, an encounter with the divine. The incident is invoked as a way of exemplifying the linked and powerful roles of spirituality and poetry in Ginsberg's poetics and also his compassion, later reflected in his own poem "Sunflower Sutra."

The second incident is far less commonly encountered in the Ginsberg canon, but several sources indicate that it was a turning point for the poet's relationship to himself and the world, and I include it here as having special relevance to the problematic of Ginsberg-as-Jewish-American. In 1953, on leaving the New York area after several years of drifting in and out of straight jobs and the demimonde, Ginsberg traveled to the Yucatán, where he worked on the plantation of a friend and, more importantly, wrote and explored Mayan ruins. In one instance of exploration, he "led" a group of indigenous Mexicans to a cavelike ruin with a great deal of confidence and was hailed by them as a kind of leader or recognized as a spiritual and brave person. Ginsberg, whose social experience up to this point did not include being recognized for leadership (quite the contrary; he'd felt like a bit of social detritus, an embarrassment to human existence), felt validated and affirmed as a man, as a spiritual being, and as an explorer. Though his explorations and leadership qualities would manifest themselves rather spectacularly (if unorthodoxly) in later years and would not involve physical bravery and indigenous people away from his own country, this moment has been credited with making him recognize that potential in himself.

We encounter here a familiar, if uncomfortable, template for the working out of Jewish ethnicity in the New World through its relationship to other ethnicities. In order for Ginsberg to feel actualized as an American male, in order for him to function meaningfully in society and feel that he had agency, he apparently needed the experience of being "in charge of," or hailed as a special person by, a group of people lower down on the social hierarchy. His assimilation, in other words, was enabled by his taking on a subject position superior to specifically designated Others, in the same way that other "white ethnics" became white through disidentification with black, the American underclass—which meant, among other things, establishing trade unions whose purpose was to keep black out. The incident resonates all too distinctly with other accounts of white explorers' being "hailed as gods" by indigenous Americans, which is, in most cases, a fabricated tale whose purpose is to ratify white supremacy and colonization. While clearly, Ginsberg's biography obviously did not develop into a record of imperialistic soldiery, and while his sympathies, like those of many American Jews, remained with the "fellahin," one cannot overlook this anecdote as symptomatic of the "whitening" of Jews in America, especially since Ginsberg credits this episode as giving him the confidence to function in the world he had felt so victimized by—even though he ultimately used this confidence to iconoclastic ends.

Ginsberg was released into the life we now know as Allen Ginsberg's by a psychiatrist: while he was living in the San Francisco Bay Area, where he had moved in 1954, holding down a "straight" marketing research job, dating a woman, and trying to toe the line, he described to his analyst the life he wanted to lead: gay, poetic, free. Unlike the stereotypical psychiatrist of the time, this one encouraged Ginsberg to go for it. Shortly thereafter, he formed a committed, serious relationship with Peter Orlovsky, who had been living with Ginsberg's friend the artist Robert Lavigne (the history of this relationship has been documented in *Straight Hearts' Delight* and *Honorable Courtship*); and in 1955, at the Six Gallery in San Francisco, he read his new poem "Howl" to the acclaim of the crowd and to the verbal accompaniment of Jack Kerouac's jazz-inspired encouraging "yeah, man" and "go, man, go." Ginsberg has said that he thought the poem would at best be privately printed by a "lavender press," an underground gay publishing house, and in fact, he did inscribe and send a copy to H. D. (Hilda Doolittle) when Lawrence Ferlinghetti's City Lights Publishers brought the book out in their new pocketbook series. Instead, the obscenity trial that followed after the book was impounded and censored and the subsequent acquittal of Ferlinghetti and his assistant Shigeyoshi Murao—and, by extension, *Howl and Other Poems*—catapulted the book and its author out of the quietly desperate closet at last and into overnight fame. "Howl" was, along with Bob Kaufman's "Abomunist Manifesto," considered the closest thing in Beat literature approximating a manifesto or an anthem, and while the latter work has until recently languished relatively unread, "Howl" is generally acknowledged to be the signature piece of Beat poetry. Its rage, hope, and incantatory, oratorical overtones still astound young readers in the 1990s with the relevance of its politics, its sexual forthrightness, its passionate advocacy for the dignity in "grunge" (to the degree that contemporary youngsters are often surprised to learn that Ginsberg became a suit-wearing elderly man—he was not freezeframed as a Beat or a hippie anymore than he was as an ancient, wrathful Hebrew patriarch).

Ginsberg died on April 4, 1997, in the Manhattan loft he had just purchased with the proceeds of the sale of his collection of memorabilia to the Stanford University Library. His death was not entirely unexpected; he had been in frail health and had just been diagnosed with liver cancer and given several months to live. At the time of his death (he suffered a stroke related to his cancer within a week of his diagnosis), he was surrounded by friends and lovers and, according to Peter Orlovsky, requested that Orlovsky put Ma Rainey on the stereo.

A Buddhist funeral ceremony was held the following Monday, and a Jewish ceremony was held the next day. In the weeks that followed, university and college campuses, arts organizations, and religious and poetic communities throughout the world held impromptu memorials, group readings, and reminiscences of this remarkable sensibility who touched our century.

MAJOR WORKS AND THEMES

Ginsberg's second book, *Kaddish and Other Poems*, is arguably stronger even than *Howl*, though the latter has accrued more notoriety because of its (largely justified) claim to generational representativeness and because of the dramatic circumstances surrounding its premier reading and its publication. Because ''Kaddish'' tells a story so familiar to Jewish Americans of the twentieth century, I will dwell at some length on the title poem, which, as that title suggests, concerns the death not only of a Jewish person but of a particular Jewish sensibility: the Eastern European, radical, leftist woman who cannot find a place in the New World. Raised in a staunchly secular household, Ginsberg had, in fact, never heard the Kaddish, the Jewish prayer for the dead, before his mother died, shock-treated and lobotomized beyond recognition, in a state psychiatric hospital when he was in his early thirties. Like Mezz Mezzrow's remarking that cantoral singing reminds him of the blues and jazz, with which he identifies, the Kaddish reminded Ginsberg of the Ray Charles he had been listening to; African-American popular culture, rather than the expressive arts of their own ethnic/ religious tradition, is the reference point for many secularized, American-born Jews. The ''Jewishness'' of ''Kaddish,'' Ginsberg's heart-wrenching lament for his mother, Naomi, and her mental illness, lobotomy and eventual death in abject circumstances, lies in the tale it tells of the trauma of displacement, relocation, and escape from Stalin's Russia to an alien world of suburbia and prosperity.

Like the protagonist of Tillie Olsen's ''Tell Me a Riddle,'' whose bitter, introverted old age is haunted by memories of a politically activist, intellectual girlhood in Russia, or like the portrait of his mother-in-law that talk-poet David Antin traces in his performance ''The Principle of Fit,'' whose hysterical blindness accompanies her ostensible assimilation and socioeconomic rise in the ''*goldeneh medineh*'' (''Golden Land''), Naomi Ginsberg represents, paradoxically, the trauma of survivor guilt, of the unresolved ''Jewish question'' being played out dramatically far from their new, putatively safe haven. Naomi's madness, which Ginsberg documents with such painful honesty that he still wept when he read the poem in the 1990s, consists in paranoid beliefs that Stalin, Hitler, and her mother are conspiring to kill her or control her mind. In 1940, the date of the central episode of the poem, this is not an entirely delusional belief; in fact, although American Jews knew that their people were victims of genocide and slave labor, the full horrors of the Holocaust, revealed after the war, exceeded in grotesquerie anything Naomi fantasized. At twelve, Ginsberg undergoes the trauma of having to take his hysterically screaming, schizophrenic mother to a sanatorium by bus—forced by circumstances to act the adult, Allen undergoes a nonreligious, harrowing bar mitzvah in which the son of the Commandment witnesses the dissolution of the rational world, of the covenant itself, and must interpret it in a way that honors his mother's reality even as, in order to care for her, he must be mindful of the enormity of her illness.

The poet, he reminds us, is a twelve-year-old child "tagging along" (213) with his out-of-control, ought-to-be caretaker, with roles violently reversed. In this child's bus ride with his crazy mother, Ginsberg links the genocide and ethnocide of Native Americans, which are embedded in the New Jersey landscape in the form of "old wampum loading the streambed" (213) and "a tomahawk or Pocahontas bone" (213), with the preparation for World War II (America's nonintervention in the war against the Jews). Ginsberg describes Naomi's delusion of being poisoned by Rockefeller with "invisible bugs and jewish sickness" (213) and his own childlike agony and desire that it all end peacefully "in a quiet room in a Victorian house by a lake" (213). If the Jewish male's rite of passage is textual interpretation, this landscape and the insane utterances of this mother comprise the text from hell, which must somehow be sacralized to be endured. The premise of Beat writing became precisely this, the sacralization of personal experience of trauma (social, sexual, emotional, spiritual, physical)—in the words of William Blake, a marriage of heaven and hell—and this happens through the imagination. (In Ginsberg's later years, the imagination as means of transforming hell to heaven cedes to the disciplined practice of meditation.)

In two of the many climactic moments of the poem (which is pitched at high urgency and emotion throughout), Ginsberg identifies himself with Israel through and to his mother, who tragically no longer recognizes him as her son ("you're not Allen") (224), by his Jewish name, Srul Avrum (Israel Abraham, which has been Americanized to Irving Allen). In the first instance, he merges her grave with his own "cracked grave! Shema Y'Israel—I am Srul Avrum— you—in death?" (221)—as he also merges their own identities to be subsumed into the idea of Israel—not the land, but the people—as victim of madness, persecution Holocaust, death. In the second, he renders biblical time contemporary, seeing her as one of the matriarchs ("Ruth who wept in America— Rebecca aged in Newark") (224) and himself as "Srul Avrum—Israel Abraham—myself—to sing in the wilderness toward God" (224)—whereon he receives the strange message of hope that ends the section: a posthumous letter from his mother, of whose death he has just learned, advising him that "the key is in the bars, in the sunlight in the window" (224).

Other poems of the early period, "America" and "To Aunt Rose" among them, also document the life of secular, highly politicized leftist Eastern European American Jews. Aunt Rose and other female relatives—Aunt Edith, Aunt Elanor—worked tirelessly to unionize the workforces of which they were members, through Yiddish-speaking labor groups and political parties. The Spanish civil war, Stalin's betrayal of the Marxist dream, the Third Reich (its anticommunism as well as its anti-Semitism), and finally the Rosenbergs' execution became touchstones, signal events around which experience was organized, as personal as his father Louis's poetry publications, Allen's confused adolescent sexuality, and family gatherings around the piano. However, what emerges from these family portraits is a profile not only of spirited political engagement but of futility and emotional unfulfillment. Rose, in the last analysis, dies as she has lived, a lonely, sexually frustrated "girl," just as Ginsberg himself was an "ignorant girl of family silence" ("To Aunt Rose," *Collected Poems 1947–1980*, 184). It is not hard to see that for Ginsberg, writing at this time, identification as the "non-Jewish Jew," as Isaac Deutscher has it, was fraught with dangers not only social but private. The cost of an engaged and public political utopianism was "family silence" and personal pain to the point of hopelessness about love and sex. Again, as Ginsberg came to see, this silence brought its own paradoxical gifts: he has on several occasions attributed the sexual and emotional candor of his poetry to his early belief that he could never publish lest his father, who was active in poetry circles, read of his "gaiety"; doomed to private expression, the young poet felt free to say whatever he needed to.

"America" is one of Ginsberg's most famous and loved poems: it puts his "Jew-commie-fag" identity in the forefront of an intimate, kvetchy dialogue with his country of citizenship. When he read this poem aloud, the rhythms of Yiddish in this one-sided, odd-couple argument were inescapable, as were its constant references to Jewish-American political life. The familial bitterness of "America I've given you all and now I am nothing" ("America," *Collected Poems 1947–1980*, 146) and "I'm sick of your insane demands" (146), juxtaposed against "I won't say the Lord's Prayer" (146), "[Scott Nearing] was . . . a real mensh . . . I once saw . . . Israel Amter plain" (147) and these, in turn, interspersed with Ginsberg's yearning to transcend the material realm in which he feels America is mired—"America when will you be angelic?" (146) and "America how can I write a holy litany in your silly mood?" (147)—make this a great comic poem as well as a political poem of lasting value, instanciating what Mark Schechner has called "Yiddish consciousness," that is, the knack of yoking the familiar, comic, and quotidian to the otherworldly and metaphysical, namely, Marc Chagall, Bob Dylan, Woody Allen, Sholem Aleichem. In its first published form (in *Black Mountain Review*), this poem had a second section that invoked the Rosenbergs but otherwise went over the top in its reliance on "mystical vibrations" as the solution to America's ills; the wise decision to drop this section saved the poem from unintentional self-parody and secured its place in Jewish-American politically engagé and comic traditions. Where Ginsberg differs from his fellow Yiddish-consciousness writers, some of whom I enumerated earlier, is in the dramatic angst with which he and other Beat writers colored this yoking of the mundane and the transcendent. The word "Beat" itself, meaning both utterly depleted and beatified/sanctified, captures, to some extent, the wild extremes of lower depths/celestial aspirations that characterized Beat thinking and writing. The sophisticated folksiness of Chagall and Aleichem is charming; "Howl" is, as its name indicates, harrowing.

Another way in which Ginsberg's "secular Jewish identity" (the phrase is Irena Klepfisz's) manifests itself is in the conversational, hyperverbal persistence of his verse. While one could accurately point to French-Canadian-American Jack Kerouac's "spontaneous bop prosody" as Ginsberg's prime influence in this realm, as well as Walt Whitman's long-line poetics and William Carlos Williams' breath-based line, there is also a Jewish tradition, both vernacular and formal, of interlocution, of commentary as a religious obligation, be it conversation with God, Torah, and Talmud study, storytelling, or contestatory debates and freewheeling discussions. As Gertrude Stein has her Jewish protagonist say in the novel *QED*, "You know I have the failing of my tribe: I believe in the sacred rite of conversation even when it is a monologue" (*Fernhurst, QED, and Other Early Writings.* New York: Liveright, 1971, p. 57). Ginsberg's stated desire to create "yak poems" anticipates David Antin's "talk-poems" and points to both the informality and obsessive-compulsiveness of the need to talk and to frame that talk as art. Daniel Boyarin has observed that the earliest uses of the verb "to read" in Hebrew texts indicate not a private act of silent reading to oneself but to "harangue" a public audience; this connotation matches Ginsberg's style and philosophy of poetry, though he tends to express this concept as Whitmanian or bardic rather than Hebraic (although, in fact, Whitman is not known for spectacular readings in the oral oracular tradition; rather, the line of his verse lends itself to declamation in the rhythm of "a man's natural breath").

"Jewishness" for Ginsberg seems to mean, to a large degree, "family." The middle period is one in which his alternative families—Beat, global, and so on—eclipse the concerns of his earlier exorcisms of family demons and secrets: his homosexuality, his mother's madness, his own fear of madness, his crushing loneliness and sense of alterity; hence, there is very little either overt or coded "Jewish" content in the poetry of the 1960s through the 1980s. Also, during this period he is searching for a meaningful spiritual practice and finding the answer in Eastern meditative traditions, particularly in the Tibetan Buddhist— vajrayana—tradition. It could be persuasively argued that this tradition, which incorporates elements of Tibetan folk religion such as flamboyant, wrathful deities, vibrant color, and esoteric ritual (unlike, e.g., Japanese Buddhism, which tends toward minimalism in its aesthetic, and an ahierarchical nondeism), may have appealed to the poet because of its resonance with the hieratic drama of the Old Testament conception of God and the ritual aspects of Judaism. However, it must be remembered that this Judaism played very little part in Ginsberg's formation, and while the possibility is worth mentioning, it is equally noteworthy that Ginsberg was always critical of Judaism's monotheism, which he sees as partially responsible for the ease with which Jewish intellectuals like the objectivist poets and many other leftist American Jews were led into supporting Stalin's dictatorship, with tragic results. At the same time, Ginsberg also sees as "Jewish" the concern with the material world that fuels the desire to realize an economically and socially just society. This is something he finds sympathetic and familiar and strove to carry into his role as public poet; he was consistently outspoken about the ills visited upon the human body and spirit by the militarism both of repressive regimes and of the rapacity of capitalism. Furthermore, this materialism, this acknowledgment of the importance of the here-and-now, has the makings of a good "American" poetics, one that is grounded in the materiality of language (he often cites William Carlos Williams' famous dictum "No ideas but in things" in this regard).

The middle period's best-known (most widely anthologized and/or most often read by the poet at readings poems are "Kral Majales," "Wichita Vortex Sutra," "Please Master," and "Hum Bom"; its major volumes include *Planet News, Airplane Dreams, The Fall of America: Poems of These States*, and, in a somewhat different mode, *First Blues* and *Mind Breaths*. In addition, an early work (*The Gates of Wrath: Rhymed Poems 1948–1951*) was published. During this time Ginsberg traveled around the world, meeting many spiritual leaders and gurus, especially in India; he also consolidated his position as representative poet of America, heir to Whitman in expansive, politically inflected, long-line erotics of democratic and critically celebratory verse. His family of origin recedes as subject matter, as does the primacy of his need to establish the Beat presence in American letters; this has been accomplished. Instead, experiments in consciousness, spiritual questing, and political observation take over as primary themes and concerns. Ever anti-identitarian, he rejected even the tenuous connections he earlier felt to certain fixed identities: though openly homosexual and "married" to Orlovsky from 1955 until his death, he did not travel with a gay crowd; though ever emancipationist in orientation, he was not affiliated with specific leftist parties as his mother and older relatives were; though Jewish culturally and affectively, he had no stake in maintaining a false solidarity with a patriarchal, heterosexist religion that he did not wish to practice. His alternative Beat "boy gang" family also fell apart in this period; the deaths of Jack Kerouac and Neal Cassady, the departure of Gary Snyder for Japan, Burroughs' flight to Morocco and then England, and his own travels (sometimes accompanied by Orlovsky, sometimes solo) point him on his own path, in the direction of Eastern spiritual practices, on one hand, to reconcile the pain of living with the potential boundlessness of human consciousness, and leftist/pacifist political intervention, on the other. Ginsberg also, in this period, seems bemusedly to relish his notoriety and to mentally experiment with it, noting the paradoxes and ironies of his position as outcast-turned-representative. The poem "Kral Majales" (King of May), for example, commemorates his being crowned King of May in a traditional Czech student Mayday festival parade and the following day expelled from Czechoslovakia for being gay (a decadent bad example for youth). "Please Master," a sadomasochistic love-sex poem to Neal Cassady, carries to exuberantly explicit extremes the sexual candor only briefly touched upon in "Howl" 's protagonists' joyful screams at being "fucked in the ass by saintly motorcyclists" (128)—which phrase was enough to have that latter poem impounded for obscenity. These middle years make it clear that the painfully silent apprenticeship of Ginsberg's youth has paid off, expressively in terms of rigorous honesty about sexuality and introspectively in terms of an ability to persevere in spiritual discipline. "Wichita Vortex Sutra" and *The Fall of America* in general document the final phases of the manic cross-country politicospiritual commentary that characterized Beat writing. (It should be noted, however, that Ginsberg consistently had a more developed political analysis of the American scene than his fellow Beats, whose verbal experiments on America often seem merely sentimental populism [Kerouac] or satirical nihilism [Burroughs].) The latter part of this era also sees his assumption (on orders from his guru Chögyam Trungpa Rinpoche) of an administrative, "establishment" position as cofounder and director of the Jack Kerouac School of Disembodied Poetics, the writing program of the Naropa Institute, Trungpa's Buddhist-inspired university in Boulder, Colorado. This new respectability, also manifest in his later position as Distinguished Professor of Creative Writing at Brooklyn College, had further developed Ginsberg's spiritual commitment to compassionate action—this time from a position of power rather than that of underdog.

Ginsberg's more recent writings, starting with *Mind Breaths* and *First Blues* and continuing into *White Shroud* and *Cosmopolitan Greetings*, have been characterized by a return to rhyme, albeit not exclusively. This time, however, the rhymed verse expresses a Blakean, hieratic, and yet playful, tribal/oral spirit rather than a desire to yoke erotic pain in the acceptable measures of his juvenalia. His verse, often printed with melody, is as ribald ("Violent Collaborations"), incantatory ("Hum Bom!"), satirical ("CIA Dope Calypso"), and didactic ("Do the Meditation Rock") as it ever was at the height of his Beat wrath and exuberance. Thematically now, however, he was much preoccupied with aging, mortality, death. Since these themes also bring back memories and anticipations of reunions with the dead—family and friends (Naomi and Louis, who died in 1977, Neal Cassady, Joan Burroughs)—and since Ginsberg's sense of Jewishness is, to such a large degree, mediated by "family," a warmer, more affirmative attitude toward Jewishness has emerged in the last two volumes, *White Shroud* and *Cosmopolitan Greetings*. The poem "White Shroud" documents a dream of Naomi and functions as an epilogue to "Kaddish," depicting a harmonious, if melancholy, reunion with the poet's mother. Though in the dream/poem she is a bag lady living on the streets (again, Ginsberg sees the mythic, the personal, and the sacred in contemporary emblems of despair), seeing her content, he has found "long-sought peace" ("White Shroud." *White Shroud* 49) and wakes "glad of life" (50). In another poem in the volume, "Going to the World of the Dead," which has a tune transcribed complete with guitar-chord changes above the staff, Stalin and Hitler, twin scourges of twentieth-century Jewry who continue to serve as Ginsberg's reference points for the nadir of human relations, are "in Bed" (33) in the world of the dead; further along in the poem, he urges—as a good Buddhist—that we/he "let go your Holy Land Let go" (34) and likewise give up Palestine—"Jews Let go" (34) of the nationalist fantasy of Israel.

Cosmopolitan Greetings is a title that, as Ginsberg glossed it at readings, basically means "Greetings of a Jew"; "cosmopolitan bohemians" or "homeless cosmopolitans" were evidently the damning epithets with which Stalin dismissed the Jews; elsewhere, in the poem "Why I Meditate" (in *White Shroud*), the poet writes that "I sit because after Lunacharsky got fired and Stalin gave Zhdanov a special tennis court I became a rootless cosmopolitan" (9). To Ginsberg and the poetic community he represents and has created for himself and others, "cosmopolitan bohemianism" is a virtue, and in embracing the label meant to confer contempt, Ginsberg is embracing a form of Jewishness not his father's or his mother's but, finally, his own. As an eminence grise of cosmopolitan bohemianism and "decadence" (homosexuality) and as a student of human consciousness, Ginsberg speaks the imperatives that give this title poem authority and resonance: "Stay irresponsible" "Cosmopolitan Greetings" (12). This poem also reiterates the axiom that Ginsberg learned the hard way, the closeted way: "That if the poet doesn't show what he's writing, he can write what he wants." In the late 1980s I heard him, at age sixty, triumphantly belt out "SH'MA, YISRAEL: ADONAI ELOHEINU, ADONAI EHAD" to an audience of post-Beat derelicts and poets, neo-Beat teens and college students, and incongruously well heeled speaker-series season-ticket subscribers at the San Francisco Jewish Community Center at a reading that showcased "Cosmopolitan Greetings." He was pretty well heeled himself, on the outside, wearing the suit and tie his guru Chogyam Trungpa Rinpoche had insisted on—but he was still shocking the bourgeoisie with that voice and that sensibility.

Another poem in the same volume, "Yiddishe Kopf" (which he translates for audiences as "smart Jew," tapping his skull and nodding his head knowingly), uses the tag phrase "I'm Jewish because" to list a number of ways in which the poet identifies as Jewish, all of them secular. They include gesture (shrug of shoulders when mad), ("Yiddishe Kopf," 71) senior citizen discounts, intellectual proclivities at tender age, ability to trace Jewish family back to Vitebsk and Kaminetz-Podolska by way of Lvov, love of stereotypical Eastern European cuisine, etc. He also, though, claims his Buddhist beliefs as Jewish—again, on a theological/religious level, he prefers nontheism. He has said that when writing this poem, he had the Yiddish rhythms of his grandmother's speech patterns in mind and also her immigrant's concern for the future of young Jews going out into the world underprepared. For Ginsberg to write an entire poem, however brief, about his Jewishness, rather than embedding it in a family drama, a political diatribe, or a generalized sensibility, indicates a less embattled relation to it than his previous work would suggest. "Salutations to Fernando Pessoa" has much of the combative humor of "America"—playing the grandiose American poet who must demonstrate his superiority to the Portuguese poet, Ginsberg trots out American nationalism (America is a larger country than Portugal, etc.) and other silly claims to greatness (such as the fact that he is taller than Pessoa) and abruptly concludes with "Pessoa Shmessoa" (*Cosmopolitan Greetings* 35), a Yiddishism that so highly qualifies the American supremacy the persona has been aiming for that the whole collapses into an excellent joke. This poem is a good counterargument to those who believe Ginsberg's talent waned after the explosive displays of *Howl* and *Kaddish*.

CRITICAL RECEPTION

As one might imagine, Ginsberg's critical reception has been mixed: his publishing career began in controversy, and while he is commonly acknowledged to be the best-known poet in America, he has continued to draw mixed fire from his readers. M. L. Rosenthal included him in *The New Poets*, an influential volume that conferred academic legitimacy by inclusion with other poets such as Robert Lowell. Helen Vendler, also a respected, conservative "gatekeeper" kind of critic, has acknowledged his importance, albeit at times grudgingly, deploring, as many did, his turn away from the psychological naturalism of "Howl" and "Kaddish" (closer in nature to traditional post-Romantic lyrics' exploration of personal feeling, though purposefully eschewing the formal control of those lyrics) to the broader sweep of politics and the documentation of travels and drug experimentation (*Planet News, The Fall of America, Angkor Wat*). In the mid-1960s, when "confessional poetry" was emerging as a serious trend with skilled, academically trained practitioners such as Robert Lowell, Sylvia Plath, and W. D. Snodgrass as well as the more popularly oriented Anne Sexton, Ginsberg was already moving away from his more confessional first two books toward a global, documentarian view. Thus, in a curious way, Ginsberg was damned when he did and damned when he didn't—initially reviled for his raw sexual honesty and grimly glamorous depictions of the "lower depths," he was then scolded for abandoning that rawness, which was at least accorded some poetic authenticity, in favor of outspoken leftist politics and Eastern religion, both of which generally seen as inimical to the cultivation of—the primary of—individual perception and emotion, on which the Western lyric tradition rests.

Later still, many of his Beat-oriented followers were turned off when he adopted the tie and suit, associating it with a worn-out spirit and hence a worn-out poetics: in short, he underwent the "sellout" critique. Some couch their critiques in terms of what they see as a shift from an early, praiseworthy anti-dogmatism to the dogmatism of Buddhism—the didactic ditties and the rhymed songs more generally display, they argue, a return to an unimaginative formalism, even though these forms are balladic and populist rather than "high"-cultural, like, for example, sonnets and villanelles. While many see him as a hero of sexual minority rights, anticipating the gay liberation movement by a decade and a half (from 1955, the first reading of "Howl," to 1969, the Stonewall uprising that catalyzed and, in the popular imagination, iconically marks the emergence of a politicized gay rights movement), in a time when overt homosexuality spelled social death in no uncertain terms, the more recent sexual abuse awareness movement has turned critical attention to his support of the North American Man-Boy Love Association (NAMBLA), which is viewed as an apologist group for pedophiles. While it can be argued that these matters are extraliterary, Ginsberg's life and poetry so reflect each other, and he is so pointedly a public poet whose creative output explicitly confronts these themes that all of these matters affect his critical reception, both popular and scholarly. However, *Howl and Other Poems* continues to be one of the best-selling poetry books in the country: "Howl" is taught in almost every survey of American poetry where it continues to shock and delight first-time Ginsberg readers, and Ginsberg received many honors from bastions of institutional conservatism, including a Distinguished Professorship at Brooklyn College, the medal of Chevalier de l'Ordre des Arts et Lettres (awarded by the French minister of culture), an honorary lifetime membership in the Modern Language Association, and membership in the American Institute of Arts and Letters. *The Fall of America* won the National Book Award in 1974, and "Howl" was issued in a large coffee-table facsimile edition in 1986. Jewish institutions which were at one time embarrassed by his antics (a shande fur die goyim [an embarrassment for Jews for the gentiles to see] perhaps), invited him to perform readings in their lecture halls. The revival of interest in radical Jewish culture has led a number of critics, including Maeera Schreiber, Steven Freedman, and Alicia Ostriker, to revisit Ginsberg's oeuvre in the context of Jewish cultural and literary theory. Poet-critic-anthologist Hayden Carruth has predicted that several hundred years hence, Ginsberg's might be the only poetic name and oeuvre of contemporary poets to survive and thrive in the common canon, and there is no reason to disbelieve him, unless sexual censorship comes back into fashion.

BIBLIOGRAPHY

Works by Allen Ginsberg

Poetry

Howl and Other Poems. San Francisco: City Lights Pocket Books, 1956.
Empty Mirror: Early Poems. New York: Totem Press, 1961a.
Kaddish and Other Poems. San Francisco: City Lights Books, 1961b.
Reality Sandwiches. San Francisco: City Lights Books, 1963.
Angkor Wat. London: Fulcrum Press, 1968a.
Planet News. San Francisco: City Lights Books, 1968b.
T.V. Baby Poems. San Francisco: Beach Books, 1968c.
Airplane Dreams. Toronto: Anansi Press; San Francisco: City Lights Books, 1968/1969.
The Fall of America: Poems of These States. San Francisco: City Lights Books, 1972.
The Gates of Wrath: Rhymed Poems 1948–1951. Bolinas, CA: Grey Fox Press, 1973a.
Iron Horse. Toronto, CA: Coach House Press, 1973b.
First Blues. New York: Full Court Press, 1975.
Mind Breaths: Poems 1971–1976. San Francisco: City Lights Books, 1978.
Plutonian Ode: Poems 1977–1980. San Francisco: City Lights Books, 1982.
Collected Poems 1947–1980. New York: Harper and Row, 1985.

White Shroud: Poems 1980–1985. New York: Harper and Row, 1986.
Cosmopolitan Greetings: Poems 1986–1992. New York: Harper and Row, 1994.

Prose

With William Burroughs. *The Yage Letters.* San Francisco: City Lights Books, 1963.
Indian Journals. San Francisco: City Lights Books, 1970.
Allen Verbatim: Lectures on Poetry, Politics, Consciousness. Ed. Gordon Ball. New York: McGraw-Hill, 1974a.
With Allen Young. *Gay Sunshine Interview.* Bolinas, CA: Grey Fox Press, 1974b.
With Neal Cassady. *Visions of the Great Rememberer.* Amherst, MA: Mulch Press, 1974c.
To Eberhart from Ginsberg. Lincoln, MA: Penmaen Press, 1976.
Journals: Early Fifties, Early Sixties. Ed. Gordon Ball. New York: Grove Press, 1977, 1992.
As Ever: The Collected Correspondence of Allen Ginsberg and Neal Cassady. Ed. Barry Gifford. Berkeley, CA: Creative Arts, 1977.
Composed on the Tongue (Literary Conversations 1967–1977). Bolinas, CA: Grey Fox Press, 1980a.
With Peter Orlovsky. *Straight Hearts Delight: Love Poems and Selected Letters 1947–1980.* Ed. Winston Leyland. San Francisco: Gay Sunshine Press, 1980b.
Howl, Original Draft Facsimile, Fully Annotated. Ed. Barry Miles. New York: Harper and Row, 1986.
Your Reason and Blake's System. New York: Hanuman Books, 1988.
Honorable Courtship. Minneapolis: Coffee House Press, 1993.
Journals Mid-Fifties (1954–1958). Ed. Gordon Ball. New York: HarperCollins, 1994.

Recordings

First Blues. Cassette Tape (Folkways/Smithsonian Records FSS 37560). 1981.
Howls, Raps and Roars. CD (Fantasy). 1993a.
Hydrogen Jukebox (opera) with Phillip Glass. CD (Elektra/Nonesuch). 1993b.
Holy Soul Jelly Roll: Poems and Songs 1949–1993. CD (Rhino). 1994.

Works about Allen Ginsberg

Bibliographies

Morgan, Bill. *The Works of Allen Ginsberg 1941–1994: A Descriptive Bibliography.* Westport, CT: Greenwood Press, 1995.
———. *The Response to Allen Ginsberg, 1962–1994: A Bibliography of Secondary Sources.* Westport, CT: Greenwood Press, 1996.

Criticism

Burns, Glen. *Great Poet's Howl.* New York: Peter Lang, 1983.
Portuges, Paul. *The Visionary Poetics of Allen Ginsberg.* Santa Barbara, CA: Ross-Erickson, 1978.
Rosenthal, M. L. *The New Poets: American and British Poetry since World War II.* New York: Oxford University Press, 1967.

Tytell, John. *Naked Angels*. New York: McGraw-Hill, 1976.
Watson, Steven. *The Birth of the Beat Generation*. New York: Pantheon, 1995.

Biographies

Miles, Barry. *Ginsberg: A Biography*. New York: Simon and Schuster, 1989.
Schumacher, Michael. *Dharma Lion: A Critical Biography of Allen Ginsberg*. New York: St. Martin's Press, 1992.

LOUISE GLÜCK   (1943–   )

Linda Rodriguez

BIOGRAPHY

Louise (Elisabeth) Glück was born in New York City on April 22, 1943, the second of three daughters in the family of Daniel and Beatrice (Grosby) Glück. Her older sister died seven days after birth. Glück, the older of the two subsequent children, was emotionally wounded by the knowledge of this earlier dead sister, whose replacement and fulfillment she believed she was expected to be, and by the unresolved grief she believed her mother suffered. This family tragedy not only permeated her childhood but is still a major theme throughout her work.

Her father, an executive, was a first-generation American and the only son among five daughters born to a prosperous Hungarian scholar who had been forced to immigrate to America and become a cigar-factory worker after crop failures bankrupted him. Glück's father had wanted to be a writer but lacked the drive his daughter would find. Before her marriage, Glück's mother, on the other hand, fought to attend Wellesley College in the days when women's education was not generally accepted.

Born into a family where "the right of any family member to complete the sentence of another was assured," Glück describes her mother's speech as "the socially acceptable form of murmur" and her father's as "performance and disguise." She notes that, in keeping with her later love of brevity and lacunae in her own work, "My response was silence" (*Proofs and Theories 5*). Primarily at her mother's urging, Glück and her younger sister were given lessons in the arts, taught to read before starting school, and urged toward high achievement in every area where they showed any interest or gift. As a preschooler, Glück throve on the stories that her father told her and her mother read aloud. Long before she entered school, she came to know and love the Greek myths that would have such an enduring impact on her poetry.

As a child, Glück read Shakespeare, Yeats, Blake, and others and felt this literary tradition to be her inheritance. Raised to value and aim for great achievement of some kind, she was never made to feel that such achievement was unobtainable for a girl. She recalls herself at this young age as being ambitiously devoted to her vocation. From this time in her life dates her view of the poet as one "attempting dialogue with the great dead" (*Proofs and Theories* 4).

Throughout Glück's childhood, her mother's judgment and high standards influenced her attempts at writing. This critical relationship with her mother was complicated by Glück's mystical sense of obligation to both her dead older sister and the mother she believed was constantly grieving. In adolescence, this troubled relationship contributed to Glück's development of anorexia nervosa, which she has come to see as an attempt to force a demarcation or boundary between herself and her mother. By the time she was beginning her senior year in high school and weighed a mere seventy-five pounds, Glück realized the gravity of her situation and requested psychoanalysis. Within months, she was removed from school and spent the next seven years in analysis.

During these years of her analysis, Glück attended Sarah Lawrence College for six weeks and later studied for two years with Leonie Adams and five years with Stanley Kunitz in poetry workshops at Columbia University's School of General Studies. During these years of analysis, paralyzing inner turmoil, and intense, artistic apprenticeship Glück wrote and published her first book.

Glück moved to Vermont in 1971 for a three-month teaching job at Goddard College in Plainfield after her first book appeared. She had suffered a two-year period during which she wrote little, then another two-year hiatus during which she wrote nothing, and she had begun to fear that she might not write again. Originally reluctant to teach, she began to write again once she started teaching. In the course of her career, Glück has taught at Goddard College, the Fine Arts Work Center in Provincetown, Massachusetts, the University of North Carolina at Greensboro, the University of Virginia at Charlottesville, Columbia University, the University of Iowa, Warren Wilson College, the University of Cincinnati, and the University of California at the Berkeley, Davis, Irvine, and Los Angeles campuses.

Glück married Charles Hertz, Jr., in 1967 and divorced him after the birth of her son, Noah, in 1973. Married in 1977 to John Dranow, a writer who is also vice president of the New England Culinary Institute, Glück now lives for half the year in Plainfield, Vermont, with Dranow and her son. She spends the other half of the year teaching at Williams College in Williamstown, Massachusetts, and boarding with an academic couple there. Glück has maintained this basic schedule for the past fourteen years.

For her poetry, Glück has received grants and fellowships from the Vermont Council for the Arts, the National Endowment of the Arts, the Guggenheim Foundation, and the Rockefeller Foundation. She won the Academy of American

Poets Prize of Columbia University, the *Poetry* Eunice Tietjens Prize, the American Academy and Institute of Arts and Letters Award in Literature, the National Book Critics Circle Award for Poetry, the *Boston Globe* Literary Press Award for Poetry, the Sara Teasdale Memorial Prize of Wellesley College, and the Poetry Society of America's Melville Kane and William Carlos Williams Awards and was a corecipient of the Bobbit National Prize. A fellow of the American Academy of the Arts and Sciences, she has been a Phi Beta Kappa Poet at Harvard University. Glück was awarded the 1993 Pulitzer Prize in poetry for *The Wild Iris*, and the following year, she received the PEN/Martha Albrand Award for Nonfiction for *Proofs and Theories*.

MAJOR WORKS AND THEMES

Louise Glück's poetry is lyrical yet reticent, cloaking the confessional in the classical, both in mythic borrowings and in outlook. She writes of the intimate drama of her family with tragedies resonating through the generations, the tragedy of alienation as well as that of untimely death. She writes of being a daughter, a niece, and a granddaughter but, above all, a sister—to her younger sister and to the older one who died after seven days of life. As her work has progressed, she explores the roles of wife and mother and the relationship between human beings and their creator, as well. Her seven volumes of poetry also represent a steady progression in style.

Her first book, *Firstborn* (1968), openly displays its roots in the intensity of the confessional mode with an almost stream-of-conscious fragmentation and an explosive load of violent, bitter emotion, all kept under the tightest control, each poem's ending a lid slammed shut and locked. Unlike the confessional poets, whose influence shows in these poems and with whom she might well have been grouped otherwise, she demonstrates even in this first book the authority and restraint that would become her hallmark. Lines, images, entire poems are so tightly structured that they threaten to burst on the page. Many of the characteristic themes of her future work make their debut in this first book: a family's inability to connect with each other, the human experience of loss in all its forms, the desire for, and resentment of, carnal love. Only her distinctive use of classical myth and her recurrent attempts to understand God are missing, though the final poem, "Saturnalia," points toward the classical motifs of the next books.

According to Glück, "Each book I've written has culminated in a conscious diagnostic act, a swearing off" (*Proofs and Theories* 17) of fragments in *Firstborn*, of a recurring vocabulary and short breath units in *The House on Marshland* (1975), of formal, declarative sentences used to distance the poem from the author in *Descending Figure* (1980). Each of her books builds on, and reacts to, the book immediately before it. To read her books in the order they were written is to follow the conscious development of an extraordinary talent.

In her earliest books, Glück's Jewish background is either invisible (in *First-*

born) or used as a storehouse of mythic images and stories, a lesser version of her beloved Greek classics, as in "The Undertaking," a poem of the infant Moses as he is placed into the basket in the water and suddenly faces a life that seemed impossible seconds earlier, and "Abishag," a perceptive rendering of the tale of the young wife of King David's old age from the unexpected viewpoint of the bride. As Glück matures as woman and artist, however, she turns more often and more deeply to her heritage. In *Descending Figure*, "Lamentations," a long poem with four parts—"The Logos," "Nocturne," "The Covenant," and "The Clearing"—is her re-visioning of the Genesis creation story. Finally, in *The Triumph of Achilles* (1985), she delves into her Jewish inheritance for a handful of remarkable poems: "Winter Morning," "A Parable," "Day without Night," and "Legend." In "Winter Morning," she looks at the Christian mythos from a liberal and sympathetic, but fundamentally skeptical, point of view. She views from outside the Christian mainstream Jesus' birth, his Crucifixion, and the accounts of his appearances after his death. In the final part, she still can't accept it as truth, though she feels the seductiveness of the whole story—as she feels the warm promise of the winter sun that vanishes and reappears (161–63).

In "A Parable," Glück touches the story of King David again, at its beginning with David's victory over Goliath and at its tragic apex with David's scheming for Bathsheba, more out of boredom than desire. Glück even creates her own ambitious midrashic interpretation of a story of the infant Moses in "Day without Night," which opens with an epigraph from the *Midrash Rabbah*. In keeping with her love of lacunae and mystery, the deliberately withheld, she finds a dark truth in the story of an angel's pushing the baby's hand away from jewels and into burning coals: the truth is inscrutable (*The First Four Books of Poems* 200). In this book, she also examines the life of her immigrant grandfather, forming under the pressure of difficult circumstances a belief in equality, justice, and honesty ("Legend" 209).

Eventually, in *The Wild Iris* (1992), Glück wrote an entire book in the voice of one of the Hebrew prophets (if one were a late twentieth-century American woman and backyard gardener). Glück was awarded the Pulitzer Prize for *The Wild Iris*, written in a two-and-a-half-month span of intense creativity. In this book, not only does she speak to God with many of the same concerns and complaints that fill the books of the prophets, but God speaks to and through Glück in resigned, tolerant, irritated, pleased, but always ironic tones. This can be seen most notably in "Retreating Light," where God explains individual choice and human tragedy as a way of giving tiresome human children their own stories to write so that God will not have to be tied down any longer telling bedtime stories. In this book and especially in this poem, we see the girl who "felt, even before I learned to read, that a book was a holy object" (*The First Four Books of Poems*, "Author's Note" xii).

Each of Glück's books is a thematically and stylistically consistent whole, an "attempt to make, of a pile of poems, a speaking whole" ("Author's note" xii). Her last three volumes of poetry succeed most completely in this self-imposed assignment. *Ararat* (1990) is a sustained reflection on mortality and grief, through the medium of her father's death and the family's reactions. Within the lens of this intense time in her own and her family's life, she examines her favorite issues of the fear and bitter reality of loss, the ambivalence of love, and the amplified echoes through the years and the generations of the pain and wounding that result from deliberate and unconscious isolation. *The Wild Iris* uses Glück's own garden—the individual plants, the necessary chores, the changing seasons—as a shaping metaphor for her unsparing exploration of humanity's situation within a created cosmos and of the questions of faith, free will, and relationship with the divine.

In *Meadowlands* (1996), she returns to the classical world, offering a vivid retelling of *The Odyssey* in terms of the breakup and reconciliation of a modern American marriage, complete with seductive sirens, a nearly grown Telemachus, and a klezmer band next door in this Ithaca. Throughout, she manages to be consistent in tone and faithful to both the myth and the modern reality, reexamining her recurring themes of the joy and ambivalence of male–female passion, the fear and reality of loss, and, through Telemachus' precociously perceptive and wry commentary on his parents' marital woes, the ways each generation unconsciously visits its pain on the next. Her tone is relentlessly assured, yet completely natural. In a departure for Glück, she writes poem after poem entirely in dialogue between the two main actors, conversations that are both natural and emblematic for the modern couple, yet still completely in character for Odysseus and Penelope. The design and execution of this ''pile of poems'' seamlessly create her desired ''speaking whole.''

In addition to her poetry, Glück has published a collection of essays about poetry and becoming a poet. *Proofs and Theories* (1994) offers insights into her own history, as well as her views on the theory and practice of the art of poetry. In this rich book, she demonstrates repeatedly her mastery of the essay form and the lucid prose sentence that is its fundamental unit. Her clarity and precision of language in these essays join with her unflinching honesty and intelligent analysis to dance to the graceful music of a poet's prose, illuminating her ''twenty years of discipline and obsession'' (*Proofs and Theories* 100) in the service of the muse.

CRITICAL RECEPTION

In the twenty-eight years Louise Glück has been publishing poetry, critics have come to recognize her as one of America's finest lyric poets. From the beginning, while recognizing such influences on her work as Robert Lowell, Sylvia Plath, and Anne Sexton, critics appreciated her advanced skills with language and form and her passion restrained by intelligence. With each book's increasing transparency of language and richness of vision, her reputation has grown. Don Bogen notes that ''Glück has never been content to stop at the

surfaces of things . . . [and] has narrowed and deepened the focus of her work,''
while Liz Rosenberg describes Glück's work as ''poems that partake of a mythic
largeness indirectly, the unexpected Jewish humor of poet-as-philosopher.''
With *The House on Marshland*, Calvin Bedient announced that Glück had entered into ''her majority as a poet'' (Rev.) while Diane Bonds remarked on the
''iconographic force'' of Glück's landscape in the same book, and Helen Vendler calls its opening poem, ''All Hallows,'' ''saturated by the poet's sense of
her own birth'' (37). Laurie George describes Glück as ''willing to dive deeply
to perform a . . . necessary critique of the wreck of western civilization'' in *Descending Figure*, and Rhoda Yerburgh put it simply: ''Glück is foremost among
her generation of poets.''

Other critics have praised her restraint and reticence, her creation of poems
that resemble myth and fairy tales, her use of mythology to illuminate the intimate secrets of both the individual heart and of the archetypal family, and her
relentless clarity. Some, however, have found her work cryptic, and others have
been bothered by her reliance on parable and fable. Strangely, for a poet known
for controlled elegance of language and luminous mystery, a common description of her work is ''harsh''; Edward Hirsch, Rush Rankin, Robert Spector,
Anna Wooten, Vendler, Bogen, and George are just a few of the critics who
have applied this term to Glück's work. Even Glück has found herself ''forced
to recognize how purposefully I had insisted on distance'' (*The First Four Books
of Poems*, ''Author's Note'' xii) in *Descending Figure* and notes that she once
believed so fervently ''that poems were like words inscribed in rock . . . that the
inaccuracies of the metaphor as description of my own experience did not occur
to me until very recently'' (*Proofs and Theories* 128). She also confesses she
has ''always been too at ease with extremes'' (105) and describes herself as a
poet addicted to paradigm, who ''aim[s] at a kind of terminal authority'' (101).

Recently, feminist critics have focused on ambiguous relationships between
men and women in Glück's work, whether between husband and wife or father
and daughter. These critics have also been interested in Glück's ambivalence
toward the figure of the mother, ''yearning backward as so many of her poems
do toward the serenity of preexistence,'' as Alicia Ostriker notes (''In Mind'').
With her latest books, Glück has earned the respect of critics from a variety of
schools. David Biespiel speaks for many when he says: ''Louise Glück ranks
at the top of the list.''

BIBLIOGRAPHY

Works by Louise Glück

Poetry

Firstborn. New York: New American Library, 1968.
The House on Marshland. New York: Ecco Press, 1975.

The Garden. Antaeus Editions, 1976. (Chapbook of five closely related poems later incorporated into *Descending Figure*.)
Descending Figure. New York: Ecco Press, 1980.
The Triumph of Achilles. New York: Ecco Press, 1985.
Ararat. New York: Ecco Press, 1990.
The Wild Iris. New York: Ecco Press, 1992.
The First Four Books of Poems. New York: Ecco Press, 1995.
Meadowlands. New York: Ecco Press, 1996.

Essays

Proofs and Theories. New York: Ecco Press, 1994.

Works about Louise Glück

Bedient, Calvin. "Birth, Not Death, Is the Hard Loss." *Parnassus: Poetry in Review* 9.1 (1981): 175.
———. Rev. of *The House on Marshland*. *Sewanee Review* (Spring 1976): 352.
Biespiel, David. Rev. of *The Wild Iris*. *Book World—The Washington Post*, November 22, 1992: 8.
Bogen, Don. "The Fundamental Skeptic." *The Nation* 242 (1986): 53.
Bonds, Diane S. "Entering Language in Louise Glück's *The House on Marshlands* [*sic*]: A Feminist Reading." *Contemporary Literature* 31.1 (1990): 58.
Boyers, Robert. "Mixed Bag." *Partisan Review* 36.2 (Spring 1969): 306.
Contemporary Authors. Detroit, MI: Gale Research, 1973: 364.
Contemporary Authors: New Revision Series. Detroit, MI: Gale Research, 1993: 170.
Dictionary of Literary Biography: American Poets since World War II. Detroit: Gale Research, 1980: 290.
Doreski, William. "The Mind Afoot." *Ploughshares* 7.1 (1981): 157.
George, E. Laurie. "The 'Harsher Figure' of *Descending Figure*: Louise Glück's 'Dive into the Wreck.' " *Women's Studies* 17 (1990): 235.
Hirsch, Edward. "The Watcher." *The American Poetry Review* 15.6 (November–December 1986): 33.
Kitchen, Judith. "The Woods Around It." *The Georgia Review* 47.1 (Spring 1993): 145.
Kuzma, Greg. "Rock Bottom: Louise Glück and the Poetry of Dispassion." *Midwest Quarterly: A Journal of Contemporary Thought* 24.4 (1983): 473.
Lesser, Wendy. "Poetic Sense and Sensibility." *Book World—Washington Post* (February 2, 1986): 11.
McClatchy, J. D. "Figures in the Landscape." *Poetry* 138.4 (July 1981): 231.
———. Rev. of *The House on Marshland*. *The Yale Review* (Autumn 1975): 99.
Meyering, Sheryl L. "Louise Glück." *The Oxford Companion to Women's Writings in the United States*. Ed. Cathy N. Davidson and Linda Wagner Martin. New York: Oxford University Press, 1995: 355.
Molesworth, Charles. "Fondled Memories."*The New York Times Book Review* (October 12, 1980): 14.
Mueller, Lisel. "Versions of Reality." *Poetry* 117.5 (February 1971): 322.
Ostriker, Alicia Suskin. "In Mind: The Divided Self and Women's Poetry."*Midwest Quarterly: A Journal of Contemporary Thought* 24.4 (1983): 351.

————. *Stealing the Language: The Emergence of Women's Poetry in America*. Boston: Beacon Press, 1986.

Pettingell, Phoebe. Rev. of *The Wild Iris. The Yale Review* 80.4 (October 1992): 114.

Rankin, Rush. "Knowing Ourselves So Fiercely." *New Letters* 1.1 (Spring 1987): 3.

Riemer, Ruby. "Women as Poets/Poets as Women." *Belles Lettres* 2.2 (November–December 1986): 6.

Robinson, James K. "Louise Glück." *Contemporary Poets*. Ed. Tracy Chevalier. New York: St. James Press, 1991: 349.

Rosenberg, Liz. "Geckos, Porch Lights and Sighing Gardens." *The New York Times Book Review* (December 22, 1985): 22.

Spector, Robert D. "Lyrics, Heroic and Otherwise."*Saturday Review* 52.11 (March 15, 1969): 33.

Stitt, Peter. "Contemporary American Poems: Exclusive and Inclusive." *The Georgia Review* 39.4 (Winter 1985): 849.

Vendler, Helen. "Flower Power." *The New Republic* 208.21 (May 24, 1993): 35.

————. "In the Zoo of the New." *The New York Review of Books* 33.16 (October 23, 1986): 47.

————. *Part of Nature, Part of Us: Modern American Poets*. Cambridge, MA: Harvard University Press, 1980.

————. Rev. of *The House on Marshland. The New York Times Book Review* (April 6, 1975): 37.

————. "Sociable Comets." *The New York Review of Books* 28.12 (July 16, 1981): 24.

Wagner, Linda W. "Idiom and Wisdom in Some Recent Collections of Poetry." *Michigan Quarterly Review* 20.3 (Summer 1981): 301.

Williamson, Alan. "The Concise and the Conversational." *Book World—Washington Post* (January 11, 1981): 6.

————. *Introspection and Contemporary Poetry*. Cambridge, MA: Harvard University Press, 1984.

Wooten, Anna. Rev. of *The House on Marshland. The American Poetry Review* (July/August 1975): 5.

Yerburgh, Rhoda. Rev. of *The Triumph of Achilles. Library Journal* 110. 15 (September 15, 1985): 84.

JORIE GRAHAM   (1951–   )

Karen Bender

BIOGRAPHY

Jorie Graham was born May 9, 1951, to a Jewish-American artist mother and an Irish-American writer father. She was raised trilingually in Italy, attended the French *lycée* in Rome, and studied philosophy at the Sorbonne. Graham returned to the United States to pursue film studies with Martin Scorsese at New York University (NYU), worked briefly in television, and went on to receive her M.F.A. from the University of Iowa.

Graham is currently a member of the permanent faculty at the University of Iowa's Writer's Workshop and is the recipient of numerous awards, including the John D. and Catherine T. MacArthur Fellowship, the Morton Dauwen Zabel Award from the American Academy and Institute of Arts and Letters, and the 1996 Pulitzer Prize for Poetry. She has edited several poetry anthologies, including *Best American Poetry 1990*, and was the poetry editor of the journal *Crazyhorse* from 1978 to 1981. Graham lives in Iowa City with her husband, James Galvin, and their daughter.

MAJOR WORKS AND THEMES

> As the imagination of *journeying* transforms itself from the rational search
> for a known destination to the dream of finding an unknown destination, it
> also transforms our lineage of objectivity and place.
> > —Graham, *Earth Took of Earth* xi–xii

Jorie Graham's work is a journey of self-invention, a mapping of her varied intellectual and aesthetic concerns as they intersect with, and respond to, worldly experience. Perhaps because of her unusual childhood, Graham is indebted to many traditions in Western thought and art—a heritage that she both acknowledges and effaces as she invokes such figures as Wittgenstein, Audubon, and Plato. Her subject matter ranges from ecphrastic to mythic, to national and political, to ecstatic, to everyday.

Graham's first book, *Hybrids of Plants and of Ghosts*, takes its title from Nietzsche's *Also Sprach Zarathustra*, where the philosopher defines man in a formula that neglects man's animal nature, rendering him a "discord" and a hybrid. Thus, Graham determines the dilemmas of her first book: patterns of transformation and mutation are central to this work. With nature as her inspiration, Graham observes the organic world's rhythms. In each blossoming and flight pattern, the poet finds postulates about the world, crafting lines as if they were philosophic assertions. She doesn't rest there, examining perceived patterns for faults the way (as in one of her favorite tropes) a knitter goes over dropped stitches.

Graham's second book, *Erosion*, takes on more ambitious subject matter such as classical painting, autopsy, saints, philosophers, even the enormity of the Holocaust itself in a poem entitled "History." Graham evokes the fractured moments that combine to form history and the debris that veils the remembrance and apprehension of the most important events. Elsewhere, she recounts the autopsy that painter Luca Signorelli performed on his young son—the action becomes a metaphor for the artist's desperate grappling with the boundaries between death and permanence.

In *The End of Beauty*, Graham introduces the use of such formal devices as algebraic variables and blank spaces to explore her continuing preoccupation with language and its failures. She creates a series of self-portraits drawn from mythological and biblical figures, as in "Self-Portrait as the Gesture between Them." In this poem, Graham retells the story of Adam and Eve in order to narrate an elliptical self-portrait. She breaks the poem into thirty-three sections (some comprising as few as five words), cutting and freezing on moments like a camera recording in slow motion.

Region of Unlikeness reveals Graham's taking on more accessible subject matter. The poem "Fission" offers not only familiar events (the John F. Kennedy assassination, the screening of the film *Lolita*) but also a specific narrator. The work effects a sort of fission in Graham's voice as she recounts events in an unusually personal—and extremely fragmented—manner. At times in the book, Graham's lines become repetitive, and the poet is criticized for using an ecstatic (some say hysterical) voice that is overly indebted to Rilke.

Materialism is an ambitious collage of Graham's own work with the sometimes lengthily excerpted writings of other thinkers. In this book, Graham quotes from the early thought of Wittgenstein, Francis Bacon's *Novum Organum*, and Audubon's hunting journals. The poems are extremely intuitive, often beginning and ending abruptly and linking unexpected subjects from the philosophical to the mundane. Graham is a poet of transformation, beginning with Nietzsche's unearthly postulate, and she arrives at materialism, the realm of the physical.

Even as she favors more personal, earthly experiences in her writing, Graham herself remains obscured. In locating Graham as a Jewish poet, one must then turn to the ideas and the thinkers that she appropriates in constructing her helix-like poems. In *Materialism*, the poet selects passages from Benjamin's *Illuminations*: "On Description": "Where we perceive a chain of events, [the angel of history] sees one single catastrophe that keeps piling wreckage on wreckage and hurls it in front of his feet. . . . He makes them transparent, and behind all of them, there appears to me the one for whom they are intended" (55). As in Benjamin's thinking, Graham's work benefits from a certain cabalistic structure—a thought process that is at once intuitive and rigorously logical. At its root, there is a certain willingness to map all events within a larger schema.

Elsewhere, she invokes Wittgenstein: "Form is the possibility of structure." Drawing from the philosopher's early thought in *Tractatus*, Graham returns again and again to the notion of a chain of being and of a latent order not yet decoded. She writes often of a story that is already written, of meaning that is built outside the subject, of man who lives within language and is himself *deciphered* ("he should read in her the rigid inscription") (56). Graham also draws from Sir Francis Bacon's *Novum Organum*: "No conflagration . . . can reduce even the smallest portion of matter to nothing . . . or prevent it from being something." The hidden structures of all things are ostensibly contained within the smallest of details: "It is what we see swelling forth making the shape we know a thing by." Like other Jewish thinkers, the poet does not name herself as author of these patterns; rather, she is a commentator and hopeful participant within them.

CRITICAL RECEPTION

Graham's work provokes strong responses for the strength of her removed voice and circumvention of a confessional style. Critics often find these depersonalized poems too obscure, overly intellectual, even downright callous. "Graham thinks before she feels . . . Her obscurity comes from too great a love of rhetoric," writes William Logan (223–24) in reviewing Graham's first book. Her aesthetic sensibility and philosophic outlook have gotten Graham into trouble as well. Graham received horrified reviews of lines where she describes the pattern of Holocaust victims' bodies as being "beautiful."

Graham is often praised for a subtlety lacking in her contemporaries. Her ecstatic voice and obsessive sensitivity to nuance attract the favor of some readers. "Miss Graham continues, with her haunting indwelling musicality, to make the pattern that constructs us as we read it," asserts Helen Vendler (*The Music of What Happens* 458), an important critic in establishing Graham's reputation. Detractors find that she uses intellectual ideas without being stringent about their content and context, rewriting them to her own ends. Mary Kinzie writes in the

American Poetry Review: "The filmy uncertainties of the verb constructions and the reaching for authority from ethical categories without being able to explore or apply them, are evidence of an undisciplined and unripe apprenticeship" (45). Most critics, however, admit to the impressive scope of Jorie Graham's projects, unparalleled in her generation of poets.

BIBLIOGRAPHY

Works by Jorie Graham

Hybrids of Plants and of Ghosts. Princeton: Princeton University Press, 1980.
Erosion. Princeton: Princeton University Press, 1983.
The End of Beauty. Hopewell, NJ: Ecco, 1987.
Region of Unlikeness. Hopewell, NJ: Ecco, 1990.
Ed. *The Best American Poetry 1990*. Hopewell, NJ: Ecco, 1990.
Materialism. Hopewell, NJ: Ecco, 1994.
The Dream of the Unified Field: Selected Poems 1974–1994. Hopewell, NJ: Ecco, 1995a.
Ed. *Earth Took of Earth: 100 Great Poems of the English Language*. Hopewell, NJ: Ecco, 1995b.

Works about Jorie Graham

Kinzie, Mary. "Pictures from Borges." *American Poetry Review* 12, No. 6, November-December 1983, 40–46.
Logan, William. "First Books, Fellow Travelers." *Parnassus: Poetry in Review* 11, No. 1, Spring-Summer 1983, 211–30.
McClatchy, J. D. "Catching the World." *The New York Times Book Review*, July 26, 1987, 9.
———. "Love, War and Leotards." *The New York Times Book Review*, July 31, 1994, 18.
Swiss, Thomas. "Moving from Station to Station." *Southwest Review* 67, No. 3, Summer 1982, 346–49.
Vendler, Helen. *The Music of What Happens*. Cambridge, MA: Harvard University Press, 1988.
———. *The Given and the Made*. Cambridge, MA: Harvard University Press, 1995a.
———. *Soul Says: On Recent Poetry*. Cambridge, MA: Harvard University Press, 1995b.

ALLEN GROSSMAN   (1932–   )

Daniel Tobin

BIOGRAPHY

Born in Minneapolis in 1932, Allen Grossman was educated at Harvard University and earned his doctorate from Brandeis University, where, from 1956 to 1991, he was the Paul E. Prosswimmer Professor of Poetry and General Education. He is presently Professor of English at Johns Hopkins University. Allen Grossman has been the recipient of a Guggenheim Fellowship, a fellowship from the National Endowment for the Arts, the Witter Byner Poetry Prize, and a fellowship from the John D. and Katherine T. MacArthur Foundation, as well as many other awards. *The Ether Dome* (1991) was a finalist for the National Book Award in Poetry.

Of the many significant American poets born into his generation, Allen Grossman has been until recently one of the least known. This may be due to the fact that, in significant ways, his work is an anomaly in the world of contemporary American poetry. For one thing, like the English poet Geoffrey Hill, Grossman largely eschews the demotic for the bardic. The style of his work has its sources in Romanticism, the High Moderns, as well as the Hebrew Bible. Grossman's gravitation to the bardic, however, is not merely question of style. Rather, for Grossman perhaps more than any contemporary American poet, the poetic voice is the expression of the poet's definition of reality. For Grossman, "the poetry of immanence" that so dominates the contemporary scene inevitably falls short because, regardless of period style, the validity of the poet's work must rest on an authoritative idea of transcendence and not just "the wish to transcend." Grossman has deep personal reasons for his stance, for, as he observes in *Against Our Vanishing*, as early as the age of ten his sense of self was shaped by his own awareness of genocide in the Holocaust, of "the extinction of persons."

That insight is carried forward to his remarks on our present nuclear culture, which, he argues, precipitates "a crisis of representation" by alienating us from our relationship to the transcendent through the threat of total extinction. In either case, the "I" of his poetry emerges from a sense of the self's obliteration or of a self that survives only by accident. Most fundamental to his work is an impulse toward transcendentalism, toward securing the value and validity of self in something invulnerable that at once lies beyond history and yet promises a compassion that transcends the human. There is in Grossman, then, by his own estimate, a profound distrust in the self and in the human family. Yet, though he distrusts the human family, Grossman nevertheless would assume the voice of the bard and would do so with the Miltonic hope of securing "the proper wealth of humanity from a space outside the human world" (*Against Our Vanishing* 83).

MAJOR WORKS AND THEMES

Grossman's work therefore begins with a rarefied understanding of the poet's desire and his object of desire and hence of the desire for transcendence. More specifically, it begins in his conception of a lineage and of the poet's relationship to that lineage. As Grossman defines it, a lineage is a story about the self that connects the self not only to the past but to the universal origin of things. Consistent with the vision of cosmogonic origins established in the Hebrew Bible, the lineage is essentially a discourse-myth, a narrative that is fundamentally about narrative, about the possibility of telling significant stories about ourselves. A person's definition of life is finally determined by the access to story, or, as Grossman suggests in "Summa Lyrica," in the *The Sighted Singer*, the poetic construction of a world like the religious history of the world is the story of the world's narratability. The poet's voice, in turn, gains authority not through the speech of the self but by letting the lineage speak through him. Grossman's understanding of the origins of his poetry is thus oracular and demonic, insofar as he seeks to join his cultural lineage with his poetic lineage. Therefore, his sense of being a poet does not depend on his having found his voice but on his being "a person whom a poetic voice has found." Despite this bardic conception, poetry is not Scripture that as a privileged text would find its linguistic source perfectly in the source of reality. Nevertheless, like Scripture, poetry announces a loss of unmediated relationship between the self and experience.

This sense of loss and the consequent desire to surmount it are already evident in "The Sands of Paran," the poem Grossman confesses was the beginning of his work. As in Pound's "Near Perigord" (ironically, given Pound's anti-Semitism), the poem follows the quest of a speaker who seeks the truth about a legendary person whose life experience is crucial for his own sense of self. In Pound's poem that person is Betrans de Born, the troubadour who inspired his work and shaped his understanding of his art; in Grossman's it is Moses, source of the poet's Jewishness, of his biblical lineage. Where Pound would establish his place in a literary heritage, Grossman seeks finally "a transcendental presence" that is mediated through the lineage he has inherited. Thus, invoking Paran, the desert around Sinai where "fear compounded deity of desire," he declares that his mind is "in the wilderness with Moses" (*Of The Great House* 58). Assuming Moses to be the paradigm for his work, Grossman sets for poetry the highest possible goal: he would recover "the complex face that talked with Moses there, and spoke on stone" (58). Poetry that would recover the confrontation with this supreme object of desire also must assume that poetry, for its very existence requires the existence of something that transcends death. There is, then, a double intention behind Grossman's work. On one hand, he would have the voice of his poems approach the purely transcendent, not a mode of being but the ground of being itself, which therefore transcends the mediatory nature of language, hence, the concern in many of his poems with "the unborn," with a "state" prior to the need for mediation. On the other hand, he would have his work bear witness to the lineage, both cultural and poetic, that establishes the human relation to the transcendent in time, indeed, through which that presence is made known despite the destructive legacy of history, hence, the eschatological imagery that runs through much of his work and especially his use of millennialism in the new poems of *The Ether Dome* (1991) and *The Philosopher's Window* (1995).

As one who would ultimately convey a communal voice and not just the speech of an individual, the poet must be conscious of the double nature of his own role. As Grossman claims in "An Inventory of Destructions," the poet is as in Shelley an "unacknowledged legislator," though with a decidedly transcendent emphasis: God speaks "first to the governor and lays his rod on him" (*Of the Great House* 82). Ever conscious of the marginal place poetry has assumed in our society, Grossman with such claims suggests that poets should attempt to offer a great hope in the face of the negations of history. To fulfill his vocation, the poet must avail himself of a historical conscience. Nevertheless, beyond this historical perspective, the poet's work should ideally shape a poetry that would comprise a vision at once alternative to, and redemptive of, history. At its best, poetry would negate the negations of history in order to, as Grossman declares in "Of the Great House," "establish rest . . . establish rest profound" (5). Such rest recalls Eliot's peace that passes understanding, and Grossman's invocation of it gives testimony to the high goals he sets for himself, goals consistent with the culture-creating aspirations of the High Modernists and, even more profoundly, with the kind of self-transcendence envisioned by the Wisdom Tradition, especially as put into poetic practice by Yeats and Crane. Grossman does not set such goals naively but with full knowledge that ultimately "the great house is not to be established / on divisible earth" (*Ether Dome* 143). Only in imagination is the world righted. Thus, while Grossman's assumptions bear witness to the highest poetic aspirations, they likewise lead him to admit that poetry of such ambition is also necessarily incomplete. In other words, the vision that would establish the great house, if only in imagination, is inevitably provisional, is always, by Grossman's own standards, a failure. Nevertheless, for Grossman, poetry is itself a journey in pursuit of truth and so, like Job, the poet in his very failure to comprehend the infinite nevertheless establishes his fragmentary link to the transcendent.

But despite Grossman's aspiration to make a poetry that serves a transcendent presence, his self-proclaimed transcendentalism reflects an equally powerful need to safeguard the value of the person. Thus, despite its marginality, poetry for Grossman situates itself within what he takes to be our civilization's central crisis, that is, "how do we know a person is present?" (*Against Our Vanishing* 17). What poetry does in Grossman's vision is to enact or model the conditions through which persons are made present to one another and to themselves. Poetry therefore has a profoundly ethical dimension, for it is ultimately concerned with human well-being. To use Sidney's words, poetry should not only create a golden world but also teach us how to live justly in this one. Grossman's conception of the person is more specified than what we find in the work of many of his contemporaries. The voice most often heard in so much contemporary poetry is that of an individual, a personal self with a particular history. By contrast, the voice Grossman would represent is that of the person as though mediating a transcendent source, like an oracle. The voice of the poem is not an instrument of self-characterization but a way of conserving the human image as encoded in the language of the poem. Selves and persons are not the same for Grossman. Whereas selves might be said to be—to use Yeats' words— "accidental," personhood is "intended." Thus, in Grossman's understanding of the term, "person" refers to the value-bearing aspect of our being, that element of each of us that would become a kind of exemplum of immortality. The person is, then, in the sense in which Simone Weil uses the word, the *decreated* self, the self that has been purged of ego. In religious terms, the person as understood by Grossman refers to the image of God. In Blake's myth it would be the equivalent of the human form divine. It is this core humanity, the encoded human image, that for Grossman poetry ultimately represents.

Yet, far from being static, the *person*, the human image or *eidos* Grossman seeks to encode in his poetry, would disclose what he calls "the drama of acknowledgement and presence" (*Against our Vanishing* 27). In articulating this fundamental poetic purpose, Grossman draws considerably from Jewish philosopher Emmanuel Levinas. For Grossman as for Levinas the valorization of the person (symbolized for Levinas by the face) is accomplished only through the recognition and preservation of the *Other*. It is through the other that we ourselves obtain presence, presence that in Levinas' eyes presupposes the transcendence of expression. Hence, there is a bond between expression and ethical responsibility, a bond that entails a mutual act of bearing witness between persons, face-to-face. Language is the medium of this most fundamental covenant, language that comes not from "my" consciousness but from the other and that ultimately bears witness to the human kinship signified, so Levinas maintains, by monotheism itself. Grossman's self-proclaimed intention to "hunt the highest object of desire equal to mind's desire for an object" (*Of the Great House* 6) represents this most essential ethical and artistic dimension of the poet's call. Because for Grossman the individual and the collective participate in one another through the act of speech, poetry as the speech-act par excellence occasions the ideal relationship among persons for it creates a "nexus of value" in which the person may become present (*Sighted Singer* 199). In the final analysis, poetry is a ceremony in which persons are "recovenanted" with one another so that the act of reading itself takes on the aspect of a personal encounter (*Sighted Singer* 284).

This drama of presence, the story of a covenant relationship that the poem would bespeak into being, discloses itself in his work through the central motifs of what I have already identified as the lineage but also that of the Beloved. In his poem "Of the Great House" Grossman vows a book "of mother and father against our vanishing" (6). Indeed, it is through mother and father that the lineage is handed down. By invoking them continually in his work, Grossman not only binds himself to his personal history but locates himself within a cultural and religious legacy. Thus, the imagined spiritual marriage of the son with his father is encoded in poems like "The Book of Father Dust" as the human image Grossman intends us to encounter. Nevertheless, the father in Grossman's poetry, especially in the sequence "Poland of Death," retains historical and not merely metaphysical significance insofar as the dramatic struggle for acknowledgment and presence takes place within a historical context. "Poland of Death," one of Grossman's major poems, may be seen as a liminal realm in which the poet quests after the embodiment in speech of the ideal that eludes total historical representation yet nonetheless promises the infinite. Similarly, in "Poland of Death" and elsewhere, at least as much significance is extended to the mother, through whom the lineage also descends. She, too, is invoked as the creatrix who gives her son access to another, golden world, a world in which the pain of history is transformed into greater consciousness through the constructive effort to tell the story of the person as exemplified by the poet.

To go further, Grossman has observed in *Against Our Vanishing* that whereas his father is associated in his mind with the frailty of the body (hence, the father's association with the befallen, with dust), his mother is associated explicitly with his discourse, with the voice of his poetry. In fact, what he takes to be the demonized speech of his poetry is more specifically in his view the speech of his mother, and this speech is ultimately what mediates that transcendental presence he would, in turn, mediate with his art. Again, poetry has power for Grossman precisely because it is not the speech of an individual. As Grossman observes, this condition of the poet's speech is signified, punningly, by the fact that the word "other" is contained within the word "mother." Poetry is not the speech of the self, "but of the other as mother, as maternal source, source of the world, as the deep source of the art, the point of intersection between nothing and something" (*Against Our Vanishing* 64). This deep association of the mother with the other, of the mother as source of creation with the voice of his poetry, establishes the paradigm of a relationship between persons that Grossman understands as the relationship to the beloved. Most immediately, then, his mother is the beloved of his poems, Beatrice, a truly Dantean figure, though she is not the sole beloved. Father, as the son's imagined marriage to him suggests, may be the beloved. Moses may be the beloved, or the yellowwoods outside the poet's window. The poet's child-self may be the beloved or his own body or his childhood nurse Pat or a dead colleague. Lovers, husband and wife, especially in the sustained book-length sequence *The Bright Nails Scattered on the Ground* (1986), may be beloved of each other. As he says in "In My Observatory Withdrawn," echoing Levinas, any face passionately imagined may be "the Beloved who hears among her stars" (*Of the Great House* 77).

In its broadest scope of significance, then, because of its protean nature, the figure of the Beloved in Grossman's work is intended to model the covenant relationship between persons. The Beloved is fundamentally the human image Grossman would encode in his poems, poems that dramatically make present the Beloved as person, as that which is revealed through interaction with the other. The audience thus, in turn, becomes not only a witness but a participant in the drama, the person to whom, in whom, or by whom the other of the poem is spoken anew. In essence, the poem models the act of civilization itself. But beyond even this, the Beloved as the figure of personhood demands that the relationship between "I" and "You" as encoded in the voice of the poem and bestowed to the reader rest on some common ground. This common ground Grossman alternately calls the intersubjective or the collective or the divine. In its furthest implication, then, the Beloved is the common place where the object equal to mind's desire of an object is obtained in a visionary act of "letting be" that looks forward even to the transcendence of language. As Grossman reminds us in his Preface to "Summa Lyrica," the poet's work, whether in poems or in prose, should give rise to thoughts about something else.

Given Grossman's obsession with such philosophical and theological concerns, it should not be surprising that the Mind itself becomes a character in his more recent work. In "Mary Snorak the Cook, Skermo the Gardener, and Jack the Parts Man Provide Dinner for a Wandering Stranger" (*Ether Dome* 26–27), the Mind itself is the stranger who wanders the world for a companion who is like himself and yet finds nothing in the world so disposed. Here again is the search for the Beloved, now a kind of Yeatsian Anti-self, comically portrayed. Beyond the mind's wandering, however, is the love of Mary Snorak for Jack the Parts Man, a love that lingers in the reader's mind at the end of the poem, a gesture that places the emphasis of the poem on "the foul rag and bone shop of the heart" rather than on the grand symbol. In a similarly seriously comic way, The Messiah is figured as a piano no one can play in "The Piano Player Explains Himself," an ars poetica that more playfully invokes Grossman's belief that the calling of the poet transcends mere aestheticism. In his most recent book, *The Philosopher's Window*, Grossman has reinvented the Romantic quest poem in the image of his own conception of the Mind's pilgrimage to attain its impossible object of desire. "The end is the destination of the Jews," he affirms, where the pilgrims sit together and bring "the world to mind" by telling true stories about the world and "the gods listen and believe" (72). But this is only one of the poem's endings, and in the end "we all have a long way to go." Thus, in a way that asks the reader to know the place again as if for the first time, Grossman's poetry once again invokes its origins in the "truth seeking journey" to Sinai. Grossman's poetic journey, which affirms transcendence as an a priori value without denying what he calls "the postcatastrophic" nature of the poet's speech, would, in the final analysis, subvert the postmodern inclination to defer meaning indefinitely, precisely by affirming that what transcends makes both speech and personhood possible. Or, as he states in more symbolic terms, Jerusalem is the city of presence. Against substantial critical, artistic, and historical pressures that would render the human image fractured or, at the least, incomplete and so with the audacity of a poet aspiring to the highest claims of his art, Grossman would in his own manner and mode contribute to the restoration of the person. Like Yeats and Stevens before him, his art ultimately composes a quest in pursuit of what will suffice.

CRITICAL RECEPTION

Despite having won several major literary awards in recent years, Allen Grossman's poetry has yet to receive wide critical recognition. David Bromwich's short essays on Grossman's early work offer strong, sympathetic, brief introductions to the poet's themes as they develop through the first three books and seek to place Grossman's poetry in the context of Robert Lowell, one of his early models. The most sustained article on Grossman's work is by fellow poet Gerald Stern, entitled "Grossman's Lament." Stern's essay examines Grossman's work in the light of the Wisdom tradition and makes particular claims for "Poland of Death" as a poem that reveals Grossman at his incantatory best. On the other hand, Lynn Emmanuel in a review of *The Woman on the Bridge over the Chicago River* claimed that "Grossman's delight in abstraction and its ability to give language a sonorous almost biblical quality are occasionally his downfall. They result in a density of image and association that makes the poems confusing rather than rich; a reader loses sight of the poem's meaning in a welter of metaphor" (1576). Emmanuel's observation stands as a fine general summary for those critics and reviewers who have found Grossman's work overly difficult, at times mystifying, and at times even bombastic. By far the most illuminating introduction to Grossman's work remains *The Sighted Singer*, which incorporates Grossman's earlier conversations with poet Mark Halliday (published under the title *Against Our Vanishing*) and adds to them another series of discussions. These conversations are laudable not only for what Grossman has to say about his own work and for Halliday's respectful, though often passionate, objections to Grossman's aesthetic but for both men's willingness to wrestle with questions of ultimate concern both for poets and for anyone interested in the fate of the human image and its representation in language.

BIBLIOGRAPHY

Works by Allen Grossman

Poetry

A Harlot's Hire. Cambridge, MA: Walker-de Berry, 1961.
The Recluse. Cambridge, MA: Pym-Randall, 1965.
And the Dew Lay All Night upon My Branch. Lexington, MA: Aleph Press, 1973.
The Woman on the Bridge over the Chicago River. New York: New Directions, 1979.
Of the Great House. New York: New Directions, 1982.
The Bright Nails Scattered on the Ground. New York: New Directions, 1986.
The Ether Dome and Other Poems: 1979–1991. New York: New Directions, 1991.
The Philosopher's Window. New York: New Directions, 1995.

Other Works

Poetic Knowledge in the Early Yeats: A Study of the Wind among the Reeds. Charlottesville: University Press of Virginia, 1970.
Against Our Vanishing. Boston: Rowan Tree Press, 1981.
The Sighted Singer. Baltimore: Johns Hopkins University Press, 1994.

Uncollected Articles

"Teaching Literature in a Discredited Civilization." *The Massachusetts Review* 20 (1969): 419–52.
"Milton's Sonnet 'On the Late Massacre in Piedmont': A Note on the Vulnerability of Persons in a Revolutionary Situation." *TriQuarterly* 7 (1970): 283–301.
"Criticism, Consciousness, and the Sources of Life: Some Tasks for English Studies." In *Uses of Literature*. Cambridge: Harvard University Press, 1973, 19–48.
"Why Is Death in Arcadia? Poetic Process, Literary Humanism, and the Example of Pastoral." *The Western Humanities Review* 41, 2 (1987): 152–88.
"Orpheus and Philomela: Subjection and Mastery in the Founding Stories of Poetic Production and in the Logic of Practice." *TriQuarterly* 77 (1989/1990): 229–48.
"The Calling of the Poet: The Constitution of Poetic Vocation, the Recognition of the Maker in the Twentieth Century, and the Work of the Poet in Our Time." *TriQuarterly* 77 (1990): 220–38.
"Inquiry into the Vocation of Sir William Topaz McGonagall, Poet and Tragedian: The Poetics of Derision and the Epistemic Nobility of Doggerel." *TriQuaterly*: 7 (1990): 239–58.
"On the Management of Absolute Empowerment: Nuclear Violence, the Institutions of Holiness, and the Structures of Poetry." *Agni* 7 (1990): 268–78.

"The Poetry of Robert Lowell." In *American Writing Today*. Troy, NY: Whitson, 1991, 315–33.

Works about Allen Grossman

Bromwich, David. "The Poetry of Allen Grossman." *The New Republic* (December 18, 1976): 24–26.

———. "Prophetic Dreaming." *Parnassus* 8, 1 (1980): 144–49.

Emmanuel, Lynn. Rev. of *The Woman on the Bridge over the Chicago River. Library Journal* 104 (August 1979): 1570.

Sroka, J. R. Rev. of *The Woman on the Bridge over the Chicago River. Choice* 16 (December 1979): 1307.

Stern, Gerald. "Grossman's Lament." *American Poetry Review* (July/August 1992): 7–13.

ANTHONY HECHT (1923–   )

Joel Shatzky and Michael Taub

BIOGRAPHY

Anthony Hecht was born January 16, 1923, in New York City to Melvyn Hahlo and Dorothea Holzman Hecht. He received a B.A. in 1944 from Bard College and an M.A. from Columbia University in 1950. Hecht has been married twice, to Patricia Harris and Jelen D'Alessandro, and has two children, Jason and Adam by his first marriage and one child, Evan Alexander, by his second.

Hecht has taught at Kenyon College, the State University of Iowa, New York University, Smith College, and Bard College, where he was associate professor of English from 1962 to 1967. In 1967, he became John H. Deane Professor of Poetry and Rhetoric at the University of Rochester. Hecht was also a visiting professor at Harvard in 1973 and Yale in 1977. He has received recognition for his work as a member of the National Institute of Arts and Letters and the American Academy of Arts and Sciences as well as the Academy of American Poets, of which he has been chancellor. Among his awards are a Prix de Rome fellowship in 1951, several Guggenheim Fellowships in 1954 and 1959, and two Ford Foundation Fellowships in 1960 and 1968. In 1968 Hecht received the Pulitzer Prize in poetry for his volume *The Hard Hours*.

MAJOR WORKS AND THEMES

Considering that he began his formative years as a poet in the 1940s and 1950s, Hecht is, in many respects, from an earlier tradition in his use of the older forms and language of poetry. His style recalls the wit and conciseness of La Fontaine, Pope, and Byron rather than such contemporaries as Allen Ginsberg.

While *A Summoning of Stones* (1954) is regarded as coming from the "courtly" tradition, *The Hard Hours* (1967) is far more spare in its language and relies less on the literary traditions of poetry and the playfulness of language than on the experiences of life. This progression and maturing of Hecht's work can be seen in *Millions of Strange Shadows* (1977), in which the directness of the poems in *The Hard Hours* is enriched by a sensibility to music reminiscent of the work of Wallace Stevens, in "the melodic intricacy of expression, and the expansive discourse that is propelled through its argument as much by the perfection of the word's sounds as by the thesis that they construct" (Madoff quoted in *Contemporary Authors*, New Revision Series, 122).

In *The Venetian Vespers* (1977), Hecht, in some ways, returns to the style of his earlier work in being more concerned again with the brilliance of language. In his ability to render the horrors of the twentieth century, as in the Holocaust poem "Rites and Ceremonies" (*The Hard Hours*), with his wonderful control of language and tone, he is of special interest to readers of this volume. In this poem he imagines himself in the same "changing room" where the Jews who are about to be sent to the gas are being prepared for their deaths. The poet addresses and questions a God who hears the prayers of the doomed and yet, implicitly, is silent in response. The poem is a vivid and chilling description of those terrible moments between the waiting for death and the closing of the death-chamber door. Yet, despite the despair of this particular work, according to the critic Brad Leithauser, Hecht manages to find some balance between good and evil, even amid the horrors of the twentieth century: "This law, or balancing, is nothing so simple as 'Bad must follow good' or 'innocence is doomed' " but "a complex deliberation on the intertwined states of innocence and evil" (12).

CRITICAL RECEPTION

From his earliest work, Hecht has gotten special attention for his technical brilliance and his mastery of earlier poetic forms. George P. Elliott observes: "Hecht's voice is his own, but his language, more amply than that of any living poet writing in English, derives from, adds to, is part of the great tradition" (quoted in *CA* 222). His first collection of poems *A Summoning of Stones*, received similar praise from Donald Davie but a warning as well: "[T]he poems are full of erudite and cosmopolitan references, epigraphs, opulent, laced with the sort of wit that costs nothing" (quoted in *CA* 222). Elliott also observes that in *The Hard Hours*, Hecht shows his development as a poet from his earlier stylistic brilliance: "One measure of Hecht's maturing as a poet is his skill at handling the ornament of poetry. His youthful verse, in *A Summoning of Stones* ... fed off poetry, skillfully and even handsomely, far more than off experience or felt thought" (quoted in *CA* 222).

Of *Millions of Strange Shadows*, Steven Madoff writes: "Effects of diction no longer call attention to themselves" (quoted in *CA* 222), and of *The Venetian*

Vespers, Michael Dirda writes: "[Hecht] . . . demonstrates again that he may be the most accomplished master of technique since Auden. The verse is musical, the diction precisely nuanced, the syntax smooth and conversational. There is never a jarring line, never a word out of place; everything fits together with the inevitable rightness of the classical poet" (quoted in *CA* 222).

In a general appreciation of his work in the *New York Review of Books*, Leithauser says: "In the four decades of his literary career, Anthony Hecht has shown himself to belong not only to the small group of truly accomplished contemporary American poets, but also to that still smaller group whose members have discovered some fruitful way to dwell upon the special horrors of the age" (12). Of Hecht's combination of controlled technique with chaotic subject matter, the critic adds: "Those same formal aspects that contrast so powerfully with his violent subject matter—the sophistication of tone and language, the intricacy of metrical and rhyme schemes—here serve to enhance innocence and render it somewhat ironic. These formal techniques distance poet from subject even while a restrained, clear, suffusing sympathy suggests deep levels of identification. Our 'distant' author begins to look like a former innocent whose knowledge has been painfully achieved" (11).

BIBLIOGRAPHY

Works by Anthony Hecht

A Summoning of Stones. New York: Macmillan, 1954.
The Hard Hours. New York: Atheneum, 1967.
Ed. with John Hollander. *Jiggery-Pokery: A Compendium of Double Dactyls*. New York: Atheneum, 1967.
Millions of Strange Shadows. New York: Atheneum, 1977a.
The Venetian Vespers. New York: Atheneum, 1977b.
Flight among the Tombs. New York: Knopf, 1997.

Works about Anthony Hecht

Contemporary Authors [*CA*]. New Revision Series 6. Detroit: Gale Research, 1982. 221–222.
Davie, Donald. Rev. of *A Summoning of Stones. Shenandoah*, Spring 1968, quoted in *CA*, 222.
Dirda, Michael. Rev. of *Venetian Vespers. Washington Post Book World*, December 30, 1977, quoted in *CA*, 222.
Elliott, George P. Rev. of *The Hard Hours. Times Literary Supplement*, November 23, 1967, quoted in *CA*, 222.
Leithauser, Brad. "Poet for a Dark Age." *New York Review of Books*, February 13, 1986, 11–12, 14.
Madoff, Steve. Rev. of *Millions of Strange Shadows. The Nation*, September 3, quoted in *CA*, 222.

MICHAEL HELLER   (1937–   )

Norman Finkelstein

BIOGRAPHY

Michael Heller, poet and literary critic, was born in Brooklyn on May 11, 1937. Heller's paternal great-grandfather, David, was a revered rabbi in the Polish city of Bialystock; his son Zalman, also a rabbi, emigrated to the United States in 1911 and settled with his family in the Williamsburg section of Brooklyn. Heller's father Philip (later, Peter) was a businessman; his mother, Martha, née Rosenthal, was a schoolteacher until a heart condition led to her early retirement. For this reason also his family moved to Miami Beach in 1943, where Heller spent most of his childhood and teenage years. Originally trained as an engineer (he received a B.S. from Rensselaer in 1959), Heller first worked as a technical writer and gradually turned to literature in his twenties. Since 1967 he has been on the faculty of New York University (NYU) and received an M.A. in English there in 1986. He directed NYU's American Language Institute from 1986 to 1991. Heller is married to the poet and critic Jane Augustine. He has one son from a previous marriage. He lives in Manhattan.

Accidental Center, Heller's first book of poems, was published in 1972; two more major collections followed: *Knowledge* (1980) and *In the Builded Place* (1990). A groundbreaking work of criticism, *Conviction's Net of Branches: Essays on the Objectivist Poets and Poetry* (1985), was given the Di Castagnola Award from the Poetry Society of America. His poetry, essays, reviews, interviews, and memoirs have appeared in mainstream publications such as the *New York Times*, scholarly journals such as *Contemporary Literature*, and many little magazines (where he has been the subject of a number of special issues). He has given readings and lectures at universities and other venues across the country.

MAJOR WORKS AND THEMES

Heller's work belongs to what could be called the objectivist tradition in modern American poetry and poetics, a tradition that begins with certain tendencies in the writing of Pound and Williams and develops fully in the objectivists of the 1930s, including Louis Zukofsky, George Oppen, and Charles Reznikoff. The objectivists, most of whom were first-generation New York Jews, wrestled with issues of cultural tradition and assimilation, a struggle compounded by their allegiance to a modernist aesthetic that stressed immediacy of perception conveyed through linguistic precision or, as Pound would have it, ''direct treatment of the 'thing' whether subjective or objective.'' As Heller observes in *Conviction's Net of Branches*, the result of this tension between historical memory and the verbal rendering of the phenomenal world is ''a kind of time-bound adeptness.'' ''[T]he impulse behind Objectivist poetics'' (105), Heller notes elsewhere in this book, ''lies not in presenting a better vision or understanding of reality, but in creating an art which aspires to complete transmissibility'' (30).

The transmissibility of culture and belief gradually takes on great importance in Heller's work, especially in his explicitly Jewish texts. *Accidental Center* contains virtually no Jewish material; rather, it is a book in dialogue with the scientific and rationalistic discourses in which he was originally trained—what Heller calls ''these later gods.'' The objectivity of science and technology, as appealing as it might be in its epistemological power, is regarded as insufficient: although it reveals us to be ''isolate particles/suspended in our fates and faiths'' (''Madness''), Heller still tries ''to pose something *as language* which gives more force to a human argument of the world'' (73). These concerns already align Heller with an objectivist aesthetic, but it is in his next book, *Knowledge*, that the ''human argument'' takes a Jewish turn. In this volume, the power of language as a means of transmissibility is fully recognized; as Heller observes, ''whether the word is found/Or finds us, it is inserted in history'' (''Objurgations'' 50). In an extraordinary sequence of poems called ''Bialystock Stanzas,'' Heller's Jewish word is inserted into Jewish history.

''Bialystock Stanzas'' (with its subtitle, ''From a Book of Old Pictures'') embodies the delicacy and horror, the precarious comfort and certain doom of European Jewry. We view these pictures through two lenses, that of the photographer and that of the next generation, the American generation, the fortunate children of those who got away. Impossibly remote, the poet still tries to get as close as he can:

> Light—
> The scene filled with photographer's light
>
> The sparsely furnished room
> In the corner of which
> A china-closet Ark

> The old men
> Under green shaded bulbs
> Reading *Torah*
>
> The prayers are simple,
> To what they think larger
> Than themselves
> —the place almost bare,
> Utterly plain
>
> The flat white light
> Adds no increment
> But attention (15, 18)

Like the photographer's "flat white light," the objectivist's attention to detail illuminates a lost world. In confronting the photograph, Heller is reminded that his experience is an extension of his people's experience and yet is incommensurate with what has gone before. The scrupulous language maintains the transmissibility of culture and faith, but the ruptures of emigration, assimilation, and genocide that largely constitute modern Jewish history are felt as a kind of palpable absence in the text, transforming it into a vessel filled only with the light of attention. Like the old men reading Torah or, as in the following poem, at prayer, Heller devoutly attends to the past, however distant he may be:

> The old bind with phylacteries
> between the leather turns
> The pinched flesh bulges, the old
> Skin, the hairs burn
>
> As if to do this is also
> For the pain
> —to explain
> To Him of what it is
> They are made
> Thus, why they fail (18)

Heller speaks to the Jewish past as the Jew in his phylacteries speaks to God. The admission of failure in both cases is inevitable, but the mitzvah, the commandment that is also a good deed, has been performed.

History, memory, and the transmissibility of Jewish life remain of great concern in Heller's most recent collection of poems, *In the Builded Place*, though the grim certainty of rupture tends to be eased by the endurance of personal relations and family ties. Two poems about Zalman Heller, "The American Jewish Clock" and "In a Dark Time, on His Grandfather," together achieve an extraordinary sense of temporal plenitude dialectically posed against the mundane realities of loss and death. Zalman, we are told, "heard the clock sounds that translate every-/ where. He had been brought into redeeming time,/ each stroke the echo of his unappearing God'' (''The American Jewish Clock,'' 60). For the devout Zalman, purported author of a lost work called *The Just Man and the Righteous Way*, redemptive time remains a certainty despite the shocks of his immigrant life. For his skeptical grandson, such cannot be the case:

> . . . Grandfather,
> What to say to you who cannot hear?
> The just man and the righteous way
> Wither in the ground. No issue,
> No issue answers back this earth. (''In a Dark Time, on His Grandfather,'' 60)

Nevertheless, in ''For Uncle Nat,'' lunch with his elderly uncle becomes for the poet a sacred moment, at least as meaningful as the remembered occasion when he allowed himself to be pulled into a 20th Street shul to become the last of ''the necessary ten'' of a minyan. The concluding stanza of the poem is one of the grandest passages in recent Jewish-American literature:

> So I ask, Nat, may I borrow you, for a moment,
> To make a necessary two? Last time we lunched,
> Enclaved in a deli, in the dim light, I saw
> A bit of my father's face in yours. Not to make
> Too much of it, but I know history
> Stamps and restamps the Jew; our ways
> Are rife with only momentary deliverance.
> May I borrow you for a moment, Nat. We'll celebrate
> By twos, the world's an Ark. We'll talk in slant,
> American accents to code the hidden language of the Word. (62)

These lines may, in turn, be glossed by a passage in Heller's recently written, still unpublished, memoir, *Living Root*:

''Can the human word,'' Gershom Scholem writes, ''contain the word of God in its pure form, or can the word of God, if it exists, express itself within the confines of the human language?'' The answer, for me, to both of these questions can only be yes. Any attempt to separate God word and human word would have no meaning or force whatsoever. The idea is one which could hold true whether one were a believer or not. . . . What is prime, the causal factor of the poem, is the world, the unnameable angel who is struggled with, in order to find the blessed name, Israel, the place of God or divinity. This much I allow myself.

Heller's understanding of the ways in which history and language are folded into poetry is, at this point in his career, shaped as much by figures such as Scholem and Walter Benjamin as by his objectivist mentors. For Heller, like the Cabalists, language is the shadow cast by divinity upon human history, and in writing the poem, we see the things of this world as both immediate material

presences and historically inscribed signs pointing to an impossibly remote redemption, "rife with only momentary deliverance."

It should come as no surprise, then, that Heller, despite his strong links to
modernist poetics, is highly critical of the various formalisms that have recently
developed in American verse, especially the avant-garde tendency known as
language poetry. In a wide-ranging essay called "Avant-Garde Propellants of
the Machine Made of Words," Heller insists that poetic meaning is grounded
in historically conditioned self-expression and that "[o]nce we try to claim for
a work that it is non-expressive or non-referential, that its resonances as language no longer matter . . . we have trivialized it out of existence" (*Sagetrieb*
20). For Heller, language in its postmodern state has undergone yet another
cabalistic breaking of the vessels, a drastic spillage not of meaning but of the
potential for meaning, so that it is the task of the poet to gather and raise the
shards or sparks. As he declares in "Through the Binoculars," one of a number
of poems in *In the Builded Place* occasioned by his father's death,

> . . . You can hear such confusion
> In the language of the fathers as they fall
> Through time. It sounds like hope haunting
>
> The epochal voices which seek a stay against
> Their time. *O keep me from this death*. Father,
> All your words have died, yet, curiously, their muses
>
> Live on. . . . (112)

CRITICAL RECEPTION

All four volumes of Heller's poetry have been well received. Writing about
Accidental Center in *Parnassus*, James Guimond noted that the "poems' structures record the mind's subtle and the heart's rushed movements toward the
world, then the mind's skeptical, meditative dis-engagements, and finally the
achievement of itself in the world which is scientifically as well as emotionally
satisfying" (106). This response is typical of the reviews of Heller's first book;
critics were quick to recognize the meditative, dialectically honed quality of the
verse as manifested in both voice and structure. His affinity to the objectivists
gradually came to be noted as well, as reviews of *Knowledge* in *Sagetrieb* indicated. Considering *Knowledge* in *The American Book Review*, Lucien Stryk
observed that what was "[m]ost admirable in *Knowledge* is the manner in which
the eye moves among harsh materials" (2). Although Stryk and Alan Williamson complained of Heller's occasional imprecision and abstraction, both reviewers acknowledged that Heller was a poet of serious ambition and importance.

With the appearance of the widely reviewed *In the Builded Place* Heller's
reputation seems to have been secured. Once again, the meditative, highly
wrought qualities of the verse were frequently observed, but this time, the scope

of the work also drew praise. "The sheer intellectual range of this book is astonishing" declared Bill Tremblay in *American Book Review* (20). For Tremblay, *"In the Builded Place* is such a vast book that it may well alter the way distinctions are made between Modernist and postmodernist theory" (20). Edward Foster, in *Sagetrieb*, perhaps summing up the overall response to Heller's accomplishment, called *In the Builded Place* "a major book, the realization of an aesthetic and a human possibility not much regarded in times when poems are written without a sense of the traditions words involve" (253).

BIBLIOGRAPHY

Works by Michael Heller

Poetry

Accidental Center. Fremont, MI: Sumac, 1972.
Knowledge. New York: Sun Press, 1980.
In the Builded Place. Minneapolis: Coffee House Press, 1990.
Wordflow: New and Selected Poems. Jersey City, NJ: Talisman House, 1997.

Criticism

Conviction's Net of Branches: Essays on the Objectivist Poets and Poetry. Carbondale: Southern Illinois University Press, 1985.
Ed. *Carl Rakosi: Man and Poet.* Orono, ME: National Poetry Foundation, 1993.

Works about Michael Heller

Finkelstein, Norman. *"Dy-Yanu*: Michael Heller's 'Bialystok Stanza.' " *Talisman: A Journal of Contemporary Poetry and Poetics* 11 (Fall 1993): 77–80.
Foster, Edward. Rev. of *In the Builded Place. Sagetrieb* 9.1 and 2 (Spring/Fall 1990): 251–253.
Frye, Richard. "The Poet as Phenomenologist." *Talisman: A Journal of Contemporary Poetry and Poetics* 11 (Fall 1993): 90–91.
Gardner, Thomas. " 'Speaking the Estranged of Things': Michael Heller." *Talisman: A Journal of Contemporary Poetry and Poetics* 11 (Fall 1993): 94–95.
Géfin, Laszlo K. "Michael Heller's Personae." *Talisman: A Journal of Contemporary Poetry and Poetics* 11 (Fall 1993): 81–85.
———. Review of *Knowledge. Sagetrieb* 3.1 (Spring 1984): 143–47.
Guimond, James. "Moving Heaven and Earth." *Parnassus* 1.1 (Fall/Winter 1972): 106–15.
Heller, Michael. "Avant-Garde Propellants of the Machine Made Words." *Sagetrieb* 10: 1 and 2 (Spring/Fall 1991): 20.
Kimmelman, Burt. "The Autobiography of Poetics: Michael Heller's *Living Root*." *Talisman: A Journal of Contemporary Poetry and Poetics* 11 (Fall 1993): 67–76.
Peterson, Jeffrey. "The Builder's Art of Michael Heller." *Talisman: A Journal of Contemporary Poetry and Poetics* 11 (Fall 1993): 96–99.
Riemer, Ruby. "Michael Heller: A Poet's Quest." *Talisman: A Journal of Contemporary Poetry and Poetics* 11 (Fall 1993): 100–102.

Schwerner, Armand. " 'Taking Up the Thread' ('Father Studies'): On the Poetry of Michael Heller." *Talisman: A Journal of Contemporary Poetry and Poetics* 11 (Fall 1993): 65–66.

Seidman, Hugh. "Eye: Void: Matter." *Talisman: A Journal of Contemporary Poetry and Poetics* 11 (Fall 1993): 105–9.

Stryk, Lucien. "Of Music and Rites." *American Book Review* 4.2 (1982): 2.

Tarn, Nathaniel. "A Letter to Michael Heller." *Talisman: A Journal of Contemporary Poetry and Poetics* 11 (Fall 1993): 86–89.

Tremblay, Bill. "America and the Vast Codependency." *American Book Review* (November/December 1990): 3, 17, 20.

Weber, Marc. "Heller's Realm: The Overlook." *Talisman: A Journal of Contemporary Poetry and Poetics* 11 (Fall 1993): 103–4.

Weinfeld, Henry. "Fragment of an Imaginary Dialogue with Michael Heller on *In the Builded Place.*" *Talisman: A Journal of Contemporary Poetry and Poetics* 11 (Fall 1993): 110–12.

Williamson, Alan. "At Borders, Think." *Parnassus* 9.2 (Fall/Winter 1981): 247–54.

EDWARD HIRSCH   (1950–   )

Joel Shatzky and Michael Taub

BIOGRAPHY

Edward Hirsch was born on January 20, 1950, in Chicago to Kurt and Irma Ginsburg Hirsch. He has a B.A. from Grinnell College (1972) and a Ph.D. from the University of Pennsylvania (1979). In 1977 he married Janet Landay, and they have one child, Gabriel.

Hirsch was an assistant professor of English at Wayne State University from 1979 to 1982 and has been at the University of Houston since 1982, becoming a professor of English in 1988. Among his many honors and awards have been several Academy of American Poets Awards (1975–1977), a National Endowment for the Arts creative writing fellowship (1982), a Guggenheim Fellowship (1985–1986), and the Rome Prize from the American Academy and Institute of Arts and Letters, American Academy of Rome (1988). In 1982 Hirsch was nominated for a National Book Critics Circle Award in poetry for *For the Sleepwalkers*, and in 1987 he received this award for *Wild Gratitude*.

He has produced four volumes of poetry: *For the Sleepwalkers* (1981), *Wild Gratitude* (1986), *The Night Parade* (1989), and *Earthly Measures* (1994). Hirsch has also contributed articles, stories, and poems to such journals and periodicals as the *New Yorker, Poetry*, the *New Republic*, the *New York Times Book Review*, and the *Nation*.

MAJOR WORKS AND THEMES

Perhaps the best description of Hirsch's work comes from his own mouth. He expresses one of the themes that one finds in so many of the poets in this book: a search for some meaning in a universe that seems bereft of God.

"If I were to describe my new work, I would say that it is 'god hungry.' *Earthly Measures* is very much about what the soul does after hungering after God and He does not come. What does one do to fill the subsequent emptiness?" (*CA* 229). In this respect, Hirsch's quest has much in common with the early writings of Robert Mezey and the questionings of the meaning one can try to derive from the Holocaust found in a number of other Jewish-American writers, such as Charles Fishman.

Hirsch's earlier poetry reflects a technical mastery of different styles. *For the Sleepwalkers* employs these techniques in suggesting the poetry of Rimbaud and Rilke as well as presenting the point of view of a painter like Matisse. But Hirsch's brilliance can also be taken to task for its tendency to become self-gratifying, in the view of a number of critics.

With his most recent book, *Earthly Measures*, Hirsch has employed his technical facility and fertile linguistic imagination in a way that speaks profoundly to the longing of Americans, American Jews especially, for spiritual meaning.

In "In the Mid-East," Hirsch suggests in the journey of the Greek hero into the modern-day "underworld" the ironies of contemporary politics where he sees the Muslims looking through barbed-wire fences in Israel as if they were Jews. This frightening analogy between the treatment of the Jews by the Nazis and what he perceives of Jewish-Palestinian relations in Israel is also reflected in his grim vision of a God-abandoned landscape in "In the Midwest" (*CA* 229): "As if God had crumbled bits of charcoal" (*Earthly Measures* 7). In this volume the poems reflect the quest for a God whose absence is far more evident in a landscape of sterility, isolation, and death than an implied presence in miracles of natural wonders.

Hirsch imagines the questioning of the philosopher Simone Weil, a victim of the Nazis despite her conversion from Judaism to Catholicism: of a God that is "clumsy and inefficient" ("Simone Weil: The Year of Factory Work [1934–1935]" *Earthly Measures* 18), but there is no answer to her ponderings in a factory camp. And in "Unearthly Voices," Hirsch speculates on the ponderings at a monastery of Hugo von Hofmannsthal, the Jewish poet who collaborated with Richard Strauss who has a vision of himself walking in a barren landscape where the angels have disappeared into the trees, and the peacefulness of the silence is of death (*Earthly Measures* 34). These visions of emptiness suffuse Hirsch's latest work with a profound sense of despair. In it he reflects the pessimism that can be found in the writing of many of his contemporary Jewish poets who question the justice of a God who seems to have abandoned his people, although Hirsch himself feels and the book concludes that "[a]rt stands against the emptiness" (qtd. in *CA* 229).

CRITICAL RECEPTION

Hirsch's poetry has been generally met with favorable reviews. Peter Stitt in *Poetry* describes him as "a poet of genuine talent and feeling" (qtd. in *CA*

228), and Phoebe Pettingell in the *New Leader* in a review of *For the Sleep-walkers* says: "I admire Edward Hirsch for his mystical vision, for the mastery he has . . . attained—and for his daring" (qtd. in *CA* 228). But *The Night Parade* had a more mixed review. Stephen Dobyns in *The New York Times Book Review* notes: "Too many poems become sentimental or seem willed rather than to come from the heart" (quoted in *CA* 228), while Pat Monaghan in *Booklist* feels that Hirsch knows the difference between "emotion and sentimentality" (quoted in *CA* 228).

Earthly Measures received highly favorable reviews that reflect Hirsch's somber and powerful impressions of the spiritual desolation he sees around him. Patricia Hampl notes how the poet "charges his poems with a luminous power," and they are "poems of immense wonder and rigor. To say they are religious poems is only to recognize their grandeur and generosity, and their heartbreaking longing" (quoted in *CA* 229). Daniel L. Guilory confirms this view and regards these works as "a profoundly spiritual quest for the absolute. There is a deep hunger for divinity here" (quoted in *CA* 229). These and the other almost uniformly positive reactions to Hirsch's poetry confirm his place as of considerable importance among the Jewish-American poets who have emerged in the last two decades.

BIBLIOGRAPHY

Works by Edward Hirsch

For the Sleepwalkers. New York: Knopf, 1981.
Wild Gratitude. New York: Knopf, 1986.
The Night Parade. New York: Knopf, 1989.
Earthly Measures. New York: Knopf, 1994.

Work about Edward Hirsch

Contemporary Authors. New Revision Series 42. Detroit: Gale Research, 228–229.

JOHN HOLLANDER   (1930–)

Mark Rudman

BIOGRAPHY

John Hollander was born in New York City into a middle-class family. His mother was a high school teacher, and his father was a research physiologist whose commitment to science made a lasting impression. Hollander's ability to move freely between science, music, and poetry was initiated early on when he attended Bronx High School of Science, then Columbia College, where he studied English literature and art history with Mark Van Doren and Lionel Trilling. Among his classmates were fellow poets and his first critics Allen Ginsberg and Richard Howard. He did his doctoral work at Indiana University and spent three years in Cambridge, where, in addition to his literary studies, he increased his involvement with music by playing in small chamber groups. Hollander has taught literature, at Yale since 1959, which, while it has cut into his own writing time, has deepened his scholarship.

MAJOR WORKS AND THEMES

In addition to writing his poetry, for which he is best known, Hollander has been active for almost forty years as an essayist, scholar, editor, and anthologist. His work as an editor would deserve its own encyclopedia entry. In the past several years, his two vastly inclusive volumes of nineteenth-century American poetry in the Library of America series appeared and should not go unremarked. Though far less demanding from a purely editorial point of view, his more recent anthology, *The Gazer's Spirit: Poems Speaking to Silent Works of Art* (1995), is worthwhile as much for his thorough and searching Introduction and discussion of individual cases as it is for the poems and juxtaposed paintings. One of the unique specimens in Hollander's body of work is his primer on poetic form, *Rhyme's Reason*, a tour de force in which Hollander composes all of the examples of all known English forms and through that process explains how to write them.

John Hollander is known as a brilliant, witty, and inventive poet. I can't think of another American poet who has so exhausted or reinvented the lexicon of forms. No statement conveys the gist of Hollander's fascination with form than one that Alberto Giacometti wrote in 1945: "[I]n every work of art the subject is primordial, whether the artist knows it or not. The measure of the formal qualities is only a sign of the measure of the artist's obsession with his subject; the form is always in proportion to the obsession." Hollander's intricate formal games or puzzle element is used in the service of an extraordinarily complex and complicated imagination. The poet who most informs Hollander's practice is W. H. Auden, who chose Hollander's first book, *A Crackling of Thorns*, for the Yale Younger Poets Series. Indeed, the Audenesque tone of "Late August on the Lido" is undeniable and, I would argue, conscious to the young poet still learning his craft, which Hollander personifies the beaches of summer as a woman whose "golden children" will leave when the season turns to fall.

It is not the pyrotechnics and speculative psychology that give the work of this polymath its claim on the reader's imagination; conversely, it enhances the formal dexterity that gives rise to his sonorous tones. His use of the eleven-syllable line in a book like *Reflections on Espionage* is a kind of formal antinomianism, since hendecasyllables in English have proved so notoriously problematic with regard to music. (Hollander's knowledge of music is not metaphorical. During graduate school at Columbia, he studied harmony, counterpoint, and the history of music and taught himself to play the lute.)

Hollander does not so much share Auden's themes or preoccupations as he does his proclivity to make each poem a distinct, formal unit, quarried from a wide array of traditional forms, from sonnets to Pindaric triads, to syllabics, to adaptations of the stanza form Fitzgerald used in the *Rubaiyat*. Or, given his obsession with the look of the poem on the page, he invents forms to create visual images. One of Hollander's signature books is *Types of Shape*: here his poems imitate the objects that they embody or describe, such as a car key, a lightbulb, or—thanks to Vicki Hearne's article in the *New Yorker*—most famously, a cat. This book is not as emotionally propelled as some of Hollander's others, but it is emblematic of his gesture in terms of the attempt to trace a figure, find a pattern. These poems, as well as *Powers of Thirteen*, use his primary unit—syllabics. In *Powers*, each poem has thirteen lines with thirteen syllables to each line, and there are 169 poems.

One of the most notable aspects of Hollander's work is the absence of sentimentality and cliché. It is consonant with his claim that his family life "lacked all but a tincture of the raw, Yiddishized culture shared by so many of [his] contemporaries" that he has few poems that can be easily categorized as "Jewish." He is perhaps the least anecdotal poet of his generation. A poem like "Cohen on the Telephone" is an anomaly in his work. But he is not remote from the idea of an accessible poetry. His translations of Moyshe-Leyb Halpern are among the best translations I know from Yiddish into English.

His surfaces and subjects are far more cosmopolitan than Jewish. Hollander's Jewishness is more apparent in his overall vision. He presents the world in almost staggering detail, yet mysteriously obscures himself behind the object.

Given the strongly empirical basis of both his poems and his prose, it follows that Hollander is adamant that it is equally important for a poet to know both poetic forms and the law behind the forms. He takes Allen Ginsberg to task for what he considers a misuse of the idea of a "kaddish" in *Kaddish*: "Whether or not one admires this poem, one must recognize that it ignores the meaning—the nature, structure, liturgical function—of the prayer after which it takes its title" ("The Question of American Jewish Poetry").

In his poetry, Hollander aspires toward elegance as much in the purely mathematical sense as in ways having to do with the beauty of language. (Another piece of the puzzle is that while now married to the sculptor Natalie Charkow, he was previously married to Anne Hollander, an astute critic who has focused her attention on fashion and its implications throughout history.) John Hollander claims that law is necessary to establish identity and moral foundation, drawing attention to both the object in isolation and the verse unit itself. His use of numbers and patterns is meant to invoke a certain design. While more the spiritual son of William James than Henry, he traces figures, but they continue to disappear in more ways than one, both subjectively and objectively, as in "The Mud Potter" in which the New Year is compared to the coil of a clay pot that has its tail in its mouth.

While Hollander is more often linked with other formalists such as James Merrill and Anthony Hecht than with other contemporary Jewish poets such as Allen Ginsberg, Philip Levine, or Gerald Stern, he is without question the most cabalistic of them all. Like Walter Benjamin, Hollander's work is very difficult to classify in terms of genre. This man, who is exceptionally knowledgeable about subjects that poets are usually ignorant of, including science and mathematics, has created an oeuvre that is as rewarding as it is difficult. The critic who reads closely demands to be read closely, and this precision of language is itself unfashionable as "dumbing down" becomes an operative phrase at the time of this writing. The author is obscured.

CRITICAL RECEPTION

Critics have tended to focus more on Hollander's skills than his substance, praising over and over again his dexterous use of one difficult form after another. Louis L. Martz goes so far as to praise Hollander for composing in "*strict eleven-syllable lines*" (*Contemporary Literary Criticism* [*CLC*] 261). This foregrounding of technique seems to invite such superacademic, as opposed to intuitive, responses to his work—which is unfortunate. Hollander's obsession with detail is also a source of much spicy critical commentary. To some, it is an irritant.

Michael Wood, in one of the more measured essays written about Hollander, upbraids him for cleverness, "diffusion, elusiveness, flippancy, and (my hand shakes as I tap out the word) insincerity" but ends with strong praise of his "fragmentary, hinting narrative" in *Reflections on Espionage*, which he finds both funny and haunting (*CLC* 263). Harold Bloom's praise of him is basically swelling rhetoric, whereas Paul Auster, J. D. McClatchy, and Richard Poirier are both positive and incisive. In one of the most insightful sentences written about Hollander, Richard Poirier praises his " 'radical self-questioning' " and maintains that he "escapes the limits of confessional poetry because he will not imagine the self—his or any other—in isolation, as a 'substantive,' to recall William James, deprived of the relational and blurring effects of 'and' and 'if,' of 'but' and 'by' " (*CLC* 264). David Lehman's "The Sound and Sense of the Sleight-of-Hand Man" is the article that, to my mind, best characterizes Hollander's work.

BIBLIOGRAPHY

Works by John Hollander

Poetry

A Crackling of Thorns. New Haven, CT: Yale University Press, 1958.
Movie-Going. New York: Atheneum, 1962.
Visions from the Ramble. New York: Atheneum, 1965.
With Anthony Hecht. *Jiggery-Pokery*. New York: Atheneum, 1966; 2d ed., 1984.
Types of Shape. New York: Atheneum 1969; 2d expanded ed. with ten new poems, notes, and Introduction, New Haven, CT: Yale University Press.
The Night Mirror. New York: Atheneum, 1971.
An Entertainment for Elizabeth (masque). *English Literary Renaissance Monographs*. Storrs, CT, 1972a.
Selected Poems. New York: Atheneum, 1972b.
Town and Country Matters. Boston: Godine, 1972c.
The Head of the Bed. Boston: David R. Godine, 1974.
Tales Told of the Fathers. New York: Atheneum, 1975.
Reflections on Espionage. New York: Atheneum, 1976.
Spectral Emanations: New and Selected Poems. New York: Atheneum, 1978.
Blue Wine and Other Poems. Baltimore: Johns Hopkins University Press, 1979.
Powers of Thirteen. New York: Atheneum, 1983.
In Time and Place. Baltimore: Johns Hopkins University Press, 1986.
Harp Lake. New York: Alfred Knopf, 1988.
Tesserae and Other Poems. New York: Alfred Knopf, 1993.
The Death of Moses (libretto). New York: Schott, 1993a.
Selected Poetry. New York: Alfred Knopf, 1993b.

Criticism

The Untuning of the Sky. Princeton: Princeton University Press, 1961.
Vision and Resonance: Two Senses of Poetic Form. Berkeley: University of California Press, 1975.

The Figure of Echo: A Mode of Allusion in Milton and After. New Haven, CT: Yale University Press, 1981a.

Rhyme's Reason: A Guide to English Verse. New Haven, CT: Yale University Press, 1981b.

Melodious Guile: Fictive Pattern in Poetic Language. New Haven, CT: Yale University Press, 1988.

William Bailey. New York: Rizzoli; Milan: Fabbri, 1990.

Edited Works

Selected Poems of Ben Jonson. New York: Dell, 1961a.

With H. Bloom. *The Wind and the Rain: Anthology of Poems for Young People.* New York: Doubleday, 1961b; latest ed., North Stratford, NH: Ayer, 1988.

American Short Stories Since 1945. New York: Harper and Row, 1968a.

Modern Poetry: Essays in Criticism. New York: Oxford University Press, 1968b.

Poems of Our Moment. New York: Pegasus, 1968c.

With R. Brower and Helen Vendler. *I. A. Richards; Essays in His Honor.* New York: Oxford University Press, 1973a.

With F. Kermode. *The Oxford Anthology of English Literature.* New York: Oxford University Press, 1973b.

Poetics of Influence: New and Selected Criticism. New Haven, CT: H. R. Schwab, 1988.

The Essential Rossetti. New York: Ecco Press, 1990.

American Poetry, the Nineteenth Century. Vols. 1, 2. New York: Library of America, 1993.

The Gazer's Spirit: Poems Speaking to Silent Works of Art. New Haven, CT: Yale University Press, 1995.

Animal Poems. New York: Knopf, 1996a.

Garden Poems. New York: Knopf, 1996b.

Works about John Hollander

Bloom, Harold. "Books Considered: 'Spectral Emanations: New and Selected Poems.' " *The New Republic* 179, No. 11 (September 9, 1978): 42–43.

Contemporary Literary Criticism, Vol. 14. Detroit: Gale Research, 1980, 262–64.

Corn, Alfred. "Water Music and the Effects of Snow." *Grand Street* 9:1 (Autumn 1989): 258–63.

Lehman, David. "The Sound and Sense of the Sleight-of-Hand Man." *Parnassus: Poetry in Review.* 12: 1 (Fall/Winter 1984): 180–212.

McClatchy, J. D. "Speaking of Hollander." *The American Poetry Review* 11:5 (September–October 1982): 23–26.

Nirth-Nesher, Hana, ed. *The Question of American Jewish Poetry. What Is Jewish Lit?* New York: Jewish Publication Society, 1994.

Stein, Lorin. "The Gazer's Spirit." *The Threepenny Review* (Spring 1996).

Wood, Michael. "Calculated Risks." *The New York Review of Books* 25, No. 9 (June 1, 1978): 27–30.

RICHARD HOWARD
(1929–)

Daniel Kane

BIOGRAPHY

Richard Howard was born on October 13, 1929, in Cleveland, Ohio, and was adopted by the Joseph family. He grew up an only child and was given every opportunity to develop cultural tastes. Howard remembers being instructed in practically all the disciplines—art, music, sports. He says, "I was the kid who was given lessons in everything." (All of Howard's statements come from a personal interview with author in 1997.)

Howard describes his extended family as a group of "vigorously integrated Jews who played golf and owned part of the Cleveland Indians baseball team." The Josephs imparted an intellectual tradition to Howard that he views as characteristic of a Jewish heritage. Indeed, Howard's family was crucial for his development as a writer and reader—his grandfather on his mother's side was an avid book collector who maintained a personal library replete with fine, first-edition books and rare manuscripts. Howard would spend many hours reading in this library, and describes the books as his "companions—there was a relationship that I didn't have with other kids but that I had with the voices that came out of those pages."

Howard's adoptive mother, Emma Joseph, was married three times. Her third marriage was to her first cousin Ralph Joseph, whom Richard Howard considers his main father figure during the crucial adolescent years. The Joseph and Feiss Company, a men's clothing factory that produced suits and army uniforms, was the Josephs' principal family business. As a group, the Josephs were considered one of the most prominent Jewish families in Cleveland and remain so to this day.

Howard attended a progressive school in Cleveland that lasted for as long as

Howard was there—from the time he entered it at two years, nine months to the end of his seventh grade year, just before the start of World War II. After that school closed, he attended Shaker Heights High School from eighth grade through graduation. Howard's best friend in high school was Rafael Silver, the son of Rabbi Hillel Silver. The rabbi was a respected and admired Zionist figure, and Howard credits his friendship at the time with kindling an interest in Zionism that was to flower during his college years.

Howard went on to Columbia University, graduating Phi Beta Kappa in 1951. While at Columbia, Howard developed friendships with a group of students and poets who are now renowned in the literary field, including John and Ann Hollander, Allen Ginsberg, and the editor Robert Gottlieb. Howard received his M.A. from Columbia in 1952, followed by studies at the Sorbonne (1953–1954).

Though Howard describes himself as the only "out" gay person in that circle at the time, he found the social life of bars and street life and the integration of being gay within the mostly straight life of the university relatively easy. Howard characterizes many of his friends from that time as secular Jews interested in Jewish issues, particularly Zionism. He attended Zionist group meetings at Columbia and refers to his actions from that time as "the thing to do if you were Jewish." However, his attention to the cause during college was the nearest Howard would ever get to organized Jewish life. Howard says that it's possible there is "a sense of convergence between one's sense of one's cultural and social identity and one's erotic identity and it all comes together—I'm gay because I'm a Jew or I'm a Jew because I'm gay, and my poetry manages to stir it up, but not much." Howard has rarely incorporated conspicuously Jewish themes into his poetry.

Howard worked as a lexicographer with the World Publishing Company from 1954 to 1955 and with Funk & Wagnalls from 1955 to 1957. Since 1957, besides writing ten books of poetry, Howard has worked as a translator for American and British publishers of over 150 works from the French. Howard cites his translation of Julien Gracq's *The Opposing Shore* as his favorite work, but he is perhaps best known for his translation of Baudelaire's *The Flowers of Evil*, for which he received several awards, including the National Book Award for Translation in 1984. With a home base in Manhattan's Greenwich Village, Howard has taught at Yale, Princeton, Johns Hopkins, and Brandeis Universities, as well as the California Institute of the Arts, the University of Texas (Austin), the University of Utah, and the University of Cincinnati. He is currently professor of English at the University of Houston. Howard has held or is currently holding many distinguished literary positions: he was the president of PEN—American Center (1978–1979), the chancellor of the Academy of American Poets since 1991, and poetry editor for *The New American Review* (nos. 11–26), *Shenandoah* (1978–1979), *The New Republic* (1983–1991), *Western Humanities Review* (1989–present), and *The Paris Review* (1992–present). His awards include a Guggenheim Fellowship in poetry (1967), a Chancellors' Fellowship for Distinction in Poetry, Academy of American Poets (1989), a position as poet Laureate of New York state (1993–1995), and a MacArthur Foundation Award (1996).

MAJOR WORKS AND THEMES

In his poetry, Howard often speaks in the dramatic voices of figures from history, art, literature, and dance. Personages as diverse as Robert Browning, Proust, Whitman, and Edith Wharton (as well as their friends and relatives) engage in extended monologues or conversations, helping to articulate one of Howard's main themes—the nature of the artistic experience. Additionally, his poetry tends toward the elegiac, effecting a consideration of impermanence and loss as significant motifs in Howard's work.

In poems from his first book *Quantities* (1962) we also begin to see signs of what would result in Howard's lifelong incorporation of the voices and experiences characteristic of gay life. The homosexual experience, particularly as it is lived within the world of art, literature, politics, and music, is a major theme throughout Howard's poetry.

In Howard's second collection, *The Damages* (1967), his dramatic monologues show increasing sophistication and an even wider range of subject matter. In *Untitled Subjects* (1969), Howard incorporates dramatic monologues throughout the entire book. The book is made up of fifteen poems, each poem representing the voice of a nineteenth-century character known in the fields of politics, painting, music, or writing, including Rossini, Carlyle, Thackeray, and Walpole. The book proved to be Howard's most popular work up to that point: *Untitled Subjects* received a Pulitzer Prize in 1970.

Where *Untitled Subjects* was a series of long poems, the poems in *Findings* (1971) were shorter and thematically unrelated. *Two-Part Inventions* (1974), comprising six long poems, builds on themes of gay sexuality, showing homosexuality as parallel to, and in some ways providing for, the development of great art. For example, the critic Michael Lynch has pointed out that in Howard's poem "Contra Naturam," we find Rodin lingering over the sight of Nijinsky, who is nude and clearly aroused—a sight that Lynch suggests forges a metaphoric link between homoeroticism and artistic inspiration.

In *Fellow Feelings* (1976), as in his other books, the themes Howard tends to register that refer to his Jewishness are those of anti-Semitism and the Holocaust, paralleled by his self-identification as a gay man. In the poem "Again for Hephaistos, the Last Time," Howard tells Auden he has dropped a mutual acquaintance due to the person's use of the pejoratives "kike" and "cocksucker." At least in his poetry, Howard is Jewish not so much because he considers himself so but because people read him as such, often in a disparaging and hateful way.

Howard's subsequent books, *Misgivings* (1979), *Lining Up* (1984), and *No Traveller* (1989), continued building on themes of sexuality, impermanence, and loss as experienced and heard by past figures of art and literature and Howard's own contemporaries. Many of Howard's recent elegies have as their subject a more imminent threat—in *Like Most Revelations* (1994), the specter of AIDS haunts various poems. In *Like Most Revelations*, the continuing theme of the poet's interconnectedness with historical figures and events and the resulting conflation of temporal space suggests Howard's ongoing concern with the past's relevance to the present, particularly when the past that is being discussed is, in some way, pertinent to the production of art. In this context, the devastating effect of AIDS on our present arts community and in the lives of Howard's own friends and loved ones is a subject that had to find its way into Howard's work.

CRITICAL RECEPTION

Not surprisingly, there has been little attention paid to Richard Howard as a Jewish poet. In fact, in his essay "The Sorrows of American-Jewish Poetry," which hypothesized that contemporary Jewish poets either evade or neglect their Jewish identity or express it in the "alienated discourse" of modernism, Harold Bloom has made a point of Howard's *nonincorporation* of Jewish material. Most critics tend to focus on Howard's mode of dramatic monologue and dialogue, pointing out Howard's indebtedness to Robert Browning. Several scholars have discussed Howard's work in terms of its being "gay poetry," particularly in journals with concerns specific to the gay academic community, such as *The Lambda Book Report* and *The Gay Academic*. Howard's "gayness" is often described in terms of his high camp tone and his articulation of voices that are homosexual or are affected by issues specific to homosexuals.

Many articles on Howard in journals and periodicals, including *Newsweek* and *The New York Times Magazine*, highlight Howard's accomplishments as a translator and lexicographer—critics theorize that this work feeds into Howard's preoccupation with adopting personae into his own poetry and his love for the *textures* and surfaces of language.

Donald Sheehan discussed Howard's talent as one that seems peculiarly novelistic. Sheehan listed the ability to record social surfaces and habits with accuracy and to make the seemingly inconsequential representative of more universal concerns as novelistic techniques that Howard lends to his poetry.

Michael Lynch discussed Howard's ouevre as a "superficial poetry" in a literal sense—poetry concerned with surface gloss and grace as opposed to the more "naked" and personal poetry of Robert Lowell or the "prophetic" work of W. S. Merwin and James Schuyler. Lynch was actually praising Howard, positing that Howard reconstructs historical voices in order to emphasize the veneer of personality and the "bundle of poses" shared by *all* these figures (6).

David Bromwich, in his review of *Two-Part Inventions*, claimed that Howard was the most original poet in the United States since Elizabeth Bishop. Unlike many critics, especially Harold Bloom, who had described Howard as a Browning for our times, Bromwich called the connection between Howard and Robert Browning "rather thin." According to Bromwich, Browning's use of dialogue tends toward dissolution and madness, whereas Howard's use of the form lends itself to a sense of aesthetic control and elegance.

Bromwich felt that Howard's poetry was in danger of becoming too coquettish for its own good but that, overall, Howard was one of the best poets writing, particularly in terms of his treatment of art.

James Longenbach considered practically all of Howard's career, including *Alone with America*, Howard's book of critical essays on forty-one American poets. He described Howard's aesthetic as being radically inclusionary of different stylistic techniques and approaches. Confronting critics who claim that Howard writes impersonal poetry, Longenbach countered that it is precisely the opposition on which the traditional meaning of the word "impersonal" depends that Howard is trying to dismantle by literally projecting his life into the voices we see in the poetry.

BIBLIOGRAPHY

Works by Richard Howard

Poetry

Quantities. Middletown, CT: Wesleyan University Press, 1962.
The Damages. Middletown, CT: Wesleyan University Press, 1967.
Untitled Subjects. New York: Atheneum, 1969.
Findings: A Book of Poems. New York: Atheneum, 1971.
Two-Part Inventions. New York: Atheneum, 1974.
Fellow Feelings. New York: Atheneum, 1976.
Misgivings. New York: Atheneum, 1979.
Lining Up. New York: Atheneum, 1984.
No Traveller: Poems. New York: Knopf, 1989.
Selected Poems. London: Penguin U.K, 1991.
Like Most Revelations. New York: Pantheon Books, 1994.

Nonfiction and Criticism

Alone with America: Essays on the Art of Poetry in the United States since 1950. New York: Atheneum, 1969; reissued, rev. and enlarged, 1980.
Preferences: 51 American Poets Choose Poems from Their Work and from the Past. New York: Viking Press, 1974.
Homosexualities. Eds. George Stambolian and Elaine Marks. Ithaca, NY: Cornell University Press, 1979.

Works about Richard Howard

Bernstein, Richard. "Howard's Way." *New York Times Magazine* (September 25, 1988): 40–44+.
Bloom, Harold. "The Sorrows of American-Jewish Poetry." In *Figures of Capable Imagination*. New York: Seabury Press, 1976.

Bromwich, David. "A Review of 'Two-Part Inventions.' " *The Georgia Review* (Fall 1975): 736–43.

Donaldson, Jeffery. "Physical Measures—*No Traveller* by Richard Howard." *Salmagundi* 88–89 (Fall 1990): 486–95.

Kinzie, Mary. "Among the Shades." *American Poetry Review* (March/April 1984): 38–47.

Lehman, David. "Across Literary Frontiers." *Newsweek* 108, No. 22 (December 1, 1986): 90A-90E.

Longenbach, James. "Richard Howard's Modern World." *Salmagundi* 108 (Fall 1995): 141–63.

Lynch, Michael. "Richard Howard's Finishes." *American Poetry Review* (November/ December 1975): 5–11.

Sheehan, Donald. "Recent American Poetry." *Contemporary Literature* (Spring 1969): 284–302.

DAVID IGNATOW   (1914–1997)

Barry Fruchter

BIOGRAPHY

David Ignatow was born in Brooklyn, New York, on February 7, 1914, to immigrants Max Ignatowsky and Yetta Reinach. He graduated from New Utrecht High School in 1932. After a series of sales jobs, young David started work at his father's commercial pamphlet bindery in Manhattan. "I Can't Stop It," his first published story, appeared in the New Talent section of O'Brien's *Best American Short Stories* in 1933. Ignatow worked as a Works Progress Administration (WPA) researcher and reporter and entered a series of relationships with literary magazines. He married the artist Rose Graubart in 1937, and they had a son, David, at the end of the year; in 1956 a daughter, Yaedi, was born.

After a long series of service and industrial jobs and a return to management of his father's bindery, Ignatow in the 1960s turned to academe. He held visiting professorships at the universities of Kentucky and Kansas and, from 1969 to 1983, a full-time teaching position at York College of City University of New York. Until the 1990's he taught part-time at Columbia University's School of the Arts. In 1981–1982 Ignatow was Poetry Society of America president. He received numerous awards, including Guggenheim and Rockefeller Fellowships, a National Institute of Arts and Letters Award, the Shelley Award, and the Robert Frost Medal. David Ignatow died on November 17, 1997.

MAJOR WORKS AND THEMES

In a recent letter, David Ignatow confirms that his early religious and social training had a major impact on his thinking and writing. "I don't doubt," Ignatow adds, "that the experience of being brought up in an East-European Jewish immigrant household has singled me out among American poets and that it has entered into an understanding and evaluation of my poems among critics and among other poets . . . pain and suffering and uncertainty are the materials with which I forge a vision within me and in my poems of survival and in an affirmation in terms of poetry of the conditions of my life" (Letter to the author; January 22, 1996). He further acknowledges his consciousness of Jewish poets as participants in the biblical prophetic tradition. However, he distances himself both from organized Judaism and from political Zionism, firmly noting that no ethnic, national, or religious group has a monopoly on virtue. He specifically criticizes those forces in Israel and in the United States responsible for fomenting attacks on Arabs and for the assassination of Yitzhak Rabin. It would seem, then, that any examination of Ignatow's "Jewishness" must skirt around any conscious identification with organized Judaism or with cultural, ethnocentric, or nationalist Jewishness. Nevertheless, Ignatow's poetry is thoroughly Jewish in consciousness and image, in the same way, he assures this writer, as Robert Bly's is Lutheran.

For analytical purposes, it is useful to organize David Ignatow's poetry around several themes, each amenable to Jewish contextualization: (1) the relation of the individual to "God" (variously defined); (2) the historical legacy of the Jews, including the burdens of persecution and of cultural transmission; and (3) the prophetic tradition.

The Individual and God

Among David Ignatow's earliest poems is "Autumn Leaves," one of his few extant pieces from the 1930s, in which the leaves are hailed as "children of the road" forced into wandering by a "depression" and become "comrades to spring." The turning point of this socially conscious elegy speaks of the wanderers as literally woven into the garment of a God who "walks by in stubble fields" wearing a crown of "unripened torn-up grain." Weather-beaten, having stalked the roads with his desolate children, God lies down in the mud "like a shriveled nut." Though he represents and leads the displaced children of "well-stocked homes," he cannot save them. God dies along with (and in) his children. The fact that the "stubble fields" may be spring lands suggests a possible resurrection, but nothing is certain here except the mortality and weakness of a once-dependable redeemer (*Poems 1934–1969*, 8).

Twenty years later in *The Gentle Weight Lifter* (1955), we find the epigrammatic "Consolation," in which God is further reduced to a ghost, a perception of "yellow pillow" meeting "blue wall" (*Poems 1934–1969*, 96). He appears as a sign not of protection from evil but of its absence or relativism. But here, too, God's presence prevents only *total* degradation, a pillow to cushion only a fatal fall. He is perceptible perhaps only in the homely aesthetic of domesticity, in the process of maintaining a family against all odds.

Like Israel himself, Ignatow's poetic persona engages directly with God and/ or his messenger, often violently. In these instances God is actually dependent on us, a thought that occurred to more than one Jewish poet after World War II. In *Say Pardon* (1961) "The Good Angel" imposes "impossible conditions" on a working man who complains bitterly. When the poet returns home from his futile quest for freedom, he finds the Angel snoring under his dining room table and kicks him furiously. The Angel leaps up into an attitude of embrace, crying "At last!" (*Poems 1934–1969*, 136–37). This is an *ange-provocateur* who could pass for a professor of management science or a Marxist revolutionary. Here, God's raison d'être is not our helping ourselves but our rebellion, our overpowering him by force of will. Yet unlike Israel, the poet here wins nothing measurable in the contest; the Angel escapes with no covenant wrung from him and his wrestling partner bears no visible wounds.

In "The Rightful One," another of God's apparitions is the communal work of the poet and his son. In this poem the son shouts, "He is here," drawing the father down the hall to his room to encounter a Being "whom [he] had neglected in [his] thoughts" but whom his sick child had long sought. God stands in the son's room, long-haired, exhausted, sad-eyed, waving off gestures of submission with the disclaimer, "I am a sufferer like yourself." At the father's confession of failure, the Rightful One reminds him that he also contains "forgiveness" and instructs him to bless his son. Then God leaves, his vestige "a power to feel free" (*Poems 1934–1969*, 145). The covenant is here reduced to God's crowning the father as king over himself. Ignatow's God is not the Almighty of Genesis but perhaps the Wanderer of the shtetl tradition, the *moshiach* (the messiah) glimpsed in shreds and patches. Here, Isaac, first glimpses the redemption and leads his doubting father—a constant theme in Ignatow's poems about both his son and his daughter.

Two much later poems encapsulate this tension between a God who goads and a God who heals. Poem 56 of *Leaving the Door Open* (*New and Collected Poems* 295) begins, "I wish a god were possible." The poet wishes for an immortality that can come only through an Other who, unlike one's mortal companions, will forever embody one's memory. Noting that this god resembles the sky, to which children sense that they belong, the poet feels himself becoming a child again. The very late poem "The Image" focuses on a man's relation to his mirror-image, which is said to be his master, as he needs it, but it does not need him. Like the Rightful One and the yellow pillow and the leaf-clothed wanderer, the image "reveals him to himself." "If there is a god," the poem ends ambiguously, "this is he" (*New and Collected Poems* 332). Yet how different from the Whitmanic yawp, "I contain multitudes"; here, in fact, the poet is contained, and his image, a distant/nearby god, that does the containing.

The Burden of the Jews

Three of David Ignatow's earlier poems—all written before 1960—exemplify his approach to modern Jewish history: the use of his own generational position as a conduit for the whole painful, modern Jewish inheritance. Sometimes, as in "Europe and America," this pain reflects the trauma of passage from the East, across Western Europe, to America. At other times, as in "We Came Naked," it touches on the ramifications, for all Jews everywhere, of the Nazi massacre. Finally, it also includes, in passing, a reckoning with anti-Semitism in its "pure American" form, as in "Harold." Since the first type is most representative of Ignatow's work as a whole, I reserve it for last, taking the three poems in reverse order.

"Harold," from Ignatow's earliest published book, profiles a poisonous Lochinvar from the American West, so down on his luck that he has to swallow his hatred of the Other by going to work in a Jewish hospital in New York. Deprived of the chance to shoot Jews down like so many racial desperadoes, he contents himself with keeping the sick and the pregnant waiting, "mouthing blasphemous phrases," farting loudly, and telling insulting jokes. Interestingly, Ignatow makes this prototype of our contemporary Western, racial supremacists pitiful—a beaten working man with illusions.

"We Came Naked," an early poem of the 1940s, both allegorizes and naturalizes the slaughter in the death camps. Beginning with a restatement of the Abrahamanic promise and Moses' prospect from Nebo, the poem proceeds into a thicket of Holocaust images: the "ash smell" that replaced "our bodies," stripped of souls, the "blackened tongues" in the earth, the "piled bodies." The destruction of Jewish flesh becomes the destruction of homes, of homelands, as Jews become so much "fuel." Homeless, bereft of foundations, the Jews turn to the one remaining source of "food," Jerusalem, "upon [whose] outstretched hand" they tread, "feast[ing] each other over the tables/Of the land" (*Poems 1934–1969*, 28). In Zion, death becomes a continuing ceremony of rebirth; the promise becomes the natural succession to the ashes left behind.

Yet the Holocaust per se and anti-Semitism as such are not major themes of Ignatow's poems, as is the relation of fathers and sons. "Europe and America," from the 1948 *Poems*, reverses the traditional posture of "rebellion." The son's voice denigrates himself and empathizes with his father in a cross-generational retrospect that bridges the gap between the titular continents. The poem turns on three sets of images. The first pivots on the antinomy work/rest. The "father brought the emigrant bundle/Of desperation," while the son is "bedded upon soft green money." The second set of images opposes the son's perceptions of America—breezes, shadows, lakes—to the father's—storms, darkness, "rough channels." The third reduces the European experience to a shambles (and, by extension, to the slaughtered animals' experiences), of hearing "the scream as the knife" (of the *shohet* or the Cossack) "fell"; the experience of the newly American son as of one who "slept/as guns pounded offshore" (*Poems 1934–*

1969, 49). In its totality "Europe and America" represents a cry of mingled envy and compassion, a last reaching out by the permanently deracinated. Significantly, though, there is *no* pledge of "return."

The Prophetic Tradition

Ignatow's ambivalent relation with Whitman, discussed at length in *The One and the Many*, also informs the bardic voice in many of his poems. However, as he said in a recent letter and has said in countless public appearances, behind the Whitmanic voice is the biblical one. Ignatow is a deutero-Isaiah as often as a Jeremiah, providing comfort—even if of a savage quality—as often as he prophesies ruin. Nowhere is this voice so painful as in the invocation of *Facing the Tree*. Its visionary opening, "Dirt and stone, if I may know you as you know yourselves," (*New and Collected Poems* 3), parallels both that of Neruda's last odes and Ignatow's own much earlier "We Came Naked"—but how changed, how both personalized and accepting as only the prophet's invitation to the god can be accepting. The poet/prophet sees himself as an outsider on the border of life and death, a representative of the living who must be reduced to "dirt and stone" and who "wants to know what home will be like there." There follows a passage of speculation in which the possibility of an "exchange program" between the living and dead elements is cause for joy, leading the living to bury their fellows "with solemn benediction on a current of joy."

But the speculation masks the poet's need for reconciliation with what he or we will become, a need expressed in the longing to be answered. The invocation ends with the thought that the poet's own flesh is silent because it is already one with the dirt and stone; he "contains multitudes," as Whitman would say, but dead multitudes to whose cases his attention has turned. "Reading the Headlines" begins, "I have a burial ground in me where I place the bodies/ . . . hundreds of thousands at a glance" (*New and Collected Poems* 4)—so the dirt and stone do speak after all, but that is only after the voice of prophecy begins to take hold, after the isolated poet's painful transition.

The title poem of *Rescue the Dead* takes this prophetic role in a different sense, albeit one equally informed by the biblical tradition of teaching the people through vision. Another of Ignatow's starkly binarist statements, "Rescue the Dead" alternates between contrasting visions: on one hand, the public, masculinized world of "living" and, on the other, the private, feminized space of "loving"; it resembles Robert Bly's famous (and contemporaneous) poem "The Busy Man Speaks," but in his typically ambiguous fashion Ignatow avoids Bly's baldly overt choices. Ignatow uses cumulative images: to let rain fall nakedly upon your head," "to respect fire," "to sign your name," "to carry a wallet." Those who love are led into a forest "where the secret grave" is created, and darkness is praised—a risk-taking echo of the deep images associated with Ignatow's "modernist" literary forebears as well as with the Holocaust, with which their images have become enmeshed. However, it ultimately leads to the prophetic vision whose dead cannot be ignored. The poet-prophet senses his coming change—"to love is to be a fish"—and reaches, again, across the gap of vision to call upon others to "rescue the dead" (*Poems 1934–1969*, 219).

Ignatow directly confronts exceptionalism, xenophobia, and racism: in both his prose and his poetry he is broadly inclusive of the human condition, of the working class, of those who suffer. This fact is clear when one considers a list of representative titles: "Statement for the Times," "Communion," "Business," "Man's Picture," "Say Pardon," "America." Similarly, his most striking poetry of self—"Sunday at the State Hospital," "The Appointment Card," "Dream," and so on—is quite emphatically *not* "Jewish" on its face. Gary Pacernick, the critic most attuned to Ignatow's heritage, suggests that Jews may have the advantage (as writers) of having learned how to verbalize suffering. Ignatow, however, neither verbalizes it in a self-consciously Jewish way nor displays the "advantage" that is allegedly his inheritance. The alienation in his poetry is, in the final instance, that of a late twentieth-century, urban man. If this is Jewish, then perhaps, as Elie Wiesel, speaking of the "Doomsday Clock," once said, "We are all Jewish."

CRITICAL RECEPTION

There have generally been two kinds of responses to Ignatow's poetry: praise for its reflection of the everyday struggles of human beings and lament over its flatness of tone. Thus, on one hand, we find William Carlos Williams, Ignatow's mentor, praising the 1948 *Poems* by remarking on their "odor, foul with love," saying that for Ignatow "language is like his skin" (quoted in Terris 138) and suggesting that the poems be mass-produced for the masses, who will understand them. On the other hand, formalist doyens like Randall Jarrell first chide Ignatow for being a mere imitator of Williams and then complain that his "temperament . . . lacks the heights and depths of Williams' " and that his poetry is "humane, unaffected, and unexciting" (*Terris* 138). There have been over twenty general references, in lengthy articles or books, to Ignatow's body of work, as well as countless reviews of particular volumes. It does the poetry the best service to summarize the three most important and developed commentaries: Michael Heller's "Typology of the Parabolist," Ralph J. Mills, Jr.'s, "Earth Hard: David Ignatow's Poetry," and Gary Pacernick's "David Ignatow: Prophet of Darkness and Nothingness."

Michael Heller considers Ignatow the consummate "parabolist." For Heller, parables are the preeminent genre for providing the secular modernist with a sense of "truths and certainties no longer available in the present" (Terris 93). While Heller sees Ignatow's poetry as deeply relevant to the experience of our times, much of its form is recyclable, relying on an attempted transformation of its material into "something unbounded in time" (Terris 97).

Mills notes that while Ignatow belongs with the great poets of his generation, such as Robert Lowell and John Berryman, he has worked apart from them, cultivating "an extraordinary firmness of purpose and direction, . . . a language and approach to experience that could derive only from the most severe demands upon himself" (Terris 13). While Ignatow's primary movement is a direct representation of his own painful self-knowledge, he is equally aware of the suffering of others. Ignatow's immersion in the world of the "actual" bears fruit in a carefully created style, "avoiding the 'poetical,' through which his urban experience could be incarnated" (Terris 17). While in so doing he creates a verse with affinities to other poetry of "location" (e.g., that of Charles Olson, Denise Levertov, and Edward Dorn), it also necessitates a plain language in which the reader can discern his own experience.

Finally, Gary Pacernick traces Ignatow's evolution from deep skepticism of his inheritance, through anguished examination of self, toward a kind of mythic affirmation of his powers. "Ignatow," he says, "is not a confessional poet" but a transformer of personal experience into prophecy through confrontations with matters of life, death, and moral judgment, enacting "the relationship between personal agony and religious memory" (Terris 65). Ignatow's Jewishness affects his work through heightening his sensitivity to the suffering that emerges from the traditional struggles between fathers and sons and generally from the lives of working people.

BIBLIOGRAPHY

Works by David Ignatow

Poems. Prairie City, IL: Decker Press, 1948.
The Gentle Weight Lifter. New York: Morris Gallery, 1955.
Say Pardon. Middletown, CT: Wesleyan University Press, 1961.
Figures of the Human: Poems. Middletown, CT: Wesleyan University Press, 1964.
Earth Hard. London: Rapp and Whiting, 1968a.
Rescue the Dead: Poems. Middletown, CT: Wesleyan University Press, 1968b.
Poems, 1934–1969. Middletown, CT: Wesleyan University Press, 1970.
Facing the Tree: New Poems. Boston: Little, Brown, 1975a.
Selected Poems. Edited with Introductory Notes and an Afterword by Robert Bly. Middletown, CT: Wesleyan University Press, 1975b.
The Animal in the Bush: Poems on Poetry. Ed. Patrick Carey. Pittsburgh: Slow Lorris Press, 1977.
Tread the Dark: New Poems. Boston: Little, Brown, 1978.
Sunlight: A Sequence for My Daughter. Brockport, NY: BOA Editions, 1979.
Conversations. New York: Survivors' Manual Books, 1980.
Ten David Ignatow Poems. New York: Silver Hands Press, 1981a.
Whisper to the Earth: New Poems. Boston: Little, Brown, 1981b.
Leaving the Door Open: Poems. New York: Sheep Meadow Press, 1984.
New and Collected Poems, 1970–1985. Middletown, CT: Wesleyan University Press, 1986.
The One and the Many: A Poet's Memoirs. Middletown, CT: Wesleyan University Press, 1988.

Despite the Plainness of the Day: Love Poems. Pittsburgh: Mill Hunk Press, 1991a.

Shadowing the Ground. Middletown, CT: Wesleyan University Press, 1991b.

If We Know. [Tuscaloosa, AL]: Polymorph Editions, 1992. Chapbook.

Against the Evidence: Selected Poems, 1934–1994. Hanover, NH: University Press of New England [Wesleyan], 1993.

I Have a Name. Hanover, NH: University Press of New England [Wesleyan], 1996.

At My Ease. Rochester, NY: BOA Editions, 1998.

Works about David Ignatow

Dickey, James. *Babel to Byzantium: Poets and Poetry Now.* New York: Farrar, Straus, and Giroux, 1968.

Lipari, Joseph A. *The Poetry of David Ignatow: An Introduction and Bibliography of Primary Sources, 1931–1978.* Ann Arbor, MI: University Microfilms, 1983.

Mooney, Stephen, ed. *David Ignatow.* Special issue of *Tennessee Poetry Journal* 3, 2 (Winter 1970).

Mills, Ralph J., Jr. "Earth Hard: David Ignatow's Poetry." In Mills, *Cry of the Human: Essays on Contemporary American Poetry,* 67–133. Urbana: University of Illinois Press, 1975.

Pacernick, Gary. "David Ignatow: Prophet of Darkness and Nothingness." In *Memory and Fire: The American Jewish Poets,* 143–63. New York: Peter Lang, 1989.

Stocking, David M., ed. *A Chapbook for David Ignatow.* Special issue of *Beloit Poetry Journal* 26, 1 (Fall 1975): 1–7.

Terris, Virginia R., ed. and Intro. *Meaningful Differences: The Poetry and Prose of David Ignatow.* Tuscaloosa and London: University of Alabama Press, 1994.

MILTON KESSLER (1930–)

Adam Schonbrunn

BIOGRAPHY

Milton Kessler was born in Brooklyn, New York, on May 9, 1930, the son of Arthur and Elizabeth Racoe Kessler. To relieve his asthma, his family moved to the Bronx a few years later, where the air was supposed to be better in the hills surrounding the Grand Concourse. Perhaps it was this early battle for breath that gave his lines their patterns of great immediacy. As a young man, the gifted singer performed the "Star Spangled Banner" for Eleanor Roosevelt at the Waldorf Astoria. In 1952 he married Sonia Berer, who is a teacher in the local elementary schools in Binghamton, New York, where they have lived since 1965 and where Kessler, until his recent retirement, was a professor of English at the State University of New York (SUNY), Binghamton. Prior to moving to Binghamton, he worked in New York as an optician, a shoe salesman, and in the garment industry. He received a B.A. from the University of Buffalo in 1957 and an M.A. from the University of Washington in 1962. From 1963 to 1965 Kessler was a lecturer at Queens College (CUNY). The Kesslers have three children: David, Paula, and Daniel.

In addition to his teaching at Binghamton, Kessler has also taught in Israel at the Universities of Be'-er Sheba in 1972 and Haifa in 1981. Between 1972 and 1980, Kessler was coeditor of the magazine he founded with John Logan, *Choice*; he also founded the Creative Writing Program at SUNY, Binghamton. He has published five books of poetry: *A Road Came Once* (1963), *Called Home* (1967), *Woodlawn North* (1970), *Sailing Too Far* (1973), and *The Grand Concourse* (1990). He has received numerous fellowships, among them a Robert Frost Fellowship and several from Yaddo and the MacDowell Foundation.

MAJOR WORKS AND THEMES

Over the years, Kessler, with his fierce integrity to line, music, visceral Judaic morality, imagism, and family has grown into a major Jewish-American poet. His poems are accessible to the simple mensch, and they bring to the ordinary moment the true joy of this poet's vision. His own rendition of his poetry in public readings can be most moving to the listener, especially in his gifted bass-baritone "cantorial" voice. Kessler does not write about feeling but with feeling. He communicates the multilayered universes of the individual working on the Concourse or Boardwalk. He never repeats himself, and the work seems to rediscover itself each time one reads it. A Whitman scholar, Kessler strikes out like Whitman to welcome the whole world:

> But I'm self-employed
> My new job's
> to wave them in.
> Hello freighter,
> hello tanker.
> Welcome, welcome,
> to New York. ("Sailing too Far," *Grand Concourse* 3)

In *Sailing Too Far*, Kessler proved his ability to weave myth and Jewish song into his work. In "Chad Gadya, One Little Goat," a song traditionally sung on the Passover, Kessler even manages to mix the surreal with the shtetl image:

> Life, life, your alley was sick
> with rats and diptheria.

The poem concludes with a more upbeat image of the shtetl:

> . . . singing in a circle,
> "one little goat, one little goat."
> The old mothers fill their windows laughing (47)

If Bernard Malamud is the master of the spoken Jewish Brooklyn idiom in the novel and short story genres, Kessler has done the same with the Bronx in poetry. But it isn't only the vernacular that he brings to his poems. It is the flavor of an old woman's babushka as she bends to sip cocoa on the Boardwalk in Brighton Beach, of "Nathan's" frankfurter stands, of the tailor and haberdashery.

Kessler is possessed of a restless and well-stocked mind, and thus his poems reveal a broad and intense intellectual appetite. He can write about any number of subjects with authority: art, poverty, the city, and even the history and suffering of the horse. The latter is a Jewish concept recorded in the laws of the

Hebrew scholar, Tzar Ba-alei Chayim: laws forbidding causing an animal to suffer. Kessler's knowledge of Jewish law enables him to create a brilliant collage, juxtaposing texts from the "Amidah"—the Eighteen Benedictions, which is an integral part of the weekday service—with a botany book. He creates new myths out of old ones; both avant-garde and accessible to the average reader.

In the poem "Right Now," one can feel his genuine and sincere concern for children growing up in a fake and plastic world. The poem follows the long-lined pattern of the Hebrew prophets as well as Christopher Smart, William Blake, and Walt Whitman. What makes this both Jewish and Whitmanesque is the expansive big-heartedness so straightforwardly expressed:

> I see children hugging their crumbling parents who hang on their tiny
> clavicles, huge smothering dolls stuffed with the poisons of the time . . .
> I see children whose male adult is every booze violent knock on the door.
> (*Grand Concourse* 76).

The late Allen Ginsberg has said: "Poet is priest." Kessler, as poet-teacher, serves as well as rabbi. In "God's Cigar," the poet communicates an era and an individual's universe, compressed into huge and urgent sentences. This poem, which was written for the poet's father, is a human catalog that cries "Yes!" to immortality. The poem concludes:

> And those who only have eyes for the tinsel
>   of the ideological angel
> what do you make of such a man
> that kinky haired sprinter on Rockaway Beach
>   Boulevard
> see him now with his limb of drenched
>   bandages
> flying in front of buses
> Without wings (*Grand Concourse* 45)

Yet another aspect of Kessler's work can be seen in a poem from *Grand Concourse*: the way he uses documentary elements as part of his objectivist technique. In "Zero," he startles the reader with a poem shaped like a horse's head: it is a catalog of the uses and misuses mankind has made of horses since "The Ch-ing Emperor's troupe of Buried horses/The visor-blind horses of the jousts" (*Grand Concourse* 71). With great humanity, Kessler gives a historical lament to the suffering these animals endured through mankind's preoccupation with war. Thus, Kessler, in his work, is at home in both traditional as well as experimental forms. He is a great master craftsman whose work should live on.

CRITICAL RECEPTION

Of *Grand Concourse*, Camille Paglia has written:

Kessler's poetry seizes my attention by its fidelity to both visual and emotional truth, a rare combination. Kessler negotiates between the outer and inner worlds; he records the day-to-day moments of truce won by our own ever-shifting consciousness. Even when he alludes to Nietzsche, Wagner, Furtwangler . . . there is nothing academic about it. His style is stripped down, abrupt, emphatic, concrete. The rhythms are spoken, flexible. All the poems in *The Grand Concourse* have a different look. The lines, the shapes vary, like our own moods. (210)

In another evaluation of this collection of his work, Arthur Miller writes of *Grand Concourse* "A good book like this is a gift to the world, a tourniquet to stanch the bleeding" (jacket cover), and Ruth Stone singles out the poem "God's Cigar" as "perhaps the most amazing modern poem I've ever read" (jacket cover). His work was also familiar to London subway riders when, in 1994, it was chosen to represent New York City in the "Poems on the Underground" project.

BIBLIOGRAPHY

Works by Milton Kessler

A Road Came Once. Columbus: Ohio State University Press, 1963.
Called Home. New York: Blackbird, 1967.
Woodlawn North. Boston: Impressions Workshop, 1970.
Sailing Too Far. New York: Harper, 1973.
The Grand Concourse. Binghamton State University of New York, 1990.

Works about Milton Kessler

Paglia, Camille. "Milton Kessler." *Sulfur*, No. 28, 1991. 210.
Schonbrun, Adam. "Interview." *Studies in Jewish-American Literature*, No. 2, 1990.

ABRAHAM MOSES KLEIN   (1909–1972)

Rachel Feldhay Brenner

BIOGRAPHY

A. M. Klein was born in Ratno, Ukraine. In 1910, his family emigrated to Canada and settled in Montreal. Klein was educated in Protestant and Jewish schools. From 1926 to 1930 he attended McGill University, majoring in classics, political science, and economics. He then studied law at the Université de Montréal and was admitted to the bar in 1933. In 1934 he established a law firm. In 1935, Klein married Bessie Kozlov, with whom he had three children. Klein practiced law while remaining an active Zionist and a prolific essayist, poet, and lecturer. In the mid-1950s, he suffered a mental breakdown. Until his death, he remained a complete recluse.

Klein was a lifelong, dedicated Zionist. As a student, he served as educational director of Canadian Young Judea and edited its monthly magazine, *The Judean*; later, he edited *The Canadian Zionist*, the Zionist Organization of Canada monthly, and from 1938 to 1955 he was the editor of *The Canadian Jewish Chronicle*; in 1949 he was sponsored by the Canadian Jewish Congress to travel to Israel, and upon his return he lectured extensively on Zionism and on the state of Israel in Canada and in the United States.

MAJOR WORKS AND THEMES

Klein subscribed to Ahad ha-Am's ideology of cultural Zionism. Like Ahad ha-Am, Klein believed in Jewish national redemption through revival and maintenance of Jewish cultural tradition, which would link the diaspora heritage with reborn Israel. The establishment of the state of Israel, therefore, seemed, for a while, to actualize Klein's hopes for the cultural center for all Jewish people,

especially in the wake of the Holocaust. The Holocaust affected Klein profoundly; he feared that the tragic annihilation of European Jewry and its culture
may have eliminated the future of the Jewish people.

It is important to note that, in contrast with the assimilationist attitudes of the
New York Jewish intellectuals at the time, Klein became aware of the Nazi
threat very early. In his editorials throughout the 1930s, he admonished the
North American Jews "happily situated in a free country on this side of the
Atlantic" against indifference regarding the suffering of Jews in Europe. In the
aftermath of the Holocaust, Klein mourned the loss of the Jewish nation and its
culture and rejoiced in the birth of the Jewish state, which he saw as a promise
of Jewish regeneration.

The state of Israel, however, did not fulfill Klein's hopes for cultural revival.
Dismayed by the Zionist position of *shelilat ha-galut* (the negation of the diaspora), Klein protested the ideology that, to his mind, sought "the nullification
of Diaspora Jewry." Significantly, Klein's last work, an essay poignantly titled
"In Praise of the Diaspora," is both a eulogy and an elegy of the Jewish 2,000-
year-long cultural tradition of the exile, which Israel failed to recognize.

Klein's own considerable contribution to Jewish culture emerges in his literary
oeuvre. In his poetry, Klein succeeded in combining the cultural particularity of
the Jewish people with the universality of the humanistic values of equality,
justice and respect for the other. Klein's two first published volumes of poetry,
Hath Not a Jew (1940) and *Poems* (1944) outline a movement from the poet's
happy childhood, to his adoption of the humanist ideal of moral regeneration,
to an increasingly pessimistic world picture in view of the rise of the fascist
movements in Germany and in Canada. In the poem "Heirloom," the poet
invokes the Hassidic inheritance of Baal Shem Tov and of the tradition of learning as "[m]y noble lineage, my proud ancestry" (158). Klein's recourse to
Spinozistic pantheism in the poem "Out of the Pulver and the Polished Lens"
(1931) signals the search for an adequate philosophical system in view of the
growing, largely unopposed menace of terror and persecution. The Zionist dream
of return to the land where "Izak and Ishmael are cousins met," however,
cannot provide the solution in a world where the tyrannical golem holds sway.
In one of his most moving poems, "Childe Harold's Pilgrimage" (1938), Klein
identifies with the German-Jewish refugees fleeing Nazi persecution: "Always
and ever have I been the Jew/Bewildered, and a man who has been tricked,/
Examining/A passport of a polyglot decision/To Esperanto from the earliest
rune-/Where cancellation frowns away permission,/and tuning in despair/To seek
an audience with the consul of the moon" (114).

The horror of the Nazi regime, however, did not condone passivity. In 1942,
Klein forcefully confronted the terror of the Third Reich in a long mock epic,
The Hitleriad, published in 1944. Practically the first North American literary
response to the Nazi regime, the epic presents a response whose crudity, ve-
hemence, and unconcealed mocking rage propose to mirror and to expose the
crass brutality of the tyrannical golem. The poem is written, for the most part,

in Augustan rhyming heroic couplets. Klein felt that Augustan poetry of "wit and wrath" was suitable for his theme. Though *The Hitleriad* was criticized for lacking the necessary historical distance and for using an inadequate form of the representation of its theme, it offers an uncommon insight into the problematics of the literary response to the Holocaust. While the rudimentary device of the invective and the mechanical repetitiveness of the rhyme echo the tyrant's destruction of humanity and humanism, the referential framework of the Enlightenment's Augustan poetry summons the pre-Hitler humanistic notion of society. The poetic form thus both acknowledges and seeks to forestall the process of dehumanization manifest in the Nazi enactment of evil.

An attempt to present an integrated, humanistic vision of the the world emerges in Klein's volume of poetry titled *The Rocking Chair and Other Poems* (1948). The volume was critically acclaimed as Klein's best poetic achievement, and it received the Governor General Award. The humanistic intent emerges in the Jewish poet's attitude of love and respect for Quebec. Indeed, in his introductory letter to the poems, Klein stated clearly that he was motivated by the fact that "we [the Jews and French Quebeçois] have many things in common: a minority position; ancient memories; and a desire for survival" (quoted in Caplan 149). The title poem commends Quebec's age-old tradition. An idealized portrayal of it emerges in the memorable depiction of Quebec's religious faith in "The Cripples," and the brotherly coexistence of Canadian ethnic minorities informs the linguistic intricacies in the poem "Montreal," while the Jewish poet's personal devotion to Quebec emerges in his childhood memories in "Winter Night: Mount Royal," "Lookout: Mount Royal," and "The Mountain."

However, the concluding poem, "Portrait of the Poet as Landscape," considered to be one of Klein's best poetic accomplishments, speaks in a different tenor. The poem, which invokes both Milton's "Lycidas" and Joyce's *A Portrait of the Artist as a Young Man*, presents a striking vision of the alienated poet. In contrast with the traditional image of the poet as a moving force of civilization and culture, the poem highlights the irrevocable split between the poet and modern society, which sees poetry as an "outmoded art." The world wishes to forget the poet, and so the poet must redefine his function. He watches the world surreptitiously, marking its moral disintegration. The reading of *The Rocking Chair* from the point of view of the "drowned," that is, invisible, poet, presents Quebec as a microcosm of the world that rejected the poet. In that sense, the volume presents a complex structure whereby the disintegration of the cultural and ethical mainstays of community life is shown in the recurring displacement of poetic conventions. Seen from this point of view, the seemingly idealized picture of Quebec transforms into a parodic and cynical vision of suffering, exploitation, and hopelessness of the underprivileged in a world that denies its poetic self.

Despite his darkening vision of the world, Klein succeeded once more in conjuring up a world of humanistic rebirth. *The Second Scroll*, Klein's last major work and his only novel, represents, in many respects, the epitome of Klein's artistic and conceptual achievement. Published in 1951, the novel originated in the poet's journey to Israel, Europe, and North Africa in 1949. *The Second Scroll* tells the story of a young Canadian Jew who sets out to the newly established state of Israel to collect and translate the new Hebrew poetry. The major part of this first-person narrative, however, focuses on the narrator's search for his uncle Melech Davidson—a former Talmudic scholar, disenchanted communist, and Holocaust survivor. Uncle Melech emerges as a Jewish Everyman, a Messianic figure who, despite his long history of suffering, rejects the temptation to convert to Christianity and makes his way to Israel at the head of a group of Moroccan Jews he has saved from the poverty and oppression of the Casablanca mellah. Upon his arrival in Israel, the nephew discovers Hebrew poetry in everyday, colloquial Hebrew discourse. He never sees his uncle; the meeting is about to take place when Melech is murdered and burned by Arab infiltrators. Nonetheless, Melech's death is presented as a symbol of rebirth: his funeral becomes a manifestation of Israel's and the world's reconstruction. On a personal level, the Canadian nephew symbolically reunites with the Holocaust survivor through the recitation of the Kaddish, the Mourner's Magnificat, at his grave.

As the title indicates, the form of the novel presents a structure analogous to the original Scroll, the Torah's Five Books of Moses. Indeed, the five chapters of the novel are named after the books of the Torah. This intricate construct indicates an attempt to delineate the historical relations and the spatial dimensions between the North American diaspora, the European and North American dispersions, and the biblical origins of the Jewish people. What emerges in this powerful text is a "new alphabet" that inscribes the Buberian I–Thou relationships of completion and reintegration. These relationships demonstrate that the diaspora past cannot be rejected; on the contrary, as the novel shows, redemption can come only through the recognition of the spiritual guidance that the past infuses into the present.

CRITICAL RECEPTION

Klein lived and died with a sense of failure to reach the general public, especially the U.S. readership, due to the conspicuously ethnic nature of his work. He himself declared, "I travel on my own passport," and he asserted that he has "a contribution to make as a Jew" and that he meets other cultures "as an equal, not as an interloper" (Caplan 149). Indeed, only a few New York Jewish intellectuals, such as Ludwig Lewisohn and Maurice Samuel, recognized Klein's unique voice and praised Klein as "the first contributor of authentic Jewish poetry to the English language" (Caplan 71). On the Canadian scene, his works were widely reviewed, though not as much and not as positively as Klein would have liked. Yet, Klein has left an indelible mark upon both the Jewish and the Canadian cultural landscape. Ironically, the stature that he had sought and deemed never to have achieved has been, in fact, in his particular position on the Jewish-Canadian scene. Klein's profound impact on Jewish-Canadian literature is evident in the tribute that Jewish-Canadian writers offered him in terms of their art. Klein was commemorated not only in the poetry of his friends, such as Irving Layton and Miriam Waddington, but also in the work of those who never met him yet were affected by his vision: Leonard Cohen, Eli Mandel, Henry Kreisel, Seymour Mayne, and others.

Posthumously, his work has been increasingly recognized. Besides the many books and articles on Klein that have appeared in recent years, it is important to note the volumes of Klein's collected prose poems that were recently published by the Toronto University Press.

BIBLIOGRAPHY

Works by Abraham Moses Klein

The Second Scroll. (Toronto: McClelland and Stewart, 1969).

The Collected Poems of A. M. Klein. Ed. Miriam Waddington. Toronto: McGraw-Hill Ryerson, 1974.

A. M. Klein, Beyond Sambation: Selected Essays and Reviews, 1928–1955. Ed. Usher Caplan and M. W. Sternberg. Toronto: Toronto University Press, 1982.

A. M. Klein, Literary Essays and Reviews. Ed. Usher Caplan and M. W. Sternberg. Toronto: Toronto University Press, 1987.

The Collected Poems of A. M. Klein. 2 vols. Ed. Zailig Pollock. Toronto: Toronto University Press, 1990.

Works about Abraham Moses Klein

Books

Brenner, Rachel Feldhay. *A. M. Klein, the Father of Canadian Jewish Literature: Essays in the Poetics of Humanistic Passion.* Lewiston, ME: Mellen, 1990.

Caplan, Usher. *Like One That Dreamed: A Portrait of A. M. Klein.* Toronto: McGraw-Hill Ryerson, 1982.

Fischer, G. K. *In Search of Jerusalem: Religion and Ethics in the Writings of A. M. Klein.* Montreal: McGill-Queen's University Press, 1975.

Marshall, Tom, ed. *A. M. Klein.* Critical Views on Canadian Writers Series, vol. 4 Toronto: Ryerson Press, 1970.

Mayne, Seymour, ed. *The A. M. Klein's Symposium, The Reappraisals.*

Pollock, Zailig. *A. M. Klein: The Story of the Poet.* Toronto: University of Toronto Press, 1994.

Canadian Writers Series. Ottawa: University of Ottawa Press, 1975.

Waddington, Miriam. *A. M. Klein.* Vancouver: Copp Clak, 1970.

Articles

Bentley, D. M. R. "Klein, Montreal, and Mankind." *Journal of Canadian Studies* 19, No. 2 (1984): 34–58.

————. "A Nightmare Ordered: A. M. Klein's 'Portrait of the Poet as Landscape.' " *Essays on Canadian Writing* 28 (Spring 1984): 1–46.

Brenner, Rachel Feldhay. "A. M. Klein and Mordecai Richler: Canadian Responses to the Holocaust." *Journal of Canadian Studies* 24, No. 2 (Summer 1989): 65–78.

————. "A. M. Klein and Mordecai Richler: The Poetics of the Search for Providence in the Post-Holocaust World." *Studies in Religion* 19, No. 2 (1990): 207–221.

Greenstein, Michael. "Canadian Poetry after Auschwitz." *Canadian Poetry*, No. 20 (Spring/Summer 1987): 1–20.

————. "History in *The Second Scroll*." *Canadian Literature*, No. 76 (Spring 1978): 37–46.

Kessner, Carole, ed. "The Intellectual as a True *Ohev Israel* [Lover of Israel]." In *The Other New York Intellectuals*. New York: New York University Press, 1994.

Irving Layton. "Personal Memoir." *Viewpoints: The Canadian Jewish Quarterly* 2, No. 4 (Spring 1981): 3–11.

KENNETH KOCH (1925–)

Joseph Lease

BIOGRAPHY

Kenneth Koch was born in Cincinnati, Ohio, February 27, 1925. After graduating from high school, he began a three-year tour of army duty (he served as a rifleman in the Pacific). Koch attended Harvard, graduating from college in 1948. He also met John Ashbery at Harvard, and his friendship with Ashbery would be tremendously important to Koch's poetry. At Harvard, Koch studied writing with Delmore Schwartz and read, under Schwartz's guidance, the poetry of William Butler Yeats and Wallace Stevens.

Koch completed his Ph.D. at Columbia University in 1959; his dissertation is entitled "The Reception and Influence of American Poetry in France, 1918–1950." He spent the 1950–1951 academic year in France, and that experience had a major effect on his poetry. Koch married Janice Ellwood in 1954; they have one daughter, Katherine. Koch joined the Columbia faculty in 1959; that same year, his first important book of poetry, *Ko, or a Season on Earth*, was published; a second collection, *Thank You and Other Poems*, was published in 1962. During the 1950s Koch developed close friendships with the poets John Ashbery and Frank O'Hara and the painters Larry Rivers and Jane Freilicher: Koch's involvement with the New York avant-garde poetry-art-music scene was a major influence on his poetry throughout the 1950s and 1960s. Like O'Hara, Koch collaborated with Rivers; Rivers and O'Hara also wrote a satirical play celebrating the New York art world and poetry scene called "Kenneth Koch: A Tragedy."

Critics have designated Koch, Ashbery, O'Hara, James Schuyler, Barbara Guest, and other poets (including Ted Berrigan, Bernadette Mayer, and David Shapiro) "the New York School of poetry." The term is general and does not designate a unitary poetic program: however, New York School poetry is principally ironic and, in a variety of modes, anticonventional. Koch's early style balances irony and attacks on academic pomposity with abstraction and, occasionally, surrealist lyricism. Like many of the poets with whom he appeared in Donald Allen's crucial 1960 anthology *The New American Poetry*, Koch was fighting to make poems that were genuinely new and that would overturn the stultifying conventions that made academic late modernism seem diminished, removed from life, and trivial. Koch was never as famous as Allen Ginsberg, Robert Creeley, Charles Olson, or Robert Duncan, but, like them, he helped to inspire a generation of poets and readers to experiment and to expect different things from American poetry. For one thing, Koch, Ashbery, and O'Hara believed that poems should surprise readers in order to delight them.

Koch's early poetry, like the poetry of Frank O'Hara and the poetry that John Ashbery wrote during the 1950s and 1960s, often fuses stream-of-consciousness so fast as to become opaque with painterly abstraction (Koch became a serious poet at seventeen, when he read the novels of John Dos Passos). Though New York School poetry is different from Beat poetry or Black Mountain poetry, it had some of the same impact during the 1960s: readers were drawn to a new sense of freedom and play and to the music of a more active immersion in language. Koch's poetry was never any more openly political than the painting of Larry Rivers (or Andy Warhol), but in the cultural context of the 1960s, it was seen as part of a broad artistic opposition to political and social conformity. In a recent (1996) interview (''Kenneth Koch''), Koch emphasizes the community he felt with Ashbery and O'Hara: ''Being together so much and talking so much and telling each other what to read so much, we were a little bit, I suppose, like members of a team, like the Yankees or the Minnesota Vikings. We inspired each other, we emulated each other, we were very critical of each other, we admired each other, we were almost entirely dependent on one another for support'' (53). During 1961–1962, Koch also edited five issues of *Locus Solus*, an important poetry journal, together with John Ashbery, James Schuyler, and Harry Matthews; the magazine was an important forum for New York School poetry and poetics.

Koch's subsequent major collections of poetry were *The Pleasures of Peace* (1969) and *The Art of Love* (1975). During the 1950s, 1960s, and 1970s, Koch also wrote numerous short plays many of which were produced off-Broadway, with sets by many of Koch's artist friends, including Larry Rivers, Roy Lichtenstein, and Red Grooms. In 1975, Koch published a novel, *The Red Robins*, which he subsequently rewrote as a play. Koch may be more widely known as a teacher of poetry than as a poet: teaching poetry (with considerable verve and creativity) to those considered to be uninterested in it or incapable of understanding it brought Koch a kind of celebrity. Koch has taught poetry writing to children in New York City public schools, an experience that inspired Koch's 1970 volume, *Wishes, Lies, and Dreams*, and his 1973 volume, *Rose, Where Did You Get That Red?: Teaching Great Poetry to Children*. Koch's experience teaching poetry in a nursing home in Manhattan resulted in the 1977 volume *I Never Told Anybody: Teaching Poetry Writing in a Nursing Home.*

Koch continued to publish books of poetry and plays during the 1970s, 1980s, and 1990s: important volumes of poetry from those years include *The Burning Mystery of Anna in 1951* and *One Train.* In 1996, Koch was awarded the Bollingen Prize. His essays and interviews were collected in the 1996 volume *The Art of Poetry.*

MAJOR WORKS AND THEMES

In a sense, Koch's central theme is his style, which is often playful and sometimes wistful, or Koch's theme is the experience of writing poetry and how poetry does and doesn't answer (or complete) life—and the delight and discovery with which poetry answers his creative desire. Kenneth Koch's poetry has been justly celebrated for its comedy: and the *issue* of comedy (and related experiences such as delight and irony) are themselves major themes in Koch's (highly self-conscious) work.

As Koch puts it in the 1996 interview:

Some readers think of a poem as a sort of ceremony—a funeral, a wedding—where anything "comic" is out of order. They expect certain feelings to be touched on in certain conventional ways. . . . I love the quality in Frank [O'Hara]'s work that makes its "message" always that life is so rich, so full of variety and excitement . . . "What spanking opossums of sneaks are caressing the routes!" . . . this cartoon-comedy vision of sneaker opossums sexily spanking their way down the highway positively sings and fizzes with something—without which poetry is a lot less than it could be. The comic in a poet like O'Hara or Wallace Stevens or Byron, Aristophanes, Shakespeare, Lautreamont, Max Jacob is a part of what is most serious for art to get to—ecstasy, unity, freedom, completeness, Dionysiac things. (52)

However, Koch's work shifts thematically in the poems of his middle period: his humor is still there, but in volumes such as *The Burning Mystery of Anna in 1951* and *Days and Nights,* it is transformed by introspection. For example, in poems such as "The Circus," "To Marina," and "Days and Nights," Koch writes in propria persona—these poems are not confessional, but they are closer to the work of poets such as Creeley and Lowell than anything Koch did before. In "To Marina" especially, Koch adopts a wistful tone, longing for vanished experience. Likewise, "Days and Nights" describes Koch's education in poetry and the excitement he felt writing his early poems.

Koch's recent poetry remains admirably varied in form and tone. The delightfully patterned "One Train," for example, returns to the scheme of repetition and variation Koch has reinvented throughout his career (most remarkably in "Sleeping with Women"). "One Train May Hide Another" is both exuberant and proverbial. (In fact, Koch has returned to the proverb as a tone, as a source of both humor and ironic wisdom, in numerous poems.) Koch's version of the proverb, which is simultaneously visionary, practical, and barbed, connects both to the Hebrew Bible and to Kafka. In *Train* Koch touches lightly (perhaps unconsciously) on Jewish Mysticism. Or, as Koch writes in "No One Else": "A bagpipe failed you like Elijah" (*Train* 50).

CRITICAL RECEPTION

Koch's poetry is marked in all of its phases by wit and inventiveness. However, because of critics' tendency to categorize him as merely another member of the New York School of poets, Koch's reputation has suffered. Such categorization has meant that Koch has been overshadowed by Ashbery and O'Hara and, more recently, Schuyler and Guest. Koch has, however, been underrated by those who have failed to recognize the visionary delight in his comic, exuberant language. Koch's early poetry is frequently about, or at least inspired by, poems, poets, and the desire to write poetry. For example, "Fresh Air" recounts in the form of a surreal and funny adventure narrative Koch's attempt to write a new poetry free of academic clichés. Similarly, poems such as "Variations on a Theme by William Carlos Williams" ("I chopped down the house that you had been saving to live in next summer") and "Mending Sump" (Koch's parody of Frost) transcend satire or mockery and rise to a kind of giddy discovery. These and related early poems (as well as Koch's droll imitation, in *Ko, or a Season on Earth*, of such models as Byron and Ariosto) led Richard Howard to describe Koch as "the best parodist of our time."

Koch's work has not been discussed in terms of a Jewish tradition in modern and postmodern American poetry. In part, this is because Koch has made little or no effort to identify his poetry with Jewish cultural themes or history. To read Koch's work in terms of Jewish poetic tradition involves making several interpretive conjectures. Theorists of ethnicity and modernist poetry have suggested, for example, that minority poets are frequently more willing to transform, ironize, and reinvent premodern forms and genres then are those poets who view themselves as part of a cultural majority. If this assertion is convincing, then Koch's playful, radical ambivalence toward "the" tradition of English poetry may be read as a sign of his poetry's Jewish dimension. Likewise, Koch's comic poems and the sharp timing he shares with, for example, Allen Ginsberg (and Lenny Bruce) provide remarkable examples of Jewish humor (as well as surrealist lyricism and narrative) in American poetry.

BIBLIOGRAPHY

Works by Kenneth Koch

Poems. New York: Tibor de Nagy Gallery, 1953.
Ko, or a Season on Earth. New York: Grove Press, 1959.

Permanently. New York: Tiber Press, 1960.

Thank You and Other Poems. New York: Grove Press, 1962.

Bertha and Other Plays. New York: Grove Press, 1966.

Poems from 1952 and 1953. Los Angeles: Black Sparrow Press, 1968.

The Pleasures of Peace. New York: Grove Press, 1969a.

Sleeping with Women. Los Angeles: Black Sparrow Press, 1969b.

When the Sun Tries to Go On. Los Angeles: Black Sparrow Press, 1969c.

Wishes, Lies, and Dreams: Teaching Children to Write Poetry. New York: Chelsea House, 1970.

A Change of Hearts: Plays, Films, and Other Dramatic Works, 1951–1971. New York: Random House, 1973a.

Rose, Where Did You Get That Red?: Teaching Great Poetry to Children. New York: Random House, 1973b.

The Art of Love. New York: Random House, 1975a.

The Red Robins. New York: Random House, 1975b.

The Duplications. New York: Random House, 1977a.

I Never Told Anybody: Teaching Poetry Writing in a Nursing Home. New York: Random House, 1977b.

The Burning Mystery of Anna in 1951. New York: Random House, 1979.

Days and Nights. New York: Random House, 1982.

Selected Poems. New York: Random House, 1985.

On the Edge. New York: Viking, 1986.

Seasons on Earth. New York: Viking, 1987.

One Thousand Avant-Garde Plays. New York: Knopf, 1988.

Hotel Lambossa. Minneapolis: Coffee House Press, 1993.

One Train. New York: Knopf, 1994a.

On the Great Atlantic Rainway: Selected Poems, 1950–1988. New York: Knopf, 1994b.

The Art of Poetry. Ann Arbor: University of Michigan Press, 1996a.

The Gold Standard. New York: Knopf, 1996b.

Work about Kenneth Koch

''Kenneth Koch: An Interview by Jordan Davis.'' *The American Poetry Review*, November/December 1996, 45–53.

RICHARD CORY KOSTELANETZ (1940–)

Chris Semansky

BIOGRAPHY

Part human being, part semiotic generator, Richard Kostelanetz embodies what remains of the avant-garde in America. Unencumbered by the demands of an academic position or the obligations of corporate patronage, Kostelanetz produces work so startlingly different and new that to classify him as a dramatist or poet or cultural critic would be to miss the point of his life's activities. Kostelanetz manipulates sign systems. He is as apt to create pieces of audio theatre or video writing or literary holography as he is to compose one-sentence novels or poems without words. Challenging ideas of artistic propriety as much as labeling systems for what passes *as* art, Kostelanetz pushes the envelope so far that even the term sui generis falls short of classifying what he does.

Born May 14, 1940, in New York City to Boris (a lawyer) and Ethel (Cory) Kostelanetz, Richard Cory Kostelanetz spent the better part of his childhood there and, later, in Westchester County, New York. After completing an A.B. in American civilization at Brown University, he studied at King's College in London before taking an M.A. in American history from Columbia, where he wrote his thesis on the African-American novel. Having failed his Ph.D. oral examination, Kosti (as he is known to friends) began publishing—books, anthologies, articles, poems, stories, plays—as well as producing films and holograms and composing audiotapes and videotapes. He is one of the few contemporary authors to occupy more than two columns in *Books in Print*. That he has been able to survive as a writer and artist outside academe speaks to the varied and various kinds of work he has produced in his career and to his tireless pursuit of funding for that work. For his graduate work he received Woodrow Wilson, New York State Regents, and International Fellowships, and in 1964–

1965 he was a Fulbright Scholar at King's College, University of London. In addition he has received personal grants for his projects from the Guggenheim Foundation, the National Endowment for the Arts, the American Public Radio Program fund, the Fund for Investigative Journalism, the Ludwig Vogelstein Foundation, the Coordinating Council of Literary Magazines, American Society of Composers, Authors and Publishers (ASCAP), New York State Council on the Arts Media Services, Kitchen Media Bureau, Inter Nationes (German translation agency), and the DAAD Berliner Kunstlerprogramm. He has also been a Pulitzer fellow in critical writing. Kostelanetz won Pushcart Prizes in 1977, 1982, and 1984 and an Ann Arbor Film Festival Prize in 1986. In 1976 *Numbers: Poems and Stories*, a collection of his "writing" composed entirely of numerals, was selected one of the Best Books of the year by the American Institute of Graphic Arts.

That so many prominent organizations have funded him speaks to the perception that his work *is* culturally relevant. That he is now publishing almost exclusively with smaller presses and in nontraditional formats and facing challenges in finding underwriters for his work suggests that there has been a genuine change in the attitude toward innovative art over the last decade in the United States.

His reluctance to work full-time in academe, however, stems not only from Kostelanetz's lack of appropriate academic credentials (neither a Ph.D. nor an M.F.A.) but from his reticence to participate in the institutionalized production of McArt, that is, writing or media work that merely reiterates rather than challenges what has already been done. Naming Edmund Wilson and Ezra Pound as his professional heroes, Kostelanetz claims that his primary reason for *not* teaching poetry or fiction writing is based on a conviction that has evolved over his years as an independent writer.

Self-described as "deliciously single for the past thirty years," Richard Kostelanetz has lived in downtown Manhattan since 1966, provoking, instigating, and entertaining as he goes about his business trafficking in the market of new ideas.

MAJOR WORKS AND THEMES

Like many Jewish writers, Kostelanetz' writing exhibits an ambivalent relation to his own ethnic identity. He is at once cognizant of the obstacles Jews historically have faced in being accepted by the literary establishments, yet he is also aware of the pitfalls that come with assertions of group importance. In *The End of Intelligent Writing* (1974), his controversial analysis of the literary cabals of the United States, Kostelanetz displays his contempt for the literary establishment's nonefforts to accommodate the "other" in the first half of the twentieth century, detailing how Jews, among other groups, were actively discouraged from pursuing careers as either writers or academics. Noting that that situation has now been largely reversed, Kostelanetz describes how both academe and publishing have adopted what Leslie Fiedler in *End of Intelligent Writing* terms a "Philo-Semitic stance" (19). Each group is a literary machine unto itself, Kostelanetz suggests, that serves to differentiate and consolidate literary reputation based on the values and literary features of that particular group. "Especially in contrast to the Southerners, the Jewish-American writers seem more cohesive, if not more truly conspiratorial, not only in defending their operation but in carving out new terrain" (25). One inherent danger in this cohesiveness, however, is the lengths to which in-group members will go to puff up writers of their own. Kostelanetz names luminaries such as Norman Podhoretz, Philip Rahv, and Isaac Bashevis Singer among those who have benefited from this puffery.

Kostelanetz not only resists being pinned down in terms of the work he creates but also shuns the labeling systems of identity politics, which attempt to generalize about a person's critical or creative activities based on their racial or ethnic heritage. "Categories function best when they describe work, not people," he writes (*End of Intelligent Writing* 23).

As apt to publish with an obscure small press in Calcutta as he is to publish with a major New York house, Kostelantez is anything but a prima donna about his work. His relentless experimentation with writing marks his own impatience with what passes as "new" in literature as it provides him with a forum for investigating the ways that the word has become wor(l)d. Kostelanetz's poetry and fiction—if one goes by the labeling mechanisms of academic naming systems or library indexes—like his dramatic pieces, exploit the visual elements of language, though as he himself has commented, it would be wrong to label such work exclusively "concrete." These visual elements are devoid of graven images and, true to one tradition of Jewish writing, remain rigorously abstract.

In the introduction to *Imaged Words and Worded Images* (1970), his groundbreaking anthology of visual poetry, Kostelanetz distinguishes between art forms that use one or the other as their base. Perhaps his own most successful "worded image" is "Tributes to Henry Ford," the triptych in which the capital letters A and T—representing successive models of automobiles—are grouped in three patterns typical of increasingly complex automotive traffic.

Believing, along with such "groups" as "language-writers," that the truly new in poetry transcends individual voice, ego, time-worn notions of realism, and the menu of formalist poetic devices that constitute them, Kostelanetz has chosen the path of *most* resistance for his work. His *Portraits from Memory* (1975) contains thirty-three sketches of lovers in shapes meant to evoke either the lover or her memory. These "fabricated," handwritten curriculum vitas (visual-verbal portraits) tell us as much about the narrator's desires as they do about the women they purport to represent.

Pitches, Arena, Fields, Turfs (1982) pushes the boundaries of the page as an organizing device for writing rather than merely serving as a "canvas" upon which pretty shapes are formed with words. Written in 1979 during his first residency at Mishkenot Sha'ananim, Jerusalem, *Pitches* takes poetry out of the realm of literature per se and reinscribes it in a continuum of art practices that are more geometric than expressive, more conceptual than concrete. With each page limited to first four, then eight, then sixteen words, arranged in rectangular patterns, the reader is challenged to develop relationships among the words, relationships that may be based on common neology, sound, imagery, or any other denominator. One is always reminded that for Kostelanetz poetics can never be merely a science of composing techniques but that it must first take into account the expectations of the reader and work with and against those expectations to both provoke and please. In his Preface to the collection, Dan Jaffe says "These aren't poems just because they don't look like poems." As is the case with much of his work, Kostelanetz takes a single text through different media, exploring possibilities intrinsic in each. Hence, *Pitches* has appeared not only as one of a series of books but as an audiotape and a videotape as well. Distinguishing in *The New Poetries and Some Old* between poetry more marked by identity politics and that marked by "genuine" innovative form, Kostelanetz claims, "Unless the word 'new' is used to refer particularly to form and style, it becomes a platitude. This debasement of critical language, mostly in the interest of exploiting the prestige of the avant-garde without delivering the goods, regrettably obscures the emergence of genuinely new poetries in North America" (122).

Like his written poetry, Kostelanetz's audio theatre emphasizes its own materiality—this time, acoustic—as well. *Kaddish* (1990), for example, an audio piece commissioned by German radio, utilizes a wide variety of declamations of the Jewish prayer for the dead to "expose" the sound of the Jewish diaspora. A range of accents and backgrounds is used for this piece. In a similar vein another audio piece, *The Eight Nights of Hanukah* (1983), employs two dozen laymen of various ages to read the familiar prayer for lighting the candle. Spoken in Hebrew in a variety of accents, the prayers are then mixed with one another into eight separate fugues of successively increasing numbers of voices. Kostelanetz's award-winning *A Berlin Lost* (1985) uses the same footage as *Ein Verlorenes Berlinin* (1983), which itself copies a film documentary about the Jewish cemetery. While images of the cemetery itself appear on screen, the voices of Berliners, in German, speak about the graveyard and its relation to the Berlin they once knew. Faces never appear on the screen, so the disembodied voices represent a kind of acoustic diaspora.

CRITICAL RECEPTION

Critics have invariably praised Kostelanetz's abilities to create innovative art forms through his intermedia practices and his interweaving of genres. In his review of *Visual Language* for *La Gazetta di Modena* Carlo Alberto Sitta writes that Kostelanetz

uses spatial form in which the sign of the writing breaks out of the arbitrariness of the alphabet to take on the shape of the idea designed from words. . . . Here . . . one sees an entirely modern conception of art as play, as irony, a demystification worked on the traditional messages of the language; a language that for the occasion could be English, or a poetics that could be centered on 'After Joyce,' the title that Kostelanetz gives to another of his concrete works, consisting of the alphabet's letters spreading outwards in concentric spirals (3).

At home in a number of languages, Kostelanetz has experimented with weaving poetic pidgins out of English, Spanish, and French, as well as other tongues. ''Kostelanetz makes his 'Franglish Interweaving' turn around another axis,'' writes Marc Dachy. ''Here the words are perpetually in search of a symmetry between the two languages''. . . . ''He has invented the first poem written simultaneously in two combined languages, a late twentieth-century transatlantic zaum containing its own translation'' (182), Writing in *The Experioddicist*, Bob Grumman names ''Iviefdea'' his favorite ''Spanglish'' interweaving, saying that it ''trembled from a live-leaf jumble (with 'idea' emerging from it) into a fascinatingly parallel concern with the inexorable pace of life/veda toward death'' (3).

Lamenting the lack of attention visual poetry has received in the United States, Bob Grumman writes in *American Book Review* that *Wordworks* (1993), Kostelanetz's compendium of poetries in different forms, ''is strong across the board—though, especially as, or about, visual poetry. When that artform finally gets its full due, this collection will surely be considered one of its primary texts'' (6).

Satisfied, to demonstrate the ways that language (verbal or iconic) functions to construct unified senses of both reader and writer amid the welter of other sign systems, Kostelanetz takes his place alongside that other twentieth-century Jewish master of poetic abstraction, Gertrude Stein.

A collection of critics' praise of his work can be found in *Ecce Kosti, Published Encomia, 1967–1995* published by Kostelanetz's own Archae Press. ''There is a paradox here,'' Kostelanetz says in the Preface, ''and a truth about being noticed in America, which is that regardless of how much scattered recognition a writer might receive, it doesn't really have much impact upon the impressionable unless orchestrated by an aggressive publisher and his publicists.''

ArtistBook International in Paris mounted an exhibition of Kostelanetz's book art in 1996.

BIBLIOGRAPHY

Works by Richard Cory Kostelanetz

Poetry

Visual Language. Brooklyn, NY: Assembling Press, 1970.
I Articulations/Short Fictions. New York: Kulchur, 1974.

Portraits from Memory. Dana Point, CA: Ardis, 1975.
Rain Rain Rain. Brooklyn NY: Assembling Press, 1976a.
Numbers: Poems and Stories. Brooklyn NY: Assembling Press, 1976b.
Illuminations. Dallas, TX: Laughing Bear, 1977a.
Numbers Two. Columbus, OH: Luna Bisonte, 1977b.
Pruning, Accruings. New York: Archae Editions, 1978.
Richard Kostelanetz. New York: Archae Editions, 1980a.
Turfs/Arenas/Fields/Pitches. High/Coo Press, 1980b.
Arenas/Fields/Pitches/Turfs. BkMk Press/University of Missouri at Kansas City, 1982.
Seductions-Relationships. New York: Archae Editions, 1983.
Fields/Pitches/Turfs/Arenas. Port Charlotte, FL: Runaway Spoon Press, 1990.
Solos, Duets, Trios and Choruses. Milwaukee, WI: Membrane Press, 1991.
Repartitions Four. Port Charlotte, FL: Runaway Spoon, 1992.
Wordworks: Poems New and Selected. BOA Editions, 1993.
MoRepartitions. Port Charlotte, FL: Runaway Spoon, 1994.

Fiction

In the Beginning. Knoxville, TN: Abyss, 1971.
Accounting. Brescia, Italy: Amodulo 1972.
Metamorphosis. Milwaukee, WI: Membrane Press, 1974.
Constructs. Reno, NV: West Coast Poetry Review, 1975.
One Night Stood. Bula Cynwyd, PA: Future Press, 1977.
Constructs Two. Milwaukee, WI: Membrane Press, 1978a.
Foreshortenings and Other Stories. Berkeley, CA: Tuumba Press, 1978b.
Inexistences: Contructivist Fictions. New York: Archae Editions, 1978c.
Milestones in a Life. Lethbridge, Alta. Canada: Lethbridge Herald, 1978d.
Tabula Rasa: A Constructivist Novel. New York: Archae Editions, 1978e.
And So Forth. Bula Cynwyd, PA: Future Press, 1979a.
Exhaustive Parallel Intervals. Bula Cynwyd, PA: Future Press, 1979b.
Constructs Three, Four, Five and Six: Stories. New York: Archae Editions, 1991a.
Fifty Untitled Constructivist Fictions. New York: Archae Editions, 1991b.
Flipping. New York: Archae Editions, 1991c.
Intermix. New York: Archae Editions, 1991d.
March. Cleveland, OH: Generator Press, 1991e.
Minimal Fictions. Paradise, CA: Asylum Arts, 1994.

Nonfiction

On Contemporary Literature. New York: Avon, 1964; Books for Libraries, 1971; rev.
    ed., Avon, 1969.
The New American Arts. New York: Horizon, 1965; New York: Collier, 1967a.
The Young American Writers: Fiction, Poetry, Drama, and Criticism. Mahwah, NJ: Funk
    and Wagnalls, 1967b.
Beyond Left and Right: Radical Thought of Our Time. New York: William Morrow,
    1968a.
*The Theatre of Mixed Means: An Introduction to Happenings, Kinetic Environments, and
    Other Mixed-Means Performances*. New York: Dial Press, 1968b.
Master Minds: Portraits of Contemporary American Artists and Intellectuals. New York:
    Macmillan, 1969.

Imaged Words and Worded Images. New York: Outerbridge and Dienstfrey, 1970a.

John Cage. New York: Praeger, 1970b.

Possibilities of Poetry: An Anthology of American Contemporaries. New York: Delta/ Dell, 1970c.

Social Speculations: Visions for Our Time. New York: William Morrow, 1971a.

Young Writers in North America. Hatfield, Eng.: American PEN, 1971b.

Breakthrough Fictioneers. New York: Something Else, 1973a.

The Edge of Adaptation: Man and the Emerging Society. Englewood Cliffs, NJ: Prentice-Hall, 1973b.

The End of Intelligent Writing: Literary Politics in America. Franklin, WI: Sheed and Ward, 1974a; republished as *Literary Politics in America: The End of Intelligent Writing*. Kansas City, MO: Andrews and McMeel, 1977.

Recyclings: A Literary Autobiography. Vol. 1, Brooklyn, NY: Assembling Press, 1974b; vol. 2, Future Press, 1984; augmented edition published as *Recyclings, 1959–61*, Bula Cynwyd, PA: Future Press, 1984.

Language and Structure in North America: The First Large Definitive Survey of North American Language Art. Kensington Arts Association, 1975.

Younger Critics in North America: Essays on Literature and the Arts. Fairwater, WI: Margins, 1976.

Esthetics Contemporary. Amherst, NY: Prometheus Books, 1978a; rev. ed. 1989.

Grants and the Future of Literature. New York: Archae Editions, 1978b.

Twenties in the Sixties: Previously Uncollected Critical Essays. Westport, CT: Greenwood Press, 1979a.

Visual Literature Criticism. Carbondale: Southern Illinois University Press, 1979b.

Author of introduction. *The Yale Gertrude Stein*. New Haven, CT: Yale University Press, 1980.

American Writing Today. 2 vols. New York: Voice of America Forum Series, 1981a; rev. ed., Whitson, 1991.

The Old Poetries and the New. Ann Arbor, MI: University of Michigan Press, 1981b.

The Avant-Garde Tradition in Literature. Amsterdam, Netherlands: Prometheus, 1982.

With Benjamin Hrushovski. *The Poetics of the New Poetry*. New York: Archae Editions, 1983.

The Eight Days of Hanukah (CBC audio disc). 1983.

A Berlin Lost (film). 1984.

The Grants-Fix: Publicly Funded Literary Granting in America. New York: Archae Editions, 1987a.

Prose Pieces/Aftertexts. San Diego, CA: Atticus Press, 1987b.

Conversing with Cage. New York: Limelight Editions, 1988.

On Innovative Music(ian)s. New York: Limelight Editions, 1989.

Gertrude Stein Advanced: An Anthology of Criticism. Jefferson, NC: McFarland Press, 1990a.

Kaddish (audio disc).

Unfinished Business: An Intellectual Nonhistory. New York: Archae Editions, 1990b.

The New Poetries and Some Old. Carbondale, IL: Southern Illinois University Press, 1991a.

Politics in the African-American Novel. Westport, CT: Greenwood Press, 1991b.

John Cage Criticism. Ann Arbor, MI: University of Michigan Press, 1992a.

On Innovative Art(ist)s. Jefferson, NC: McFarland, 1992b.

Partitions. Reno, NV: Patagonia, 1992c.

An ABC of Contemporary Reading. San Diego, CA: San Diego State University Press, 1995.

Ecce Kosti, Published Enconomia: 1967–1995. New York: Archae Press, 1995;

Works about Richard Cory Kostelanetz

Berman, Ronald S. *America in the Sixties.* New York: Free Press, 1967.

Bory, Jean-François, ed. *Once Again.* New Directions, 1968.

Dachy, Marc. In *Gertrude Stein Advanced,* 180.

Grumman, Bob. *The Experioddicist.* March 1995, 3.

Hassan, Ihab. *Contemporary American Literature, 1945–1972.* New York: Ungar, 1973.

May, Charles E. *Short-Story Theories.* Columbus, OH: Ohio University Press, 1976.

McCaffery, Larry, ed. *Postmodern Fiction: A Bio-Bibliographical Guide.* Westport, CT: Greenwood Press, 1986.

Myers, George, Jr. *An Introduction to Modern Times.* Grosse Pointe Farms, MI: Lunchroom Press, 1982.

Parker, Peter, ed. *A Reader's Guide to Twentieth-Century Writers.* New York: Oxford, 1995.

Robson, Ernest. *Poetry as Performance Art on and off the Page.* Minneapolis, MN: Primary Press, 1976.

Sitta, Carlo Albert. "Una vecchia favola riportata e realto storica." *Gazetta di Modena.* March 4, 1973, 3.

Woodress, James, ed. *American Literary Scholarship, 1980.* Durham, NC: Duke University Press, 1981.

AARON KRAMER (1921–1997)

Tamra Plotnick

BIOGRAPHY

Born to Hyman and Mary (Click) Kramer in Brooklyn, New York, in 1921, Aaron Kramer became a prolific poet and a major translator of Yiddish literature. In addition to authoring numerous books, both scholarly and poetic, he collaborated on books, scripts, and musicals, contributed to literary and scholarly journals, and edited anthologies and editions, which he also translated. Additionally, he recorded his poems, both on albums and for the Library of Congress. Aaron Kramer held a B.A. (1941) and M.A. (1951) from Brooklyn College and a Ph.D. from New York University (1966). His career as a poet and translator was complemented by his work as a professor and lecturer at various colleges and as a pioneer in the field of poetry therapy.

Starting in 1961, Aaron Kramer climbed the ranks from associate professor to graduate professor, 1975–1978, at Dowling College, Oakdale, New York. Previously, he had lectured and been the director of dramatics at the New York Guild for the Jewish Blind. He was also a high school instructor of English in Bogota, New Jersey. Otherwise, he lectured in English at Queens College of the City University of New York, 1966–1968, and in Shakespearean studies at the University of Guanajuanto, 1974. He also served as guest poetry teacher at various schools and colleges.

As a forerunner in the field of poetry therapy, Aaron Kramer created a program at Hillside Hospital in Glen Oaks, New York. He went on to direct that program and the poetry therapy units at Cleary School for the Deaf in Ronkonkama, New York, and Central Islip State Hospital, 1956–1960. He published articles on the subject in a number of journals.

Between 1940 and 1997 Aaron Kramer published forty books, twenty-seven of which were volumes of his own poetry, three of which contained his essays, criticism, and scholarship, nine of which were translations (from German and Yiddish), and one of which was an anthology of American protest poems (*On Freedom's Side*, 1972). As a writer he belonged to a decade of organizations, including PEN and the International Academy of Poets, and received at least a dozen awards, such as the Hart Crane Memorial Award (in 1969 for "A Hundred Planets") and the Memorial Foundation for Jewish Culture fellowship (1978–1979). He contributed to a multitude of journals and newspapers, including *Carleton Miscellany, Massachusetts Review, Prairie Schooner, San Francisco Review, Midstream, Mediterranean Review, Modern Poetry Studies, Journal of Humanistic Psychology, Denver Quarterly, Kenyon Review, Poet Lore, New England Review, Psychiatry, New York Times, Poetry Northwest, Harlem Quarterly, Sing Out, Village Voice, Jewish Currents*. His work is anthologized in *Treasury of Jewish Poetry, The Jews in the United States*, and *Poems of the United Nations*, among other places.

Evident in his coediting of *West Hills Review: A Whitman Journal* is Aaron Kramer's commitment to poetry and fascination with Walt Whitman. He authored several essays pertaining to Walt Whitman and was the Walt Whitman Birthplace Association trustee beginning in 1980. He promoted poetry by producing poetry programs on radio and judging many contests like those of the Poetry Society of America (1948–1958) and *Lyric* (1974). His voice can be heard reading his and others' works on "Serenade," a Folkways album, and "On Freedom's Side: The Songs and Poems of Aaron Kramer," a Freneau album. Through his translations, he brought works of Yiddish poets like Dora Titelboim, Abraham Reisen, and Morris Rosenfeld as well as the German poetry of Heinrich Heine, Rainer Maria Rilke, Goethe, and Schiller to English-speaking readers. To top off a prolific career with poetry at its heart, Aaron Kramer allowed many composers and choreographers to use his poems in their artistic works.

MAJOR WORKS AND THEMES

A writer imbued with global vision, Aaron Kramer communicates a passion for poetry, humanity, and Jewishness in his life's work. His Jewishness (rather than Judaism) plays an integral role in his writing, both in his observations in poetry and essays and in his volumes of translations by Yiddish authors. This writer's wide-ranging concern for people from Brooklyn to Pretoria asserts itself in his books.

In the Introduction to *Indigo and Other Poems*, Richard E. Braun states that "the formal verse of Aaron Kramer has tended to simplify or ignore the powerful and seemingly inescapable connotations of religious reference" (*Indigo* 21). Jewishness, not Judaism, compels Kramer. He is, as Thomas Yoseloff dubs him, "the Jewish wanderer, seeking the meaning and the destiny of the diaspora" (*The Burning Bush* 15). Kramer writes about his discovery of Jewish ghosts on his travels in Greece in an essay that appears in *The Burning Bush*. He stumbles upon the Square of Hebrew Martyrs on the island of Rhodos. Upon investigating, he uncovers the fact that 6,000 Jewish families who resided there had been swept away one night by the Germans during World War II. Kramer is drawn back to the square to write about it. Here he explains the difference between his attraction to the place and that of the Scandinavian tourists: "what the blondes took to be shade was in reality ghost blood; what for them was the delicious ululation of sea was for me the last moan, drawn out unto eternity, of the Jews of Rhodos" (*The Burning Bush* 231). Clear in this passage is Aaron Kramer's embracing of Jewishness. In his writings never do we see the Jewish self-loathing that has gone in and out of vogue in literature.

Yet, Aaron Kramer's vision extends beyond the Jews. He is aware, for example, that "the Holocaust. . . . huge as it was, is only one chapter, and not the main chapter, except for other Jews, in the ongoing hellishness of twentieth-century history" (*The Burning Bush* 232). He speaks out against the aparthied government in South Africa in his poem "For Benjamin Moloise, Hanged in Pretoria Prison" (*Indigo* 83). In the final stanza, which he addresses to "the White Minority of South Africa," he writes that the poet may be killed by the state but that his words will outlive it. Here we see Kramer grappling with the enormous issue of aparthied in his poetry.

Although he occasionally takes on aparthied, the Holocaust, and the depression, most of Kramer's poems tend to begin in moments of everyday life. He writes about a man waiting for a woman in the "Dress Department." The theme seems mundane until the manikin transforms into Michael and each "aching . . . , each sin" of shoppers is "taken in/to the breast of the manikin as if he were Abraham (*The Burning Bush* 35–36). Although decidedly nonreligious, Aaron Kramer's works emanate a sense of secular sanctity.

Like Whitman, Kramer sings of the everyday. He is influenced by Whitman and writes an essay called "1881: Whitman's Impact on American Jewish Poetry" (*The Burning Bush* 218). In this essay Kramer claims that "Whitman's personal attitude, his cosmic embrace" greeted American's influx of Jews fleeing pogroms and echoed in the writings of Emma Lazarus, I. J. Schwartz, L. Miller, Morris Rosenfeld, Z. Weinper, Chaim Schwartz, Isaac E. Ronch, and Joseph Bov Shover (*The Burning Bush* 218–27). Characterizing the resonance found in the works of these Jewish immigrants and Whitman, Kramer writes that the immigrants "shared—perhaps more passionately than 'the native-born'—his yearning for the ideal America, and their young intellectuals—as soon as they had mastered the new tongue—would recognize Whitman as their poet, both for the biblical cadence of his lines and the affirmation of individual dignity they had come so far so desperately to enjoy" (*The Burning Bush* 218).

Kramer's artistic, historical, and blood understanding of these immigrant writers is partially responsible for his numerous translations of Yiddish poetry. Without his artistic renderings of the works of Morris Rosenfeld (*The Teardrop Millionaire*, 1955), Abraham Reisen (*Poems by Abraham Reisen*, 1971), and

Dora Teitelboim (*All My Yesterdays Were Steps*, 1995) and the works of 138 Yiddish poets (*A Century of Yiddish Poetry*, 1989), many of these poems would have remained entombed in a sadly dying language. Perhaps as it did to Dora Teitelboim, Aaron Kramer heard the wind speak in Yiddish. It would have him tell the world in English what it said to Dora in Yiddish. "The ash of Treblinka—that's what we are."

CRITICAL RECEPTION

Unfortunately, there is scarce criticism of Aaron Kramer's large body of work. In a review of *The Golden Trumpet* (1949), the author's seventh volume of poetry, in *Furioso* (Fall 1949), Reed Whitemore criticizes the writing as both polemic and naive. Whitemore's brief, abstrusely worded article lumps Kramer together with two other poets, Milton Blau and Thomas McGrath. This reviewer seems to particularly relish tearing apart the three left-leaning writers by quoting statements on poetry by Marx and Engels and trying to prove that the poetry falls short of the standards set by the radical pundits. Besides calling Kramer's work simplistic, Whitemore claims that it is biased. Whitemore uses only two short quotations from *The Golden Trumpet* and may, in fact, have his own ax to grind.

In the Foreword to Aaron Kramer's *Indigo and Other Poems* (1991), Joseph Wershba praises the poet for being at "the height of his poetic power" (15). According to Wershba, the leitmotif of Aaron Kramer's lifetime work can be encapsulated in the phrase *compassion never contempt*. Wershba alludes to Kramer's adeptness at transforming mundane topics into sublime themes that are musical on the page. Kramer's interest in everyday experience demonstrates his poetic ties to Whitman. Heinrich Heine, whom Kramer later translated, can also be cited as a literary influence of Kramer, says Wershba.

Thomas Yoseloff points out Aaron Kramer's "poet's eye for the multiplicity of the world's pains, . . . problems, . . . defeats, and . . . victories" (13) in the Foreword to *The Burning Bush* (1983), a collection of some of Kramer's Jewish writings. Writers Mark Van Doren, Louis Untermeyer, Howard Fast, and Charles Fishman, among others, have acclaimed Kramer's works. Shaemas O'Sheel, the Irish nationalist, writes of Aaron Kramer (in a publication that includes Kramer, Langston Hughes, and others) that he commands a wide gamut of poetic powers for the voicing of his consuming hatred of fascism in all its forms. "There is the tumult of war and horror in these poems, but a great wind of vision and hope sweeps through them, too" (*The Burning Bush* 14).

BIBLIOGRAPHY

Works by Aaron Kramer

Anthologies

The Prophetic Tradition in American Poetry. Cranbury, NJ: Associated University Presses, 1968.

Melville's Poetry: Toward the Enlarged Heart. Cranbury, NJ: Associated University Presses, 1972.

The Burning Bush. Cranbury, NJ: Cornwall Books, 1983.

Indigo and Other Poems. Cranbury, NJ: Cornwall Books, 1991.

Poetry

Another Foundation. 1940. New York: Edward Rosner Co.

Seven Poets in Search of an Answer. 1944. New York: Beechhurst Press.

'Til the Grass Is Ripe for Dancing. 1944. Kingston, ONT: Harbinger House.

Thru Our Guns. 1945. Privately printed.

The Glass Mountain. 1946. New York: Beechhurst Press.

The Thunder of the Grass. 1948. New York: International Publishers.

The Golden Trumpet. 1949. New York: International Publishers.

Thru Every Window! 1950. Privately printed.

Roll the Forbidden Drums! 1954. San Francisco, CA: Cameron & Kahn.

A Ballad of August Bondi. 1955. Privately printed.

The Tune of the Calliope. 1958. New York: Yoseloff.

Moses. 1962. New York: O'Hare Books.

Rumshinsky's Hat and House of Buttons. 1964. New York: Yoseloff.

Henry at the Grating. 1968. Mount Vernon, VA: Folklore Center.

On the Way to Palermo. 1973. Fort Ann, NY: A. S. Barnes.

O Golden Land! 1976. Decatur, GA: Dowling College Press.

The Dance. 1978. Port Jefferson, NY: Street Press.

Carousel Parkway. 1980. Fort Ann, NY: A. S. Barnes.

In Wicked Times. 1983. Winterville, GA: Ali Baba Books.

Regrouping. 1997. Northport, NY: Birnham Wood Graphics.

Scholarly Writing

Neglected Aspects of American Poetry. 1997. Oakdale, NY: Dowling College Press.

Edited Works

On Freedom's Side (an anthology of American poems of protest). 1972, New York: Macmillan.

Translations

The Poetry and Prose of Heinrich Heine (German). 1948. Secaucus, NJ: Citadel Press.

The Teardrop Millionaire (Morris Rosenfield, Yiddish). 1955, Emma Lazarus Federation.

Songs and Ballads: Goethe, Schiller, Heine (German). 1963. New York: O'Hare Books.

Rainer Maria Rilke: Visions of Christ (German). 1967. Boulder, CO: University of Colorado Press.

Poems by Abraham Reisen (Yiddish). 1989. Decatur, GA: Dowling College Press.

Edited and Translated Works

A Century of Yiddish Poetry. Cranbury, NJ: Cornwall Books, 1989.

All My Yesterdays Were Steps: The Selected Poems of Dora Teitelboim. Hoboken, NJ: Ktav Publishing House, 1995.

STANLEY KUNITZ   (1905–   )

David Caplan

BIOGRAPHY

Stanley Jasspoon Kunitz was born on July 29, 1905, in Worcester, Massachusetts. His parents, Solomon Z. Kunitz and Vetta Helen Jasspoon Kunitz, were Jewish Lithuanian immigrants. Six weeks before Kunitz was born, his father committed suicide, an act at least partly motivated by the recent bankruptcy of the family dress manufacturing business. In bitterness and anger, his mother forbade mentioning her deceased husband's name in her presence. When Kunitz was eight, his mother married a second time, to Mark Dine, who died six years later. As a boy, Kunitz also endured the early deaths of his two older sisters, his only siblings.

The 1923 Worcester Classical High School class valedictorian, Kunitz matriculated at Harvard and lived next door to J. Robert Oppenheimer. After graduating summa cum laude, he pursued graduate studies, but, after realizing that anti-Semitism would significantly hamper his academic career, he left Harvard with an A.M., but not a Ph.D. A stint as a newspaper reporter for the *Worcester Daily Telegram* followed, during which he covered the Sacco-Vanzetti case. In 1928, he started working for the W. H. Wilson Company as an editorial assistant. "Dilly Tante," the pseudonym he used for the first volume he edited, suggests his attitude toward this job.

In 1930, Kunitz married Helen Pierce and moved to a 100-acre farm in Connecticut. The marriage, Kunitz's first of three, ended in divorce in 1937. In 1939, he married Eleanor Evans. They had a daughter, Gretchen, and divorced in 1957, after which he married Elise Asher, a painter and poet.

Kunitz was drafted in 1943. After declaring himself a pacifist and refusing to bear arms, he edited a camp newspaper, which subsequently won the army's award for best publication. Kunitz was offered and refused a commission as an officer.

After the war, Bennington College hired Kunitz as a replacement for Theodore Roethke, a longtime friend who, in the midst of a severe manic attack, refused hospitalization unless the college named Kunitz as his replacement. For the next several decades, Kunitz worked as an untenured professor. In addition to Bennington, Kunitz taught at Potsdam State Teachers College (now SUNY), the New School, Queens College, Brandeis, Columbia University.

In 1958, after the publication of *Selected Poems 1928–1958*, Kunitz's life experienced a dramatic change. Suddenly considered an important poet, he won several major awards, including the 1959 Pulitzer Prize. Better teaching posts allowed him to stop working as a consultant for the W. H. Wilson Company. In 1968, he helped found the Fine Arts Work Center in Provincetown, Massachusetts, a fellowship designed to provide artists free time to devote to their work. Also, Kunitz judged the Yale Series of Younger Poets from 1969 to 1977. In addition to his nine books of poetry, Kunitz has published translations of Anna Akhmatova, Andrei Voznesensky, and Ivan Drach, criticism, and a collection of interviews.

MAJOR WORKS AND THEMES

Much of Stanley Kunitz's poetry considers a few major issues. Among these preoccupations are the anguished and impossible search for the lost father and the metaphysical debates of body and soul. Yet, while remaining fixed on many of the obsessions his early work establishes, Kunitz's later poetry shows a consistent progression toward increased tenderness and intimacy and away from unnecessary ornament and pretensions. Like Yeats, he presents an inspiring example of a poet who writes with greater and greater effect by continually paring down his work until only the essential remains.

Although it included a section of poems from the already out-of-print *Intellectual Things* (1930), Kunitz's second book, *A Passport to the War* (1944), signaled a change from apprentice to mature work. Abandoning some, although by no means all, of the currently fashionable metaphysical conceits, paradoxes, and mannerisms, this book showed Kunitz's poetry moving toward a more forthrightly autobiographical, less convoluted style. "Father and Son," perhaps the best-known poem in *A Passport to the War*, ends with a son's anguished plea for the father to "teach me how to work and keep me kind" (7). The father's unsatisfying response is to show "his face white with ignorance" (7). In "Father and Son" and the other poems in *A Passport to the War*, Kunitz establishes his fundamental belief that a poet must explore his deepest injuries, his "wounds," to use one of Kunitz's favorite terms. As a consequence, his work consistently returns to the childhood traumas of his father's suicide, his mother's reaction to it, and, more obliquely, his stepfather's death.

As he has asserted in many interviews, Kunitz does not possess a conventional

Jewish faith but rather a wide-ranging spiritualism influenced by Jewish culture and ethics. Several of his poems use the language of Judaism to express his spiritual longings. Most notably, "An Old Cracked Tune" in *The Testing-Tree* (1971) transforms an anti-Semitic street song into a celebration of survival. "The Wellfleet Whale" from *Next-to-Last Things* (1985) is Kunitz's most extended and profound meditation upon his relationship with the divine. The poem contemplates a whale that washes up on a Cape Cod beach and the range of responses it elicits from the townspeople who gather to watch it. While swimming in the bay, the whale presented an awe-inspiring image of strength and power. The poet, however, feels a closeness with the mythic animal only after it is trapped on the sand. Humiliated by its blunder and about to die, the whale no longer remains godlike—or rather becomes godlike in a way that the poet can appreciate. Humbled by experience, the beached whale turns into a divinity that he can pray both to and with.

Several other poems included in *Next-to-Last Things* show Kunitz reworking familiar themes to great effect. "Passing Through" with its subtitle of "—on my seventy-ninth birthday" is a tender love poem that grapples with the poet's keen sense of his mortality and the legacy of his father's suicide. Like "River Road" from *The Testing-Tree*, the prose poem, "The Old Darned House," describes the painful failure of Kunitz's first marriage.

During the first four decades of his poetic career, Kunitz published a book every fourteen years. However, *The Testing-Tree* signaled an era of greater productivity. Other volumes of poetry followed at a pace that even Kunitz found somewhat amazing: *The Terrible Threshold: Selected Poems, 1940–1970* (1974), *Next-to-Last Things* (1985), and *Passing Through* (1995). Kunitz also published *A Kind of Order, A Kind of Folly: Essays and Conversations* (1975) and *Interviews and Encounters with Stanley Kunitz* (1993).

The best poems of the most recent third of Kunitz's career balance a sense of personal injury with an understanding of others' pain. "The Magic Curtain" describes a boy's youthful infatuation with Frieda, his German nursemaid, who eventually runs away with a married man. The poem would have been a beautifully nostalgic, if somewhat slight, remembrance of childhood fancies, if it had omitted a simple detail mentioned in the poem's final lines. Years later, after World War I, the boy receives a postcard from Frieda in Dresden. The mention of this city which World War II would soon destroy broadens the scope of the boy's and the poem's discovery of the impermanence of childhood pleasures. Not only love but war and death take people away, the poem implies.

The title poem of *The Testing-Tree* provides perhaps the best and best-known example of Kunitz's ability to fuse personal anguish and a sense of social injustice. As the poem suggests, to turn away from the nightmares of childhood is to flinch from the "the deeper dark." Instead, the poet must relentlessly explore the source of his pain. What saves this poem and much of Kunitz's mature work from solipsism is the recognition that the poet is not alone in his suffering. Instead, "The Testing-Tree" argues that the poet's torments are part of the "murderous time." To live in such an era is to endure, by necessity, its miseries. This knowledge makes the voice of "The Testing-Tree" both personal and prophetic, using particular experience in order to understand the processes of grief and life, how one's heart / . . . "lives by breaking" (62). A fine tribute to this poem is Tony Kushner's decision to use several lines as an epigraph to his Pulitzer Prize-winning play *Angels in America: A Gay Fantasia on National Themes* (Part One). Kushner's drama of the politics of AIDS greatly differs from "The Testing-Tree"; yet the two works contemplate the similar problem of living in a "murderous time."

The new poems in *Passing Through* show Kunitz starting his ninth decade at the height of his poetic powers. In particular, "Touch Me," the final poem in the volume, exemplifies the strengths of his later work. The opening, "Summer is late, my heart" (158), quotes "As Flowers Are," a poem that Kunitz wrote more than forty years before and collected in *This Garland, Danger* from *Selected Poems 1928–1958*. Except during a brief undergraduate infatuation with modernism, Kunitz bitterly disagreed with Eliot and the New Critical valorization of artistic impersonality. However, "As Flowers Are" affirms Eliot's motto that poetry ought to be difficult. With its punning, metaphysical conceits, and philosophical language, the verse more challenges than invites a reader. Although a love poem, "As Flowers Are" displays, like much American verse written in the 1930s and 1940s, a deeper passion for Donne than the lover it addresses.

In contrast, "Touch Me" ends with lines that are half prayer, half lover's plea and moving in their tenderness and honesty. Addressing his wife, the elderly poet asks for her touch to "remind me who I am" (159). The three-stress lines are more conversational than Kunitz's earlier, accentual-syllabic verse; their tone is both relaxed and passionate. As such, the differences from "As Flowers Are" and "Touch" not only represent the maturation of Kunitz's work but also follow the general trend in post–World War II American poetry, as poets diverse as Robert Lowell, James Wright, and Adrienne Rich moved from metrical to less densely restrictive verse forms.

At the heart of "Touch Me," however, is the most traditional of metaphysical subjects: the dialogue of body and soul. In Kunitz's early work, this conversation generally occurs within the poet and in isolation from others. In contrast, in "Touch Me," the poet wants—in fact, needs—his wife to affirm his identity. Only her touch can remind him who he is. By alluding to his life and, indeed, centering the poem around it, Kunitz makes his biography relevant in ways that Eliot would find disagreeable. For example, the scene's poignancy is deepened by the fact that Kunitz wrote this love poem in his late eighties. The physical love he yearns for is possible only because of the hard-won wisdom gained from the disappointments of an earlier, failed marriage and a mature appreciation of the frailty of human mortality and the almost overwhelming force of desire. This is the poetry of a grown man of knowledge and experience. It is, in the best sense of the word, personal.

CRITICAL RECEPTION

In 1929, two weeks after he submitted his first book, *Intellectual Things* (1930), to Doubleday Doran Publishers, Kunitz received a call from Ogden Nash, the poetry editor, accepting it. This flattering response made Kunitz believe that his literary career would progress smoothly; unfortunately, nearly thirty frustrating years would pass before Kunitz's work received the acclaim it deserved.

Both *Intellectual Things* and Kunitz's second book of poetry, *Passport to the War* (1944), enjoyed little critical attention during their initial publications and soon were out of print. However, Kunitz had earned a modest reputation as "a poet's poet," with admirers including W. H. Auden and Marianne Moore. Of the two, Moore had the more direct impact on Kunitz's life, by accepting several of his poems for the *Dial* and obtaining a Guggenheim Fellowship for him in 1945. The lack of interest that Kunitz encountered when trying to find a publisher for his *Selected Poems, 1928–1958* suggests the general neglect his work suffered from at the time. Several publishers refused to print the book; several others even refused to consider it. However, in 1958, when the Atlantic Monthly Press released *Selected Poems, 1928–1958*, Kunitz began to receive widespread recognition as a major poet. Among others, John Ciardi highly praised the book in print and correctly predicted that it would win Kunitz a greater readership and more widespread attention.

In 1959, Kunitz won the Pulitzer Prize in poetry and the National Institute of Arts and Letters grant in poetry, and his work began to appear regularly in major anthologies. Each of Kunitz's subsequent books dependably won prestigious awards. In 1971, *The Testing-Tree* solidified Kunitz's reputation, with several reviewers praising it for exemplifying the virtues of Kunitz's later, more open style. Robert Lowell—who had previously written a widely noticed appreciation of "Father and Son" and a blurb for *Selected Poems, 1928–1958*—published a glowing review of *The Testing-Tree* on the front page of the *New York Times Book Review*. In 1974, Kunitz was appointed consultant in poetry to the Library of Congress, a post many felt was long overdue.

Since the late 1970s, Kunitz has been considered a distinguished elder statesmen of poetry. In 1986, *A Celebration for Stanley Kunitz on His 80th Birthday* (Skillings) collected tributes from a wide range of poets, including Robert Hass and Michael Ryan (both of whom Kunitz had selected as Yale Younger Poets Series more than a decade before), Stanley Moss, Joyce Carol Oates, Galway Kinnell, W. S. Merwin, and Kenneth Koch. Also, a wide variety of Kunitz's former students paid tribute to their former teacher, including Louise Gluck and Jack Gilbert. *Passing Through: The Later Poems*, a collection of selections from *The Testing-Tree, The Poems of Stanley Kunitz, 1928–1978*, and *Next-to-Last Things* and nine new poems, won the 1995 National Book Award.

Kunitz's other honors include an honorary doctor of letters degree from Clark

University, the Brandeis University Medal for Achievement, a Ford Foundation grant, and the Fellowship Award from the Academy of American Poets.

BIBLIOGRAPHY

Works by Stanley Kunitz

Intellectual Things. Garden City, NY: Doubleday, 1930.
Passport to the War: A Selection of Poems. New York: Holt, 1944.
Selected Poems, 1928–1958. Boston: Atlantic Monthly/Little, Brown, 1958.
The Testing-Tree: Poems. Boston: Atlantic Monthly/Little, Brown, 1971.
The Terrible Threshold: Selected Poems, 1940–1970. London: Secker and Warburg, 1974.
The Poems of Stanley Kunitz, 1928–1978. Boston: Atlantic Monthly/Little, Brown, 1979.
The Wellfleet Whale and Companion Poems. Riverside-on-Hudson, NY: Sheep Meadow Press, 1983.
Next-to-Last Things: New Poems and Essays. Boston: Atlantic Monthly Press, 1985.
Passing Through. New York: W. W. Norton, 1995.

Works about Stanley Kunitz

Davidson, Peter. "Be Patient with My Wound: Stanley Kunitz, 1958–9." *The Fading Smile: Boston Poets from Robert Frost to Sylvia Plath*. New York: Alfred A. Knopf, 1985.
Friedman, B. H. "Tribute to a Survivor." *A Celebration for Stanley Kunitz On His Eightieth Birthday*. Riverdale-on-Hudson, New York: Sheep Meadow Press, 1986.
Glück, Louise. "To My Teacher." *Interviews and Encounters with Stanley Kunitz*. Ed. Stanley Moss. Princeton: Princeton University Press, 1993.
Hass, Robert. "What Furies." *Twentieth Century Pleasures/Prose on Poetry*. New York: Ecco Press, 1984.
Hénault, Marie. *Stanley Kunitz*. Boston: Twayne, 1980.
Lowell, Robert. "The Testing-Tree." *The New York Times Book Review*, March 21, 1971: 1, 18.
———. "Stanley Kunitz's 'Father and Son.' " *Collected Prose*. New York: Farrar, Straus, and Giroux, 1987.
Orr, Gregory. *Stanley Kunitz: An Introduction to the Poetry*. New York: Columbia University Press, 1985.
Rudman, Mark. "Thursday, October 17; Worcester, Massachusetts." *A Celebration for Stanley Kunitz on His Eightieth Birthday*. Riverdale-on-Hudson, NY: Sheep Meadow Press, 1986.
Ryan, Michael. "Life between Scylla and Charybdis." *Interviews and Encounters with Stanley Kunitz*. Ed. Stanley Moss. Princeton: Princeton University Press, 1993.
Skillings, Roger. "Early Days at the Fine Arts Center." *A Celebration for Stanley Kunitz On His Eightieth Birthday*. Riverdale-on-Hudson, NY: Sheep Meadow Press, 1986.

IRVING LAYTON   (1912–)

Caren Irr

BIOGRAPHY

Born Israel Lazarovitch in Romania, Layton emigrated to Canada with his parents at the age of one. His family settled in Montreal, where his mother ran a shop from their home, and his father studied Talmud and made cheese. The economic hardships of this childhood often figure in Layton's poetry.

Layton attended high school, but conflicts with teachers led to his being expelled in 1930. With the help of novelist A. M. Klein, he enrolled at Macdonald College, an agricultural school outside Montreal. While writing on socialism for the college paper, he began using the name Irving Layton. After graduating in 1939 and serving in the army during World War II, Layton earned an M.A. in economics and political science at McGill in 1946. For the next thirty-three years, he was a popular teacher at Herzliah Junior High School and Sir George Williams College in Montreal and York University in Toronto. During 1981–1982, the University of Toronto appointed him writer-in-residence.

In the mid-1940s, Layton, Louis Dudek, and John Sutherland edited *First Statement*, a literary periodical devoted to modern, international, and politically engaged writing. In 1944, Layton composed his first major poem, ''The Swimmer.'' His first collection, *Here and Now*, appeared the following year, and since 1948 he has published at least one book a year.

In the early 1950s, Layton corresponded with the U.S. poet Robert Creeley, who offered him a teaching position at Black Mountain College in North Carolina. However, the U.S. government's decision that Layton was an undesirable alien made accepting this position impossible. Layton toured Europe and Asia in the 1960s and 1970s. Among the honors Layton has received are two Canada Council grants (1959 and 1973), a Governor General's Award (1959), several honorary degrees, and the Order of Canada (1976). He was nominated for the Nobel Prize in 1981.

Layton has been married four times and has two sons and two daughters. He lives in Montreal.

MAJOR WORKS AND THEMES

In his Foreword to *The Collected Poems of Irving Layton* (1971), Layton asserts that "a poet has his images and symbols handed to him very early in life; his later poems are largely explorations he makes into the depths of his unconscious to unravel their meanings." Accordingly, Layton has used images of sensual women, joyless scholars, Gothic cemeteries, and mechanization throughout his career—from his early social realist poems, to the surrealist and polemical work of his middle phases, to his most recent satirical lyrics. Of these images, those associated with Judaism have become increasingly important to Layton.

Many of Layton's social realist poems appear in *Red Carpet for the Sun*. "Cote de Neiges Cemetery," for example, illustrates how the religious, ethnic, and economic distinctions that segregate Montrealers survive after death. Frequently, the sociological poems describe what being a Jew means to Layton. In "Gothic Landscape," he feels menaced by trees that resemble "penitential Augustines" (*Collected Poems* [*cp*] 368), and in "On Seeing the Statues of Ezekial and Jeremiah in the Church of Notre Dame" he is moved to sympathy for the prophets. The narrator promises to rescue them from the context of Catholicism by occasionally bringing them his "hot Hebrew heart . . . in aching confraternity" (*CP* 138). Sandwiched between the Catholic French and the Protestant English, Layton identifies neighborhood with nation. Being Jewish in these poems means finding his home in the ghetto, rather than in the larger abstraction of "Canada."

Still, home does not mean comfort to Layton, as his poems about family demonstrate. He sees in other people's families occasional sparks of genuine love ("Madonna of the Magnificat"), but generally he is cynical about the family and the ethnic community it grounds. " '[T]hank heaven/ I'm not/ Jesus Christ—/ I don't have to love them' " (*CP* 203), he remarks dismissively in "Family Portrait." Even his parents' deaths inspire little sentiment. In "Death of Moishe Lazarovitch," Layton expresses some anguish, mixed with suspicion of a corpse "arrogant with new life" (*CP* 36). The corpse retains scholarly qualities that Layton dislikes, and it warns him away from the hermeneutical side of Judaism. Layton prefers to inherit his mother's cursing and "proud carnal assertion," as described in "Keine Lazarovitch, 1870–1959" (*CP* 244). This strong, angry woman is the most powerful of Layton's many Liliths; she recalls the popular, Yiddish side of the ghetto. In these Kaddish poems and in writings about his wives and children, Layton openly prefers the secular aspect of Jewish life.

In his second, surrealist phase, the content of Layton's poems often asserts the irrelevance of religion in a materialistic world, but their focus on violence and pain foreshadows his later Zionism. Typically, the surrealist poems make the self a site of suffering, as in "Me, the P.M. and the Stars," "The Dwarf," "In the Midst of My Fever" and "The Improved Binoculars." The poet witnesses violence too severe for realist description. Though angered, he cannot actively prevent atrocities and resorts to an inadequate, almost scholarly empathy; his only weapon is a set of "improved binoculars" for viewing the ironies of destruction.

Since the poet cannot vanquish suffering, he turns to eros. In two of his more light-hearted, surrealist poems, "The Day Aviva Came to Paris" and "Why I Don't Make Love to the First Lady," Layton imagines sensuality disrupting the public, political order. Disenchanted with the socialism of his youth, Layton finds in eros a source of worldly redemption. See, for example, "For Mao Tse-Tung: A Meditation on Flies and Kings":

> They dance best who dance with desire,
> Who lifting feet of fire from fire
> Weave before they lie down
> A red carpet for the sun (*CP* 215)

Since the late 1960s, this Nietzschean theme has been central to Layton's interpretation of twentieth-century history. He identifies suffering specifically with the Holocaust and casts himself as poetic champion of the state of Israel; rejecting the academic modernism of Yeats, Pound, Eliot, and Auden, he favors a more straight-shooting, polemical style. Many of the poems in *The Shattered Plinths* (1968) and *For My Brother Jesus* (1976) echo the sentiments of "Who Will Give Me Back"; here, Layton contrasts the "lovely emotions" of reading Shelley to the necessity of torturing Arabs and annihilating Russians and Chinese. Further, in "For My Two Sons, Max and David," he urges his children to reject quietist stereotypes of Jewish behavior and "be gunners in the Israeli Air Force" (*A Wild Peculiar Joy* 151–52). This admonition signals Layton's solution to his dilemma as a late twentieth-century Jew. Although plagued by an unrepresentable memory of genocide—a memory that necessarily ties him to the past—he chooses to foreground the struggle to survive in the present. He proposes compensating for past suffering with present aggression.

While identifying militant Zionism with social renewal, Layton also associates Christianity with necrophilia. "The gentiles have poured your rich blood/into their boredom and futility," he laments in "Shlemihl (in *A Wild Peculiar Joy*). Like the English-Canadian professors and poetasters he loves to ridicule, Christians in general seem life-denying to Layton, and their ubiquity leads him to wonder whether any form of idealism can survive the modern age. He concludes in "Dracula" that the vampire is the dominant symbol of the century and that "we must kill one another and die" (*A Wild Peculiar Joy* 180).

The gruesome imagery of the Zionist poems—emaciated bodies, charred bones, and human lampshades—have given way to more generic representations of suffering in Layton's recent work, no doubt because, as many commentators have remarked, such imagery usually pales beside the horror of the real Holocaust. From *For My Neighbors in Hell* (1980) to *Final Reckoning* (1987), his latest poems describe life as a whole, though it's "not worth a frog's fart," according to the title poem of the latter collection. But, even in these late poems, death remains a moral, rather than a religious, question for Layton. He does not turn to faith to lessen the horror of dying. Instead, he continues to magnify the contrast between aesthetics and human cruelty. According to "The Carved Nakedness," (in *Final Reckoning*), Layton forges his poetry from the lava of life, the "scalding dross" that kills and maims but can, perhaps, be finally rendered beautiful through art.

CRITICAL RECEPTION

Since Irving Layton's first publications, critics have disagreed strongly about the value of his work. Canadian writer A. M. Klein reviewed his first volume, *Here and Now*, positively in the *Canadian Forum*, praising the "refreshing cynicism" he attributed to Layton's Jewishness (47). Yet, in the same periodical, the prominent literary critic Northrop Frye objected to Layton's militant rhetoric and repetition of themes, concluding that he was "fettered by a moral conscience" (262).

These differences of opinion grew more acrimonious during the 1950s and early 1960s. On one hand, U.S. writers such as Black Mountain poet Robert Creeley hailed him as "the first Great Canadian Poet" (Mayne 35). William Carlos Williams wrote an enthusiastic Introduction to *The Improved Binoculars* in 1956, and literary critic Hugh Kenner found Layton's poetry strong and pleasingly varied (Mayne 52–53, 65). His work was mentioned in the same breath with Ezra Pound, Friedrich Nietzsche, and Walt Whitman. Yet, on the other hand, other critics, including his friend and coeditor Louis Dudek, called Layton "the most over-rated poet anywhere" and denounced his sensationalism and limited symbolic vocabulary (review of *Red Carpet for the Sun*, in Mayne, 89–92). Since Dudek also complained that Layton did not show enough "Christian humility," religion was clearly a factor in Layton's critical reception.

Layton's Judaism inspired even more controversy in the 1960s and 1970s. Fellow poet A. W. Purdy wrote in *Canadian Literature* that Layton was "a moralist," as righteous as "a megalomaniac god" (81). Christopher Levenson claimed Layton explored violence because it was a Jewish theme (272); Patrick O'Flaherty objected to the "obnoxious chauvinism" of *For My Brother Jesus* (30); and Suniti Namjoshi disliked Layton's reliance on the stereotype of the sensitive Jew in *The Pole Vaulter* (19). Some of the same reviewers also found an "artistic clumsiness" in Layton's work of this period (Skelton 63–65). At the same time, critics such as Skelton commented on Layton's "sexual simplicities.'' Often, Layton's depictions of women provoked as much hostility as his politics.

Since the early 1980s, however, Layton's place in Canadian literary history has been assured. Scholarly works devoted to his career place him in a Jewish-Canadian literary lineage between A. M. Klein's modernism and Leonard Cohen's postmodernism (Greenstein 1–16). Pro-Layton scholars emphasize his humanism, Nietzschean energy and courage in addressing major moral issues (Wiens 1–20; Kertes, 32–42; Lemm, 1986). Meanwhile, an anti-Layton contingent objects to the starkness of his oppositions between Jews and Gentiles and between men and women. Michael Andre Bernstein has even gone so far as to call *Fortunate Exile*, a collection of Layton's writings on Jewish themes, ''an appalling volume imaginatively, morally and technically'' (214). On a similar note, Joanne Lewis finds that ''Layton's poetry . . . degrades both women and human sexuality'' (144).

Most controversy about Layton's work has concentrated on content rather than style. This may be partly due to Layton's fondness for dramatic overstatement, but it may also suggest that it is in content that Layton takes his biggest risks. In his role as coxswain for North American Jews, Irving Layton demands strength, virility, and commitment—values at odds with his post-Holocaust world.

BIBLIOGRAPHY

Works by Irving Layton

Here and Now. Montreal: First Statement, 1945.
Now Is the Place (stories and poems). Montreal: First Statement, 1948.
In the Midst of My Fever. Montreal: Divers Press, 1954.
The Blue Propeller. Toronto: Contact, 1955a.
The Cold Green Element. Toronto: Contact, 1955b.
The Bull Calf. Toronto: Contact, 1956a.
The Improved Binoculars: Selected Poems. Highlands, NC: Jonathan Williams, 1956b.
Music on a Kazoo. Montreal: Contact, 1956c.
A Laughter in the Mind. Highlands, NC: Jonathan Williams, 1958.
A Red Carpet for the Sun. Toronto: McClelland and Stewart, 1959.
The Swinging Flesh (poems and stories). Toronto: McClelland and Stewart, 1961.
Love Where the Nights Are Long. Toronto: McClelland and Stewart, 1962.
Balls for a One-Armed Juggler. Toronto: McClelland and Stewart, 1963.
The Laughing Rooster. Toronto: McClelland and Stewart, 1964.
Collected Poems of Irving Layton. Toronto: McClelland and Stewart, 1965.
Periods of the Moon. Toronto: McClelland and Stewart, 1967.
The Shattered Plinths. Toronto: McClelland and Stewart, 1968.
Selected Poems. Toronto: McClelland and Stewart, 1969a.
The Whole Bloody Bird: obs aphs and pomes. Toronto: McClelland and Stewart, 1969b.
Nail Polish. Toronto: McClelland and Stewart, 1971.

Engagements: The Prose of Irving Layton. Toronto: McClelland and Stewart, 1972.

Lovers and Lesser Men. Toronto: McClelland and Stewart, 1973.

The Pole Vaulter. Toronto: McClelland and Stewart, 1974a.

Seventy-Five Greek Poems, 1951–1974. Athens: Hermias, 1974b.

The Darkening Fire: Selected Poems, 1945–68. Toronto: McClelland and Stewart, 1975a.

The Unwavering Eye: Selected Poems 1969–1975. Toronto: McClelland and Stewart, 1975b.

For My Brother Jesus. Toronto: McClelland and Stewart, 1976a.

The Uncollected Poems 1936–1959. Oakville, Ontario: Mosaic, 1976b.

The Covenant. Toronto: McClelland and Stewart, 1977a.

The Poems of Irving Layton. Toronto: McClelland and Stewart, 1977b.

The Selected Poems of Irving Layton. New York: New Directions, 1977c.

Taking Sides: The Collected Social and Political Writings (prose). Oakville, Ontario: Mosaic, 1977d.

Irving Layton. Carlo Mattioli, tredici. Milan: II Bicordo, 1978a.

Love Poems of Irving Layton. Toronto: Canadian Fine Editions, 1978b.

The Tightrope Dancer. Toronto: McClelland and Stewart, 1978c.

Droppings from Heaven. Toronto: McClelland and Stewart, 1979a.

For My Neighbors in Hell. Oakville, Ontario: Mosaic, 1980a.

An Unlikely Affair (correspondence). Oakville, Ontario: Mosaic, 1980b.

Europe and Other Bad News. Toronto: McClelland and Stewart, 1981.

Shadows on the Ground. Oakville, Ontario: Mosaic, 1982.

A Wild Peculiar Joy: Selected Poems 1945–1982. Toronto: McClelland and Stewart, 1982.

The Gucci Bag. Oakville, Ontario: Mosaic, 1983.

Waiting for the Messiah, a Memoir (autobiography). Toronto: McClelland and Stewart, 1985.

Dance with Desire: Love Poems. Toronto: McClelland and Stewart, 1986.

Final Reckoning: Poems 1982–1986. Oakville, Ontario: Mosaic, 1987.

Fortunate Exile. Toronto: McClelland and Stewart, 1987.

Wild Gooseberries: The Selected Letters of Irving Layton. New York: Macmillan, 1989.

Irving Layton and Robert Creeley: The Complete Correspondence, 1953–1978. Montreal: McGill-Queen's, 1990a.

Nazi Airmen. Vancouver: Colophon, 1990b.

Butterfly on Rock. Vancouver: Colophon, 1991.

Works about Irving Layton

Bennett, Joy. *Irving Layton: A Bibliography, 1935–1977.* Montreal: Concordia, 1979.

Bernstein, Michael André. "Usurpations: A Poetics of Catastrophe and the Language of Jewish History." *TriQuarterly* 79 (1990): 214.

Cameron, Elspeth. *Irving Layton, a Portrait.* Toronto: Stoddart, 1985.

Creeley, Robert. In Mayne, 35.

Dudek, Louis. Rev. of *Red Carpet for the Sun.* In Mayne, 89–92.

Francis, Wynne. *Irving Layton and His Works.* Montreal: ECW Press, 1984.

———. "Layton and Nietzsche." *Canadian Literature* (1967): 39–52.

Frye, Northrop. *Canadian Forum* 31 (1952): 262.

Greenstein, Michael. "Canadian Poetry after Auschwitz." *Canadian Poetry* 20 (1987): 1–16.

Kenner, Hugh. In Mayne, 52–53, 65.

Kertes, Joseph. "Brief Are the Days of Beauty." *Canadian Literature* 105 (Summer 1985): 32–42.

Klein, A. M. Rev. of *Here and Now. Canadian Forum* 24 (1945): 47.

Lemm, Richard. "Polished Lens and Improved Binoculars." Ph.D. thesis, Dalhousie, 1986.

Levenson, Christopher. Rev. of *Collected Poems. Queens Quarterly* 79 (1972): 272.

Lewis, Joanne. "Irving's Women." *Studies in Canadian Literature* 13 (1988): 144.

Mandel, Eli. *Irving Layton.* Toronto: Forum House, 1969.

Mayne, Seymour, ed. *Irving Layton: The Poet and His Critics.* Toronto: McGraw-Hill, 1978.

Namjoshi, Suniti. Rev. of *The Pole-Vaulter. Canadian Forum* (November 1974): 19.

O'Flaherty, Patrick. Rev. of *For My Brother Jesus. Canadian Forum* (October 1976): 30.

O'Rourke, David. "The Lion in Winters: Irving Layton at York." *Canadian Literature* (1987): 52.

Purdy, A. W. Rev. of *Balls for a One-Armed Juggler. Canadian Literature* 16 (1963): 81.

Skelton, Robin. Rev. of *The Laughing Rooster. Canadian Literature* 23 (1965): 63–65.

Wiens, Erwin. "From Apocalypse to Black Mountain." *Canadian Poetry* 16 (1985): 1–20.

DENISE LEVERTOV (1923–1997)

Karla Alwes

BIOGRAPHY

Denise Levertov's father, Paul Peter Levertoff, was a descendant of a Russian rabbi, Schneour Zaimon, renowned as a Hasid, a member of the Jewish mystical movement that began in the eighteenth century. Levertov's mother, Beatrice Adelaide Spooner-Jones, was a descendant of the Welsh tailor and mystic Angel Jones. Although born Jewish, Levertoff became a convert to Christianity as a young man. He nurtured a desire, throughout his life, to unite the two religions and eventually went to England to become an Anglican minister. Levertoff attempted to create unity between Judaism and Christianity by writing a narrative of the life of St. Paul in Hebrew and by translating into English parts of the Jewish mystical work the *Zohar* (Ellmann 1056).

Born at llford, Essex, on October 24, 1923, Denise Levertov enjoyed an erudite childhood provided by her parents; however, she never received a formal education. Both she and her sister Olga received ''sporadic religious training'' from their father, and both were educated by their mother until the age of thirteen. Levertov decided at five years of age to become a poet and wrote juvenilia that showed the beginnings of her poetic style and intensity of grace, making clear how important her early home environment was to her later poetic success. At the age of twenty-five Levertov came to the United States from England to live (*Contemporary* 5).

Levertov was married in 1947 to writer Mitchell Goodman, with whom she had a son, Nikolai Gregor. Levertov and Goodman were divorced in 1972, but during their marriage Levertov, with Goodman, vigorously protested the involvement of the United States in Vietnam and the prolonged war that ensued.

As Levertov's social consciousness began to inform her identity as an individual, her protests against the political status quo frequently took the form of poetry, including many expressions of sympathy with, and empathy for, the victims of war. Her poem "During the Eichmann Trial" was composed at the time as an expression of protest. While her wartime service includes three years working as a civilian nurse at hospitals in the London area from 1943 to 1945, Levertov was also active in the movement against nuclear proliferation and was one of the founders (with poet Muriel Rukeyser) of Writers and Artists Protest against the War in Vietnam in 1965. Levertov was briefly jailed on numerous occasions for civil disobedience during the Vietnam War era, and more recently she spoke out against the continued proliferation of nuclear weapons and U.S. aid to El Salvador. The central piece in the collection *A Door in the Hive* is "El Salvador: Requiem and Invocation," written as a requiem for Archbishop Romero and four American women who were killed by death squads in El Salvador.

Levertov received numerous awards and honors, including the Guggenheim Fellowship (1962); the American Academy and Institute of Arts and Letters grant (1965); the Morton Dauwen Zabel Memorial Prize, from *Poetry* magazine (1965); the D. Litt. from Colby College (1970), University of Cincinnati (1973), Bates College (1984), and Saint Lawrence University (1984); the Lenore Marshall Poetry Prize (1976); the Elmer Holmes Bobst Award (1983); the Shelley Memorial Award from Poetry Society of America (1984); the Robert Frost Medal (1990); National Endowment for the Arts Senior Fellowship (1990); and the Lannan Award (1993).

Levertov wrote and translated a myriad of poems since her first collection, *The Double Image*" (1946). She was a member of the American Academy and Institute of Arts and Letters and a contributor to numerous poetry anthologies and journals, as well as poetry editor for *Nation* (1961–1962) and *Mother Jones* (1976–1978). Further, Levertov made various sound recordings of her poetry in order to keep the voice, as well as the image, alive.

Levertov's career was as an educator as well as a poet, critic, and translator. She taught English in Holland for three months in 1964; was a teacher of poetry craft in the YM-YWCA poetry center in New York City in 1964 and was a visiting lecturer/professor-and-poet-in-residence at several colleges and universities between the years of 1964 and 1981. In 1981 she became professor of English at Stanford University.

Writer and critic Doris Earnshaw comments that Levertov "was fitted by birth and political destiny to voice the terrors and pleasures of the twentieth century. . . . [Her poetry] speaks of the great contemporary themes: Eros, solitude, community, war (*Contemporary* 5). Jean Gould called Levertov "a poet of definite political and social consciousness" (Contemporary 5). She remained, however, strictly independent, and her work manifests the essence of a creativity and intensity born of the humanity and consciousness of both individual and collective concerns. Levertov died on December 20, 1997.

MAJOR WORKS AND THEMES

Levertov's poetic themes range from issues of marriage to the protest of inhumanity and war, with all aspects of life contained within the two poles. Her first collection of poems, *The Double Image*, published just after the war, shows little focus on the war itself and no direct evidence of the immediate events of the time. Instead, the collection is true to the "British neo-romanticism of the 1940s," with its "recurrent sense of loss" and a "germ of personal mythology." Gould asserts the collection revealed at least "one thing for certain: the young poet possessed a strong social consciousness and . . . showed indications of the militant pacifist she was to become" (*Contemporary* 6).

The personal mythology that emanates from the loss that Levertov explores in her poetry finds exquisite expression in poems that later focus on the victimization of war. The disparate identities and places in the soul of "self" and "other" emerge in the poetry that weeps for the victims; "During the Eichmann Trial," for example, finds "a mystery,/a person, an/other, an I" (16–18), which pushes open the horror to find a "pitiful man whom none/pity" (2–3). "Corpse-like" (24) evolves into the "yellow" of the Jewish identification by the Nazis and becomes the "yellow sun" (32) and the "yellow of autumn leaves in/ Wienerwald" (28–29). Myth is created in order to understand, with precision, the horror of the reality of violence. The theme of private obedience, in the face of what should be public protest, is a theme in Levertov's poetry about war: "Pity this man who saw it/ whose obedience continued" ("Eichmann" 63–64). Clear and unflinching, the poetry about war and violence underscores the psychical as well as physical bloodletting: "I see/ a spring of blood gush from the earth—/ Earth cannot swallow/ so much at once" (55–58). We the survivors, the writers of truth when the lies are dead, are "an apparition/telling us something he does not know: we are members/one of another" ("Eichmann" 70–72).

As an epigraph to her collection of poems titled *The Jacob's Ladder*, Levertov reprints a quote of Rabbi Moshe from Martin Buber's *Tales of the Hasidim: Later Masters*. The words focus on the human, expressed as "one of the countless shards of clay," and the transcending angels: "my soul reaches to heaven; 'and behold the angels of God ascending and descending on it'—even the ascent and descent of the angels depend on my deeds." The division of human from angel and the exquisite, transcendent duality that emanates from such division recur in the collection's poems, as the person and the other, the teller and the hearer. (Later in the collection, in "Merritt Parkway," "the people—ourselves!" [11] will be "the humans from inside the/cars, apparent/ only at gasoline stops" [12–14]). The angel, "the yellow star within him," from "During the Trial of Eichmann," that defines our humanity all the more by focusing on our inhumanity, is, in "The Jacob's Ladder," an ascension of human poetry. The angels fly down the ladder, "giving a little/lift of the wings":

and a man climbing
must scrape his knees, and bring
the grip of his hands into play. The cut stone
consoles his groping feet. Wings brush past him.
The poem ascends. (14–20)

Levertov's religious topics are paralleled in passion and determination by her obvious condemnation of violence. Like her poetry, Levertov seems to "ascend" when she focuses on the transcendence of the human, through the pain of violence.

In the poem "Illustrious Ancestors," from *The Jacob's Ladder*, Levertov speaks of "The Rav/of Northern White Russia" (1–2), an obvious reference to the Jewish mystic from whom her father descends, and "Angel Jones of Mold, whose meditations/were sewn into coats and britches" (11–12), the Welsh mystic who was Levertov's mother's own illustrious ancestor. The illustrious ancestors become mythical in the poetry, as "Rav," or rabbi, opens the poem of ancestry, of ascension.

One of Levertov's books of prose, *Tesserae* (1995), takes its name from the individual pieces of glass or stone that form mosaic, a fitting way to identify the various aspects in the individual pieces of prose that make up the book. *Tesserae* is made up of memoirs that focus on Levertov's family, her childhood, and herself. The memories become themes in her poetry. One such instance occurs in the prose piece titled "Cordova," a memoir of Levertov's childhood:

My mother lets me help by giving me a stack of freshly-ironed handkerchiefs to take upstairs to the bedroom chests of drawers where they belong—I . . . I am a messenger with important secret papers to deliver. It is a long, dangerous journey. (16)

Her family's Jewish roots and the cultural anti-Semitism, which would play a role in Levertov's poetry of protest and violence, are discussed in a story about her father and his baptism into Christianity, titled "A Minor Role." A pastor's daughter, whose father had assisted at Mr. Levertoff's baptism, had "an eye" for Levertoff, and, remarks the writer Levertov, "it is possible that she was not sorry his nose had a quite non-semitic shape" (9).

In the piece "What One Remembers," Levertov confides that the childhood memories she speaks of "give me a sense of linkage, however flimsy." One such "link," she continues, is "knowing that Israel Zangwill told my Welsh mother, to her delight, that she had 'a Jewish soul' " (142). As a poet, Levertov's own links to the soul of humanity are created, in large part, by her poignant protest and antiwar poems. It is a protest that grows out of the creation of personal myth to counterbalance the collective horrors.

From "A Lost Poem," the final piece in *Tesserae*, Levertov's mythmaking abilities are made clear. Reminiscent of T. S. Eliot, to whom she turned as a very young poet and with whom she is frequently compared, Levertov talks about a poem she remembers writing but has lost, "Cathedral of Pearls":

What remains with me is not the idea—though that cannot fail to occur—that the poor would be less poor if the cathedral were stripped bare and the pearls sold, but the sense of the murky darkness of the city even in daylight, the darkness of the stone in which the pearls were embedded, the glimmering beauty of the pearls—magical barnacles upon a great vessel risen from the sea—and the deep pleasure that beauty was to those who passed and repassed. (148)

The "deep pleasure," the "ascent," as Levertov calls it in "The Jacob's Ladder," comes from the beauty of the poem's protest against religion's inability to feel and create—in this case, the cathedral becomes a scene from *Revelation*, but transcendence is no more than "murky darkness." Because poetry can ascend, however, protection is afforded the poet and the idea, which becomes the myth incarnate.

"The poet's task," Levertov asserts, "is to hold in trust the knowledge that language . . . is not a set of counters to be manipulated, but a power" (*The Poet in the World* 54). This knowledge lies at the soul of Levertov's poetics: "Writing poetry . . . parallels what, in a person's life, is called individuation: the evolution of consciousness toward wholeness, . . . a touching, a 'being in touch' " (54). Wholeness comes, as her mentor Eliot asserts in his poetry, from the discovery and reassertion of meaning and of love. Levertov's themes are those that restore meaning and re-create love in order to ascend with the angels.

CRITICAL RECEPTION

In a moving discussion of poet Anne Sexton and her death, Levertov asserts that "we who are alive must make clear, as [Sexton] could not, the distinction between creativity and self-destruction" (*Light Up the Cave* 80). It is this distinction, finely honed and preserved by Levertov, that critics recognize and exult. *World Literature Today* reviewer Daisy Aldan calls Levertov's collection *Evening Train*: "an important transition toward what some have called 'the last plateau': that is, the consciousness of entering into the years of aging, which she experiences and expresses with sensitivity and grace" (*Contemporary* 9). It is this world of transition that Levertov mourns for Sexton and creates for others to experience in her poetry.

Although most of the criticism of her poetry is favorable, some critics see the sociopolitical and protest poems as "distaste[ful]," noting that they resemble prose more than poetry (*Contemporary* 7). Other critics, such as Marjorie G. Perloff, call much of Levertov's antiwar poetry "bad confessional verse" (7). Some critics find these poems "preachy" and suffering from "a tendency toward sentimentality" (7). On the other hand, James F. Mersmann, in his study *Out of the Vietnam Vortex: A Study of Poets and Poetry Against the War* praises

Levertov's protest poems and calls her poetry "balanced and whole," suggesting further that her work "reaches to the heart of things, finds out what their centers are" (quoted in *Contemporary* 8).

Levertov herself often ponders poetry as a craft in her prose works. In *The Poet in the World*, for example, she discusses some "habitual preoccupations" in her career as a poet, including the questions, "What is the task of the poet? What is the essential nature of [her] work?" (43–44). The preoccupations lead to the essence of Levertov's poetics and politics: "All the thinking I do about poetry leads me back, always, to Reverence for Life as the ground for poetic activity; because it seems the ground for Attention" (54).

In a discussion of her own task as a poet, in the Preface of *The Poet in the World*, Levertov reiterates the sharp and uncontrived style she is known for when she condemns the scholarly use of documentation and sources: "Are not exhaustive notes of the pedantic kind somewhat a product of that dubious aspect of 20th-century education which makes of literature grist for the graduate-school mill rather than the common nourishment and conversation of a civilized people?" (ix–x). While the poet goes on to explain away her condemnation as "only half sincere" (x), it is a stunning example of the type of unfettered knowledge and sentiment Levertov wishes to convey in her writing.

The "common nourishment" Levertov speaks of is also a product of her poetry that focuses on aspects of religion. Poet Diane Wakoski calls this poetry "American mysticism, . . . the discovery of God in [the poet] herself, and an attempt to understand how that self is a 'natural' part of the world, intermingling with everything pantheistically, ecologically, socially, historically and, for Levertov, always lyrically" (*Contemporary* 9).

Throughout Levertov's poetic career critics and reviewers consistently spoke of the "spirituality" of her poetry, a spirituality that began in her childhood, growing up with two parents who claimed mysticism as ancestral, and remained throughout the poetry of protest in her maturity. Levertov sees into the hearts and minds of the suffering and sees through the eyes of the victims in poems that range from Eichmann to El Salvador. Such poems of human protest have been criticized as "narrow," but critic Gould says of Levertov and of poetry in general: "History does, after all, prefer those who take stands" (*Contemporary* 7–8). Denise Levertov's poetry continues to stand firm.

BIBLIOGRAPHY

Works by Denise Levertov

The Double Image. Philadelphia: Cresset Press, 1946; Waldron Island, WA: Brooding Heron Press, 1991.
Here and Now. San Francisco: City Lights, 1957.
Overland to the Islands. San Francisco: Jargon Press, 1958.
With Eyes at the Back of Our Heads. New York: New Directions Press, 1959.

The Jacob's Ladder. New York: New Directions Press, 1961.
O Taste and See: New Poems. New York: New Directions Press, 1964.
Three Poems. San Francisco: Perishable Press, 1968.
The Cold Spring and Other Poems. New York: New Directions Press, 1969.
Relearning the Alphabet. New York: New Directions Press, 1970.
The Poet in the World. New York: New Directions Press, 1973.
Light Up the Cave. New York: New Directions Press, 1981.
Candles in Babylon. New York: New Directions Press, 1982.
New and Selected Essays. New York: New Directions Press, 1992.
Tesserae: Memories and Suppositions. New York: New Directions Press, 1995; reprinted, 1996.
Sands of the Well. New York: New Directions Press, 1996.
El Salvador: Requiem and Invocation. New York: William B. Ewert, 1984.
A Door in the Hive. New York: New Directions Press, 1989.

Translations

Black Iris by Jean Joubert. Port Townsend, WA: Copper Canyon Press, 1988.
Selected Poems by Eugene Guillevic. New York: New Directions Press, 1969.

Translated and Edited Work

With Edward C. Dimock, Jr. *In Praise of Krishna: Songs from the Bengali*. New York: Doubleday, 1967.

Works about Denise Levertov

Contemporary Authors: New Revision Series. CD-Rom. Detroit: Gale Research, 1996: 5–9.
Ellmann, Richard, and Robert O'Clair. *The Norton Anthology of Modern Poetry*. New York: Norton, 1973.

PHILIP LEVINE   (1928–   )

Steven Schreiner

BIOGRAPHY

Philip Levine was born January 10, 1928, in Detroit, Michigan, the first of identical twins, to Russian-born parents Harry Levine and Esther Priscol. Harry Levine ran an auto parts business until his death in 1933. Although the family had been comfortably middle-class, after the death of the poet's father they moved socially downward, eventually settling in a small brick home on the outskirts of the city. The poet's mother worked as a stenographer and later as an office manager. In the wooded edges of his neighborhood, Philip Levine as a young boy spoke his first poems to the moon, trees, and stars.

In spite of the Whitmanian oneness he felt with the natural world, the poet recalls growing up in a "viciously anti-Semitic community in a particularly anti-Semitic era" (*The Bread of Time* 39). He notes that, from a nearby suburb, "the rantings of Father Coughlin were broadcast every Sunday . . . and urged [the] expulsion" (39) of Jews from Europe. He saw the invasions and annexations of World War II as "revenge against the Jews" (39) and perhaps as a result came to the conclusion that "there was no God or any chosen people" (81).

In fact, the poet's inclination was to feel a solidarity toward oppressed people everywhere, and he describes an "epic event in his young life" (44) as occurring when the Spanish civil war broke out. He was quick to recognize in the working people of Detroit the same spirit of the anarchists fighting in Europe against the forces of fascism and injustice, and he formed his political persuasion, his love of working people, and his hatred of prejudice during this time. He began composing poems when, at the age of thirteen, he felt himself becoming "one man in a sea of men and women . . . who came together to form a brotherhood and sisterhood of all those beings with souls'' (44).

Before, during, and after attending high school and college in Detroit, Levine worked at various blue-collar jobs, including a soap factory and Chevy Gear & Axle. He enlisted in the armed services, but the war ended before his induction.

Philip Levine attended Wayne State University (then Wayne University: B.A., 1950; M.A., 1954) and later the University of Iowa Writers Workshop (M.F.A., 1957), where he studied with John Berryman, a singularly important influence on the poet. In 1954, he began publishing his poems in *Poetry, Beloit Poetry Journal*, and other magazines. After attending Stanford University on a fellowship, he accepted a teaching position at the University of California, Fresno, in 1958, which he held until retirement in 1992. In the 1960s, he lived and studied in Spain during sabbaticals, working on translations of Spanish poets and commemorating in his own poems martyrs of the Spanish civil war.

As a visiting writer, Levine has taught at Tufts University, New York University, Princeton, and Columbia, as well as at the National University of Australia at Canberra. He has been married twice; with his second wife, Frances Artley, whom he married in 1954, he has three sons and lives in Fresno.

Levine's first book, *On the Edge*, was published in 1963, with *Not This Pig* (1968) marking his first success with a university press. In 1972, he published *They Feed They Lion*, one of his most important books, and since that time he has published twelve more books of poetry, as well as books of essays, interviews, and translations. His poetry has been awarded the American Book Award (*Ashes*), National Book Critics Circle Award (*Ashes* and *Seven Years from Somewhere*), The National Book Award (*What Work Is*), and the Pulitzer Prize (*The Simple Truth*). He has won the National Endowment for the Arts Fellowship three times and the Guggenheim Fellowship.

MAJOR WORKS AND THEMES

Philip Levine's work can be broken down into three major periods. During the early period, he explored the political disfranchisement of his subjects; in the middle period, he sang elegiacally about lost relatives and the defeated Spanish civil war heroes; in his latest period, he has moved toward metaphysical examination of mortality (Buckley v–vi). Yet through fifteen books of poetry, Levine has kept faith with his commitment to speak for those individuals, usually workers, who would otherwise remain silent.

Known widely as a poet of Detroit, Levine's favored themes become most visible in the poetry he wrote for his second book, *Not This Pig*, in which he began to praise the unacknowledged worker. He honors ''a black man whose / name I have forgotten who danced/all night at Chevy/Gear & Axle'' (''Silent in America'' 48) as well the figure who ''fights back'' (''Baby Villon''). The determined pig of the title poem utters an emblematic cry of resistance that shapes the poet's work: though on its way to market, the pig will not go gladly nor "turn like a beast" on the boy who drives him along. The final line is a triumphant, of sorts, motto: "No. Not this pig" (48).

In the title poem of one of his most important books, Levine confronts himself as the outsider coming home to Detroit after the riots or "Great Rebellion" of 1965. "They Feed They Lion," written in the anaphoric style of the Bible and of Whitman and inspired by Lorca's poetry, combines prophetic imagery with the powerful colloquial idiom of American speech to create Levine's most strident tones yet. The shock of returning to Detroit, seeing neighborhoods near his and businesses like the one his brother now ran burned, stressed upon Levine the power of a righteous cause.

Although Levine is characterized as global, scattered throughout his poetry are references to his workplace encounters with anti-Semitism. He has known the coarse, bigoted driver who says he only sleeps with Jews, then includes the poet's sister ("Making Soda Pop" in *One for the Rose*) and the tired figure on the assembly line who drank and cursed those in his hearing with racial and religious epithets ("Sweet Will" in *Sweet Will*). Nevertheless, the incidents form part of a larger drama, in which the poet reveals a solidarity among individuals facing the struggles of daily toil.

"What Work Is," the title poem of a recent volume, addresses both the solidarity among workers and the need to redeem the cost of work with love. Though "we stand in the rain in a long line" to learn that the factory is not hiring, the dehumanizing aspects of work form the backdrop to the poet's desire to affirm the abundance within those who know work and its indignities intimately. Having failed to offer his love to his brother, whom he imagines standing ahead of him in line, the poet recriminates himself for not knowing what work is.

In his eloquent poems about the loss of his father, relatives, and the heroes of the Spanish civil war, which comprise two books of his middle period, *1933* and *The Names of the Lost*, Levine fulfills his pledge "never to forget" ("Gift for a Believer"). It is important to honor the lost, in part, because the poet has noted, "I don't hear the music of a farther life beyond ("Jewish Graveyards, Italy").

In his three most recent books, *A Walk with Tom Jefferson, What Work Is*, and *The Simple Truth*, the poet again focuses on the fact that we must endure despite hardship. "Tom Jefferson," who has survived dehumanizing labor and unemployment as a black man in America, speaks for the poet's first love, a garden that renews hope with each planting. The poet notes that Tom Jefferson is a believer, because "you can't plant winter vegetables if you aren't." But the poet finally questions and speculates rather than affirms, as Tom does, what it means to describe suffering and survival as "biblical." At the last, Levine recognizes that the simple truth is that which we cannot express in words.

CRITICAL RECEPTION

Philip Levine is one of the most acclaimed contemporary American poets, whose work has long been identified by "an incapacity for indifference" and its commitment "to the failed and lost, the marginal, the unloved, the unwanted" (Hirsch 35). He is recognized as a Whitmanian poet, a voice both rhetorical and believable, and his work has been likened to that of William Carlos Williams, which celebrates in colloquial language the American common man in the city.

His status as an American poet of the first order was established by *They Feed They Lion*, and other books singled out for acclaim include *1933, A Walk with Tom Jefferson*, and *The Simple Truth*. His earliest work has been praised for its skillful use of metrical and syllabic verse. Levine's middle and later poetry is identified by long, flowing narrative poems written in short, free verse lines. In moving from the earlier, elegiac mode to a reliance on the later narrative style, Levine has drawn criticism along with ample praise. For some critics, his realism suggested prose (Vendler), and his use of surrealistic imagery in his earlier work could be exotic or strained (Zweig). Levine's work has continually developed and varied, and, in particular, his tone has progressed from anger to compassion (Buckley, "Preface" viii).

Levine's first *Selected Poems* illustrates well the poet's "acquired, somewhat defensive cover of hurt and bitter realism" (Parisi) through which readers came to recognize the poet's sensitivity to people trapped in their lives (Mills). For all of its attention to the working-class individual, Levine's poetry successfully resists caricature. Yet in relentlessly addressing the cause of oppressed people, the poet has been faulted for a tone sometimes "maudlin" and not sufficiently modulated (Pinsky). Nevertheless, the "fire" in Levine's work, of "individual spirit taking hold of the world despite hardship or even privilege" (Buckley, "Extension" 230), makes the work enduring.

A Walk with Tom Jefferson again pays unflinching attention to the common person; Tom Jefferson may be "Levine's most heroic individual to date" (Pettingel 247). In *What Work Is* Levine confronts the conditions of American labor with powerful clarity, and the collection may be "one of the most important books of poetry of our time" (Baker 173). *The Simple Truth*, which won the Pulitizer Prize for 1995, is more subdued than his previous work. The poems are often meditations on mortality and the meaning of our lives. This most recent book finds the poet looking back wistfully in deeply felt poems that continue to move us. Still seeking to reveal the dignity in lives that often pass unacknowledged, Philip Levine fulfills the role of a major American poet.

BIBLIOGRAPHY

Works by Philip Levine

Poetry

On the Edge. Iowa City, IA: Stone Wall Press, 1963.
Not This Pig. Middletown, CT: Wesleyan University Press, 1968.
Pili's Wall. Greensboro, NC: Unicorn Press, 1971a.
Red Dust. Santa Cruz, CA: Kayak, 1971b.
They Feed They Lion. New York: Atheneum, 1972.
1933. New York: Atheneum, 1974.
The Names of the Lost. New York: Atheneum, 1976.
Ashes: Poems New and Old. New York: Atheneum, 1979a.
Seven Years from Somewhere. New York: Atheneum, 1979b.
One for the Rose. New York: Atheneum, 1981.
Selected Poems. New York: Atheneum, 1984.
Sweet Will. New York: Atheneum, 1985.
A Walk with Tom Jefferson. New York: Knopf, 1988.
New Selected Poems. New York: Knopf, 1991a.
What Work Is. New York: Knopf, 1991b.
The Simple Truth: Poems. New York: Knopf, 1994.

Edited Works

Translator with Ernesto Trejo. *Tarumba: The Selected Poems of Jaime Sabines,* by Jaime
    Sabines. San Francisco: Twin Peaks Press, 1979.
Translator with Ada Long. *Off the Map: Selected Poems,* by Gloria Fuertes. Middletown,
    CT: Wesleyan University Press, 1984.
The Essential Keats. New York: Ecco Press, 1987.

Other

Don't Ask (interviews). Ann Arbor: University of Michigan Press, 1979.
The Bread of Time: Toward an Autobiography (essays). New York: Knopf, 1994.

Recording

The Poetry and Voice of Philip Levine. Caedmon, 1976.

Works about Philip Levine

Baker, David. "Against Mastery." *Kenyon Review* (Summer 1992): 166–73.
Buckley, Christopher. *On the Poetry of Philip Levine: Stranger to Nothing.* Ann Arbor:
    University of Michigan Press, 1991.
———. "The Extension of Method and Vision in Philip Levine's *Sweet Will.*" In Buck-
    ley, 228–43.
Contemporary Authors: New Revision Series. Vol. 52. Detroit: Gale Research, 1996.
Contemporary Literary Criticism. Vol. 2 (1974); vol. 5 (1976); vol. 9 (1978); vol. 14
    (1980); vol. 33 (1984). Detroit: Gale Research.

Dictionary of Literary Biography. Vol. 5: *American Poets since World War II.* Detroit:
    Gale Research, 1980.
Hirsch, Edward. ''Naming the Lost: The Poetry of Philip Levine.'' In Buckley, 344–52.
Mills, Ralph J., Jr. *Cry of the Human.* Champaign: University of Illinois Press, 1975.
Molesworth, Charles. *The Fierce Embrace: A Study of Contemporary American Poetry.*
    Columbia: University of Missouri Press, 1979.
Parisi, Joseph. ''Selected Poems.'' In Buckley, 194.
Pettingell, Phoebe. ''Voices for the Voiceless.'' In Buckley, 189–93.
Pinsky, Robert. ''The Names of the Lost.'' In Buckley, 107–9.
Vendler, Helen. ''From 'All Too Real.' '' In Buckley, 172–75.
Zweig, Paul. ''From 'I + I + I + I + I.' '' In Buckley, 27–30.

LYN LIFSHIN

(1944–)

Hugh Fox and Joel Shatzky

BIOGRAPHY

Lyn Lifshin was born on July 12, 1944, in Burlington, Vermont, to Ben and Frieda Lazarus Lipman. Her mother was American-born, and her father came from Vilnius, Russia. Lifshin grew up in a small town where there were few Jews. She heard her grandparents say: "When you are Jewish in a small town, you have to be especially careful." Excluded from the social life of the Catholic and Protestant children in her neighborhood, she read so voraciously that she skipped several grades and actually graduated from Syracuse University with a B.A. in 1960 at the age of sixteen. She received her M.A. from the University of Vermont in 1963.

While at Syracuse, where she majored in English, she tried to learn Yiddish phrases from her roommate. Her M.A. thesis was on Dylan Thomas, but while attending Brandeis University, she began writing after auditing a class of Allen Grossman's. Lifshin married Eric Lifshin in 1963 and tried to finish her Ph.D. at SUNY, Albany, on the poetry of Thomas Wyatt but left before finishing her last qualifying exam.

From the 1960s on, Lifshin has been a remarkably prolific poet with over sixty volumes of poetry to her credit, as many as five being published in a single year. She has been poet-in-residence at Mansfield State University, Rochester University, SUNY, Albany, Union College, and many writing workshops as well as having read at over 500 universities, libraries, and writing centers. She also edited three major anthologies of women's literature: *Tangled Vines* (1978), *Ariadne's Thread* (1982), and *Lips Unsealed* (1990). Her poetry dealing with her Jewish background has been published in several volumes, and her poetry has been found in such Jewish journals as *Lillith, Davka, Jewish Currents, Israel Horizon, Tikkun*, and *Agada*.

MAJOR WORKS AND THEMES

When Lifshin exploded on the literary scene in the 1960s, she was first known—despite her earliest political and socially relevant poems—as a love poet. From the start of her career, however, she moved between very personal poems and family poems, including some of her recent work involving the relationships between mothers and daughters, as well as poems that have a very clear persona, such as Marilyn Monroe, or ethnic identity, like Native Americans and women in early Plymouth. In *Blue Tattoo* (1995), perhaps her most important work to readers of this volume, Lifshin wrote about the various stages of anti-Jewish sentiment in Europe during the 1930s that led to the Holocaust.

Blue Tattoo is written in a format similar to war news fragments, with typeface from the period, and is often a first-person narration. Lifshin, in discussing her own experience as a child growing up after the Holocaust, reveals that she had been told by a baby-sitter when she was six about the tortures that Jewish children endured during World War II and, as a result, ended up having nightmares for more than a year. She was also very much affected by the film *Night and Fog* when she saw it in the 1960s.

Lifshin's workshops on mother–daughter relationships and feelings about women's sexuality led to her doing workshops about the Holocaust. Much of the impetus for this came from people whose parents had survived the Holocaust and wanted to keep the memory of those experiences alive through the written word. In teaching these workshops, Lifshin became immersed in the literature and history of the Holocaust. When first contacted by the publishers of *Blue Tattoo*, Lifshin sent the editors over 1,000 poems. They came from dreams, interviews, readings, telephone calls, films, and many other sources. Since its publication, she has been told that some of her work comes from accounts she read in other works about the Holocaust and films such as *Shoa*.

Lifshin concludes, in this promotional note to *Blue Tattoo*:

[T]he voices in *Blue Tattoo* are based on the voices of those who had been involved in the Holocaust. I know some people believe that one who has not participated directly in the Holocaust should not write about it. Others feel that poetry and fiction should come from these experiences. But I feel that keeping the memory alive, relating the experiences and the suffering, and drawing upon the real words of real people who knew the Holocaust first hand, is a legitimate way to remember and honor those who were its victims.

This collection of poetry is assembled in the spirit of countless survivors who intoned, "Lest they forget," as they painfully told of their experiences. As a member of the surviving Jewish culture, though not literally a Holocaust survivor, for me their anthem translates "Lest *we* forget." I will continue to do workshops to assure that we do not.

A typical Lifshin poem is a small work, consisting of a few words per line and rarely more than thirty lines in length. In common with haiku and other short poetic forms, Lifshin's lean and concise poems are especially suited for re-creating a single moment or emotion or describing a particular place. Her best work, many critics believe, is found in her poems about historical subjects. Some of these pieces are collected in *Shaker House Poems* (1976), in which Lifshin writes about the women of the Shaker religious communities in early America; she visited many of the original historical settlements before writing her book.

Lifshin's feminist concerns are also evident in her popular ''Madonna'' poems, each of which describes a modern female archetype in a terse, often humorous manner, including ''Minestrone Madonna,'' ''Channuka Madonna'' ''Blood Red Nail Polish Madonna,'' ''Non Returnable Bottle Madonna,'' and ''Madonna Who Shifts for Herself.''

Lifshin's first book of poems, *Why Is the House Dissolving?* (1968), is an ''angry'' book. This anger, the author believes, came from Lifshin's failure to pass her oral examination for a doctorate. As a result, she rejected the formal, academic writing in favor of a personal poetry. Her poetry has a great deal of spontaneity, her rejection of ''academic watch-making'' for an expression of a ''primal interior howl.'' Although she has written extensively of many cultures, including Eskimo, Shaker, and Native American, *Blue Tattoo* is of greatest interest to readers of this volume. Several poems illustrate her approach:

> The huge dome
> of stained glass—
> cherry, lime, guava
> and raspberry—
> shatters,
> a snow of glass ankle deep
> in jagged pieces.
> Then they throw
> the Torah in the air,
> saying,
> *Wipe your asses with it!* (''Torah'' 5)

> Thousands
> stand in front of stores
> to get rations
> after seven days of hunger.
> People greet one another,
> wish each other well
> for the New Year
> like after an earthquake
> or shipwreck.
> Did you get through?
> Who was taken?

My brother. My mother.
My parents. My children. ("The Greeting" 24)

In the blunt power and the cumulative effect of these poems Lifshin demonstrates her technique of allowing the facts of the language to have their greatest
force. Considering the powerful nature of these descriptive works with titles like
"For Years Her Parents Never Said a Word about It" or, simply, "Freight" or
"There Were Screams through Double Doors," Lifshin's artistry is clearly seen
in what she chooses and what she leaves out. Like the novelist Aharon Appel-
feld, what she leaves out is as telling as what she includes.

Besides poetry, Lifshin has also shown a marked interest in journal and diary
writing and teaches classes and workshops on the subjects. She keeps a diary
herself and has drawn upon its entries for some of her poems. *Ariadne's Thread:
A Collection of Contemporary Women's Journals* presents a wide spectrum of
women's emotions and ideas on such subjects as relationships, work, families,
death, and birth.

CRITICAL RECEPTION

One of the most prolific poets in the United States, Lyn Lifshin has published
in virtually every poetry and literary magazine. A critic for the *San Francisco
Review of Books* calls Lifshin, "one of the most distinctive, prolific, and widely
published poets of all time . . . and very popular with readers" (quoted in CA,
262). Kenneth Funsten of the *Los Angeles Times Book Review* explains that
Lifshin "writes poems both spontaneous and sure of their mark" (CA, 262). A
critic for the *North American Review*, referring to the speed with which a Lifshin
poem can be read, calls her "Queen of the quickies"(*CA*, 262).

In a review of *Shaker House Poems*, the critic in *Choice* remarks that Lifshin
"very successfully captures the spirit, the mood, the mystique of the Shakers,
through magnificently crafted poems, terse as needlework" (*CA* 262). Her collection *Leaning South* (1977) contains poems about sites in New England and
about the early Eskimo culture of the Arctic. Peter Schjeldahl, reviewing the
book for the *New York Times Book Review*, finds the Eskimo poems to be
especially well done. These poems, Schjeldahl, writes, evoke "in fantasy, but
with a lot of anthropological detail, the world of the ancient Eskimos. Here
[Lifsin's] clipped line takes on a chantlike undertone, as of native voices themselves singing from the beyond, that is very pleasing" (*CA* 262).

In recent years Lifshin has emerged as one of the most recognized woman
poets in the country. She has given over 500 poetry readings and participated
in mixed media theatre performances as well. In 1988, Karista Films released a
documentary of Lifshin, *Not Made of Glass*, which shows her typical working
day, a visit she made to the Yaddo writing colony, and a reading she gave at a
local coffeehouse. Lifshin also appears on the "First American Poetry Disc," a
laser disc recording of readings given by the University of Texas at Austin and

by Temple University. Janice Eidus notes in the *Small Press Review* that Lifshin "continues to explore her poetic obsessions with her unique poetic voice and her unique sensibility" (*CA* 262).

BIBLIOGRAPHY

Works by Lyn Lifshin

Poetry Collections

Why Is the House Dissolving? San Francisco: Open Skull Press, 1968.

Femina 2. Madison, WI: Abraxas Press, 1970a.

Leaves and Night Things. West Lafayette, IN: Baby John Press, 1970b.

Black Apples. Dogpatch, AR: New Books, 1971a; rev. ed., Trumansburg, NY: Crossing Press, 1973.

Lady Lyn. Milwaukee, WI: Morgan Press, 1971b.

Forty Days. Apple Nights. Milwaukee, WI: Morgan Press, 1972a.

I'd Be Jeanne Moreau. Milwaukee, WI: Morgan Press, 1972b.

Love Poems. Durham, NH: Zahir Press, 1972c.

The Mercurochrome Sun. Tacoma, WA: Charas Press, 1972d.

Moving by Touch. Traverse City, MI: Cotyledon Press, 1972e.

Tentacles, Leaves. Bellmont, MA: Hellric, 1972f.

All the Women Poets I Ever Liked Didn't Hate Their Fathers. Gulfport, FL: Konglomerati Press, 1973a.

The First Week Poems. Durham, NH: Zahir Press, 1973b.

Museum. Albany, NY: Conspiracy Press, 1973c.

The Old House on the Croton. San Lorenzo, CA: Shameless Hussy Press, 1973d.

Blue Fingers. Bolinas, CA: Shelter Press, 1974a.

Mountain Moving Day. Trumansburg, NY: Crossing Press, 1974b.

Plymouth Women. Milwaukee, WI: Morgan Press, 1974c.

Poems. Gulfport, FL: Konglomerati Press, 1974d.

Selected Poems. Trumansburg, NY: Crossing Press, 1974e.

Thru Blue Post. New Mexico. Fredonia, NY: Basilisk Press, 1974f.

Walking thru Audley End Mansion Late Afternoon and Drifting into Certain Faces. Long Beach, CA: Mag Press, 1974g.

Green Bandages. Geneseo, NY: Hidden Springs, 1975a.

Old House Poems. Santa Barbara, CA: Capra Press, 1975b.

Paper Apples. Stockton, CA: Wormwood Review Press, 1975c.

Upstate Madonna: Poems. 1970–1974. Trumansburg, NY: Crossing Press, 1975d.

Naked Charm. Evergreen, CO: Fireweed Press, 1976a.

North Poems. Milwaukee, WI: Morgan Press, 1976b.

Shaker House Poems. Chatham, NY: Sugarin Press, 1976c.

Some Madonna Poems. Buffalo, NY: White Pine Press, 1976d.

Crazy Arms. Chicago: Ommation Press, 1977a.

The January Poems. Cincinnati, OH: Waters Journal of the Arts, 1977b.

Leaning South. New York: Red Dust, 1977c.

Mad Girl Poems. Wichita, KS: Out of Sight Press, 1977d.

Pantagonia. Bend, OR: Wormwood Review Press, 1977f.

Blue Dust, New Mexico. Fredonia, NY: Basilisk Press, 1978a.

Early Plymouth Women. Milwaukee, WI: Morgan Press, 1978b.

Glass. Milwaukee, WI: Morgan Press, 1978c.

35 Sundays. Chicago: Ommation Press, 1979b.

Lips on the Blue Rail. San Francisco: Lion's Breath, 1980.

Colors of Cooper Black. Milwaukee, WI: Morgan Press, 1981a.

Doctors and Doctors of English. Santa Barbara, CA: Mudhorn Press, 1981b.

In the Dark with Just One Star. Milwaukee WI: Morgan Press, 1981c.

Finger Prints. Stockton, CA: Wormwood Review Press, 1982a.

Hotel Lifshin. Eureka, CA: Poetry Now, 1982b.

Leaving the Bow. New York: New World Press, 1982c.

Lobster and Oat Meal. Boston: Pinchpenny, 1982d.

Mad Girl. Peninsula, OH: Blue Horse, 1982e.

Reading Lips. Milwaukee, WI: Morgan Press, 1982f.

Wants Ads. Milwaukee, WI: Morgan Press, 1982.

Madonna Who Shifts for Herself. Long Beach, CA: Appelzaba, 1983.

The Radio Psychic Is Shaving Her Legs. Detroit: Planet Detroit, 1984.

Kiss the Skin Off. Silver Spring, MD: Cherry Valley Editions, 1985b.

Remember the Ladies. East Lansing, MI: Ghost Dance Press, 1985c.

Camping Madonna at Indian Lake. Portlandville, NY: MAF, 1986a.

With others. *Eye of the Beast.* El Paso, TX: Vergin Press, 1986b.

Madonna (bound with Vergin Mary by Belinda Subraman). El Paso, TX: Vergin Press,
    1986c.

The Daughter May Be Let Go. Clock Harbor Beach, FL: Radio Press, 1987a.

Red Hair and the Jesuit. Park Dale, OR: Trout Creek Press, 1987b.

Dance Poems. Chicago: Ommation Press, 1988a.

Many Madonnas. St. John, KS: Kindred Spirit Press, 1988b.

The Doctor Poems. Long Beach, CA: Applezaba, 1989a.

Not Made of Glass: Poems. 1968–1988. Ed. Mary Ann Lynch. Introduction by Laura
    Chester. Greenfield Center, NY: Combinations Press, 1989b.

Reading Lips. Milwaukee, WI: Morgan Press, 1989c.

With Belinda Subraman. *Skin Divers.* Leeds, England: Krax, 1989d.

Under Velvet Pillows. Ashvelot Village, NH: Four Zoas Press, 1989e.

With Belinda Subraman. *The Innocents.* San Jose, CA: Buzzard Roost Press, 1991.

Appleblossoms. East Lansing, MI: Ghost Dance Press, 1993.

Marilyn Monroe. Portland, OR: Quiet Lion Press, 1994a.

Parade. Stockton, CA: Wormwood, 1994b.

Blue Tattoo. Desert Hot Springs, CA: Event Horizon, 1995a.

Color and Light. Chester Spring, PA: Lilliput Press, 1995b.

Mad Girl Drives in a Daze. Arcandia, FL: JVC, 1995c.

Mad Girl Poems. Milwaukee, WI: Morgan Press, 1995d.

Editor

Tangled Vines: A Collection of Mother Daughter Poems. Boston: Beacon Press, 1978;
    new ed. San Diego and New York: Harcourt, 1992.

Ariadne's Thread: A Collection of Contemporary Women's Journals. New York: Harper,
    1982.

Lips Unsealed. Santa Barbara, CA: Capra, 1990.

Works about Lyn Lifshin

Contemporary Authors [*ca*], Newly Revised Series, 50. Detroit: Gale Research, 1996.
Contemporary Authors Autobiography Series. Vol. 10. Detroit: Gale Research, 1993.
Eidus, Janice. *Small Press Review* (May 1990).
Fox, Hugh. *Lifshin: A Critical Study.* Troy, Whitiston Press, 1985.
Los Angeles Times Book Review. September 23, 1984.
North American Review. March 1985.
Rev. of *Shaker House Poems. Choice* (March 1977).
San Francisco Review of Books. (Fall 1985).
Schjeldahl, Peter. Rev. of *Leaning South. New York Times Book Review.* December 17, 1978.

ALLEN MANDELBAUM   (1926–   )

Henry Weinfield

BIOGRAPHY

Poet, translator, essayist, scholar, and educator, Allen Mandelbaum is the quintessential man of letters, a writer of enormous range and linguistic gusto whose sensibility is at once indelibly Jewish and yet tinctured with the many worlds he has embraced and translated into a vision of his own. The son and grandson of orthodox rabbis (his grandfather's house in Jerusalem was the site of what later became known as the Mandelbaum Gate), Mandelbaum was born in Albany, New York, in 1926. His father had emigrated to the United States in 1917 and, though previously ordained, was one of the first English-language-speaking graduates of Yeshiva University (he was also, as the poet describes him, one of the first *unbearded* orthodox rabbis in the country). The family lived in Albany, Louisville, and Chicago before settling in New York City when Allen was thirteen.

Mandelbaum himself studied at Yeshiva, graduating from high school at fourteen and taking the B.A. in 1945 at the age of 18. He then moved on to Columbia University, where he received an M.A. in 1946. He taught at Cornell from 1946 to 1947, at Yeshiva (both English and Hebrew literature) from 1947 to 1949, and at Hunter College from 1949 to 1950. In 1947 he married Marjorie Bogat, and a son, Jonathan, was born in 1953. Between 1950 and 1951, he was a Rockefeller Fellow in Humanities. He received the Ph.D. in English in 1951 from Columbia, with a dissertation entitled "Stasis and Dynamis: Two Modes of the Literary Imagination (Crashaw, Hopkins, Joyce and T. S. Eliot)," and subsequently spent three years (1951–1954) as a member of the Society of Fellows at Harvard.

The years from 1954 to 1964 were passed mainly in Italy, first in Florence and then in Rome, where Mandelbaum was the director for a time of the printing firm Tipografica. For a poet of such linguistic exuberance as Mandelbaum was then in the process of becoming, this concrete involvement with the craft of printing—in other words, with the *letter*—was by no means an extraneous experience, and throughout his entire career Mandelbaum has been intimately involved with the design and typesetting of his books, often collaborating with such well-known artists as Barry Moser and Marialuisa de Romans. During this Italian sojourn Mandelbaum completed the first in the remarkable series of translations for which he is best known and that have made him one of the most eminent translators of our century: his versions of the twentieth-century Italian poets Giuseppe Ungaretti and Salvatore Quasimodo, which were published in 1958 and 1960, respectively. Many of the poems included in his first collection, *Journeyman* (1967), were also completed during this period.

When Mandelbaum returned to the United States in 1964, he taught at Sarah Lawrence College for a time and was invited to be part of the nucleus of the English Department of the newly formed Graduate Center of the City University of New York. He later served as the chairman of the Graduate Center, English Department, and both in this capacity and in his wide-ranging courses on literary history and literary theory he exerted a profound influence on the doctoral students who came within his orbit. In the late 1970s and early 1980s, he served as the poetry editor of the Jewish Publication Society (with Yehuda Amichai). In recent years, Mandelbaum has taught at Wake Forest University as the William R. Kenan Professor of Humanities. He continues to spend part of every year in Italy and is currently Professor in Poetics *per chiara fama* at the University of Turin. He has received honorary doctor of letters degrees from Purdue University, the University of Turin, and the University of Cassino. He has also been the recipient of the Italian Mondello, Leonardo, Biella, and Lerici Prizes and was a finalist for the Pulitzer Prize in poetry in 1994 for his translation of the *Metamorphoses*.

MAJOR WORKS AND THEMES

Mandelbaum's translation of Virgil's *Aeneid* was published in 1972 and won the National Book Award in 1973. In his Introduction to that work, reflecting on Ungaretti's volume *La Terra Promessa*, which he had already translated, Mandelbaum described how, for Ungaretti, "the promised land of Virgil fuses with the promised land of the Bible and with the terminus of all desire" (vii, Bantam edition). Perhaps in this deceptively simple statement we can find a key to Mandelbaum's accomplishment as a literary intellectual; for what is most striking—and even exemplary—about Mandelbaum's work is the way in which a distinctly Jewish ethos or sensibility has striven to assimilate all that is worth preserving in the non-Jewish world. This is an act of "translation" that is profoundly original, whether manifested in this author's actual translations or in his "original" poetry and essays. Perhaps also we can see from that statement why

Mandelbaum would have begun his series of epic descents with the "pious Aeneas" before moving on to the more parochial Dante and finally to Homer's "wily Odysseus," who, though closer in time to the world of Abraham and Moses, may be all the more remote from them (and us) because of that temporal propinquity. In any event, in the triad that stretches from Homer through Virgil to Dante—a triad that Mandelbaum is alone in encompassing as a translator—Virgil was again assigned the role of mediator—not solely, this time, in his capacity of connecting pagan Greece with medieval Christianity, as had been the case for Dante, but, more complexly for the modern Jewish poet-translator, in his capacity of connecting each with the spirit of ancient Judaism and with post-Enlightenment modernity as well as with the other.

Mandelbaum's translation of the *Aeneid* led him forward and backward in time: forward to the three canticles of Dante's *Commedia* and then backward to Homer's *Odyssey*. But at the same time as he was charting this itinerary, Mandelbaum was also mining his own poetry; and it is particularly interesting that during the arduous early years of his work on Dante—the period of the mid-1970s—Mandelbaum was developing a book-length poetic sequence that centered on a conception of the diaspora that was at once historically grounded and at the same time woven around the multiple strands of "text and talk" unloosed from the corners of Jewish lore and the poet's own imagination. This was the remarkable *Chelmaxioms: The Maxims, Axioms, Maxioms of Chelm* (1978). Mandelbaum's Chelm is not the Chelm of *Yiddishkeit*, but, as his spokesman, the Hoarse Savant, tells us in the Preface to the work, "the *echt* Chelm, the meandering Chelm . . . of talk of talk and talk of text, which mime the riverlike careers of the Oral Law and the Written Law but carry a cargo of alegalities—the divagations, digressions, the discreet and indiscreet parentheses native to talmudic/midrashic exegesis" (xvi). Comic and serious by turns, the sequence gives ample scope to Mandelbaum's linguistic garrulousness; yet it is perhaps most moving when it allows itself to be turned aside and chastened from its "talk of talk and talk of text"—as in this extraordinary passage from its "Fifth Finding":

> Do not defend the ways of men
> to God and not the ways of God
> to men for each of them has turned
> aside and each has found it hard
> to listen when the other was
> the one who was in question and
> for each the one atonement is:
>   begin again.
>
> A son of Chelm had written these
> wallwords on entering an oven
> and whispered them again when he
> had let me dream of him within

my room above the Isar when
the waters crossing Munich seemed
to murmur, asking if one can
begin again and answering
within a voice they took from him:
    Begin, begin. (87)

These lines, antithetical as they are to the most prevalent stance in post-Holocaust Jewish poetry—one characterized by despair, by the sense that one cannot begin again, and even that "lyric poetry after Auschwitz is barbaric" (Adorno)—nevertheless indicate that Mandelbaum's is a crucial voice in the dialogue.

"The men of Chelm do not despair; / They lift their lances in the air / and leave them there" (15). Partly, this is because of their obsession with the Perfect Woman. Indeed, perhaps the most fully realized poem in *Chelmaxioms* occurs when "The Perfect Woman Reads a Page of Kant" lifts itself out of the narrative. Here is the first stanza of that magisterial poem:

The perfect woman reads a page of Kant.
She thinks upon the mauve invariants
of later August and the pregnant branch
of slender gestruemia, on the *Selbst-
erkenntniss* of this island in the lake,
upon the arbor and the silent wakes
of silent boats, of all that need not take
hellways to find their godliness but glide
or rest or hover on the silent waters
and do not shudder at the fate of fire. (97)

"Regret, the final flower found by Kant" (97), with which "The Perfect Poem" concludes, marks Mandelbaum as a lyric son of Mallarmé, one who, like Wallace Stevens, has "studied the nostalgias." Yet we should remind ourselves that when he wrote these charming lines, lines that "need not take / hellways to find their godliness," Mandelbaum was already approaching Dante's *Inferno*, "prepared to undergo the battle, / both of the journeying and of the pity" (II.4–6). Mandelbaum's translation of the *Inferno* was published in 1980, and it was followed, at two-year intervals, by the *Purgatorio* and the *Paradiso*. The final result is a version of the *Commedia* that is at once deeply responsive to the groundswell of Dante's poetry and at the same time more clear, more alert to the philosophic, thematic, and linguistic nuances of Dante's thought than any other verse-translation in English.

That Mandelbaum should have begun his Introduction to the *Inferno* by referring to Dante as "an exiled, aggressive, self-righteous, salvation-bent intellectual . . . at once our brother and our engenderer" (ix, Bantam edition) is not surprising if one considers the complex vectors of affiliation and ambivalence leading from the thirteenth-century Tuscan to a Jewish-American poet who, on the one side (as we noted), was the son and grandson of orthodox rabbis and, on the other, the inheritor of the modernist legacy of Joyce, Pound, and Eliot, writers for whom Dante was nothing less than the center of the European canon. Yet—and this testifies to the complexity of Mandelbaum's perspective, as well as to his deep erudition—that he should then have proceeded to draw on the resonances of Aquinas' meditation on love (in the *Summa Theologica*) to describe a Dante who was finally transformed by his encounter with Beatrice: this is a much less predictable side to the story.

From a prosodic point of view, Mandelbaum's Dante is notable for its dignity and its grave stateliness, effects achieved by the use of assonance and the slow, careful drawing out of syllables. Here is an example from the opening of Canto VIII of the *Purgatorio*:

> It was the hour that turns seafarers' longings
> homeward—the hour that makes their hearts grow tender
> upon the day they bid sweet friends farewell;
>   the hour that pierces the new traveler
> with love when he has heard, far off, the bell
> that seems to mourn the dying of the day. (VIII.1–6)

The bell that pierces the new traveler with love tolls also in *The Savantasse of Montparnasse*, a second book-length poetic sequence that Mandelbaum began around the time he was completing his labors on the *Paradiso* and that he published in 1988. In the opening quatrains,

FIRSTLIGHT

>   descends the serpent Seine.
> It fords two shuttered panes and then
> my dim divan in this Hôtel
> du Mi-Chemin near Rue Grenelle.
>
> *La nuit s'en va, et ses chandelles* . . .
> Some ninety lines away, a bell-
> tower wakes. It tolls. My tale's
> impatient incipit impels. (11)

The poet, having completed his work on Dante or just about to complete it, finds himself "in this Hôtel/ du Mi-Chemin" (or, in other words, if one were to translate Paris to Times Square, in a sort of Midway Motor Inn), in medias res but at a new beginning, embarked on a new set of wanderings. Where the "Hoarse Savant" of *Chelmaxioms* had served as the narrator of that work, the "Savantasse" (the French word means "pedant," but this is terribly unfair) is at once narrator and protagonist—and this allows the poet to move closer to his own essential experience than in the earlier work, while still maintaining an ironic distance from it. The Savantasse is a Wandering Jewish Poet/Scholar, and the Montparnasse he is always leaving and to which he is always returning (in a movement that is at once centrifugal and centripetal) is not only a beloved Paris of the mind (that Paris that Walter Benjamin called the "capital of the nineteenth century") but the history of poetry itself; for Montparnasse is also "Mon Parnasse" in the poem. Pascal's melancholy dictum, that the problem with human beings is they have never learned to sit quietly in a room, penetrates the entire sequence, as does the famous opening of Mallarmé's "Brise Marine": "La chair est triste, hélas! et j'ai lu tous les livres" (The flesh is sad, alas, and there's nothing but words!). But in counterpoint to the melancholy or nostalgic strains that run throughout the work, there is also a deep vein of comedy, and the poem is enlivened by the many female figures in whom the Savantasse takes refuge: Frau Perforce, Signora Enthymeme, Angélique Abri, and so on. Mandelbaum's material in *Savantasse of Montparnasse* is extraordinarily rich, and it may be that in this work a fully European sensibility is brought to bear upon a modern American poetic idiom for the first time.

The Savantasse of Montparnasse was followed by Mandelbaum's translations of Homer's *Odyssey* (1990) and Ovid's *Metamorphoses* (1993), both of them inevitable extensions of this writer's oeuvre and both of them prepared by a lifetime of experience and study. Perhaps we can see in Mandelbaum's rendering of the "Prologue" to the *Metamorphoses* a microcosm of his extraordinary contribution to poetry and of his continuing struggle to encompass "the world's beginning to our day" in a seamless song:

> My soul would sing of metamorphoses.
> But since, o gods, you were the source of these
> bodies becoming other bodies, breathe
> your breath into my book of changes: may
> the song I sing be seamless as its way
> weaves from the world's beginning to our day. (3)

CRITICAL RECEPTION

Of Mandelbaum's National Book Award-winning version of the *Aeneid*, Bernard Knox wrote, "A brilliant translation, the only one since Dryden which reads like English verse" (private letter). Similar praise was accorded his *Odyssey* by Joseph Coates in the pages of the *Chicago Tribune*: "At last . . . Homer's muse has found the voice to sing in English verse for the first time since the 18th century." Mandelbaum's translations have been frequently praised not only for the quality of his versification (hence the references to Dryden and the eighteenth century) but also for their readability and accuracy. John Ahern, in the *New York Times Book Review*, wrote of Mandelbaum's rendering of the *Divine Comedy*: "Not one of the 90 other English translations, verse or prose, is more literally accurate or readable." Some critics, however (and they are in the minority), have complained of Mandelbaum's iambic rhythms and his heavy reliance on internal rhymes in his translations.

Mandelbaum's two book-length poetic sequences, *Chelmaxioms* and *The Savantasse of Montparnasse*, have been lavishly praised by a number of critics, but, unfortunately, they have not yet found the wide audience they deserve. Paul Mariani, writing in the pages of *Parnassus*, called *Chelmaxioms* "[a] brilliant arabesque of a poem . . . exhilaratingly exact . . . one of the most intriguing and truly distinctive poetic sequences in all modern poetry." Richard Moore, writing on *The Savantasse of Montparnasse* in *American Book Review*, noted that "[t]his grand and marvelous book . . . reminds me in its inexhaustible outlandish zest for all things . . . of no one so much as Rabelais" (14). *Choice* called it "[o]ne of the most original and most important poems written in English during the last 50 years . . . [a]lmost overpowering in its sweep of language and idea and its sustained level of intensity, [a poem that] breaks new poetic ground." Ivan Arguelles, writing in *Library Journal*, concurred that it is an "astonishingly original poem" and wrote that its "multilingual and punning nature invites comparison with *Finnegans Wake*." "Mandelbaum understands literature better than most writers today," remarks Arguelles, "and his poem reverberates with references to Pascal, Leopardi, and Heidegger in its frequent meditations on the infinite. For its metric coherency, internal rhythms and, above all, kaleidoscopic language, this is nothing short of a tour de force."

BIBLIOGRAPHY

Works by Allen Mandelbaum

Poetry

Journeyman. New York: Schocken Books, 1967.
Leaves of Absence. New York: Living Hand, 1976.
Chelmaxioms: The Maxims, Axioms, Maxioms of Chelm. Boston: Godine, 1978.
The Savantasse of Montparnasse. New York: Sheep Meadow Press, 1988.

Verse Translations/Editions

Life of a Man by Giuseppe Ungaretti. New York: New Directions, 1958.
Selected Writings of Salvatore Quasimodo. New York: Farrar, Straus, and Cudahy, 1960.
The Aeneid of Virgil. Berkeley: University of California Press, 1972; Bantam paperback ed., 1981.
Inferno of Dante. Berkeley: University of California Press, 1980; Bantam paperback ed., 1982.
Purgatorio of Dante. Berkeley: University of California Press, 1982; Bantam paperback ed., 1984.
Paradiso of Dante. Berkeley: University of California Press, 1984; Bantam paperback ed., 1986.
The Odyssey of Homer. Berkeley: University of California Press, 1990; Bantam paperback ed., 1991.
Metamorphoses of Ovid. San Diego: Harcourt, Brace, 1993.

Works about Allen Mandelbaum

Ahern, John. Rev. of *The Divine Comedy. New York Times Book Review* 9 (April 21, 1985): 12.

Arguelles, Ivan. Rev. of *The Savantasse of Montparnasse. Library Journal* 113 (July 1988): 83.

Choice 26. Rev. of *The Savantasse of Montparnasse*: (November 1988): 491.

Coates, Joseph. Rev. of *The Odyssey. Chicago Tribune* 14 (December 9, 1990): 10.

Finkelstein, Norman. *The Ritual of New Creation: Jewish Tradition and Contemporary Literature*. Albany: SUNY, 1992.

Mariani, Paul. Rev. of *Chelmaxioms. Parnassus* 5 (Spring/Summer 1977): 33.

Moore, Richard. Rev. of *The Savantasse of Montparnasse. American Book Review* 10 (January/February 1988): 14.

ROBERT MEZEY   (1935–   )

Joel Shatzky and Michael Taub

BIOGRAPHY

Robert Mezey was born on February 28, 1935, in Philadelphia, the son of Ralph and Claire Mandell Mezey. When he was in his teens, he hitchhiked to St. Elizabeth's Hospital in Washington, D.C., and visited Ezra Pound. He attended Kenyon College, served in the military from 1953 to 1955, received a B.A. from the University of Iowa in 1959, and did graduate study at Stanford University. He married Olivia Simpson in 1963, and they have two children: Naomi and Judah. Mezey also has another daughter, Eve, by an earlier marriage.

A former probation officer, psychology technician, social worker, and advertising copywriter, Mezey held his first full-time teaching position at Western Reserve University (now Case Western), in 1963–1964. He was poet-in-residence at Franklin and Marshall College and then held positions at Fresno State College and the University of Utah before he went to Pomona College, where he has taught since 1976.

Among his awards are the Lamont Poetry Award for *The Lovemaker* (1960), an Ingrahm-Merrill Foundation grant (1973, 1986), a Guggenheim Fellowship (1977–1978) and an American Academy of Arts and Letters Award in 1982.

MAJOR WORKS AND THEMES

Mezey's early work dealt with biblical texts and the impact of the Shoa. His more recent poetry centers on loss, but of a less specifically personal nature, yet he feels that his earliest influences still have a profound effect upon his mature work. In an early sonnet, Mezey brilliantly employs the section of the Bible describing the contest between Jacob and the angel, using the metaphor of a love poem:

That love which once was nearest to my heart
And pressed against my arm and forehead too,
Is gone and you went with it. We are two,
You have your legends, I an empty heart . . .
Unaging ghost, you never said your name—
You only came to wrestle, and I lost. ("Vetus Flamma," *The Lovemaker* 57)

This sense of the sacred and the earthly intermingled can be seen in another early work, "Part of a Journey," where the poet questions the possibility of an afterlife:

Here in the environs of God's winter home,
The spirit sags with flesh, the giddy mind
Beats weakly at its bowl of narrow bone
With broken wings. (*The Lovemaker* 58)

Mezey's reaction to the Shoa can also be seen in his challenging the existence of a merciful God:

Sometimes, at noon, the dull sun seems to me
A jahrzeit candle for the millions gone,
—As if that far, indifferent fire could be
Memorial to the black, disrupted bone!

Tempted and fallen, the Lord God is brooding
Over the ashes where Job sat in pain.
And yet his tribe is ashes, bleeding
And crying out to the sun and to the rain. ("The Wandering Jew," *The Door Standing Open* 10)

In "To Levine on the Day of Atonement" Mezey even muses, with wit and humor, on how secular the lives of the two poets have become:

Impenitent, we meet again,
As Gentile as your wife or mine,
And pour into a jelly glass
The cheapest California wine.

Jewless in Gaza, we have come
Where worldly likenesses commence
And gather fury, but still keep
Some dark, essential difference. (*The Door Standing Open* 6)

But in his later work, the poet refines the elements of the formative influences of his life into a more complex vision. In "Twilight Under Pine Ridge," he conjures up a heterodoxical image of an all-pervasive God:

On every slope great trees are flowering
in beautiful relation and yet
all solitary. In the early darkness
clear voices leave off
and fold inward toward sleep.
The grass
parts.
Lord God slides forward on his belly (*Evening Wind* 11)

In this poem Mezey conveys the multitude of manifestations of the Godhead, yet a profound bleakness is reflected in ''The Silence,'' a poem that recalls the spiritual darkness of an early Ingemar Bergman movie:

How many times God will remember
the silence of the beginning,
that silence which even God himself couldn't endure,
which was finally to blame for our being here now—
he lost his head, and clawing at the earth, picked up some mud and made us.

And thus ended the silence,
and then began the howling,
interrupted now and then by a faint chattering
when we make love in our sleep. (*Evening Wind* 16)

On the other hand, Mezey can regard the silence as a sign of redemption:

In an orgy of silence the moon rose
And we sat and looked up. Then the wind
Swaying the flowers with a gentle force
Broke open its sweetness on our foreheads. . . .
Mercy, she said. Now I remember.
And we say quiet, under a listening sky.
For a moment it seemed we held it all in our hands,
Then let it go, and that was the best of all (''Mercy,'' *Evening Wind* 24)

Perhaps the best expression of Mezey's poetic vision can be found in his own words in reference to a departed friend, the poet Burt Meyers. He feels that this description is appropriate for him as well:

He is not able to forget his intimations of the Garden where truth and beauty are one—a realm of the imagination, ceaselessly undermined by reality. His poetry is one long dance of praise and lament, now one, now the other, often both at once. He [is] continually seeking images that might express the inexpressibly beautiful and lost, images of the physical world through which we can glimpse ''ordre et beauté,/ calme et volupté,'' images that might contain the bottomless sorrow of our exile. (Personal note to author)

CRITICAL RECEPTION

The most comprehensive single article on Mezey is by Ralph J. Mills, Jr., in a 1974 issue of *American Poetry Review*. Mills points out in reviewing *The Door Standing Open* several of Mezey's poems that pertain to his ambiguous feelings about his Jewish identity:

"To Levine on the Day of Atonement," and "The Wandering Jew," emphasize Mezey's fundamental sense of alienation in his life. The alienation is actually of a double character. "The Wandering Jew" formulates a stark, powerful record of the poet's youthful orthodoxy which conferred upon him a feeling of selective identity as a Jew in a world filled with enemies and universally corrupt. . . . Wretchedness, injustice, oppression, and suffering make the paternal concerns of God even more dubious, or at least undermine traditional laws, definitions, and concepts. (18)

In his images of the Shoa Mezey finds "another sort of identity," in Mills' words. But it is this sense of profound alienation from what is seen as a cruelly indifferent God that leads to a deeper sense of the root of the poet's identity.

The profane means of survival are elaborated . . . in "To Levine on the Day of Atonement." Here . . . he delineates through some ordinary particulars the shape of the secular, alienated existence both of them pursue. Yet it is clear, this existence qualifies itself everywhere by the rememberance of Jewishness. Each simple act—the drinking of a glass of wine—recalls acts hallowed by religion, ritual, and law, so that the inheritance seems always there, abandoned but unforgotten. Mezey declares, it forms the very structure of the person, determining to an extent his nature. (18)

This sense of a core of identity, even in the most seemingly ordinary acts and gestures, what is called the *"pintele yid"* (the "Jewish kernal"), is beautifully and, in some sense, sorrowfully reflected in these poems. In the growth and added complexity of Mezey's later work he gives us both a more enriched, yet sparer, vision of the difficulties of maintaining this core Jewish identity in a world that is rapidly stripping us of the spiritual dimensions of human existence.

BIBLIOGRAPHY

Works by Robert Mezey

The Lovemaker. Iowa City, IA: Cummington Press, 1961.
White Blossoms. Iowa City, IA: Cummington Press, 1965.
The Door Standing Open: New and Selected Poems. New York: Houghton Mifflin and Oxford University Press, 1970.
Small Song. Grand Rapids, MI: Humble Hills Press, 1970.
Poems from the Hebrew. New York: Thomas Y. Crowell, 1973.
Couplets. Salt Lake City, UT: Westigan Press, 1978.

Selected Translations 1960–1980. Grand Rapids, MI: Westigan Press, 1981.
Evening Wind. Hanover, NH: Wesleyan University Press, 1987.

Work about Robert Mezey

Mills, Ralph J., Jr. " 'A Voice in This Life': The Poems of Robert Mezey." *American Poetry Review*, September/October 1974: 17–21.

STEPHEN MITCHELL (1943–)

Stephen Monte

BIOGRAPHY

Stephen Mitchell was born in Brooklyn, New York, in 1943. He studied at Amherst College, the University of Paris, and Yale University. He has claimed in an interview that all of his books have been the result of falling in love, beginning with a relationship that ended in 1965 while he was a first-year graduate student in comparative literature at Yale. After this "first serious love affair," he spent seven years wrestling with the Hebrew of the Book of Job and six years practicing Zen under the Korean master Seung Sahn. He currently lives with his wife, Vicki Chang, an acupuncturist and healer, in Berkeley, California.

MAJOR WORKS AND THEMES

To read Stephen Mitchell's work is to read at the same time the work of other writers, from Lao-tzu and the author of Job to Rainer Maria Rilke and Dan Pagis, for Mitchell is best known as a translator and an anthologist, though he is also the author of a book of poems, a children's book, and a book on the teachings of his Zen master, Seung Sahn. In order to place recurrent themes of his work in perspective, one needs to consider the variety of his output, but concentrating on his translations neither misrepresents his interests nor disparages his abilities as a writer. Mitchell expresses many of his concerns through the texts he chooses to translate, and his best translations are achievements stunning enough to remind one of an easily forgotten truth about translation: the art depends as much on the translator's ability to manipulate the language in which he is writing as the quality of the original.

Mitchell's English versions of Rilke are undoubtedly his most celebrated translations and are most readers' introduction to his other works. Beginning with a *Selected Poetry of Rainer Maria Rilke* (1982), Mitchell has published translations of *The Notebooks of Malte Laurids Brigge* (1983), *The Lay of the Love and Death of Cornet Christoph Rilke* (1983), *Letters to a Young Poet* (1984), and *The Sonnets to Orpheus* (1985). His *Selected* is probably the single most popular book of Rilke translations in English, and deservedly so. Mitchell's selection of Rilke lyrics is generous and judicious; it underrepresents perhaps only the early poems of *The Book of Hours* and *The Book of Pictures*. Some eighteen poems from *New Poems* are included, all of the *Duino Elegies* (including the important first version of the tenth elegy), fifteen of the *Sonnets to Orpheus*, the long poem "Requiem for a Friend," prose poem selections from *The Notebooks of Malte Laurids Brigge*, and numerous uncollected poems. Add to this a biographical and literary-historical essay by Robert Hass and informative, but unobtrusive, notes in the back of the volume, and one can begin to see why Mitchell's book has become the introduction to Rilke for so many American readers.

Mitchell translates Rilke in what Dryden might have called the middle style: most poems stay close to the original and yet are clearly intended to be read as poems, not as cribs for the facing German. Mitchell is at his best with the longer, discursive poems—the *Duino Elegies*, "Requiem for a Friend," "Orpheus. Eurydice. Hermes"—and the prose works.

One can learn a lot about Mitchell's own preoccupations by glancing through the different works he has chosen to translate and anthologize. The Rilke translations emphasize the spiritual and philosophical sides of the poet. It is hard not to read the *Duino Elegies* as the core of the *Selected*, for example, and some of Mitchell's selections, such as "Buddha in Glory," seem dictated more by the concerns of the author of *Dropping Ashes on the Buddha* than by their importance in the Rilke canon. The translations of the prose works, Rilke's novel *The Notebooks of Malte Laurids Brigge* and the *Letters to a Young Poet*, suggest another concern of the translator: *Bildung*. Brigge's notebooks are, at one level, the young Rilke's therapy for his solitary, exilelike life in Paris; they close with a version of the parable of the Prodigal Son. Rilke's letters to Kappus are even more directly concerned with personal and poetic development.

Mitchell's interests in *Bildung*, spirituality, and, in general, living life can also be found in his translations of *The Book of Job* (1979), *Tao Te Ching* (1988), *The Gospel According to Jesus* (1991), and *Genesis* (1996). Choosing to translate these works, in however literary a style, implies an interest in recovering ancient wisdom for the modern reader. As with the Rilke translations, Mitchell supplies just enough background information and translates conversationally, yet faithfully, so that a general reader can better appreciate the power and relevance of the works. In his translation of *The Book of Job*, for example, Mitchell not only aids the reader with the apparatus of "introduction in front, notes in back" but divides the Book of Job into reader-friendly sections that are, for all practical purposes, the products of his editorial decisions: a prose prologue and epilogue envelop the verse sections "The Curse," three rounds of arguing between Job and his neighbors, "The Summation," and "The Voice from the Whirlwind." The presence of the editor is even more palpable in *The Gospel According to Jesus*, where the 28-page translation of "the gospel" is sandwiched between a 62-page essay and a 150-page commentary. The gospel itself is a blend of passages from different New Testament books; Mitchell's primary criteria for selection have to do with historical accuracy (what Jesus said and taught) but are based ultimately on "spiritual value," as he makes clear in his Introduction (6). In a similar way, the *Genesis* translation removes the sections written by the "P" or "priestly" writer—one of several "authors" of *Genesis*, according to biblical scholars—on aesthetic grounds. The *Tao Te Ching* translation is sleeker, as if to suggest that the words of Lao-tzu require not so much a scholar's mediation as the reader's open-mindedness. Mitchell is, above all, concerned with Lao-tzu as teacher, frankly admitting, "If I haven't always translated Lao-tzu's words, my intention has always been to translate his mind" (Introduction x). The *Tao Te Ching*, after all, does not so much preach as suggest a way of understanding through claiming repeatedly it can only explain what it *cannot* do.

The variety of religious texts Mitchell has chosen to translate—Judeo-Christian, Christian, and Taoist—itself suggests that his own sense of the spiritual is eclectic. His *Gospel*, for example, is intended for "believers and unbelievers," according to the subtitle. Mitchell opens this work with a revealing description of his study:

One of the icons on the walls of my study is a picture of Thomas Jefferson, an inexpensive reproduction of the portrait by Rembrandt Peale.... among the other icons on my wall are the beautiful, Jewish, halo-free face of Jesus by Rembrandt from the Gemäldegalerie in Berlin; a portrait of that other greatest of Jewish teachers, Spinoza; a Ming dynasty watercolor of a delighted bird-watching Taoist who could easily be Lao-tzu himself; a photograph, glowing with love, of the modern Indian sage Tamana Maharshi; and underneath it, surrounded by dried rose petals, a small Burmese statue of the Buddha, perched on a three-foot-tall packing crate stenciled with CHUE LUNG SOY SAUCE, 22 LBS. (3)

Reading through Mitchell's published works, one does not sense that his eclecticism stems from a vague set of core beliefs—quite the contrary. A healthy skepticism of fixed dogma mixes with a curiosity about living life in this world and an appreciation of aesthetic experience. As with the criticism of Walter Benjamin and the poetry of Wallace Stevens, one can find affinities to certain rabbinical traditions of thought in his translations and commentaries. Parables, questioning, and opposing views play important roles in his work.

The most obvious examples of eclecticism (or perhaps syncretism) in Mitchell are his two anthologies *The Enlightened Heart* (1989) and *The Enlightened Mind*

(1991). The former anthology is of sacred poetry; the latter of sacred prose. *The Enlightened Heart* is dedicated to the Zen master Seung Sahn, who, Mitchell says, taught him everything he doesn't know. The selections range from passages from *The Upanishads*, *The Book of Psalms*, Lao-tzu, and *The Bhagavad Gita*, to Hildegard of Bingen, Francis of Assisi, Dante, Shakespeare, and Basho, and then to Blake, Hopkins, Yeats, Rilke, and Jeffers. *The Enlightened Mind* is similarly ambitious in its historical and cultural range. The effect of bringing together so many different writers in one volume is mixed. Looking at familiar texts in a new light can be eye-opening, as can discovering unfamiliar works with familiar concerns. But Mitchell's anthologies are also designed to raise some eyebrows. Is, say, Yeats' ''Lapis Lazuli'' really a sacred poem? Does not the inclusion of so many writers primarily influenced by *literary* traditions make one question whether Mitchell has paid enough attention to the historical and cultural use of the texts he anthologizes, not just their content? But then again, Mitchell seems to tell us, if these anthologies make you question categories of the sacred, they are doing their work.

Mitchell's translations of two more contemporary figures, the Israeli poets Dan Pagis and Yehuda Amichai, are of a different order than his anthologies and translations of older writers: one cannot assume that these translations tell us much about Mitchell himself. The editorial and translation duties of *The Selected Poetry of Yehuda Amichai* (1986) are split between Mitchell and Chana Bloch (Mitchell translates all poetry up to the year 1969). Both volumes are thin on notes and introductions, not simply because modern writers demand less background information. The translations of Pagis and Amichai are poetic introductions to Israeli writers who have not yet received their due in the English-language world. In contrast to the Rilke translations, for example, there is no facing original text in these volumes. Mitchell is also more likely to translate the rhymed poems (there are many in the Amichai) into rhyme. In the Rilke volume, he generally substitutes half rhymes or avoids rhyme altogether.

As central to his identity as a writer as Mitchell's translations and anthologies are, an estimate of his work would not be complete without an examination of his book of poems, *Parables and Portraits* (1990). More so than in his book for children, *The Creation* (1990), or in his work on his Zen master, *Dropping Ashes on the Buddha* (1976), Mitchell's preoccupations receive their fullest expression in his poems. As the title of the collection indicates, Mitchell's poems can be divided into portraits and parables. The former are of some writer, artist, philosopher, or teacher and are generally in verse; the latter are often a variation on a literary or religious story and generally in prose. The opening of the poem ''Jerome'' is typical of the portraits in that it is an ecphrasis of someone else's portrait:

> In Dürer's engraving
> you sit hunched over your desk,

> writing, with an extraneous
> halo around your head. (13)

Mitchell's attitude toward his subject matter comes through with his adjectives—the halo is ''extraneous''—and reveals him to be the sort of person his translations have led us to expect: someone interested in different ways of knowing and living, someone who does not believe in a single notion of the sacred. The parables approach their subject matter in a gently ironic vein, as in the opening of ''The Prodigal Son'' and the close of ''Job'':

Sometimes, after a day among the swine, he would be afraid to lie down in his wretched hut. Actually, the swine weren't bad company. (''The Prodigal Son'' 23)

''In any case,'' the friends said on their way home, ''his offensiveness has not diminished. A miracle is no cure for bad breath.'' (''Job'' 19)

As with the selections in his anthologies, Mitchell is asking us to look at the familiar in a new light. The morals to his parables are always ambiguous. His most successful poem is probably the ''Vermeer,'' which closes the volume and whose painting of the milkmaid he reprints on the cover of the book. Other poem titles recall the range and eclecticism of his other work: ''Tao-Chi,'' ''Zen Master,'' ''Spinoza,'' ''Through the Eye of the Needle,'' ''Kafka,'' ''Orpheus,'' ''A Reluctant Bodhisattva.'' The collection provides a convenient way of summarizing what is distinctive about Mitchell. If, in translating Rilke, Mitchell balances fidelity to the original against the need to render poems as poems, his own poetry suggests that he is concerned as much with the accuracy of the portrait-maker as he is drawn by the parable's ambiguous answers and questions.

CRITICAL RECEPTION

What critical literature exists on Mitchell is in the form of reviews. While the critical reception of Mitchell has been generally favorable, there have been some differences of opinion with regard to his method of translation. It is Mitchell's gift to make whatever he is translating sound as if it were written in English, but this facility causes some reviewers to question his accuracy. The debate is best illustrated by the reactions of reviewers to his translation of *Genesis*. Mitchell's translation was published almost simultaneously with a translation made by his longtime friend Robert Alter, and these two versions of *Genesis* have come to represent something like poetic license and scholarly fidelity. (Mitchell and Alter have even discussed their translations on National Public Radio.) In Phyllis Trible's *New York Times* review, Alter is praised for staying close to the Hebrew, and Mitchell upbraided for bowdlerizing *Genesis* and producing ''an adaptation rather than a translation'' (7). In Jacob Neusner's *National Re-*

view article, Mitchell is the "poet" who "avoids jarring the reader while still singing to him," while Alter is "mannered and condescending" (62). These poles of criticism are fairly representative, though the issues of fidelity and license have tended to receive more prominence when religious or historical texts are at issue.

BIBLIOGRAPHY

Works by Stephen Mitchell

Translations

Poems by Dan Pagis. Oxford, England: Carcanet Press, 1972.

Selected Poems of T. Carmi and Dan Pagis. Baltimore: Penguin, 1976.

Points of Departure: Poems by Dan Pagis. Introduction by Robert Allen. Philadelphia: Jewish Publication Society of America, 1981.

The Selected Poetry of Rainer Maria Rilke. New York: Random House, 1982; rpt. New York: Vintage, 1989; also rpt. as *Ahead of All Parting: The Selected Poetry and Prose of Rainer Maria Rilke*, New York: Modern Library, 1995.

The Lay of the Love and Death of Cornet Christoph Rilke. San Francisco: Arion Press, 1983.

The Notebooks of Malte Laurids Brigge. New York: Random House, 1983; rpt. New York: Vintage, 1990.

The Sonnets to Orpheus. New York: Simon and Schuster, 1985.

The Selected Poetry of Yehuda Amichai. Ed. and trans. with Chana Bloch. New York: Harper and Row, 1986; newly rev. and expanded ed., Berkeley: University of California Press, 1996.

Letters to a Young Poet. New York: Random House, 1984; rpt., New York: Vintage, 1987.

Tao Te Ching, a New English Version. New York: Harper and Row, 1988.

Variable Directions: The Selected Poetry of Dan Pagis. San Francisco: North Point Press, 1989.

The Gospel according to Jesus: A New Translation and Guide to His Essential Teachings for Believers and Unbelievers. New York: HarperCollins, 1991.

The Book of Job. New York: Harper Perennial, 1992; Rpt., San Francisco: North Point Press, 1987 and *Into the Whirlwind: A Translation of the Book of Job*, Garden City, NY: Doubleday, 1979.

The Duino Elegies. New York: Random House, 1992.

Genesis: A New Translation of the Classic Biblical Stories. New York: HarperCollins, 1996.

The Selected Poetry of Dan Pagis. Introduction by Robert Alter. Berkeley: University of California Press, 1996.

Anthologies

The Enlightened Heart: An Anthology of Sacred Poetry. New York: Harper and Row, 1989.

The Enlightened Mind: An Anthology of Sacred Prose. New York: HarperCollins, 1991.

Into the Garden: A Wedding Anthology (poetry and prose on love and marriage). Ed. with Robert Hass. New York: HarperCollins, 1993.

For Children

The Creation. Trans. and adapted from the Book of Genesis. With paintings by Ori Sherman. New York: Dial Books, 1990.

Poetry

Parables and Portraits. New York: Harper and Row, 1990.

Other

Dropping Ashes on the Buddha: The Teaching of Zen Master Seung Sahn. New York: Grove Press, 1976; distributed by Random House; Rpt; New York: Harper and Row, 1988.

Works about Stephen Mitchell

Donoghue, Denis. "Transforming the World into Feeling." Rev. of *The Selected Poetry of Rainer Maria Rilke*. New York Times, January 30, 1983, Section 7:9.

Gross, John. Rev. of *The Book of Job*. *New York Times*, September 25, 1987, Section C: 36.

Hirsch, Edward. "In Language Torn from Sleep." Rev. of *The Selected Poetry of Yehuda Amichai*. *New York Times*, August 3, 1986, Section 7: 14.

Hofmann, Michael. "Achievements of a Lifelong Guest." Rev. of *The Sonnets to Orpheus*. *New York Times*, September 21, 1986, Section 7: 18.

Neusner, Jacob. "Genesis: A Living Conversation." Rev. of *Genesis: A New Translation of the Classic Biblical Stories. National Review* 48, No. 23 (December 9, 1996): 61–62.

Rev. of *The Book of Job*. *Book World* 22 (April 19, 1992): 1+.

Rev. of *The Book of Psalms*. *Library Journal* 118 (June 1, 1993): 132.

Rev. of *The Creation*. *Library Talk* 4 (March 1991): 43.

Rev. of *The Enlightened Heart*. *Book World* 23 (September 26, 1993): 12.

Rev. of *The Gospel according to Jesus*. *New Age Journal* 10 (Winter 1993): 43.

Rev. of *Parables and Portraits*. *Tikkun* 6 (January 1991): 81.

Trible, Phyllis. "Unauthorized Versions." Rev. of *Genesis: A New Translation of the Classic Biblical Stories. New York Times*; December 15, 1997, Section 7: 7.

Williamson, Alan. "Pasts That Stay Present." Rev. of *Points of Departure*. *New York Times*, May 1, 1983, Section 7: 15.

HOWARD MOSS (1922–1987)

Burt Kimmelman

BIOGRAPHY

Howard Moss was born on January 22, 1922, in New York City to David Leonard Moss, who had immigrated from Lithuania, and Sonya (Schrag) Moss. Howard grew up in Rockaway Beach, in the borough of Queens; this locale fostered a deep affinity in him for the ocean, which manifested in early poems like "Waterwall Blues" and "Around the Fish: After Paul Klee" (from *The Wound and the Weather*, his first book, published in 1946) and in later works such as the childhood memoir "Long Island Springs" (from *Selected Poems*, 1971), the autobiographical "Shorelines" (from *Buried City*, 1975), and "Miami Beach" (from *Rules of Sleep*, 1984, his final original collection). The shore, Moss has said, was "where I first fell in love [and] first was overcome by things like moonlight and the smell of lilacs . . . when books first started to mean something to me, and friends, and the world was a great enigma almost as mysterious as myself" (Leiter 31).

Moss began college in 1939 at the University of Michigan, but in 1940 he transferred to the University of Wisconsin, where he completed a B.A. degree in 1944. He also spent the 1942 summer at Harvard. Upon graduation, he returned to New York, to work first as a copy boy and subsequently as a book reviewer for *Time* magazine. His desire to be a poet received great encouragement when he won the Janet Sewall David Award, bestowed by *Poetry Magazine*, in that same year. By 1946, he had returned to formal study, at Columbia University, but soon lost interest in securing an M.A. "Most of [the curriculum] was pretty dull stuff," he later recalled. "Literature was being taught as if it were history—the history of ideas. We read everything but the texts themselves" (Leiter 27). Even so, Moss was to remain connected to academe. From 1944 to 1946, he taught English at Vassar College. "Those two years were an extraordinary education for me," he recalled. "I think I read more in two years than I had the rest of my life" (27). Subsequently, until nearly the end of his life, he was to teach, albeit for short stints, at Washington University in 1972, Barnard College in 1975, Columbia in 1977, the University of California at Irvine in 1979, and the University of Houston in 1980.

His Columbia experience, however, influenced him sufficiently to choose a career in publishing. After *Time*, Moss went to *Junior Bazaar* as its fiction editor—to publish fiction by college students in this "junior" version of *Harper's Bazaar*—and then, in 1948, he became a fiction editor at the *New Yorker*. In 1950, he became its poetry editor and served in that capacity until his death. Moss's long reign at the *New Yorker* allowed him the opportunity to help shape literary taste, insofar as the magazine was a presence on the post–World War II American poetry scene. He was also to serve as a judge for the National Book Awards in 1957 and again in 1964 and at various times for the University of Michigan Avery Hopwood Awards and the Brandeis University creative writing awards. In 1968 he was inducted into the prestigious American Academy and Institute of Arts and Letters. In 1972 he won a grant from the Ingram Merrill Foundation and the National Book Award for poetry for his *Selected Poems*. His subsequent *New Selected Poems* (1985) was awarded the Lenore Marshall *Nation* Poetry Prize in 1986; in this year he also received a fellowship from the Academy of American Poets. Additionally, Moss was a member of PEN as well as of the Authors Guild.

These honors were well deserved, yet they were hard won. Moss published *The Wound and the Weather* when he was only twenty-four. The book garnered mixed reviews. All the same, it was becoming clear that Moss was a poet to be taken seriously. *The Toy Fair* appeared eight years later, followed by ten more books of verse. He also published a great many essays and four books of criticism, including studies of W. H. Auden, Elizabeth Bishop, Elizabeth Bowen, Proust, and Chekhov. Moss was also a dramatist whose work was often performed and then published belatedly.

Moss died on September 16, 1987, at St. Vincent's Hospital in New York City. The cause of death was cardiac arrest. The most poignant of the many obituaries that marked his passing was printed in the *New Yorker*, where, using that magazine as a kind of headquarters, he had spent the greater portion of his life. The magazine's remembrance describes Moss as "able to concentrate [his] whole [life] on poetry." This quality was perhaps most evident in person. "In public, he read his poems quietly; and the voice in the poems is a quiet one, though warm with compassion and shared pain. . . . It was not simply our offices but the office of poet that he graced with his life" ("Howard Moss" 128).

MAJOR WORKS AND THEMES

All of Moss's work has the quality of *finish*. His poems are constructed with care. At the start and throughout the middle of his career, his poems were end-rhymed and metered; yet even when, in later life, Moss switched to free verse, there was in each of his lines a regularity that declared a love of order and ultimately of form itself. As might be expected of just about any poet's work, his early pieces can be awkward in their attempts to make statement and syntax adhere to pattern—so that the feeling of "natural talk" has been sacrificed. Dana Gioia has shrewdly observed that "[a]ll of Moss's best early work is formal, but here he merely fills in forms rather than reinvents them in his own image" (99). In later years, in contrast, Moss was able to achieve a complementarity of form and language in which his statements are often held together by an extraordinarily subtle wit. Punning could extend well beyond merely incidental wordplay, as in "At the Fire Fountain":

> Here, the fountain's question marks of haze
> No longer glaze the marble. Winter's spare,
> Bone monuments of stone and glass appraise
> Themselves across the plaza, the evening air
> Holds up the starlight in that silent, queer
> Moment of perfection when each thing assays
> Its selfhood only, and perception stays. (*Finding Them Lost* 30–31)

This stanza contains a number of startling mixtures of perception, such as the textual "question marks" that shape the primal "haze" of a fountain and measured permutations of sound, such as the progression of "haze," "glaze," "glass," "plaza," and "assays," which drives the action of the poem forward toward the summary remark that "perception stays." However, the stanza is unified because of a deeper source. Even more dazzling and moving, as Richard Howard has pointed out, is this stanza's concern for "the doubleness of existence [and] the duplicity of being" that are brought together in the phrase "the evening air holds up the starlight"; the duality here of "*supports by its cold weight* and *retards by its cold obstruction*, as in a hold-up, is an enunciation of [Moss's] theme, the cyclical nature of reality" (453).

As his craft was refined, Moss was able to move into the formality visible in his early work until its formalness completely disappeared; his poems were always structured, but the work of making one or another poetic form operate felicitously was less and less obvious. In fact, reading some of his work, one may be quite unaware of its regularity—that is, up to a point where a tension between the freedom of idea and the discipline of sound as well as image is established. "Moss did not as a rule," writes Bruce Bawer, "go in for radical experiment or spectacular effects. (When he did, on one occasion, write a poem that represented a radical departure from his usual manner, he called it 'Radical Departures' [1971])" (35). John Hollander notes that "Moss's unfailing iambic verse was, in his earlier poems, an instrument of wry searching, of celebration of picture and of place. In his later work, it pierces even the deeper patterns he was so good at tracing to stir up the eternal but Protean fables of love, idleness, hope, and regret" (247). Stylistically, Moss's verse is akin to that of contemporaries like Richard Wilbur, Anthony Hecht, and Howard Nemerov. These formalists featured a decidedly intellectual discourse full of ironies. Yet Moss, while equaling them as craftsmen, could be softer in tone, more willing to employ colloquial diction, and less willing to provide pyrotechnic displays.

Another identifying sign of a Moss poem—and one of his great strengths— was the apparent ease with which the poetic voice can conflate perceptions of natural and artificial objects and forces, for example, in "Standards" (1980):

> Sadly among the patient standards
> Of trees the twirlers arrive to conduct
> The last of the summer's orchestral pieces.
> The garden's icetray of seeds is about
> To swing back into its glacial room. (*Notes from the Castle* 58–59).

A number of Moss's poems are about art. Aesthetics, like technology, does not have to be set apart from the natural flows of life. Moss has said, "What my poems are really about . . . is the experience of hovering between the forms of nature and the forms of art. My work is the response of someone who is equally *moved* by nature and art" (Leiter 29). Moss was known as a poet of the city— for the most part, because of his poems about New York—but his urbanity is particularly vivid in the most unlikely settings.

His sense of himself as a Jew was also blended into distinctly secular venues, so much so that Jewish life, for Moss, exists only at the periphery of his experience. The poem "Saratoga" wishes to make this very point in its efforts to indicate how protean and heterogeneous this upstate New York city, best known for its restorative springs, opera, and horse racing, can be. On a trip there, from the nearby Yaddo artist colony, Moss observes Saratoga's many quick changes, as if no identity can really suit it. There is something genuine about it, finally, but it is unbecoming, and yet Moss embraces it. There is a seediness beyond the city's main street. Overall, the changing faces of the tourists contrast with, and may inflect, the life of a variety of nontransients. Moss is shocked and perhaps perversely delighted by what he finds after the pomp and otherwise high culture have moved on and before the horsey set has arrived:

> Who would dream there is a street of Chasidic Jews
> Left over among the mineral waters,
> Black-bearded, black, among the cures of summer,
> In rows of rooming houses gone to seed
> Braced by vines in which they seem suspended?
>
> This is a country of seconds—a kind
> of bucolic, demented Garment District:
> Landscapes and yardgoods going for a song—
> Windfalls of shirts on the cheap at the mill,
> Factories where hands still touch the fabric.

The hills are overstocked with sunsets.
Cemeteries are they housing projects
For never enough? Or too much of everything? (*New Selected Poems* 197–
    98)

If there is a nostalgia here, then it is for the details of an at times difficult Jewish assimilation, which have marked Moss' own life as well as those within his purview.

No poem of his sets out specifically to explore Jewish identity—with the possible exception of "Long Island Springs." Even here, however, the discussion of a child's conflict about his Jewish roots and his present existence within a Gentile milieu is rendered obliquely in relation to, simply, Moss' poignant remembrance of his grandparents, his acknowledged debt to them for the love they gave him. He remembers with a mixture of pain and warmth his grandmother's growing and preparing her own horseradish, her afternoons with her friends playing bridge and mah-jongg. More movingly and getting to the point of this poem as it nears its central lines is this apostrophe:

Grandpa, forgive me. When you called for me
At school in a sudden rain or snow, I was
Ashamed that anyone should see your beard
Or hear you talk in broken English. You
Would bring a black umbrella, battle-scarred,

And walk me home beneath it through the lots,
Where seasonal wild roses took a spill
And blew their cups, and sumac bushes grew
Up from the sand, attached to secret springs,
As I was secretly attached to you. (*New Selected Poems* 203)

Still, the ideas and rhetoric of Hebrew Scripture permeate a lot of Moss' writing; they are present, though, with such delicacy that they do not call attention to their origins.

The prevalent themes in Moss's work include what is most fundamental to a person's life—change itself, human relationships, death, and loss; there are "the difficulty of love, the decay of the body, the passing of time, and the inevitability of death," all counterpointed against "the inexhaustible beauty of the natural world" (Gioia 102). Most of all, especially in Moss's mature writings, there is a profound awareness of how life is conditioned by decay and mortality. Indeed, Moss was one of our great elegists. He can render attachment and loss with an at times wrenching acuity through graphic simplicity that moves steadily toward bitter irony. Hence, "Elegy for My Sister" (1980) begins,

Getting out of bed one day, you broke
Your leg simply by standing up,

> The bones too frail, the marrow gone,
> Melted into a kind of eggshell sawdust,
> The Crab, and chemotherapy against it,
> The cure as killing as the pain it cured . . .
>
> Why torture myself? Or you?—sailed into
> The port of Nothing or that Elysium
> Of childish happiness the heart sets story by. (*Notes from the Castle* 41)

A similar treatment of loss of a loved one is to be found in the earlier "Elegy for My Father" (1954), where the end of life is marked by intense pain and where both the dying and the bereft who remain alive are set together as physically separate but merged in psychic distress:

> Above you, the white night nurse shook
> His head, and moaning on the moods of luck,
> We knew the double-dealing enemy:
> From pain you suffered, pain had set you free.
>
> Down from the ceiling, father, circles came:
> Angels, perhaps, to bear your soul away.
> But tasting the persisting salt of pain,
> I think my tears created them, though in vain,
> Like yours, they fell. All losses link: the same
> Creature marred us both to stake his claim. (*New Selected Poems* 21)

CRITICAL RECEPTION

Moss's early poetry was greeted with both acclaim and censure, sometimes by the same critic. It was clear, nonetheless, that Moss was to become a significant literary voice when in *The Atlantic Monthly* Howard Nemerov called *The Toy Fair* (1954) "one of the most accomplished collections of lyric poetry to appear since the war"; the book contained a "sinewy flowing of figure and intellectual control" (247). Conversely, Donald Justice, in reviewing *A Swimmer in the Air* (1957) for *Poetry* magazine, observed that in one or another of its poems Moss's wit "disintegrates into willfully cute fooling around with the sounds of words" (76). Similarly in 1960, Thom Gunn, analyzing *A Winter Come, a Summer Gone: Poems 1946–1960* for the *Yale Review*, objected to the "slickness and empty gesturing" of some of the verse (76).

With the publication of *Finding Them Lost* in 1965, however, the take on Moss became more uniformly positive, and when his *Selected Poems* was brought out in 1971, the general reaction was widely enthusiastic. The *Virginia Quarterly Review* said that "Moss has come the necessary distance and is now well into that harder realm of realization he has worked for, that realm beyond technique. It is a labor that should not go unnoticed or unrewarded" (clxiv). Laurence Lieberman noted in the *Yale Review* that "Moss has trimmed back

old work in the light of advancing craft and widening vision [which] has had a
liberating effect'' (94). The widespread opinion was, as Edmund White put it
in *Poetry*, that Moss had ''proceeded from being a gifted poet to being an
accomplished one'' (350).

Moss had arrived. Nevertheless, while future reviews would be full of praise,
some of the old criticisms also continued to make their way into print. In commenting on *Buried City* (1975), Michael Lally wrote in the *Washington Post*
that ''sometimes the technical defenses created to defend the success of the
poem become so elaborate and contrived they end up falling of their own weight
and burying the poem'' (4). Even so, in *The New Republic*, Harold Bloom said
of the book, it would ''give deep pleasure to any reader searching for a mature
art that addresses itself to the observed, urban world'' (25). Likewise, Richard
Howard, writing in *The Georgia Review*, compared Moss favorably with James
Merrill, and he especially praised the Valery translations that appeared first in
Buried City (207). In the *New York Times* Helen Vendler opined, ''Intellectuality
is still present, in the form of wit, but language empties itself of intellectual
reference and of ambitious or equivocal diction'' (22).

When *Notes from the Castle* (1979) appeared, the public reaction was even
more adulatory. Dave Smith in *American Poetry Review* called it ''more than
ever attentive, perhaps even reverential, toward the natural world which [Moss]
regards both as a mirror and a window. The elements and forms of nature have
become almost a dramatic script from which it is his task to tease out human
meaning. Moss repeatedly portrays the poet as translator of nature by rendering
through simile and metaphor the natural particular in a literary, artistic, or craft
term.'' More than in the past, too, Moss was ''[allowing] himself the fuller and
more musical resources of line, image, and rhetorical variation.'' Ultimately,
Moss's ''power, and his poetic signature'' had become the capacity ''to continue
fitting the world's fragments into the order of formal beauty'' (38).

A number of critics have considered *Notes from the Castle* Moss's finest
volume. Yet his next book of poems, *Rules of Sleep* (1984), earned its own high
marks. The book revealed a more finely honed ''sense of mortality,'' according
to Phoebe Pettingell in *The New Leader* (18). Moss's last book of verse was
New Selected Poems (1985). Perhaps critics of the time were sensing a closure
to his career (Moss had suffered a heart attack prior to the appearance of his
previous collection). With summation and the tone of respect afforded an elder
statesman, Peter Stitt proclaimed in the *New York Times Book Review* that ''Mr.
Moss works his miracles with a quiet subtlety. Perhaps it is that quietness that
has made him so relatively neglected as a poet, when reputation is measured
against that talent'' (11). In a similar vein, Ashley Brown, in *World Literature
Today*, spoke of Moss's ''generosity'' that can allow him to ''generate a real
power from trivial, almost journalistic material'' (109). Moss's penchant for the
peripatetic and seemingly insignificant detail and in a way his like penchant for
poetry crafted to the ultimate degree may account for the continued impatience
on the part of reviewers throughout Moss's career, who nevertheless saw the

genuine truth peeking through his artifice and at times saw the artifice, so finely rendered, as a profound truth in itself.

BIBLIOGRAPHY

Works by Howard Moss

The Wound and the Weather (poetry). New York: Reynal and Hitchcock, 1946.
The Folding Green (drama). 1954a. Unpublished.
The Toy Fair (poetry). New York: Scribners, 1954b.
A Swimmer in the Air (poetry). New York: Scribners, 1957.
A Winter Come, a Summer Gone: Poems 1946–1960. New York: Scribners, 1960.
The Magic Lantern of Marcel Proust (criticism, poetry). New York: Macmillan, 1962; London: Faber and Faber, 1963.
Finding Them Lost and Other Poems. New York: Scribners, 1965; London: Macmillan, 1965a.
The Oedipus Mah-Jongg Scandal (drama). 1965b. Unpublished.
Second Nature (poetry). New York: Atheneum, 1968.
Writing against Time: Critical Essays and Reviews. New York: Morrow, 1969.
Selected Poems. New York: Atheneum, 1971.
Chekhov (criticism). New York: Albondocani Press, 1972a.
The Palace at Four A.M. (drama). 1972b. Unpublished.
Travel: A Window (poetry). New York: Albondocani Press, 1973.
Instant Lives (prose satire). New York: Saturday Review Press/Dutton, 1974.
Buried City (poetry). New York: Atheneum, 1975.
A Swim off the Rocks (poetry). New York: Atheneum, 1976.
Tigers and Other Lilies (juvenile poetry). New York: Atheneum, 1977.
Notes from the Castle (poetry). New York: Atheneum, 1979.
Critical Conditions (criticism). New York: Atheneum, 1980a.
Two Plays (drama). New York: Sheep Meadow Press/Flying Point Books, 1980b.
Whatever Is Moving (criticism). Boston/Toronto: Little, Brown, 1981.
Rules of Sleep (poetry). New York: Atheneum, 1984.
New Selected Poems. New York: Atheneum, 1985.
Minor Monuments (criticism). New York: Atheneum, 1986.

Works about Howard Moss

Bawer, Bruce. "The Passing of an Elegist." *The New Criterion* 6.3 (November 1987): 35–37.
Bloom, Harold. Rev. of *Buried City*. *The New Republic* (29 November 1975): 25.
Brown, Ashley. Rev. of *New Selected Poems*. *World Literature Today* 60.1 (Winter 1986): 108–109.
Gioia, Dana. "The Difficult Case of Howard Moss." *The Antioch Review* 45.1 (Winter 1987): 98–109.
Gunn, Thom. *The Yale Review* (September 1960): 38–41.
Hollander, John. Rev. of *Selected Poems*. *Harper's Magazine* (July 1971): 72–76.
"Howard Moss." *The New Yorker* 63.33 (October 5, 1987): 126–128.

Howard, Richard. *Howard Moss, Alone with America: Essays on the Art of Poetry in the United States since 1950.* Enlarged New York: Atheneum, 1980, 450–465.

————. Rev. of *Buried City. The Georgia Review* (Spring 1976): 205–208.

Justice, Donald. Rev. of *A Swimmer in the Air. Poetry* (October 1957): 76–78.

Lally, Michael. "A Gathering of Moss." *Washington Post Book World* (August 24, 1975): 4.

Leiter, Robert. "Howard Moss: An Interview." *American Poetry Review* 13.5 (September/October 1984): 27–31.

Lieberman, Laurence. Rev. of *Selected Poems. The Yale Review* (Autumn 1971): 23–27.

Nemerov, Howard. Rev. of *The Toy Fair. The Atlantic Monthly* (September 1954): 51–53.

Pettingell, Phoebe. "Through Memory and Miniatures." *The New Leader* 67.15 (August 20, 1984): 17–18.

Rev. of *Selected Poems. Virginia Quarterly Review* 47.4 (Autumn 1971): 67–70.

Smith, Dave. "Castles, Elephants, Buddhas: Some Recent American Poetry." *American Poetry Review* 10.3 (May/June 1981): 37–42.

Stitt, Peter. "Poets Witty and Elegiac." *New York Times Book Review* (September 1, 1985): 11.

Vendler, Helen. Rev. of *Buried City. New York Times Book Review.* (April 18, 1976): 23.

White, Edmund. "Midas' Touch." *Poetry* (March 1974): 350–353.

HOWARD NEMEROV   (1920–1991)

Miriam Marty Clark

BIOGRAPHY

Howard Nemerov was born on February 29, 1920, in New York City. Nemerov's paternal grandparents, Meyer and Fanny Nemerov, were Orthodox Jews who had emigrated from Kiev in the early 1890s and ran a struggling grocery store on Manhattan's Lower East Side. His maternal grandfather, Frank Russek, was a Polish immigrant who became a successful bookie and later a prosperous Fifth Avenue furrier. Howard's father, David Nemerov, began as a window dresser and a tailor at Russek's; within a few years he had married Russek's daughter Gertrude and overseen the expansion of Russek's into an elegant department store, which he ran with energy and flair through the depression and into the late 1950s. As an adult, Howard Nemerov found both amusement and anxiety in comparing his own mysterious and relatively unprofitable literary career to his father's business pursuits.

The Nemerov children grew up in affluent surroundings, in Park Avenue and Central Park West apartments populated by nannies, cooks, and chauffeurs. The most comprehensive and detailed account to date of this part of Nemerov's life is provided by Patricia Bosworth in her biography of the poet's younger sister, the photographer Diane Arbus. Although their parents were generally distant and preoccupied, Bosworth observes, there was a strong bond between Howard and Diane, both of them gifted, artistic, and intense children. Bosworth mentions young Howard's athleticism and good looks as well as his lofty aspirations— to be a tenor or a psychoanalyst. Nemerov was also a reader, she notes, "of bird books, flower books, tree books, star books" and eventually of Freud's writings. These particular interests, along with the habits of naming and knowing, persist even many years later in Nemerov's poems.

Nemerov attended Harvard University, where he wrote a prizewinning essay on Thomas Mann and began to publish short stories in the *Harvard Advocate*. During this time he also read the modern poets—T. S. Eliot, William Carlos Williams, Ezra Pound, Archibald MacLeish—who would powerfully influence his early work. Following his graduation from Harvard in 1941, he became a fighter pilot in the Royal Canadian Air Force and later in the U.S. Eighth Army Air Force. These experiences, too, would have a bearing on his poems, especially in the early volumes. During his military years he continued to read widely, making his way through periods of deep depression by reading Nabokov, Proust, and other great moderns. In 1944, during his Royal Air Force (RAF) service, he married Margaret Russell, an Englishwoman. They were married for forty-seven years and had three sons.

Shortly after the war, Nemerov accepted a position teaching returning veterans at Hamilton College in New York. In 1948 he moved to Bennington College in Vermont, where he remained for nearly twenty years. After a brief appointment at Brandeis University, he joined the English faculty of Washington University in St. Louis, where he taught from 1969 until his death in 1991. An unsparing critic and a demanding teacher, Nemerov became legendary among his students for his gruff style, his prickly dedication to the art of poetry, and his willingness to let grudging admiration turn into generous encouragement of gifted younger writers.

MAJOR WORKS AND THEMES

Between 1948 and 1991, Nemerov published twenty-six books. The most significant of these are his thirteen volumes of poetry: *The Image and the Law* (1947), *Guide to the Ruins* (1950), *The Salt Garden* (1953), *Mirrors and Windows* (1958), *New and Selected Poems* (1960), *The Next Room of the Dream* (1962), *The Blue Swallows* (1967), *Gnomes and Other Occasions* (1973), *The Western Approaches* (1975), *Collected Poems* (1977), *Sentences* (1980), *Inside the Onion* (1984), and *War Stories* (1987).

Early in his career he also wrote fiction, largely as a way to see himself through dry spells between volumes of poetry. He published three novels: *The Melodramatists* (1949), *Federigo, or the Power of Love* (1954), and *The Homecoming Game* (1957). In 1960 *The Homecoming Game* was made into a film, *Tall Story*, which was moderately successful and provided Nemerov with a steady income in royalties. In addition he published two collections of short fiction: *A Commodity of Dreams* (1959) and *Stories, Fables, and Other Diversions* (1971). In all of his fiction, Nemerov explores difficult, unclear boundaries: between dream and myth and reality, between good and evil, strangeness and familiarity, timelessness and the present moment.

Nemerov also wrote essays and criticism. His nonfiction prose is collected in *Poetry and Fiction* (1963), *Reflexions on Poetry and Poetics* (1972), *Figures of Thought* (1978), *New and Selected Essays* (1985), and *The Oak in the Acorn*, a series of lectures on Proust (1987). In the essays, which are Nemerov's best form after his verse, he ranges broadly, writing extensively and acutely about poets and poetry but also taking up science, nature, politics, psychology, music, and art. He uses the essay form to venture explanations and metaphors, to inquire acerbically or courageously into the human condition.

During his lifetime Nemerov garnered many prizes and honors. He won the Blumenthal Prize from *Poetry* magazine (1958), the Theodore Roethke Memorial Prize (1967), the National Book Award and the Pulitzer Prize (both for *The Collected Poems*); he also won the Bollingen Prize for Poetry, a Guggenheim Fellowship, and the first Aiken Taylor Award for Modern American Poetry. In 1963 he was consultant in poetry to the Library of Congress, and in 1988 he returned to Washington for a two-year appointment as poet laureate of the United States. At the time of his death he was Edward Mallinkrodt Distinguished University Professor of English at Washington University.

Such honors reflect but do not fully encompass his contributions to American literature—particularly to American poetry—in the second half of the twentieth century. Situated between the high modern poets of the 1920s and 1930s and the uncertainties of the late century, Nemerov's verse is reasoned and lucid, often complex and sometimes difficult but never willfully obscure. He approaches objects and ideas with deceptive modesty, his powers of mind disclosed in graceful, formal stanzas or comic, pithy epigrams. His subjects include the everyday suburban world of storm windows, telephones, and seaside vacations, but he also writes with uncommon clarity and intelligence about the mysteries of the world and of human thought, the "inward of the mind," as he calls it in one poem.

About his Jewishness Nemerov was generally wry. He was raised in a secular household, only rarely going to temple or visiting his Orthodox paternal grandparents. At Harvard, where Jewishness was less a matter to be taken for granted than it had been at home, Nemerov briefly contemplated a conversion to Catholicism. Eventually, he came to see the influence of high church modernists Eliot and Auden in this, as he saw it in his early poems. Late in his life he described himself sardonically as "an old Jew whose only religion is the joke." All the same, Nemerov's Jewishness plays a vital role in his work, particularly his poetry.

In the first place, it affords him an ironic stance toward some aspects of American culture. As a Jew he can be a skeptic about civic pieties (in "Amnesty," "On an Occasion of National Mourning," and many of his short, comic poems); he can count himself a bemused outsider to mainstream suburban religiosity of the kind he satirizes in "Boom!" where 1950s families trek to church in the same way they trek to the beach and the filling station. Nemerov is also a satirical observer of the American way of Christmas in poems such as "Eve," "Christmas Morning," "The Night before Christmas," and "Santa Claus." "Somewhere on his travels," the latter poem begins,

> the strange Child
> picked up with this overstuffed confidence man,

Affection's inverted thief, who climbs at night
Down chimneys, into dreams, with this world's goods.
He teaches the innocent to want, thus keeps
Our fat world rolling. (*Collected Poems of Howard Nemerov* 238)

At the same time, his use of "we" and "our" in these poems is an acknowledgment that he, too, takes some part in American culture, its platitudes and peculiar practices.

Despite his skepticism about religion and religious practice, however, Nemerov finds the Hebrew Scriptures a rich source of images and narratives. His verse dramas "Endor" and "Cain" and dramatic poems like "Moses," "Nebuchadnezzar, Solus," and "Lot's Wife" give an interior—and a modernist—dimension to Bible stories. In shorter lyrics the Scriptures frequently provide a way of talking about the human predicament; this is true in "On a Text: Jonah IV, xi," "The View from Pisgah," "The First Day," "Small Moment," "A Song of Degrees," "To the Babylonians," and many others. These considerations may be comic, as they are in the Nebuchadnezzar poem, which begins,

Seven years I had to think it over;
Or not to think, I couldn't, but to yield.
Seven years on all fours and in clover,
Taking a nosedown closeup of the field. (*Collected Poems* 458)

Later, after the king's rehabilitation and "submission to the Will" he sometimes wishes "[t]o be my animal again and still." Nemerov ends by noting and defying Nebuchadnezzar's edict: "I forbid all men from making ballads / About my seven years spent browsing salads" (*Collected Poems* 458).

They can also be quite serious, as when in "The Icehouse in Summer" Nemerov turns to Amos' terrifying prophecy for Israel at the end of a dark meditation on class and wealth. A boy visiting a luxurious "great house" in summer is shown the icehouse, its walls "great blocks of ice" cut and hauled in winter for "the summer's keeping." A servant tells him of a team and driver drowned while crossing the frozen lake during a spring thaw and adds, darkly, that "the man's cry melting from the ice that summer/frightened the sherbet-eaters off the terrace" (*Collected Poems* 232). This story converges in the boy's mind with Bible stories and prophecies:

Dust of the cedar, lost and evergreen
among the slowly blunting water walls
where the blade edge melted and the steel saw's bit
was rounded out, and the horse and rider drowned
on the red sea's blood, I was the silly child
who dreamed that riderless cry, and saw the guests
run from a ghostly wall, so long before

the winter house fell with the summer house,
and the houses, Egypt, the great houses, had an end. (*Collected Poems* 233)

This fusion of personal experience and social commentary with a source narrative—biblical, mythological, literary—is a common strategy in Nemerov's
work and reflects his sense of the vitality of texts and traditions in the present
moment.

If the Hebrew Scriptures provide subjects and strategies for some of Nemerov's poems, however, the *law* as an idea is crucially important from his first
volume to his last. The law—which begins in Judaic law but extends to natural,
mathematical, and scientific law—is everywhere in tension with what Nemerov
calls *the image*. By *law* he refers to first principle, final cause, originating Word,
governing truth, abiding form. "To lay the logarithmic spiral," he writes in
"Figures of Thought,"

> on
> Sea-shell and leaf alike, and see it fit,
> To watch the same idea work itself out
> In the fighter pilot's steepening, tightening turn
> Onto his target, setting up the kill
> And in the flight of certain wall-eyed bugs
> Who cannot see to fly straight into death (*Collected Poems* 472)

The *image*, on the other hand, is the particular, the unruly, the unpredictable,
even the chaotic. The world of images is a "storm of photons," "blind and
blinding myriads" of snowflakes, the "chaotic scrawl of upper branches."

For Nemerov, the tension between the image and the law is most vividly
expressed in the natural world of leaf and shell and in the thought of those
invisible worlds of cell and photon that underlie them. But the image and the
law are also the subjects of his most profound meditations on the perceiving,
creating mind. In these poems the Genesis story of creation—the formless void
into the world of things and beings—figures crucially as mystery and metaphor.
In "The First Day," for instance, he reflects on the division of darkness from
the light, using the movies as his metaphor. "That was the first day," he concludes,

> and in that day
> Of pure distinction, movies were without color, without sound.
> Much later, words began to issue from the silence, and
> The single light broke into spectral iridescence;
> Meanwhile, in black and white and meddling into gray
> Results, the Fall already is recorded on the film. (*Collected Poems* 345)

In "The Painter Dreaming in the Scholar's House," he considers the painter's
mind using the language of genesis and Genesis. He ponders how from the

"Dark silence of the Absolutely Not, / Material worlds arise" (*Collected Poems* 434). Then, turning again and again to the myth of Creation, he summons his own vision of how the painter's eye sees the world: the chaotic energies of the Void, the emergence and elaboration of forms, the proliferation of images. The painter, he notes, thinking of modernist painters Paul Klee and Paul Terence Feeley, sees

> a single energy
> Momently manifest in every form,
> As in the tree the growing of the tree
> Exploding from the seed not more nor less
> Than from the void, condensing down and in,
> Summoning sun and rain. He views the tree,
> The great tree standing in the garden, say (*Collected Poems* 433–34)

There is an implicit paradox here in that the law that (as word and Word) speaks the world into existence also enjoins the making of images. But Nemerov's painter is no mere engraver of images, no clever copyist. Although he lives in the visible world—of "mountain, flower, cloud, and tree"—his work is to render visible the "secret history of the mind" (432). He "makes his world," Nemerov writes, "Not imitates the one before his eyes."

> He is the painter of the human mind
> Finding and faithfully reflecting the mindfulness
> That is in things, and not the things themselves. (*Collected Poems* 433)

Thus, the painter is godlike in the moment of creation, reckoning the energies and potentialities of the void into pure forms, silence into speech, darkness into worlds.

"The Painter Dreaming in the Scholar's House" is among the most difficult and beautiful lyric poems of the twentieth century. In it a set of essentially modernist concerns—the nature of art and of representation, the experience of the artist, the inward life of the mind—are articulated with a Judaic sense of the world. Nemerov's Jewishness, often approached with levity in the poems, is here a point of elegant gravity.

CRITICAL RECEPTION

"For good or for ill," Nemerov once remarked, "no one seems to have much to say *about* what I write." There is some validity in Nemerov's complaint; even now the body of Nemerov criticism is quite small in proportion to his writing. Nevertheless, Nemerov has been the subject both of insightful reviews by his contemporaries and of more thorough consideration by a handful of academic critics and literary scholars. None of these have addressed in a sustained way Nemerov's Jewish themes and perspectives.

Reviewers of Nemerov's early volumes of poetry found him promising, even occasionally brilliant but complained that he was too ironic, too mannered, and too much in thrall to his modernist predecessors Eliot, Auden, and Stevens. Randall Jarrell found *The Image and the Law* (1947) and *Guide to the Ruins* (1950) "tight, dry, and uneasy," always in pursuit of a subject and a final irony (Duncan 81–82); I. L. Salomon complained that the second book exploits "not the excellences but the defects of his masters" and that it "lacks originality and discipline" (Duncan 76). Although Nemerov's work continued to receive mixed reviews, there was strong critical consensus that his middle volumes represented important growth and development. Jarrell characterized *The Salt Garden* (1953) as the work of "a late-blooming, youthful-seeming poet from whom one can expect, soon, poems even better" (Duncan 84). Reed Whittemore noted the emergence of Nemerov as nature poet in *Mirrors and Windows* (1958) and describes him as "mellower, humbler, wiser—like one of Shakespeare's good dukes, though without a country to govern" (Duncan 90). Reviewers of the later volumes are reliably (and perhaps purposefully) goaded by Nemerov's little poems and wicked ironies; at the same time they praise his powers of description, his apt metaphors and surprising turns, his fluent formality, his mastery of a variety of tones and techniques. Wyatt Prunty admires his "dark reserve" and his "powerful sense of compassion grounded in and resultant from his austere vision of the world" (265, 270). In his obituary for Nemerov, Willard Spiegelman remarks on Nemerov's Horatian sense of balance and moderation, his learnedness, his modest, but assured, way of being in the world (76–80).

Nemerov's essays met with enthusiasm from reviewers who had already come to admire his poems. Louis Rubin found the essays in *Poetry and Fiction* "marked by good sense, an unswerving belief in the necessity for close reading, a conviction of ultimate worth of imaginative literature, and the unity that comes from the internal consistency of a good mind" (Duncan 127). R. W. Flint, reviewing *Reflexions on Poetry* and *Poetics*, finds in Nemerov a "straightness of eye and obliquity of mind" (30) as well as "admirable high spirits" (31) and the capacity for "scintillating analysis" (34). Nemerov's fiction, while it received some favorable notices and provided a measure of financial security, was treated as a less significant contribution than the poetry or the essays.

Nemerov's poems are now widely anthologized and widely taught. Among academic critics, however, he has received relatively little attention; there are at present only a handful of scholarly books devoted to his writing. Mary Kinzie's 1977 essay for *Parnassus* offers perhaps the best assessment of Nemerov's career and the most illuminating analysis of his themes and influences.

BIBLIOGRAPHY

Works by Howard Nemerov

Collected Works

A Howard Nemerov Reader. Columbia: University of Missouri Press, 1991.
The Collected Poems of Howard Nemerov. Chicago: University of Chicago Press, 1977.

Poems

The Image and the Law. New York: Henry Holt, 1947.
Guide to the Ruins. New York: Random House, 1950.
The Salt Garden. Boston: Little, Brown, 1953.
Mirrors and Windows. Chicago: University of Chicago Press, 1958.
New and Selected Poems. Chicago: University of Chicago Press, 1960.
The Next Room of the Dream. Chicago: University of Chicago Press, 1962.
The Blue Swallows. Chicago: University of Chicago Press, 1967.
Gnomes and Other Occasions. Chicago: University of Chicago Press, 1973.
The Western Approaches. Chicago: University of Chicago Press, 1975.
Sentences. Chicago: University of Chicago Press, 1980.
Inside the Onion. Chicago: University of Chicago Press, 1984.
War Stories. Chicago: University of Chicago Press, 1987.

Novels

The Melodramatists. New York: Random House, 1949.
Federigo, or The Power of Love. Boston: Little, Brown, 1954.
The Homecoming Game. New York: Simon and Schuster, 1957.

Short Stories

A Commodity of Dreams and Other Stories. New York: Simon and Schuster, 1959.
Stories, Fables, and Other Diversions. Boston: Godine, 1971.

Essays

Poetry and Fiction: Essays. New Brunswick, NJ: Rutgers University Press, 1963.
Reflexions on Poetry and Poetics. New Brunswick, NJ: Rutgers University Press, 1972.
Figures of Thought. Boston: Godine, 1978.
New and Selected Essays. Carbondale: Southern Illinois University Press, 1985.

Literary Criticism

The Oak in the Acorn. Baton Rouge: Louisiana State University Press, 1987.

Works about Howard Nemerov

Batholomay, Julia. *The Shield of Perseus: The Vision and Imagination of Howard Nemerov*. Gainesville, FL: University of Gainesville Press, 1972.
Bowers, Neal. "An Interview with Howard Nemerov." *Massachusetts Review* 22.1
   (1981): 43–57.

Burris, Sidney. "A Sort of Memoir, a Sort of Review." *Southern Review* 28 (1992): 185–201.

Clark, Miriam Marty. " 'Between the Wave and Particle': Figuring Science in Howard Nemerov's Poems." *Mosaic* 23.4 (1990): 37–50.

Duncan, Bowie, ed. *The Critical Reception of Howard Nemerov: A Selection of Essays and a Bibliography.* Metuchen, NJ: Scarecrow Press, 1971.

Flint, R. W. "Holding Patterns." *Parnassus: Poetry-in-Review* 3.2 (1975): 27–34.

Holinger, Richard. "Impressions of Nemerov." *Southern Review* 23.1 (1987): 5–24.

Kiehl, James M. "The Poems of Howard Nemerov: Where Loveliness Adorns Intelligible Things." *Salmagundi* 22–23 (1973): 234–57.

Kinzie, Mary. "The Signature of Things: On Howard Nemerov." *Parnassus* 6.1 (1977): 1–57.

Labrie, Ross. *Howard Nemerov.* Boston: Twayne, 1980.

———"Howard Nemerov in St. Louis: An Interview." *Southern Review* 15 (1979): 605–16.

Meinke, Peter. *Howard Nemerov.* Minneapolis: University of Minnesota Press, 1968.

Mills, William. *The Stillness in Moving Things: The World of Howard Nemerov.* Memphis: Memphis State University Press, 1975.

Nemerov, Alexander. "Modelling My Father." *American Scholar* 62.4 (1993): 551–61.

Potts, Donna. *Howard Nemerov and Objective Idealism.* Columbia: University of Missouri Press, 1994.

Prunty, Wyatt. "Permanence in Process: Poetic Limits That Delimit." *Southern Review* 15 (1978): 265–70.

Spiegelman, Willard. "Alphabeting the Void: Poetic Diction and Poetic Classicism." *Salmagundi* 42 (1978): 132–45.

———. "In Memoriam: Howard Nemerov, 1920–1991." *New Criterion* (December 1992): 76–80.

GEORGE OPPEN   (1908–1984)

Kenneth Sherwood

BIOGRAPHY

Born in New Rochelle, New York, George A. Oppen was raised in San Francisco. He entered college in Oregon in 1926 and there, in a poetry class, met his future wife, Mary Colby. During the late 1920s, the Oppens lived for a time in Dallas, Texas, and eventually migrated east to New York City; the Oppens made the last leg of this journey, from Detroit, in a small sailboat across the Great Lakes and through the Erie Canal. The poet Louis Zukofksy, a crucial friend and early New York influence, soon published Oppen's early poems in the special objectivist issue of *Poetry* (February 1931). Between 1930 and 1933, the young Oppens relocated to rural France, from where, with Zukofsky's help in New York, To Publishers issued work by Ezra Pound and William Carlos Williams, as well as *An "Objectivists" Anthology*. At the same time, Oppen was composing many of the poems subsequently to appear in his important and self-published first volume of poetry, *Discrete Series*.

Upon returning to New York in 1934, the Oppens became involved in leftist politics and labor organizing there and later in Detroit. By all accounts, Oppen abstained from writing poetry during this period in favor of direct political action. After he served in World War II, the Oppens settled briefly in California, where intrusive government investigations into their political past forced them into exile in Mexico City. They did not return to the United States until 1958, whereupon George resumed writing poetry. Between 1962 and 1978, seven well-received volumes appeared, including *Of Being Numerous*, which was awarded the Pulitzer Prize in 1969. Always travelers, George and Mary Oppen made their first and only trip to Israel in 1975.

MAJOR WORKS AND THEMES

George Oppen emerged in the 1930s with the objectivist poets, whose sharp-edged, optical poetry aimed to use "the image as a test of sincerity" ("Three Oppen Letters with a Note" 83). According to Oppen, "objectivist" poetry was a response to the imagists' "liquidation of poetry into . . . sentimentalism," but the term itself was coined by Louis Zukofksy in the pages of the historic February 1931 issue of *Poetry*, which included Oppen's first two published poems (83). Zukofksy initiated Oppen into the antisymbolist poetics of clarity that he was then developing, teaching the younger poet the "necessity for forming a poem properly, for achieving form" (Dembo).

Zukofksy was interested in a writing "which is the detail, not the mirage, of seeing, of thinking with the things as they exist, and of directing them along a line of melody" (Zukofksy 273). The idea that poetry could be made from details, from particular things as they existed, would fit well with Oppen's own determined pattern of travel and exploration. Oppen himself insisted that one needed to achieve the form of a poem, clearly echoing Zukofsky's more famous qualification of the objectivist poem as that which valued "sincerity as craft" (Zukofksy 284). Of the seminal and initially intense relationship between Zukofsky and Oppen, Mary Oppen later acknowledged that "George has said many times, 'I can never repay my debt to Zukofksy, he taught me everything' " (Mary Oppen 91).

Oppen was by this time working on the poems that would appear in *Discrete Series* (1934), to be published by the Objectivist Press, successor of To Publishers. Oppen explained that the volume's title refers to "a series of terms each of which is empirically derived, each of which is empirically true. And this is the reason for the fragmentary character of those poems" (Dembo). This slim, sometimes overlooked volume is, in many, ways a surer fulfillment of objectivist notions than any single volume by Zukosfky or the other objectivist poets.

Oppen's craft, his attention to the poem as "achieved form" and "empirical statement," is dramatically evident in this first volume. The terse poems are shaped to accord with the sharpness of individual perceptions, through compressed lines and syntactic fragmentation. As the book's title promises, the poems are derived from empirical observation, which for Oppen meant that they are sincerely seen.

> White. From the
> Under arm of T
>
> The red globe.
>
> Up
> Down. Round

Shiny fixed
Alternatives

From the quiet

Stone floor (*Collected Poems of George Oppen* 3)

Punctuated as if it were itself a complete statement, ''White.'' suggests something of the radical poetics of Oppen's project. Once the reader arrives at the image here depicted—the stylish indicator of an art deco elevator—its initial obscurity vanishes. Left are the dynamized particulars that compose the poem—''Up / Down. Round''—and that become metonyms for the whole skyscraper, details, as Zukofsky was quick to recognize, seen from the inside.

The careful placement of poems, one to a page (in the original edition of *Discrete Series* but not the *Collected Poems* reprinting) highlights Oppen's formally innovative seriality. Each poem can be read as a discrete entity or as linked to the others and composing a single, book-length serial poem. This fragmented structuring gains its effect by translating to the page something like the perceptual experience of emerging randomly from subway stations. Each neighborhood, each station, each poem is itself discrete—yet ineluctably connected to the others by the structure of the system. On the page facing the proceeding poem, the following poem, dealing also with the mechanical and social, is visually, numerically, and thematically paired:

2
Thus
Hides the

Parts—the prudery
Of Frigidaire, of
Soda-jerking———

Thus

Above the

Plane of lunch, of wives
Removes itself
. . . .
big-Business (*Collected Poems* 4)

The objects seen are not simply described for their own sake; still less are they evoked as symbols (e.g., the ''stone floor'' echoing economic crash). Rather, the buildings of ''big-Business'' literally sit atop the ordinary activity of a street-level soda shop. In ''objectivist'' fashion, the poem seizes upon the actual, observable relation between objects rather than spinning a metaphoric one.

Most often, when people figure into these poems, they are shown in relation to a general, mechanized condition. Even a poem like the notably erotic "Near your eyes" thinks in these terms:

> . . . .
> We slide in separate hard grooves
> Bowstrings to bent loins,
>   Self moving (*Collected Poems* 11)

Written partly upon the Oppens' return to New York City after the 1929 crash of the stock market, these early poems begin only obliquely to register the painful historic conditions of that moment.

> Bad times:
> The cars pass
> By the elevated posts
> And the movie sign.
> A man sells post-cards. (*Collected Poems* 13)

Mary Oppen describes the tremendous shock the Oppens experienced on returning to New York as though they "were in a nightmare, [their] fathers impoverished" (*Meaning* 144). The catastrophe of the depression for them was the way it impoverished "grown men, respectable men"—a spiritual as much as a financial crisis. Encountering a changed world, Oppen's poetry had as yet no real way to engage it socially; and yet he felt compelled to engage it.

Shortly after the publication of *Discrete Series*, both the Oppens became politically involved, joining the Communist Party and becoming organizers for the Workers Alliance in Brooklyn in 1935. The turn toward political activism, though it seems sudden in hindsight, was in fact, gradual. When they first met Ezra Pound in Rapallo, Italy, they were dismayed to find that the man whose poetry they so admired and had published referred to Mussolini, almost fondly, as "the boss." They were struck not only by Pound's emerging fascism but that he was apparently unaware of the word's negative connotations, of the antipathy between Americans and their bosses. When Pound took them to the beach, pointed to the wrong direction, and announced, "from here came the Greek ships," he dramatized the danger of disconnection from the actual world, something Oppen could accept neither as navigator nor as poet.

For Oppen, not just poetry but one's mode of living was, in Zukofsky's words, bound "inextricably [to] the direction of historic and contemporary particulars" (Zukofsky 268). It would be twenty-eight years before Oppen's next book. "There are situations that cannot honorably be met by art," he wrote, offering partial explanation (Oppen, "The Mind's Own Place" 136). Although future poems would draw on this experience, Oppen had given up writing to work as a labor activist for a time. "The break in the poetry," he later explained, "was a political break. But I think it would have come anyway.... And it's necessary to explain that the Depression, it was not something in the newspapers. There were actually hungry people in the street under one's window. . . . You either did something or you didn't do something'' (''Three Oppen Letters with a Note'' 23).

In 1962, George Oppen's second volume, *The Materials*, was published. Written beginning just prior to his return to the United States in 1958, it marks an expansion of the poem's domain, from the objective world to an inclusion of the social. The book's epigraph suggests as much—''We awake in the same moment to ourselves and to things. Maritain.'' Where the poet of *Discrete Series* was awake to things, he had not been able to assimilate the self or the selves of those many others in an always political world, into his poems.

The former ''objectivist'' commitment to the contemporary particular came to include the political and social. The poems of the second period are less ''discrete,'' the syntax less fragmented, but the concerns and craft are clear extensions of the earlier poetry, however modified by the experiences of the intervening years. As if acknowledging the insufficiency of a strict objectivism, Oppen writes, ''The image of the engine // That stops./We cannot live on that'' (''Image of the Engine,'' *Collected Poems* 19).

Beginning to write again ''in time of the breaking of nations,'' Oppen engages the crises of the age, alienation and ethical responsibility toward the other— ''And we have become the present. . . . But we abandon one another'' (''Leviathan,'' *Collected Poems* 68). Amid this alienation, Oppen also locates a necessary, sometimes burdensome connectedness among people—''Their weight is part of mine'' (*Collected Poems* 36). Matured through poverty, war, and exile, the poems of this volume insist on the ethical necessity of recognizing a shared, if shipwrecked, humanity.

Alone to ocean

Save we are
A crowd, a population, those
Born, those not yet dead, the moment's
Populace (*Collected Poems* 22)

The early commitment to sincerity—which for Oppen meant an antirhetorical poetry of discovery—made it impossible for him to write straightforward political poetry during his activist years. Even afterward, these events continued to block any easy return to ''pure'' poetry. ''And the world changed. / There had been trees and people,'' he writes of the war in ''Survival: Infantry'' (*Collected Poems* 60). The task for poetry would not be light, but there was a demand to make words work somehow: ''We were ashamed of our half life and our misery: we saw that everything had died./ And the letters came. People who addressed us thru our lives/ They left us gasping'' (*Collected Poems* 60). For Oppen, the tragic facts of history make poetry even more essential. As he would later write of this paradox, "There are words that mean nothing/ But there is something to mean" ("The Building of the Skyscraper," *Collected Poems* 131).

Balancing what might count as a tone of despair in this first postexile volume, brief moments of hope are offered, often derived from the appreciation of beauty. Oppen writes, for instance, to his wife, Mary, "After these years/ I write again/ Naturally, about your face" ("O Western Wind," *Collected Poems* 53); and in another poem, "In some black brick/ Tenement, a woman's body// Glows," which is "The City's/ Secret warmth" ("The Source," *Collected Poems* 55). The encounter of humans with disastrous shipwrecks of various sorts would be continuous themes—

> From disaster
>
> Shipwreck, whole families crawled
> To the tenements, and there
> survived by what morality
> Of hope (*Collected Poems* 29)

—standing in for particulars like the Holocaust, Vietnam War, poverty of the Great Depression, racial oppression.

In contrast to the directness of fellow objectivist Charles Reznikoff, who shapes the testimony of victims into poems, Oppen refuses to name the Holocaust. In many poems he chooses, instead, to gesture toward it while respecting the unrepresentability of such losses. In *This in Which* (1965), "The fact is/ It is not his world," Oppen writes of a nameless man:

> He thinks of murders and torture
> In the German cellars
> And the resistance of heroes
>
> Picturing the concrete walls. (*Collected Poems* 108)

Without clarifying whether this man is a survivor or war veteran, he conveys the sense that it is our situation to have lived out "a ruined ethic" whose "myths/ Have been murderous" (*Collected Poems* 76).

A separateness from family, class, and culture had been Oppen's since he first set out to write. The experiences of organizing, the war, and forced exile crystallize the issue, forging lived conditions into poetic themes. Despite alienation, he and we share a common fate: "We are pressed, pressed on each other/ . . . . / Crusoe// We say was/ 'Rescued.'/ So we have chosen" ("Of Being Numerous," *Collected Poems* 150). That is, we have already chosen the mutual responsibilities of civilization and nation over shipwreck.

In the title of his third book, *Of Being Numerous* (1968), Oppen recognizes the paradox of the individual and poet—that one can be neither among nor apart from people. *Being numerous* is the condition of being simultaneously alienated from, and linked with, others, most evident in urban living. In addressing the city, Oppen proposes an ethic of mutual responsibility based on the simple recognition of those around us. "We encounter them. Actually/ A populace flows/ Thru the city.// This is a language, therefore, of New York" "Of Being Numerous," *Collected Poems* 149).

Developed from a shorter sequence in the prior volume, "The Language of New York," the thirty-page "Of Being Numerous" is generally regarded as Oppen's most important engagement with the self in society. "There are things/ We live among 'and to see them/ Is to know ourselves.'// Occurrence, a part/ Of an infinite series" (*Collected Poems* 147).

This same sense of compelled responsibility surfaces in Oppen's reflections on the war: "I cannot even now/ Altogether disengage myself/ From those men/ / With whom I stood in emplacements. . . . /. . . . How forget that? How talk// Distantly of 'The People' " ("Of Being Numerous," *Collected Poems* 157). The distancing effect of a phrase like "The People" dissatisfies Oppen because he believes that, however bewildered we are "By the shipwreck/ Of the singular," our fate is to "have chosen the meaning/ Of being numerous" ("Of Being Numerous," *Collected Poems* 151).

Consistent with the secular, humanist quality of a concept like "numerousness," Oppen's apparent identification with his own Jewishness in writing was faint. Instead, evocations of shipwreck or an unbelonging singularity, from which he broke only in isolated lines, dominate the poetry. "Semite: to find a way for myself," he writes, tentatively associating the exile and searching of his own life history with a generalized Jewish condition ("Historic Pun," *Collected Poems* 181). A characteristically Jewish dimension to Oppen's work is difficult to isolate. In a 1978 letter, Oppen wrote: " 'Jew' means: those to whom these things happen." Following his own broad definition, a Jewish dimension to his themes of despair or disaster can be discerned.

> Imagine a man in the ditch,
> The wheels of the overturned wreck
> Still spinning—
>
> I don't mean he despairs, I mean if he does not
> He sees in the manner of poetry. ("Route," *Collected Poems* 191)

Persisting from the early *Discrete Series*, seeing "in the manner of poetry" has more clearly become seeing-as-a-way-of-being, transforming literal into spiritual disaster.

The eye is now capable of turning from the particular and individual to a historic scale: "Ours aren't the only madmen tho they have burned thousands / of men and women alive, perhaps no madder than most" ("Route," *Collected Poems* 196). With a title that puns on "sea," "see," and "eye," Oppen's

Seascape: Needles Eye (1973) echoes Oppen's own encounter with moral disaster:

> No man but the fragments of metal
> Burying my dogtag with H
> For Hebrew in the rubble of Alsace ("Of Hours," *Collected Poems* 211)

Wounded by shrapnel in the war, Oppen divests himself of his Hebrew "H" as a sign for the destruction of the Holocaust. Yet the gesture suggests Oppen's sense of the danger of identifying oneself with a narrow or, particularly, nationalist *communitas*.

Fusing the political, moral, and aesthetic, Oppen looks back on his own life and work, historical events, and his predecessors' work; he associates the overreaching cultural ambition of modernist poetry with the error of authoritarian politics. In the section of new poems first published in the 1975 American edition of *Collected Poems*, "Myth of the Blaze (1972–1975)," Oppen suggests, presumably with the example of Ezra Pound in mind, that the effort to impose coherence risks insincerity. "The Speech at Soli" concludes:

> mad kings
>
> gone raving
>
> war in incoherent
> sunlight it will not
>
> cohere it will NOT that
> other
>
> desertion
> of the total (*Collected Poems* 235)

At best a provisional coherence applies to the aesthetic object as well as to the self and the community, always threatening to return to fragments. Despite the promise of the title in the poem "Semite," Oppen writes of an identity that will not cohere, a self of negation: "sung to all distances// my distances neither Roman// nor barbarian the sky the low sky." Desertion and distance cannot be overcome, because one only has to "think also of the children/ the guards laughing" (*Collected Poems* 266–67).

Appearing after his *Collected Poems* and, Oppen's final book, *Primitive* (1978), takes its title from an earlier poem and draws its contents from various books. Though still not prominent, a concern with Jewish identity grows relatively more apparent in Oppen's late work, culminating in this last volume. While Oppen received no formal religious instruction as a child, he visited Israel with Mary in 1975. Isolated lines like these suggest he was not altogether content to accept his own distance: "to whom and// to what are we ancestral" "Dis-

asters'' 11. Oppen's daughter, Linda Oppen Mourealatos, has described his Jewishness as being self-chosen. Perhaps he felt, as his contemporary Edmond Jabès
put it, that "being Jewish means exiling yourself in the word and, at the same
time, weeping for your exile."

In "Populist," Oppen writes of bridging distance—"I dreamed myself of
their people, I am of their people,/ I thought they watched me that I watched
them" (20)—as if to answer the question earlier posed in *Of Being Numerous*:
"How talk// Distantly of 'The People.' '' Such a resolution of the crises of
"being numerous," of Jewishness, and of distances is also implied in the late
poem "If It All Went Up in Smoke," which concludes:

> help me I am
> of what people the grass
>
> blades touch
>
> and touch in their small
>
> distances the poem
> begins (*Primitive*, 18)

Beginning in pursuit of a modernist aesthetic, turning to politics, and enduring
forced exile, Oppen's poetry, if not Oppen the man, comes to rest with this
resolve.

CRITICAL RECEPTION

In the Preface to Oppen's self-published first book, *Discrete Series* (1934),
Ezra Pound recognized Oppen's artisanal ethic, concluding famously: "I salute
a serious craftsman, a sensibility which is not every man's sensibility and which
has not been got out of any other man's books." Thirty-five years later, Oppen's
craft was recognized with a Pulitzer Prize for *Of Being Numerous*.

Critical appreciation of Oppen's work has reflected his sporadic publishing
history. The limited edition *Discrete Series* was republished after some thirty
years, meaning that Oppen's most important objectivist poems would be thoroughly assessed only by later generations of critics and poets. Critic Marjorie
Perloff appreciates these early poems in formal terms, noting their skill in "rup-
turing the very sentence and phrasal units in which the image appears" (80).

The poems of Oppen's postexile phase have received numerous reviews and
critical essays, as well as influencing a subsequent generation of poets. In these
poems, Burton Hatlen observes, it seemed as if in exile "Oppen [had] prepared
himself to create a new kind of poetry which would steer a path between the
Scylla of a vacuous populist rhetoric and the Charybdis of an arid elitism" 335.
As a linguistically experimental poetry occupied with Romantic themes, Oppen's
work continues to be appreciated and influential in diverse aesthetic circles.

Many assessments of Oppen's late work have noted their deeply philosophical base, a reflection of Oppen's reading of Heidegger, among other philosophers. A poet and one of the foremost Oppen scholars, Michael Heller notes Oppen's distinctive employment of ideas from philosophy, which had nonetheless "been tested . . . in some way within his experience and against his experience" ("An Interview with Michael Heller" 51). In addition to receiving the Pulitzer Prize, Oppen was nominated for the National Book Award for *Collected Poems of George Oppen* (1976); he received the American Academy and Institute of Arts and Letters Award in 1980.

BIBLIOGRAPHY

Works by George Oppen

Poetry

Discrete Series. New York: Objectivist Press, 1934; reprinted, and distributed by Asphodel Book Shop, 1966.
The Materials. New York: New Directions, 1962.
This in Which. New York: New Directions, 1965.
Of Being Numerous. New York: New Directions, 1968.
Alpine: Poems. Mount Horeb, WI: Perishable Press, 1969.
Collected Poems. London: Fulcrum Press, 1972.
Seascape: Needle's Eye. Freemont, MI: Sumac Press, 1973.
The Collected Poems of George Oppen. New York: New Directions, 1975.
Primitive. San Francisco: Black Sparrow Press, 1978.

Other Works

An "Objectivists" Anthology. Ed. Louis Zukofsky. New York: To Publishers, 1932.
Active Anthology. Ed. Ezra Pound. London: Faber and Faber, 1933.
"The Mind's Own Place." Montemora 1 (Fall 1975).
Selected Letters of George Oppen. Ed. Rachel Blau DuPlessis. Durham, NC: Duke University Press, 1990.
From the Other Side of the Century: A New American Poetry 1960–1990. Ed. Douglas Messerli. Los Angeles: Sun and Moon, 1995a.
Poems for the Millennium: The University of California Book of Modern and Postmodern Poetry. Ed. Jerome Rothenberg and Pierre Joris. Berkeley: University of California Press, 1995b.

Works about George Oppen

Dembo, L. S. "George Oppen" (interview). *Contemporary Literature* 10 (Spring 1969): 160.
Hatlen, Burt, ed. *George Oppen: Man and Poet*. Orono, ME: National Poetry Foundation, 1981.
Heller, Michael, ed. *Conviction's Net of Branches: Essays on the Objectivist Poets and Poetry*. Carbondale: Southern Illinois University Press, 1985.

————. "An Interview with Michael Heller." *Talisman* 11 (Fall 1993): 51.

"Three Oppen Letters with a Note." *Ironwood #5: George Oppen Issue* (1975).

Oppen, Mary. *Meaning a Life: An Autobiography*. Santa Barbara, CA: Black Sparrow Press, 1995.

Perloff, Marjorie. *Radical Artifice: Writing Poetry in the Age of Media*. Chicago: University of Chicago Press, 1991.

Zukofsky, Louis. "Program 'Objectivists' 1931." *Poetry: A Magazine of Verse* (February 1931): 268–84.

JOEL OPPENHEIMER   (1930–1988)

Lyman Gilmore

BIOGRAPHY

Joel Oppenheimer was born in Yonkers, New York, on February 18, 1930. One of Joel's earliest memories was being held and rocked by an old, white-bearded man, his mother's father, Samuel Rossenwasser, the family patriarch who is reported to have emigrated from the village of Stropkov in what is now eastern Czechoslovakia in the 1880s. Although Joel's father had left school in sixth grade to help support his family, he was known in the family as a self-educated man who read books incessantly. Joel asserted that although his mother observed the formalities of Jewish faith, his seemingly agnostic father was the more deeply religious Jew. Throughout his life Joel spoke of an incident during his infancy that alienated him from his mother and contributed two of the major themes in his work, isolation and ambivalence toward women. His father had returned from France after World War I with lungs damaged from German gas, and by the time Joel was born, the condition had worsened so that he was confined for several months to a tuberculosis sanitarium in upstate New York. Joel's mother hired a maid to care for Joel while she visited his father, and from that moment Joel accused her of abandoning him.

Joel was raised with two older brothers and four cousins in an affectionate, middle-class, Jewish family in a multiethnic neighborhood. "In that structured society, smart Jewish boys had their life cut out for them. Study was in, athletics out, dating was confined to 'good girls,' and masturbation was rampant" ("Drying Out," 3, Unpublished ms., Joel Oppenheimer Archive, Dodd Research Center, University of Connecticut, Storrs). His school record from elementary through high school was exemplary, but he flunked out of both Cornell University and the University of Chicago within a year and a half. Joel claimed that he had wanted to become an architect, but his mother discouraged this choice as difficult for Jews and encouraged engineering, in which he floundered at Cornell. The following fall he went to Chicago, but, displeased with what he described as the arrogance of his fellow students, he went home for Thanksgiving and never returned. Before he left, he saw his first psychiatrist and wrote a seminal poem, "awful and predictable, but by god I was writing. In it I was a young man who rode the giant worm amongst the other worms and read the Rubaiyat" ("Drying Out" 7).

In February 1950 Joel went off to his last chance at higher education, Black Mountain College in rural North Carolina. "Black Mountain became my first home in the true sense of the word" ("Drying Out" 12). During his three years there Joel married his first wife, Rena Furlong, learned the craft of printing that supported him for the next sixteen years, discovered a poetic father in William Carlos Williams, and became a poet studying with Charles Olson. In 1951 Joel printed and hand-bound his *Four Poems to Spring* and saw as his first official publication *The Dancer*, a broadside with a drawing by Robert Rauschenberg published as *Jargon 2*. In February 1953, miserable from his failing marriage, Joel left Black Mountain, spending several months in Olson's Washington, D.C., house before finding work as a printer in Rochester, New Hampshire, and then, in June, taking a similar job in Provincetown on Cape Cod. During the summer, his pregnant wife joined him, and they were reconciled.

The fall of 1953 Joel lived with his parents in New York and worked in the advertising department at Macy's Department Store while Rena returned for her final semester at North Carolina Women's College in Greensboro. Nicholas Oppenheimer was born March 3, 1954, and in the fall Rena and the child joined Joel in his single-room, five-floor walk-up tenement apartment on Manhattan's Lower East Side. Joel was as delighted as his mother was chagrined with their living in the poor immigrant neighborhood from which her relatives had struggled so hard to move away. In November 1955 their son Daniel was born, and in early 1956 Joel's first major book, *The Dutiful Son*, was published.

Joel had begun drinking in high school, and he consumed increasing amounts of alcohol at Cornell and Chicago. At Black Mountain drinking became a daily habit, and by the mid-1950s alcohol played a central and intrusive role in his and his family's lives. In the fall of 1959, the marriage dissolved, with his wife's taking the children to live in New Mexico and Joel again living alone.

After a period of melancholy following the breakup of his marriage, Joel enjoyed a freedom he had never before known. Respected as a typographer, his print shop jobs improved steadily. Having been sexually inexperienced when he met Rena, he relished his many affairs with women, including two or three serious relationships amid the plethora of brief encounters. The result of one relationship was that Joel and the well-known poet and nonfiction writer Margaret Randall had a son, Gregory, who was born October 14, 1960. Randall and Gregory left New York for New Mexico and ultimately Cuba, and it was years before Joel and Gregory established a close relationship. Joel and Robert Creeley maintained a voluminous correspondence about life and literature, and his steady production of poems culminated in his second major work, *The Love Bit and Other Poems* (1962). However, it was the publication two years earlier of five Oppenheimer poems in Don Allen's famous *The New American Poetry: 1945–1960* that brought Joel serious recognition and a wide readership as a "Black Mountain poet" (1960). On November 18, 1961, Joel's satiric play about movie westerns, *The Great American Desert*, appeared to positive reviews as the first production of the Judson Poets' Theater at the Judson Memorial Church in Greenwich Village. Joel had two more of his plays produced in New York, a musical, *Miss Right*, at the Judson in 1963 and *Like a Hill* at the Hardware Poets' Theater in 1964.

In the summer of 1966 Joel married Helen Bukberg and gave up printing to accept the directorship of the new federally financed Poetry Project at St. Marks Church in the Bowery. Funded under an Office of Equal Opportunity grant to bring arts to inner-city youth, the Poetry Project became one of the major centers of nontraditional poetry in the United States. As director, Joel's job was to plan and oversee weekly readings by local poets as well as nationally known figures and to administer the free poetry workshops taught by experienced writers, including himself.

Joel's fourth son, Nathaniel, was born November 23, 1966. In the summer of 1967 one of Joel's strongest poems and one that has powerful Jewish resonance, *Sirventes on a Sad Occurrence*, was published as a chapbook. Increasingly, Joel gave paid readings throughout the eastern United States and Canada, and when he left the Poetry Project in August 1968, these were a major source of income. Joel was director of the Teachers and Writers Collaborative from December 1968 to August 1969, when he began his twelve-year position as a writer-in-residence at City College of New York (CCNY). In March 1969 Joel published the first of his 300 witty and wise columns in the alternative weekly newspaper the *Greenwich Village Voice*.

Before his father died in August 1969, Joel was proud to show him a hardbound copy of his third volume of poems, *In Time: Poems 1962–1968* (1969). Beginning in 1966 Joel had become a regular at the Lion's Head, a bar in Greenwich Village's Sheridan Square, famous for its hard-drinking writers and newspapermen. At the Lion's Head his drinking finally caught up to him, and in August 1970, after the terrifying realization that his mind was failing, a doctor's cirrhosis diagnosis, and an emergency stay in Roosevelt Hospital's detox unit, he gave up alcohol completely and never had another drink. Joel's fifth son, Lemuel, was born August 15, 1971.

Two important books came out of his new sobriety, *The Wrong Season* (1973), a wry combination of autobiography and baseball, and his first collection of poems that deal with a single theme, *The Woman Poems* (1975), Joel's passionate account of male–female conflict, including the unraveling of his and Helen's marriage. Two other books that had been written earlier were published during this period, the poetry collection *On Occasion* (1973) and a collection of short stories written at the time of the breakup of his first marriage, *Pan's Eyes* (1974).

When Joel and Helen's marriage ended in 1975, Joel found himself in the unfamiliar and time-consuming role as single parent and housekeeper. Regretting the loss of his first family fifteen years earlier, Joel applied himself assiduously to the care of his two young sons while maintaining his teaching at CCNY, writing his regular *Village Voice* column, producing poems of increasing quality such as *Acts* (1976) and *names, dates, and places* (1978), and finding time daily for schmoozing with friends over soda water at the Lion's Head. From 1975 to 1978 he was part-time visiting professor of English at the College of New Rochelle; winter terms from 1977 to 1982 he taught poetry workshops at St. Andrews Presbyterian College in Laurinberg, North Carolina; and during the summers of 1977 and 1978 he was visiting teacher of poetry at the College of the Atlantic in Bar Harbor, Maine.

In 1977 he and his first wife, Rena, were finally reconciled at the wedding of their son Nicholas, and on this occasion Joel wrote a poem considered to be among his best, ''Houses'' (1981). For his son Nathaniel's bar mitzvah in 1979, Joel published *On the Giving of the Tallis*. In 1981 he published a popular biography of Marilyn Monroe, *Marilyn Lives!*, and a year later his long poem *At Fifty* appeared. A heavy smoker since adolescence, Joel was diagnosed with cancer in the summer of 1982 and had a lung removed. That fall Joel replaced Russell Banks as writer-in-residence at New England College in Henniker, New Hampshire, and when he moved there, he was accompanied by his new partner and imminent wife Theresa Maier. After two series of lectures and readings in 1978 and again in 1980 at Buffalo State College in celebration of Black Mountain College, Joel published a book of workshop transcriptions and poems that contains the most complete description of his poetics, *Poetry, The Ecology of the Soul: Talks and Selected Poems*.

Joel's final six years were happy and productive. At New England College, his first full-time teaching position, students revered him, and faculty sought his council. He brought many nationally known poets to the college for readings, and he wrote a popular weekly column for the statewide *New Hampshire Times*. During the 1984–1985 academic year he was appointed Gannett Professor at the College of Liberal Arts, Rochester Institute of Technology (RIT) in Rochester, New York, where on November 4, 1984, he and Theresa were married. In April 1985, Joel organized and moderated a major two-day conference at RIT on the ''Poetry of Place,'' which included discussions and readings by noted writers, scholars, and critics on ''the growing body of American and other poetry in which poets return to the use of the 'local' as the starting point of their work'' (Conference brochure, RIT). Joel's cancer worsened, and after more surgery and chemotherapy, he wrote what some have said is the ultimate cancer poem, *The Uses of Adversity* (1987). Joel died in his home in New Hampshire, October 11, 1988.

MAJOR WORKS AND THEMES

The major themes in Joel's poetry include the discovery of significance in ordinary daily life, the importance of family and friends, the struggle between solipsistic isolation and love, the fear and necessity of facing oneself honestly, sexual passion as our most natural act, justice and dignity as rights of every individual, the importance of play in poetry and life, and simply getting along day after day. An obvious feature of Joel's work is his nearly exclusive use of lowercase letters; he always strove for a "flat line," and capitals intruded. Most of Joel's poems are admittedly autobiographical, and each of his major books expresses a single theme having to do with his life at the time. The poems in *The Dutiful Son* (1956) concern personal relationships in general and marriage and the family in particular. Their tone is as ambiguous and ambivalent as the marriage of which most of them were bred. A poem that is characteristic of this tone begins the book (no pagination):

THE LOVER

> every time
> the same way
> wondering when
> this when that.
> if you were a
> plum tree. if you
> were a peach
> tree.

The Love Bit (1962) contains poems in which the author speaks both wistfully and bitterly of tenderness between a man and a woman as their relationship diminishes. Written in the months before the breakup of his first marriage, they present a fearful, yet hopeful, marital ambivalence (no pagination).

THE LOVE BIT

> the colors we depend on are
> red for raspberry jam, white
> of the inside thigh, purple as
> in deep, the blue of moods, green
> cucumbers (cars), yellow stripes down
> the pants, orange suns on ill-
> omened days, and black as the
> dirt in my fingernails.
> also, brown, in the night,
> appearing at its best when
> the eyes turn inward, seeking

seeking, to dig everything but
our own. i.e. we make it crazy or
no, and sometimes in the afternoon.

In Time: Poems 1962–1968 (1969) is a complex collection including poems
of yearning for love, confused relationships, lost love, albas in which lovers part
at dawn, and sirventes, poems modeled on satiric French troubadour songs. One
of Joel's longest and most powerful poems is "Sirventes on a Sad Occurrence,"
in which the poet is walking down his Lower East Side tenement stairs when
an old woman struggling her way up to her apartment loses control of her bowels
and defecates on the stairs. The old woman cannot move, and her daughter is
embarrassed and frightened, but the poet empathizes with the old woman's
plight:

and on top of it, as you clung to
the banister at the top step, almost
around, fifteen feet from your
door, to face me suddenly, coming
down from one flight up, my hat no
longer swinging but over my head,
over my thin bearded face, my god
the moan then, even your daughter
scared by it, i thought you were
dying 'til i found out the truth:
me a tall skinny bearded eyeglassed
hollow-eyed ascetic jew, big
hat, you were back in poland—but
i am no rabbi, and it is no sin,
i am not the chasid or simple
ashkenazi reb you knew and
danced before, around, the psalms
went high to god, david i am
not, there's no cause for the
alarm, i'm so far removed from
it, all i could think was old
lady i wish i knew how to say
aspeto in yiddish, and couldn't. (215)

The Woman Poems (1975) was the first book of poems that Joel wrote after
he stopped drinking, and it was his only book of serial poems in which each
poem is linked to a single topic, the myth of the Great Mother. It is a painful,
wrenchingly beautiful book in which he confronts all of his demons: alcohol,
feelings of abandonment by his mother and other women, the confusions of love
and sex, and his own sanity, as in "Screaming Poem"

the woman inside me
does not murmur she
screams. it has
been so ever since
i gave up breast for
bottle, the geometry
of shapes for the
algebra of numbers.
this woman claws at
my innards (12)

Five years after *The Woman Poems* Joel produced another collection of linked verse that he referred to as one long poem, *At Fifty: A Poem* (1982). The theme here is ''the ecology of lives and the necessity to make endless adjustments in order to get along with people'' (Bertholf, ''Joel Oppenheimer'').

Joel believed that ''occasional poems'' were of the highest order, and he wrote many of them in books such as *On Occasion* (1973), *names, dates and places* (1978), and *Just Friends/Friends and Lovers: Poems 1959–1962* (1980).

Two of Joel's finest poems appear in *New Spaces: Poems 1975–1983* (1985): ''Cacti'' and ''Houses.'' Both are meditative as the poet reflects on his life. In ''Cacti'' he regrets:

and i have watched
all the flowering plants
of my life
wither and die
because i did not
handle them
properly (127)

But he has come to self-knowledge:

i am learning
i am neither rose
nor weed of the field
but did not know that
and suffered long
trying to be such
trying to grow that way (136)

In the long and exquisitely controlled lyrical poem ''Houses,'' Joel reconciles with his first wife eighteen years after their separation when he visits her house in New Mexico for the marriage of their first son. He remembers some of the verses he wrote to her so long ago, but he is not sentimental:

    i thought how all
    that i have loved
    all that i have missed
    is in this house
    don't misunderstand me
    i am not speaking
    of romance
    or rekindled love
    or even second chances (139)

In the intervening years he has learned to understand in himself what he did not
when they had been together:

        i am a man
    i need a woman's touch
    might be the pity of it
    but i've learned to build
    without it
        but now can see
    how pleasant such things are
    and where they come from
    in me
        that is what
    i did not know
            and what
    i now do know
    and will remember. (147–48)

Joel's poetic mentors and teachers were not Jewish, and most critics fail to
mention Jewish elements in his work. However, at least three acute readers
acknowledge his Jewish roots. Joel's good friend, the classical scholar and poet
Sam Abrams, has said that Joel thought of himself as a Jewish poet and that
"he prided himself on being a *yiddishche kopf*, a real jewish head" (8). Michael
Joyce's description of Joel includes: "for this is a student and a jew, a passionate
jew, student/dutiful son of Hillel" (129). Hayden Carruth compares Joel's poetry
with that of William Carlos Williams: "Their poems move in the same way.
Oppenheimer's poems on the whole are simpler, their humor is more abundant
and distinctly Jewish, their sexuality is far more evident; but the rhythms and
phrasings are noticeably similar" (194). In his *Village Voice* columns and poems, Joel frequently referred to himself as a Jew, as in his delightful poem to
Marilyn Monroe: "i am a/ sport-loving jewish/ intellectual/ writer." ("Dear
Miss Monroe," *In Time* 107).
    Joel was not a practicing Jew in any religious sense, but all his life he proudly
acknowledged his Jewish heritage and culture. Generally, he did not focus on
Jewish themes, although occasionally his work dealt with Jewish content, as in

"Anti Semitism" and "My Wife's Grandfather, Dead" from *On Occasion* and in his *Voice* columns "Poet Gets Hair Cut, Retains Strength" (June 21, 1976) and "Funny, We Don't Look Jewish" (November 8, 1976). "Sirventes on a Sad Occurrence" (*In Time*) is Joel's poem that most clearly and powerfully evokes Jewish themes in terms of its setting in a Lower East Side tenement, its protagonist an old Jewish woman, its Yiddish diction and rhythms, its humor in making fun of "this is your/ son the doctor riverside/ drive," its profoundly moral emphasis on human dignity and justice, its gruff, but caring, rabinnical admonition to the old woman, and its acceptance of the injunction to perfect the world.

When Joel was in his forties, he made a point of including Jewish culture in the raising of the last two of his five sons. Lem, the youngest, says that Joel raised him "a complete Jew," and when Nat insisted on celebrating his bar mitzvah, the ceremony was at least as important to Joel as Nat. As Joel wrote in his *Voice* column: "So we joined a synagogue, and he went to Hebrew school and finally, a date was set . . . the studying began in earnest, and my anxieties began also. I wanted it to be right for him, but it couldn't be a parodic bar mitzvah either" ("Rite of Passage," *Village Voice*, December 17, 1979).

ON THE GIVING OF THE TALLIS

this shawl, son,
this wrap, this
fringed garment
is your sign

you have come
of age
        you may
read the words
and live by them

you may approach
the book and read

you may carry
the words with you
wrapped in you
as you in this shawl

it is of the desert
and it has covered us
everywhere
        we start
from nothing, from
the dry dust
        we grow

with the word
until we flower

flower well my son
    for nathaniel ezra oppenheimer
    his bar mitzvah, 1 december 1979

CRITICAL RECEPTION

Although reviews of his work were generally positive, Joel went to his death disappointed and puzzled that his writing had not received more attention. Critics of Joel's work often cite his lucidity, the clarity of his language, and his simplicity. Hayden Carruth said that "Oppenheimer's poems were always direct and clear . . . literally, a refreshment. They combined the most ordinary language to make poems that were natural and tricky at the same time, as all really fine poems are" (193). Robert Bertholf describes Joel's grace: "He trusts simple vocabulary and the everyday commerce between people. . . . There is an unhurried mildness, an unstudied repose—grace, it might be called—to the poems. That, along with their inherent warmth, the perception of and defense of such human values as independence, fairness, tolerance, frankness, are their most admirable qualities" ("Joel Oppenheimer" 2). In an early review, Donald Phelps spoke of Joel's rhythm: "The motion of his poetry, whether playful, elegiac or erotically yearning, is always the same ruminative tempo, like the bobbing of an elephant's head: heavy, delicate, tentative." Phelps goes on to address "that sweet, and rueful hopefulness of Oppenheimer's voice . . . one of our outstanding monologists" (28–29).

In an important essay on "The Objectivist Tradition," Charles Altieri places Joel firmly in the company of Pound, Zukofsky, Olson, Ignatow, Duncan, and Rakosi. Altieri's acute analysis of Joel's poem "Houses" describes how it "engages themes of loss while risking the refusal to admit any turns toward eloquence or interpretation that might alter a concrete sense of the speaker's energies in an immediate act of composition. In this poem, in fact, hesitancies that counter-balance the effort of naming serve rich mimetic functions because the focus of the poem is on the care to get things right, to clean up eighteen years of confusion and evasion that followed his divorce by showing the consequences of love and respect as they warrant direct speech." He ends his essay by stating in "Houses," "Objectification in poetry becomes, on many levels, the means for committing the self to relationships that master time and loss" (21–22).

Aside from David Thibodeaux's insightful analysis of Joel's poetry, plays, fiction, and journalism in his published doctoral dissertation *Joel Oppenheimer: An Introduction* (1986), William Corbett's convincing demonstration of Joel's "essential use" in his Introduction to the selected early work *Names and Local Habitations*, Leverett T. Smith's acute critique of the work before 1980, Robert

Bertholf's close reading of the entire oeuvre in *The Dictionary of Literary Biography*, and David Landrey's brief, but brilliant, Introduction to *Poetry, the Ecology of the Soul*, the liveliest critical appraisal is Michael Joyce's "Getting It Right: Joel Oppenheimer's Poetry." Joyce asserts that Joel "takes, yes, 'delight in the ordinary,' but not—and here is where it is important to be careful—not any ordinary delight. The day to day graces of Oppenheimer so often depend on his attempts to learn how to get it right, this living in a world of ordinary delights, how to live a life as a man and father in a city" (128). Joyce sees the essence of Joel's work in his unique language: "And this, I think, is what forms the center in Oppenheimer's writing, how he mines this language of kinship in the places he best knows it, family and love, all knotted up" (131).

BIBLIOGRAPHY

Works by Joel Oppenheimer

The Dancer. Highlands, NC: Jonathan Williams, 1951a.
Four Poems to Spring. Black Mountain, NC: Privately printed, 1951b.
The Dutiful Son. Highlands, NC: Jonathan Williams, 1956.
The Love Bit and Other Poems. New York: Totem/Corinth, 1962.
The Great American Desert. New York: Grove Press, 1966.
Sirventes on a Sad Occasion. Madison, WI: Perishable Press, 1967.
In Time: Poems 1962–1968. Indianapolis and New York: Bobbs-Merrill, 1969.
On Occasion: Some Births, Deaths, Weddings, Birthdays, Holidays, and Other Events. Indianapolis and New York: Bobbs-Merrill, 1973a.
The Wrong Season. Indianapolis and New York: Bobbs-Merrill, 1973b.
Pan's Eyes. Amherst, MA: Mulch Press, 1974.
The Woman Poems. Indianapolis and New York: Bobbs-Merrill, 1975.
Acts. Driftless, WI: Perishable Press, 1976.
names, dates, and places. Laurinburg, NC: Saint Andrews Press, 1978.
Just Friends/Friends and Lovers: Poems 1959–1962. Highlands, NC: Jargon Society, 1980a.
The Only Anarchist General. Rocky Mount, NC: Arthur Mann Kaye, 1980b.
Houses. Buffalo: White Pine Press, 1981a.
Marilyn Lives! New York: Delilah Books, 1981b.
At Fifty: A Poem. Laurinburg, NC: Saint Andrews Press, 1982a.
del quien lo tomlo: A Suite. Minor Confluence, WI: Perishable Press, 1982b.
The Ghost Lover. Rocky Mount, NC: Arthur Mann Kaye, 1983a.
Poetry, the Ecology of the Soul: Talks and Selected Poems. Ed. David Landrey and Dennis Maloney. Buffalo, NY: White Pine Press, 1983b.
Notes toward a Definition of David. Minor Confluence, WI: Perishable Press, 1984.
New Spaces: Poems 1975–1983. Santa Barbara, CA: Black Sparrow Press, 1985a.
Why Not. Rochester, NY: Press of the Good Mountain, 1985b; republished, Buffalo, NY: White Pine Press, 1987.
The Teacher. Rocky Mount, NC: Arthur Mann Kaye, 1986.
The Debt. Annandale-on-Hudson, NY: Bard College, 1987a.

The Uses of Adversity. Vandergrift, PA: Zealot Press, 1987b; republished, New York: Oncology Service of Yonkers General Hospital, 1988.

Names and Local Habitations: (Selected Earlier Poems 1951–1972). Winston-Salem, NC: Jargon Society, 1988.

New Hampshire Journal. Perry Township, WI: Perishable Press, 1994.

Papers

Joel Oppenheimer's papers are in the Special Collections, Dodd Research Center, University of Connecticut, Storrs.

Works about Joel Oppenheimer

Abrams, Sam. "The Only Anarchist General, Joel Oppenheimer." *and.* 2, 4 (Fall/Winter) 1988): 8–10.

Altieri, Charles. "The Objectivist Tradition." *Chicago Review* 30, 3 (Winter 1979): 5–22.

Beach, Christopher. "Interview with Joel Oppenheimer." *Sagetrieb* 7, 2 (Fall 1988): 90–130.

Bertholf, Robert. "Joel Oppenheimer." *Dictionary of Literary Biography.* American Poets Since World War II (5th Series). Ed. Joseph Conte. Detroit: Gale Research.

———. "On The Great American Desert and The Woman Poems." *Credences* 2 (July 1975): 26–35.

Butterick, George. "Earned Reality: Man as Cactus." *Exquisite Corpse* 4, 3 (March/April 1986): 23.

———. "Joel Oppenheimer: A Checklist of His Writings." Storrs: University of Connecticut Library, 1975.

Carruth, Hayden. "Joel Oppenheimer." *Suicides and Jazzers.* Ann Arbor: University of Michigan Press, 1992, 193–98.

Coombs, S. Maxine "A Study of the Black Mountain Poets." Ph.D. diss. University of Oregon, 1967.

Gilmore, Lyman. "Don't Touch the Poet." *North Carolina Literary Review* 11, 2 (1995): 68–83.

"Interview with Poet Joel Oppenheimer." *Noiseless Spider* 1 (Spring 1972): 2–5.

Jones, F. Whitney. "An Interview with Joel Oppenheimer." *St. Andrews Review* 4 (Spring-Summer 1977): 45–54.

Joyce, Michael. "Getting It Right: Joel Oppenheimer's Poetry." *North Dakota Quarterly* (Fall 1987): 123–52.

Owens, William L. "Joel Oppenheimer at Storrs, Conn." *Credences* 2 (July 1975): 13–25.

Phelps, Donald. "The Simple Ecology of the Soul." *For Now* 11 (1970): 28–31.

Smith, Leverett T. "The Poetry of Joel Oppenheimer." *St. Andrews Review* 5, 4 (Spring/Summer 1980): 127–40.

Stephens, Michael. "Joel Oppenheimer." *The Dramaturgy of Style: Voice in Short Fiction.* Carbondale and Edwardsville: Southern Illinois University Press, 1986, 68–77.

Thibodeaux, David. *Joel Oppenheimer: An Introduction.* Columbia, SC: Camden House, 1986.

"Three Versions of the Poetic Line." *Credences* 4 March 1977): 55–60.

ROBERT PINSKY   (1940–   )

Charles S. Berger

BIOGRAPHY

Robert Pinsky was born in Long Branch, New Jersey, in 1940. He received a B.A. in 1962 from Rutgers University and a Ph.D. in English from Stanford in 1966. He has taught at Wellesley College, the University of California at Berkeley, and Boston University. He has served as poetry editor of *The New Republic*. Among his prizes and awards are the Artists Award from the American Academy of Arts and Letters, a Guggenheim Fellowship, the Saxifrage Prize, and the William Carlos Williams Prize. In 1997 he was named U.S. poet laureate.

Pinsky has been associated with poets such as Robert Hass (who preceded him as U.S. poet laureate) and Frank Bidart. He and Hass have translated the poetry of the Polish poet and Nobel Prize laureate Czeslaw Milosz, who resided in Berkeley at the same time as Pinsky and Hass.

The influence of Judaism on Pinsky's life is best illustrated by remarks he made in an interview published in *TriQuarterly*. The passage amounts to an autobiographical credo for the ''secular,'' Jewish-American literary imagination:

For me, God is an important episode in the history of creation. Possibly having been raised as an Orthodox Jew, which is to say with considerable separation from the majority culture, has contributed to my interest in making. . . . The experience of a gorgeous, fading European reality—the rich, lower class Eastern European Judaism and its culture, which were still present and very European in my childhood—must have had an impact upon me that I can't fully understand. . . . As the oldest child, the oldest son in the family, I was expected to go to synagogue every Saturday. The musaf, the Orthodox service, lasts three, maybe three-and-a-half hours. . . . What happens is an accumulation of prayers and rituals, a liturgy that feels medieval. . . .

The religion is kind of a surrounding reality, no more "losable" in its own terms than the color of your eyes, or the force of gravity. It's like having faith in the universe, for the Jew to have "faith in" Judaism: it's just there. . . .

So Judaism was in large measure a powerful boredom for me, but it was a very powerful boredom: a serious and for me stifling force. And the force of that boredom, no mere ennui but a desperate, animal sense of being caged and trapped, left me, I think, with a feeling about the majority culture that makes me feel both more inside it than I might have been otherwise—because I chose it, I might not have, but I chose the majority culture and I like it—yet by the same process also more outside it, in my feelings, than I might be otherwise. There are special ways in which a secularized Jew feels both additionally in the new culture, compared to others, and outside it. Terms like "assimilation," or numbering generations from the first act of immigration, do not begin to deal with these intricacies.

MAJOR WORKS AND THEMES

Since the publication of his first book of poems, *Sadness and Happiness* (1975), Pinsky has been a strong voice in American poetry but a difficult one to characterize. Though he displayed a preference for formal structure and "didactic" poetry, Pinsky always resisted aesthetic smugness. From the beginning, there has been a hard-edged, worldly quality to his work, coupled with an unpredictability of subject matter that has made his poetry almost antiaesthetic, despite its formal polish. Pinsky thrives in the precincts of both high and low culture. In *The Want Bone* (1990) and the "New Poems" section of his collected poems, *The Figured Wheel* (1996), Pinsky has also become a poet much more concerned with writing about, and defining, his sense of himself as a Jew.

From the beginning of his poetic career, Pinsky has written with diamond clarity about persons, places, and things. He has dared to be unfashionable in his strict rendering of subjects that most other poets would veil in a haze of mystification. When he writes about people, as in the well-known, early "Poem about People" *(Sadness and Happiness)*, he delineates them with unforgettable precision, right up to the point where he confesses that what most interests him about others is their awful unknowability, their hungry desperation to be known. Poems such as "Lair" and "Memorial," from the volume *An Explanation of America* (1979), remain exact and heartbreaking in their discriminations of the world's beauty and pain. No reader of "Lair," with its achingly sharp parsings of early light, ought to have been surprised that Pinsky would eventually prove such a distinguished translator of Dante.

Pinsky's longer poems—"Sadness and Happiness" (1975), "Essay on Psychiatrists" (1975) both in *Sadness and Happiness*, and the book-length *An Explanation of America*—dare to be openly didactic because they remain so cunningly eccentric. Pinsky tells the truth but tells it slant. His explanations are only version, filled with private angles that manage to assume public status. As its title indicates, *An Explanation of America* is both modest and audacious. A three-part, twelve-section poem written in blank verse, it takes the loose, epistolary form of a letter written to the poet's daughter "explaining" the vastness and the idiosyncrasy of America, its promise and its repressiveness, its narratives of justification and self-criticism. Pinsky tells his daughter a version of the American story that crosses national borders, bringing in cognate stories from Gogol, Horace, Shakespeare, Homer. Of American writers, interestingly enough, Willa Cather comes to mean the most for Pinsky in this long poem. Only an alert, leisurely reading of *An Explanation of America* will convey a sense of the ground it traverses and the importance of its subtle arguments about American character and identity.

One thing not to be found in the poem, however, is an account of ethnic identity. Until *The Want Bone*, Pinsky preferred to dwell on themes drawn from popular culture as a way to spice up the melting pot, though he was always aware of how popular forms actually help induce a sense of American solidarity. If there is any meaning to the concept of a popular sublime, then surely it would be found in the opening sections of "History of My Heart" (1984), where the poet imagines his primal scene of conception to have originated with his mother's sighting of Fats Waller playing a toy piano at Macy's: "She put into my heart this scene from the romance of Joy."

The Want Bone marks something of a stylistic break in Pinsky's career, as well as a turn to religious, or explicitly Jewish, subjects. Two poems in particular illustrate the range of Pinsky's tonal and thematic concerns. "The Uncreation" is a hymn in praise of human song in all its manifestations, from "Take Me Out to the Ball Game" to "Kol Nidre." Pinsky displays a cosmological imagination in this poem, as he imagines us teaching the gods how to sing, so that they might inherit the world we have created and deformed. "The Night Game" is an inspired marriage of Judaism and popular culture—baseball, to be specific. The poem is a funny and brilliant ode to Sandy Koufax, the great Dodger lefty who refused to pitch in a World Series game on Yom Kippur. Pinsky renders a cunning comparison between Koufax and the Yankee left-hander Whitey Ford, whom the poem comes to treat as an archetypal Gentile figure. Two other poems from the volume, "From the Childhood of Jesus" and "Visions of Daniel," brood on Jewish identity in a more historic or prophetic mode.

The Figured Wheel: New and Collected Poems 1966–1996 opens with a section of sixteen new poems that have struck reviewers as being among Pinsky's finest. These new poems show Pinsky's mastery of two distinct styles of lyric: one exemplifies a strict, impersonal voice, appropriate to a near-prophetic survey of the world and its conceptual structures; the other displays a penchant for narrative truths, especially those with autobiographical, Jewish ties. "City Elegies," a six-part meditation on the archaic, universal power of the city, its ubiquitous settings of desire and destitution, is written with fused and sensuous precision but expands at every point so that it connects with many other city poems written by figures such as Blake, Crane, or Cavafy. Near the end of the poem, Pinsky writes: "and now we are the city."

The best examples of the more narrative, "colloquial" lyrics (though these poems are no less steeped in the history of poetry) can be found in two extraordinary elegies, "The Ice-Storm" and "Impossible to Tell." As with the best elegies, these poems reinterpret and expand the boundaries of the genre. Both poems are masterpieces of Jewish-American imagination, incorporating liturgy, history, sheer ethnic jokiness into the running idiom of high-vernacular American poetry that Pinsky mastered from the very beginning of his career. "The Ice-Storm" grows out of Pinsky's Dante translation, for it adopts the form of an address to the poet from beyond the grave. The speaker of the poem is a scientist, a friend, who instructs the poet in remembrance, whether biblical or personal, telling him that "*Yisgadal V'yiskadash*" [opening words of the Kaddish, the prayer for the dead] is part of the tenuous nature of life. The closing lines of this poem will be read as a permanent addition to the storehouse of elegiac tropes of death and survival, transience and permanence: "Lifespan of the ice-storm the week after I died."

"Impossible to Tell" is, indeed, that, for it must be the only elegy ever written that structures itself upon the Jewish joke, a category recognized by Freud as being synonymous with wit itself. Most elegies try to raise the dead, in one way or another, but none attempt it through Jewish burlesque. This is a five-page, encyclopedic poem, binding together many of Pinsky's driving obsessions, from high to low. Indeed, the poem erases hierarchical distinctions altogether, insisting only on "the secret courtesy" of the perfectly performed routine and on the chain of living voices forged by swapped jokes and poems. The outrageous, but convincing, linkages made by the poem map the mind's power to save and connect—an essential part of elegiac work.

CRITICAL RECEPTION

The publication of *The Figured Wheel*, coming just after his Dante translation and coupled with his appointment as U.S. poet laureate, moves Pinsky into the front ranks of American poets. In addition, he is writing the Jewish-American experience in new and brilliant ways that will prove highly influential for younger poets.

BIBLIOGRAPHY

Works by Robert Pinsky

Poetry

Sadness and Happiness Princeton, NJ: Princeton University Press, 1975.
An Explanation of America. Princeton, NJ: Princeton University Press, 1979.
History of My Heart. New York: Ecco Press, 1984.
The Want Bone. New York: Ecco Press, 1990.
The Figured Wheel: New and Collected Poems, 1966–1996. New York: Farrar, Straus, 1996.

Criticism

Landor's Poetry. Chicago: University of Chicago Press, 1968.
The Situation of Poetry. Princeton, NJ: Princeton University Press, 1977.
Poetry and the World. New York: Ecco Press, 1988.

Translations

The Separate Notebooks, by Czeslaw Milosz. New York: Ecco Press, 1983.
The Inferno of Dante. New York: Farrar, Straus, 1994.

Works about Robert Pinsky

Bedient, Calvin. Rev. of *The Want Bone. Salmagundi*, Spring/Summer 1991, 212–30.
"A Conversation with Robert Pinsky." *TriQuarterly*, Winter 1994/1995, 21–37.
Cotter, James Finn. Rev. of *History of My Heart. Hudson Review*, Autumn 1984, 496–507.
Longenbach, James. "Robert Pinsky and the Language of Our Time." *Salmagundi*, 157–77.
Sacks, Peter. " 'Also This, Also That': Robert Pinsky's Poetics of Inclusion." *Agni*, No. 36, 1992, 272–80.

CARL RAKOSI

(1903–)

Steve Shoemaker

BIOGRAPHY

Born in Berlin on November 6, 1903, Carl Rakosi has so far lived a life roughly coeval with the twentieth century. In 1904 his parents separated, and his mother returned with Carl and his brother to her parents' home in Baja, Hungary, while his father emigrated to the United States. In Hungary, Rakosi has recalled, he was raised primarily by his grandmother, without ever really knowing his mother. One of his earliest memories records his mother's conspicuous absence:

I am in a very long room, so long that I can not see its end. There is very little furniture. The ceiling is very high and vast. There are shadows. The further away they are, the longer and heavier. There is no one there. I lie in my crib. No one comes. The silence is all there is. The nothing is oppressive. Hours go by and it becomes harder and harder to bear. There is no end. There is only the silence. And nothing. But beyond what I can see is Something ominous looming. (Buckeye 457)

This memory of absence is at least partially balanced by a memory of his grandmother's luminous presence, of whom he has written, "My grandmother . . . was my mother, only more gentle and kind than a mother":

Her presence has always been with me. The eyes are sad and reflective, the face tired, beginning to show wrinkles, but the mouth smiles and an incomparable sweetness, her character, exudes from her, holding nothing back, and envelops me. She leans towards me, attentive, smiling, and I respond in like, as I had learned to do from her, also smiling, all inside me light. (*Collected Prose* 85)

For Rakosi, who was later trained in both social work and psychotherapy, these two opposing memories are both primary and primal, and we can see his work registering a related tension of opposites—of absence and presence, of looming strangeness and benevolent lightness.

At the age of six, Rakosi was taken to Chicago to live with his father, a watchmaker, now remarried. His father, Rakosi recalls, first introduced him to "political thinking": "He was really a beautiful socialist, in the sense that he was all idealism. And what seemed to him most noble was the man who was concerned about society and put it on the line, fought for social justice and social reform" (Hatlen 109). As his father struggled in business, the family moved first to Gary, Indiana, and then to Kenosha, Wisconsin. In 1920, Rakosi attended the University of Chicago and began to write poetry. The following year he transferred to the University of Wisconsin, where he eventually became editor of the *Wisconsin Literary Magazine*. By comparison to the "blond young Babbits. . . . fed on fresh country milk and Iowa corn" who made up the majority of the student population, Rakosi seemed to himself to cut the figure of a "poor little Jewish boy, stewing in an inner life, sensitive, mystical, full of Tolstoy and Nietzsche, feeling as if I had been branded by a stigma" (*Collected Prose* 90). At this time, however, he also became close friends with the writers Margery Latimer and Kenneth Fearing, in whose company he found refuge. In later years, after having lived in the Midwest for much of his adult life, Rakosi's early sense of alienation would give way to a certain admiration for the "stable and homogeneous" quality of the region, with its strong sense of place and identity: "its spirit—the farmlands, the plains, the flatness, a certain humor and macho quality in the men that I like and find interesting, that's a part of me, a universal neighborliness" (Evans and Kleinzahler 63).

After graduation from the University of Wisconsin, Rakosi embarked on a search for steady employment. During the years from 1924 to 1932 he worked as a social worker, as a messboy on a merchant ship to Australia, as a psychologist, and as an English teacher. He also studied first law and then medicine, both at the University of Texas. For professional reasons he changed his name legally to the less "foreign"-sounding Callman Rawley, retaining Carl Rakosi as his pen name. By 1931 he was "in despair," having "tried every occupation I could think of in which I could make a living and still have the time and mental energy to write without success." At this time he was contacted by Louis Zukofsky, who would initiate his involvement with what came to be known as the "objectivist" movement in poetry. That contact was, for a time, a kind of rescue, infusing new energy into Rakosi's poetry and instigating an important phase of artistic development. The search for steady employment, however, continued to exert its strain throughout the 1930s. After his money ran out, Rakosi withdrew from medical studies in Texas and returned to social work in Chicago, having made his way north by riding freight cars (Buckeye 467). From this time forward Rakosi pursued social work as a profession, though continuing to move about and change jobs with some frequency. His studies in social work were carried out at the University of Chicago, at Tulane University, and finally at the University of Pennsylvania, which granted him a master of social work degree. From 1940 to 1968, he worked as a social worker, first in St. Louis at Jewish Family Service, then at a residential treatment center for disturbed children in Cleveland, and finally as executive director of Jewish Family and Children's Service in Minneapolis, where he continued from 1945 until his retirement in 1968. He also worked as a psychotherapist in private practice during this period.

Sometime around 1939, Rakosi fell silent as a writer. He would not resume writing until he neared retirement. This long silence (of about twenty-seven years) makes up a kind of absent center to Rakosi's writing career. It resulted from a complex entanglement of personal and political causes, and Rakosi has vacillated over the years as to which of these causes played the larger role. Having married in 1939, he felt more keenly than ever the difficulty of balancing professional, artistic, personal, and now familial demands, finding it almost impossible to write while also meeting his other responsibilities. During this same period (the 1930s) he had been politically radicalized by his experience of the Great Depression, a process that culminated in his joining the Communist Party and in his Marxist conviction that lyric poetry was inadequate to the exigencies of the age. Finally, Rakosi has also spoken and written of another cause antecedent to these factors, describing an ''inertness of . . . will'' that seems to have plagued his attempts to write almost from the start (*Collected Prose* 88). During his period of poetic silence, however, Rakosi did not abandon writing completely. He published many professional articles on social work and psychotherapy and found himself fascinated ''by people'' and ''the process of helping.'' He has summed up the significance of this time away from poetry by saying, ''This was not a dead period for me. It was tremendously alive,'' and by pointing out that ''[f]or a writer [social work is] a great opportunity because people open up to you endlessly'' (Hatlen 113). Even so, it remains an irony of Rakosi's career that it would take so many years for this ''opportunity'' to manifest itself in poetry.

MAJOR WORKS AND THEMES

The trajectory of Rakosi's life is worth dwelling on because it so dramatically influences the shape of his writing career, with its three rather sharply marked stages of writing, silence, and resurgence. As a young writer in the 1920s, Rakosi had some notable successes, placing poems in two of the most important little magazines of the international avant-garde, *The Little Review* (edited by Margaret Anderson and Jane Heap) and *The Exile* (edited by Ezra Pound). Probably through seeing his work in *The Exile*, Louis Zukofsky first became aware of Rakosi. As Zukofsky edited a special ''objectivist'' number of Harriet Monroe's *Poetry* magazine (which would appear in February 1931), followed by the book-length *An "Objectivists" Anthology* (1932), the two men entered into a period of intensive correspondence. Zukofsky commented on Rakosi's work in

meticulous detail, helping to free the poetry of certain too-dominant early influences (especially T. S. Eliot and Wallace Stevens) and facilitating the emergence
of Rakosi's own distinctive style. As we have already seen, Zukofsky's interest
and recognition came at an important moment, when Rakosi was near despair
and already close to giving up writing. Rakosi benefited from the attention and
found it exciting to be part of a ''movement,'' even if the nature of that movement was far from coherent. In later years, however, Rakosi has often responded
with demurrals when asked about the significance of the movement, pointing to
the rather arbitrary manner of its coming into being (which initially involved
Harriet Monroe's insistence that Zukofsky have a ''movement'' for his special
number of *Poetry*). At one extreme, he has suggested that the movement really
existed only in Zukofsky's head. On the other hand, Rakosi has frequently noted
that the term ''objectivist'' and the aesthetic concerns associated with it seemed
to him ''useful'': ''It conveyed a meaning which was, in fact, my objective: to
present objects in their most essential reality and to make of each poem an
object'' (''A Note on the 'Objectivists' '' 36).

Upon closer examination this ''meaning'' reveals itself to be double, indicating both (1) a devotion to ''objective'' as opposed to purely ''subjective''
reality, the latter being the realm of ''personal vagueness; of loose bowels and
streaming, sometimes screaming, consciousness'' (''A Note'' 36), and (2) a
desire to present the poem itself *as an object*, one obeying the laws of linguistic
and formal necessity. As it turned out, the term was similarly useful to the other
members of the core group of objectivists that emerged from Zukofsky's anthologies, including Zukofsky himself, Charles Reznikoff, and George Oppen.
Rakosi felt a direct artistic affinity only with the work of Reznikoff, but each
of these four writers seems to have continued to think about the ''objectivist''
principles originally formulated by Zukofsky and to have applied his own interpretations of these principles to his work. This process of thinking with the
term ''objectivist'' (a variation of what Zukofsky called ''thinking with the
things as they exist'') produced a repertoire of related individual responses to a
shared set of aesthetic concerns. This ''objectivist'' field of production can be
thought of as consisting of various works displaying distinctive ratios of individuality and interconnectedness. The calculation or examination of such ratios
would have to take into account not only purely ''aesthetic'' concerns but also
publishing activities (specifically, the operations of To Publishers and the Objectivist Press). In any event, the term has proven inescapable for Rakosi, significantly affecting both his early career and the reception of his work upon his
return to writing in the 1960s.

The difficulties surrounding the term ''objectivist'' seem no more than appropriate, since Rakosi's writing has been fraught by conflict and contradiction
almost from the start. Even before his entanglement in the conflict between art
and social action reached its peak in the late 1930s, his poetic practice had been
haunted by difficult oppositions. First among these oppositions was what might

be described as a conflict between symbolist and objectivist modes. Under the influence of both Eliot and Stevens, Rakosi found himself as a young poet "very much seduced by the elegance of language, the imaginative associations of words" (Dembo interview 195). As Rakosi has described it, his intense involvement in this "language world—a little like the world of Wallace Stevens" existed in tension with the devotion he also felt toward "social reality" (195). Accordingly, much of Rakosi's early poetry manifests a certain volatility and instability, displaying an affinity for elusively ironic stances and fantastic journeys into bizarre landscapes, as if such imaginary zones might accommodate in their plasticity the tensions and oppositions that his poems could not escape.

One poem in particular, "Orphean Lost," can give us some important insight into both Rakosi's early poetic stance and his development into an objectivist writer:

> The oakboughs of the cottagers
> descend, my lover,
> with the bestial evening.
> The shadows of their swelled trunks
> crush the frugal herb.
> The heights lag
> and perish in a blue vacuum.
>
> And I, my lover,
> skirt the cottages,
> the eternal hearths and gloom
> to animate the ideal
> with internal passion. (*Poems 1923–1941* 78)

Rakosi has written in retrospect that this poem "recalls . . . [his] deepest inner tone," evoking "[t]he bestial evening of insecurity and alienation, of mysterious depths and longing" (*Collected Prose* 93). As it happens, this most typically "Rakosian" poem was also deployed as an exemplar of objectivist qualities. Zukofsky printed it as the lead-off poem of the objectivist number of *Poetry*—only here it appeared with a difference. Zukofsky installed the poem as part of a series including three other Rakosi poems, all appearing under the common heading "Before You" (and culminating with the poem of that title). As a consequence of this arrangement, Rakosi's "subjective" stance of "insecurity and alienation" (the lonely "I" addressing his "lover") is decentered, made to participate in a more wide-ranging play of different voices. The individual and alienated lyric scene gives way to serial engagement with a variegated topography. This was one way to contain, or disperse, the appeals of "streaming, and sometimes screaming, consciousness," but still to be dealt with were the seductions of the Stevensian "language world" ("The heights lag / and perish in a blue vacuum").

Another poem, first published in 1933, two years after the objectivist number of *Poetry*, demonstrates a counterresponse to the Stevensian mode. This poem, "The Lobster," which was dedicated to William Carlos Williams when it first appeared, has often been discussed as Rakosi's objectivist poem par excellence. Here is an excerpt:

> Young sea-horse
> Hippocampus twenty
> minutes old—
>
> nobody has ever
> seen this marine
> freak blink
>
> It radiates on
> terminal vertebrae
> a comb of twenty
>
> upright spines
> and curls
> its rocky tail.
>
> Saltflush lobster
> bull encrusted swims
> backwards from the rock. (*Collected Poems* 84–85)

Here Rakosi shows the influence of Williams (and also Marianne Moore), adopting a mode of hard-edged and precise objectivist description and displacing the lyric "I" completely in favor of particularities of the physical scene. In Rakosi's later work this mode seldom expresses itself so purely, but the penchant for precise quasi-"scientific" observation becomes an enduring element of his poetic repertoire.

In the second half of the 1930s, however, the conflict of symbolist and objectivist modes receded before the struggle between the aesthetic and the political, between literary production and social action. With the help of Andrew Crozier's invaluable edition of the *Poems 1923–1941*, which recovers much early material that had been either completely lost or transformed beyond recognition, it has become possible to trace the process by which Rakosi's poetry of the late 1930s enacts its own dissolution, tenaciously grappling with the conflicts and contradictions of its age as it slowly and painfully argues itself into silence. In an abandoned longer work entitled "The Beasts," partially reconstructed by Crozier (and considered by him to be a lost "modern masterpiece"), Rakosi shifts his focus from imaginary and fantastic scenes to the modern urban landscape, with its displays of power:

> This way the channeled ceiling
> luminaires
>   of the National

> Bank of Commerce
> metal finish crystal ground floor
> and small grilled windows,
> the banking hours.

and its rapid shifts of scene:

> Immigrants from Lodz
> in a furnished room
> close to the stores.
> Porcelain pitcher,
> bath and hand towels
> on the bed rails.

> A new sign goes
> into the window *Smocking
> Hemstitching, Rhinestone Setting.* (*Collected Poems* 152–54)

Here Rakosi juxtaposes the facades of wealth to those of the more modest "enterprises" of urban immigrants. The poem as a whole moves toward an examination of the forms of life under capitalism, a system experiencing world-wide crisis in the 1930s. Here Rakosi's work parallels moves made by the other objectivists toward a poetics of topography, a large-scale grappling with "historic and contemporary particulars."

Despite its sophisticated and promising response to the historical situation, however, "The Beasts" was never completed, and Rakosi continued the process of self-interrogation that would eventually lead to his poetic silence. In "Surrealists (1930)" Rakosi had approached his difficulties ironically, mixing surrealist imagery and vaudevillian cross talk in an exchange on the responsibilities of the poet. A skeptical interlocutor squares off against the poet, who asserts his artistic imperatives:

> I don't get you.
> Why don't you talk English?

> You don't get me?
> I have the blues, I have to tear. (*Collected Poems* 166)

As the poem continues, the poet is faced with, and rejects, a whole range of social responsibilities, as in this sample exchange:

> But somebody has to drive the spikes,
> pitch the gears, oil the cams.

> Not me brother! I'm inside waiting for a surprise,
> I'm in love with a girl on the Wabash,

I'm alone with a hand in my hand
and a pair of wonderful eyes. (*Collected Poems* 166–67)

Here the poet fends off the demands of the social "machine" by comically
invoking the poetic prerogatives of sentiment. But the dialogue continues, ending in a standoff as a direct appeal to principles of social solidarity ("Say, could
you stand an old man to a cup of coffee?") is rebuffed ("Listen, old man! I
draw a sweet note out of myself / and have no time for other strangeness" 167).
The tension here between social obligations and the poet's own "sweet note"
is sounded in poem after poem from the 1930s. In "Declaration," the poet
surrenders, putting aside his art to take up the social struggle:

I shall put away my purity now
and find my art in other men
before I end up like a taper
in the bedroom of an old maid.

. . . .

This is no time for looking backward.
I am for public action and public hate
and I am impatient to declare myself. (*Collected Poems* 142)

The poet decisively rejects the feminized world of poetry for the masculine arena
of politics, but as the historical situation worsened in the 1930s, the realm of
"public action and public hate" proved an extremely dangerous place. In an
unpublished manuscript from 1938 (cited in the notes to *Poems 1923–1941*)
bearing the twin titles "On the Proposed Partition of Czechoslovakia" and
"Black Day," Rakosi laments a world where "whole nations know no justice"
(199) and professes a sense of explicitly sociopolitical bewilderment ("this can
not be 1938, this is not my city, not my land" 199) and fear ("I am back in
the Ghetto / with a yellow Jewsign on my back" 200). The identity of ethnic
Jew, which had permitted a special, if difficult, angle of vision on the modern
scene, is now stamped upon the poet like a brand. At the same time, the poem
registers an atmosphere in which the very possibility of sincerity seems to be
undermined by a politically and ethnically tinged paranoia and suspicion:
"Every honest word = Red / & every intense passion Jewish" (200). It may
be that Rakosi, damned as both communist and Jew, records in this manuscript
the final double bind from which it seemed, for a time, that no argument could
extricate him.

    After nearly three decades of silence, Rakosi *did* extricate himself, and he
has produced another three decades or so of writing since his return to the field.
One culmination of this activity was reached with the publication of his *Collected Poems* in 1986, in the composition of which Rakosi proceeded "as if . . .
making up a book for the first time, with the parts before me, the individual

poems'' (17). The intended result was that the poems would be more than ''just an aggregation,'' that a ''larger and perhaps different meaning'' would ''be found . . . in the arrangement'' (17). Here Rakosi's lifelong habit of obsessive revision found expression in a complete reworking of his poetic oeuvre. This re/visionary approach to poetry may perhaps be seen as the sign of a perpetual dissatisfaction addressed not only to whether a particular poem is ''good'' or ''bad'' but to a shifting sense of the aims and purposes of poetry itself. The resulting textual instability is matched, on a historical scale, against the insta-bilities and dislocations of the modern world itself, the twists and turns through which the century has unfolded. Thus, Rakosi's poetics of re/invention takes on a mimetic function, reflecting the multiple and shifting strategies of reading and living called forth by the modern and postmodern conditions.

An examination of Rakosi's *Collected Poems* permits a more complex view of his characteristic modes, themes, and concerns—including his attitudes to-ward his Jewishness—to emerge. Rakosi has said that he started out with ''very little sense of Jewish identification'' (Hatlen 107), but we have already seen evidence of the sort of terror-ridden ''identification'' forced from without by the events of the fascist 1930s. More positively, Rakosi notes that he developed a stronger sense of Jewish identity through his connection to Jewish social agen-cies, which involved working with, and living in, Jewish communities. In con-sidering the role played by Jewishness in the work of the objectivists, Rakosi identifies four relevant characteristics: ''very great seriousness,'' ''a sense of moral purpose,'' an ''existential intensity,'' and ''humor and irony,'' with this last pair of qualities belonging more particularly to ''the modern Jew living in the diaspora'' (Hatlen 108). Sharon Dolin points out that a significant number of Rakosi's poems are marked by explicit biblical references and argues for a connection between Rakosi's Jewishness and his use of the ''dyadic strophe.'' According to Dolin, this strophe allows for the expression of a particularly Jewish concern, the ''dialogical, interrogative relationship with the divine'' (293). Rakosi's ''Services'' is an example of the use of the dyadic strophe to address a Jewish subject:

> Hush!
> The rabbi walks in thought
>   as in an ordained measure
> to the Ark
>   and slowly opens its great doors.
>
> The congregation rises
>   and faces the six torahs
> and the covenant
>   and all beyond.
> The Ark glows.
>   Hear, O Israel! (*Collected Poems* 126)

A citation from Rakosi's "Americana" series may serve to indicate how seriousness and irony often go hand in hand for Rakosi and how he is always attuned to the revelations of voice and idiom:

> I'll bet you dollars to doughnuts
> the Vincents hit us tonight.
> The village chief just took off,
> claiming he had business in Danang.
>
> I'd like to take off myself,
> all the way to Flint, Michigan.
> For openers I'd show up at the airport
> with a big sign, GET THE MARINES OUT OF VIETNAM.
> Under that in smaller letters:
> > *starting with me.*
> ("A Mustache Drawn on Captain Patterson" *Collected Poems* 358)

Finally, we might point to the way the struggle with contradiction and conflict so characteristic of Rakosi's early poetry might be said to mature into an engagement with paradox and the play of multiple and simultaneous possibilities in his later work. Here an example of Rakosi's epigrammatic prose, which sometimes runs very close to poetry, should serve:

Are God and man streaming in opposite directions? . . . man towards the grand, the universal—mystical because it is not attainable—and God, since He is already in possession of that, towards the elementary particles of matter and the bursting inexhaustibility of a moment.
   The forces are too powerful for love.
   The poet has a sense of both vectors. (*Collected Prose* 119)

CRITICAL RECEPTION

As we have seen, Rakosi's early poems were well received, but until recently they remained scattered in the pages of the ephemeral little magazines of the modernist era. His first book, *Selected Poems*, did not appear until 1941, after Rakosi had already stopped writing, and it seems to have gone largely unnoticed. Rakosi himself, unhappy with his reworkings and abridgments of earlier poems for that volume, would later call the book "a disaster" (Hatlen 101). *Amulet* (1967), the book that marks his return to writing, was met with critical praise, with John Hall, for example, describing the verse as "meditative poetry which avoids the sentimental," also calling it "graceful in language" and "exact" (cited in Buckeye 471). Other critics praised the lightness and irony of the poetry, but Jim Harrison thought Rakosi's lyric strength came without the "range" of Williams or Zukofsky (cited in Buckeye 470). Between 1967 and 1983 Rakosi published four more books of poetry—*Ere-Voice* (1971), *Ex Cra-*

nium, Night (1975), *Droles de Journal* (1980), and *Spiritus, I* (1983)—all appearing to generally good reviews, with some dissenting voices. Significant critical overviews and evaluations of Rakosi's career began to appear with the publication of the *Collected Poems* (1986), followed by a collection of critical essays edited by Michael Heller in 1993 (as part of the important *Man/Woman and Poet* series from the National Poetry Foundation, which has also devoted volumes to the other objectivists). In the Heller volume, David Zucker explores the important role of "wit" in Rakosi's poetry, which Zucker finds "crucial not only to tone but to the structure of his thought, his way of approaching the organization of the poem as well as his response to the world" (359). Of special importance is Jeffrey Peterson's long, wide-ranging, and provocative essay, which explores such diverse concerns and issues as the figure of the poet-as-scientist, the "biomorphic" interpenetration of body and machine, and the relationship between social work and poetry.

Andrew Crozier's reconstruction of Rakosi's early body of work in *Poems 1923–1941*, with its introductory essay and editorial apparatus, remains one of the most significant interventions in the reception and production of Rakosi's poetry. That volume is supplemented in the Heller collection by two additional essays on Rakosi's early poetry by Crozier, "Carl Rakosi in the 'Objectivists' Epoch" and "Remembering Carl Rakosi: A Conjectural Reconstruction of 'The Beasts.' " However, an important question about Rakosi's status as a primarily "lyric" poet is raised both by Crozier's "reconstruction" of "The Beasts" and by the possibility of reading the *Collected Poems* as one long, serial work. That question is of relevance not only to the evaluation of Rakosi's work but to the criticism of poetry more generally: Should we read the body of Rakosi's poetry looking for a "masterpiece" in the form of a major work of significant length (another candidate here is "The Old Poet's Tale"), or should we heed Rakosi's frequently reiterated defenses of the importance of the short lyric taken on its own terms? It has been observed that Rakosi's affinity for the "microcosmic," in both subject and form, links him to the great traditions of Chinese and Japanese poetry (Clark, cited in Buckeye 485). Rakosi himself has written of the paradoxically "epic" power the small, unassuming lyric can have, because it has "sifted out the essence of a thing" (*Collected Prose* 41). At present, though, academic criticism in America seems ill prepared to carry out an evaluation of poetry operating in this mode (the difficulty is relevant to the work of Charles Reznikoff as well). Despite the longevity of Rakosi's career, the problem remains an open one, since the serious critical estimate of his work is only just beginning.

BIBLIOGRAPHY

Works by Carl Rakosi

Two Poems. New York: Modern Editions Press, 1933.
Selected Poems. Norfolk, CT: New Directions, 1941.

Amulet. New York: New Directions, 1967.
"A note on the 'Objectivists.'" *Story Brook* 3: 4 (1969): 36–37.
Ere-Voice. New York: New Directions, 1971.
Ex Cranium, Night. Los Angeles: Black Sparrow Press, 1975.
Droles de Journal. West Branch, IA: Toothpaste Press, 1980.
The Collected Prose of Carl Rakosi. Orono, ME: National Poetry Foundation, 1983.
Spiritus, I. New York: New Directions, 1983.
The Collected Poems of Carl Rakosi. Orono, ME: National Poetry Foundation, 1986.
"George Oppen: The Last Days." *Talisman: A Journal of Contemporary Poetry and Poetics* (1989): 82–89.
Poems 1923–1941. Los Angeles: Sun and Moon Press, 1995.

Works about Carl Rakosi

Buckeye, Robert. "Materials towards a Study of Carl Rakosi." In Heller, 451–88.
Chilton, Harrison Randolph, Jr. *The Object Beyond the Image: A Study of Four Objectivist Poets.* Diss., Ann Arbor: UMI, 1981.
Crozier, Andrew. "Carl Rakosi in the 'Objectivists' Epoch." In Heller, 95–114.
———. "Remembering Carl Rakosi: A Conjectural Reconstruction of 'The Beasts.'" In Heller, 213–32.
Dembo, L. S., and Cyrena N. Pondrom, eds. "Interview with Carl Rakosi." *The Contemporary Writer: Interviews with Sixteen Novelists.* Madison: University of Wisconsin Press, 1972.
Dolin, Sharon. "Carl Rakosi's Dyadic Strophe." In Heller, 285–306.
Evans, George, and August Kleinzahler. "An Interview with Carl Rakosi." In Heller, 61–92.
Hatlen, Burton. "Interview with Carl Rakosi." *Sagetrieb: A Journal Devoted to Poets in the Pound–H. D.–Williams Tradition* 5: 2 (1986): 95–123.
Heller, Michael, ed. *Carl Rakosi: Man and Poet.* Orono, ME: National Poetry Foundation, 1993.
Peterson, Jeffrey. "'The Allotropes of Vision': Carl Rakosi and the Psychology of Microscopy." In Heller, 119–92.
Sharp, Tom. *"Objectivists" 1927–1934: A Critical History.* Diss., Stanford University, 1982. Ann Arbor: UMI, 1982.
Shoemaker, Steve. "Interview with Carl Rakosi." *Sagetrieb: A Journal Devoted to Poets in the Pound–H. D.–Williams Tradition* 11: 3 (1992): 93–132.
———. *Of Being Numerous: The Modernist Revolution, the "Objectivist" Vortex, and the Poetry of Survival.* Diss., University of Virginia, 1997. Ann Arbor: UMI, 1997.
Zucker, David. "'A Small Metaphysical Lamp': Carl Rakosi's Wit." In Heller, 359–68.

CHARLES REZNIKOFF (1894–1976)

Genevieve Cohen-Cheminet

BIOGRAPHY

Charles Ezkiel Reznikoff was born in Brownsville, Brooklyn, a Jewish neighborhood, in 1894, and he grew up in New York City. Both his parents, Sarah Yetta Wolwovsky, a seamstress, and Nathan Reznikoff, a sewing machine operator, were Yiddish-speaking Russian Jews. Family history left a significant imprint on Reznikoff. He read his own predestined vocation in the fate of his maternal grandfather, who had been torn between his professional duties and his need to write Hebrew poetry. When his grandfather's widow heard he had died on a business trip, she burned his manuscripts for fear that the czarist police would deem the Hebrew writings subversive. Hence, publication remained Reznikoff's primary concern.

Reznikoff graduated from Brooklyn Boys' High School in 1910, then went to the Missouri School of Journalism. However, realizing that "journalism was more concerned with news than with writing" (*Complete Poems* [*CP*], 233) or literature, he enrolled in New York University's Law School in 1912. While studying law, he discovered James Joyce's *Portrait of the Artist as a Young Man*, the review *The Egoist*, and the writings of Robert Frost, T. S. Eliot, William Carlos Williams, Marianne Moore, Wallace Stevens, and D. H. Lawrence. Later he turned to Ezra Pound and Wyndham Lewis' *Blast*, Joyce's *Ulysses*, Eliot's *The Waste Land*, and Gaudier-Brzeska's statues.

He was admitted to the bar of the state of New York in 1916 but practiced only long enough only to lose a family trail and make the choice that governed his life. He would not be tied down by a career. He would be a poet, much to his parents' dismay. He published a few poems in Harriet Monroe's *Poetry*

(1917) and became a traveling salesman for his father's business. This allowed him time to walk—"he saw, felt, wrote" (Syrkin in Hindus 42)—and to print *Rhythms* (1918) privately.

In the late 1920s, Reznikoff met William Carlos Williams, George and Mary Oppen, and Louis Zukofsky, who launched the Objectivist Press. In 1927 he met Marie Syrkin, the daughter of Russian-Jewish intellectuals Basya and Nachman Syrkin, one of the founders of Labor Zionism. In 1930, Marie Syrkin married him:

a neatly dressed, moderately nice-looking young man, average in height, with no striking features and nothing in his appearance to suggest bohemian non-conformity; in fact very unlike [her] vision of a literary man; . . . But . . . he rejected the basic conventions of how life should be led. He would assume no obligations, such as support of a family that might hamper his true vocation. (Syrkin in Hindus 39–40)

Due to the 1929 depression, Reznikoff worked as editor for the *Corpus Juris* law encyclopedia but was fired for being too slow and meticulous. He read German poetry and Japanese and French poetry translations while Marie was involved with the Zionist cause. Their personalities often clashed. Though deeply Jewish, Reznikoff "[was] neither an observant Jew nor a nationalist with political affiliations" (Hindus 55). In 1933, Marie Syrkin took a trip to Palestine without Reznikoff, as "he had not yet explored Central Park to the full" (Hindus 44). He continued writing and had *Testimony* (1934), *In Memoriam* (1934), *Jerusalem the Golden* (1934), and *Separate Way* (1936) printed privately.

In 1938, needing money to live and publish, Reznikoff put his talents to script writing thanks to an oldtime friend, Albert Lewin, a Hollywood producer. When that failed, he decided writing would come first, no matter how strained his circumstances were. He had *Going To and Fro and Walking Up and Down* (1941) printed privately. Odd jobs from the Jewish Publication Society of America helped but also kept him away from poetry (*The Lionhearted, a Story about the Jews in Medieval England*, 1944). When their marriage broke down, Marie went to Brandeis University as assistant professor in 1950, while entrusting Reznikoff with editing jobs for *Jewish Frontier*. New Directions published *By the Waters of Manhattan* (verse) in 1962.

Public recognition came late. At sixty-nine Reznikoff received the 1963 Morton Dauwen Zabel Award for Poetry from the National Institute of Arts and Letters.

To CHARLES REZNIKOFF,
born by the waters of Manhattan. Mr. Reznikoff was educated for the law but has instead dedicated his life to giving sworn testimony in the court of poetry against the swaggering injustices of our culture and on behalf of its meek wonders. (May 26, 1971. William Maxwell. San Diego Archives, Box VIII)

At seventy-seven, he was awarded the 1971 Jewish Book Council of America's Award. New Directions published the first volume of *Testimony: A Recitative, the United States, 1885–1915* (first printed 1965), but Reznikoff had the second volume printed privately (first printed 1968). To see Black Sparrow Press publish *By the Well of Living and Seeing, New and Selected Poems 1918–1973* (1974), *Holocaust* (1975), and *The Complete Poems* (Seamus Cooney, ed., 1976) was thus a long-awaited reward.

On January 22, 1976, after an early dinner, Reznikoff told Marie Syrkin, "You know I never made money but I have done everything that I most wanted to do," and died of a heart attack. In his papers, Marie Syrkin found the manuscript of a novel, *The Manner Music*, later published by Black Sparrow Press. In the Old Mount Carmel Cemetery, Brooklyn, walkers can read his epitaph taken from *Separate Way*, "And the day's brightness dwindles into stars" (*CPI* 167).

MAJOR WORKS AND THEMES

A story told by a French Talmudist, Marc-Alain Ouaknin, insightfully points to some of the issues related to poetry and Judaism. See how Rabbi Bounam welcomed his new disciples at their first meeting with the following parable:

In Cracow, there lived a Jew named Rabbi Eisiq, son of Rabbi Yankel. One night, he dreamed of a man telling him: "Go to Prague, walk up to the bridge which leads to the Royal Castle, dig under the third pillar, and there you will find a treasure." Eisiq did not pay much heed to this dream, but when it occurred again, he left for Prague. Upon reaching the bridge, he meant to start digging but the captain of the guards called him out and asked him:

"What are you doing? What are you looking for?" And Rabbi Eisiq told him his dream. The captain of the guards burst out laughing:

"Poor fellow, he said, you walked all the way from Cracow to Prague just for a dream! What if I too listened to my dreams? Last night I dreamed that I had to go to Eisiq's, son of Yankel, because I would discover a great treasure under his stove."

Rabbi Eisiq, son of Yankel, smiled, thanked the captain and returned to Cracow where he found the treasure hidden under his stove. (Ouaknin and Rotnemer 30–31)

In the journey from Cracow toward Prague I read the necessary dialogue with the Other, which helps one understand one's own discourse. This dialogical detour transforms the walker who does not return to Cracow as he left it. Furthermore, read within the context of a master-disciple relationship, this story performatively enacts a displacement between what is given and what is received, between transmission and interpretation. In Jewish tradition, the meaning of canonical texts is not a sacred truth to be authoritatively delivered whole to a passive disciple. It results from an individual engagement with texts and from "the disengagement of the master" ("l'effacement du maître," Ouaknin 26), who becomes a dialogical go-between linking discipline and texts. The trope of the journey is thus the paradigm of an open interpretation, which refuses an idolatrous transmission of meaning and which conjoins genealogy with fracture.

I suggest we address Reznikoff's relation to Judaism within this context of an "atheistic interpretation" (Atlan 86), of a detour and an appropriation of American and Jewish narrative chains. This detour could be termed hermeneutical, in the sense given by contemporary French philosopher Paul Ricoeur when he defined hermeneutics as "the very deciphering of life in the mirror of the text" ("le déchiffrage même de la vie au miroir du texte," Ricoeur 377). The mirror metaphor should not be understood as meaning that the poetical text is the mirror of the world. Paul Ricoeur used the Latin meaning of mirror, *speculum*, thus referring to writing as a speculative experience correlating a text to other texts. My overall thesis is that the originality of Reznikoff's speculative journey into Judaism lies in the fact that he is part and parcel of American culture while "deciphering" the New World "in the mirror of the texts" of the Old World. Let us see how Reznikoff looks "at the world through printed pages" (*Collected Poems* 159).

An appraisal of a poet's relation to Judaism necessarily implies that one should look into the influence and import of tradition in his writing. Ever since Walt Whitman, the canonical image of the American poet has been that of a rebel breaking away from an exhausted tradition. Hence, Reznikoff has been shown as a nonobservant Jew, a Marxist activist of the 1930s, and recent anthologies that mention him (Eliot Weinberger's, Douglas Messerli's) quote *Holocaust* and *Testimony* because they seem to confirm "Charles Reznikoff's radical or Marxist politics" (Blasing 16). However, beneath the stereotype of modernism as rebellion, there lies the idea of a linear, teleological progress of literary history. Albert Gelpi's *A Coherent Splendor* or, more recently, Mutlu Konuk Blasing's *Politics and Form in Postmodern Poetry* both hold as methodologically irrelevant

the prevailing assumption that experimental forms signify political opposition while traditional forms are politically conservative. Such essentialist alignments of forms with extraformal values, and the oppositional framework of innovation versus conservation that they yield, reflect modernist biases inappropriate for reading postwar poetry. (Blasing, Foreword)

Blasing and Gelpi uncover both tensions and continuities between premodernist and modernist poetry. This more subtle epistemological groundwork allows us to assess Reznikoff's poetical modernity in his renewed relation to the Jewish tradition. "*Luzzato*," a poem from *Jerusalem the Golden*, exemplifies this point:

78
Luzzato Padua 1727

The sentences we studied are rungs upon the ladder Jacob saw;
the law itself is nothing but the road;

I have become impatient of what the rabbis said,
and try to listen to what the angels say.
I have left Padua and am in Jerusalem at last, my friend;
for, as our God was never of wood or bone,
our land is not of stone or earth. (*CPI*, 127)

In Luzzato's departure from Padua to Jerusalem, Reznikoff read an exemplary Jewish attitude toward canonical texts, which emphasizes a thorough knowledge of texts and a call for heterodox interpretations. Talmudic hypertexts ("the sentences we studied"), their misreading ("I have become impatient of what the rabbis said"), and the dialogue they raise ("my friends") are Reznikoff's chosen land.

A second misunderstanding has predictably surrounded the academic usage of Judaism as a critical tool. What is at stake is not so much folkore or ethnicity, that is, the predictable argument of a cultural tension between minority and majority groups, but Judaism as a specific textual space, delineated by a corpus of canonical texts and their interpretations, a corpus of source texts (hereafter called hypotexts) that make up what Harold Bloom rightfully called "the Jewish textual difference" (Bloom 205). What was Reznikoff's relation to this hypotextual space? He certainly was not born into it. He learned with T. S. Eliot that between a textual heritage and an inheritor there is no continuity, no *mnemne*, but a generational fracture in transmission, an *anamnesis*, and an effort of reappropriation: "[Tradition], cannot be inherited, and if you want it you must obtain it by great labour" (Eliot 14). Reznikoff's forceful singularity was to anticipate in the genealogical fracture a future process of words inseminating words (in Hebrew *Zakhor*, memory is related to *Zekhar*, semen).

This inseminating process is metaphorically at work in poems like "We Have a Print of Marc Chagall's Picture of a Green-Faced Jew" (*CPII*, 121), which correlates fracture and Jewish endurance, or "A Compassionate People," which sets within contingent historical ruptures the future dissemination of Jewish discursive chains.

As when a great tree bright with blossoms and heavy with fruit,
is cut down and its seeds are carried far
by the winds of the sky and the waves of the streams and seas,
and it grows again on distant slopes and shores
in many places at once,
still blossoming and bearing fruit a hundred and a thousandfold,
so, at the destruction of the Temple
. . . , ten thousand synagogues
took root and flourished
in Palestine and in Babylonia and along the Mediterranean;
so the tides carried from Spain and Portugal
a Spinoza to Holland
and a Disraeli to England.

> *God, delighting in life,*
> *You have remembered us for life. (CPII, 60)*

The metaphor of the tree felled in full bloom associates destruction with the unpredictable, secret, and aleatory growth of seeds that will be disseminated by the wind and sea. They will grow and multiply far from their land of origin, in an ectopic move. Fracture is thus dialectically overcome by a future fertile scattering, whose biological/discursive nature ensures the perennial Jewish philosophical agenda.

Two side points here: to associate destruction with scattering and discursive rebirth implicitly points to a teleological view of history in which moments of darkness become an anticipation of light, as described in this poem:

> If there is a scheme,
> perhaps this too is in the scheme,
> as when a subway car turns on a switch,
> the wheels screeching against the rails,
> and the lights go out—
> but are on again in a moment. (CPI, 120)

The first religious hypothesis of a divine scheme, of the "continuing intervention of God in history" ("la continuité de l'intervention divine dans l'histoire" (Yerushalmi *Zakhor* 41), runs parallel to the second hypothesis of a predestined poetical vocation (my interpretation of "this too"). Uncertainty is a moment of darkness recorded in a temporal continuum (the speed of the train rolling on its rails). The train metaphor implies a starting point as well as a final station, a *telos*. The paratactic dash dramatizes the waiting period, enacting in reading time this suspension of signification and direction. It works in parallel with the suspension of faith in the intervention of God in history but also attests to two inevitable and consecutive moments in the historical continuum of the Bnei Israel's lives. In this poem, as in "A Compassionate People," Reznikoff associates temporal consecutiveness, direction, and signification. Destructions are thus seen as historically contingent and temporary, bound to be overcome by discursive rebirth in another land. This I find consonant with entire volumes like *Holocaust* or *In Memoriam: 1933*, which performatively asserts that although Jerusalem has been trampled down, "when [oppressors] have become a legend/ and Rome a fable, that old men will tell of at the city's gate,/the tellers will be Jews and their speech Hebrew" (*CP*, 145). This leads to my second side point: the process of dissemination-insemination described in "A Compassionate People" is quite etymologically a diaspora, a discursive sowing ("*Yzre'el* literally means 'God sows,' " Modrzejewski 6). Thus, writing itself becomes invested with a diasporic dimension since Reznikoff's poems grow out of a hypotextual soil.

> Of all that I have written
> you say: "how much was poorly said."
> But look!
> The oak has many acorns
> that a single oak might live. (*CPII*, 209)

Biological growth and poetical reactivation, exile, and dissemination thus converge. I therefore argue that Judaism in Reznikoff's poetry is more than a thematic network of references. It pertains to the discursive nature of his writing, which is consistently reader-oriented. How, then, does the reader notice the presence of Jewish canonical hypotexts?

The reader is usually alerted by paratextual notations, titles, and epigraphs. They point to source hypotexts and reveal a discursive fathering/mothering process.

Reznikoff reactivated biblical, American, and European narrative chains by removing them from their first enunciative contexts and then rooting them in his own discourse. At times, the source hypotexts are both readable and visible, as in "Salmon and Red Wine," which genetically links the holy book, the *Mishnah* (*Aboth* 6: 4) to Reznikoff's situation in New York.

> Salmon and red wine
> and a cake fat with raisins and nuts:
> no diet for a writer of verse
> who must learn to fast
> and drink water by measure.
>
> Those of us without house and ground
> who leave tomorrow must keep our baggage light:
> a psalm, perhaps a dialogue—
> brief as Lamech's song in *Genesis*,
> even Job among his friends—
> but no more. (*CP*, 76)

Reznikoff is a traveler rooted in New York City, a sedentary nomad, this oxymoron being balanced by the poetic learning of measure. The same readability and visibility are to be noted in *The English in Virginia, April 1607*, whose paratextual note says: "Based upon the *Works of Captain John Smith*, edited by Edward Arber" (*CPI*, 122). The reader also masters the context of the detour in the case of volumes like *Holocaust* and *Testimony*, whose incipits clearly mention easily accessible European and American judicial archives. A limited example of readability and visibility would be *The Fifth Book of the Maccabees* (*CPII*, 179), where Reznikoff upturns this pattern of discursive fathering/mothering. A missing fifth book is added to the four biblical hypotexts, instead of being fathered/mothered by the *Four Books of the Maccabees* or Josephus' *The Jewish War* and *Antiquities of the Jews*. This is no pastiche but a creation upturned toward its hypotextual source. Here again the reference is stable, legible, and announced.

At other times, the hypotext is legible but unreadable to the reader who is not cognizant with Hebrew basics, as in "A Compassionate People," in which you may or may not have recognized a *Beracha* (a prayer of blessing) in italics (*God, delighting in life, You have remembered us for life. CPII*, 60). The poem does not grow out of the hypotext as previously shown but includes its own Hebrew textual seed.

Seen from the reader's side, poems are moved away from their own Reznikoff's enunciative space toward their discursive sources. A few lines from "Day of Atonement" typify this move or detour:

> If only I could write four pens between five fingers
> and with each pen a different sentence at the same time—
> but the rabbis say it is a lost art, a lost art.
> I well believe it. (*CP*, 67)

The four pens of appropriation point to a refusal of linearity, totality, closure, and exclusive meanings and guide the reader toward canonical hypotexts. But again, a uniquely objectivist, proletarian view of Reznikoff would be oblivious to these pens. Further, holding Reznikoff's poems together with their source hypotexts turns attention toward the issue of stasis and movement, rootedness and perambulation. I will now argue that this textual detour metaphorically pulls writing and reading away from their familiar and comfortable American grounds.

A last poem will guide my reading:

> A hundred generations, yes, a hundred and twenty-five,
> had the strength each day
> not to eat this and that (unclean!)
> not to say this and that,
> not to do this and that (unjust!),
> and with all this and all that
> to go about
> as men and Jews . . .
> Whatever my grandfathers did or said
> for all of their brief lives
> still was theirs,
> as all of its drops at a moment make the fountain
> and all of its leaves a palm.
> Each word they spoke and every thought
> was heard, each step and every gesture seen,
> by God;
> their past was still the present and the present

a dread future's.
But I am private as an animal.

I have eaten whatever I liked,
I have slept as long as I wished,
I have left the highway like a dog
to run into every alley;
now I must learn to fast and to watch.
I shall walk better in these heavy boots
than barefoot.
I will fast for you, Judah,
and be silent for you
and wake in the night because of you;
I will speak for you
in psalms,
and feast because of you
on unleavened bread and herbs. (*CP*, 24–25)

As I have already tried to establish, genealogy and fracture are concomitant, the generational break occuring in the very stanza devoted to the metaphors of an organic Jewish identity. In addition, I now wish to underline the two metaphors of tradition as prescriptive law, those of the road and of the awakening. In Reznikoff's work, the law is always associated with movement, exile, the desert ("Exodus, Joshua at Sechem," *CP*, 126) or with Abraham leaving Ur for an unknown Promised Land. In his relation to the Jewish tradition, in the city as well as in his text, Reznikoff values departure from familiar American grounds, "from the warm and comfortable ark" (*CP*, 23), over rootedness as a form of idolatry. This ethical stand maintains movement within stasis and favors an ethical attention to the world, to the faces of tramps in Central Park, to the plight of immigrants in sweatshops, to the suffering of a child crushed by a machine, to the actions of thieves and murderers, or to the fate of a doomed community. The complementary metaphor of the awakening, present at the end of this poem as in "Exodus," throws light on this ethical point. The poet in heavy boots is kept awake by his responsibility toward the Other, both individual and universal (the ambiguous doublet of You-Judah). The poet-walker does not face Nature but the Other, and his poetical discourse will feed on the ancestral words. Feeding upon the Law, "tasting in each syllable," is a poethical activity:

The Indian of Peru, I think,
chewing
the leaf of a shrub
could run all day.
I, too,
with a few lines of verse, only two or three,
may be able
to see the day through. (*CP*, 62)

In short, the detour through Judaism read as a specific textual space reveals that Reznikoff's writings are oriented toward the "ethical utopia" that defined Judaism for Maurice Blanchot. In their textual direction and signification, poems are at the crossroads of the particular and the universal. On the reader's part, they call for neither an ideological recognition nor an ethnic recognition but for a conscious act of cognition. Charles Taylor's well-known distinction between works of recognition and works of cognition allows one to understand that Reznikoff is a mediator helping the reader discover or rediscover past, forgotten, unknown texts. He pulls his reader away from "the warmth and comfort" of New York City, in a detour through Cracow and Prague.

CRITICAL RECEPTION

Charles Reznikoff has been largely ignored, and despite occasional recognition from writers (William Carlos Williams' Easter Monday letter, Djuna Barnes' November 1959 letter, Paul Auster's September 1975 letter, Cynthia Ozick's February 1976 letter, Archives, Box VIII) and academics (Milton Hindus, Brandeis University, L. S. Dembo, University of Wisconsin). Significantly, "Helen Vendler's *Harvard Anthology of Contemporary American Poetry* simply erases without comment the whole Objectivist tradition" (Golding 148). Harold Bloom equally overlooked Reznikoff: "[T]hough it [caused him] grief to say this, the achievement of American-Jewish poets down to the present moment remains a modest and mixed one" (Bloom 1976, 247).

To understand why Reznikoff did not enter the American poetic canon sooner, my contention is that one should go beyond the idea of [a contemporary] critical neglect of poetry in favor of prose forms (usually fiction) that have a superficially more "direct connection to social and historical reality" (Golding xiii). One should address some of the critical assumptions that have consistently shaped the reception of Reznikoff's writings. My starting point is Barbara Gitenstein's 1986 *Apocalyptic Messianism and Contemporary Jewish-American Poetry*, which outlined the history of Jewish-American poetry from Emma Lazarus and Penina Moise to the present. She mentioned Reznikoff while associating him with "the Modernists and Experimentalists" Louis Zukofsky, Carl Rakosi, and George Oppen (Gitenstein 4). My overall thesis is that this association with objectivism is one of the reasons so little attention has been paid to Reznikoff.

Most critics think of Reznikoff as an objectivist disciple of Ezra Pound, never fully maturing out of Pound's overwhelming orbit, forever prisoner of a pioneering group whose reaction against imagism paved the way to poetic modernism (Gray 66). A promising young figure in the 1930s, Reznikoff remained in the footnotes of objectivism when newer poetical trends came to the fore. Literary history and its concept of a 1930s poetic renaissance have henceforth trapped Reznikoff in the anonymous depths of the origins of poetic modernism.

A second invidious reading screen routinely shrinks Reznikoff to an objective walker-poet-witness-reporter of the real holding up a mirror to nature. Objectivism being defined by an acute attention to the world, Reznikoff is read through his context (Robert Franciosi, Linda Simon, Burton Hatlen), through his Jewish urban immigrant experience:

[This is] a poetry that alerts us to the loneliness, the small ironies and amusements, and the numbness of the immigrant in the urban tenement. . . . In the best of his earlier, shorter poems Reznikoff refuses to moralise, to withdraw from the experience in order to comment on it or "place" it; the lives of the poor in the city possess an integrity that he chooses simply to respect and record. (Gray 66)

or through his biography (Syverson 136). This contextualist approach can be traced both in the praise bestowed on poems noticed for their detached observation of the banal, the commonplace, and the "mere" (Quatermain 148) and in the rejection of blindingly simple poems blamed for being "*near*-poems, narrow misses" (Quartermain 148), uninteresting or lacking in depth. In its reaction to imagism, objectivism further maintained that the poet's self was not to interfere in his writings. Reznikoff is thus said to be intent on showing "particulars" as they are, concerned with rendering American reality as objectively, that is, as self-lessly, as possible: "Reznikoff effaced himself as thoroughly as any lawyer writing a brief" (Watson 663). Indeed, Reznikoff opted for conciseness and linguistic fasting ("a writer of verse/who must learn to fast/and drink water by measure," *CPII*, 76). But when he expounded the idea of "a forgetfulness of self" (Archives, Box III, no. 32, "First there is the need . . . ," Drafts of Essay), he also eschewed his status of author as bearer of explicit intentions. He did not posit the possibility of an overlapping between the poet's signifying intentions and the language he uses. Harrison R. Chilton nonetheless uses this intentionalist approach to denounce what he reads as a contradiction:

At the same time, we can now note at least one apparent contradiction in Reznikoff's poetic sensibilities. On the one hand, he wishes to avoid "the rainbow of connotations," and goes so far as to suppress metaphorical complexity in his sparsest verse. On the other, he is clearly interested in conveying feelings by association; in fact, the details he selects for his poetry are significant precisely because of the emotional association he makes with them. (Chilton 158)

Objectivism has inadequate explanatory powers when applied to the specifics of Reznikoff's poems and only pits the critic against the aporia of an enunciation without enunciator. There is no contradiction between playing with connotations and wishing to limit a metaphorical outpour. This incidentally reveals that most readers reject as nonpoetical a discourse that has none of the normative signs of poetry, namely, metaphor, analogy, symbolism, or depth. Besides, to excise the self from the poem and to transcribe a pure, uncontaminated experience into words would mean Reznikoff treated poetry as a form dissociated from content (perceptions). This would imply a theory of language in which the poem is on the side of the signified while the form is a residual, "redundant" shell. "Redundant" refers to William Carlos Williams' remark, that the importance of a poem "cannot be in what the poem says, since in that case the fact that it is a poem would be a redundancy. The importance lies in what the poem *is*" (Conte 124). Reznikoff's meticulous care in writing and weaving poems, in organizing them into "discrete series" (George Oppen), rather points to a modernist approach that made "the poem itself an object of experience" (Gelpi 421).

Objectivism as an academic concept finally fosters a sociological interpretation through context and political commitment and favors a moralizing approach of Reznikoff "the didactic public moralist" (Quartermain 151). Critics discard Reznikoff's personal rejection of militant action, disregard his expressed distrust of social realism:

> Young men and women in a ballet
> on the platform:
> how romantic!
> And a young man is climbing a shaky ladder
> to photograph it:
> this is realism. (*CPII*, 210),

and read *Testimony* as an indictment of industrial destructiveness set in the days when America was changing from an agrarian republic to an industrial superpower (Shevelow 293; Franciosi 177). This contextualist approach is well grounded, though disqualified by Reznikoff's diffidence toward the realist fallacy, toward the confusion between the world and its literary referent.

Contextualist critics equally blame Reznikoff for his "social commentary" (Quartermain 151) and for his absence of moral vision (Robert Alter, Sidra DeKoven Ezrahi). That Reznikoff's authorial presence/absence should be both conspicuous and devoid of a moral message cannot be accounted for by objectivism. To me, one quotation from nineteenth-century French historian Adolphe Thiers sums up the critical belief that has hampered assessments of Reznikoff's poems: "To be simply true, to be what things themselves are, to be nothing more than them, to be nothing but through them, like them, as much as they are." That defined the realist fallacy for Roland Barthes (Barthes 90).

To conclude, no outline of critical trends would be complete without a special mention of recent developments in Reznikoff's studies. Different avenues for thought have been suggested by Charles Bernstein at SUNY, Buffalo, and Geneviève Cohen-Cheminet in Sceaux, France. Recent research addresses Reznikoff's Judaism and textual work.

BIBLIOGRAPHY

All material housed in the Archives for New Poetry, Mandeville Department of Special Collections (University of California, San Diego, La Jolla) are cited as "Archives," followed by the box number. All quotations from Reznikoff are from the 1989 edition of the *Complete Poems*, unless otherwise specified. They are abbreviated as *CPI* or *CPII*.

Works by Charles Reznikoff

Poetry

Rhythms. New York: Charles Reznikoff, 1918.

Rhythms II. New York: Charles Reznikoff, 1919.

Five Groups of Verse. Printed Privately, 1927.

By the Waters of Manhattan. Introduction by Louis Untermeyer. New York: Charles Boni Paper Books, 1930.

In Memoriam: 1933. New York: Objectivist Press, 1934.

Jerusalem the Golden. New York: Objectivist Press, 1934a.

Testimony. Introduction by Kenneth Burke. New York: Objectivist Press, J. J. Little and Ives, 1934b.

Separate Way. New York: Objectivist Press, 1936.

Going To and Fro and Walking Up and Down. New York: Futuro Press, 1941.

Inscriptions: 1944–1956. New York: Shulsinger Brothers, 1959.

By the Waters of Manhattan. Introduction by C. P. Snow. New York: New Directions and San Francisco Review, 1962.

By the Well of Living and Seeing and the Fifth Book of the Maccabees. New York: Charles Reznikoff, 1969.

Holocaust. Los Angeles: Black Sparrow Press, 1975.

Te Deum. New York: Menard Press, 1976.

Testimony: a Recitative, the United States 1885–1915. Vol. 1. Ed. Seamus Cooney. Santa Barbara, CA: Black Sparrow Press, 1978.

Testimony: a Recitative, the United States 1885–1915. Vol. 2. Ed. Seamus Cooney. Santa Barbara, CA: Black Sparrow Press, 1979.

The Complete Poems of Charles Reznikoff 1918–1975. Ed. Seamus Cooney. Black Sparrow Press, 1989.

Theatre

Nine Plays, Uriel Accosta, Abram in Egypt, Chatterton, Meriwether Lewis, Captive Israel, The Black Death, Coral, Rashi, Genesis. New York: Charles Reznikoff, 1927.

Historical Writings

The Lionhearted, a Story about the Jews in Medieval England. Philadelphia: Jewish Publication Society of America, 1944.

The Jews of Charleston, a History of an American Jewish Community. With the collaboration of Uriah Z. Engelman. Philadelphia: Jewish Publication Society of America, 1950.

Ed. *Louis Marshall, Champion of Liberty, Selected Papers and Addresses*. Introduction by Oscar Handlin. Philadelphia: Jewish Publication Society of America, 1957.

Family Autobiography

By the Waters of Manhattan, a Novel. New York: Charles Boni, 1930.

Early History of a Sewing—Machine Operator and Needle Trade by Nathan and Charles Reznikoff. New York: Schulsinger Brothers, 1929, 1936, 1963.

Trans. *Family Chronicle, Early History of a Seamstress* by Sarah Reznikoff. New York: Schulsinger Brothers, 1929, 1936, 1963.

Trans. *Early History of a Sewing-Machine Operator* by Nathan Reznikoff. New York: Objectivist Press, 1936.

Family Chronicle, an Odyssey from Russia to America. With Nathan and Sarah Reznikoff. Ed. Jonathan D. Sarna. Introduction by Milton Hindus. New York: Markus Wiener, 1988.

Nonhistorical Prose

The Manner Music, a Novel. Introduction by Robert Creeley. Santa Barbara, CA: Black Sparrow Press, 1977.

First, There Is the Need. Sparrow 52, a publication of Black Sparrow Press. Santa Barbara, CA: Black Sparrow Press, 1977.

"Ezra Pound." *Encyclopaedia Judaica.* Jerusalem: Ketev Publishing House, 1974, 407–8.

"Louis Zukofsky." *Encyclopaedia Judaica.* Jerusalem: Ketev Publishing House, 1974, 409.

Personal Correspondence

Hindus, Milton. *The Collected Letters of Charles Reznikoff.* Los Angeles: Black Sparrow Press, 1997.

Works about Charles Reznikoff

Atlan, Henri. "Niveaux de significations et athéisme de l'écriture." *La Bible au présent*, Actes du Colloque des Intellectuels juifs de langue française. Paris: Gallimard, 1982, 82–87.

Barthes, Roland. "l'effet de réel." In *Littérature et réalité.* Barthes, Bersani, Hamon, Riffaterre, Watt. Paris: Seuil, 1982, 81–90.

Bernstein, Charles. "Reznikoff's Nearness." *Sulfur*, no. 32 (Spring 1993): 6–38.

Hamon, Riffaterre, Watt. Paris: Seuil, 1982, 81–90.

Blanchot, Maurice. *L'entretien infini.* Paris: Gallimard, 1969.

Blasing, Mutlu Konuk. *Politics and Form in Postmodern Poetry.* New York: Cambridge University Press, 1995.

Bloom, Harold. "La culture juive contemporaine au point de vue pragmatique." In John Rajchman. *La pensée américaine contemporaine.* Trans. A. Lyotard-May and Cornel West. Paris: PUF, 1991. (*Post-Analytic Philosophy*, 1985). 195–218.

———. *Figures of Capable Imagination.* New York: Continuum Book, Seabury Press, 1976.

Boyarin, Daniel. *Intertextuality and the Reading of Midrash.* Bloomington: Indiana University Press, 1994.

Cohen-Cheminet, Geneviève. "L'Entretien infini: modernité poétique et tradition appropriée dans l'oeuvre de Charles Reznikoff." Villeneuve d'Ascq: P U du Septentrion, 1998.

Conte, M. Joseph. *Unending Design: The Forms of Postmodern Poetry.* Ithaca, NY: Cornell University Press, 1991.

Eliot, Thomas S. "Tradition and the Individual Talent." *Selected Essays 1917–1932.* London: Faber, 1951.

Ezrahi, Sidra DeKoven. "The Grave in the Air: Unbound Metaphors and Poets—Holocaust Poetry." In Saul Friedlander, ed., *Probing the Limits of Representation: Nazism in Art.* Cambridge, MA: Harvard University Press, 1992, 259–276.

Franciosi, Robert M. *A Story of Vocation: The Poetic Achievement of Charles Reznikoff.* Ph.D., University of Iowa, 1985, Ann Arbor: UMI 5814 DEU 85-18828 DA8518828. (265 pages). *Dissertation Abstracts* 46/06a, 1623.

Gelpi, Albert. *A Coherent Splendor: the American Poetic Renaissance 1910–1950.* Cambridge: Cambridge University Press, 1987, 1990.

Gitenstein, Barbara. R. *Apocalyptic Messianism and Contemporary Jewish-American Poetry.* Albany: State University of New York Press, 1986.

Golding, Alan. *From Outlaw to Classic, Canons in American Poetry.* Madison: University of Wisconsin Press, 1995.

Gray, Richard. *American Poetry of the Twentieth Century.* Albany, NY: Longman, 1990.

Gutmann Allen. *The Jewish Writer in America, Assimilation and the Crisis of Identity.* New York: Oxford University Press, 1971.

Hatlen, Burton, ed. Charles Reznikoff Issue. *Sagetrieb A Journal Devoted to Poets in the Pound, H. D., Williams Tradition* 13, Nos. 1, 2 (Spring, Fall 1994).

Heller, Michael. *Conviction's Net of Branches: Essays on the Objectivist Poets and Poetry.* Carbondale: Southern Illinois University Press, 1985.

Hilton, Harrison R. "The Object Beyond the Image: A Study of Four Objectivist Poets." Unpublished Ph.D. diss., University of Wisconsin, 1981.

Hindus, Milton, ed. *Charles Reznikoff Man and Poet.* Orono: University of Maine, 1984.

Hollander, John. "The Question of American Jewish Poetry." *Tikkun* 3, No. 3, 1988, 33–37, 112–16.

Messerli, Douglas, ed. *From the Other Side of the Century, a New American Poetry 1960–1990.* Los Angeles: Sun & Moon, 1994.

Modrzejewski, Joseph Mélèze. "Les Juifs dans le monde gréco-romain, racines et antécédents d'une pensée juive du christianisme." *Les Nouveaux Cahiers.* no. 113, (Summer 1993): 5–13.

Ouaknin, Marc-Alain. *Le livre brûlé, lire le Talmud.* Paris: Lieu Commun, 1986.

———. Rotnemer, Dory. *Le grand livre des prénoms bibliques et hébraïques.* Paris: Albin Michel, 1993.

Quartermain, Peter. *Disjunctive Poetics: From Gertrude Stein and Louis Zukofsky to Susan Howe.* Cambridge: Cambridge University Press, 1992.

Ricoeur, Paul. "Préface à Bultmann." *Le conflit des interprétations, essais d'herméneutique.* Paris: Seuil, 1969, 373–92.

Shevelow, Kathryn. "History and Objectivation in Charles Reznikoff's *Documentary Testimony* and *Holocaust.*" *Sagetrieb* 1:2 (Fall 1980): 209–306.

Syverson, M. A. "The Community of Memory, Reznikoff Family Chronicle." *Sagetrieb* 2:1–2 (Spring–Fall): 127–170.

Taylor, Charles. *Multiculturalisme, différence et démocratie.* Paris: Aubier, 1992.

Watson, Benjamin. ''Reznikoff Testimony.'' *Law Library Journal* 82:101 (December 1990): 647–671.

Weinberger, Eliot, ed. *American Poetry since 1950, Innovators and Outsiders.* New York: Marsilio, 1993.

Yerushalmi, Yosef Hayim. *Zakhor, histoire juive et mémoire juive.* Vigne, Eric, trans. Paris: La Découverte, 1984.

ADRIENNE RICH   (1929–   )

Jonathan Gill

BIOGRAPHY

Adrienne Cecile Rich was born on May 16, 1929, in Baltimore to a Jewish father, Arnold Rich, one of the first Jewish faculty members in the Pathology Department at Johns Hopkins Medical School, and a Protestant mother, Helen Rich (née Jones), a classical pianist. Rich's paternal grandfather, Samuel Rich, an Ashkenazic Jew from the former Austro-Hungarian empire, had come to the United States after the Civil War and settled in Birmingham, Alabama. He married Hattie Rice, a Sephardic Jew from Vicksburg, Mississippi. Living in the South during a period of public animosity toward Jews, Rich's paternal grandparents elected to assimilate—a choice that would have enormous significance for the poet's personal life and career.

Rich was educated at the nondenominational Roland Park Country School in Baltimore (1938–1947) and sent to Episcopalian church services, "as a kind of social validation, mainly as protection against anti-Semitism," as she later observed (*What Is Found There* 1993). Rich recalls in her 1982 essay "Split at the Root: An Essay on Jewish Identity" that she was baptized and confirmed as an Episcopalian, "though without belief" (*Blood, Bread, and Poetry* 105). Rich's father was a self-described "deist" who never spoke of the anti-Semitism he might have encountered in his native Birmingham, during his schooling in North Carolina and at the University of Virginia, or at Johns Hopkins. As Rich has explained, her father had consciously rejected his religious heritage and kept his oldest daughter ignorant about Judaism, teaching her "to study but not to pray" (*Your Native Land, Your Life* 9). Rich never entered a synagogue while she lived with her parents, and her inquiry about the events portrayed in a 1946 film she saw about the Allied liberation of Nazi death camps was met with denial and disapproval on the part of her parents. Just as Rich found herself "utterly disaffected from Christianity" (*What Is Found There* 1953), so, too, did she eventually come to question her father's way of life as "the floating world of the assimilated who know and deny they will always be aliens" (*Your Native Land, Your Life* 9).

Rich's departure for Radcliffe College at Harvard University marked a turning point in her identity. There she encountered other Jews of her own generation for the first time and began to learn from them about their religious and cultural values and practices. Also during this time Rich learned that her patrilineal heritage made her non-Jewish in the eyes of Orthodox Judaism tradition, a status she seems to have temporarily embraced. As if obeying her mother's warning to avoid Jews—advice recounted in the 1990 poem "1948: Jews"—Rich denied her Jewish heritage in response to the private inquiry of a Jewish seamstress and Holocaust survivor. The confusion and shame of that encounter sparked a confrontation with her father over his failure to teach her about Judaism.

Rich graduated from Radcliffe with honors in 1951. That same year Rich, who at the urging of her father had been writing poems and plays since childhood, won the prestigious Yale Younger Poets Award. That honor meant the publication of her first volume of verse, *A Change of World*, which was well received by critics and marked the beginning of Rich's emergence as one of the most significant poets of the postwar era. After a period of travel in Europe and England, funded by a Guggenheim Fellowship (1952–1953), Rich resettled in Cambridge, Massachusetts, and married Alfred Conrad, a Harvard economist in 1953. That event forced another confrontation with her parents, who refused to attend the wedding because Conrad was "a real Jew" (*Blood, Bread, and Poetry* 115)—that is, born in Brooklyn to immigrants from Eastern Europe. During the early years of her marriage, when she was raising three sons—David (born 1955), Paul (born 1957), and Jacob (born 1959)—Rich was less active as a poet.

After a brief residence in the Netherlands in the early 1960s, Rich and her family moved to New York. Her experience as a teacher—at the YM-YWHA Poetry Center in New York (1966–1967), Swarthmore College (1967–1969), Columbia University (1967–1969), and the City College of New York (1968–1975)—along with the climate of the civil rights, anti-Vietnam War, and women's liberation movements led Rich to increasingly radical political views and more open and vocal explorations of male power, feminism, and female sexuality. What is perhaps Rich's most widely recognized public act came after her 1973 volume *Diving into the Wreck* won the 1974 National Book Award. In a now-famous gesture, Rich rejected the award as an individual but accepted it along with two other nominees, the African-American writers Audre Lorde and Alice Walker, in the name of "all women, of every color, identification or derived class" (qtd. in Martin 204).

Rich's identification with feminism was matched by her growing interest in Jewish history and culture in the 1970s, but Rich became best known as a lesbian poet during this time, when she publicly declared her lesbianism and began living with her partner, the Jamaican-born writer Michelle Cliff. In 1979 Rich moved from New York City to western Massachusetts, becoming involved with a Jewish lesbian study group, exploring what she later termed ''the terrain of North American Jewish experience'' (*Blood, Bread, and Poetry* xiii), and rejecting what she called in her poem ''Sources'' the ''rootless ideology'' advocated by her father (*Your Native Land, Your Life* 8). In the 1980s she became active in New Jewish Agenda and served on its national board. The 1990s have been among Rich's most productive years, both politically and artistically. During this time Rich has remained a prolific and celebrated poet, essayist, lecturer, editor, and teacher. Her *Collected Early Poems* was published in 1993 and the following year she received a MacArthur Fellowship. In 1996 she received the Dorothea Tanning Prize ''for mastery in the art of poetry.'' Rich served as coeditor of *Sinister Wisdom* (1980–1984) and on the editorial board of *Bridges: A Journal; for Jewish Feminists and Our Friends* (1989–1993). Since 1984, Rich, who has received numerous awards and honorary degrees, has lived in northern California.

MAJOR WORKS AND THEMES

While Rich's early poems nominally focus on love, marriage, travel, and motherhood, they also treat subjects that Rich would later identify as crucial to her Jewish identity. The theme of the outsider is already on display in ''By No Means Native,'' from her first book, *A Change of World*. In that poem Rich explores the character of a ''minor alien'' (*Collected Early Poems* 13). Another important theme, which Rich would later call the ''passionless respectability'' (*What Is Found There* 193) of Protestantism, is handled in another poem from *What Is Found There*, ''A View of the Terrace.'' The poem ''The Uncle Speaks in the Drawing Room,'' also from the same volume, with its explorations of ''the frailties of glass,'' might be read as implicitly treating *Kristallnacht*: ''We stand between the dead glass-blowers/And murmurings of missile throwers'' (*Collected Early Poems* 24).

Judaism occupies an increasingly important place in the writing that follows Rich's first volume, especially in *The Diamond Cutters and Other Poems* (1955) and *Snapshots of a Daughter-in-Law* (1963). In the 1955 poem ''At the Jewish New Year,'' Rich speaks of ''our kind/Over five thousand years,/The task of being ourselves'' (*Collected Early Poems* 198)—for the first time explicitly using the first-person plural to place herself within the Jewish community. *Snapshots of a Daughter-in-Law*, the volume that marked Rich's emancipation from her early formalist literary influences, contains ''Readings of History,'' an important early discussion of the complications of identity (*Collected Early Poems* 165). The fifth section of the poem, which dates from 1960, explores the anxiety of her personal identity: ''Split at the root, neither Gentile nor Jew'' (*Collected Early Poems* 164). In ''Necessities of Life,'' collected in the 1966 volume of the same name, Rich alludes to Jews in biblical slavery, making bricks for their Egyptian rulers.

Rich has also forged connections with other Jewish women poets like Muriel Rukeyser, whom Rich has praised for her unapologetic discussions of Jewishness and female sexuality. Just as important was Rich's increasing interest in women writing in Yiddish, which Rich recognizes as a "female" counterpart to Hebrew and therefore a natural birthright for Jewish feminists. In 1968 Rich translated two poems by Kadia Molodowsky: "White Night" for Eliezer Greenberg and Irving Howe's *A Treasury of Yiddish Poetry* (1969) and "There Are Such Springlike Nights," which was published in Rich's own 1969 volume *Leaflets*.

Not surprisingly, as a feminist, Rich has struggled with her father's status as a male and as a Jew. As Rich later remembered, she was given the intellectual upbringing of a son and encouraged by her father to write from an early age. However, in the 1970s Arnold Rich came to represent patriarchal authority—what she later termed "the power and arrogance of the male" (*Your Native Land, Your Life* 9)—which she came to understand as inherently oppressive. As such, the struggles to understand the two aspects of her identity—the Jewish and the female—increasingly resembled one single enterprise. Rich conceived Judaism as essentially part of a larger patriarchal system enforcing compulsory heterosexuality through the distinctions and hierarchies of essentialist dogma. Her 1973 volume *Diving into the Wreck* uses Rich's status as an outsider to treat such issues as male power, feminist history, and violence against women with grace and audacity. That volume's title poem, perhaps Rich's best-known work, uses deep-sea exploration as an extended metaphor for the search for identity within culture and history. Ultimately, the diver gives up the sense of gender itself in the hold of the sunken vessel, surrounded by the now-ruined ship's instruments.

If, in the early 1970s, which saw the publication and enthusiastic reception of *The Will to Change* (1971), Rich was still subordinating her Jewish identity—she claimed in her 1971 essay "When We Dead Awaken: Writing as Re-Vision" that "My own luck was being born white and middle-class" (*On Lies, Secrets, and Silence* 38)—in the volumes that followed, including *The Dream of a Common Language* (1978), *A Wild Patience Has Taken Me This Far* (1981), *Sources* (1983), and *The Fact of a Doorframe: Poems Selected and New 1950–1984* (1984), she reconciled herself to ambivalence. While Judaism had always provided an important thematic undercurrent in Rich's writing, her interest in her Jewish heritage underwent another transition starting in the Foreword to *Blood, Bread, and Poetry*, her 1986 collection of essays: "The woman who seeks the experiential grounding of identity politics realizes that as Jew, white woman, lesbian, middle-class, she herself has a complex identity" (xii). Not surprisingly, Rich's 1984 essay "Notes toward a Politics of Location" specifically looks to the Holocaust as a way to revise her 1971 self-description:

"The body I was born into was not only female and white, but Jewish . . . I was a *Mischling*, four years old when the Third Reich began" (*Blood, Bread, and Poetry* 216).

Rich's interest in the Holocaust is crucial to her most important poetic statement about Judaism, "Sources," a twenty-three-part poem dating from 1981–1982 and contained in the collection *Your Native Land, Your Life*. In "Sources" Rich argues that in her Jewish heritage "There is something more than food, humor, a turn of phrase, a gesture of the hands" (19) and struggles to claim it: "Old things, diffuse, unnamed, lie strong/across my heart./This is from where/ my strength comes" (4). Rich also notes the continuity of her endeavor over more than three decades, asking, "*With whom do you believe your lot is cast?/ From where does your strength come?*" and answering, "I think somehow, somewhere/every poem of mine must repeat those questions" (6). Although the poet admits, "There is a *whom*, a *where*/that is not chosen/that is given and sometimes falsely given" (6), she emerges triumphant in the belief that she remains without a faith/you are faithful" (26).

In *Your Native Land, Your Life* and in her other volumes since then, including *Time's Power* (1989), *An Atlas of the Difficult World* (1991), and *Dark Fields of the Republic* (1995), Rich recognizes the inevitable complexity of her identity, the fact that Judaism can be perceived as a problem within the larger problem of feminism. In "Yom Kippur" (1984), Rich declares that: "to be with my people is my dearest wish/but that I also love strangers/that I crave separateness" (*Your Native Land, Your Life* 77). Rich, who has in recent years self-consciously added her voice to Jewish thinking, especially Jewish feminist thinking, has also gone so far as to add the question, "If not with others, how?" (*Blood, Bread, and Poetry* 209) to Hillel's famous three questions and revised the traditional Jewish prayer for the dead in "Tattered Kaddish" (*An Atlas of the Difficult World* 45). In a later essay, "A Leak in History," Rich quotes in English translation the traditional Hebrew blessing over wine as example of the place of "sensual vitality" in modern life (*What Is Found There* 77). In recent years Rich has continued to draw from the example of Jewish women, taking inspiration from figures such as Rosa Luxemburg, Hannah Arendt, and Ethel Rosenberg and contemporary poets like Irena Klepfisz and Dahlia Ravikovitch.

CRITICAL RECEPTION

Although Rich's frank and uncompromising treatments of marriage, gender politics, and female sexuality have been frequently anthologized and studied, scholars have rarely acknowledged her struggle "to explore the meanings of Jewish identity from a feminist perspective" (*Bread, Blood, and Poetry* 162), a theme that has always animated her writing. In his Introduction to *A Change of World*, W. H. Auden, the British poet who for many years judged the Yale competition, found that Rich's poems "speak quietly but do not mumble, respect their elders but are not cowed by them, and do not tell fibs" (qtd. in *Martin*

127)—ironic praise, given the literary and cultural resistance that Rich's later works would demonstrate and advocate. If in the 1960s and 1970s Rich was celebrated by critics specifically as the most significant lesbian-feminist poet of her generation and credited mainly for revising the traditional thematic and formal boundaries of poetry written by women, in the 1980s and 1990s her more general achievements as one of the most accomplished and influential American poets of the post–World War II era have been acknowledged. Often placed in the poetic tradition of feminist refusal and creativity embodied by Anne Bradstreet, Emily Dickinson, and H. D.—Wendy Martin has called Rich "midwife to a new age" (qtd. in Gelpi and Gelpi 189)—Rich has nonetheless been read with increasing frequency outside strictly feminist contexts. Albert Gelpi has written of Rich's investment in a literary culture that considers "the poet as prophet and the prophet as scapegoat" (qtd. in Gelpi and Gelpi 148). For Claire Keyes, although "Rich's sex is at the root of her aesthetic" (10), she can be understood to be issuing a more general critique of society, "an indictment of the times, specifically those power structures that limit and dehumanize us all" (14). With the publication of *Dark Fields of the Republic*, Rich's status as one of the most crucial voices of twentieth-century poetry in America was secure, with frequent critical comparisons to Wallace Stevens and William Blake.

BIBLIOGRAPHY

Works by Adrienne Rich

Poetry

A Change of World. New Haven, CT: Yale University Press, 1951.
The Diamond Cutters and Other Poems. New York: Harper, 1955.
Snapshots of a Daughter-in-Law. New York: Harper and Row, 1963.
Necessities of Life. New York: Norton, 1966.
Selected Poems. London: Chatto and Windus, 1967.
Leaflets. New York: Norton, 1969.
The Will to Change. New York: Norton, 1971.
Diving into the Wreck. New York: Norton, 1973.
Poems: Selected and New. New York: Norton, 1975.
Twenty-one Love Poems. Emeryville, CA: Effie's Press, 1976.
The Meaning of Our Love for Women Is What We Have Constantly to Expand. New York: Out and Out, 1977.
The Dream of a Common Language. New York: Norton, 1978.
A Wild Patience Has Taken Me This Far. New York: Norton, 1981.
Sources. Woodside, CA: Heyeck, 1983.
The Fact of a Doorframe: Poems Selected and New 1950–1984. New York: Norton, 1984.
Your Native Land, Your Life. New York: Norton, 1986.
Time's Power: Poems 1985–1988. New York: Norton, 1989.
An Atlas of the Difficult World: Poems 1988–1991. New York: Norton, 1991.

Collected Early Poems 1950–1970. New York: Norton, 1993.
Dark Fields of the Republic: Poems 1991–1995. New York: Norton, 1995.

Essays

Of Woman Born: Motherhood as Experience and Institution. New York: Norton, 1976.
On Lies, Secrets, and Silence: Selected Prose 1966–1978. New York: Norton, 1979.
Blood, Bread, and Poetry: Selected Prose 1979–1985. New York: Norton, 1986.
What Is Found There: Notebooks on Poetry and Politics. New York: Norton, 1993.

Works about Adrienne Rich

Alkalay-Gut, Karen. "Adrienne Rich." *Jewish American Women Writers: A Bio-Bibliographical and Critical Sourcebook.* Ed. Ann R. Shapiro. Westport, CT: Greenwood Press, 1994, 333–41.

Bennett, Paula. *My Life a Loaded Gun: Female Creativity and Feminist Poetics.* Boston: Beacon Press, 1986.

Cooper, Jane Roberta, ed. *Reading Adrienne Rich: Reviews and Re-Visions, 1951–1981.* Ann Arbor: University of Michigan Press, 1984.

Des Pres, Terrence. "Adrienne Rich, North America East." In *Praises and Dispraises: Poetry and Politics, the 20th Century.* New York: Viking, 1988, 187–224.

Diaz-Diocaretz, Myriam. *The Transforming Power of Language: The Poetry of Adrienne Rich.* Utrecht, Netherlands: HES, 1984.

———. *Translating Poetic Discourse: Questions on Feminist Strategies in Adrienne Rich.* Amsterdam, Netherlands: Benjamins, 1985.

Gelpi, Barbara Charlesworth, and Albert Gelpi, eds. *Adrienne Rich's Poetry.* New York: Norton, 1975.

Herzog, Anne. "Adrienne Rich and the Discourse of Decolonization." *The Centennial Review* 33, No. 3 (Summer 1989): 258–77.

Keyes, Claire. *The Aesthetics of Power: The Poetry of Adrienne Rich.* Athens: University of Georgia Press, 1986.

Martin, Wendy. *Adrienne Rich's Poetry.* New York: Scribner's, 1978.

———. "Another View of the City upon a Hill: The Prophetic Vision of Adrienne Rich." In *Women Writers and the City.* Knoxville: University of Tennessee Press, 1984, 249–64.

Montenegro, David. "Adrienne Rich: An Interview by David Montenegro." *American Poetry Review* 20 (January–February 1991): 7–14.

Smith, Joan. "Poetic Justice." *San Francisco Chronicle* (June 19, 1994): B13.

Templeton, Alice. *The Dream and the Dialogue: Adrienne Rich's Feminist Poetics.* Knoxville: University of Tennessee Press, 1994.

Werner, Craig Hansen. *Adrienne Rich: The Poet and Her Critics.* Chicago: American Library Association, 1988.

DAVID ROSENBERG (1943–)

Joel Shatzky and Michael Taub

BIOGRAPHY

David Rosenberg was born August 1, 1943, in Detroit. The son of Herman and Shifra Rosenberg. He received his education at the University of Michigan, where he earned a B.A. in 1964; Syracuse University, where he received an M.F.A. in 1966; and the University of Essex, England, 1970–1972, and Hebrew University, Jerusalem, 1980–1982.

Rosenberg as an undergraduate worked as an assistant to Robert Lowell at the New School, 1961–1962, and later as a lecturer in English and creative writing at York University in Toronto, 1967–1971, and as an editor, 1981–1987, at Hakibutz Hameuchad/Institute for the Translation of Hebrew Literature in Tel Aviv, the Jewish Publication Society of Philadelphia, and Harcourt Brace Jovanovich. Among Rosenberg's awards is the Hopwood Special Award for Poetry from the University of Michigan, 1964, a graduate fellowship in poetry from Syracuse University, 1965–1966, and a PEN/Book-of-the-Month-Club Translation Prize in 1992.

Since the late 1980s, Rosenberg has become increasingly involved in research into the natural world. He was writer-in-residence at the Fairchild Tropical Garden in Miami in 1992 and has been a Field Bridge fellow of the National Tropical Botanical Garden in Miami since 1994.

MAJOR WORKS AND THEMES

David Rosenberg is probably best known for his work as a translator of Harold Bloom's interpretation of the first five books of Moses, *The Book of J*. Rosenberg's work as a biblical scholar and translator is also reflected in his translation of the Psalms and other books and passages from the Bible, including *Blues of the Sky: Interpreted from the Original Hebrew Book of Psalms* (1972), *Job Speaks: Interpreted from the Original Hebrew Book of Job* (1977), and *Lightworks: Interpreted from the Original Hebrew Book of Isaiah* (1978). He has also provided original translations of the Haggadah and the ''Scroll of Paradise,'' a creation story in which he added a fictional character, a woman scholar from ancient Jerusalem, Devorah Bat-David. This original interpretation of the story of Adam and Eve, *The Lost Book of Paradise: Adam and Eve in the Garden of Eden* (1993), reveals Rosenberg's scholarly abilities as well as his gifts as a translator and imaginative interpreter of biblical texts.

Rosenberg's most controversial work, his translation of *The Book of J.*, was a reading of one of what biblical scholars consider to be the four sources of the Pentateuch, the first five books of the Bible. This source, which is referred to as the ''Yahwist'' or ''J.,'' was extracted and translated by Rosenberg, and Bloom provided the commentary. It proved to be a controversial work that gave a fresh and, to believers, shocking interpretation of the Bible.

Another example of Rosenberg's daring interpretations and translations of biblical texts is in his approach to the story of the Garden of Eden in *The Lost Book of Paradise*. In his version, the garden is inhabited by two serpents, one male and one female; it is the female serpent, rather than Eve, that tempts Adam. Like Ellen Pagels' interpretations of the New Testament through *The Gnostic Gospels*, Rosenberg's disclosures of the variant meanings of ancient biblical texts present new and exciting challenges to both theologians and the faithful.

Yet another area that David Rosenberg has enriched with his knowledge and involvement in Jewish scholarship and history is in two books he has edited: *Congregation: Contemporary Writers Read the Jewish Bible* (1987) and *Testimony: Contemporary Writers Make the Holocaust Personal* (1989). The first demonstrates the impact that the Bible has had on the thinking of writers today; the second consists of twenty-seven essays by writers almost all of whom experienced the Holocaust secondhand but still felt its influence upon them. Although not noted as much for his own original poetry as he is as a translator, David Rosenberg's work has given to Jewish-American literature new and original ways of viewing its earliest literary heritage.

CRITICAL RECEPTION

Rosenberg's translations, especially of *The Book of J.*, have met with generally positive criticism, despite the controversial nature of the work. Frank Kermode, in his review in the *New York Times*, marveled: ''In *The Book of J* bright ideas gleam, vanish and are replaced by more. . . . Believers, fundamentalists, may be shocked, but the effect on others will surely be refreshing, with just a little of the jolt that one sometimes gets from looking at a familiar painting newly cleaned'' (qtd. in *Contemporary Authors* [CA] 384). Barbara Probst Solomon regarded the work as a ''bold and deeply meditated translation [that] attempts to reproduce the puns, off-rhymes and wordplay of the original'' (qtd. in *CA* 384).

Robert Taylor, in *The Boston Globe*, was as favorably impressed with *The Lost Book of Paradise*. ''Rosenberg blends Devorah Bat-David's commentary on the Book of Paradise with his own remarks, framing a lucid prose poetry that conveys the sense of the story as both extremely old and intensely immediate. . . . Here and there the earnestness of its critical discourse infiltrates the poetry and mars its spontaneity''; still, ''however problematic, Rosenberg's innovative mix of poetry, exegesis and speculation reveals the story's enduring capacity to speak to the present and replenish the meanings of Eden'' (qtd. in *CA* 384).

Although poets who have been primarily noted for their translations are normally not included in this volume, David Rosenberg's significant contributions to the modern understanding and interpretations of biblical texts give him a special place in the canon of Jewish-American literature. His skill and creative insight give traditional texts from the Bible new and freshly stimulating meaning to his contemporaries.

BIBLIOGRAPHY

Works by David Rosenberg

Poems and Translations

Disappearing Horses. Toronto: Coach House Press, 1969.

Headlights. Toronto: Weed/Flower Press, 1970.

Paris and London. Vancouver, B.C.: Talonbooks, 1971.

Leavin' America. Toronto: Coach House Press, 1972.

The Necessity of Poetry. Toronto: Coach House Press, 1973.

Blues of the Sky: Interpreted from the Original Hebrew Book of Psalms. New York: Harper, 1976.

A Blazing Fountain: A Book for Hannukah. New York: Schocken Books, 1978a.

Job Speaks: Interpreted from the Original Hebrew Book of Job. New York: Harper, 1978b.

Lightworks: Interpreted from the Original Hebrew Book of Isaiah. New York: Harper, 1978c.

Chosen Days: Celebrating Jewish Festivals in Poetry and Art. With decorations by Leonard Baskin. New York: Doubleday, 1980.

Congregation: Contemporary Writers Read the Jewish Bible. Ed. San Diego: Harcourt, 1987.

Testimony: Contemporary Writers Make the Holocaust Personal. Ed. New York: Times Books, 1989.

The Book of J. Interpreted by Harold Bloom. New York: Grove Press, 1990.

A Poet's Bible: Rediscovering the Voices of the Original Text. New York: Hyperion, 1991.

The Movie That Changed My Life. Ed. New York: Viking Press, 1991.

The Lost Book of Paradise: Adam and Eve in the Garden of Eden. New York: Hyperion,
    1993.
Communion: Leading Writers Reveal the Bible in Their Lives. New York: Anchor Press,
    1995.
The Book of S. The First Novel Restored. New York: Hyperion, 1998.

Works about David Rosenberg

Contemporary Authors, 147, 383–85. Detroit: Gale Research, 1994.
Kermonde, Frank. Rev. of *The Book of J. New York Times Book Review*, September 23,
    1990, 1, 24.
Lehman, David. Rev. of *Congregation. Newsweek*, January 18, 1988, 72.
Milton, Edith. Rev. of *Testimony. New York Times Book Review*, January 28, 1990, 27.
Solomon, Barbara Probst. Rev. of *The Book of J. Washington Post Book World*, Septem-
    ber 16, 1990, 5, 14.
Taylor, Robert. Rev. of *The Lost Book of Paradise. Boston Globe*, September 22, 1993,
    36.
Zavatsky, Bill. Rev. of *Blues of the Sky. New York Times Book Review*, December 14,
    1975, 16.

M. L. ROSENTHAL (1917–1996)

William Harmon

BIOGRAPHY

M. L. Rosenthal was an important presence on the world literary scene since the 1950s, known best as a helpful and wide-ranging historical critic of modern and postmodern poetry in English. But he was more than a critic: he also turned in distinguished work as translator, editor, anthologist, essayist, teacher, champion of the arts, and—not least among his many achievements—himself a respected original poet.

He was born Macha Louis Rosenthal (the first names consistently reduced to initials on title pages) in Washington, D.C., in 1917 and raised in various places in the Northeast and Midwest. His main education was at the University of Chicago, which he entered at a most advantageous time from the student's point of view. In his work for the bachelor's and master's degrees, finished in 1937 and 1938, Rosenthal enjoyed a complete range of available styles and attitudes, represented at Chicago in ways that no other school before World War II could match. To begin with, Rosenthal was exposed to conventional academic scholarship in the persons of Tom Peete Cross (a Celticist and medievalist) and Gerald Eades Bentley (an Elizabethan and Jacobean scholar). Then there were R. S. Crane, Norman Maclean, and other members of a militantly Aristotelian camp soon to be known as the Chicago Critics. Sui generis, there was Thornton Wilder, who taught creative writing in a way that must have been most inspiring and most influential. Beyond these English Department associations, Rosenthal also got to know members of the larger academic community who were making Chicago one of the most progressive, creative, and experimental of universities: Robert Maynard Hutchins, Mortimer Adler, and Joseph J. Schwab. Amid these diverse and often contradictory influences, Rosenthal formed habits of eclecticism and pluralism that stayed with him through a long career of versatile activities. At Chicago, furthermore, his own creative energies were first challenged, so that he became a practicing poet himself. One does not have to be a poet to know what poetry is all about, but it certainly cannot do any harm if someone teaching students about sonnets has at least tried at one time or another to write two or three.

During World War II, reasons of health keeping him from serving actively, he taught at Michigan State College (later, Michigan State University). After the war, he finished his doctorate at New York University (degree awarded in 1949) and served as a member of that school's English Department from 1946 onward. During his academic career he made a specialty of travel in diverse countries and lectured or taught in England, France, Spain, Pakistan, China, Poland, Bulgaria, Rumania, and Switzerland. Similarly, his poetry has been augmented by numerous translations or adaptations from poems in German, Catalan, Urdu, Italian, Spanish, and Chinese, earning Rosenthal a place in the guild of polyglot translators along with Ezra Pound, Kenneth Rexroth, John Frederick Nims, and W. S. Merwin.

MAJOR WORKS AND THEMES

Modern American poet-teacher-critics are called on to perform a variety of functions, and Rosenthal seems to have taken a turn at most of them. Alone or in company, he edited anthologies: coeditor, with Gerald DeWitt Sanders and John Herbert Nelson, of *Chief Modern Poets of England and America* (1962); editor of *The New Modern Poetry: An Anthology of American and British Poetry since World War II* (1967); general editor of *Poetry in English: An Anthology* (1987), also specifically editing the early modern section. *Exploring Poetry* (1955), which Rosenthal wrote in collaboration with A. J. M. Smith, is a reinforced anthology in the genre established by Cleanth Brooks and Robert Penn Warren in *Understanding Poetry* (1938).

Rosenthal's general critical books include *The Modern Poets: A Critical Introduction* (1960); *The New Poets: American and British Poetry since World War II*; and *The Modern Poetic Sequence: The Genius of Modern Poetry* (with Sally M. Gall, 1983). *The Poet's Art* (1987) has to do with details of rhetoric, diction, tone, and music. *Poetry and the Common Life* (1974) and *Our Life in Poetry* (1991) belong more in the category of miscellany, including some memoirs and autobiographical essays alongside more conventional essays, articles, and reviews.

Rosenthal has served as guide to a number of challenging modern poets. *A Primer of Ezra Pound* (1960) introduces the American poet who poses the most problems for many readers. Rosenthal edited *The William Carlos Williams Reader* (1966) and *Selected Poems and Three Plays of William Butler Yeats* (1986). *Randall Jarrell* (1972) is a pamphlet in a series published by a university press. Rosenthal's continuing engagement with Yeats is shown also in *Sailing into the Unknown: Yeats, Pound, and Eliot* (1978) and *Running to Paradise: Yeats's Poetic Art* (1994).

Rosenthal's influence has been strongest in two areas: the classic or High Modern poets who have come to constitute the central tradition: Hardy, Yeats, Williams, Pound, and Eliot; and somewhat younger poets much closer to his own age: John Berryman (1914–1972), Randall Jarrell (1914–1966), and Robert Lowell (1917–1977). Lowell's *Life Studies* provoked one of Rosenthal's most suggestive critical observations, first articulated in 1959 in a review called "Poetry as Confession" and later elaborated in *The New Poets* in two chapters that extend the "confessional" label from Lowell to Sylvia Plath, Allen Ginsberg, Theodore Roethke, John Berryman, and Anne Sexton. A later suggestive observation makes sense of much poetic activity since the career of Walt Whitman, especially the tendency of poets to produce sequences that fall between the realms of the brief lyric and the extended narrative or epic.

The interaction between what Rosenthal preaches and what he practices can be unmistakably witnessed in poems of his own that are organized into sequences and so subtitled: "Beyond Power: A Sequence," "His Present Discontents: A Sequence," "Power: A Sequence," and *She: A Sequence of Poems*. The critic-as-poet can also be glimpsed in such poems as "Visiting Yeats's Tower" and "To William Carlos Williams in Heaven" (a title that echoes one of Williams': "To Ford Madox Ford in Heaven"). Although it may not be a stellar achievement, it is to Rosenthal's abiding credit that he kept a place in his heart for poets who, without being of the first rank, do not deserve oblivion: Ramon Guthrie, Edwin Muir, John Montague, and many another.

CRITICAL RECEPTION

As a thinker and a writer, Rosenthal was consistently objective; his schooling at the University of Chicago and his experience as a poet predisposed him to regard an artwork as an object distinct from its maker, so that he seldom wrote from a perspective that could be labeled as authentically Jewish. He was incapable of following the example of his contemporary Karl Shapiro, who titled a book *Poems of a Jew* and, as a Jew, objected to the inflated reputations of Ezra Pound and T. S. Eliot. Rosenthal was also incapable of letting his love of poetry be diverted or diluted by his knowledge of the ideological positions of the poets, even of those notorious for, or charged with, anti-Semitism, as is the case with Pound, Eliot, and Imamu Amiri Baraka. That is not to say that Rosenthal ignored the issues. In *A Primer of Ezra Pound*, he explains his position in detail:

It is impossible to say that Pound's record . . . is without stain. His specific commitments to Mussolini's methods and his anti-Semitism (see Canto 52, for instance), which not even admirers as intelligent and well-informed as Wykes-Joyce, Hugh Kenner, and Brian Soper can very convincingly discount or explain away, remain the terrible aberrations of a man of genius. Yet in the face of these imponderables and of his own insufferable dogmatism, we are compelled to recognize, in his poetry at its best, the humane motives and the moral and intellectual power of his essential outlook. (20–21)

Later, in *Poetry and the Common Life*, Rosenthal took a careful look at ''a deliberately political poem by Imamu Amiri Baraka, attacking whites generally and liberals and Jews especially'': ''Baraka's poem is infantile and repulsive in its attitudes, but that is not the end of the matter. It still expresses a real state of mind that, since people do entertain it, must be recognized as present in our lives'' (116). Rosenthal was a courageous participant in a debate that is continuing.

BIBLIOGRAPHY

Works by M. L. Rosenthal

Exploring Poetry. With A. J. M. Smith. New York: Macmillan 1955.
The Modern Poets: A Critical Introduction. New York: Oxford, 1960a.
A Primer of Ezra Pound. New York: Macmillan, 1960b.
Ed. with Gerald DeWitt Sanders and John Herbert Nelson. *Chief Modern Poets of England and America.* New York: Macmillan, 1962.
Blue Boy on Skates (poems). New York: Oxford, 1964.
The William Carlos Williams Reader New York: New Directions, 1966.
The New Modern Poetry: An Anthology of American and British Poetry since World War II. New York: Oxford, 1967a.
The New Poets: American and British Poetry since World War II. New York: Oxford, 1967b.
Beyond Power: New Poems. New York: Oxford, 1969.
Randall Jarrell. Minneapolis: University of Minnesota Pamphlets on American Writers, No. 103, 1972a.
The View from the Peacock's Tail (poems). New York: Oxford, 1972b.
Poetry and the Common Life. New York: Oxford, 1974.
She: A Sequence of Poems. Rochester, NY: BOA Editions, 1977.
Sailing into the Unknown: Yeats, Pound, and Eliot. New York: Oxford, 1978.
Poems 1964–1980. London: Oxford, 1981.
With Sally M. Gall. *The Modern Poetic Sequence: The Genius of Modern Poetry.* New York: Oxford, 1983.
Selected Poems and Three Plays of William Butler Yeats. 3d ed. New York: Collier, 1986.
As for Love: Poems and Translations. New York: Oxford, 1987a.
Ed. *Poetry in English: An Anthology.* New York: Oxford, 1987b.
The Poet's Art. New York: Norton, 1987c.
Our Life in Poetry: Selected Essays and Reviews. New York: Persea, 1991.
Running to Paradise: Yeats's Poetic Art. New York: Oxford, 1994.

JEROME ROTHENBERG (1931–)

Pierre Joris

BIOGRAPHY

Jerome Rothenberg was born on December 11, 1931, in New York City and spent his early years in the Bronx. His parents were first-generation Jewish immigrants who had arrived in the New World from Poland in 1920. He himself describes his parents as of "a secular democratic-socialist orientation," though his grandfather on his father's side (after whom he was named) was a Hasid— connected to the same Hasidic rebbe as I. B. Singer's father. Yiddish was Rothenberg's mother tongue, with American English picked up only later on the street and in school. Literary interests came early, and as a young teenager he discovered and became fascinated with poets such as Gertrude Stein and e. e. cummings while also absorbing "a certain amount of undigested Joyce." Also at that time he first came across the work of the Spanish poet Frederico Garcia Lorca, who, like Stein, would remain a lifelong influence.

In the late 1940s he enrolled as an undergraduate at CCNY, an environment he did not find very congenial, his own budding sense of the kind of innovative poetry he was interested in clashing with the then-canonical New Criticism and its attendant poetries, which he saw as a closed, oppressive situation. Already present were the desire to break with those academic modes and the determination to make the new grounds of poetry perfectly apparent and open. This feeling was shared by other young poets who met concurrently at CCNY, a number of whom—such as David Antin, Robert Kelly, Jack Hirschman—would remain friends or associates over the next decades. After graduating from CCNY in the spring of 1952 and marrying Diane Brodatz (a son, Matthew, would be born in 1965), Rothenberg moved to Ann Arbor, where he earned an M.A. from the University of Michigan. Drafted into the army upon his return to New York, he spent most of the two next years in Germany, where he was able to investigate the young German poetry that would eventually lead to his first published book. Upon his return to New York he took on various clerical—and later, teaching and translation—jobs, while beginning to define his own practice as a poet. What came to be known as "the New American Poetry" was by this time in full swing, and Rothenberg and his associates were able to draw on that energy as well as on their own investigations and discoveries of poetries from outside America to start to define their own directions. By the end of the 1950s, his first book of translations, *New Young German Poets* had been published in San Francisco by City Lights Books, and he himself had founded a small press— that essential tool for experimental and avant-garde poets—with the Yeatsian name of Hawk's Well Press. Under this imprint he published his own first book, *White Sun Black Sun* in 1960, as well as the first books of Robert Kelly, Diane Wakoski, Armand Schwerner, and Rochelle Owens. Simultaneously, he edited the magazine anthology *Poems from the Floating World* (1959–1963), in which his concerns with tribal poetries find a first locus, before leading to the groundbreaking anthology *Technicians of the Sacred*, published in 1967. The 1960s also saw Rothenberg publishing a further ten collections of his poetry, besides several volumes of translations. His involvement with tribal or so-called primitive poetries grew, and in the winter of 1967 he made his first "field trip" to the Seneca Nation in Salamanca, New York, where he and Diane would be living from June 1972 to the summer of 1974. For the following two years the Rothenbergs made their home in Milwaukee, where he taught at the Center for Twentieth Century Studies at the University of Wisconsin.

During the 1970s, the formidable rate of production did not abate: besides several further groundbreaking gatherings early in the decade *Shaking the Pumpkin*, (1972); *America a Prophecy*, with George Quasha, 1973; *Revolution of the World* 1974), he published the extraordinary anthology *A Big Jewish Book: Poems and Other Visions of the Jews from Tribal Times to the Present* in 1978, edited in collaboration with Harris Lenowitz (a shortened version, under the title *Exiled in the Word*, came out in 1989). This was also the decade of the ethnopoetics journal *Alcheringa* (1970–1976), coedited with Dennis Tedlock, followed by the magazine *New Wilderness* (he published some fifteen books and chapbooks of poetry, including, most notably, the various installments of the *Poland/1931* series, an exploration of his ancestral Jewish roots). Toward the middle of that decade, New Directions became his main publisher and has remained so since, though Rothenberg continues to bring out books with many small, avant-garde poetry and art presses.

From Milwaukee he moved into the San Diego area of southern California, which has remained his home base ever since, except for a few years in the mid-1980s, when he was based briefly in Albany, attached to the New York State Writers Institute as visiting writer-in-residence (1986), followed by two years in the Department of English at SUNY, Binghamton. Since 1989 he has held a joint appointment in literature and the visual arts at the University of

California in San Diego. During the 1980s he published several major volumes of poems—*Vienna Blood, That Dada Strain, New Selected Poems (1970–1985)*—closing the decade with the volume *Khurbn*, the title poem sequence being maybe his single finest achievement to date. The 1990s have so far produced several further volumes of poems as well as a *PPPPPP: Selected Writings of Kurt Schwitters* (with Pierre Joris) and the two-volume anthology *Poems for the Millennium: The University of California Book of Modern and Postmodern Poetry* (also with Pierre Joris). During all these years Rothenberg has been a constant and brilliant performer of his work as well as an unremitting traveler, crisscrossing not only these States but also Mesoamerica, Europe East and West, and, more recently, the Far East (Taiwan, Japan).

MAJOR WORKS AND THEMES

"I believe that everything is possible in poetry, & that our earlier 'western' attempts at definition represent a failure of perception we no longer have to endure" (*Poems for the Game of Silence* 122)." Thus, said Rothenberg, relatively early in a career now spanning some forty years in poetry, a career that can, indeed, be seen as the single-minded pursuit of expanding and renewing the possibilities of contemporary poetry through the inextricably related actions of writing, performing, and translating and of creating circumstances—anthologies—in which to present those findings and workings. But even as "everything" may be possible in poetry, Rothenberg privileges specific directions, prefacing a 1979 interview thus: "The only absolutes for poetry are diversity & change (& the freedom to pursue these); & the only purpose, over the long run, is to raise questions, to raise doubts, to put people into alternative, sometimes uncomfortable situations" (*Pre-Faces* 217). The urgency is clear and finds its roots in the need to challenge the most widely held preconception in our culture, namely, "that 'Western man' is the culmination of the human evolutionary process" (*Pre-Faces* 224). The thrust is therefore, from the very start, toward a transformational poetics, a poetics of changes ("I will change your mind," he says in his 1966 "Personal Manifesto" see *Pre-Faces* 51) based on the belief that art is fundamentally subversive and has to aim at an open-ended and continuous revolution—not a revolution in style or taste (and thus his fierce opposition to officially sanctioned 1950s American poetry as spearheaded, ever so bluntly, by the "New Critics," both as commentators and as poets) but one in the deep structures of our imaginings of the world. This vision includes a complex feedback historicity: changes effected in the present, he insists, are significant if they also change our concept of the past.

How is this put into effect in the poetics themselves? From the start there are several areas of exploration; one such area can be summed up as the "deep image" workings (*White Sun Black Sun* is exemplary here), where perception is seen/used as an instrument for a deeper vision arising in the unfolding of the poem. Martin Buber's distinction between "husk" and "kernel," the phenomenal world and the hidden depth, is used by the poet to make the point that the deep image is "at once husk and kernel, perception and vision, and the poem is a movement between them" (*Pre-Faces*). A second area involved the exploration of what one could call more syntagmatic or constructivist language concerns, arising, in great part, from his involvement with the writings of Gertrude Stein and related modernist experimenters, as well as with performative concerns, which see the poem as a mapping for ritual, a score for live performance. This double thrust cannot be assimilated to some difference between depth and surface or content and form, however, but needs to be seen as two related investigatory modes toward elaborating a poetics of presentation rather than of re-presentation—what Charles Olson called "language as the act of the instant" as against "language as the act of thought about the instant" (*Collected Prose 156*). His 1981 collection *Pre-Faces and Other Writings* usefully gathers his various writings and most important interviews on poetics.

These concerns for a visionary poetics of presentation are both old and new. To make his point Rothenberg calls on William Blake and Tristan Tzara and includes in this community of visionary seekers the oldest paleolithic shamans, the cabalistic tradition of Jewish mysticism as well as, say, a contemporary brujera poetics of healing such as that of the Mazatec shamaness Maria Sabina; Frederico Garcia Lorca and Paul Celan, among many other European poets; his own American contemporaries and peers such as David Antin, Jackson Mac Low, Robert Kelly, Clayton Eshleman, and others; the international practitioners of concrete and visual work as well as the performers of traditional oral and contemporary sound poetries.

The work of recovery and translation that starts in the early 1960s and comes to be known as "ethnopoetics" (Rothenberg's term) culminates in a series of brilliant anthologies (*Technicians of the Sacred*, and *Shaking the Pumpkin*, among others); their mapping of unknown and/or previously excluded areas of poetry has radically altered the way in which to conceive of what poetry is today—and even of what it was in the past. They should also be read as an integral part of his own poetic oeuvre—using the collage and constructivist methods of modern, avant-garde poetry, they are epic-sized intertextual compositions. This gathering/assembling activity has been constant, starting with the anthology/magazine *Poems from the Floating World* in 1960–1964 and reaching its present apogee in the two-volume *Poems for the Millennium* (1995/1998), a global anthology of twentieth-century avant-garde workings, coauthored with Pierre Joris. If the concerns have usually been "global," specific and particular thrusts have also been evident, from *America a Prophecy*, which sets out to trace a Pan-American inheritance in innovative and visionary writing, to *A Big Jewish Book*, which charts a specifically Jewish *poesis* from prebiblical times until today, with particular attention to those traditions that would be seen as noncanonical or even heretical (such as mystical and apocalyptic visionary works, cabala from Simon bar Yohai to Sabbatai Zevi and Jacob Frank).

For Rothenberg's poetry and thought, as for Ezra Pound's, "all ages are

contemporaneous''—but with the major proviso that for Rothenberg the horrors
of history (which Pound's exacerbated aestheticism elides) are inalterable presences: the Jewish and Native American genocides crystallize as omnipresent
black suns churning at the heart of the work. A first full realization of Rothenberg's poetic powers is the complex of poems assembled under the title *Po-
land/1931*. This ''surrealist yiddish vaudeville'' is Rothenberg's experimental
attempt to explore and recover his own ancestral sources in the world of ''Jewish
mystics, thieves and madmen.'' Its rhythmical measures are, as the critic Eric
Mottram noted, ''unique in American 20th century poetry . . . a recovery of a
rhetorical music fit to carry multilevelled action: ecstatic, critical and humorous—a sense of alienation with an excitement over new-found inheritance''
(*Vort* no. 1 177–78). This excitement comes through on the page for the reader
but reaches its culmination in live readings of the work by the poet, when the
nature of the poem as score for performance becomes clear. The work itself
moves from Jewish life in Poland to Jewish life in America, where, in a mas-
terful comic apotheosis, the Jewish exile—in the form of ''Cokboy,'' the Baal
Shem Tov reborn as a beaver (just as Rothenberg himself was initiated into the
Seneca Beaver clan)—meets the Native American exile high up in the Rockies
''on a mountain & kept from/true entry to the west true paradise'' because
''America disaster/America disaster'' (*Poland/1931*, 151).

This is Rothenberg's most profound wisdom: the Black Sun of History is
always already lodged in the heart of the White Sun of Innocence. There are
no pure, uncontaminated origins that could somehow be regained by an act of
human will—as Rothenberg, recalling the poem ''Seeing Leni Riefenstahl's *Triumph of the Will*'' from his first book (*White Sun Black Sun*), says in the title
poem of the 1980 volume *Vienna Blood*: ''o triumph of the will—disasters of
the modern state'' (19). The human condition is always already postlapsarian.
In a poem honoring his son Matthew's bar mitzvah, reminiscing about the coincidence of Matthew's birth and the poet's brother's death, he writes: ''the
mystery thus thrust/into our thoughts/—of light & dark/co-equals'' (*Vienna
Blood* 33).

If Europe is the black sun (and Rothenberg repeats this again and again
throughout the work, e.g., in the poem ''Europe,'' which speaks of ''the death
of Europe'' and accumulates images of death, satan, skulls, dead rabbis, ghosts,
exile, failure, etc.), then the American possibility is marred from the beginning
by the European seed. But again, Rothenberg's workings are all but simplistic:
his involvement with Native American cultures, while always sympathetic and
emphatic, does not merely pitch those supposedly state-less and history-less
cultures as utopian Rousseauistic alternatives. His knowledge is much too accurate for such oversimplifications, as is made clear by the poems assembled in
A Seneca Journal (1978), the ''shaman's notebook'' of his two-year stay on the
Allegheny Seneca Reservation in western New York.

In Rothenberg's work geography, as it is always traversed by history, can
never be a purely Euclidean space or obey Euclidean laws of linearity. All

places/spaces are mixed; they touch and cut through all other spaces. An early Rothenberg volume was entitled *Between*, and if that word was meant more in its temporal than in its spatial sense in that context, it is nevertheless emblematic of the poet's stance. As he writes in *Vienna Blood*, meditating on concepts from the anthropologist Victor Turner's writings: "the liminal he writes/or 'place between'/ & sees suddenly/ the terror of that situation" (21)—a terror that has to be dealt with and, first of all, looked squarely in the face. In the "finale" section of the poem "Seneca Journal 6" he puts it this way: "there are such mysterious comings & goings/ across so many oceans/ the good & the bad are changing places/ always" (*A Seneca Journal* 80).

But the absolute bad, the Shoa, if always present *behind* the various works, was still waiting to be dealt with head-on. Rothenberg does so in the sequence "Khurbn" written between 1987 (the date of his first trip to Poland) and 1989, when it was collected in the book of the same title. In the prose prolegomenon he explains the choice of the title word *khurbn*, Yiddish for "total destruction," via his dislike of, for him, the inaccurate term Holocaust: "A word with which I never felt comfortable: too Christian & too beautiful, too much smacking of a 'sacrifice' I didn't & still don't understand" (3). Clayton Eshleman has described "Khurbn" as Jerome Rothenberg's "masterpiece . . . the great middle-length poem of our time." After some thirty books of poems, Rothenberg brings all his creative powers and accumulated knowledge of poetry to bear, and, as he says in the prose prolegomenon: "The poems that I first began to hear at Treblinka are the clearest message I have ever gotten about why I write poetry. They are an answer also to the proposition—by Adorno & others—that poetry cannot or should not be written after Auschwitz" (*Khurbn* 4). The most recent collection, *Seedings* (1996), continues the meditation on the Holocaust with "14 Stations," a sequence of poems composed to accompany Arie Galles' monumental charcoal drawings derived from World War II aerial views of the principal Nazi extermination camps. This time, however, the poet decided to use gematria, the technique of traditional Hebrew numerology based on the fact that to every letter of the Hebrew alphabet corresponds a specific number, so that words and phrases the sums of whose letters are equal are at some level meaningfully connected. He had already used gematria previously as a compositional method in such books as *Gematria* (1993) and did so in this case in order to "objectify" and to determine the words and phrases that would make up the poems. As he explains it: "The counts were made off the Hebrew and/or Yiddish spellings of the camp names, then keyed to the numerical values of words and word combinations in the first five books of the Hebrew Bible" (*Seedings* 100). If that sequence closes the book, another, more personal meditation on death opens it: the title poem "Seedings" speaks to and of those other, now departed, close companions in the life of poetry: Robert Duncan, George Oppen, and Paul Blackburn. But perhaps the title of middle section of the book most accurately describes Rothenberg's concerns over the years: "Twentieth Century Unlimited." That at the end of this century poetry can still be the central, vibrant core of imaginative activity—of this Jerome Rothenberg is living proof and testimonial.

CRITICAL RECEPTION

The critical reception of Rothenberg's work—some fifty books of poems, anthologies, and translations—if sympathetic and positive in the main, has been, in quantitative terms, far below what such an oeuvre should command by right. This, however, is not suprising if one considers the fact that most U.S. criticism and book reviewing in the established press and journals are either openly hostile to, or incapable of, dealing with innovative, avant-garde work. The most sympathetic, open, and intelligent reception has therefore come from his peers and from the handful of critics able to deal with his wide-ranging experimental concerns. Thus, Kenneth Rexroth wrote: "Jerome Rothenberg is one of the truly American poets who has returned U.S. poetry to the mainstream of international modern literature." Rexroth goes on to call him "a swinging orgy of Martin Buber, Marcel Duchamp, Gertrude Stein and Sitting Bull" (*Vort*, no. 7, 127). Early on, David Antin, writing in *Chelsea*, compares Rothenberg favorably to Paul Celan, suggesting that Rothenberg is even clearer and more musical than the great Bukovinian poet. By the early 1970s, Rothenberg's renown as poet and anthologist/translator had breached the frontiers of the United States and allowed the Canadian poets Steve McCaffery and bpNichol to write: "Rothenberg stands at a unique crossroads in the history of modern poetics; his achievement is to synthesize Williams' 'variable foot,' Olson's 'projective verse,' the collaborative emphasis and spontaneity of Dada and Surrealist poets, and the discovery (by concrete and sound poets) of an effective application of visual form to an oral poetic" (50). In 1975 the magazine *Vort* devoted an issue to Rothenberg and Antin, including important interviews with the poets and several groundbreaking essays on Rothenberg's work by critic such as Eric Mottram and Kevin Power. One also needs to mention the *Boundary 2* issue on David Antin and Jerome Rothenberg, with articles by Kevin Power, George Economou, and Dennis Tedlock, plus an important interview with Rothenberg by William Spanos, reprinted in *Pre-Faces*. A few years later, in 1984, Eric Mottram was the instigator of a collection of interviews with Rothenberg, edited by Gavin Selerie and published in England in book form under the title *The Riverside Interviews 4*. In 1986 Sherman Paul published *In Search of the Primitive*, which devotes some 110 pages to Rothenberg's work, constituting an excellent, if somewhat idiosyncratic, close reading of the books of poems published up to that date. Paul sums up the achievement by calling it "*a poetry of changes* . . . that offers us the chance to see America with new eyes (170)." Published the same year, Barbara Gitenstein's study *Apocalyptic Messianism and Contemporary Jewish-American Poetry* investigates more specifically the Jewish roots of Rothenberg's writings. Frederick Garber in his 1995 book *Repositionings: Readings of Contemporary Poetry, Photography and Performance*

Art deals at some length with notions of performance and narrative history as they unfold in Rothenberg's work. There are also worthwhile recent studies and reviews by Hank Lazer, Paul Christenson, Geoffrey O'Brien, and others. Finally, a most useful book for the serious Rothenberg reader or scholar is Harry Polkinhorn's *Jerome Rothenberg: A Descriptive Bibliography*.

BIBLIOGRAPHY

Works by Jerome Rothenberg

Poetry

White Sun Black Sun. New York: Hawk's Well Press, 1960.
The Seven Hells of the Jigoku Zoshi. New York: Trobar Books, 1962.
Sightings I-IX. New York: Hawk's Well Press, 1964.
The Gorky Poems. Mexico City, Mexico: El Corno Emplumado, 1966.
Between: Poems 1960–1963. London: Fulcrum Press, 1967.
Poems 1964–1967. Los Angeles: Black Sparrow Press, 1968.
Poems for the Game of Silence. New York: Dial Press, 1971.
Poland/1931. New York: New Directions, 1974.
A Seneca Journal. New York: New Directions, 1978.
Vienna Blood. New York: New Directions, 1980.
That Dada Strain. New York: New Directions, 1983.
New Selected Poems 1970–1985. New York: New Directions, 1986.
Khurbn and Other Poems. New York: New Directions, 1989.
The Lorca Variations. New York: New Directions, 1993.
Gematria. Los Angeles: Sun and Moon Press, 1993.
Seedings and Other Poems. New York: New Directions, 1996.

Translations

The Deputy, by Rolf Hochhuth (American Playing Version). New York: Samuel French, 1965.
The Book of Hours and Constellations, by Eugen Gomringer. New York: Something Else Press, 1968a.
Cotranslator with Hans Magnus Enzensberger and Michael Hamburger. *Poems for People Who Don't Read Poems*, by Hans Magnus Enzensberger. New York: Atheneum, 1968b; London: Secker and Warburg, 1968.
New Young German Poets. San Francisco: City Lights Books, 1959.
The Seventeen Horse Songs of Frank Mitchell (Navajo, with prints by Ian Tyson). London: Tetrad Press, 1970.
The Suites, by Federico Garcia Lorca. In *Collected Poems*. New York: Farrar, Straus, and Giroux, 1991.
With Pierre Joris. *PPPPPP: Poems Performance Pieces Proses Plays Poetics of Kurt Schwitters*. Philadelphia: Temple University Press, 1993.

Anthologies

Ritual. New York: Something Else Press, 1966.

Technicians of the Sacred. New York: Doubleday-Anchor, 1967; rev. ed., Berkeley: University of California Press, 1985.

Shaking the Pumpkin. New York: Doubleday-Anchor, 1972; rev. ed., Albuquerque: University of New Mexico Press, 1991.

With George Quasha. *America a Prophecy*. New York: Random House, 1973.

Revolution of the Word: A New Gathering of American Avant-Garde Poetry 1914–1945. New York: Seabury-Continuum, 1974.

With Harris Lenowitz. *A Big Jewish Book: Poems and Other Visions of the Jews from Tribal Times to the Present*. New York: Doubleday-Anchor, 1978; abridged and reprinted as *Exiled in the Word*, Port Townsend, WA: Copper Canyon Press, 1989.

With Diane Rothenberg. *Symposium of the Whole: A Range of Discourse Toward an Ethnopoetics*. Berkeley: University of California Press, 1984.

With Pierre Joris. *Poems for the Millennium: The University of California Book of Modern and Postmodern Poetry*. Vol. 1: *From Fin-de-siecle to Negritude*. Berkeley: University of California Press, 1995. *Poems for the Millennium*. Vol. 2: *From Postwar to Millennium*. Berkeley: University of California Press, 1998.

With David Guss. *The Book, Spiritual Instrument*. New York: Granary Books, 1996.

Essays

Poems for the Game of Silence. New York: Dial Press, 1971.

With Gavin Selerie, ed., and Eric Mottram. *The Riverside Interviews 4: Jerome Rothenberg*. London: Binnacle Press, 1984.

Theater

That Dada Strain. Music by Bertram Turetzky. Center for Theater Science and Research, San Diego, and Lexington, NY, 1985, 1987.

Poland/1931. Adaptation by Hanon Reznikov. New York: Living Theater, 1988.

"Khurbn/Hiroshima." Texts by Jerome Rothenberg (poet) and Makoto Oda (novelist) and music by Charlie Morrow; produced by Bread and Puppet Theater, August 26–27, 1995.

Works about Jerome Rothenberg

Alpert, Barry, ed. David Antin/Jerome Rothenberg Issue. *Vort*, No. 7, 1975.

Antin, David. *Chelsea* 7(1960): 114–117.

Christensen, Paul. "Some Bearings on Ethnopoetics." *Parnassus* 15, No. 1 (1989).

Garber, Frederick. "Chapter 2: The Histories and Poetics of Jerome Rothenberg." In F. Garber, *Repositionings: Readings of Contemporary Poetry, Photography, and Performance Art*. University Park: Pennsylvania State University Press, 1995.

Gitenstein, Barbara. *Apocalyptic Messianism and Contemporary Jewish-American Poetry*. Albany: State University of New York Press, 1986.

Lazer, Hank. "Thinking Made in the Mouth: The Cultural Poetics of David Antin and Jerome Rothenberg." In William G. Doty ed., *Picturing Cultural Values in Postmodern America*. Tuscaloosa: University of Alabama Press, 1994.

McCaffery, Steve, and bpNichol. "Some Notes on Jerome Rothenberg and Total Translation." In *Rational Goemancy: The Collected Research Reports of the Toronto Research Group*. Vancouver: Talonbooks, 1992.

Mottram, Eric. "Where the Real Song Begins: The Poetry of Jerome Rothenberg." *Dialectical Anthropology* 2, Nos. 2–4 (1986). 171–177.

Olson, Charles. *Collected Prose*. Berkeley: University of California Press, 1977.

Paul, Sherman. *In Search of the Primitive: Rereading David Antin, Jerome Rothenberg and Gary Snyder*. Baton Rouge and London: Louisiana State University Press, 1986.

Perloff, Marjorie. "Soundings: Zaum, Seriality and the Discovery of the 'Sacred.' " *American Poetry Review* (February 1986).

Peters, Robert. "Jerome Rothenberg: That Dada Strain." In *Great American Poetry Bakeoff*, 3rd series. Lanham, MD: Scarecrow Press, 1987.

Polkinhorn, Harry, ed. *Jerome Rothenberg: A Descriptive Bibliography*. Jefferson, NC, and London: McFarland, 1988.

Rasula, Jed. "On Rothenberg's Revised 'Technicians of the Sacred.' " *Poetics Journal*, No. 6 (1986).

Rexroth, Kenneth. "Re: Jerome Rothenberg." *VORT* no.7 3:1 (1975): 127.

Sayre, Henry M. *The Object of Performance: The American Avant-Garde since 1970*. Chicago: University of Chicago Press, 1989.

Selerie, Gavin. *Jerome Rothenberg* (Book-length Interview, Riverside Series). London: Binnacle Press, 1984.

Weinberger, Eliot. "Rothenberg: New York/1968." In *E. W., Poetics Politics Polemics*. New York: Marsilio, 1996.

MARK RUDMAN

(1948–   )

Theodore Blanchard

BIOGRAPHY

Mark Rudman was born on December 11, 1948, in Manhattan; his father's family were Russian Jews, and his mother came from a mixed Russian/Alsace-Lorraine Jewish background. The class tensions between them were "terrific (and destructive)," and they stayed together for only a year and a half. Even during this time, his mother whisked him away often to southern California, where her people were, and these frequent journeys set up in the boy an enduring internal dialectic of East and West, to which his poetry would later resonate: the restless trope of the quest, the odyssey from the desert—the ancient site of solitary revelation—to the city, and back again.

His father had ambitions to be a composer and studied at New York University (NYU) but was drawn toward the world of advertising. He worked at the famous firm Grey Advertising and was involved in the application of psychological aptitude testing to the business, and he did very well. In 1954 his mother married the rabbi she had been dating—the stepfather who would become "the Little Rabbi," the occasional interlocutor of *Rider* and *The Millennium Hotel*: a presence that a recent *Village Voice* review, choosing *The Millennium Hotel* as one of the "Best 25 Books of 1996," termed the "spectral inquisitor." Shortly thereafter, the new family left Manhattan (where Mark had attended L'Ecole Française for preschool and kindergarten) and headed west to Illinois.

These were harder times: the constant moves, as the rabbi took pulpit after new pulpit; young Mark's dual identity—"Rudman" at school, "Strome" in the synagogues; asthma, which came suddenly; and the beginnings of a difficult and adversary relationship with school that would persist until he entered college (during this period, he had sessions with "a famous child psychiatrist" in Chicago). Eventually, having dropped out of one high school (in Salt Lake City) and attended a boarding school in Arizona for a while, he received his degree and went to the Seminar College at the New School—back to Manhattan.

Although he pursued an eclectic course of study there—which was to contribute to his later affinity for the mosaic form and his penchant for blurring the poetry-prose distinction—Rudman did not write poetry until after he graduated. Having read an article by Kenneth Koch about teaching poetry to children, he called the poet to ask how one might find a job in that field. Koch steered him to the Poets and Writers Collaborative, and after a year of teaching in the New York public schools he applied and was accepted to Columbia's School of the Arts' Graduate Program in Writing.

Receiving encouragement from Stanley Kunitz, Mark Strand, and already-publishing older students like Mei-Mei Bersenbrugge and Gregory Orr, Rudman soon began publishing poems in journals like *The Atlantic Monthly* and *Harper's* and writing critical essays for editors such as Philip Rahv. Also at this time he set himself to translation as part of his poetic apprenticeship, translating first from the French—Apollinaire, Char, Reverdy, and others—and later from Slavic and other languages, in collaboration with native speakers. In 1983 he published a translation (done with Bohdan Boychuk) of Pasternak's *My Sister—Life*, for which he received the Max Hayward Translation Award. In 1997, University of Pennsylvania Press published his version of Euripides' *Daughters of Troy*, done with Katharine Washburn and David Slavitt. His first original collection, *In the Neighboring Cell*, was published in 1982; there followed two chapbooks, *The Mystery in the Garden* (1985) and *The Ruin Revived* (1986). These were eventually collected together (along with other poems) in *By Contraries* (1986).

In 1986, Rudman's father committed suicide, an act that he documented in a series of poems published in *The Nowhere Steps* (1990), his second major collection. The year this book was published, his stepfather, "the Little Rabbi," died. These two events proved to be catalytic for the new form that Rudman adopted for the writing of *Rider* (1994) and its sequel, *The Millennium Hotel* (1996). The dominant opposites of his life—father and stepfather, city and desert, Jew and non-Jew (in an American context)—are reflected and amplified clearly in the back-and-forth rhythm, the mundane-and-metaphysical pendulum swings of *Rider* and *The Millennium Hotel*, to be continued in his conclusion to this trilogy, *Provoked in Venice* (1998). He has also published two books of essays, critical and otherwise: *Diverse Voices* (1993) and *Realm of Unknowing* (1995).

The summer before he began study at Columbia, he met his future wife, the mathematician Madelaine Bates. In 1985, their son, Samuel, was born. They live on the Upper West Side. Mark has taught at the graduate and undergraduate level at NYU and Columbia (both School of the Arts and General Studies). Since 1985 he has been the editor of *Pequod*, having been poetry editor since 1976. He has consistently received prestigious prizes for his work, beginning with the Academy of American Poets Prize at Columbia and including a PEN

Translation Fellowship in 1976, an Ingram Merril Fellowship in 1983, a National Endowment for the Arts Fellowship in Poetry in 1994, and a Guggenheim Fellowship in 1996. In 1994 he was given the National Book Critics' Circle Award for Poetry for *Rider*.

MAJOR WORKS AND THEMES

One of Mark Rudman's earliest published poems, "In the Neighboring Cell," was written, he attests, in reaction against the idea of confessional poetry and intended, indeed, "to parody the autobiographical poem" (*By Contraries* 31). Yet his most successful and mature works, the book-length poems *Rider* and *The Millennium Hotel*, as well as earlier poems like "Casket Closed," have a strong current of autobiography; more, they are built with it, using not just images and themes from the poet's life but the structure of events, the palpable force of memory. Is this not "confession"? The question is useful only up to a point. The primacy of a kind of testimony in Mark Rudman's work is linked inextricably to the loose, but particular, form he has arrived at and made his own: a certain type of dialogue.

It begins with the idea of movement, as against stasis. In "Mosaic on Walking," an essay in *Diverse Voices*, Rudman's award-winning prose "rumination," the form of movement—the walking of the title—becomes explicit in the subject of the writing. "Great poetry has always been about this," he says, "—ambulatory movement" (*Diverse Voices* 11). His practice in this piece and in many poems is an accumulation of moments that force movement, like the still frames of a film (Rudman has, in fact, written extensively about the films of Michaelangelo Antonioni, Godard, and others and acknowledges these directors as influences as important as his more specifically poetic sources of inspiration). "Language describes a possibility and it is possible to be myself once I give up the need for unity, for consistency" (*Diverse Voices* 25). The choice of the dialogic form flows naturally from this movement toward plurality. "It's no accident that much of Shakespeare's 'poetry,' in the plays, is *dialogue*; even in the soliloquies, which are what they are because the audience, the 'other,' is *there*" (*By Contraries* 28).

Through the dialectic of such experiments Rudman came to dialogue as a fertile way to respond to the pressure of autobiography. "An interrogative voice asserted itself," he says, "and I was compelled to answer its questions. This resulted in *Rider*" ("Self-Interview" 4). The language in many of his poems, culminating in *Rider* and *The Millennium Hotel*, is structured by this implicit and explicit use of the dialogic form and becomes almost incantatory at times; at others it is verbatim recording of conversation, stripped of almost all ritual. This play of contraries brings to mind the poet's habitual blurring of the line between poetry and prose: he points out that Joyce and Woolf and Malcolm Lowry are more "poetic," in the sense of the lyrical use of language, than a lot of poetry and that many poets use a pared-down narrative that is almost

explicitly novelistic. Necessarily, this insistence on the recognition and absorption of contraries is unstable. "*You are torn at every moment in time, aren't
you?*" Rudman's interrogator asks. "Nearly," comes the answer. "*When will
you rest?*" Then silence (*Rider* 25).

The power of dialogue, the back-and-forth movement, is linked also to wan-
derlust (recalling the poet's own early and frequent migrations)—the obsessive
need, the *human* need, to explore—and especially to forced explorations and
permanent journeys, like the diaspora. This inherited restlessness becomes implicitly and sometimes explicitly Jewish, this notion that the proper structure for
exploring life in all its aspects is conversation: question and answer. Shakespeare
is the great forebear of the form in poetry; but, further back, the literary ritual
of the Jewish holy service, the sacred conversation between congregation and
leader, provides the eternal, enshrined echo of celebrant and congregation. "*All*
of my poems," Rudman says, "are dialogues," the "diasporian white particles"
(*Rider* 19), interacting to produce the snowstorm. In these poems the rhythmic
cadence of the conversation, of the temple ceremony, underlies the music of the
words and the meaning and gives the poems form.

"A lot of poems exclude too much," says Rudman in *By Contraries*. "Rather
than moving up and down and around, following the sentences as they back-
track, get lost, dissolve, are reborn, a lot of poems construct a stance toward
reality ('love poem,' 'pastoral,' etc.)" (*By Contraries* 28). The process, he seems
to be saying, is more important that the decisions made prior to embarkation.
There is an implicit trust here in reality itself, in the idea that the world need
not be constructed per se but only followed to its logical, mysterious conclusion.
"But this is what really happened in Oshkosh," says Rudman in *Rider*, discussing an awakening in childhood. "I sensed clues and signs, keys to the
mystery, scattered everywhere, each one radiant and strange, yet by itself impoverished. In Oshkosh I felt my brain begin to curl around an idea, to comprehend the seizure" (*Rider* 6). The mind's seizure, the world's seizure, is the
poem's seed.

Within the deep source of his powerful and moral yearning toward motion
lies also a certain bone-weariness—a desire to stop—which becomes the bare,
tense skeleton of "The Dancing Party" (Rudman's only dream poem: an exploration of the tension between a stasis of casual evil and movement—the
Dance—which is painful but morally unavoidable. This was the earliest poem
Rudman chose to include in his later collection). In *The Millennium Hotel*, there
is a moment of bursting in the dialogue, of tired rage, in which the poet-speaker
conjures the futility of speaking into the void of the world: "Don't ask me
what/ I'm getting at," the narrator anticipates his interrogator. "What is there
to get/ at, where/ is there to go?/ Space,/ is a grid of limits,/ . . . / Heaven is
what does not go on in the physical world" (59).

The poet's anger rises against official justifications and explanations, against
the facile linking of physical and spiritual. The poetic crime of the Jews—of

himself—is having too much faith and in the wrong things: "praying to an invisible,// and therefore invincible,/ God./ . . . / Crossroads, not crosses" (59). Focused on the journey, instead of on the final proof of God, seeing the divine as a process rather than an end, the Jews with their wanderings threaten the very existence of those who yearn toward fixity, a sureness. For all his millennial foreboding, Yeats didn't have it quite right: "The problem/ was never that the best/ lacked conviction but that// they needed it to override uncertainty/ and live as if life was not pure/ chance or a mad, wild game of charades/ in the dangerously volatile/ hands of shape-shifting maniacs" (60).

In the central section of *The Millennium Hotel*, Rudman takes his young son on a sort of vacation of luxurious exile, to the Hotel Millennium in lower Manhattan, in search of a space in which order, however temporary, does not contain its own implicit and immediate destruction. It is "our winter's luxury, escape, and splurge," as Rudman "patiently shouts" at his mother (who is shocked by the room-service bill) (56). This episode provides the book's fulcrum, and the sections before and after—detailed memories of past lovers, restlessly remembered journeys, evocative nights and days long ago in Brooklyn, Utah, Soho, Mazatlán—are all tinted with the cold, blue winter light of that one weekend at the Millennium. In spite of the respite, the poet cannot avoid contemplation of decay: there is more than a hint here of eschatological bracing. "[B]ecause I live here," he says, nervous and aware, "I must/ be part of the storm watch" (34). One can hear faint echoes of the millennialist cults described by Gershom Scholem; a terrified fascination with the approach of the End Days.

This sense of inevitability, this series of revelations of things that *had* to be done, leads to a fertile contradiction and a durable insight into the heart of the condition of poet and man: "Beyond religion," Rudman insists in *The Millennium Hotel*, lies "the gift/ of chance./ It's why diaspora ought to signify/ semaphore, open door,/ all who wander/ and come to be here, here,/ in the fullness of nowhere;/ to be in/ unyielding// chaos" (60). The steps leading nowhere have pointed the way to the journey leading nowhere. It is the journey that, as it has throughout Rudman's poetic odyssey, has proved to be most worth taking.

CRITICAL RECEPTION

Although not widely reviewed, Rudman's work has been highly praised, evidenced by his reception in 1995 of the National Book Critics Circle Award for Poetry for *Rider*. A good summary of the critics' opinion, however, is expressed in a review of *By Contraries*: "A sentient self emerges clearly in Mark Rudman's work—complex, despairing, speaking to confront the contradictions offered up by the contemporary urban life. . . . He displays considerable craftsmanship and control over his material as he confronts a complex world with a sensitivity that is acute, subtle, and entirely unshielded. He and the City are well matched" (Ullman).

BIBLIOGRAPHY

Works by Mark Rudman

Poetry and Translations

Trans. with Bohdan Boychuk. *Square of Angels: The Selected Poems of Bohdan Anto-nych*. Ann Arbor, MI: Ardis, 1977.

Trans. with Bohdan Boychuk. *Orchard Lamps Poems*. by Ivan Drach. Ed. Stanley Kunitz. Riverdale-on-Hudson, NY: Sheep Meadow Press, 1978.

In the Neighboring Cell. New York: Spuyten Duyvil, 1982.

Trans. with Bohdan Boychuk. *My Sister—Life and the Sublime Malady*, by Boris Pasternak. New York: Sheep Meadow Press, 1990.

The Mystery in the Garden. New York: Spuyten Duyvil, 1985.

The Ruin Revived: A Chapbook of Poems and Prose. Illustrated by Susan Laufer. Brookline Village, MA: Branden Press, 1986.

By Contraries and Other Poems, 1970–84, Selected and New. Orono, ME: National Poetry Foundation, 1987.

Ed. and cotrans. *Memories of Love: The Selected Poems of Bohdan Boychuk*. New York: Sheep Meadow Press, 1989.

The Nowhere Steps. New York: Sheep Meadow Press, 1990.

Rider. Middletown, CT: Wesleyan University Press, 1994.

The Millennium Hotel. Middletown, CT: Wesleyan University Press, 1996.

Trans. with Katharine Washburn. *Daughters of Troy*. Philadelphia: University of Pennsylvania Press, 1997.

Provoked in Venice. Middletown, CT: Wesleyan University Press, 1998.

Other Works

Robert Lowell: An Introduction to the Poetry. New York: Columbia University Press, 1983.

Ed. and contributor. *Secret Destinations: Writers on Travel*. Northridge, CA: Pequod Press/Persea Books, 1986.

Ed. *Literature and the Visual Arts*. Northridge, CA: Pequod Press, 1990.

Diverse Voices: Essays on Poets and Poetry. Ashland, OR: Story Line Press, 1993.

Realm of Unknowing: Meditations on Art, Suicide, and Other Transformations. Middletown, CT: Wesleyan University Press, 1995.

Works about Mark Rudman

Orr, Leslie. "Form and the Father: On Mark Rudman's Poetry." *Agni* 34 (1992).

Revell, Donald. "Rose as Decoy, Beauty as Use." *Ohio Review*, No. 53 (1995).

Slavitt, David. "Two Jewish Ironists." *New England Review* 17, No. 3 (Summer 1995).

Ullman, Leslie. "Conjuring Up Paintings and Light Shows." *New York Times Book Review*, October 16, 1988.

Ullman, Leslie. Rev. of *By Contraries*. *New York Times Book Review*, October 16, 1988, 42.

MURIEL RUKEYSER (1913–1980)

Michele S. Ware

BIOGRAPHY

The oldest daughter of a wealthy Jewish family, Muriel Rukeyser was born in New York in 1913. She experienced from a very young age the physical comforts of a privileged life in New York City, attending the School of Ethical Culture in Manhattan and the Fieldstone School. She spent two years studying at Vassar, when her father's financial ruin forced her to withdraw from college. Rukeyser was acutely aware fairly early of something missing in her life amid "the maids and nurses and chauffeurs, those who most talk to you, who give you books to read" (*The Life of Poetry* 192). During her teens, she questioned the closed world of her parents and began to reject the culturally impoverished and conservative materialism of her family. On the eve of attending college, Rukeyser began to recognize how limited her childhood and adolescence had been: "I learned that I had been brought up as a protected, blindfolded daughter, who might have finally learned some road other than that between school and home, but who knew nothing of people, of New York, or of herself" (*Life* 205). By 1933, Rukeyser had left Vassar, in part because of her father's bankruptcy and in part because of her desire to write, and she set about learning that other road with a passion, going to Alabama to report on the Scottsboro trial, in which nine African-American youths were wrongfully convicted of raping two white women. There, at the age of nineteen, Rukeyser was arrested, she contracted typhoid fever in an Alabama police station, and she began in earnest a life of political activism.

Her early writing career combined a love of poetry and a penchant for journalism, and she contributed regularly to two communist publications, the *Student Review* and *New Masses*. Rukeyser's sympathies with the political Left drew her in 1936 to Gauley Bridge, West Virginia, to investigate the appalling conditions of the miners there who were dying of silicosis. In the same year, she traveled to Spain to report on the antifascist Olympics in Barcelona. Although her trip was cut short by the beginning of the Spanish civil war, Rukeyser wrote a number of overtly political poems about that experience and the consequences of the conflict. As Kate Daniels notes, however, in her Introduction to *Muriel Rukeyser: Out of Silence*, by 1939, with the publication of *A Turning Wind*, Rukeyser's "natural abhorrence of violence against human beings eventually overruled her interest in revolutionary politics" (xi). But Rukeyser maintained a politically engaged stance throughout her career, even when it cost her in terms of her relationship with her family and others. She was disowned by her father; she had a disastrously short marriage to painter Glyn Collins in 1945, which was annulled in the same year; and in 1947, she bore a son, William Laurie Rukeyser, out of wedlock and raised him alone as a single parent, never publicly revealing the name of his father. In spite of an often chaotic and peripatetic life, Rukeyser established herself as a devoted teacher, first at Vassar College, then at the California Labor School, and finally at Sarah Lawrence College. In 1964, Rukeyser was temporarily incapacitated by her first stroke. Yet in spite of that extended illness, she published *The Speed of Darkness*, one of her most powerful books of poetry, in 1968. In the late 1960s, her political activism surfaced with a renewed energy and commitment. Rukeyser traveled to North Vietnam on a peace mission with Denise Levertov in 1972 (Daniels xiv), and she was arrested in Washington for protesting against the war. As president of the American Center of PEN, she went to South Korea in 1975 on behalf of dissident poet Kim Chi-Ha and stood outside the gates of his prison in silent protest. Her final book of new poems, *The Gates*, published in 1976, emerged from that experience. Rukeyser found out after many years the far-reaching consequences of her political engagement when she confirmed, in 1978, that she had been under surveillance by the Federal Bureau of Investigation (FBI) for more than forty years. Rukeyser's life of struggle, achievement, and artistic creation came to a close in February 1980, when she died after a long illness. She was only sixty-six years old, yet when she described herself in "Breaking Open" as a "rare battered she-poet," Rukeyser must have realized that she would leave behind the enduring legacy of her art.

MAJOR WORKS AND THEMES

Muriel Rukeyser was a revolutionary and visionary poet in terms of both her poetic form and her subject matter. One of the most important female poets of the twentieth century, her career spanned almost fifty years, during which she produced seventeen volumes of poetry, beginning with *Theory of Flight* (1935), which won the Yale Series of Younger Poets Prize, and ending with *The Collected Poems of Muriel Rukeyser* (1979), published just a year before her death. Additionally, she translated the work of other poets and wrote biographies, children's books, plays, a novel, and a prose defense of her art, *The Life of Poetry* (1949). She insisted on the prophetic role of the poet in society and on sustained formal experimentation in poetry, and this insistence poses some difficulty in categorizing Rukeyser's work within a modernist poetic tradition. Although she wrote a number of short lyric poems, Rukeyser's formal preference was for the long poetic sequence, and throughout her career, almost all of her important poems are in this form.

Rukeyser wrote from personal experience, and her energetic activism became an essential part of her creative life. The social and political concerns she had in the beginning of her career are the same preoccupations of her later poetry. Rukeyser's political activism led her to write in her first volume of poetry, "Not Sappho, Sacco," rejecting the classical for the revolutionary ("Poem Out of Childhood," in *Theory of Flight* 28), and such would be her focus for most of her career. *Theory of Flight* describes her awakening political consciousness, her willingness to speak for those who have no voice. Like Walt Whitman, a poet whose profound influence is obvious in Rukeyser's work, she removes the veil of aesthetic distance in poetry, striving for an immediacy drawn from her own personal act of witness. In "The Trial," the third section of her sequence "The Lynchings of Jesus," the poet describes the interior of the courtroom in Scottsboro, Alabama:

> John Brown, Nat Turner, Toussaint stand in this courtroom,
> Dred Scott wrestles for freedom there in the dark corner,
> all our celebrated shambles are repeated here: now again
> Sacco and Vanzetti walk to a chair, to the straps and rivets
> and the switch spitting death and Massachusetts' will. (28)

Rukeyser links the fate of the "Nine dark boys" (55) in the Scottsboro trial to the historic injustices suffered in the struggle against prejudice and racial and ethnic hatred. She announces in this first volume of poetry her drive to expose and correct such injustice. With *Theory of Flight*, Rukeyser places herself firmly at the forefront of a defiant, passionately engaged, and openly political strain of American poetry. "We are talking about," she explains, "the endless quarrel between the establishments and the prophets, and I hope to be forever on the side of the prophets." This endless quarrel permeates her poetry, from the first volume to the last.

"The Book of the Dead" in Rukeyser's second volume of poetry, *U.S. 1*, chronicles her experience in Gauley Bridge, West Virginia. In this poem, she draws on reportage, documentary evidence, congressional reports, and interviews with miners, as well as on her lyric gift, to expose the tragic loss of life to silicosis, the greed of corporate mine owners, and the destruction caused by technology gone mad. In that same volume, she writes, too, of her journey to Spain, a trip cut short by the beginning of the Spanish civil war. In such poems

as "Cruise" and "Mediterranean," her sympathies with the Spanish Republican
cause are clear, as is her fear of the repercussions of this war:

> I saw Europe break apart
> and artifice or martyr's will
> cannot anneal this war, nor make
> the loud triumphant future start
> shouting from its tragic heart. ("Mediterranean," Section V 141)

Rukeyser explores her own particular position in history in "Poem," from
The Speed of Darkness (1968). She points to her obligation, her mission as a
poet in troubled times:

> To construct peace, to make love, to reconcile
> Waking with sleeping, ourselves with each other,
> Ourselves with ourselves. We would try any means
> To reach the limits of ourselves, to reach beyond ourselves,
> To let go the means, to wake.
>
> I lived in the first century of these wars. (451)

Her efforts to construct peace and to reach beyond the limits of the self in her
poetry drew considerable fire from the critical establishment of the 1940s and
1950s, when the proponents of the New Criticism valued a more inner-directed
and less explicitly political poetry. But Rukeyser refused to be silenced and
continued writing as a witness to injustice and a fighter for social change. Her
title poem from *The Gates* (1976), written very late in her life, is a poignant
and powerful recollection of her seemingly futile attempt to secure the release
of Kim Chi-Ha from a Korean prison.

Like many American women poets who came after her, Rukeyser believed
that the personal was always political, and she wrote openly of her own life as
a woman, articulating the struggles and joys of her existence. Her poem "Desdichada," from *Breaking Open* (1973), describes her triumphant self-discovery
in spite of the pitfalls of being rejected by her family, experiencing a disastrous
marriage, and raising a child alone:

> Disinherited, annulled, finally disacknowledged
> and all of my own asking. I keep that wild dimension
> of life and making and the spasm
> upon my mouth as I say this word of acknowledge
> to you forever. *Ewig*. (494)

Rukeyser found enormous strength in speaking and writing the truth, in the
role of artist as activist. As she wrote in "Käthe Kollwitz," her biographical
poem in praise of the sibylline power of the female artist: "What would happen

if one woman told the truth about her life? The world would split open" (III 482). Rukeyser's poetry kept that wild dimension of life alive and encouraged other women to explore and celebrate their own lives. She broke down the barriers of patriarchal mythology in "The Poem as Mask" from *The Speed of Darkness*, declaring, "No more masks! No more mythologies!" (435). Instead, Rukeyser created a woman-centered mythology, focused on self-exploration and understanding, linking her own life to the lives of others. The final result of telling the truth about her life is to discover her singular identity as a woman, poet, and agent of change.

Adrienne Rich argues that a significant aspect of the poet's self-portrayal includes her Jewish heritage, writing that Rukeyser was "a secular visionary with a strongly political sense of her Jewish identity" (xiv). However, Rukeyser rarely addresses or explores her own Jewishness in depth, except as a corollary to her awareness of injustice, prejudice, and exclusion or as a reference to her personal family history. In an early poem, "The Lynchings of Jesus," she calls upon her Jewish heritage in the second section, "The Committee Room," where she invokes the religious past in sharp contrast to the material present:

> Those people engendered my blood swarming
> over the altar to clasp the scrolls and Menorah
> the black lips, bruised cheeks, eye-reproaches
> as the floor burns, singing Shema (*Collected Poems* 25–26)

Her reference to singing Shema, traditionally recited before death and especially for martyrdom, shows her sense of the tragedy of contemporary society, the death of spirituality, and the losses associated with it. Rukeyser took great pleasure and pride in her mother's revelation of their family's ancestral connection to Rabbi Akiba, which she describes in *The Life of Poetry*:

> A silver goblet, hearsay of a cantor's songs, is all you know; then a gap of two thousand years until the Ancestor, Akiba, who fought to include the Song of Songs in the Bible, who was smuggled out of Jerusalem in a coffin by his disciples, who believed in Bar Cochba's revolution, who was tortured to death by his friend, the Roman general Rufus. (193)

We can discern the poet's yearning for a connection with her Jewish ancestry, forgotten or ignored by her family. Rukeyser wrote "Akiba," one of her biographical poems in the sequence *Lives*, for *The Speed of Darkness* (1968), and she informs the reader in a footnote that "Akiba is the Jewish shepherd-scholar of the first and second century, identified with the Song of Songs and with the insurrection against Hadrian's Rome.... The story in my mother's family is that we are descended from Akiba—unverifiable, but a great gift to a child" (473–74). Especially powerful in this family story is Rabbi Akiba's link to poetry and political rebellion, a story in which Rukeyser finds an ancestral confirmation of her lifelong concerns.

Although Rukeyser writes infrequently of Judaism, she declared in an essay in 1944 that Jewishness was an elemental part of her being: "My themes and the use I have made of them have depended on my life as a poet, as a woman, as an American, and as a Jew" (qtd. in Rich xiv). One poem in particular describes Rukeyser's sense of what it means to be a Jew. In "Letter to the Front," from *Beast in View* (1994), Rukeyser devotes an entire section of a long sequence to reflection and meditation on the special responsibilities of being Jewish in contemporary history:

> To be a Jew in the twentieth century
> Is to be offered a gift. If you refuse,
> Wishing to be invisible, you choose
> Death of the spirit, the stone insanity.
> Accepting, take full life. Full agonies:
> Your evening deep in labyrinthine blood
> Of those who resist, fail, and resist; and God
> Reduced to a hostage among hostages.
>
> The gift is torment. Not alone the still
> Torture, isolation; or torture of the flesh.
> That may come also. But the accepting wish,
> The whole and fertile spirit as guarantee
> For every human freedom, suffering to be free.
> Daring to live for the impossible. (239)

Clearly, Rukeyser has accepted the gift of her Jewishness, taking the expression of "full life" and "full agonies" as her personal vocation. As she notes in this sonnet, the gift is not an easy one, but the rewards are great. Although she doesn't write explicitly, for example, of the atrocities of the Holocaust or about anti-Semitism, her encompassing, optimistic, incantatory vision reveals her poetic goal—to fight for human freedom, to live for the impossible.

"Breathe-in experience, breathe-out poetry," Rukeyser wrote in "Poem Out of Childhood" (*Collected Poems* 3). From her first published volume of poetry to her last, Muriel Rukeyser attempted to encompass all experience in her poetry, to ground her poetry in the physical world around her while suggesting her own attachment to history and the past as well as her excitement about what was to come. Rukeyser combines a public and private voice to accomplish what she envisioned as her related goals—self-knowledge within a specific political and historical milieu and cultural and political transformation. She felt that there ought to be no split between art and life, and her art is a tribute to that vision. Her poetry conveys her generous optimism about the possibility of individual expansion and social change, her persistent and unwavering belief in human potential. Rukeyser's prophetic poetry was an inspiration to an entire generation of poets, and the resurgent critical interest in her writing demonstrates the continuing power and authority of her pioneering voice.

CRITICAL RECEPTION

After enjoying an initial decade of popular and critical acclaim, Rukeyser's poetry suffered an extended period of neglect from the critical establishment. From 1940 to 1975, only six major scholarly articles were published on Rukeyser's poetry. Louise Kertesz's *The Poetic Vision of Muriel Rukeyser* (1980) is the only book-length study of the poet's work at this writing (Ware 307). Scholars have speculated about the reasons for the decline of Rukeyser's reputation; certainly, her overt and radical political engagement damaged her reception in the 1940s and 1950s, but her lifelong defiance of formal and aesthetic conventions also contributed to her critical neglect. The fullness and intensity of her poetic expression confused proponents of the New Criticism and encouraged many critics to dismiss her work as "muddy emotionalism" (Rosenthal 203). Only recently has her poetry received the wider critical attention it deserves. Her oracular voice and her prophetic vision speak volumes to a contemporary audience, and her robust feminism and energetic activism mark her as the first in a long and distinguished tradition of American women's political poetry or, as Anne Sexton called her, "beautiful Muriel, mother of everyone" (Kertesz 389). Although most of Rukeyser's poetry remains out of print, two editions of her selected works have been published recently, Kate Daniels' 1992 collection of her poetry, *Muriel Rukeyser: Out of Silence*, and Jan Heller Levi's *A Muriel Rukeyser Reader* in 1994. Rukeyser's prose manifesto, *The Life of Poetry*, based on various lectures she gave during the 1940s, was reissued by Paris Press in 1996, and two biographies are in progress, one by Kate Daniels and another by Jan Heller Levi. As Jane Cooper writes in her Introduction to *The Life of Poetry*, "a grand process of reclamation is under way" (xxviii). Such renewed critical attention ensures that an important and influential American poet will not be silenced.

BIBLIOGRAPHY

Works by Muriel Rukeyser

Theory of Flight. New Haven, CT: Yale University Press, 1935.
U.S. 1. New York: Covici-Friede, 1938.
A Turning Wind. New York: Viking, 1939.
Wake Island. Garden City, NY: Doubleday, Doran, 1942a.
Willard Gibbs. New York: Doubleday, Doran, 1942b.
Beast in View. Garden City, NY: Doubleday, Doran, 1944.
The Green Wave. Garden City, NY: Doubleday, Doran, 1948.
Elegies. Norfolk, CT: New Directions, 1949a.

The Life of Poetry. New York: Current Books, 1949b; reissued Ashfield, MA: Paris Press, 1996 with Foreword by Jane Cooper.

Selected Poems. New York: New Directions, 1951.

One Life. New York: Simon and Schuster, 1957.

Body of Waking. New York: Harper, 1958.

The Colors of the Day. Poughkeepsie, NY: Alumni Association of Vassar College, 1961.

Waterlily Fire: Poems, 1935–62. New York: Macmillan, 1962.

The Orgy. New York: Coward-McCann, 1965.

The Outer Banks. Santa Barbara, CA: Unicorn Press, 1967.

The Speed of Darkness. New York: Random House, 1968.

The Traces of Thomas Hariot. New York: Random House, 1971.

"Craft Interview with Muriel Rukeyser."*New York Quarterly* 11 (1972a): 14–37.

29 Poems. London: Rapp and Whiting; London: Deutsch, 1972b.

Breaking Open. New York: Random House, 1973.

The Gates. New York: McGraw-Hill, 1976.

The Collected Poems of Muriel Rukeyser. New York: McGraw-Hill, 1978.

Out of Silence: Selected Poems. Ed. and introduction by Kate Daniels. Evanston, IL: Tri-Quarterly Books, 1992.

Works about Muriel Rukeyser

Kertesz, Louise. *The Poetic Vision of Muriel Rukeyser.* Baton Rouge: Louisiana State University Press, 1980.

Levi, Jan Heller, ed. *A Muriel Rukeyser Reader.* New York and London: W. W. Norton, 1994.

Rich, Adrienne. Introduction to *A Muriel Rukeyser Reader.*

Rosenthal, M. L. "Muriel Rukeyser: The Longer Poems." Ed. James Laughlin. *New Directions in Prose and Poetry* 14 (1953): 202–29.

Ware, Michele S. "Opening 'The Gates': Muriel Rukeyser and the Poetry of Witness." *Women's Studies: An Interdisciplinary Journal* 22 (1993): 297–308.

DELMORE SCHWARTZ   (1913–1966)

Jennifer Lewin

BIOGRAPHY

Delmore Schwartz was born on December 9, 1913, in Brooklyn, New York, to middle-class, Jewish parents, Rose and Harry Schwartz. His father was a real estate agent. Delmore graduated from George Washington High School in 1931. After briefly attending the University of Wisconsin, he received a B.A. in philosophy from New York University in 1935 and went on to study philosophy at the graduate level at Harvard. In 1938 he left Harvard, published his first book, *In Dreams Begin Responsibilities*, with New Directions Press and married Gertrude Buckman. Two years later he won a Guggenheim Fellowship and started teaching composition at Harvard, a job that lasted seven years and during which he published the verse play *Shenandoah* (1941) and began editing *Partisan Review*. He left Cambridge in 1947. Schwartz married Elizabeth Pollet (his first marriage ended in divorce in 1944) and lectured on T. S. Elliot at Princeton for the Christian Gauss Seminars in 1949. He won an award from the National Institute of Arts and Letters in 1952; in 1959 he won the Bolligen Prize for *Summer Knowledge*; and in 1960 he won the Shelley Memorial Prize. He was a poetry editor and film critic of the *New Republic* from 1955 to 1957 and taught intermittently at Kenyon College, Indiana University, University of Chicago, and University of California. From 1962 to 1965 he was visiting professor at Syracuse University. On July 11, 1966, he died in a room at the Columbia Hotel in Times Square.

MAJOR WORKS AND THEMES

Allen Tate (in *Atlas* 129, quoted from a letter to Schwartz from Tate, January 5, 1939) famously called Delmore Schwartz's work ''the first real innovation that we've had since Elliot and Pound.'' While his literary reputation rests largely on his poetry and essays like ''The Isolation of Modern Poetry'' (1941) and ''The Present State of Poetry'' (1958), Schwartz had a unique relationship to Judaism. Unlike other poets who consistently incorporate Jewish themes and Yiddishkeit in their work, Delmore's Jewishness surfaces in his literary endeavors only in isolated places—it is to be discovered in his fiction and some of his essays and letters and only occasionally in his poetry, both published and unpublished. If one were to rely solely on the popular anthology pieces such as ''In the Naked Bed, in Plato's Cave'' and ''The Heavy Bear Who Goes with Me,'' one might never know that beneath the surface of Schwartz's philosophically inflected, analytical, Eliotic mind is a psyche torn between his poetic influences and the cultural heritage of his immigrant Jewish parents. Still, while his lyric voice does not overtly explore Judaism, Bruce Bawer has noted that ''his sense of alienation, which he shares with the other Middle Generation poets, stems also from his sense of Jewishness; more accurately, from the painful meaning that Jewishness held for him'' (8). Schwartz was acutely aware of his Judaism, encountered a lot of anti-Semitism, and felt that it was a social stigma both while at Harvard and throughout his life. Like other writers of his generation and after, like Karl Shapiro and Irving Feldman, he also became fascinated by the special Jewish relation to the American-English language. The following is a telling excerpt from his conference paper ''On American Literature and the Younger Generation of American Jews,'' as quoted by James Atlas, Schwartz's biographer and editor:

To be the child of immigrants from East Europe is in itself a special kind of experience: and an important one to an author. He has heard two languages through childhood, the one spoken with ease in the streets and at school, but spoken poorly at home. Students of speech have explained certain kinds of mispronunciation in terms of this double experience of language. To an author, and especially to a poet, it may give a heightened sensitivity to language, a sense of idiom, and a sense of how much expresses itself through pronunciation; a hesitation in speech; and a sharpened focus upon the characters of the parents. (*In Dreams Begin Responsibilities* xix)

Schwartz's work in its most autobiographical moments bears witness to this last dimension of urban immigrant life, as ''a sharpened focus upon the characters of the parents'' is characteristic of the writings that I explore: two early short stories in *Shenandoah* and *Genesis*.

Schwartz published his first piece, the short story ''In Dreams Begin Responsibilities,'' at the ripe age of twenty-four. It appeared in the inaugural issue of the revived *Partisan Review* in 1937 and immediately established his as a formidable young voice in urban literary circles. The story is a sequence of dreamlike episodes from the courtship of the narrator's parents that seem ''as if'' they are being viewed by him in a movie house. The year might be 1909, in the summertime. His mixed reactions to seeing his father visiting with, and thinking about, his mother include guilt, pity, and resentment. But the son-narrator has access to the thoughts of other characters, too, such as his maternal grandfather and his mother. Irving Howe has said of it that "the tone of 'In Dreams Begin Responsibilities' is distinctively urban. It speaks of Brooklyn, Coney Island, and Jewish immigrants fumbling their way into the new world, but also of their son, proudly moving toward the culture of America and finding there a language for his parents' grief" (*In Dreams Begin Responsibilities* ix). One of the story's most striking features is its deft weaving in and out of the narrator's recognition that "this is only a movie-dream"—he consistently pushes the boundaries of the real and illusionary and gets frustrated by his helplessness in the face of their quarrels, danger, estrangement.

Another story dealing more overtly with Jewish themes is "America! America!" which was first published in 1948 in the collection *The World Is a Wedding*. The collection's title is taken from a section of the Talmud that Schwartz was reading while teaching at Harvard; he admired it for its rich metaphorical implications. This story about the Baumann family is being told by his mother to Shenandoah Fish, a young, jaded man just back from a trip to Paris. For some years the Fish and Baumann families had been close, and Mrs. Fish's recounting, in excruciating detail, of the Baumanns' misfortunes seems to be a cautionary tale for her son's benefit. The story centers on Mr. Baumann, an immigrant insurance businessman, and his sincere, but intellectually misdirected, wife. Their sons, Dick and Sidney, attempt to adopt their father's successful business sense but gravely and miserably fail, at the time of the Great Depression. Their inability to emulate their father becomes the most important source of bitterness and tension for the entire family; no one seems to know whom to blame or how to solve the problem. Mrs. Baumann, for example, is quite confused: "What Mrs. Baumann did not understand and sought to explain to herself and Mrs. Fish was the paradox that her sons, who had a good bringing-up unlike many successful young men, had made out so poorly in comparison with most of them" (*In Dreams Begin Responsibilities* 29). While hearing the story with great interest, Shenandoah Fish, an onlooker, meditates on his wavering sense of repulsion and identification: "He reflected upon his separation from these people, and he felt that in every sense he was removed from them by thousands of miles, or by a generation, or by the Atlantic Ocean." (*In Dreams Begin Responsibilities* 28). His literary world does not intersect with the Baumanns', yet their origins are strikingly similar, and he begins to feel guilt and self-hatred for snobbishly isolating himself from their world: "He felt that the contemptuous mood which had governed him as he listened was really self-contempt and ignorance. He thought that his own life invited the same irony" (*In Dreams Begin Responsibilities* 32). The poem's movement from mockery to sympathy is one of its fine achievements.

Schwartz explores Judaism in verse in his play *Shenandoah* (1941), the epic poem *Genesis 1* (1943), and the unfinished, posthumously published, *Genesis: Selections from Book II* (1989). Like the stories, these works bear distinct traces of his childhood in a home troubled by his parents' separation. Of the play, whose title character is the same as the one in "America! America!" he wrote to Dwight Macdonald in 1941: "Though obviously personal in a painful way, I feel that the dramatic idea is sufficiently generalized" (*Letters* 107). In the same year he called it "a problem play" (*Letters* 115) to his good friend James Laughlin. *Shenandoah* dramatizes the naming and circumcision of a Jewish, newborn boy. The title character acts as narrator-chorus, revisiting the scene of this important ceremony twenty-five years later. The setting is his parents' home, which contains the proper, almost contemptuous cultural capital: "Look at the cut glass bowls on the buffet/They are the works of art of these rising Jews" (*Shenandoah* 8). Despite his mockery, he pities them for their Old World sadness. Shenandoah's temporal and psychic distance from the chaotic, tense scene is marked by his speaking in blank verse, while the others—family and guests— speak in prose. The play chiefly concerns the boy's name, about which the family is very upset. Shenandoah, like the narrator in "In Dreams," pities his mother for her husband's cruelty (this theme, as one might imagine, is autobiographical). The paternal grandfather objects, in accordance with Jewish law, to giving the baby his names; children are not to be named after living relatives. Shenandoah, throughout the play, provides commentary on the dialogue. Finally, Mrs. Fish gets a tip to look in the society pages, and she finds the right name (she comes across "Delmore," too, another hint at the author's preoccupation), and the skeptical, querulous father relents. The play ends with the ritual circumcision, and Shenandoah responds to his infant self's crying in pain by warning of greater sorrows to come—the awareness of mortality, for one—and by offering the suggestion of Aristotelian "transient release" "in the darkened theater's plays."

Schwartz put more of his literary energies into his next semiautobiographical project. Critical of his own reflections, the epic poem *Genesis* betrays his anxiety of influence with regard to the ghost of T. S. Eliot. Bruce Bawer has said that "clearly Schwartz is trying to reconcile the notion of writing a poem about his personal life and feelings with the tenets of Eliot, which demand that the poem be an intellectual contemplation of the variety and complexity of modern civilization" (78). In his letters from the early 1940s Schwartz wrote of the poem incessantly, attempting to ensure it would be reviewed well and by the right people. In a letter to Dwight Macdonald he called *Genesis* "the big frog" and defended its theme and structure against the imagined accusation that Eliot would have done better: "Eliot never wrote a long narrative poem, nor tried to use prose and verse with each other, nor made the effort at directness and clarity which I make, nor was motivated by the alienation which only a Jew can suffer, and use, as a cripple uses his weakness, in order to beg" (*Letters* 185). Two years earlier he had felt less confident about the project, however, writing to John Berryman in 1940: "Every time I read or see the long poem as a whole, my hair stands on end at my own daring or shamelessness, or whatever quality of character moves me to do what I am doing!" (*Letters* 91) and calling it "my

Leviathan/Frankenstein/Iliad'' (*Letters* 109). *Genesis* is about the first fourteen
years in the difficult life of the fictional Jewish Hershey Green, whose father
and mother came to America at the turn of the century and who meets with
awful anti-Semitism on the streets. Hershey tells his life story to a series of
ghosts entering his room and playing the role of a Greek chorus, empathic but
powerless. Near the end of the poem one says, ''The history of Life repeats its
endless circle, over and over and over again,/In the new boy, in the new city,
in the time forever new, forever old'' (*Genesis* 208). Like Shenandoah Fish,
Hershey speaks in blank verse, none of it terribly good as poetry. The focus is
on Hershey himself, whose inner torment is shown to be a product of conceptual
forces bearing down on modern, urban humankind. Hershey's escape from these
deterministic pressures is depicted as the purifying appearance and effects of
snow, rain, and other meteorological elements of city life capable of providing
rejuvenation: ''the rain on roofs makes cracks of sound,/The driving autumn
rain in the sick city!'' (*Genesis* 125). Like the previously discussed protagonist,
he suffers from witnessing his parents' abusive marriage. This idea permeated
Schwartz's relation to Judaism and his cultural heritage.

The short stories helped to establish Schwartz's literary fame, but *Shenandoah*
met with diverse reactions. Oscar Williams, Theodore Spencer, and Mary Colum
praised it, while Louise Bogan and Babette Deutsch found it flat. Schwartz's
ambivalence about *Genesis* seems to have been mirrored in the poem's very
mixed critical reception. While good reviews came in from Allen Tate, Richard
Eberhart, and his lifelong friends Meyer Schapiro and R. P. Blackmur, James
Bogan and Paul Goodman (who said it contained a ''combination of ineptitude
and earnestness'[*Letters* 172n]) did not care for it. A labor of too many years
and too much effort, *Genesis* never lived up to its author's expectations. Not
unlike Melville's *Clarel*, considered somewhat of an oddity by contemporary
audiences but with moments of excellent poetry, *Genesis* is still viewed as an
anomaly. James Atlas nicely summarizes its strengths and weaknesses better
than any other contemporary reader of Delmore Schwartz: ''When he strove for
grandeur and significance, *Genesis* became ponderous, overly solemn, freighted
with didactic argumentation; when he gave expression to the fantastic wit and
irony that characterized his conversation, and exercised his genius for detecting
the forces of history in the particular incidents of a like, the poem worked''
(231).

BIBLIOGRAPHY

Works by Delmore Schwartz

In Dreams Begin Responsibilities. Norfolk, CT: New Directions, 1938.
A Season in Hell. Translation of Rimbaud's *Saison en Enfer*. Norfolk, CT: New Direc-
    tions, 1939.
Shenandoah, A Verse Play. Norfolk, CT: New Directions, 1941.

Genesis I. New York: J. Laughlin, 1943.

The Imitation of Life. Norfolk, CT: New Directions, 1943.

The World is a Wedding. Norfolk, CT: New Directions, 1948.

Vaudeville for a Princess. New York: New Directions 1950.

Selected Poems: Summer Knowledge. Garden City, NY: Doubleday, 1959.

Successful Love and Other Stories. New York: Corinth Books, 1961.

Syracuse Poems 1964. Syracuse, NY: Dept. of English, Syracuse University, 1965.

Selected Essays of Delmore Schwartz. Edited by Donald A. Dike and David H. Zucker. Chicago: University of Chicago Press, 1970.

What is To Be Given: Selected Poems. Introduction by Douglas Dunn. Manchester, NH: Carcanet New Press, 1976.

The Letters of Delmore Schwartz. Edited by Robert Phillips. New York: Persea Books, 1984.

Portrait of Delmore: Journals and Notes of DS, 1939–1959. Edited by Elizabeth Pollet. New York: Farrar, Straus and Giroux, 1986.

The Ego is Always at the Wheel: Bagatelles. New York: New Directions, 1986.

Genesis: Selections from Book II. New York: New Directions, 1989.

Last & Lost Poems of Delmore Schwartz. Edited by Robert Phillips. New York: New Directions, 1989.

Delmore Schwartz and James Laughlin: Selected Letters. Edited by Robert Phillips. New York: W. W. Norton, 1993.

Works about Delmore Schwartz

Atlas, James. *Delmore Schwartz: The Life of an American Poet.* New York: Farrar, Straus and Giroux, 1977.

Bawer, Bruce. *The Middle Generation: The Lives and Poetry of Delmore Schwartz, Randall Jarrell, John Berryman and Robert Lowell.* Hamden, CT: Archon Books, 1986.

Deutsch, R. H. ''Poetry and Belief in Delmore Schwartz.'' *Sewanee Review* 74 (1966): 915–24.

McDougall, Richard. *Delmore Schwartz.* New York: Twayne, 1974.

New, Eliza. ''Reconsidering Delmore Schwartz.'' *Prooftexts 5* (1985): 245–62.

Simpson, Eileen. *Poets in Their Youth: A Memoir.* New York: Noonday Press, 1990.

Valenti, Lila L. ''The Apprenticeship of Delmore Schwartz.'' *Twentieth Century Literature* 20 (1974): 201–16.

Zucker, David. ''Alien to Myself: Jewishness in the Poetry of Delmore Schwartz.'' *Studies in American Jewish Literature* 9 (1970): 151–62.

———. ''Self and History in Delmore Schwartz's Poetry and Criticism.'' *Iowa Review* 8 (1974): 95–103.

HOWARD SCHWARTZ   (1945–   )
Michael Castro

BIOGRAPHY

Howard Schwartz was born on April 21, 1945, in St. Louis, Missouri, to Nathan and Bluma (Rubin) Schwartz, the eldest of three children. Except for several extended visits to Israel, he has remained in St. Louis, where he lives with his wife, Tsila, a calligrapher, and his three children, Shira, Nathan, and Miriam. Both of his grandfathers were of Russian origin and escaped from the czar's army, and both of his grandmothers were of Polish descent. His father was a watchmaker, jeweler, and antique dealer. The family attended a Conservative synagogue, where Schwartz had his bar mitzvah. He attributes his strong sense of Jewish identity to his father, who, while not especially observant, transmitted the sense of being Jewish "by osmosis." Schwartz later attended Washington University in St. Louis, and he has taught courses in creative writing, Jewish studies, and modern literature at the University of Missouri-St. Louis since 1970.

Schwartz has published more than twenty books, all but one in the field of Jewish literature or folklore. He has received a number of awards, including an Academy of American Poets poetry award (1969), a Poetry Fellowship from the St. Louis Arts and Humanities Commission (1981), the American Book Award of the Before Columbus Foundation (1984), an American Librarian Associate Notable (1991), the Sydney Taylor Book Award (1992), the National Jewish Book Award (1996), and the Aesop Prize of the American Folklore Society (1996). He has also received an honorary doctorate from Spertus Institute of Judaica (1996).

MAJOR WORKS AND THEMES

Poetry and Fiction

Schwartz's writings fall into three primary categories: his own poetry and fiction, his edited collections of modern literature, and his collections of Jewish folklore.

In the essay "How I Became a Writer" (in *Sugarin Review*) Schwartz indicates that he first began to write poetry at the age of twenty and that the writing of poetry was and has remained his first love. His first book of poems, *Vessels*, was published in 1977 and was hailed by poets such as Yehuda Amichai, James Wright, Charles Simic, and David Meltzer. His second book of poems, *Gathering the Sparks*, was published in 1979, and his third book of poems, *Sleepwalking Beneath the Stars*, in 1992. He has recently completed a volume of new and selected poems, entitled *Signs of the Lost Tribe* (as yet unpublished).

Schwartz's poems are, above all, an exploration of the myths and archetypes of the inner life. Many of the poems draw upon dream imagery (he has recorded his dreams for more than thirty years), and the influence of Jewish legend is clearly evident. Many of the poems also demonstrate a distinct liturgical nature. In her book *Apocalyptic Messianism and Contemporary Jewish-American Poetry*, R. Barbara Gitenstein describes Schwartz as "quite a competent liturgical poet." Gabriel Levin, in *The Jerusalem Post*, describes Schwartz as "enchanted by the parabolic, by the illusive and evanescent, by origins and the dark side of the moon." Nancy Schapiro, in *The Jewish Quarterly*, describes the poems as "dream vessels, containing the strange figures and mysterious images that wander the nighttime world." Rochelle Ratner, in *Library Journal*, describes the poems as "carrying the reader toward a sympathy with the biblical figures and their archetypes within each of us." Perhaps Schwartz's best-known poem is "Our Angels," which is read in Yizkor services in a great many congregations:

> Our angels
> Spend much of their time sleeping
> In their dreams
> They tear down the new houses by the sea
> And build old ones
> In their place.
>
> No matter how long they may sleep
> One hundred two hundred years
> Ten centuries is not too much
> The first to wake up
> Takes the torch that has been handed down
> Adds a drop of oil to the lamp
> Blesses the eternal light
> And then recalls the name

Of every other angle
And one by one as they are remembered
They wake up

For them
As for us
There is nothing more beautiful
Then memory. (*Vessels* 13)

Although Schwartz first defined himself exclusively as a poet, he began to write short prose parables in 1968, many of which, like his poems, were based on his dreams. Schwartz's first book, *A Blessing over Ashes* (1974), collected thirty-one of these early parables, showing the influence of Zen, Sufi, and Hasidic tales, as well as the writings of Franz Kafka and Jorge Luis Borges. About half of the parables in this collection draw on Jewish tradition and clearly establish Schwartz's identity as a Jewish writer. In 1976 Schwartz subsequently published *Midrashim*, a volume of these parables exclusively devoted to Jewish themes.

A major turning point in Schwartz's fiction was the publication in 1983 of *The Captive Soul of the Messiah*. Here Schwartz's fascination with Rabbi Nachman of Bratslav, the greatest Hasidic storyteller, resulted in a full-length collection of stories, in the Hasidic mode, about Rabbi Nachman. Cynthia Ozick wrote of this collection: "Howard Schwartz's own enchantments and weavings, under the spell of Jewish dream and legend, have yielded a magical treasury of parable and fable unlike any other written in English." From this point on, the imprint of Rabbi Nachman on Schwartz's writings and anthologies is readily apparent.

In *Adam's Soul* (1993) Schwartz gathered the best of his original midrashim, the tales about Rabbi Nachman, and other original tales in the Hasidic mode. This was followed, in 1995, by *The Four Who Entered Paradise*, a midrashic fantasy based on the brief, but enticing, Talmudic legend about four great sages who journeyed into Paradise, where one lost his life, one lost his mind, one lost his faith, and only Rabbi Akiba "ascended and descended in peace." Steven M. Rossman wrote of this novella in *Jewish Book World*: "Those who have come to know Schwartz through his poetry and popular anthologies will recognize, I am sure, his vivid narrative style, his concern for scholarly illumination, his ability to weave strands of disparate literary traditions into a cohesive tapestry of impressive art, and his *neshamah*—his good-hearted, warm soul. This is a complex and intricately crafted book, replete with allusions to the lore, legend and sacred thought of the Jewish people" (29–30).

Anthologies

Schwartz's first anthology, *Imperial Messages: One Hundred Modern Parables* (1976), was the first to gather and identify stories by modern authors such as Franz Kafka, Jorge Luis Borges, and Italo Calvino as modern parables. This landmark collection received a warm critical reception and is currently in its third edition. Although it is Schwartz's only general, rather than Jewish, book, it indicates a great deal about his literary influences, editing ability, and future direction. Above all, *Imperial Messages* bears the hallmark of Schwartz's subsequent collections in the keen eye it demonstrates in the selection of stories, which, when brought together, provide an irrefutable case for the existence of the genre of the modern parable. Robert Kirsch, writing in the *Los Angeles Times*, wrote of *Imperial Messages*: "The collection is, in effect, a vast library of fictions—imaginative, significant, mysterious, free-ranging as dreams" (34).

Indeed, seeking out unrecognized genres has been the hallmark of Schwartz's editing career. His subsequent collections include a volume of modern midrashim (*Gates to the New City*) and three collections of Jewish folklore, each of which defines one specific type of Jewish tale: the fairy tale (*Elijah's Violin*), the Jewish tale of the supernatural (*Lilith's Cave*), and the Jewish mystical tale (*Gabriel's Palace*).

For readers of Jewish poetry, Schwartz is best known for his landmark collection *Voices within the Ark: The Modern Jewish Poets*, coedited with Anthony Rudolf and published in 1980. Gitenstein describes *Voices within the Ark* as "the largest collection of contemporary Jewish poetry in English," and credits Schwartz for "almost creating the poetic canon" (91). This 1,200-page anthology includes 400 poets, writing in more than twenty-two languages. It is divided into four smaller anthologies, of poets writing in Hebrew, Yiddish, English, and other languages. The book is also distinguished by the high quality of its selections and translations, making it an indispensable work.

In 1983 Schwartz published a major anthology of Jewish fiction, *Gates to the New City: A Treasury of Modern Jewish Tales*. As *Imperial Messages* demonstrated how modern authors have drawn on the ancient form of the parable, so *Gates to the New City* demonstrates how modern Jewish writers have drawn on traditional Jewish sources. Writing in *The Nation*, Brina Caplan said of this book: "This collection qualifies as a heavyweight, but it has a light touch and a gentle soul."

Collections of Folklore

In 1983 Schwartz also published *Elijah's Violin and Other Jewish Fairy Tales*, the first of several volumes of Jewish folklore that he has collected and retold. This marked a major transition in Schwartz's career, in that he appears to have shifted his focus from modern Jewish literature to rabbinic and Jewish folklore of ancient, medieval, and more recent origin. It is important to note that *Elijah's Violin* was the first collection of Jewish folklore in English to combine traditional Jewish tales with those tales collected orally in Israel by the Israel Folktale Archives. Here Schwartz demonstrates that these oral tales, collected in Israel, blend seamlessly with those from traditional, written sources. Schwartz has continued to draw upon all of these written and oral sources in his subsequent folklore collections.

Elijah's Violin was followed in 1986 by *Miriam's Tambourine*, a potpourri of Jewish folktales of many types. In 1987 he published *Lilith's Cave: Jewish Tales of the Supernatural*, which collects the dark tales of Jewish tradition about demons and spirits and especially about the exploits of Lilith, the archetypal Jewish demoness. In 1993 Schwartz published *Gabriel's Palace: Jewish Mystical Tales*, defining the range of the Jewish mystical tale just as he had previously done with the fairy tale and Jewish tale of the supernatural. Many readers regard this four-volume set of Jewish folktales as Schwartz's premier accomplishment. It is for these four volumes of Jewish folklore that Schwartz is best known. Marc Bregman, writing in *The Jewish Book Annual* on these four volumes, comments that "Schwartz has given a new and powerful expression to the ancient voice of the traditional Jewish storyteller" (178).

Schwartz also participated in an unusual collaboration with Rabbi Zalman Schachter-Shalomi, whose tales he collected and retold in *The Dream Assembly*, published in 1987.

Beginning in 1991 with *The Diamond Tree*, Schwartz has also published a series of children's books of Jewish tales, which have been exceptionally popular and well received. Other of these children's books include *The Sabbath Lion* (1992), *Next Year in Jerusalem* (1996), and *The Wonder Child and Other Jewish Fairy Tales* (1996).

Most recently, Schwartz has published *Reimagining the Bible: The Storytelling of the Rabbis* (1998), a collection of twelve essays. Marc Saperstein says of this book that Schwartz "reveals the diversity of Jewish narrative imagination and its rootedness in a common source of inspiration: the Hebrew Bible."

CRITICAL RECEPTION

The critical reception to Schwartz's books has been consistently positive. Because of the effort he has devoted to editing, collecting, and retelling traditional Jewish tales, Schwartz is better known as a folklorist and anthologist than he is as a poet and writer of fiction. But most critics have recognized how Schwartz's role as a poet and storyteller has greatly enhanced his abilities as a transmitter of Jewish lore. Gershom Scholem wrote of Schwartz: "Howard Schwartz has a very remarkable personal contact with the imaginative elements in the Jewish tradition. His literary efforts consist in a personal further development of such motifs, of which Jewish tradition is overflowing. . . . I find his efforts very stimulating and take a decidedly positive view of this side of his work." Cynthia Ozick, who has referred to Schwartz as "an American Hans Christian Andersen," writes of *Gabriel's Palace*: "In recent years Howard Schwartz, combining the accumulative skills of scholarship with the lucently pure voice of the storyteller, has become the preeminent Jewish folklorist in

America.'' Charles Guenther, writing in the *St. Louis Post-Dispatch*, describes Schwartz as ''one of the world's foremost storytellers and folklorists writing today'' (5D).

BIBLIOGRAPHY

Works by Howard Schwartz

Poetry

Vessels. Greensboro, NC: Unicorn Press, 1977.
Gathering the Sparks. St. Louis: Singing Wind, 1979.
Sleepwalking beneath the Stars. Kansas City, MO: BkMk Press, 1992.

Fiction

The Captive Soul of the Messiah: New Tales about Reb Nachman. New York: Schocken Books, 1983.
Adam's Soul: The Collected Tales of Howard Schwartz. Northvale, NJ: Jason Aronson, 1993.
The Four Who Entered Paradise. Northvale, NJ: Jason Aronson, 1995.

Anthologies

A Blessing over Ashes. Berkeley, CA: Tree Books, 1971.
Imperial Messages: One Hundred Modern Parables. New York: Avon Books, 1976; 2d ed., New York: Overlook Press, 1992.
Midrashim. London: Monard Press, 1976.
Voices within the Ark: The Modern Jewish Poets. With Anthony Rudolf. New York: Avon Books and Pushcart Press, 1980.
Elijah's Violin and Other Jewish Fairy Tales. New York: Harper and Row, 1983a.
Gates to the New City: A Treasury of Modern Jewish Tales. New York: Avon Books, 1983b. 2d ed., Northvale, NJ: Jason Aronson, 1991.
Miriam's Tambourine: Jewish Folktales from around the World. New York: Free Press, 1986.
Lilith's Cave: Jewish Tales of the Supernatural. San Francisco: Harper and Row, 1987.
The Dream Assembly: Tales of Rabbi Zalman Schachter-Shalomi. Warwick: Amity House, 1987; 2nd ed., Nevada City, CA: Gateways, 1990.
Gabriel's Palace: Jewish Mystical Tales. New York and Oxford: Oxford University Press, 1993.

Essays

''How I Became a Writer,'' *The Sagarin Review* 5, 1995, 126–33.
Reimagining the Bible: The Storytelling of the Rabbis. New York and Oxford: Oxford University Press, 1998.

Works about Howard Schwartz

Bregman, Marc. ''The Art of Retelling.'' *The Jewish Book Annual*. New York: Jewish Book Council, vol. 53, 1995–1996, 177–82.

Caplan, Brina. *The Nation*, December 24, 1983, 19.

Gitenstein, R. Barbara. *Apocalyptic Messianism and Contemporary Jewish-American Poetry*. Albany: SUNY Press, 1986, 9.

Guenther, Charles. *St. Louis Post-Dispatch*, November 7, 1993, 5D.

Kirsch, Robert. *Los Angeles Times*, November 23, 1976, 3.

Levin, Gabriel. *Jerusalem Post*, January 26, 1979, 16.

Ozick, Cynthia. Back cover comments, *The Captive Soul of the Messiah, Lilith's Cave*, and *Gabriel's Palace*.

Ratner, Rochelle. *Library Journal*, June 1, 1997.

Rossman, Steven M. *Jewish Book World* 14, No. 1, Spring 1996, 29–30.

Saperstein, Marc. Back cover comment, *Reimagining the Bible*.

Schapiro, Nancy. *The Jewish Quarterly* 25, No. 4, Winter 1977/1978, 55.

Scholem, Gershom. Back cover comment, *Adam's Soul*.

ARMAND SCHWERNER (1927–   )

Norman Finkelstein

BIOGRAPHY

Born in Antwerp, Belgium, on May 11, 1927, Armand Schwerner came to the United States with his mother and two siblings in 1936, his father having emigrated the previous year. The Schwerners made their home in New York City, and though he has lived elsewhere during certain periods of his life, Armand Schwerner is very much a New Yorker, the city's vast cultural resources proving essential to the development of his work. Schwerner's first language was French, and though all of his major works are in English, it could be argued that the linguistic shift he was required to make as a boy has made translation, in its broadest as well as its more specific meanings, one of the central aspects of his career.

Schwerner entered Cornell University in 1945 as a premed student but soon left to serve for a year as U.S. Navy musician. (Schwerner trained as a clarinetist; he has since mastered numerous single- and double-reed instruments, including woodwinds from a variety of cultures, which he occasionally plays during presentations of his works.) He returned to Cornell, spent a year at the Université de Genève, and completed a B.A. in French from Columbia. Schwerner stayed at Columbia for graduate work, spending two years studying anthropology before changing his field and receiving an M.A. from the Department of English and Comparative Literature in 1964. That year he began teaching at Staten Island Community College; he taught there until 1976, when he took his current post as professor of English at CUNY's College of Staten Island. Schwerner has been a resident of Staten Island for many years. He was married from 1961 to 1974; the couple had two sons, Adam (b. 1961) and Ari (1964–1996).

Schwerner's work began appearing in literary journals around 1960; he is the author of approximately twenty books of poetry, prose, and translation; he has contributed to numerous important collections (including Jerome Rothenberg's crucial ethnopoetics anthologies); he has been awarded numerous grants and fellowships; and he has read and performed extensively in the United States and Europe. Yet Schwerner's work has entered the cultural mainstream very slowly: the American literary establishment's suspicion of (if not hostility toward) an aggressively avant-garde stance like Schwerner's has, arguably, kept his work from the circulation it deserves. Yet this may be changing: the widely read *American Poetry Review* recently ran an extensive feature on Schwerner, including a long interview and a canto from his bold new translation of Dante's *Inferno*.

MAJOR WORKS AND THEMES

Although Armand Schwerner has been associated throughout his career with the ethnopoetics movement in modern poetry, his first book, *The Domesday Dictionary* (1963), coauthored with psychoanalyst Donald Kaplan, is a satire on the Cold War. Yet there is a link between Schwerner's early attack on the global perversions of technocracy and his more typical concerns with native cultures and languages, the play of discourses in common speech, the fundamental ground of the human body, and the synchronicity of the archaic and the modern. At the heart of Schwerner's multifaceted project is the desire to articulate a radical, indeed, an ecstatic alternative to the homogeneity and artificiality of our violent, death-ridden society. His early poetry, in *The Lightfall* (1963), (*if personal*) (1968), and *Seaweed* (1969), presents an extraordinary range of forms; but what is to be found consistently in this work is the underlying assumption that language embodies a kind of primacy that, when discovered anew (a discovery that is to be made endlessly), can restore a fundamental sense of wonder to human existence in the material world—hence, the particular importance of what Schwerner calls, in a 1986 interview with Lee Bartlett, "the immediacy of the oral, which is the immediacy of the tribal, the archaic, the so-called primitive, which was gone for a long time" (81).

The magic of language is most apparent through the discoveries of the spoken word; thus, in poems such as "*daddy, can you staple these two stars together to make an airplane*," "Poem at the Bathroom Door, by Adam," and "What Ari Says When He's Five" (all in *Seaweed*), the speech acts of Schwerner's young sons take on, as one of the boys' names appropriately implies, the Adamic quality of primal naming:

> push-car woman do you love me
> watch woman do you love me
> iron woman do you love me
> bye woman do you love me
> happy woman do you love me

store woman do you love me
bird with a heart in his mouth and a kiss in his mouth
present woman do you love me
ask woman do you love me
that's all I can think of ("Poem at the Bathroom Door," *Seaweed* 23)

The chantlike quality of the verse, the use of repetition and variation, and the play of parts of speech are all reminiscent of the poetry of "primitive" cultures, but rather than sentimentalize either the childlike or the primitive, the poem *enacts* the oral immediacy that Schwerner finds so valuable. As he says in the same interview quoted earlier, "The question of poems as oral transmission from one generation to another for hundreds, even thousands of years, is a question of a buried tradition, a 'whispered tradition,' the Tibetans sometimes say, the stuff of one being connected to another being."

This same sense of immediate connectedness—of sincerity, that quality so valued by objectivists such as Louis Zukofsky and George Oppen, whom Schwerner knew personally—is also to be felt when the poet speaks in his own voice. "Bar-Mitzvah Poem for My Son Adam" (from *Sounds of the River Naranjana and the Tablets I–XXIV*) ends with these lines:

bar mitzvah, son of a good deed
I was told, life-bearer, man of red earth,
pri haadamah fruit of yourself, we can only know
present moments calm decisions to cut off the snapper's head
when the hook is irretrievable, gullet
beyond repair son of your finite seconds
you touch the living world gently
as a man in a fullness learns. you are earning
your face, you are this man.
love, father (5)

The play on the Aramaic *bar mitzvah* (son of a good deed) and the Hebrew *adam* (red) and *pri haadamah* (fruit of the earth) links the ritual moment to any moment when the young man may know the world in its fullness and, in effect, give birth to himself. For Schwerner, as for the other poets of his generation who are influenced by objectivism, poetry's linguistic immediacy provides an understanding of life as "fatal," in the sense of fate as a succession of unknowable moments of surprise. As the poet observes in "the boat" (also from *Sounds of the River Naranjana*):

. . . It's not dramatic,
just fatal, a vivid life like the life
of the poem is the life
of the senseless calm surprise, the profound greeting
in the kitchen and the streets and the field

to the not-known unpredictable in the beings
and to the call within the burnished and rusty things
of this world. (36)

The poem's invocation of "the not-known" or "no-mindfulness" indicates the
way in which the epistemological and phenomenological concerns of objectivism coincide, in Schwerner's work, with his extensive studies of Buddhism. It
is a coincidence out of which has come some of his most lyrical work, as in
this brief passage from the serial poem "sounds of the river Naranjana":

for a week watch the river Naranjana flowing
for a week, walk, and for a week watch
the bark of the balsam fir. now
the red-wing lights on it. now
the river eddies, now when you walk you walk. (24)

The voice speaking here is that of a sage instructing us on the path of enlightenment, which is an experience of the totality in and of every present moment. In many respects, it is similar to Schwerner's translation of the Yiddish
poem by Peretz Markish that appears in Jerome Rothenberg's and Harris Lenowitz's remarkable anthology of Jewish texts, *Exiled in the Word*:

. . . *Now*

is my name. I spread my arms, my hands
pierce the extremes
of what is. I'm letting my eyes roam around
and do their drinking from the fountains
of the world

eyes wild, shirt ballooning,
my hands separated by the world, I don't know
if I have a home
or have a homelessness
or am a beginning or an end. (151)

With this passage in mind (and in the context of this volume), we are led to
ask in what ways Schwerner, given the extraordinary range of the work's multicultural references as well as the sense of groundlessness or homelessness that
permeates the writing, is a specifically Jewish poet. In a certain respect, we have
just answered our own question: since much secular Jewish literature of the last
century has dealt with the groundlessness of Jews in diaspora, it could be argued
that the ethnopoetics of Schwerner and his colleagues is, in effect, the counter-
force to this groundlessness. To be rooted or at home in even the most remote
cultural practices is a feeling that need not be limited to Jewish writers. But

given Schwerner's biography, a predisposition to a global, culturally polyvalent stance makes a great deal of sense.

Thus, when we turn to Schwerner's masterpiece, the ongoing serial poem called *The Tablets*, we encounter a work that is altogether true to the universalist spirit of ethnopoetics yet altogether ironic in its expression of that spirit. As a number of critics have pointed out, *The Tablets* is, on one level, a Joycean hoax: it is a sequence of texts that purports to be translations of Sumerian/Akkadian clay tablets more than 4,000 years old. Riddled with signs indicating untranslatable or missing passages, filled with commentaries, notes, and speculations in a variety of real and fictive languages, the texts are the work of the "Scholar/ Translator," an eccentric, perhaps even mad figure in constant dialogue with the endless voices of the archaic past as well as the equally strange tradition of research from which he comes. Much of the weird humor of the work arises from the manic discrepancies between the Scholar/Translator's observations and the material he has managed to decipher. As Schwerner observes in the "Journals/Divagations" appended to the latest edition of the poem, "Prose is eloquence, wants to instruct, to convince; wants to produce in the soul of the reader a state of knowledge. Poetry is the producer of joy, its reader participates in the creative act. Thus Commentary and Text in *The Tablets*? (103) (Is that distinction stupid?)."

Certainly not: the uncanny relationship of prose to poetry, present to past intensifies as the sequence proceeds from the translation/commentary format of the earlier *Tablets* to what in *Tablet XXVI* is called "The Laboratory Teachings Memoirs of the Scholar/Translator." The Scholar/Translator's digressions and meditations expand, and the incorporation of (computer-generated) glyphs drawn from the original artifacts further litter and decenter the text. This fundamental lack of temporal and discursive stability distinguishes *The Tablets* from other literary works of an "archaeological" nature: as Brian McHale notes in a paper comparing Schwerner's poem to Geoffrey Hill's *Mercian Hymns* and Seamus Heaney's bog poems, *The Tablets* "represent no artifact or found object, rather they are themselves that found object, or at least they purport to be. There is no primal scene here of an archaeologist examining an artifact, because we readers enact that scene every time we look into *The Tablets*, every time we turn its pages." (103).

The readers' endless enactment of the "primal scene" of archaeology may be related, I believe, to Schwerner's vexed attitude to what Harold Bloom has ruefully called "The Sorrows of American-Jewish Poetry." In a letter to me, Schwerner notes, "My profound disinterest in almost all manifestations of 'Jewish' Americana is one of the factors that led me 5,000 years back to find, represent and embody my relatives the Akkadians." Dissatisfied with the nostalgia and sentimentality of so much Jewish-American culture, Schwerner has, in effect, produced his own Dead Sea Scrolls (or Mosaic tablets)—but rather than offer up the work in a quasi-sacred fashion (as is the case, perhaps, of the "Talmudic" books of French poet Edmond Jabés), Schwerner insists on the resolute security, the Rabelaisian profanity of his ancient "relatives." From *Tablet V*:

is the man bigger than a fly's wing?   what pleasure!
is he much bigger than a fly's wing?   what pleasure!
is his hard penis ten times a fly's wing?   what pleasure!
is his red penis fifteen times a fly's wing?   what [pleasure]!
is his mighty penis fifty times a fly's wing?   what pleasure!
does his penis vibrate like a fly's wing?   what terrific pleasure! (19)

CRITICAL RECEPTION

In 1989, writing in *Parnassus* (where Schwerner's work has most often been reviewed over the years), Paul Christensen noted that "Schwerner appropriates formalities and patterns that conceal his own voice . . . it is his reluctance to have a voice of his own that makes him a unique writer—the avoidance of a 'style' that would emphasize ego over the 'nature' of imagination." (154). Because Schwerner's work is always difficult to categorize in terms of style and school and because it is resistant to the conventional idea of poetic voice, Christensen's observation accounts, I think, for both the neglect of, *and* the attention to, Schwerner's work since he began publishing. The early poetry received scattered reviews, most written by fellow poets who sympathized with Schwerner's project. A rare exception of a review in the mainstream literary media is Hugh Kenner's 1978 *New York Times Book Review* piece on *the work, the joy and the triumph of the will*, in which Kenner compares Schwerner's translation of *Philoctetes* to Pound's *Women of Trachis*: high praise from one of the greatest critics of the modernist tradition and perfectly appropriate, given the importance of translation in Schwerner's canon and in modernist writing overall. But the one full-blown response to Schwerner's work so far is Sherman Paul's 1986 study *In Love with the Gratuitous: Rereading Armand Schwerner*, which provides close readings of over twenty years of writing as well as a thorough contextualization through Schwerner's literary precursors and contemporaries.

Naturally enough, *The Tablets* have attracted the most critical attention, especially in recent years. Kathryn Van Spanckeren's article "Moonrise in Ancient Sumer: Armand Schwerner's *The Tablets*" is a remarkably comprehensive introduction that not only analyzes the structure and procedures of the poem but usefully orients it in terms of cross-cultural genre and belief. For Van Spanckeren, the poem "is a self-reflexive or deconstructive exploration of Western consciousness. The Tablets revel in the condition of brokenness, illegibility, and loss" (15). Rachel Blau DuPlessis' short, but provocative, review uses *The Tablets* to reflect on the evolving concerns of the ethnopoetics movement, as the text moves from "the search for origins or primary emotional and cultural ground" to "the nature, functions, ideologies, and interests at stake in the transmission and the transmitter." But as is often the case, it could be that with

Schwerner, the poet is his own best critic: his interviews as the poem has proceeded over the years have consistently clarified without simplifying the challenges he has posed in his text. As he says of his Scholar/Translator in a conversation with Willard Gingerich, "The S/T has an inclination towards meaning, but he's got a problem which he avows covertly and indirectly and with pain. He has a suspicion that his inclination towards meaning must find other paths from those he has been given by his own modes of scholarship and research, his own culture, his own theological antecedents. And that's the main problem; that's also the problem of Western civilization" (32). What is remarkable about Schwerner is that he may have found one means of addressing this problem.

BIBLIOGRAPHY

Works by Armand Schwerner

With Donald Kaplan. *The Domesday Dictionary*. New York: Simon and Schuster, 1963a.
The Lightfall. New York: Hawks Well Press, 1963b.
(if personal). Los Angeles: Black Sparrow Press, 1968.
Seaweed. Los Angeles: Black Sparrow Press, 1969.
the work, the joy and the triumph of the will. New York: New Rivers Press, 1978.
Sounds of the River Naranjana and The Tablets I–XXIV. Barrytown, NY: Station Hill, 1983.
Exiled in the Word . . . Now: Poems & Other Times to the Present. Ed. Jerome Rothenberg and Harris Lenowitz. Port Townsend, WA: Copper Canyon Press, 1989.
Tablets I–XXVI. London: Atlas Press, 1989.
The Ogre of Information/the Fiend of Silence: Selected Essays, Interviews, Letters. Albuquerque: University of New Mexico Press. Series: "Studies in Twentieth Century Poetry and Poetics," forthcoming.

Works about Armand Schwerner

Alpert, Barry. "Armand Schwerner: An Interview." *Jackson Mac Low and Armand Schwerner: Interviews and Critical Essays"* (Special Issue). *Vort* 8 (1975): 101–25.
Bartlett, Lee. "A Conversation with Armand Schwerner." *American Poetry* 4: 3 (Spring 1987).
Bloom, Harold. "The Sorrows of American-Jewish Poetry." In *Figures of Capable Imagination*. New York: Seabury, 1976, 247–62.
Christensen, Paul. "Ethnopoetics." *Parnassus* 15 (1989): 154–59.
Doria, Charles. " 'The Poetry of Memory: Armand Schwerner's *the work, the joy & the triumph of the will*, with a translation of Sophocles' *Philoctetes*." *Parnassus* 7: 1 (Fall/Winter 1979): 257–66.
Duplessis, Rachel Blau. "Armand Schwerner." *Sulfur* (Fall 1991): 212.
Gingerich, Willard. "Interview #1 with Armand Schwerner." *Hambone* 11 (Spring 1994).

————. "Interview #2 with Armand Schwerner." *American Poetry Review* (September/ October 1995): 12–32.

Heller, Michael. "Schwerner's Poetry." *Sagetrieb* 3: 3 (Winter 1984): 129–34.

Kenner, Hugh. "Schwerner's *the work, the joy & the triumph of the will*, with a translation of Sophocles' *Philoctetes.*" *New York Times Book Review*, February 12, 1978, 13.

Lavazzi, Thomas. "Editing Schwerner: Versions of Armand Schwerner's 'Design Tablet.' " *Text* 8. Ann Arbor: University of Michigan Press, 1996.

McHale, Brian. "Archaeologies of Knowledge: Geoffrey Hill's Hymns, Seamus Heany's Bog People, Schwerner's Tablets." In *The Obligations toward a Difficult Whole.* Durham, NC: Duke University Press, 1996.

Paul, Sherman. *In Love with the Gratuitious: Rereading Armand Schwerner.* Grand Forks, ND: University North Dakota Press, 1986.

Van Spanckeren, Kathryn. "Moonrise in Ancient Sumer: Armand Schwerner's *The Tablets.*" *American Poetry Review* 22 (July/August 1993): 15–18.

————. "Schwerner's The Tablets." *Dialectical Anthropology* 2: 214 (Winter/Spring 1986): 381–88.

ALAN SHAPIRO

(1952–)

Richard Chess

BIOGRAPHY

Alan Shapiro was born in 1952 in Boston. He received his B.A. from Brandeis University in 1974 and was a Stegner Fellow in poetry at Stanford University in 1975. Shapiro is the author of five books of poetry, including *After the Digging* (1981), *The Courtesy* (1983), *Happy Hour* (1987), which was nominated for the National Book Critics Circle Award and was the recipient of the prestigious William Carlos Williams Award of the Poetry Society of America, *Covenant* (1991), and *Mixed Company* (1996). He is also the author of a critical study, *In Praise of the Impure: Poetry and the Ethical Imagination* (1993) and *The Last Happy Occasion* (1996), as well as a memoir, *Vigil* (1997). He is series editor of Phoenix poets, published by the University of Chicago Press. He has been a recipient of grants from the National Endowment for the Arts (1984 and 1991) and the John Simon Guggenheim Memorial Foundation, and he received a Lila Wallace–Reader's Digest Award in 1991. Shapiro teaches poetry and creative writing at the University of North Carolina, Chapel Hill. He lives with his wife and two children in Chapel Hill.

MAJOR WORKS AND THEMES

Alan Shapiro's poetry illuminates the complexities and ambiguities of romantic and married love, family life, parenthood, and social relations, in particular, relations between Jews and Gentiles, whites and blacks. Early and late, the Jewish-American experience deeply informs his work. Directly and indirectly, Shapiro concerns himself with the uneasy relationship between Jew and other, the defining impact of the Holocaust on postwar American Jews, the psychological and emotional effects of assimilation, and the resistance to Judaism as a religion.

These themes are intertwined. For instance, linked as it is to the Holocaust, the seder on the first night of Passover, which happens to have been the eve of the Warsaw ghetto uprising, affords Shapiro an opportunity to reflect on the meaning of God after the Holocaust. Thinking in particular about the cup of wine set aside for the prophet Elijah, whose appearance, according to tradition, will signal the coming of Elijah, the young speaker of "On the Eve of the Warsaw Uprising" can't help but wonder, " 'Where was Elijah?'/Nobody in the room had ever asked" (*The Courtesy* 5). The speaker's skepticism about the religion results, in part, from holding religious beliefs up to historical facts.

Among the few rituals that survive among assimilated Jewish Americans, the Passover seder is one, and the bar or bat mitzvah, a coming-of-age ritual for boys and girls on the occasions of their thirteenth birthdays, is another. Rarely, however, does the ceremony mark a meaningful rite of passage for an American boy or girl. For many young men and women, the more significant rites of passage include getting one's driver's license or experiencing sex for the first time or being included in adult talk at a job. Thus, in "Manufacturing" (*Mixed Company*), Shapiro marks a thirteen-year-old boy's coming-of-age as the time when he first hears his father say in front of him various profanities ("Who'd diddle Abramowitz/and Saperstein? Those cocksucking sons of bitches,/cut their balls off if they fuck with us" [61]). This "must have meant/I was a man now too" (62). What does he learn about manhood? "Being a man was something that you did/to other men"; "either you gave a fucking, or you took one" (62). This code of behavior is the antithesis of one of the central teachings of Judaism: love your neighbor as yourself.

The precarious relations between Jews and non-Jews cause a certain amount of self-consciousness in Jews about belonging or not belonging. This, indeed, is the predicament of the speaker of "The Christmas Story," a boy envious of his Christian friend on Christmas morning (*Happy Hour*). Caught "carol[ing]" to his Christian friend a "holy/inventory" of toys he, the Jewish boy, claims to have received, the boy is admonished by his father, "[Y]ou want to be a goy, be a goy," and sent to his room for "the whole day/where it was Channukah" (*Happy Hour* 32). But the boy's actions are not motivated by envy alone. He also feels a "vague desire/to make amends, to glorify the baby Jesus/with my friend Charlie (who said the Jews had killed him)." Historically unaware, the boy believes he is guilty as charged and turns against himself and his people.

His Jewish identity is strongest when he sees himself in relation to non-Jews. When he sees himself in relation to certain older Jews obsessed with anti-Semitism, he wishes to be free of any traces of a Jewish identity. This is the situation in the poem "Simon, the Barber" (*The Courtesy*). Simon, the barber, one of two main characters in the poem, warns his customer, a young American postwar Jew, that the goyim are "Jew haters, remember. God forbid you should forget" (21). Tragically, the barber one day comes to regard his own son, "ar-

rested in a drug raid,'' along with the other Jewish children of his son's generation, as ''enemies more dangerous than any/[the barber] had fled—your
children, your own seed'' (23).

Perhaps in holding the actual world as he experiences it up to the ideals,
beliefs, and practices of Judaism, Shapiro finds reason enough to reject or resist
the religion. When he sees his father observing ''Yahrzeit'' (a memorial service
on the anniversary of the death of a relative) for Amos, his father's brother
''who died hating him and being hated,'' what troubles him is the appearance
of his father's hypocrisy (*The Courtesy* 30). Prayer, however, ''melts'' the
''golden calf/of grievances their anger forged'' and ''gives back to him unhin-
dered love, another/family.'' Sadly enough, it may be that his father experiences
brotherly love only in the act of prayer, ''here in these syllables, if no where
else.'' Most importantly, the speaker characterizes the mourner's prayer as
''anonymous, inextinguishable sorrowing.'' While ''anonymous'' can have the
negative connotation of lacking identity, it can also have the positive connotation
of overcoming one's identity as an individual, a separate self, achieving instead
a sense of communal identity.

In Shapiro's poems, religion poses a serious threat to one's independence.
Religion is also implicitly criticized for being based on superstition. Both these
ideas provide the dramatic tension for ''Mezuzah,'' a poem in which a young
boy smashes open a mezuzah, all the while knowing the superstition that ''whoever breaks open the Mezuzah and removes the sacred scroll will incur God's
everlasting retribution.'' But as a result of his actions, ''nothing happened,''
nothing but the continuation of the daily routines around the house: ''the washer
jerked/into its spin'' (*The Courtesy* 7). Only in the poem's conclusion does the
child discover ''God's wrath,'' ''His retribution coiled,/forever,/in my questioning.'' Ironically, this act of defiance leads the speaker to a deeper, more mature,
and more Jewish relationship to Judaism, a relationship based on questioning.
Rather than signaling a turning away from Judaism, ''Mezuzah'' signifies a
furious turning toward it.

''Furious,'' in part, because Shapiro's God is a wrathful God. Like the father
in ''Perfect Son,'' God is ''aloof and unappeasable,'' an inscrutable God who
''will not say again what you have done, how you have offended,'' this post-
Holocaust father, post-Holocaust God (*The Courtesy* 29). Shapiro's is the God
of the Egyptian plagues, against whom a father, desiring to protect his newborn
child, prays, ''Lord,/Jealous Chooser, Devouring Law, keep/away from them
[mother and child], just keep away'' (''In the Kingdom of Pleasure,'' *Covenant*
66). Given this negative portrayal of God, we can see clearly why Shapiro would
not be likely to embrace him.

If not in God, Shapiro finds one of his strongest ties to Jewish life in history,
Jewish history, the Holocaust in particular. Shapiro's link to that defining event
of Jewish life is through other Jews he meets, such as Simon, the barber, or
Helen, the German-Jewish nanny (''my personal link to what I can't imagine''),
a survivor who worked for the family of one of his good friends (''The Base-

ment,'' *Mixed Company* 67). In addition to these individuals he happens to meet, Shapiro establishes imaginary contact with the ghosts of Holocaust victims in the poem "Mud Dancing'' (*Covenant*). Set at Woodstock in 1969, this visionary poem brings the "anonymous,'' "the unhallowed dead'' to the famous music festival, where they see America's idealistic and rebellious youth dancing naked "knee deep in mud'' and think it could have been themselves, the Holocaust victims, were it not that the kids danced "unpoliced and under no one's orders'' (*Covenant* 15). Also unlike the American youth, the victims of the Holocaust had their identities stripped from them; they didn't shed them willingly.

While the synagogue might once have offered Jews a refuge from the horrors of history, today many Jews do not look to the synagogue for sanctuary. This does not mean, however, that the need for such a place no longer exists. Interestingly enough, Shapiro finds his sanctuary on the urban basketball court. There "the out of work, the working, students/and dropouts'' gather and "forget/what they forget'' as "a slow, impersonal music winds/through their voices'' ("The Courts at Lawton Street,'' *The Courtesy* 12). This is similar to the language Shapiro uses to describe prayer in "Yahrzeit.'' It is also similar to the image of a congregation worshiping together, as Shapiro envisions it in his recent essay "Fanatics'': "freed from the daily drudgeries of getting and spending, from profane worries and ambitions and petty egotisms,'' the worshipers "fix their minds as one mind upon sacred matters, ultimate mysteries, upon being itself . . . an image I find more and more attractive'' (*The Last Happy Occasion* 145).

Even considered as a sanctuary, however, Shapiro's basketball court in the 1990s does not offer much hope for the improvement of race relations. Between assassinations, the court, like the synagogue, is a place that enables one to see one's communal failings, in the largest sense of the community of men and women, a place where one momentarily forgets "old burning certitudes we can't/stoke high or hot enough, yet won't stop ever stoking/until whatever it is we think we are anneals/and toughens into an impenetrable shield'' ("Between Assassinations,'' *Mixed Company* 79). While the basketball court may seem an odd analogy to a synagogue, the "cease-fire'' he finds there, even if it is dwindling, affords a sense of the timeless *in* time, the very thing one hopes to find in a synagogue.

Through examining his own life, Shapiro illuminates some of the defining problems of this period of American life, including the problem of what to make of Judaism after the Holocaust, after assimilation.

CRITICAL RECEPTION

Shapiro's work has been well received by a number of notable critics, few of whom comment on the Jewish concerns of his writing. One critic who does note those concerns, briefly, is Emily Grosholz. Comparing Shapiro's first book, *After the Digging*, to his second, *The Courtesy*, she writes:

After the Digging treated the troubles and diaspora of the Irish. I think [Shapiro] saw an analogy between their sufferings and those of his Jewish forebears; but the translation entailed so much distancing that the characters were obscured. In . . . *The Courtesy* he returns to the Jewish neighborhood of his youth. One particularly memorable figure captured by Shapiro's smooth and well-controlled blank verse is "Simon the Barber." (650)

In the *New York Times Book Review*, J. D. McClatchy says the poems in *Happy Hour* "are not likely to be forgotten" and characterizes Shapiro as "a shrewd and sympathetic moralist."

Covenant, Shapiro's fourth book, received even higher praise. David Barber, in *Poetry*, characterizes *Covenant* as a "remarkable collection," noting Shapiro's "knack for rendering the muddle of selfhood and the riddle of human affections" (232–33). Writing in *The Yale Review*, Robert Pinsky says, "Shapiro is one of the young American poets who have been doing their work, quietly attracting readers and breaking through to new levels of art, while publicity was focused elsewhere" (242).

BIBLIOGRAPHY

Works by Alan Shapiro

After the Digging. Chicago: Elpenor Books, 1981.
The Courtesy. Chicago: University of Chicago Press, 1983.
Happy Hour. Chicago: University of Chicago Press, 1987.
Covenant. Chicago: University of Chicago Press, 1991.
In Praise of the Impure: Poetry and the Ethical Imagination: Essays, 1980–1991. Evanston, IL: TriQuarterly Books, 1993.
Mixed Company. Chicago: University of Chicago Press, 1996.
The Last Happy Occasion. Chicago: University of Chicago Press, 1996.
Vigil. Chicago: University of Chicago Press, 1997.

Works about Alan Shapiro

Barber, David. "Short Reviews." Rev. of *Covenant*. *Poetry* 160.4 (July 1992): 219–36.
Chappell, Fred. "Once upon a Time: Narrative Poetry Returns?" Rev. of *Covenant*. *The Georgia Review* 46.2 (Summer 1992): 366–79.
Ellis, Steven R. "Mixed Company" (book review). *Library Journal* 121.5 (March 15, 1996): 75.
Grosholz, Emily. "Family Ties." Rev. of *The Courtesy*. *The Hudson Review* 37 (Winter 1984/1985): 647–59.
Hellerstein, Kathryn. "Pleasures of Restriction." Rev. of *Happy Hour*. *Partisan Review* 56.4 (Fall 1989): 677–82.
Hudgins, Andrew. "What's My Line? A Poetry Chronicle." Rev. of *Happy Hour*. *The Hudson Review* 40 (Autumn 1987): 517–27.

McClatchy, J. D. "Catching the World." Rev. of *Happy Hour. New York Times Book Review* (July 26, 1987): 9.

Pinsky, Robert. "Poetry in Review." Rev. of *Covenant. The Yale Review* 80.1–2 (April 1992): 236–54.

Williamson, Alan. "Stories about the Self." Rev. of *Covenant. The American Poetry Review* 22.2 (March/April 1993): 33–35.

DAVID SHAPIRO (1947–)

Thomas Fink

BIOGRAPHY

Born in Newark, New Jersey, in January 1947, David Shapiro was deeply influenced by close family members to immerse himself in literature and music.
His maternal grandfather, Berele Chagy, represented as a mythic figure in such
recent poems as "The Dead Will Not Praise You" (*After a Lost Original* 36)
and "The Seasons" (*After a Lost Original* 87), was a noted cantor and composer
who, apparently, died directly after performing a liturgical rite in his synagogue.
Between the ages of four and ten, David Shapiro read and memorized sizable
chunks of the writings of Shakespeare, Milton, and Blake. At ten, he memorized
much of Eliot's *The Waste Land*.

A violin prodigy, Shapiro appeared on the *Voice of America* program at five.
In the next eleven years, he played violin with several orchestras, including the
American Symphony, under Leopold Stokowski. At nine, Shapiro wrote his first
poem; publication soon followed. When he was still in high school, the Jewish
theologian Arthur A. Cohen, an editor at Holt, Rinehart, and Winston, accepted
January (1965), his first book, which garnered enthusiastic advance comments
from "New York School" poets John Ashbery and Kenneth Koch, who had
offered him significant encouragement, and from Kay Boyle, Jack Kerouac, and
Kenneth Rexroth. *January*, the publication of which influenced Shapiro to make
poetry and not the violin his primary focus, includes love poems, family poems,
and quasi-mythical moments. Critic Stephen Paul Miller characterizes this early
work as "expressive surrealism." He also considered the art critic Meyer Schapiro to be the most influential person in young adulthood. All Shapiro's art criticism has been a footnote to this great pluralist and friend of poets.

As a Columbia senior, Shapiro participated in the April 1968 protests against the Vietnam War; in an oft-reprinted photograph, he is seen sprawling in Columbia's president's chair and smoking one of his cigars. After receiving his B.A. from Columbia and the prestigious Kellett Fellowship, he earned an M.A. in literature at Cambridge University, began a secondary career as an art critic, and published his second book, *Poems from Deal* (1969), which uses a collage technique that remained a prominent part of his work of the 1970s. Returning to Columbia in 1970, where he earned a Ph.D. in English in 1973, he married Lindsay Stamm, an architect, designer, and architecture professor, and published a third book, *A Man Holding an Acoustic Panel* (1971), which was nominated for the National Book Award. His dissertation, published as a book in 1979, was the first full-length study of John Ashbery's poetry.

From 1973 to 1980, Shapiro was an assistant professor of English at Columbia, during which time *The Page-Turner* (1973) and *Lateness* (1977) appeared. In 1977, he received the American Academy and Institute of Arts and Letters' Morton Dauwen Zabel Award. In 1980, Shapiro began teaching art history at the William Paterson College of New Jersey. Now a full professor at Paterson, he regularly teaches Advanced Concepts: Architectural History and Poetry at Cooper Union, where his close associate John Hejduk is dean of architecture.

In his two books of the 1980s, *To an Idea* (1983) and *House (Blown Apart)* (1988) and in *After a Lost Original* (1994), Shapiro consolidates the gains of his earlier experimentations while also developing a meditative approach. Shapiro considers the Hebrew Bible to have greatest influence on his work.

David and Lindsay Shapiro's son, Daniel, was born in 1984; father and son have published several collaborative poems in literary magazines.

MAJOR WORKS AND THEMES

Especially in his work of the late 1960s and 1970s, David Shapiro pursued experiments with language as a dominantly nonreferential or even *anti*referential medium. In such works as the title poem of *Poems from Deal*, there is a collaging of disparate linguistic elements (from a wide variety of sources) without the writer's supplying a unifying device other than the recurrence of a particular tone or set of images: "You take back./ The hot shower drum roll./ In that echo chamber, musicians have/ showered. Evenings they swing up the vulture's/ beak" (24). While these poems never emerge as "readable" in a traditional sense, they force the reader to examine his or her presuppositions about the nature of linguistic coherence and the limits of context.

In later poems that utilize such strategies, Shapiro allows readers to use their imagination more freely. "Commentary Text Commentary Text Commentary Text," for instance, reaches out to the present/absent reader: "No man's land and no mistake. No wonder./ Noah's ark nocturne./ Inferno black Purgatorio matte gray Paradise is almost white/ *Present I flee you/ Absent I have you/* Your name like landscape written across the middle of the page" (*To an Idea* 24).

In many poems of the last two decades, Shapiro has been deeply involved with the effort to explore the limitations of poetry in rendering the "real world." This preoccupation, of course, has been central to "postmodern" American writing in general; Shapiro's scholarship on the highly self-reflexive art of Jasper Johns as well as his interest in Ludwig Wittgenstein and recent continental philosophers like Gilles Deleuze and Felix Guattari, Jacques Derrida, and Jean-François Lyotard have influenced his poetic forays in this area. In the title poems of *To an Idea* and *After a Lost Original*, questions of origin and originality play a significant role in the treatment of issues of representation, as they do in the meditative texts of two of Shapiro's major poetic precursors, Wallace Stevens and John Ashbery.

"To an Idea" begins with an expression of the desire for a Creation without an antecedent, but it does so in the past tense—thus creating some distance between the poem's speaker and the desire—and paradoxically: "I wanted to start *Ex Nihilo*/ I mean as a review of sorts" (15). The poem turns out to be a brief review of different "sorts" of ways to attempt the impossible project, including the "vicious/ doctrine" of perspective in the visual arts and the reduction of perception to an aura of nothingness. Knowing "nothing" but caught in the desire "to taste something, dazzled by absence," the speaker comes to a point where he is dazzled by mediations, the spaces between absence and presence: "Now the cars go past the lake, as if copying could exist./ The signs shine, through the Venetian blinds" (15).

The reader of "To an Idea" and numerous other poems of the 1980s and 1990s views palimpsests, which do not disclose an absolute "Truth" on the basis of accretion or any other principle but allow him or her to experience the interaction of different layers of representation in history as an ongoing process of disclosures and concealments. Another powerful poem in this vein is "The Lost Golf Ball," which begins with a rather startling (and ironic) statement of loss—"Part of the universe is missing/ Sings or says the newspaper, and I believe it./ Even most of it. . . . / And it won't do to go looking for holes/ Or changes in the constitution of matter" (*House [Blown Apart]* 35). The concept of the universe itself seems exposed as an inadequate explanatory term, since the perceptual apparatus of scientific experimentation—in the post-Heisenbergian era characterized by talk of "black holes"—cannot account for the complexities of space/time. The degree of abstract calculation needed even to estimate what is "missing" may exceed human capacity. In the second half of the poem, Shapiro moves from a consideration of the macrocosm to the microcosm of an individual human mind and then of an artwork. He ends with the realization that a title's ability to order or "contain" an aesthetic work is about as genuine as the ability of a two-dimensional pattern on the ceiling of someone's room to offer a full representation of the universe: "The title itself is a ceiling for/ stars that shine at night, will not fade, and stick by themselves/ like a slogan/ 'You have made my room a universe,' as you said you would" (36).

The concepts in Shapiro's poems about representation are equally charac-ter-

istic of his love poems, which often parody naive attempts to develop a tran-
scription of unexpressible erotic bliss, refuse to "capture" the "mystery" of
the "Other," and debunk male prerogatives in heterosexual relationships. In
"An Exercise in Futility" (*To an Idea* 17–18), he compares and parodies the
quests for intellectual and carnal knowledge as statically and ahistorically defin-
able entities: "I met an university professor in an antique land/ Who said: In
my hand is a cartographer's dream,/ The country which blurred genres" (17).
While, in the long history of patriarchal discourse, woman is almost always
assigned the status of a passive object and man that of an active subject, the
woman in "An Exercise in Futility" is an active participant in a relationship;
the poet speaks of the possibility of a shared interiority with the beloved and
yet still outside—still at a threshold: "You whom I had loved for years like a
monumental door leading to/ An exterior interior: to get to this door you climbed
a tiny, tinny podium/ And there two mirrors poured into each other" (17).
Deploying the binary opposition, inside/ouside, in various intricate ways within
the short space of a few lines, this passage illustrates Shapiro's ability to create
complex tropes that speak to the heart of contemporary intellectual concerns.

In each of his books since the third in 1971, Shapiro has included either a
long poem or one or more poetic sequences that weave together multiple themes
and aesthetic strategies. The title sequence of *A Man Holding an Acoustic Panel*
includes surreal moments of danger, hints of family history in a context of
current uncertainty, disjunctive "losses scattered erratically in the sky" (16),
the dizzying experience of synesthesia, "the lottery of heredity" (27), and a
brief, moving political elegy for the Czech martyr Jan Palach. This eighteen-
section sequence, which (the poet has mentioned) continually moves among
several geographical scenes, can be read as a "catalog" of the unfamiliar.

"About This Course," which concludes *The Page-Turner*, is a long, massive
poem. Beginning with a villanelle describing a "leaf" that "twists and turns,
then floats down the drain" (49), the poem then moves on to long-lined, un-
rhymed, fluid strophes that include several "children's" physics experiments,
fragmentary scenes of flight and a boat ride, extended biological metaphors, and
finally, the illusion of scientific (or erotic) control. "The Devil's Trill Sonata,"
a thirty-two-page poem, occupies nearly two-thirds of *Lateness*. Divided into
three sections, the quatrain-dominated poem keeps the reader perpetually off
balance by leaping from one topic to another without transitions. There are
elements of erotic poetry, elegy, wild tropes of physical and surreal transformation, direct citations of earlier Shapiro poems, such as "About This Course,"
joyful and unsatisfactory child's play, a cluster of re-creations of the Hamlet/
Ophelia story, fragments of political protest about Vietnam and Watergate, parodies of rigid philosophical stances, and abundant "meta-commentary."

In *To an Idea*, the sequence "Friday Night Quartet" hauntingly demonstrates
Shapiro's mastery of the elegiac mode. Written about the poet's mother, the
poem refers openly (and frequently in what appears to be her own voice) to
specific aspects of her final illness, including the indignities of being treated as

a "helpless" patient, humorous and poignant family memories, a fantasy of transcendence of suffering through music, and Shapiro's desire to ask his "Mother for a new form/ from Paradise" (75). The title sequence of *House (Blown Apart)* moves among metaphysical speculations, articulations of aesthetic desires, expressions of the left-liberal poet's disenchantment at the age of Reagan, and meditative love poetry.

Shapiro's most recent volume, *After a Lost Original*, reflects his Jewish origins. It is dominated by the poetic sequences "After a Lost Original" (9–22), "Broken Objects, Discarded Landscape" (23–38), "House" (39–51), and "Voice" (53–72) and the long poem "The Seasons" (79–88). In "After a Lost Original," Shapiro explores ideas of origin and originality and presence/absence, possible reinterpretations of the oedipal myth, aesthetic filiations, the problematics of heterosexual love, and repressive violence. In the elegiac prose poetry of "Walter Benjamin: A Lost Poem," he pays homage to two central Jewish intellectuals of the twentieth century: "Unfortunately many of Benjamin's remarks on poetry were now simple scratches on the cover of the book. . . . Scholem said, There was nothing like being alone with Walter Benjamin. *It made one want to read.* The source of that remark is also lost" (13). "In Germany" provides oblique references to the difficulty of aesthetic representation and religious faith after the Holocaust: "Language in your mouth—fiery as a tongue/ Like a flower deleted by a whirling pencil// We are the sculptors now, making our own doors/ The words remain, but the gods are gone for good// The idea remains, but the words are gone like gods" (14).

Inspired by Jasper Johns' paintings of the same name, "The Seasons" probes the intricacies of representation while considering such topics as one's relation to ancestors, the deadening effects of kitsch in our culture and heroic aesthetic resistances to it (including, as noted before, the image of his grandfather the cantor), the dangers of eros, the work of mourning, and fluctuations in the stages of the father–son relationship. Using numerous lines from his early, unpublished work and some lines from other parts of *After a Lost Original* itself, Shapiro in "The Seasons" reflects about the failures, dangers, and opportunities of appropriating, collaging, or "tracing" in a "late" era. Shapiro resists the kinds of "tracing" that disparage past cultural accomplishment and foster an ahistorical smugness and an unthinkingly absolutist relativism, but he is also hopeful that collage can help transform "the ruins of poetry" (81) into elements of aesthetic and social reparation, instructive pleasure, and reflection on the consequences and challenges of representation.

CRITICAL RECEPTION

Various reviews of David Shapiro's books have focused on the relation of making connections and the disruption of sense in his poetry. In the October 1970 issue of *Poetry*, philosopher and poet John Koethe praises *Poems from Deal* for Shapiro's "incredible mastery of the language and an ear sensitive to every nuance of idiom and rhythm'' and stresses the work's musical quality, ''for the poems seem to flow in a continuous wave which the poet gently modulates rather than consciously orders'' (56–57. Koethe ably describes the ''defamiliarizing'' impact of Shapiro's most experimental work:

His power stems from his ability to ride the tide of the language and then suddenly thwart, both metrically and semantically, the expectations this induces in us. The polarization of language has the effect of transforming entire lines and phrases into meaningless blocks of words, where, paradoxically, each word seems to vibrate with the bewitching fiction of its ''essential meaning.'' (56)

In the October 1974 issue of *Poetry*, Jerome McGann's review of *The Page-Turner* reads Shapiro's writing in the (anti-)tradition of Mallarmé: ''Fountains, stars, soup, dropping barometers, falling leaves: in Mallarmé's sense, these things 'exchange gleams' and 'flame out.' They are the correspondence of and between both listener and sender, reader and writer'' (51). Reviewing *To an Idea* in the *New York Times Book Review* ten years later, Jorie Graham presents a somewhat different perspective on the reader–writer relationship: ''Mr. Shapiro thinks of every reader as a 'writing reader,' and because he often refuses to make certain choices about meaning, he compels us to make them'' (14).

Stephen Paul Miller's 1983 master's thesis, ''Jasper Johns and David Shapiro: An Analogy,'' comprises the first extended treatment of Shapiro's work. Miller asserts that because ''Shapiro adapts [Frank] O'Hara's use of personal associations but deletes from them all hint of what they refer to,'' he emphasizes ''the poem and process of writing a poem . . . over anything the poem describes'' (19). Articulating the central analogy of his thesis, Miller states that ''Shapiro causes his readers to perceive the difference between the word and its meaning just as Johns stresses the distinction between sign and representational illusion when he, for instance, paints the stenciled letters ''R-E-D'' over a yellow patch of color in his 1959 *False Start*'' (37).

In a 1995 review of *After a Lost Original* in *Lingo*, Chris Stroffolino observes ''the theme of father and son as a grid which so much of western culture clamps onto interpersonal or intertextual relationships'' and suggests that Shapiro opens this theme ''up to a range of non-patriarchal possibilities'' (74).

BIBLIOGRAPHY

Works by David Shapiro

January. New York: Holt, Rinehart, and Winston, 1965.
Poems from Deal. New York: E. P. Dutton, 1969.
Ed., with Ron Padgett. *An Anthology of New York Poets*. New York: Random, 1970.
A Man Holding an Acoustic Panel. New York: E. P. Dutton, 1971.
The Page-Turner. New York: Liveright, 1973.

Lateness. Woodstock, NY: Overlook Press, 1977.

John Ashbery: An Introduction to the Poetry. New York: Columbia University Press, 1979.

Jim Dine: Painting What One Is. New York: Harry N. Abrams, 1981.

To an Idea. Woodstock, NY: Overlook Press, 1983.

"Art as Collaboration: Toward a Theory of Pluralist Aesthetics." In *The Artist as Collaborator.* Ed. Cynthia Jaffee McCabe. Washington, DC: Smithsonian Institute Press, 1984a: 1–28.

Jasper Johns Drawings 1954–1984. New York: Harry N. Abrams, 1984.

House (Blown Apart). Woodstock, NY: Overlook Press, 1988.

"Fury and Indestructibility: Notes after the Holocaust." In *Testimony: Contemporary Writers Make the Holocaust Personal.* Ed. David Rosenberg. New York: Times Books, 1989: 456–74.

Mondrian's Flowers. New York: Harry N. Abrams, 1991.

After a Lost Original. Woodstock, NY: Overlook Press, 1994.

Works about David Shapiro

Cohen, Arthur A. "David Shapiro." In *Contemporary Poets*, 3d ed. Ed. James Vinson. New York: St. Martin's Press, 1980: 1375–76.

Fink, Thomas. *The Poetry of David Shapiro.* Rutherford, NJ: Fairleigh Dickinson University Press, 1993.

———. "The Poetry of David Shapiro and Ann Lauterbach: After Ashbery." *American Poetry Review* 17.1 (January/February 1988): 27–32.

———. Rev. of *House (Blown Apart). Minnesota Review* 32 (Spring 1989): 157–59.

———. "Tracing David Shapiro's 'The Seasons.' " *Contemporary Literature* 37.3 (Fall 1996): 416–38.

Graham, Jorie. "Three Poets Wondering Who They Are" (including rev. of *To an Idea). New York Times Book Review*, March 4, 1984: 14.

Koethe, John. "Freely Espoused" (including a rev. of *Poems from Deal). Poetry* 117.1 (October 1970): 56–57.

McGann, Jerome J. "The Importance of Being Ordinary" (including a rev. of *The Page-Turner). Poetry* 125.1 (October 1974): 50–52.

Miller, Stephen Paul. "Jasper Johns and David Shapiro: An Analogy." Master's thesis, City College of New York, 1983.

Stroffolino, Chris. Rev. of *After a Lost Original. Lingo* 4 (1995): 72–80.

HARVEY SHAPIRO   (1924–   )

Robert S. Friedman

BIOGRAPHY

Though Harvey Shapiro was born in Chicago, January 27, 1924, New York has been the main source of his poetry's evocative, concrete imagery. This city frames personal responses to such disparate influences as Hasidism and Zen Bhuddism, war experiences and interpersonal tumult, and an unforgiving muse. Shapiro's objectivist poetry details the attempt to balance daily urban tensions with an adherence to what Buddhists call the Way, a positive ethos. Growing up in an Orthodox Jewish household on Long Island, Shapiro was drawn to the vital experiences of New York as a teenager. In an interview in the journal *Undine*, he recalls that he would go "to the Village on Sunday afternoons [to hear] all the top jazz players over at the Village Vanguard. I had a notion of myself as a poet, sitting at the bar with paper and pencil" (94). Before serving in the Army Air Force in World War II, where he won the Distinguished Flying Cross, he was a Yale undergraduate. There he published a few short stories, yet it wasn't until after the war, when he attended Columbia University to earn his M.A. in English (1948), that he considered himself a poet.

The 1950s were productive and defining years for Shapiro, who was a creative writing fellow at Bard College (1950–1951) and on the editorial staff at *Commentary* (1955–1956) and *The New Yorker* (1956–1957). His first volume of poems, *The Eye* (1953), received the Swallow Press Award (1954). In his essay "I Write Out of an Uncreated Identity," Shapiro says he began by writing "only on Jewish themes and published only in Jewish magazines and conceived of my audience as being different from that of other poets. . . . But my ghetto was not real and my audience, such as it was, and mostly it wasn't, was not Jewish. And so I had to enter the dangerous world" (22). The danger is, in large part, born of a sense of distance from the traditions of religious orthodoxy and an immersion in the daily experience of urban life. "A middle-aged man wanders about the city looking for the Way. He seems harassed by the life he leads, but he takes joy in much of what he sees—until he remembers that there is no real joy for the man who cannot figure things out. He could be a Jew" (22–23).

After beginning his career at the *New York Times* as assistant editor of the *Times Magazine*, Shapiro published *mountain, fire, thornbush* (1961). In his "Appreciation," David Ray quotes Shapiro as stating, "I approached a definite theme, and I knew it was a way of rescuing myself from being literary" (12). These efforts have an even more definite shape in seven subsequent volumes published over the past thirty years, the most recent being *A Day's Portion* (1994). Throughout these works, Shapiro examines the tensions that exist among his secularized, urban environment, his roles as father and husband, his experience of Jewish culture and religion, and his simultaneous questioning and commitment to a personal quest for existential enlightenment.

MAJOR WORKS AND THEMES

In *Battle Report* (1966) Shapiro depicts the processes of history and accepts, in "His Life," distance and disorder without feelings of despair or alienation:

> When he writes about his life
> He just rakes it back
> And forth. It's still
> His life, so he rakes it. (19)

Many of these poems, such as "Pharoah," address ancient Jewish and classical texts as roads toward introspection:

> "Reverencing the place in which
> The light of interpretation
> First shone forth."
> A god was translated
> By those rabbis.
> The sibylline oracles
> Spoke Messianic prophecies.
> The gates of allegory
> Are never closed. (51)

The experience of a life in New York fills the pages of *A Day's Portion* (1994), perhaps best captured by "City Ethic":

> In New York
> at the end of the day
> if you are pleased with yourself

and the human condition
and feel no survivor's guilt,
you have added to the darkness. (16)

The sum of understanding that follows this experience is concisely expressed at
the close of the title poem:

There are the ecstatic endings
and there are the endings that make sense. (91)

Illumination is both the method and result of Shapiro's craft and vision. The
search is not for satiation but for the opportunity to celebrate the presence of
mysticism, the strength of tradition, and the desire for experience.

CRITICAL RECEPTION

In his review of *Battle Report* (1966), David Ignatow praises Shapiro for
effectively moving between sacramental and symbolic expression with "the
measure of the traditional and majestic iambic foot, rhymed," to language that
is "[d]irect, plain, matter of fact in tone, without flourish or apology." In his
book Shapiro subordinates his established reverence for Elizabethan and metaphysical poets, so noticeable in much of his early work, to "ordinary, quotidian
circumstantial text." Ignatow captures the dialectical nature of the later poems:
"They spring from a dual vision in the poet of disillusionment, and regeneration
born from disillusionment. . . . The permanent and immutable are to be found in
the processes of life itself of which we are one expression, no matter what form
of it we take" (531).

Jascha Kessler's review of *This World* (1971) in the journal *Midstream* is an
extensive and positive discussion of the developing conciseness of Shapiro's
lines and his sharpening perspective on "the very few valid things one really
has" (72). Like Ignatow, Kessler praises Shapiro for his ability to confront "the
question of life itself and its relation to this world and the world of the spirit
[which]. . . . casts its shadow over his days and works, and that shadow is the
terror of the metaphysical absolute, gratuitous as it can be, but terrible nonetheless. In Shapiro's poetry that terror is constantly faced and handled or expressed
through a variety of plain sentences" (72–73).

David Ray, in his review of *The Light Holds*, describes Shapiro's work as
"clearly striv[ing] for simplicity of statement, dealing with the familiar rather
than inaccessible scenes." His poems are "pious remnants of an earthly life"
(26). In his "Harvey Shapiro—An Appreciation," Ray cites the influence that
William Carlos Williams, Charles Reznikoff, and David Ignatow have had on
Shapiro's spare constructions. Katherine Washburn, in her review of *National
Cold Storage Company* (1988), calls this collection "a monument to death that
gives these poems the ethos of classical Stoicism: virtue based on knowledge,

leading to a self-knowledge that . . . widens into an engaging and authentic self-mockery.'' He allows ''himself the formal play and controlled elegance of his line [and] has managed to keep sending his urgent and necessary telegrams from chaos'' (22).

Yet Shapiro's ''direct and accessible style . . . also mark[s] the limits of his work. What is missing from these poems is the rage and fury that leaked steadily and disturbingly from those of his models [David Ignatow, Charles Reznikoff, and Frank O'Hara]'' (30). For Matthew Flamm, however, A Day's Portion ''finds Shapiro mellowing out, the late-years mood bringing an almost celebratory lightness to the poems.'' He views Shapiro's poetry as ''packed with hard-earned ruefulness, their punishing compression as expressive in its way as any more explosive language'' (839).

With A Day's Portion comes praise for Shapiro's continuing ability to evoke the frenetic tenor of New York while maintaining an urbane wit and realistic, often self-deprecating sense of self. Michael Collier sees Shapiro as ''fundamentally a New York poet. The poems about the city use its tumult as a metaphor for the chaos of our individual lives.''

BIBLIOGRAPHY

Works by Harvey Shapiro

The Eye. Denver: Alan Swallow, 1953.
The Book and Other Poems. Cummington, MA: Cummington Press, 1955.
mountain, fire, thornbush. Denver: Alan Swallow, 1961.
Battle Report: Selected Poems. Middletown, CT: Wesleyan University Press, 1966.
This World. Middletown, CT: Wesleyan University Press, 1971.
Lauds. New York: Sun Press, 1975.
Lauds and Nightsounds. New York: Sun Press, 1978.
The Light Holds. Middletown, CT: Wesleyan University Press, 1984.
National Cold Storage Company. Middletown, CT: Wesleyan University Press, 1988.
''I Write Out of an Uncreated Identity.'' The Writer in the Jewish Community. Ed. Richard Siegel and Tamar Sofer. Cranbury, NJ: Associated University Presses, 1993.
A Day's Portion. Brooklyn: Hanging Loose Press, 1994.

Works about Harvey Shapiro

Collier, Michael. ''These Are the Streets.'' New York Times Book Review 99 (September 25, 1994): 30.
Flamm, Matthew. ''I Sing the City Eclectic.'' The Nation 258 (June 13, 1994): 839.
Ignatow, David. ''The Past Reordered.'' The Nation 204 (April 24, 1967): 531–32.
Interview. Undine; A Literary Journal. (1974): 92–103.
Kessler, Jascha. ''Rebels in the Kingdom.'' Midstream 28:4 (April 1972): 70–75.

Ray, David. "Harvey Shapiro—An Appreciation." *New Letters Review of Books* 2:1 (1988): 4, 12.

———. "Urban Despair, Urban Miracles." *New York Times Book Review* 89 (April 1, 1984): 26.

Washburn, Katherine. "Memories and Unholy Joys." *New York Times Book Review* 93 (December 11, 1988): 22.

KARL (JAY) SHAPIRO   (1913–)

David R. Slavitt

BIOGRAPHY

Karl Shapiro was born on November 10, 1913, in Baltimore. His career as a poet has been a peculiarly American phenomenon. With Stanley Kunitz, who was eight years older, and Delmore Schwartz, who was a month younger, Shapiro can be said to have invented the category of the Jewish-American poet, a creature that had been, before their appearance, all but unimaginable. (Muriel Rukeyser was born the same month as Schwartz was inventing the even farther-fetched category of *female* Jewish-American poet.) In his Introduction to *The Letters of Delmore Schwartz*, Shapiro writes:

We [Schwartz and I] were almost exact contemporaries and grew up under the same spheres of influence. Jewish, Depression, intellectual, poetic, but with strongly marked differences in our voyages. He was a literary prodigy; I was not. He was a New Yorker; I was a Baltimorean, a ''Southerner.'' He was well educated; I was educated cosmeti-cally. He was an activist on the attack; I was a spectator without a cause. He fought like a pit bull to avoid the uniform; I accepted conscription with a shrug. He equated literary success with power; I ridiculed literary power. He belonged to the Euro-cultural dispen-sation; I was a Whitman-Williams isolationist. And so on. He was suspicious of my literary successes, as he was of everybody's and accepted me as an equal belatedly. (38)

The other great difference between them, of course, is that Schwartz went mad, while Shapiro remained relatively sane—or as close to it as anyone could who had won the Pulitzer Prize in 1945, when he was in his early thirties.

That prize, which it became his habit later to call ''the golden albatross,'' categorized him, making him an object of admiration but also of envy, making him, in other words, a target. If Delmore Schwartz was to suppose toward the end of his life that Nelson Rockefeller was beaming evil rays into his brain from the top of the Empire State Building, Karl Shapiro had a not altogether different idea that there were enemies out there, but he couldn't be sure whether or not to hope he was just imagining them. Along with the Jewishness and the prize, he had also become, from 1950 to 1956, the editor of *Poetry* and then, for the next ten years, the editor of *Prairie Schooner*. Poetry is not a chummy or collegial racket, and, as anyone ought to be able to figure out, a poetry editor with any clout at all, accepting one poem for every twenty he rejects, is making a score of steadfast new enemies for each new casual friend.

His childhood in Baltimore was a kind of preliminary bout before the fight that would be going on for the rest of his life between assertiveness and withdrawal. As he says in *The Younger Son*, the first volume of his two-part autobiography:

He was born a year and five days after his brother, the second child, "a defect in manufacture" his father used to joke when he was old enough to understand the words, not wanted but not necessarily acceptable he would tell himself, and worse than that a middle child. The brother was born famous, as it were, what with the father's winning photograph of the most beautiful baby or baby picture or both in the Baltimore newspapers, the enlargements decorating the house and spoken of endlessly. A royal-send-off that never let up. For a middle-class Jewish child to be a news item continuously was unheard of, but there it was, the brilliant as well as photographically winning, even in the Baltimore newspapers which considered Jews as a cut above Negroes but not much. (41)

A mixed bag, then, as was the Pulitzer Prize. About that, he says in *Reports of My Death*, the second volume of that life story:

He could never decide whether he was really happy to have the Prize. Like every writer he wanted, demanded recognition from his fellows the writers and was delighted to have a passport to the ordinary world which the Prize provided, but he had always held the Prize in low esteem. It was a middlebrow honor at best and it had always been given to *intelligible* writers, those with a large reading public, and he knew that a large reading public was the most suspect readership of all, especially in America where the reading level was never above the sixth grade even among college graduates. (15)

What it probably did on the plus side was to enable Shapiro to find jobs in universities, which wasn't so easy a thing for a poet to do in those days. There weren't, in the 1940s and early 1950s, all those creative writing courses and programs and even departments. Shapiro, as a Pulitzer laureate, was chosen to be the consultant in poetry at the Library of Congress in 1946 and then was able to get himself a tenured appointment at Johns Hopkins, which he held from 1947 to 1950. It also gave him the confidence to be able to walk away from that snug berth. He has since then taught at the University of Wisconsin (1948), Loyola University, Chicago (1951–1952), the University of California (UC),

Berkeley and Davis (1955–1956), University of Indiana (1956–1966), University of Illinois (1966–1968) and then at UC, Davis (1968 to 1985, when he retired).

MAJOR WORKS AND THEMES

It looks to be a fairly restless series of peregrinations, but that has been his way in writing, too. As he explained in his essay "Is Poetry An American Art?" in *The Poetry Wreck: Selected Essays 1950–1970*, there seem to be, in our country, "a poetry of violence and a poetry of wit." Neither is entirely satisfactory. The poet of the barbaric yawp "is committed to cursing a society he does not know," while "the academic poet is committed to cursing the street. Or rather, he does not curse; he witticises and versifies. . . . But I cannot be content with either poetry."

Indeed, if there is one constant in Shapiro's life and work, it is this refusal to be content, to settle down and be comfortable, to pursue what works and make a career of it. He began as a dexterous craftsman, better trained than most of his peers in the subtleties of formal poetry. That interest manifested itself in *English Prosody and Modern Poetry*, a critical study he undertook and published in 1947, and *A Bibliography of Modern Prosody*, 1948. It also produced the elegant and witty performances for which he is perhaps still best known, such pieces as "Auto Wreck," "The Leg," and "Elegy for a Dead Soldier."

It would have been perfectly acceptable and even, in some ways, admirable to persist in this kind of polished work—as, say, Richard Wilbur has done. But for Shapiro, there was an ambition or perhaps an inner need to move on, experiment, and see whether he would take his readers along with him or lose them. He had to test that uneasy relationship, either verify it somehow or get out of it, and to this end he adopted a more Whitmanian approach. His uneasiness with the New Criticism he proclaimed in *In Defense of Ignorance* (1960) and in his poetry from *Trial of a Poet* (1947), *Poems of a Jew* (1958), and *The Bourgeois Poet* (1964). If, technically, he was playing around now with prose poems, that was only one aspect of his more general need to be self-assertive and even provocative. It was an enormous leap for so careful a practitioner, as he said in *The Bourgeois Poet*:

Lower the standard: that's my motto. Somebody is always putting the food out of reach. We're tired of falling off ladders, Who says a child can't paint? A pro is somebody who does it for money. Lower the standards. Let's all play poetry. Down with ideals, flags, convention buttons, morals, the scrambled eggs on the admiral's hat. I'm talking sense. Lower the standards. Sabotage the stylistic approach. Let weeds grow in the subdivision. Putty up the incisions in the library facade, those names that frighten grade-school teachers, those names whose U's are cut like V's. Burn the *Syntopicon* and *The Harvard Classics*. (10)

It is important to remember that this is not a proposal but a poem, an exhibition of personality, a psychological and aesthetic response to a complicated series of cultural and social stimuli.

The impulse, over and over again, is to say the unsayable and to do so in an unfashionable way. This, of course, he had always been doing, from *Person Place and Thing*, which came out in 1941, when Shapiro was serving overseas in New Guinea. In this extraordinary collection he starts "University" by declaring: "To hurt the Negro and avoid the Jew is the curriculum" (*Collected Poems* 10). Such other titles as *Adult Book Store* or *White-Haired Lover* invite us or challenge us to accept him as he is. In *Poems of a Jew* and in various pieces throughout his career, he uses his Jewishness to keep away the kind of audience he'd rather not be bothered with. Even Jews have to make an adjustment, for Shapiro, who is never sentimental, even keeps members of the tribe at a certain distance when he says, in "My Father's Funeral":

> The rabbi's eulogy is succinct
> Accurate and sincere, and the great prayer
> That finishes the speech is simply praise
> Of God, the god my father took in stride
> when he taught us to learn Hebrew and shorthand,
> Taught us to be superior, as befits
> A nation of individual priests.
> At my sister's house, we neither pray nor cry
> Nor sit, but stand and drink and joke,
> So that one of the youngsters says
> It's more like a cocktail party.

CRITICAL RECEPTION

This almost quixotic insistence on truth-telling has not made Shapiro an easy poet for readers to cozy up to. Unlike Robert Frost, who was so cagey that most of his readers had no idea that he was saying quite dark and even depressing things about the world, Shapiro has never deigned to such an accommodation. He's what the young people call "in your face." His publishing history is an outward sign of his changing fortunes, those fluctuations from esteem to disesteem in which editors—looking to the public, the temperature of whose enthusiasm they are forever taking—have held him.

Up until 1978, he was a Random House poet, which was as good as you could be. Knopf had its poets, and Atheneum had its nest of singing birds, but Random House had W. H. Auden, Robert Penn Warren, Karl Shapiro, and almost nobody else. These were not only poets of undeniable quality but writers whose books could make their way in the marketplace! He was, in other words, a heavyweight, with the Pulitzer in 1945 and then the Bollingen Prize in 1969. But the weather changed, or his belligerence finally caught up to him. Random House kept his book in print, in a theoretical way, but it was impossible to order it and actually buy it. Shapiro became a kind of nonperson who couldn't even demand the rights back and go elsewhere.

After some complicated and protracted negotiation, Shapiro was able at last to get free and go to Stuart Wright in Winston-Salem, North Carolina, which maintained a small press that did a lot of broadsides and on occasion even published books. Wright is a bibliographer and book collector, and he is smart about recognizing quality, but he is not easy about letting go of things. He brought out *Love and War, Art and God*, but it was all but impossible actually to buy one. Shapiro's mood was not improved by the difficulty he was having at this period in finding a publisher for his autobiography, which Algonquin Books of Chapel Hill finally issued in 1988 and 1990. He had never been comfortable with that damned prize, and now he had another more fundamental complaint with it—it wasn't working anymore. It was as if he'd had his moment of celebrity and lost it. He'd piddled it away; he'd failed!

Almost anyone else would have been depressed in such a predicament, and Shapiro had his less than cheerful moments. But he also took a perverse pleasure in being so unfashionable, for in our society and culture, that is almost a hall-mark of seriousness. The appearance of his *New and Selected Poems 1940–1986* in 1987 from the University of Chicago Press was a signal of his return from the outer darkness.

He is hardly back at the hot center of the literary world, however. His latest collection of verse, *The Old Horsefly* (1992), came out not from Chicago but from Northern Lights in Orono, Maine, an outfit of such modesty that directory assistance is not able to find a telephone listing for them. It is unlikely that even an ornery cuss like Shapiro would have preferred them to Chicago as another way of keeping those pesky readers at a decent distance. I saw only one review of that latest book—a dismissive couple of paragraphs by some young punk trying to look smart. But it doesn't matter. Shapiro's place in our culture is secure, partly because of the extraordinary quality of some of his poems, partly because of his charming perversity and crankiness, but also because of his place in our literary history. When Erica Jong called Muriel Rukeyser "the mother of us all," I saw just what she meant and, even though Jong is not my favorite poet or critic, had to acknowledge the acuity of her remark. By that measure, Kunitz, Shapiro, and Schwartz are our patriarchs. Of the three, I think Karl Shapiro's path has been the most adventurous, the most interesting, and the most humane.

BIBLIOGRAPHY

Works by Karl (Jay) Shapiro

Poetry

Poems. Baltimore: Waverly Press, 1935.
With others. *Five Young American Poets*. New York: New Directions, 1941.
Person Place and Thing. New York: Reynal, 1942a; London: Secker and Warburg, 1945.

The Place of Love. Melbourne: Comment Press, 1942b.
V-Letter and Other Poems. New York: Reynal, 1944; London: Secker and Warburg, 1945.
Essay on Rime. New York: Reynal, 1945; London: Secker and Warburg, 1947.
Trial of a Poet and Other Poems. New York: Reynal, 1947.
The Thin Bell-Ringer. Privately printed, 1948.
The House. Privately printed, 1957.
Poems of a Jew. New York: Random House, 1958.
The Bourgeois Poet. New York: Random House, 1964a.
Poems 1940–1953. New York: Random House, 1964b.
With others. *Ligature 68*. Chicago: Madison Park Press, 1968a.
Selected Poems. New York: Random House, 1968b.
White-Haired Lover. New York: Random House, 1968c.
Auden (1907–1973). Davis: University of California Library Associates, 1974.
Adult Book Store. New York: Random House, 1976.
Collected Poems 1940–1978. New York: Random House, 1978.
Love and War, Art and God. Winston-Salem, NC: Stuart Wright, 1984.
Adam and Eve. Lewisburg, PA: Press Alley, 1986.
New and Selected Poems 1940–1986. Chicago: University of Chicago Press, 1987.
The Old Horsefly. Orono, ME: Northern Lights, 1992.

Fiction

Edsel. New York: Bernard Geis Associates, 1971.

Nonfiction

English Prosody and Modern Poetry. Baltimore: Johns Hopkins University Press, 1947.
A Bibliography of Modern Prosody. Baltimore: Johns Hopkins University Press, 1948a.
With others. *Poets at Work*. Ed Charles D. Abbott. New York: Harcourt, 1948b.
Beyond Criticism. Lincoln: University of Nebraska Press, 1953; as *A Primer for Poets*, 1965.
In Defense of Ignorance (essays). New York: Random House, 1960a.
With James E. Miller, Jr., and Bernice Slote. *Start with the Sun: Studies in Cosmic Poetry*. Lincoln: University of Nebraska Press, 1960b.
With Ralph Ellison. *The Writer's Experience*. Washington, DC: Library of Congress, 1964.
With Robert Beum. *A Prosody Handbook*. New York: Harper, 1965.
Randall Jarrell. Washington, DC: Library of Congress, 1967.
To Abolish Children and Other Essays. Chicago: Quadrangle, 1968.
The Poetry Wreck: Selected Essays 1950–1970. New York: Random House, 1975.
The Younger Son. Chapel Hill, NC: Algonquin Books of Chapel Hill, 1988.
Reports of My Death. Chapel Hill, NC: Algonquin Books of Chapel Hill, 1990.

Works about Karl (Jay) Shapiro

Bartlett, Lee. *Karl Shapiro: A Descriptive Bibliography*. New York: Garland, 1979.
Reino, Joseph. *Karl Shapiro*. Boston: Twayne, 1981.
Walker, Sue B., ed. *Seriously Meeting Karl Shapiro*. Mobile, AL: Negative Capability Press, 1993.

LOUIS SIMPSON (1923–)

Blossom Steinberg Kirschenbaum

BIOGRAPHY

Born in Kingston, Jamaica, West Indies, Louis Aston Marantz Simpson is the younger son of Aston, a successful lawyer of Scottish-French mixed background, and a Russian-Jewish mother, Rosalind Marantz, who as a girl had worked in New York's garment district before going to Jamaica as one of Annette Kellerman's bathing beauties. Socially, she played down her Jewishness but at home told stories of her Russian girlhood that stirred her son's imagination with their vivid images, sense of community, and blend of sorrow and humor— as later poems attest. Her love of singing passed to him, too, as love of opera. The family's privileged white society, with servant-companions in middle-class homes, rested, sometimes uneasily, on a black or "colored" majority, at the bottom of which were descendants of slaves who worked the cane fields and banana plantations and broke stone for roads. There were colored professionals, too, however, for in this class structure, money modified the color factor. When Louis Simpson was about seven, his parents divorced; his mother had to leave; and he was sent to his father's Presbyterian relatives, an active happy family. (Years later a cousin became Jamaican ambassador to the United States.) His mother visited intermittently and sent books. His father remarried, to the stenographer with whom he had been having an affair, and the boys lived with them during school vacations, rather as outsiders, in a new house by the sea.

At age nine Louis Simpson was sent to the English-style boarding school his brother Herbert, five years older, already attended—cold sheets and rough blanket, emphasis on sports, compulsory Latin and chapel, disdain for Jamaica even as the colonial system was beginning to crumble. They were "being fitted for a life that we would never have and being made to understand that the life we did have was inferior'' (*North of Jamaica* 47–48 [*NJ*]). Much later he read about Jews in the West Indies. He excelled in English and French, thrilled to Shakespeare, and learned that the key weapon of a ruling class is language. Published essays twice won prizes; poems and stories appeared in the late 1930s in a weekly that favored Jamaican independence.

He was sixteen when his father died; the entire inheritance went to the second family. War was imminent. In 1940 Simpson went to his mother's family in New York and to Columbia University. Jewish according to the law, he didn't feel Jewish, but not Christian either: ''There is nothing like a religious upbringing for making you bored with religion for the rest of your life. Moreover, I hadn't noticed that Christianity made people tolerant and kind. I did not think that I would lose much by not being a Christian'' (*NJ* 87–88). Of his observant grandmother, who spoke English with a Yiddish accent, he says, ''She wept for her people in Russia, and trusted in God and Franklin Delano Roosevelt'' (*NJ* 89).

His mother, who had sold Elizabeth Arden products in Toronto, in 1945 gained rights to sell Helena Rubinstein cosmetics in Venezuela. In Caracas she met and married Renato Barsanti, one of six brothers from Viareggio whose family's property had been confiscated by Mussolini. The eldest brother had prospered as an engineer in Argentina. When Rosalind retired, she and Renato moved to Italy. The poet has published accounts of his visits to her in Italy.

In 1943 Simpson joined the U.S. Army. After basic training in Texas he served three years, mostly in glider infantry, the 101st Airborne Division, which fought in Normandy, Holland, Belgium, and Germany. He was wounded; had his feet frozen at Bastogne; won the Bronze Star and the Purple Heart; and got his American citizenship at Berchtesgaden. Poems and prose convey the immediacy and intimacy of war. From *Riverside Drive*: ''[The area] was a masterpiece of rage. Mutilated bodies, twisted torsos and limbs, hands grasping, teeth grinning, a welter of rotting cloth and rusting weapons. The bodies began to swell; every time I crossed the field, they had become more grotesque'' (54). *North of Jamaica* describes feelings of military servitude, of being shelled and bombed, insulted and bored. He remembers a colonel at Fort Dix who told the troops when they were discharged that some day they would look back on their wartime experiences as the best days of their lives; for the colonel, he thought, that was probably so: his orders were obeyed, his bed made, his sense of importance flattered. He imagined such men, after the war, wanting to perpetuate the conditions of war and changing the United States into the fearful postwar nation it became.

He has recorded his return to Columbia, postwar breakdown, hospitalization (he saw a young patient kicked to death), job as a copyboy, travel to France on the G. I. Bill, and writing war poems and love poems there (the affair described in *Riverside Drive*). A first book, *The Arrivistes*, printed in Paris, was favorably reviewed by Randall Jarrell in *The Nation*.

In New York again, he married and became the father of Louis Matthew. For five years (1950–1955) under head editor Hyram Hayden he read and edited manuscripts for Bobbs-Merrill by day, met other writers (mainly novelists), wrote at night, and supplemented earnings by teaching at the New School for Social Research and at Columbia's General Studies. A second book of poems, rejected by publishers, won the Borestone Mountain Poetry Award, promising publication and money; but the award was withdrawn, perhaps because, as Simpson claims, judge Robert Lowell changed his mind. The pain, worse than that of simple rejection, came just when his marriage had broken; he was paying alimony and child support. After that, prizes seemed suspect, though he has himself served on Pulitzer Prize juries. Scribner's later took the second book.

In 1955, remarried, he began working toward a doctorate; a year later his daughter, Anne Borovoi, was born. In 1957–1958 came the double reward of the Rome Prize (first word of this from his teacher Mark Van Doren) and a Hudson Review Fellowship. Residing outside the walls of the American Academy in Rome on the Janiculum, freed from teaching duties, he went to Edinburgh to do research and finished his dissertation on James Hogg, the Ettrick Shepherd. Meanwhile, with Donald Hall and Robert Pack he edited *The New Poets of England and America* (1957). This anthology was considered to have a "traditionalist bias" compared with Donald Allen's *New American Poetry 1945–60*, representing the "enemy camp," including the Beat poets. Allen veered away from "English" influences, rejected qualities typical of academic verse, and excluded *every one* of the poets in the other anthology. Considered as rivals, these anthologies fueled controversy between "palefaces" and "redskins."

In the summer of 1959, after birth of son Anthony Rolf, the family moved to California and their own house in the Berkeley hills, to stay until 1967. Four more books issued. A third influential movement in American poetry was being led by Robert Bly, about whose great influence Simpson has written in *North of Jamaica*. Bly contrasted poems of "outwardness" or "objectivism" (written by "the generation of 1917" and poets influenced by them) with a new "subjectivity" found in Spanish-language poets (Lorca, Juan Ramon Jiminez, Pablo Neruda, Vallejo) and also in Rilke—an alternative both inward and revolutionary, the "deep image." Minnesotans Bly, James Wright, and William Duffy were joined by New York poets Robert Kelly and Jerome Rothenberg in agreement about needing freer forms and a new sound. They differed from each other, but all differed from both those who followed the New Critics and those who were Beat and/or confessional. After 1959 Simpson's work had affinities with theirs. *At the End of the Open Road* (1963) won the Pulitzer Prize. He was invited to give readings and traveled widely. After the American invasion of Vietnam, during the Berkeley years, though settled to job and family and shrinking from politics, Simpson was drawn into the anti–Vietnam War movement, first through a committee to help arrested students, then as speaker. Yet he remained skeptical about activists and flower children, uncomfortable about criticizing the United States, and averse to those who enjoyed doing so.

In 1967 he accepted an offer from the State University of New York at Stony Brook, on Long Island's north shore and sixty miles from New York City. In 1970 a Guggenheim took him to England for a year, extended to two years, and he published his autobiography there, as well as *Adventures of the Letter I*, which issued in the United States only in paperback and so was not reviewed. In London, Fay and Ron Weldon were next-door neighbors. He met other poets and gave readings and lectures. (One was at Westminster Synagogue, where he saw the collected 1,564 sacred scrolls, each representing a destroyed community in Czechoslovakia; damages were being repaired so that scrolls could be given to fulfill requests from synagogues worldwide.) He became interested in Buddhism too, an interest reflected in *Searching for the Ox*. He felt lucky in having chosen New York over London; but once back in Stony Brook he felt isolated and so dove into writing literary criticism. He rewrites a lot and finds prose, unlike poetry, exhausting.

He says he wants to write poems for people who love their lives, and he is one of them. Responding in 1975 to Saul Bellow's novel *Humboldt's Gift*, based on the life of Delmore Schwartz and showing the self-destructive artist as scapegoat, Simpson points out that the myth of the self-destructive artist as scapegoat serves to reassure the middle class of its values: "Art strikes the middle class as an aberration, a kind of insanity. And some poets have . . . played out a middle-class idea of the life of art" ("Ghost" 52). He nevertheless insists on writing from within the middle class. *Caviare at the Funeral* got the 1981 Jewish Book Council Award for Poetry.

He remained at Stony Brook. His second marriage ended in divorce. In June 1985 he married Miriam Bachner. They reside in Setauket, with their dogs, not far from the Hamptons and "artists and many who liked the noise of art." From there they have traveled through California and in Europe. Simpson continues to write dense, moving, humorous poems (and prose, too) about the local people, most of them not the sort who read poetry, to show life as it is, and to bring a sort of community into being. As state bureaucracy burgeons, he holds, poetry increasingly expresses the life of an individual; but since the individual cannot speak for an entire society, the personal voice will express not the society, not the ego or the merely private self, but character forged in service of the work of art; thus, the portrait of the artist may function to create a community of spirits.

Half a century after leaving there, Louis Simpson has gone back to Jamaica. This last visit, long dreamed, described in "Going Back" (in *The King My Father's Wreck*), was precipitated by his lawyer-cousin's inviting him to guest-lecture at the university in Kingston. Simpson found the economy in decline, its main industry tourism; the population swelling and unemployment rife; but the cousin had served as senator and minister in the Jamaican government and as ambassador to the United States. Photographs reveal that Simpson's paternal grandfather, with spectacles and a mustache, appears "a bit dusky," and his wife is "of mixed Caucasian and Negro ancestry" (*The King* 170). Among places he visits are his father's house, where squatters live, and his father's grave; belatedly, there is more ancestry to explore. In May 1996, to commemorate their first National Poetry Month, the Jamaican consulate feted Simpson. In a September 1996 *New York Times* interview Simpson likens his growing self-awareness to the Russian nesting dolls of his childhood (Duncan 15)—and startles the interviewer with his report of being rebaptized at the Caroline Church in Brookhaven.

MAJOR WORKS AND THEMES

Simpson's 1983 selection *People Live Here* disrupts chronology of composition, rearranging poems to highlight themes: "The Fighting in Europe," "A Discovery of America," "Modern Lives," and "Volhynia Province." Other major themes have evolved: concern with community, domesticity, the poet's role, and a spiritual alternative to the boredom and restlessness of suburban entrapment.

War, a major theme in *The Arrivistes*, is treated in the sorrowful ballad "Carentan O Carentan" with poised detachment and understatement as the contrast to "the old days" of peace when the land was soft and bright, and strolling lovers in the lane could watch farmers at work; now lessons in murder have taken a toll on both sides, superior officers no longer answer, and at Carentan the speaker has learned "what death could do." This poem leads the *Selected Poems* and sets a tone for the much later *People Live Here*. In *Good News of Death*, "The Battle," laconic and matter-of-fact, implies deadening and dismemberment, depersonalization and disappearance; it concludes with fatigue and dwindling, thin hands cupped around a cigarette. In "The Heroes," an ironically rollicking meter, jingly internal rhyme, and mocking alliteration cast pain into starker contrast, after "The heroes were packaged and sent home in parts" (*Collected Poems* [*CP*] 54). "The Ash and the Oak" encapsulates a history of war, from times when motive was blunt, combat close, and virtue linked with manly valor—through nineteenth-century ideals—to impersonal attack with long-range weaponry, and failed ideals of World War I when "A hero was a fool" (*CP* 55). Compression, poised control of narrow stanzas, and a contemporary voice make "Early in the Morning" (*Selected Poems* 1965, 27), about the defeat of Antony and Cleopatra, an even more succinct history of war, in which victory implies not only the defeat of one or the other army but also downfall of love. Simpson's military service was well behind him when in Rome in December 1957 he finished a long, fictional, narrative poem, "The Runner" (*Selected Poems* 1965, 52–78), about a soldier in his division; but the attempt at a bridgehead across the Rhine at Arnhem in the Netherlands is factual, as are preparations against a German attack around Bastogne. Running ammunition up to the mortars, racing through darkness and brambles away from the enemy's challenge, screaming the password as "[r]ed tracers streaked the air" (*Dream* 51; *CP* 112), hearing the ominous remark, "Everyone else is pulling out but us'' (*CP* 120; *Dream* 61), defying a tank that seems animate as it shudders, lurches around, trembles with explosions, and pours smoke, running messages even as the poem ends, the poem re-creates a foot soldier's survival under fire. War persists as a theme in *In the Room We Share* as by moonlight the Volksgrenadiers sit up, and while one gathers his slippery intestines, the other gropes in the surrounding dirt for his arm tattooed "mit zwei Herzen . . . (with two hearts . . .) 'Fritz und Elsa' '' (*In the Room* 23).

War as contest for domination flows from deep dreams; in *A Dream of Governors*; the title poem bears an epigraph from Mark Van Doren, "The deepest dream is of mad governors" (6; *CP* 84). While some suffer, others are enchanted in love's mythic constancy and self-absorption; thus, the shepherd and shepherdess ignore time while the speaker calls attention to one disaster after another, how arrows rain, molten lead pours, and "Down from a turret seven virgins fall,/Hands folded, each one praying on her head" ("The Green Shepherd," *A Dream of Governors* 3). One set of images alarms by its obliviousness, the other by cumulative destructions; the equilibrium of painterly images is richly allusive—and funny. More ironic but likewise painterly and likewise contrasting pastoral obliviousness and denial with military disaster, its rhythmic and neatly rhymed quatrains alternating lines of five beats and two as it describes a dance, is "The Riders Held Back," from *At the End of the Open Road*; knights seduced by Graces wake to a distant trumpet's blast only when it is too late, when there are "many slain/In the dark fields" (*At the End of the Open Road* 60; *CP* 158). This volume also contains "A Story about Chicken Soup," which deals with the Holocaust. Safe in his American grandmother's home but linked to the European past as both victorious American and mourning Jew, the poet begins to come to terms with what people prefer not to discuss: "I know it's in bad taste to say it,/But it's true. The Germans killed them all" (*Open Road* 25; *CP* 144). "The Bird" presents the Holocaust through the persona of Heinrich, who sings that he wishes he were a bird while he learns to sort clothing in a concentration camp; he survives the Nazi defeat, evades capture, and goes on singing the song "so sadly/It makes his children cry." Another poem is called "The Silent Generation."

Increasingly, Simpson identifies with the oppressed and violated. During the 1950s, when outrageous Allen Ginsberg published *Howl*, Simpson parodied it (first in *Hudson Review* in 1957, then in *North of Jamaica*) as "Squeal"; but "Itzel" in *Adventures of the Letter I* presents sympathetically a figure like Ginsberg "with his beads and black-rimmed spectacles" and Simpson allies with him against attack as citizens shout abuse. "Sea of Grass" in *In the Room We Share* is dedicated to painter Jimmy Ernst, a Long Island neighbor; the speaker understands that if a Jew wants to know which transport his mother was on, it is possible to consult a French railroad list: "Jimmy showed me the name of his:/'Lou Straus-Ernst . . . Transport 76.' '' Quoting Flaubert's "Work! God wants you to," Simpson surely intends reference to the sign "Arbeit macht frei" (work makes you free).

In "To the Western World" Simpson begins to shift focus, treating the New World as extension of European wars and failed Eden from the start. He addresses Walt Whitman at Bear Mountain; but having reached California and seen the redwoods, he has also "Pacific Ideas—A Letter to Walt Whitman" (*Selected Poems* 121). Simpson moves away from tight lyrics to a freer verse as he confronts the question of a poetry adequate to the continental expanse. *At the End of the Open Road* contains his six-line much-quoted "American Poetry" (it served as epigraph for A. Poulin, Jr.'s, 1971 anthology *Contemporary American Poetry*):

> Whatever it is, it must have
> A stomach that can digest
> Rubber, coal, uranium, moons, poems.
>
> Like the shark, it contains a shoe.
> It must swim for miles through the desert
> Uttering cries that are almost human. (*Open Road* 55; *CP* 154)

He has written "On the Neglect of Poetry in the United States" (*Ships Going into the Blue*, 85–93); and in "O What Can Ail Thee, Knight at Arms?" (from *In the Room We Share*) the speaker quotes a girl: "I like poetry, she said./I just don't have the time for it." Yet Simpson continues to write poetry and discuss work of other poets, and the rationale for his persistence and for his simple (but not simplistic), lucid, direct, colloquial, broadly accessible style, all its effort and struggle cleansed away, is another major theme.

Simpson had treated biblical subjects (as in "The Man Who Married Magdalene" and "John the Baptist" from the 1955 volume) and subjects from Greek myth (as in the two Opheus poems from the 1959 book), and *Searching for the Ox* (1976) deals with a series of pictures based on eleventh-century Chinese poems that Simpson describes in his *Contemporary Authors* essay—Jack Kerouac described them, too, in *Dharma Bums*.

By 1963, however, "My Father in the Night Commanding No" (*Selected Poems* 1965, 109–10) signaled a family man's return to materials from his own childhood, whose images are eternalized in the theatre of the psyche, as the first poem "Working Late" in *Caviare at the Funeral* signaled a continuing preoccupation with the father's role as still having an influence on the poet.

Ancestral ruminations inspire other imagery—Old Russia and English colony must be reconciled with the American West. *Adventures of the Letter I* collects a group of poems about his mother's native Volhynia province; harking back to captivating, snow-filled, Cossack-riding tales of childhood, tales of his grandmother, too, and stories by Chekhov, he imagines that he loves Dvonya in Odessa, though he has never been in Odessa, for as cousins they understand each other perfectly—though they are now only fragments of the imagination.

Still recounting history as in the Haggadah—this is what happened to *me*—he tells of Avram, the only Jewish sergeant in the Czar's army, who married a rich widow and lived well but was nevertheless taken away by the Germans along with a Gentile retainer who claimed to be a Romanov. He writes of the students Chaim Baruch and Meyer, of anarchist Isidor, who evades the inspector by hiding in the oven, of the man who on his way home to supper meets a wolf; his mother's family forever sits around the kitchen stove, arguing. He reclaims a Russian landscape and literary tradition and also the sort of humor that lights up a comic side to sorrow, laughter through tears. The section on Indian country however, features the different landscape and ancestors of an adopted land and considers, for instance, the tribe that claimed Mt. Shasta. Back-and-forthing in chronological time, the poet singles out individuals but mistrusts ideologues. Irony both undercuts and enlarges a toothache on Thanksgiving. Addressing Russian poet Andrei Voznesensky, who once told him about the Russian lake built to cover up bodies of dead Jews, he tells of being haunted by the cold wind from the shtetl, of hearing the train bound for Random, for Jerusalem:

> In the night where candles shine
> I have a luminous family . . .
> people with their arms round each other
> forever. (*Selected Poems* 1965, 92)

"In the Suburbs" heralded a new emphasis on daily life. Gary Pacernick noted (84), "Like Renzikoff, Zukofsky, and other Jewish poets of memory, Simpson's imaginative remembrance of the spiritual past often clashes with his perceptions of the secular present dominated by images of shallow materialism." At the same time, contemporary Americans lead extraordinary lives just as Chekhov's villagers and countryfolk did, and the shady lane of "Carentan O Carentan" becomes "The Foggy Lane" (*People Live Here* 1983, 182) of Long Island, where an insurance salesman advises him that he needs "more protection." There are always interludes; thus, he imagines Hannibal's sojourn at Trasimeno and his, or anyone's, nocturnal return to barbarian ways. Far-ranging in time and space, Simpson lives more fully at home, considering "How to Live on Long Island," "The Previous Tenant," "Quiet Desperation," "Periodontics"—these are poem titles from *The Best Hour of the Night* (1983). Adultery, poker games, commuting, stripping paint, sawing logs, walking the dog, paying bills, sitting through a meeting of the village board, taking out the garbage—these mundane events are all the drama the narrative poems need for their lean, ironic, empathic commentary, for the battle of Iwo Jima comes right into the living room ([H]e's seen the movie" ["Quiet Desperation," *Best Hour of the Night* 16, *CP* 334]) and at home he remembers staying at the Grand Hotel at Beaulieu, his mother staying at the Manor House in Kingston, and redwoods keep growing while a family out shopping walks past "Wise Shoes, Regal Shoes,/National Shoes, Naturalizer Shoes,/Stride Rite, Selby, Hanover," where "The Mall is laid out like a cathedral/with two arcades that cross" ("The

Beaded Pear,'' *Caviar at the Funeral* 35, *CP* 279). ''Car Trouble,'' A ''Fuse Link,'' and ''Waiting in the Service Station,'' from *In the Room We Share*, respond to the ubiquitous, necessary automobile. What makes the suburbanites sympathetic is their discontent, a need to escape entrapment even as they perpetuate its illusion of safety. The lucky ones are like the Jim who goes fishing in Alaska and then returns home. Others are encapsulated in the poem ''In the Suburbs,'' whose six lines are like a pendant to ''American Poetry'':

> There's no way out.
> You were born to waste your life.
> You were born to this middleclass life
>
> As others before you
> Were born to walk in procession
> To the temple, singing (*Open Road* 12; *CP* 136)

Stephen Stepanchev saw ''a new realism'' that asks us to ''cultivate our gardens in full awareness of the imminence of death'' (*American Poetry since 1945*, 199) Simpson's poems respect unfinished lives full of possibilities but rue the substitutions for fulfillment.

There You Are renders our accelerated times (''More things happening every second/in New York, than Lutsk for a year'' [''Al and Beth,'' *There You Are* 12]) by spotlighting individuals, especially workingpeople: Uncle Al who worked in a drugstore and lived on Kingston Avenue, Brooklyn, all his life with the wife he chose, oyster-eyed Walter, the office manager, a dental assistant; a yardman; a bayman. He writes of divorced and alcoholic Mike, who married a German woman so that she could gain citizenship, later married an heiress, still later confessed to the speaker his little betrayals, gratitude, and affection: ''Where we live/there are no legends, only gossip'' (''The Cabin,''*There You Are* 41). Imagination and language exalt these subjects. In the last poem, ''A Clearing,'' set in Australia, the poet ceases to exist as a vaster cosmos speaks through him.

The collections of 1990 and 1995 continue the use of narrative structure and simple, proselike diction, but the poems are elliptical, allusive, and they find epiphanies in daily life. Matter-of-fact storyteller Simpson manipulates complex tonalities and astonishing juxtapositions, elusive moments, remembered phrases—and the resulting collage reflects back, distilled, who we are as a people.

CRITICAL RECEPTION

Eleven reviews greeted *The Arrivistes*, few neutral. Gerard Previn Meyer praised the poems as dramatic, controlled in their irony; Randall Jarrell found them outstandingly promising and called the poet ''genuinely wild''; a single carping comment referred to ''meretricious doggerel''; and Babette Deutsch, assuming the Jamaican poet was black, suggested that he learn from Villon to distinguish vulgarity from "healthy coarseness." Later (1966), Seamus Heaney noted that "Carentan O Carentan" "accumulates menace yet proceeds with all the grace of a minuet"; and C. B. Cox, also singling out "Carentan O Carentan," referred to "clear images which confuse and disturb."

Reviewers of *Good News of Death* emphasized technical virtuosity. William Arrowsmith, noting excitement and promise, found traditional elements worked into personal mythology and praised the book in *Hudson Review*. John Ciardi saw beyond seeming simplicities and felt the "miracle" of "gooseflesh." In 1969 Richard Howard referred to his admiration for this book twenty years earlier.

With *A Dream of Governors*, command of emotional range was recognized by Anthony Hecht, Daniel Hoffman (who called the book "durable"), and other contemporary poets. Robert Bly had already noted Simpson's "wry and compassionate view of people, which does not exclude humor or tenderness" (Lazer 247); he went on to praise the "hallucinatory power" of "The Runner" and lauded the poet's courage in dealing with war's atrocities—and integrating ghastly facts into mundane settings. Also lauded is integration of American history into the current scene: "In his tragic feeling he is alone in his generation."

That *At the End of the Open Road* constitutes a stylistic break has been generally noted, as has its attempt to define America: formative traditions, myths, geography, and people. William Stafford called the book "a resounding achievement" and Duane Locke focused on the subjective "I." Influence of, and distinctiveness from, other poets, including Bly, James Wright, and W. S. Merwin, were pointed out. Ronald Moran and others praised restrained diction and acute sense of timing, especially effective in flat statements. Richard Howard marveled that "a poet could speak so harshly of these States and still be prized by them" (Lazer 226; from *Alone with America*).

Donald Hall, reviewing *Selected Poems*, called Simpson "the Columbus of an inward continent," and James Dickey lauded him for seeing it all, "not just the promise, not just the loss and the 'betrayal of the American ideal,' . . . but the whole 'complex fate,' the difficult and agonizing *meaning* of being an American," when a man may be "all his life comfortable and miserable, taken care of and baffled" (Lazer 75). Seamus Heaney finds reconciliation of Paleface and Redskin in a position he terms "blood brother" (Lazer 80–82).

Ian Hamilton called *Adventures of the Letter I* Simpson's best book to date, dispensing with "Blyish wistfulness," its style suited to preoccupation with origin and ancestors—and with "his own ambivalent Americanism"; the conversational manner is "disciplined both by a fairly strict intelligence and by a responsible regard for the line by line shaping of each poem," (Lazer, 83). Grevel Lindop found directly political poems less successful—and the poet aware of his own flaws, including a distrust of ideas, but also honest, humorous, commonsensible, and technically adroit (Lazer 85–86). Terry Eagleton found "slightly disappointing" the criticism of American society "enlivened with a wry, defeatist, Jewish humour" and felt that the "almost pastoral directness and lyricism" conventionally opposing nature and culture resulted in "occasional lack of energy" (Lazer 87). Dave Smith noted the dream-logic and "heroic quest for an idealized America" (Lazer 89) and the achievement of a resolved and stable self in "Sacred Objects." Reviewer Anthony Rudolf says of the poems in *North of Jamaica* that "roots are at one with routes" (Lazer 105).

Comparing *Searching for the Ox* to stories by I. B. Singer or a novel by Saul Bellow, its style "plain, direct and relaxed" (Lazer 117), Peter Stitt comments on the quest to unite sensual and intellectual motives. Grotesque and appealing peer-examples are described lovingly and a direct parallel—man of the world who wants to study Torah—appears in "Baruch"; a solution is celebrated in the title poem; and the book conveys "the subtle assurance of a poet superbly in control of his craft" (Lazer 119). Stanley Plumly notes that Simpson becomes an actor in his own narratives about parallel island lives (Long Island and Jamaica), and the title poem "arrives where it started, knowing the place, as always, for the first time" (Lazer 123). In England, C. B. Cox called the book "the best book of poetry published in 1976" (Lazer 124).

"Essentially urban and Jewish," Paul Breslin said in reviewing *Caviare at the Funeral*, whose poems achieve effect "by concision, exactness of detail and a subtle heightening of language at the moments of greatest intensity" (Lazer 137). Here "Russia means suffering and persecution but it is also the 'far place the soul comes from,' more richly human than America" (138). Those who define soul are described in language "savagely banal" (Lazer 139)—with perhaps too ready judgment when the poet misses the grief. But G. E. Murray sees the same elements, even the roadside junkyards, shopping malls, and real estate agencies, as transmuted into radiance (Lazer 141–42). Douglas Dunn finds narratives seeming to follow the advice of a Chekhov character: "Keep it short and skip the psychology" (Lazer 144). For Peter Makick the book shows "an ability to accommodate the humorous, the terrible and the lyrical almost simultaneously" (Lazer 147); absurdist drama leaves ample room for the respondent. Makuck is reminded of one of Pascal's pensées: that the only thing that consoles us for our miseries is distraction—which is itself our greatest misery (Lazer 150).

The poet's "deadpan" attitude in *The Best Hour of the Night* and the selected poems in *People Live Here* is noted by Richard Tillinghast, who finds Simpson "by turns satirical, bemused, sorrowing, disdainful, sympathetic, wry" (Lazer 159)—engaged but alien, and he "does not avoid the iffy area of morality" (Lazer 160). Richard Howard, a Columbia classmate who has followed Simpson's career since first revelation of "all the stunning insolence of talent" (Lazer 215), interprets the doubleness another way: "war poetry as a version of pastoral, and his poems about America . . . as a collection of military tattoos" (Lazer 210). According to Alan Williamson, who has followed "the correct but amazingly precocious young Briton from Jamaica" as he became a "shrill convert to the school of Robert Bly'' and evolved into the ''wonderful poet'' who ''tells the whole truth about the mean emotional bargains people strike with themselves'' (Lazer 164), most of the suburbanites are sympathetic in their discontent. All Simpson's work, says M. L. Rosenthal, is ''based on the lesson that the powers that be, on whatever side, care nothing for the 'man on the ledge' '' (Lazer 167). Simpson has the talent, says Yohma Gray, ''to generalize his experience without diminishing its concreteness'' (Lazer 180); his art ''imposes order from within on chaos without, gives meaning to the apparently meaningless, suggests fresh vantage points from which to probe experience'' (Lazer 191). David Wojahn calls him ''one of our most moral and convincingly humanitarian writers'' (Lazer 19).

BIBLIOGRAPHY

Works by Louis Simpson

Poetry

The Arrivistes: Poems, 1940–49. Privately printed in Paris; distributed by Fine Editions Press, New York, 1949.

Good News of Death and Other Poems (in *Poets of Today II*). Ed. John Hall Wheelock. New York: Charles Scribner's Sons, 1955.

A Dream of Governors. Middletown, CT: Wesleyan University Press, 1959.

At the End of the Open Road. Middletown, CT: Wesleyan University Press, 1963.

Selected Poems. New York: Harcourt, Brace, and World, 1965; London: Oxford University Press, 1966.

Adventures of the Letter I. New York, Evanston, IL, San Francisco, and London: Harper and Row, 1971; paperback, 1974; London, Bombay, and Melbourne: Oxford University Press, 1971.

Searching for the Ox. New York: Morrow, 1976.

Armidale. Brockport, NY: BOA Editions, 1979a.

Out of Season. Deerfield, MA: Deerfield Press, 1979; Dublin: Gallery Press, 1979b.

Caviare at the Funeral. New York and Toronto: Franklin Watts, 1980.

The Best Hour of the Night. New Haven, CT, and New York: Ticknor and Fields, 1983a.

People Live Here: Selected Poems, 1948–1983. Brockport, NY: BOA Editions, 1983; London: Secker and Warburg, 1985b.

Collected Poems. New York: Paragon House, 1988.

In the Room We Share. New York: Paragon House, 1990.

There You Are. Brownsville, OR: Story Line Press, 1995.

Literary Criticism

James Hogg: A Critical Study. New York: St. Martin's Press, 1962; Edinburgh: Oliver and Boyd, 1962.

''The Ghost of Delmore Schwartz.'' *New York Times Magazine* (December 7, 1975): 52.

Three on the Tower: The Lives and Works of Ezra Pound, T. S. Eliot, and William Carlos Williams. New York: Morrow, 1975.

A Revolution in Taste: Studies of Dylan Thomas, Allen Ginsberg, Sylvia Plath, and Robert Lowell. New York: Macmillan, 1978; also published as *Studies of Dylan Thomas, Allen Ginsberg, Sylvia Plath, and Robert Lowell.* London: Macmillan, 1979.

A Company of Poets. Ann Arbor: University of Michigan Press, 1981.

The Character of the Poet. Ann Arbor: University of Michigan Press, 1986.

Selected Prose. New York: Paragon House, 1989.

Ships Going into the Blue: Essays and Notes on Poetry. Ann Arbor: University of Michigan Press, 1994.

Translations

"Four Poems by Marceline Desbordes-Valmore." *The New Criterion* 14: 3 (November 1995), 34.

"Robert Desnos: Seven Poems Translated by Louis Simpson." *American Poetry Review* 25: 1 (January–February 1996a), 25–26, 29.

"Stephane Mallarme: Four Poems Translated by Louis Simpson." *American Poetry Review* 25:1 (January–February. 1996b), 23–25.

Modern Poets of France with English Translations. Brownsville, OR: Story Line Press, forthcoming.

Fiction

Riverside Drive. New York: Atheneum, 1962.

Autobiography

North of Jamaica. New York, Evanston, IL, San Francisco, and London: Harper and Row, 1972.

"Louis Simpson, 1923–   ." *Contemporary Authors Autobiography Series.* Vol. 4. Ed. Adele Sarkissian. Detroit: Gale Research, 1986, 285–299.

The King My Father's Wreck. Brownsville, OR: Storyline Press, 1995.

Anthologies

With Donald Hall and Robert Pack, eds. *New Poets of England and America.* Introduction by Robert Frost. Cleveland and New York: World (Meridian), 1957; Canada: Nelson, Foster, and Scott, 1957.

An Introduction to Poetry. New York: St. Martin's, 1967; 2d ed., 1972; London and Melbourne: Macmillan, 1968.

Sound Recordings

Physical Universe. Washington, DC: Watershed Tapes, 1986.

Spoken Arts Treasury of 100 Modern American Poets Reading Their Poems. Vol. 15. New Rochelle, NY: Spoken Arts.

Today's Poets. Vol. 1. New York: Scholastic.

Yale Series of Recorded Poets. Carillon.

Works about Louis Simpson

Arrowsmith, William. Rev. of *Good News of Death.* *Hudson Review* 9 (Summer 1956): 291–93.

Bly, Robert. "A Wrong Turning in American Poetry." *Choice* No. 3 (1963), 33–47.

Burt, Stephen. "Putting Down Smoke." (rev. of *Ships Going into the Blue*). *Times Literary Supplement*, No. 4813 (June 30, 1995), 25.

Ciardi, John. Rev. of *Good News of Death*. *New York Times Book Review* (August 14, 1955): 4.

Cox, C. B. Rev. of *Searching for the Ox*. *Critical Quarterly* 19 (Spring 1977):3.

Cox, James M. "Re-Viewing Louis Simpson." *Southern Review* 31:1 (Winter 1995), 180–90.

Deutsch, Babette. Rev. of *The Arrivistes*. *Yale Review* 39 (Winter 1950): 363.

Dickey, James. "In the Presence of Anthologies" and "Louis Simpson" (the latter a review of *Selected Poems*). *Babel to Byzantium: Poets and Poetry Now. Byzantium* New York: Grosset and Dunlap, 1967; Universal Library paperback, 1971, 3–13, 195–97.

Dobyns, Stephen. "Will You Listen for a Minute?" (rev. of *In the Room We Share.) New York Times Book Review* (September 2, 1990), 5.

Duncan, Erika. "Once an Outsider, Poet Unravels His Life." *New York Sunday Times* (Long Island edition) (September 15, 1996), LI 1:1, 15.

Gunn, Thom, and Ted Hughes, eds. *Five American Poets: Edgar Bowers, Howard Nemerov, Hyam Plutzik, Louis Simpson, William Stafford*. London: Faber and Faber, 1963.

Hall, Donald. Rev. of *Selected Poems*. *New York Herald Tribune Book Week* (December 5, 1964): 44.

Heaney, Seamus. Rev. of *Selected Poems*. *London Times Literary Supplement* (June 9 1966): 512.

Hecht, Anthony. Rev. of *A Dream of Governors*. *Hudson Review* 12: 4 (Winter 1959–60).

Hirsch, Edward. "Better to Stay Than to Leave" (rev. of *Collected Poems*). *New York Times Book Review*, (November 13, 1988), 32.

Hoffman, Daniel. Rev. of *A Dream of Governors*. *Sewanee Review* 68 (Autumn 1960): 677–79.

Howard, Richard. "Louis Simpson." *Alone with America: Essays on the Art of Poetry in the United States Since 1950*. New York: Atheneum, 1969, 451–70.

Hungerford, Edward, ed. *Poets in Progress: Critical Prefaces to Thirteen Modern American Poets*. Evanston, IL: Northwestern University Press, 1967.

Jarrell, Randall. "Poetry Unlimited" (rev. of *The Arrivistes) Partisan Review* 17 (February 1950): 189.

Lazer, Hank, ed. *On Louis Simpson: Depths Beyond Happiness*. Ann Arbor: University of Michigan Press, 1988. Includes 48 reviews, 11 essays, and a conclusion; 389 pp. with bibliography and index.

Locke, Duane. Rev. of *At the End of the Open Road*. *dust* 1:3 (Fall 1964): 67–69.

"Louis (Aston Marantz) Simpson. 1923–   ." *Contemporary Literary Criticism*. Vol. 32. Ed. Jean C. Stine and Daniel G. Marowski. Detroit: Gale Research. 1985.

Mason, David. "Louis Simpson's Singular Charm." *Hudson Review* (Autumn 1995), 499–507.

McDowell, Robert. "A Sky Lit with Artillery: The Poems of Louis Simpson." *Hudson Review* 42: 1 (Spring 1989), 158–64.

Meyer, Gerard Previn. "A Sampling of Pound and Modern Man" (rev. of *The Arrivistes*). *Saturday Review* (24 December 1949): 14.

Moran, Ronald. *Louis Simpson.* New York: Twayne, 1972.

Pacernick, Gary. "Louis Simpson." *Memory and Fire: Ten American Jewish Poets.* New York: Peter Lang, 1989.

Perkins, David. *A History of Modern Poetry: Modernism and After.* Cambridge and London: Harvard University Press, 1987.

Pratt, William. Rev. of *Ships Going into the Blue. World Literature Today* 69: 3 (Summer 1995), 594.

Rev. of *The King My Father's Wreck. Virginia Quarterly Review* 71: 3 (Summer 1995), SS 89.

Richardson, Alice. "Jamaican Consulate Honors Louis Simpson, Pulitzer Poet." *Amsterdam News,* 28: 3 (May 18, 1996).

Roberson, William H. *Louis Simpson: A Reference Guide.* Boston: G. K. Hall, 1980.

Solomon, Charles. Rev. of *The King My Father's Wreck. Los Angeles Times Book Review* 13: 2 (April 30, 1995).

Stitt, Peter. "Louis Simpson's Best Hour." *Georgia Review* 37 (Fall 1983), 662–675.

Stepanchev, Stephen. "Louis Simpson." *American Poetry since 1945: A Critical Survey.* New York, Evanston, IL, and London: Harper and Row, 1965; Harper Colophon paperback, 1967, 198–200.

Taylor, Henry. "Great Experiments: The Poetry of Louis Simpson." *Hollins Critic* 27: 3 (June 1990), 1–12.

MYRA SKLAREW   (1934–   )

Joshua Saul Beckman

BIOGRAPHY

Myra Sklarew was born in Baltimore, December 18, 1934, to Jewish-American
parents, Samuel Myer Weisberg and Anne Wolpe Weisberg. Her father, whose
first language was Yiddish, was a biochemist and "something of a poet himself." He was brought up in an Orthodox and Yiddish-speaking Rumanian family in Boston. Her mother, the daughter of Lithuanian *Mitnagdim* (holymen—
Hasids), was pivotal in shaping Sklarew's Jewish identity and zeal for learning
through her own devotion to books, learning, and Jewish tradition.

One of three daughters, Myra Sklarew spent much of her early life ill and at
home from school. There she read her way through her parents' library and
began to discover and express through poetry and essays the world that was
beginning to take shape within her. Her mother, like all the daughters in that
family, had been taken out of school at the age of thirteen to go to work, and
spent much of her adult life setting up Jewish libraries in synagogues wherever
she lived. She inspired in Sklarew a belief in learning and the notion that we
must find our own way to becoming educated.

When she was eight years old, her third grade teacher "often went to the
window to cry." Whether this was because she had lost brothers during World
War II or for other reasons was never clear. But Sklarew discovered that she
could assuage her teacher's sorrow by writing stories, often animating the natural
world (ants who shielded themselves from the weather by crawling under mush-
rooms or mysterious, miniature people). Here the powerful impetus to use language to shape story took root.

At age eleven, Sklarew attended an accelerated summer program at Johns
Hopkins University, and seven years later, in 1952, she left for Tufts College

in Medford, Massachusetts, where she earned her bachelor of science degree in biology. There she first encountered a small community of people interested in poetry and a teacher who was to have a profound effect upon her as a poet, the late New England poet John Holmes. In 1954, *Five New Poets* was published at Tufts, an anthology that included her first published poems. While at Tufts, she married and, after graduating, went on to work as a research assistant at Yale University School of Medicine's Department of Neurophysiology, studying frontal lobe function and memory in Rhesus monkeys. In 1957 her daughter Deborah was born, and within two years, her son Eric. After receiving an M.A. degree from the Writing Seminars at Johns Hopkins University in 1970, she taught at George Washington University and American University. From 1970 to 1987, Myra Sklarew served on the faculty of American University. She was president of the Corporation of Yaddo, an artists' community established in 1900 in Saratoga Springs, New York, from 1987 to 1991. In 1992, she returned to Washington and to American University's Department of Literature, where she served as department chair from June 1, 1995, to July 31, 1996. She is currently professor of literature.

MAJOR WORKS AND THEMES

Though Myra Sklarew wrote and published for a number of years—poetry, essays, prose, science articles—it was not until the publication of her first full-length collection, *From the Backyard of the Diaspora* (1976, 1981) that she made explicit the central issue of her work. The notion of home and what it is to be at home in a place works in concert with the resonance of dispersion, exile, and return, a major theme throughout Jewish history. Just as the giving of the commandments at Sinai is seen as an event that continues to take place, so that all who have ever lived as well as all who shall ever live experience it as their own, so in her work does Sklarew view her ancestral history as part of her own contemporary experience. Much of the struggle—as in Jacob's wrestling with the angel—has to do with the reclamation of the past in her work and the admonition of contemporary life, which constantly urges one to forget the past.

In *The Science of Goodbyes* (1982, 1983), which takes its title from Mandelstam's "Tristia" ("I have studied the science of goodbyes") Sklarew begins to solidify her ongoing struggle with history. In her work she is constantly aware of the impact of memory and the importance of being one who remembers. The cry of post-Holocaust Jewry has been not to forget. Always near, but never finding the moment of freedom from the past, in *The Science of Goodbyes*, she writes:

> I seldom mention Rome nor do I own the sea
> or history or my language, but I poke

> in the ashes of old words like a finger
> sorting through the basket of buttons ("Because I am a Woman" 29)

In the same way that the diaspora has grown to be a home, the sorting through ashes has become a way of life for Sklarew.

Both *The Travels of the Itinerant Freda Aharon* (1985)—a female, contemporary version of the travels of Benjamin of Tudela, a wanderer who went in search of Jewish communities during the Middle Ages—and *Altamira* (1987) mark a midpoint in Sklarew's work. In these works, her concerns as a writer and as a Jew come together in the form of poetry. She expresses what it is to be a person whose "way to be alive in the world" is to write. The protagonist in *The Travels* who bears Sklarew's Hebrew name never actually leaves her home but instead explores the world of her couch and her navel, trying to grasp the "diversities of kingdoms" within the confinement of her rooms. In *Altamira*, she broadens her scope somewhat by not only working through her relation to self and place but also moving on to investigate other writers' works and lives. Many (if not all) of the poems in *Altamira* are about coming to a sense of the forms of writing (as prayer, as commentary, as song) and realizing these forms as part of the daily life of the world.

For Jews, finding a home in the late twentieth century means coming to terms with the notion that the Earth is filled with the recently murdered, and to make a home anywhere is to make one over a sacred burial site. This, our curse and our fate, is a primary concern of Sklarew's as she navigates her readers through a life that is surprisingly met at the most intimate of times with the unbelievable familiarity of genocide. In the title poem in one of her most recent books, *Lithuania: New and Selected Poems* (1995, 1997), Sklarew finds a place for the coming together of her many concerns. This poem is the manifestation of years of interest in the physiology of memory. As the poem makes its way through the graveyard of facts, it becomes clear that the notions of what we remember and what we are not able to remember are part of a complex web. In this poem and in many others in this collection, Sklarew concerns herself with the notion of a homeland and of the return to homeland. Yet she denies any sense of permanency as she did first in *From the Backyard of the Diaspora*. "For Jewish history is contained in time, not in space. Time is our real homeland," says Sklarew. As Cynthia Ozick once wrote to her, in regard to her concern for the transmission of Judaism to her children after her mother's death: "We are poured like wine without its vessel all the way from Sinai to here" (private letter).

CRITICAL RECEPTION

Although not widely critiqued, Sklarew's work has been given favorable notices by discerning critics. In her review of *Backyard of the Diaspora*, Julia Morrison observes: "These terse, brief poems, with a minimum of punctuation, are arresting and often very effective in their overtones and reverberations. . . . Sklarew uses the Jewish experience without melodrama or sentimentality in some of poems . . . to which she brings added irony.'' Of the same collection of poems, a critic in *Choice* remarks: ''Many readers may find that one of Sklarew's unifying strengths is a sense of the past, of mankind's pilgrimage, the Jewish experience, and growth. I like best her direct approach and unexpected imagery.''

It is clear, however, that Sklarew's sense of Jewish identity and the importance of cultural inheritance, which has been blighted by genocide, are a major part of her work. The transmission of this inheritance serves as an act of defiance against the horrors of the past but also gives courage to those who must face the ambiguities of the future of the Jewish people.

BIBLIOGRAPHY

Works by Myra Sklarew

In the Basket of the Blind. Cherry Valley, NY: Cherry Valley Editions, 1975.

From the Backyard of the Diaspora. Washington, D.C., and San Francisco: Dryad Press, 1976, 1981.

Blessed Art Thou, No-One. Wollaston, MA: Chowder Chapbooks, 1982.

The Science of Goodbyes. Athens: University of Georgia Press, 1982, 1983.

The Travels of the Itinerant Freda Aharon. New York: Watermark Press, 1985.

Altamira. Washington, DC: Washington Writers Publishing House, 1987.

Like a Field Riddled by Ants. (Fiction). Providence, RI: Lost Roads, 1988.

Eating the White Earth. Tel Aviv, (new and selected poetry in Hebrew translation). Israel: Tag, 1994.

Lithuania: New and Selected Poems. Washington, DC, and Falls Church, VA: Azul Editions, 1995, 1997.

Holocaust and the Construction of Memory (forthcoming).

Works about Myra Sklarew

Hayerushalmi, Levy Yitzhak. ''A Burden of Exile and an Expedition to Judaism and Mysticism: Myra Sklarew—*Eating the White Earth.*'' *Davar,* September 23, 1994.

Jason, Philip K. ''A Poet's Parables in Prose.'' Rev. of *Like a Field Riddled by Ants. Washington Jewish Week,* July 21, 1988.

Morrison, Julia. Rev. of *From the Backyard of the Diaspora. Library Journal,* August 1976, 1640.

Prothro, Nancy. Rev. of *From the Backyard of the Diaspora. Sibyl-Child* 2: 2, 1977.

Ramsey, Paul. ''Faith and Form: Some American Poetry of 1976.'' Rev. of *From the Backyard of the Diaspora. Sewanee Review,* Summer 1977.

Rev. of *Altamira. American Book Review,* September-October, 1988.

Rev. of *From the Backyard of the Diaspora. Choice,* November 1976, 1140.

GERALD STERN (1925–)

Harriet L. Parmet

BIOGRAPHY

Gerald Stern, American poet and essayist, was born February 22, 1925, in Pittsburgh to a second-generation, East European, working-class Jewish family whose original name was the Russian Dogipyat. His maternal grandfather, whose childhood influence on Stern was very strong and accounted for many of his Jewish attitudes that he holds to this very day, had been a rabbi and shochet (a kosher animal slaughterer) in Bialystok, Poland, and in Pittsburgh after immigrating to the United States. Stern's father, Harry, the son of a Ukrainian immigrant, was a clothing retailer; Stern's mother was Ida Barach Stern. The death of his only sibling, Sylvia, at the age of nine from spinal meningitis impacted greatly on Stern, who was eight years old at the time. His mother, after a prolonged and excessive period of grieving, refused to accept her daughter's death and became a chronic depressive. Stern became the outlet for Ida Stern's shattered affection. The poet tells of his mother's taking him to her bed, weeping and crying "Sylvia, Sylvia, Sylvia." He did not ultimately reject this role, assuming the embodiment for her loss, while searching for an outlet to grieve himself. Poetic expression for this loss is to be found in "Joseph's Pockets" (*The Red Coal*, 1981) and in "Sylvia" (*Bread Without Sugar*, 1992), and Sylvia is referenced in "The Expulsion" (*Leaving Another Kingdom* 1984).

The Pittsburgh public library, the city streets, the public schools, and the river provided the venue for Stern's early education. His college years were spent at the University of Pittsburgh, where he studied literature, graduating with a B.A. in English in 1947. Subsequently, he took a year off to read. Specializing in counterintelligence, he served a year in the U.S. Army from 1946 to early 1947. In 1949 Stern entered Columbia's graduate program in English, earning an M.A.

in 1950. Stern then toured Europe with two fellow poets from Pitt, Jack Gilbert and Richard Hagely, who would remain lifelong friends. He returned to Columbia to work for a Ph.D. in literature. The bureaucracy, intellectual pretense, and dispassion of academe prompted Stern to leave the program.

Stern married Patricia Miller on September 12, 1952. (They had two children, David and Rachel and were divorced in the late 1980s.) He and Patricia traveled in Europe for three years, making Glasgow their base, where Stern taught high school English. Home from Europe, Stern's first college teaching appointment was at Temple University in 1957. For the next twenty years he balanced a virtually unrecognized writing career with teaching English at Indiana University of Pennsylvania and Somerset County College in New Jersey and guest professorships at Sarah Lawrence College, Columbia University, University of Pittsburgh, Princeton, and New York University. He held a tenured position at the University of Iowa Writers' Workshop (probably the leading creative writing program in the United States), teaching poetry from 1982 until his retirement in 1995.

Gerald Stern has published nine major books of poetry. It took twenty years before Stern's *Lucky Life* won the Lamont Poetry Prize in 1977; he was fifty-two years old. *The Red Coal* received the Melville Caine Award in 1982. A dramatic poem, "Father Guzmann," won the Bernard F. Connors Prize given by the *Paris Review. Leaving Another Kingdom* gained a 1991 Pulitzer Prize nomination, and *Bread Without Sugar*, the 1993 Poetry Prize. Additionally, he is the winner of the Bess Hoskin Award for Poetry, the Paterson Poetry Prize, and the Jerome J. Shestack Poetry Prize, as well as a Guggenheim Fellowship and grants from the National Endowment for the Arts. Assuredly, he has won his place among our principal American poets, receiving the Ruth Lilly Poetry Prize in the spring of 1996. As Stern would in all probability say: "lucky life is like that." He does say, however, in a poem from *The Red Coal* "that nothing was wasted, that the freezing nights were not a waste, that the long dull walks" and what he felt of boredom were not wasted on him. Out of those "long dull walks" has come a poetry of hard-won blessings, of character, generosity, and wisdom. Of Stern's artistry, Muriel Rukeyser has said, it is the poetry of a "grown man" and "a profoundly realized life."

MAJOR WORKS AND THEMES

Continuity, tradition, myth, all interwoven, interconnected, constitute one of Stern's central themes. The Jewish sources of his affectionate reverence for heritage, culture, and learnedness are accented by strong Hebrew biblical echoes in the phrasing and structure of his poems. Mystical and spiritual overtones are dominant in his poetry. Stern has been likened to the Cabalists of old rather than the Aggadic rabbis, since his imagination is not essentially moral, although the message is there. In an interview (*Missouri Review*) with Sanford Pinsker, Stern says that he wants to teach "about how to live, how to survive" (32). There is a subtlety to Stern's social, psychological, and political agenda. Overarching these issues is spiritual survival. The past for Stern provides a transcendence through spiritual connection.

Nostalgia is the key to unlock the redemptive past, as Stern defines it. The impulse behind all art is trivial, sentimental nostalgia. This essential nostalgia is "a search for the permanent." It is "a combination of absence and presence, the far and the near, the lost and found." It is that charged memory in which are found the unbearable pain of separation and the sweetness of remembered union ("Notes from the River").

Nostalgia reminds us of lost perfection, as we envision it at the extremes of experience, in garden beginnings and messianic finality. Paradise, however lost, as well as suffering are fortuitous; knowledge of this provides the base for our humanity. Stern identifies with Ovid as the model of the suffering poet in "The Same Moon above Us" (*Paradise Poems*, 19–22). Since paradise is the construct of humankind, buried deep within us, it can be recovered through participation in recurrence, possible when we do not feel cut off from the past.

The garden is often the center for a Stern poem, emblematic of both the permanent perfection of Eden and the cyclical recurrence of it in death and rebirth. Here the gardener-poet recognizes that he is not Adam but man: "I walk/ like man, like a human being, through the curled flowers" ("Two Trees," *Paradise Poems*, 69).

Transcendence is the reinvention of paradise, a redemptive interval of harmony when the distance between subject and object, past and present, the visible and the historic is annulled. It is also a lament, offering catharsis: "Lament, lament, my father and I are leaving Paradise" ("The Expulsion," *Leaving Another Kingdom*, 180, 181). Yet we must prepare for this, through intellect, emotion, memory—everything we have and are, a bearing and a dissolution in the presence of an unnamed conviction. Through poetry, the poet receives, records, and makes the supranatural happen in the poem. In Stern the transcendence is often achieved through the fusion of the visible world with the art and culture of the past. His poetic double dances to the tune of Magritte, Oscar Schlemmer, and Pablo Picasso:

> I dance on the road and on the river and
> in the wet garden, all the time living in Crete
> and pre-war Poland and outer Zimbabwe,
> as through my fingers and my sparkling hair
> the morning passes, first the three loud calls
> of the bluejay, then the white door slamming,
> then the voices rising and falling in sudden harmony. ("Magritte Dancing,"
>   *Leaving Another Kingdom*, 79)

Related motifs present in Stern are death, burial, and rebirth; the angel; music; the dream and the secret; friendship; the idea of America; the Holocaust and his Jewishness.

Gerald Stern expounds on his view of himself as being an outsider in exile:

I'm in exile from the Christian world insofar as I'm a Jew and I'm in exile from the Jewish world insofar as I've broken away from Judaism. I'm in exile from the bourgeois Jewish world from Pittsburgh that I was expected to flourish in because when I was 19 or 20 I rented a room and started to read books and became a crazy poet. . . . And I feel I'm in exile from the connection or community that I had with my sister. . . . so often I feel that I'm writing for her and about her, and that my life is a debt that I owe to her. I'm also in exile from the six million Jews who were killed. Now, at my age, I'm studying Yiddish, which is an expression of that exile and an attempt to redeem that exile simultaneously. (Moyers 379).

On poetry and religion Stern states that "my poetry is a kind of religion for me. It's a way of seeking redemption for myself, but just on the page. It is finally, a way of understanding things so that they can be reconciled, explained, justified, redeemed" (Moyers 383).

Stern's meditative essay "What Is the Sabbath?" brings the distillate of his Jewish self into focus. Stern begins, "I think of lying on my back listening to Brahms and looking at the cracks in the ceiling. Or it could be Vivaldi, or Schumann. I am a recumbent angel" (17). The Sabbath foreshadows paradise, in which Stern's shoes are off, he wears the thinnest of T-shirts, and there are bird sounds. He announces that the Sabbath as a day for man is a "dream . . . a work of art . . . a poem" (19). Stern's yearning for a more attractive world, his obsession with messianism (17, 18), his sharing the fate of his fellow Jews, and, most of all, remembering place him within the Jewish experience.

Sanford Pinsker ("Weeping" 194) considers "Behaving like a Jew" a signature piece. In this poem, Stern stops his car for a "dead opossum" on the road and takes a negative position against a culture in which "the spirit of Lindbergh" dominates everything. Bill Moyers questions the meaning of "I am going to behave like a Jew." Stern replies,

I'm declaring an act of mourning. In staring into that opossum's eye, I became that opossum and, identifying with him, I became a Jew. I identified with his whiskers, his round belly, his little dancing feet. Maybe I'm also claiming something for Jews that shouldn't be claimed for them, but for all thinking people, all feeling people. Maybe I'm claiming feeling for the Jew even though there are as many unfeeling Jews as there are unfeeling gentiles. I'm sensitive about arrogating feeling to the Jews, but at that point in that poem, I was claiming feeling, tenderness, elegy, love, memory—memory for that absurd little animal. (386)

Stern saw the Jew as ethnic victim and Charles Lindbergh as politically right-wing, even fascist, an isolationist who urged the United States to remain neutral toward the Nazis before World War II.

Stern, according to Richard Chess "is the post-Holocaust Jew standing up against the forces of evil residing not in man's technological inventions but in the very spirit of man himself. Stern stands determinedly opposed to a society that chooses to ignore the consequences of its behavior, a society that indulges in a 'philosophical understanding of carnage' '' (152).

Of the Holocaust, Stern said that ''it belongs to me, the particular tragedy of the Jewish people, an extension of persecution and man's inane stupidity'' (personal communications, August 7, 1996). There is a strong sense of guilt about having lived in the United States during that horrendous time in safety and in peace, evident in ''The Dancing'' and in ''Hot Dog.'' Stern sees poetry as one way of opening dark curtains and making the light come. He still views himself as a scholar manqué. His love affair with Judaism is very deep and abiding— a special way of looking at life and human existence. The biblical cadences, the rhythm of prayer, the rage of Amos, Ezekiel, and Isaiah, the exquisiteness of the Psalms have affected him greatly. Stern views ''Jewishness'' as being possessed of curiosity, compassion, justice, kindness, and affection. Historical connectiveness is paramount with the Jewish people demonstrative of a dramatic mission and a unique direction. There is a quality, an essence, to being Jewish. Poland of old, that awful place of Jewish decimation, is a metaphor for a world no longer extant and appears in many of his poems, notably, ''Bread without Sugar.''

In ''Four Sad Poems on the Delaware'' (*Lucky Life*), Stern writes about four plants growing along the towpath in back of his home. The fourth one was a black locust, a species of a tree of the poor. It is used for fence posts, torn down, replaced by other trees—because of its rigidity and short life. To Stern this is the most beautiful of trees—blooming in extraordinary color and possessing an incomparable smell. In this poem, Stern compares himself to the locust, describing himself as ''growing more and more Jewish as his limbs weaken'' (25). Even though the Jews are no longer locusts, he remembers them that way. That's his kind of Jew, at times abandoned but always tested. ''Becoming an 'Old Jew'—being able presumably to trace his troubles back to the destruction of the Temples—is to live both in the world and within history. It also means knowing the secrets of life'' (Pinsker, ''Weeping'' 173).

In *Leaving Another Kingdom*, Jewish wonder, mysticism, and philosophical speculation are artfully conveyed: ''The Blessed,'' ''Three Skies,'' and ''Three Tears.'' Biblical themes emerge repeatedly: ''The Sensitive Knife,'' ''Strauss Park,'' ''Joseph's Pockets,'' and ''Angel Poem.'' All of his Holocaust poetry is an anguished response. ''The War against the Jews,'' a conscious appropriation of Lucy Davidowicz's pioneering study, describes a wood carving, set in a Polish town square, of Jews about to be arrested by a German soldier. Stern begs for a reversal of history for the Jews and for the soldier. This cry, desperate and pitiful, cannot intervene to save either the Jews or the soldier. ''He was carved while he could still remember his mother's garden/ How glad he was to go to Poland/How young he felt in his first pair of boots'' (14) are the innocent words of the young soldier.

Another leap into the irreversible fantastic is ''Soap.'' This poem is offensive to those who bespeak a respectful silence. To write of green Jews and blue

Jews—human beings metamorphosed into fancy, beautiful soap—is to pile the grotesque on top of grotesque. It has images so stark, so shrill that Richard Chess brands the entire poem a selfish act of invention, an easy method of purging oneself of guilt (152). On the other hand, the "weeping and wailing" of this poem, its song of lament (a constant Stern theme), are for those "who remember the eighteenth century." "Those European Jews, born in 1865 or 1870," are the "ones who listened / to heavenly voices, they were lied to and cheated" (*Leaving Another Kingdom*, 152). The poem is also for Stern's alter ego, the secret sharer and blood brother, who was born in 1925 in Poland, deprived of his books, like the victims of the Holocaust, unable to run away and live.

In the powerful "Adler" (*Leaving Another Kingdom* 177–79), Stern authoritatively writes about the life of the Jewish-American immigrants of the Lower East Side of New York and about King Lear. When he presents the Holocaust—comparing certain characters and actions in the Shakespearean tragedy as adapted for the Yiddish stage—he is careful to qualify his knowledge of that event as secondhand. This places Stern in a different position regarding the Holocaust and frees him from including the gruesome images of emaciated/murdered Jews. By this refusal to transport us imaginatively to the camps and by its concentrating on the life of Jewish-American immigrants prior to the war, this honest and profound poem successfully captures the grief and pain particular to the Jewish-American experience of the Holocaust (Parmet 83).

This poem is first a homage to Jacob Adler, luminary of the Yiddish stage whose talents were recognized and celebrated by Jew and Gentile alike. That Adler achieved fame beyond the ghetto is central to the poem, suggestive of the respect with which Yiddish theatre and Jewish cultural life were regarded by upper-echelon Gentile society. Congenial relations between Jewish and Anglo-American culture, as established through artistic exchange, are contrasted sharply with relations between Jewish and German culture.

Early in the poem, after the Jewish King Lear whispers his vision of the future in his daughters' ears, Regan and Goneril "look at him/ with hatred reminiscent of the Plains of Auschwitz-Buchenwald- and drive him mad/ an inch at a time" (*Leaving Another Kingdom* 177). Stern also notes a connection between Gloucester and one of the "famous pictures" from the Holocaust.

As the poem continues, the parallels become more awesome. "I think when they saw him put / a feather over her lips they were relieved to see her dead" (*Leaving Another Kingdom* 178). Stern concludes that murder was ritualized and carried out with sense of decorum "for the sake of art."

"The Yiddish King Lear" is life-affirming, offering its audience an opportunity for catharsis. "When sometimes he comes across the stage/crowned with burdocks and nettles and cuckoo flowers/ we forget it is Adler, we are so terrified, we are so touched by pity" (*Leaving Another Kingdom* 178). This is the universal response to tragedy. The Jews leave the theatre with renewed energy to face the traumatic difficulties of their days.

On stage, Adler as Lear is larger than life. For the audience of his day, he was "a monster of suffering, so many holes/ that he is more like a whistle than/ a king" (*Leaving Another Kingdom* 177). To today's reader, as well, he assumes monumental properties—"a monster of suffering" representative of the 6 million Jews, now "so many holes" (177) in the cloth of Jewish life.

CRITICAL RECEPTION

The numerous poetry awards Gerald Stern has received attest to the special place he holds in American letters. C. K. Williams, poet, professor, and editor, has written of Stern:

The gratitude we feel toward Gerald Stern's work doesn't just have to do with his originality, although surely there has never been anything quite like his poetry. Nor is it merely a matter of his capacious feelings, though who in our time welcomes more of true, sad reality in his voice? Perhaps it's listening in amazement as he resurrects our histories for us to sing, perhaps it's how he finds the joy in our grief, the unsuspected ecstasies inhabiting the mundane. Whatever the reasons, Stern is one of those rare poetic souls who makes it almost impossible to remember what our world was like before his poetry came to exalt it" (unpublished speech).

At once affirmative and apocalyptic, Gerald Stern's vision makes him, as *The Georgia Review* has noted, "a very brilliant, moving poet . . . the most expansively celebratory poet in years—almost a spiritual reincarnation of Whitman." To which Edward Hirsch adds, "a late ironic Jewish disciple of Whitman" (56).

Peter Balakian, reviewing *The Red Coal*, tells us that Stern "reinvests pluralistic America with idealism and faith, an urban Jew roaming the market places of America's cosmopolitan center." Stern offers a "consummate vision of an America in which he still believes—a grand place of individualism and universal brotherhood." (21).

Richard Chess does not praise Stern's Holocaust poetry unconditionally. Of "War against the Jews" he writes that this " 'leap into fantasy' is, finally, sentimental and exploitative, for it resolves on a note of historical impossibility, a 'wooden' cry, as it were ('O wooden figures, go back, go back'), and it will not suffice" (152). Of Stern's invention of his Jewish counterpart in "Soap," Chess comments that "this invention offers Stern to do what he's wanted to do all along—beg his 'little brother, if I/ should call him that' for forgiveness. After all, Stern confesses, it is the counterpart who 'died instead of me.' But a selfish act of invention is an easy method of purging oneself of guilt, and this poem too will not suffice" (152). Chess, however, does choose "Adler" as the "most powerful, most fully rendered, and most original Holocaust poem" (153).

Sanford Pinsker offers a statement about Gerald Stern and the modern Hasidic movement: "In important though not specific ways, Stern can count himself in their number, just as Stern counts himself in the minyan of those performing the ritual of Tashlikh (a ceremony in which one's sins, in the form of bread, are cast into a body of running water on the first day of Rosh Hashanah) (''Weeping'' 195).

No matter—dance and prayer, prayer and dance—weeping and wailing, if you will—it comes to the same thing. In the middle-Europe of the nineteenth century it was called ''behaving like a Jew,'' and Gerald Stern's poetic songs are very Jewish indeed.

BIBLIOGRAPHY

Works by Gerald Stern

Lucky Life. New York: Houghton Mifflin, 1979.
The Red Coal. New York: Houghton Mifflin, 1981.
''Notes from the River.'' *American Poetry Review*, September/October 1983a.
''Some Secrets.'' In *Praise of What Persists*. Ed. Stephen Berg. New York: Harper and Row, 1983b, 113–82.
Leaving Another Kingdom. New York: Harper and Row, 1984a.
Paradise Poems. New York: Random House, 1984b.
Rejoicings. Los Angeles: Metro Book, 1984c.
''What Is the Sabbath?'' *American Poetry Review* 13 (January/February 1984d): 17–19.
Lovesick. New York: Harper and Row, 1987a.
''What Is This Poet?'' *Essays from the Eleventh Alabama Symposium on English and American Literature*. University of Alabama Press (1987b), 145–56.
Bread without Sugar. New York: W. W. Norton, 1992.
Odd Mercy. New York: W. W. Norton, 1995.

Works about Gerald Stern

Balakian, Peter. ''Review of The Red Coal.'' *The American Book Review* 5, No. 2 (January/February 1983): 21.
Chess, Richard. ''Stern's Holocaust.'' *Poetry East* (Fall 1988): 150–59.
Hirsch, Edward. ''A Late Ironic Whitman.'' The *Nation* 240, No. 2 (January 1985): 55–58.
Moyers, Bill. *The Language of Life: A Festival of Poets*. New York: Doubleday, 1995, 375–90.
Parmet, Harriet L. ''Selected American Poets Respond to the Holocaust: The Terror of Our Days.'' *Modern Language Studies* 24, No. 4 (1994): 82–84.
Pinsker, Sanford. ''The Poetry of Constant Renewal and Celebration: An Afternoon's Chat with Gerald Stern.'' *Missouri Review* 13, No. 2 (1984): 32–40.
———. ''Weeping and Wailing: The Jewish Songs of Gerald Stern.'' *Studies in American Jewish Literature* 9, No. 2 (1990): 186–96.
Somerville, Jane. ''Gerald Stern: The Poetry of Nostalgia.'' *The Literary Review* 28, No. 1 (Fall 1984): 95–104.
———. *Making the Light Come*. Detroit: Wayne State University Press, 1990.
Stitt, Peter. ''Engagements with Reality.'' *Georgia Review* 35, No. 4 (1981): 874–82.

MARK STRAND   (1934–)

Neil Arditi

BIOGRAPHY

Mark Strand was born in Summerside, Prince Edward Island, Canada, on April 11, 1934, to Robert Joseph and Sonia Apter Strand. His mother was descended from Rumanian and Russian Jews; his father's father came to America from Czechoslovakia (the original family name, "Stransky," was changed by immigration officials). Because of his father's work, the family was often in motion. Strand's childhood was divided among Halifax, Montreal, New York, Philadelphia, and Cleveland—the one constant being the vacations the family took in Nova Scotia on St. Margaret's Bay. Strand's teenage years were spent in Colombia, Peru, and Mexico.

In 1954, Strand entered Antioch College in northern Ohio, where he came under the influence of Nolan Miller, his freshman English instructor. After graduating, he studied painting at Yale with Joseph Albers but found himself increasingly obsessed with poetry. He spent a year in Florence studying nineteenth-century Italian poetry on a Fulbright Scholarship and later studied at the Iowa Writer's Workshop, where he was subsequently hired as an instructor. In 1961 he married Antonia Ratensky; they had one child together, Jessica. After leaving Iowa in 1965, Strand taught for a year as a Fulbright lecturer in Brazil, where he met the American poet Elizabeth Bishop (already a large influence on his work) and first read Carlos Drummond de Andrade, a Brazilian poet he would follow Bishop in translating.

With his second and third volumes of poetry, *Reasons for Moving* (1968) and *Darker* (1970), Strand established his reputation as a major American poet. He has taught at a number of colleges and universities, including Princeton, Columbia, University of Virginia, Yale, and Harvard. In 1973, Strand was divorced from his first wife. In 1976, he married Julia Rumsy Garretson. They have one son, Thomas Summerfield. Shortly after the publication of his *Selected Poems* (1980), Strand accepted a full-time position at the University of Utah, Salt Lake City, where he remained until 1993. In 1990, Strand was named poet laureate of the United States. In addition to his eight volumes of verse, Strand has published children's stories, a collection of short fiction, and a substantial body of art criticism. He is currently Elliott Coleman Professor of Poetry at Johns Hopkins University. Strand was awarded the Pulitzer Prize for Poetry in 1999.

MAJOR WORKS AND THEMES

Unlike John Hollander and Allen Grossman, poets with whom he shares a family resemblance, Mark Strand has never been overtly Jewish in his thematic concerns. With regard to his work, Strand does not think of himself as a ''Jewish-American poet.'' Being Jewish, Strand has remarked in an interview, is ''not central to my identity as a poet. . . . It's part of my moral makeup'' (Kelen 64).

Strand's qualification notwithstanding, his poetry is deeply inflected by European Jewish culture. The largest Jewish influences on his work are Kafka and Freud and, later, Bruno Schultz, the Polish short story writer, artist, and translator of Kafka. Sometimes the borrowings are explicit; in ''The Tunnel,'' for instance, Strand offers a lyric version of Kafka's ''The Burrow.'' In a more general sense, Kafka, Freud, and Schultz, among others, seem to have instructed Strand in a particular kind of strangeness, in which nothing can be interpreted accurately, or everything cries out for endless interpretation, which comes to much the same thing. This strangeness is related to dreams and nightmares and to a complex mode of humor (in Freud, a theory of humor) that can accompany the most painful revelations. It is also related, at least in Strand, to a radical sense of exile.

Some of Strand's early poems express this sense of exile in nearly theological terms. In ''Keeping Things Whole,'' published in Strand's first book of poems, *Sleeping with One Eye Open* (1964), and reprinted in Strand's second book, *Reasons for Moving*, the poet asserts:/ I am what is missing'' (*Selected Poems* 105). Strand's negation inverts (the Divine:) *ehyeh asher ehyeh* (''I am that I am'' or ''I will be present wherever and whenever I will be present''). If one wanted a more precise theological analogy for Strand's negation, one would have to turn to late cabalistic accounts of the Creation, in which God withdraws, or limits himself, in order to create a space outside himself in which Creation can unfold. For, as if enacting some primordial *tsimtsum*, Strand withdraws or negates his presence, defining himself as an absence, itself ensconced in an abyss of ''air.'' By moving through that abyss, Strand explains, the poet keeps ''things whole,'' which otherwise would be broken. But the poetic self is never healed or fulfilled. It is, at best, movingly sustained.

Most of the poems in *Darker* (1970), Strand's third volume, return to the subject matter of "Keeping Things Whole," often in litanies or chants modeled on the poetry of Whitman and Christopher Smart. These poems demonstrate, line by line, Strand's mode of procedure, repeatedly giving the self up or emptying the self. In "The Remains," Strand empties himself not only of other people's names but also of his own name, which follows his words (and his wife's) downwind like puffs of smoke. In some of the most striking lines he has written, the poet confronts his parents' mortality. He watches them rise from their thrones and wonders how he can sing of their deaths (*Selected Poems* 151). Strand's sense of exile is not geographical but internal and largely self-willed. For Strand can sing only by emptying himself, even of his own identity. Indeed, in another poem, "My Life by Somebody Else," Strand wryly suggests that his poetry is written by an alien self who must be seduced with offerings and sacrifices.

In 1973 Strand published his fourth volume of poems, *The Story of Our Lives*, a book dominated by four long poems. Strand no longer admires *The Story of Our Lives*, but at least three of its long poems—"Elegy for My Father"; the title poem; and "The Untelling"—are memorable works of art. They are also difficult works to excerpt, because their effect is largely cumulative. Yet, what accumulates is not precisely narrative. "Elegy for My Father," the long poem in sections that opens the volume, moves forward, almost exclusively, through repetition. In "The Story of Our Lives," narrative is baffled by the speaker's pervasive sense that everything already has happened, and nothing new is ever said or written. Here and elsewhere in the volume, the theme of domestic unhappiness is prevalent, but Strand's sense of decorum and his aesthetic detachment protect him from the charge of self-pity.

In 1978, Strand published two books, *The Monument* and *The Late Hour*, only the latter of which was included, along with five "new poems," in his *Selected Poems*. They are remarkably different works. *The Monument* is funnier than anything Strand had written previously. His obsessive concern, which he mocks throughout, is literary immortality. Strand addresses himself to the future translator of *The Monument* (the book he is writing) in fifty-two chapters or prose poems, almost all less than a page, and these, in turn, incorporate quotations from Whitman, Nietzsche, Stevens, Unamuno, and Sir Thomas Browne, among others. Also present, though more deeply submerged in the text, is the voice of Elizabeth Bishop, author of "The Monument," a curiously Hebraic poem.

In *The Late Hour*, Strand returned to the short lyric, but with a difference. The surrealism of the early poetry has receded almost entirely. In addition, many of the poems have specific occasions that involve other selves. "The Coming of Light," the short poem that opens the volume, celebrates "the coming of love" and ultimately belongs to the tradition of the Song of Solomon. The content of Strand's vision is still a kind of wintry vacancy, but the darkness of his early poetry is largely displaced by a conviction of interconnectedness. Strand's transformation is clearest in "White," one of the most memorable poems in *The Late Hour*. "At the middle of my life," the poet begins, "all things are white," even "death" and "sorrow."

After the publication of his *Selected Poems*, Strand stopped writing verse for five years. He stopped, he has explained, because he no longer believed in the autobiographical poems he was writing. In particular, Strand seems to have turned away from a study of his own nostalgias, for a number of poems in *The Late Hour* and all five of the new poems Strand included in his *Selected Poems* are self-elegies structured around a childhood memory. During his period of silence as a poet, Strand wrote children's stories, art criticism (his essay on the painter William Bailey is a seminal expression of his own aesthetics), and a book of short fiction, *Mr. and Mrs. Baby* (1985).

The fables in *Mr. and Mrs. Baby* are more exuberantly comic than Strand's previous work, with the exception of *The Monument*. In "Dog Life," for instance, a man describes to his wife, one night before bed, his past life as a very poetic collie. Like "Dog Life," many of Strand's stories affectionately parody suburban life; others, like "More Life" and "Killer Poet," explore the more troubling implications of what Freud called "family romance." Bruno Schultz, the most pervasive influence on *Mr. and Mrs. Baby*, seems to have provided Strand with a less daunting model than Kafka in the mode of domestic mythmaking. Strand has remarked that he was drawn to Schultz's portrait of the father, which is gentler than Kafka's. Strand's own portrait of the father, most fully rendered in "More Life," is certainly closer to Schultz's fiction than to Kafka's. Most crucially, Strand learned from Schultz's example how to incorporate baroque, lyric digressions in narrative prose. Indeed, *Mr. and Mrs. Baby* is almost a book of prose poetry. But in another sense, Strand seems to be parodying his lyricism in these fables.

Strand returned to poetry in 1985. He was reading Robert Fitzgerald's translation of *The Aeneid* when he began to compose "Cento Virgilianus." The title of Strand's first poem in five years refers to the late classical practice of reassembling lines of Virgil to produce an independent work. In light of Strand's anecdote, "Cento Virgilianus" describes the poet's return to poetry in terms of the arrival of Aeneas and his men on a mysterious shore after their exodus from Troy. Like the other poems in *The Continuous Life* (1990), "Cento Virgilianus" is a new beginning for Strand. His lines are long and full of color, touched by the epic sublimity of the classical poets and perhaps reflecting, in some measure, the mountainous landscape in Utah, where they were composed. By comparison, Strand's previous poetry can seem rhetorically impoverished. But continuities persist. Most crucially, Strand's sense of vacancy and exile abides, even in the midst of his new rhetorical splendor. The first poem in the volume, "The Idea," is almost a manifesto on the topic. The poet approaches a cabin in the distant reaches of the north and imagines entering it and warming his hands by the fire but recognizes that it must remain unoccupied.

Strand's next and most recent volume of poetry, *Dark Harbor: A Poem*, was published in 1993. It is composed of cantos of varying numbers of three-line stanzas, one of the many respects in which it resembles the long poems of Wallace Stevens. In *Dark Harbor*, the poet wanders through a ghost town of the imagination brooding on desire, poetry, and death. The degree of irony varies greatly from canto to canto. In Canto 8, the poet sits in a diner, sipping a bowl of soup, across the table from his death, a macabre figure with bleached hair. The poet pleads with her for a sign that he is chosen, that his poetry will live. In the final canto, Strand finds himself in a misty realm where he is told of the many dead poets. The scene is reminiscent of Dante's visit to limbo, eternal resting place of poets of antiquity. As Strand approaches, the dead poets tuck their heads beneath their wings. But Strand, the perpetual exile, clearly feels at home in the realm of these seraphic influences. As he joins himself to his chosen company, an angel—"one of the good ones"—begins to sing.

CRITICAL RECEPTION

Strand's first book of poems, *Sleeping with One Eye Open*, was privately printed; his second and third books of poetry, *Reasons for Moving* and *Darker*, reached an unusually wide audience of readers and established Strand's reputation as a major American poet. Donald Justice, Robert Penn Warren, and Harold Bloom were among Strand's earliest and most outspoken admirers.

In 1973, Strand published *The Story of Our Lives*. In a review of the volume, later reprinted in *Alone with America*, Richard Howard considered it Strand's best work to date. *The Story of Our Lives* was awarded the Edgar Allan Poe Award by the Academy of American Poets in 1974. In 1978, Strand published his fifth volume of poems, *The Late Hour*, and an experimental prose work titled *The Monument*. The latter was published by Ecco Press after being turned down by Strand's publisher at Atheneum. In a review printed in *The New Republic*, Harold Bloom hailed both installments as permanent contributions to American literature. In 1980, Strand published his *Selected Poems*, which included five new poems. Reviewing the volume in *The New York Review of Books*, Irvin Ehrenpreis admired Strand's prosodic mastery but considered the poet's solipsism a weakness. For most readers, however, the publication of Strand's *Selected Poems* confirmed his status as one of the most original and haunting poets of his generation. Strand's *Selected Poems* was named one of the American Library Association's Notable Books for 1980.

Strand's next major literary effort was *Mr. and Mrs. Baby*, a book of short fiction. Reviews were mixed. Some complained that Strand's surrealistic fables were insubstantial or morbid. Others admired Strand's overt lyricism and praised him for his comic inventiveness.

In 1990, Strand was chosen by the Library of Congress to succeed Howard Nemerov as poet laureate of the United States. In the same year, he published *The Continuous Life*, his first book of poems to appear in five years. The poet George Bradley, reviewing the volume for the *Partisan Review*, considered Strand's new work a major breakthrough and perhaps his best collection to date.

Similar judgments can be found in reviews by Alfred Corn, Charles Berger, and Harold Bloom. *The Continuous Life* went into a second printing within a year of its publication.

Strand's most recent volume, *Dark Harbor: A Poem*, was awarded the Bollingen Prize for 1993. Reviewers have praised it for confidently engaging the most profound poetic themes.

In addition to the honors already mentioned, Strand has been the recipient of fellowships from the Ingram Merrill, Rockefeller, and Guggenheim Foundations and from the National Endowment for the Arts. In 1979, he was awarded the Fellowship of the Academy of American Poets. In 1987, he received a John D. and Catherine T. MacArthur Fellowship.

BIBLIOGRAPHY

Works by Mark Strand

Poetry

Sleeping with One Eye Open. Iowa City: Stone Wall Press, 1964.
Reasons for Moving. New York: Atheneum, 1968.
Darker. New York: Atheneum, 1970.
The Story of Our Lives. New York: Atheneum, 1973.
The Late Hour. New York: Atheneum, 1978.
Selected Poems. New York: Atheneum, 1980.
The Continuous Life. New York: Knopf, 1990.
The Monument. New York: Ecco Press, 1991.
Dark Harbor. New York: Knopf, 1993.
Blizzard of One. New York: Knopf, 1998.

Prose

The Monument. Hopewell, NJ: Ecco Press, 1978.
Mr. and Mrs. Baby. New York: Knopf, 1985.

Children's Stories

The Planet of Lost Things. New York: C. N. Potter, 1982.
The Night Book. New York: C. N. Potter, 1985.
Rembrandt Takes a Walk. New York: C. N. Potter, 1986.

Translations

The Owl's Insomnia (poems by Raphael Alberti). New York: Atheneum, 1973.
Traveling with the Family (poems by Carlos Drummond de Andrade, with Thomas Colchie). New York: Random House, 1987.

Art Books

Art of the Real: Nine American Figurative Painters. New York: C. N. Potter, 1983.
William Bailey. New York: Abrams, 1987.
Hopper. New York: Ecco Press, 1994.

Anthologies

The Contemporary American Poets: American Poetry since 1940. Cleveland: World, 1969.

New Poetry of Mexico. New York: Dutton, 1970.

With Charles Simic. *Another Republic: 17 European and South American Writers.* New York: Ecco Press, 1976.

The Best American Poetry of 1991. New York: Simon and Schuster, 1991.

The Golden Echo Anthology: 100 Great Poems of the English Language. New York: Ecco Press, 1994.

Works about Mark Strand

Berger, Charles. "Poetry Chronicle." *Raritan* 10:3 (Winter 1991): 119–33.

Bloom, Harold. "Dark and Radiant Peripheries: Mark Strand and A. R. Ammons." *Southern Review* 8 (Winter 1972): 133–41.

———. Rev. of *The Monument* and *The Late Hour. The New Republic* 179 (July 29, 1978): 29–30.

———. "Mark Strand." *Gettysburg Review* 4: 2 (Spring 1991): 247–48.

Bradley, George. "Lean and Lush." *Partisan Review* 58 (Summer 1991): 564–65.

Corn, Alfred. Rev. of *The Continuous Life. New York Times Book Review* 96 (March 24, 1991): 26–27.

Crenner, James. "Mark Strand: *Darker.*" *Seneca Review* 2 (April 1971): 87–97.

Donaldson, Jeffrey. "The Still Life of Mark Strand's Darkening Harbor." *Dalhousie Review* 74 (Spring 1994): 110–24.

Ehrenpreis, Irvin. Rev. of *Selected Poems. New York Review of Books* 28 (October 8, 1981): 45.

Gregorson, Linda. "Negative Capability." *Parnassus: Poetry in Review* 9 (1981): 90–114.

Howard, Richard. "Mark Strand." *Alone with America: Essays on the Art of Poetry since 1950.* Enlarged ed. New York: Atheneum, 1980.

Kelen, Leslie. "Finding Room in the Myth: An Interview with Mark Strand." *Boulevard* 5–6: (Spring 1991): 61–82.

Kirby, David. *Mark Strand and the Poet's Place in Contemporary Culture.* Columbia: University of Missouri Press, 1990.

Lieberman, Laurence. Rev. of *Reasons for Moving. Yale Review* 58 (1968): 147–49.

Miller, Nolan. "The Education of a Poet" (interview). *The Antioch Review* 39 (1981): 106–118.

NATHANIEL TARN　　　　　　　　　(1928–)

Joel Shatzky and Michael Taub

BIOGRAPHY

Nathaniel Tarn was born on June 30, 1928, in Paris. His mother, Yvonne Cecile Leah, was originally Romanian. His father, Mendel Meyer Tauriger, was of Lithuanian stock. In 1936 the family moved to Belgium, and in 1939, to England. Tarn attended boarding schools, wrote his first poems, painted, and visited London bookstores, even as bombs were falling on the city. He studied English literature at Cambridge. In 1949, Tarn returned to Paris and did his B.A. equivalent in anthropology under the guidance of such leading figures in the field as Claude Lévi-Strauss, Marcel Griaule, and Paul Levi. He moved in ''heady'' circles that included George Bataille, Marcel Jacno, Andre Breton, Octavio Paz, and scores of other brilliant artists and intellectuals.

During these years he developed a fascination with primitive and archaic cultures, Maya studies, and the sociology of Buddhist institutions. In 1951 he came to America and began graduate studies at the University of Chicago, from which he got a Ph.D. in anthropology in 1957. An expert in Southeast Asian anthropology, he traveled extensively to Burma, India, Cambodia, Nepal, and Thailand. In the 1960s Tarn returned to London to write and publish his poetry and his research in Asia. At the time he created Cape Editions and the Cape Gollard Poetry Press at Jonathan Cape Publishers. In England he forged friendships with George Steiner, Ted Hughes, Arnold Wesker, and Christopher Middleton. But Charles Olson, Robert Duncan, and Louis Zukofsky were Tarn-the-poet's main inspiration and influence. Back in the United States he taught at various universities until Rutgers in 1970 offered him a permanent position in the Department of Comparative Literature. In 1985 he took early retirement and went to live near Santa Fe, New Mexico, with his second wife, Janet Rodney. There, among others, Tarn befriended Henry Roth.

MAJOR WORKS AND THEMES

In *Old Savage/Young City*, Tarn's first book of poetry, Jewish themes appear in the context of verses about contemporary life—"Israel in the Park" and "A Rabbi's Dream," as well as in verses about Jewish mysticism—"Shimon Bar Yochai," "The Master of the Name," and others. These poems were inspired by readings of Martin Buber, Gershom Scholem, and Raphael Patai, leading authorities of Hasidism, Cabala, and folklore.

His third book, *The Beautiful Contradictions*, is filled with the spirit of the prophets. In one poem an Eichman-like figure answers an interrogation about his role in the Holocaust. Another poem begins in an old synagogue in Prague and laments the elimination of the Jews in Central Europe. A love poem contrasts the "blind" synagogue at Strasbourg Cathedral and the "Church Triumphant" at the same site. (In medieval sculpture, the synagogue is often represented as a blind young woman with a broken staff or lance.) The figures of Mahler, Kafka, and other Jewish artists are invoked in this work.

In *New Lyrics for the Bride of God*, Tarn writes about "Shekhina" (the Bride of God), as one fulfilling her ultimate cabalistic task: the return of the holy sparks, dispersed among humankind at the creation, to their original source. The bride changes identities, race, and color, as well as mythological and historical settings. Through her actions the poet raises a whole host of ecological, political, and gender-related questions.

Tarn is the translator of numerous poets, among them Neruda. He coedited several books of translated poetry. He appeared in many anthologies, here and abroad. He contributed to such periodicals as *Sulphur, Times Literary Supplement, New York Times*, and others. He published many important anthropological studies on Maya culture, Buddhism, and other subjects. He received many awards, including Ford and Rockefeller Fellowships and a Guiness Prize for Poetry.

CRITICAL RECEPTION

There are countless tributes to Tarn's distinguished career as poet, editor, translator (of Spanish, French, Native American, Mayan, and Buddhist works), and teacher. Distinguished critic Eliot Weinberger is amazed by Tarn's range, his "ecstatic vision, his continuing enthusiasm for the stuff of the world. It is a poetry whose native tongue is myth, and it rolls out in long lines of sacred hymns that oscillate between the demonic and the hieratic" (53).

Weinberger cites literary kinships with McClure, Rexroth, Donne, Blake, Whitman, and Neruda, whom Tarn had translated. On the same page, he describes Tarn as a "nomad" longing for the idea of home as both the embodiment of the American and Jewish spirit.

BIBLIOGRAPHY

Works by Nathaniel Tarn

Old Savage/Young City. New York: Random House, 1965.
The Beautiful Contradictions. New York: Random House, 1970.
A Nowhere for Vallejo. New York: Random House, 1971.
Narrative of This Fall. Santa Rosa, CA: Black Sparrow Press, 1975a.
New Lyrics for the Bride of God. New York: New Directions, 1975b.
The House of Leaves. Santa Rosa, CA: Black Sparrow Press, 1976.
Birdscape with Seaside. Santa Rosa, CA: Black Sparrow Press, 1978.
Seeing America First. Minneapolis: Coffee House Press, 1989.

Works about Nathaniel Tarn

Carruth, Hayden. *Harper's Book Letter*, October 13, 1975.
Economou, George. *Sulphur*, No. 14, 1985.
Enslin, Theodore. *American Book Review*, July–August 1980.
Fish, Harold. *The Dual Image: The Figure of the Jew in English and American Literature.* London: World Jewish Library, 1971.
Holmes, Richard. *The London Times Saturday Review*, June 7, 1969.
O'Brien, Geoffrey. *The Village Voice Literary Supplement*, February 1986.
Thomas, D. M. *The Times Literary Supplement*, May 20, 1977.
Weinberger, Eliot. "An Aviary of Tarns." In *Written Reaction.* New York: Marsilio, 1996.

Bibliographies

Contemporary Authors Autobiography Series. Vol. 16. Chicago: Garland Press, 1992.
Nathaniel Tarn: A Descriptive Bibliography. Jefferson, NC: McFarland, 1987.

LOUIS ZUKOFSKY (1904–1978)

Dror Abend-David

BIOGRAPHY

To many, Louis Zukofsky is one of the most significant modernist American poets. The founder of the objectivist movement, the winner of numerous awards, and the author of forty-nine books, his intricate and compound poetry won him the admiration of many poets, critics, and scholars who never ceased to praise the fine touches of irony and aesthetics in his work. Nevertheless, Louis Zukofsky was never a popular poet. Writing in *Parnassus: Poetry in Review*, Guy Davenport refers to Zukofsky as a ''poet's poet's poet,'' one whose work is intended for a selected audience of connoisseurs (23).

Much of the intricacy of Zukofsky's work can be explained by the multiplicity of cultures, languages, and disciplines that governed his own life. He spent most of his life in New York City, where he was born on January 23, 1904, to Pinchos and Chana Pruss Zukofsky. His native language was Yiddish, and his schooling, which also took place in Yiddish, included the Yiddish theatre as well as the plays of William Shakespeare in their Yiddish adaptations. He received his master's degree from Columbia University in 1924 to become a professor of English at the University of Wisconsin and later at the Polytechnic Institute in Brooklyn. Zukofsky was very conscious of the duality of his cultural identity and referred to it in his poetry, reflecting on the Eurocentric tradition of American education. Certainly, Zukofsky's short-term friendship with Ezra Pound, between 1931 and 1935, demonstrated not only the extent to which Zukofsky was able to become a part of the Anglo-American hierarchy of the 1920s and 1930s but also the political price that he had to pay in order to become a part of that institution. By 1935 Pound became impatient with Zukofsky, and after he had solicited and included his work in a number of publications, he rejected new work by Zukofsky that was submitted to Pound's *Active Anthology*. His comment, which parodies the style of Zukofsky's poetry, was: "the next anthology will be econ/ conscious and L/Z wont be in it" (Helming 428). But Zukofsky's cultural and political agenda was in no way the solitary drive of his poetry. On August 20, 1939, Louis Zukofsky married Celia Thaew, a composer. Together with their son, Paul Zukofsky, who grew up to be a famous violinist, Thaew inspired in Zukofsky's poetry an aesthetic inclination that made it so different from the modernist poetry of its time. Zukofsky died in 1978. He had published poetry, short fiction, and critical essays. Some of his awards include the National Endowment for the Arts Grants in 1967 and 1968, the National Institute of Arts and Letters Grants in 1976, and an honorary doctorate from Bard College in 1977. Although he was not a popular poet, he has still been a linguistic, literary, political, and Jewish hero to many.

MAJOR WORKS AND THEMES

The most noticeable manifestation of Zukofsky's unique intricacy is his epic poem *A*. *A*, a poem of enormous magnitude, was written in twenty-four parts throughout Zukofsky's lifetime, leaving room for innumerable intricate and highly diverse interpretations. Hugh Kenner, writing in the *New York Times Book Review*, refers to *A* as "the most hermetic poem in English" (6–7), while Guy Davenport uses a hermetic analogy of his own as he writes in *Agenda*: "*A* is something of a paradox, for the poem is as spare and weightless as a bicycle wheel" (130). Most critics point to the intricate relation between music and poetry throughout the poem, which, as Steven Helmling writes, merge in the second half of the work to symbolize the harmony of music and poetry in Zukofsky's own household (430). But *A* is not only a poem about aesthetic fusion.

Zukofsky began *A* in 1929, when he was a young socialist and Jewish student at Columbia University. The issues of political and economic justice appear, accordingly, as an important part of the first sections of *A*. When, in the first section, the scene moves from the concert hall to the street, filled with poverty, hardship, and strife, the poet explores the relation between politics and art. According to Helmling, "Art's 'Desire longing for perfection' seems compromised by a social milieu that reduces art to a mere . . . amusement for an elite leisure class" (431).

Zukofsky is also interested in issues of ethnicity, and in his 1928 epic "Poem Beginning 'The,' " he writes of his experiences as a student in Columbia. In this poem, the speaker paraphrases the character of Shylock in *The Merchant of Venice*, as he threatens to execute "the villainy" that he is taught in Gentile colleges. Zukofsky's emphasis in the poem that such revenge will "go hard with them" is particularly noteworthy, as it implies a characteristic of a new generation of Jewish Americans who are able to deal with non-Jews on equal terms.

Zukofsky's interest in ethnicity extends beyond the fate of American Jews. Elsewhere in the poem, he stresses the common fate of American minorities as he draws a heartfelt comparison between his own mother and a Chinese immigrant, their common struggle to feed their children, and their continuous, nerve-racking struggle to achieve goals in a foreign world.

Most of all, Zukofsky is a student of relationships: ethnicities, economic classes, family members, words, music, politics, and art all come together in a fusion, which, in *A 12–24*, represent the coexistence that Zukofsky envisioned for these diverse parts of his life.

CRITICAL RECEPTION

Certainly, Zukofsky's aesthetic inclination made him the cultural hero of literary connoisseurs. Projects such as his 1969 translation of Catullus—in which he retains the rhythm and the actual syllables of the original—won him incredible admiration as well as objection on the part of literary critics. Burton Raffel criticizes Zukofsky's *Catullus*, calling it a "never-never land of phonetic aping" (441). On the other hand, both Thomas A. Duddy, and Guy Davenport, (*New York Times Book Review* 5, 31) are only two of many who refer to the same project with admiration. Davenport also refers to a similar translation by Zukofsky of the great speech of God in the Book of Job. But even at its highest praise, Zukofsky's ironic study of canonized sounds is looked at by Davenport as nothing more than an impressive wordplay, "a feat so astounding as to seem mad" (*Contemporary Authors*, Vols. 9–12: 994). Indeed, Zukofsky is often regarded as a "mad" poet of abstractions whose work bears little political and social meaning. Gilbert Sorrentino writes, "I have been reading Zukofsky for 20 years and flatter myself that I have begun to understand how to read him." Davenport, who in 1969 called Zukofsky "a Lu Chi, a Lichtenberg, a Bashô, a Mallarmé" (*New York Times Book Review* 5), is probably most blunt in denying the social value of what he sees as the "glittering themes" of *A*. He writes in *Parnassus*, reminding his readers that Zukofsky was not admitted to the Communist Party, that he, in fact, was not considered "CP [Communist Party] material but a young man ambitious to move to the West Side." Accordingly, Zukofsky's discussion in *A* of "Jew: Christian. Christ on the cross: industrial workers crucified on their machines" is labeled by Davenport as secondary: "This inwardness is the ground for all the glittering themes and their variations which dance in *A*. Dance, for the essence of the poem is in play, intellectual play, a play of words and music" (18).

The insistence on seeing Zukofsky's work mainly as intellectual play characterizes most of the critical reception of his work. By doing so, most critics free themselves from dealing with Zukofsky's social agenda. His highly political epic "Poem Beginning 'The' " is rarely mentioned in reviews, and his recurring themes of ethnicity and economics are often neglected in favor of praise of his technique and style. It is possible that a number of reviewers attempted to protect Zukofsky from being labeled a communist during and after the communist scare of the 1950s. Moreover, as Steven Helmling implies, it may be that toward the later part of his lifetime, Zukofsky's social and ethnic passions subsided or were integrated more deeply with other aspects of his work (432). Yet, as one of few recognized Jewish modernist poets in the United States (along with Allen Ginsberg and Adrienne Rich), it seems that Zukofsky was forced to leave his ethnic baggage at the doorstep of American poetry. Being justly labeled "the patient craftsman of American poetry" (Davenport, *New York Times Book Review* 5), Zukofsky was never recognized as the historical, political, social, personal, and Jewish poet that he was.

BIBLIOGRAPHY

Works by Louis Zukofsky

Poem Beginning "The." Exile, 1928. Privately printed.
An Objectivist Anthology. Le Beausset, Var, France, and New York: To Publishers, 1932.
Active Anthology (includes poems and a note by Zukofsky). Ed. Ezra Pound. London: Faber and Faber, 1933.
Le Style Apollinaire by Zukofsky and Rene Tauppin. Paris: Le Presses Modernes, 1934.
First Half of A 9. New York: Privately printed, 1940.
Fifty-five Poems. Prairie City, IL: Decker, 1941.
Anew: Poems. Prairie City, IL: Decker, 1946.
A Test of Poetry. New York: Objectivist Press, 1948; London: Routledge, 1952.
Some Times/Short Poems. Highlands, NC: Jargon, 1956.
Five Statements for Poetry. San Francisco: San Francisco State College Press, 1958.
Barely and Widely. New York: Celia Zukofsky, 1958.
A 1–12. Kyoto, Japan: Origin Press, 1959; London: Cape, 1966; Garden City, NY: Doubleday, 1967.
It Was. Kyoto, Japan: Origin Press, 1961.
Sixteen Once Published. Edinburgh: Wild Hawthorn Press, 1962.
Bottom: On Shakespeare. Austin: Ark Press/University of Texas Press, 1963a.
I's Pronounced "Eyes." New York: Trobar Press, 1963b.
After I's. Pittsburgh: Boxwood Press/Mother Press, 1964a.
Found Objects 1962–1926. Georgetown, KY: H. B. Chapin, 1964b.
Finally a Valentine. Stroud, Gloucestershire, U.K.: Piccolo Press, 1965a.
I Sent Thee Late. Cambridge, MA: Privately printed, 1965b.
Iyyob. London: Turret, 1965c.
A Libretto. New York: Privately printed, 1965d.
An Unearthing: A Poem. Cambridge, MA: Privately printed, 1965e.
All: Collected Short Poems 1923–1958. New York: Norton, 1965; London: Cape, 1966a.
A 9. Cologne: Hansjorg Mayer, 1966b.
A 14. London: Torret, 1967a.
All: Collected Short Poems 1956–1964. New York: Norton, 1966; London: Cape, 1967b.
Little, a fragment. San Francisco: Black Sparrow Press, 1967c.
Prepositions: Collected Critical Essays of Louis Zukofsky. London: Rapp and Caroll, 1967d; New York: Horizon Press, 1968.

Ferdinand, Including It Was. New York: Grossman, 1968a; London: Cape, 1968.
From Thanks to the Dictionary. Buffalo, NY: Gallery Upstairs, 1968b.
A 13–21 (Garden City, NY: Doubleday, 1969c; London: Cape, 1968.
Catullus. New York: Grossman, 1969a; London: Cape Goliard, 1969.
Catullus Fragmenta. London: Turret, 1969b.
Autobiography. New York: Grossman, 1970a.
Little. New York: Grossman, 1970b.
All: The Collected Shorter Poems 1923–1964. New York: Norton, 1971.
A 24. New York: Grossman, 1973.
"Addenda to Prepositions." *Journal of Modern Literature* 4 (September 1974): 91–108.
A 22 and 23. New York: Grossman, 1975.
A. Berkeley: University of California Press, 1978a.
Eighty Flowers. Lunenburg, VT: Stinehour Press, 1978b.

Works about Louis Zukofsky

Ahearn, Barry. "The Adams Connection." *Paideuma* 7 (Winter 1978a): 479–93.
———. "The Aesthetics of A." Ph.D. diss., Johns Hopkins University, 1978b.
———. "Notes on a Convocation of Disciplines." *Montemora* 4 (1978c): 251–59.
———. "Origins of A: Zukofsky's Materials for Collage." *ELH* 45 (Spring 1978d): 152–76.
Booth, Marcella. *A Catalogue of the Louis Zukofsky Manuscript Collection.* Austin: University of Texas Press, 1975.
Byrd, Don. "The Shape of Zukofsky's Canon." *Paideuma* 7 (Winter 1978): 455–77.
Carruth, Hayden. "The Only Way I Get There from Here." *Journal of Modern Literature* 4 (September 1974): 88–90.
Chatters, Samuel, "Essay Beginning 'All.'" *Modern Poetry Studies* 3 (1973): 241–50.
———. *Contemporary Authors.* Vols. 9–12: 994. Detroit: Gale Research, 1974.
———. "Conversations with Celia Zukofsky." *Paideuma* 7 (Winter 1978): 585–600.
Corman, Cid. "The Transfigured Prose." *Paideuma* 7 (Winter 1978): 447–53.
Cox, Kenneth. "A-24." *Agenda* 11 (Spring-Summer 1973): 89–91.
———. "Louis Zukofsky." *Agenda* 4 (Summer 1966): 45–48.
Davenport, Guy. Rev. of *Catullus. New York Times Book Review.* September 17, 1970, 5, 31.
———. "Scripta Zukofskii Elogia." *Paideuma* 7 (Winter 1978): 394–99.
———. "Zukofsky's A 23–21 and Catullus." *Agenda* 8 (Autumn-Winter 1970): 130–37.
———. "Zukofsky's A 24." *Parnassus* 2 (Spring-Summer 1974): 15–24.
Dawson, Fielding. "A Memoir of Louis Zukofsky." *Paideuma* 7 (Winter 1978): 571–79.
Dembo, L. S. "Louis Zukofsky: Objectivist Poetics and the Quest for Form." *American Literature* 44 (March 1972): 74–96.
Duddy, Thomas A. "The Measure of Louis Sukofsky." *Modern Poetry Studies* 3 (1973): 250–56.
Duncan, Robert. "As Testimony: Reading Zukofsky These Forty Years." *Paideuma* 7 (Winter 1978): 421–27.
Ginsberg, Allen, Robert Creeley, Hugh Seidman, and Celia Zukofsky. "Memorial Cel-

ebration for Louis Zukofsky." *American Poetry Review* 9 (January–February 1980): 22–27.

Gordon, David. "Zuk and Ez at St. Liz." *Paideuma* 7 (Winter 1978): 581–84.

Harmon, William. "Eiron Eyes." *Parnassus* 8 (Spring-Summer 1979): 5–23.

Hatlen, Burton. "Catullus Metamorphosed." *Paideuma* 7 (Winter 1978): 539–45.

Helmling, Steven. "Louis Zukofsky." *Dictionary of Literary Biography.* Vol. 5. 422–34. Detroit, MI: Gale Research, 1974.

Ignatow, David. "Louis Zukofsky: Two Views." *Paideuma* 7 (Winter 1978): 549–51.

———. "Interview with Louis Zukofsky." *Contemporary Literature* 10 (Spring 1969): 155–219.

———. *A Homemade World: The American Modernist Writers.* New York: Knopf, 1975: 162–63.

Kenner, Hugh. "Bottom on Zukofsky." *Modern Language Notes* 90 (December 1975): 921–22.

———. "Love in Brooklyn." *Paideuma* 7 (Winter 1978): 413–20.

———. *New York Times Book Review*, March 14, 1976, 6–7.

———. "Louis Zukofsky: All the Words." *Paideuma* 7 (Winter 1978): 386–89.

Lang, P. Warren. "Zukofsky's Conception of Poetry and a Reading of His Poem of a Life A.' " Ph.D. diss., Indiana University, 1974.

Mandell, Stephen Roy. "The Finer Mathematician: An Introduction to the Work of Louis Zukofsky." Philadelphia, PA: Temple University Press, 1976.

Oppen, May. *Meaning of Life: An Autobiography.* Santa Barbara, CA: Black Sparrow Press, 1978.

Quatermain, Peter. "I Am Different, Let Not a Gloss Embroil You." *Paideuma* 9 (Spring 1980): 203–10.

———. "Recurrences: No. 12 of Louis Zukofsky's Anew." *Paideuma* 7 (Winter 1978): 523–38.

Raffel, Burton. "No Tidbit Love You Outdoors Far as a Bier: Zukofsky's Catullus." *Arion* 8 (Autumn 1969): 435–45.

Schimmel, Harold. "Zuk. Yehuash David Rex." *Paideuma* 7 (Winter 1978): 559–69.

Seidman, Hugh. "Louis Zukofsky at the Polytechnic Institute of Brooklyn (1958–61)." *Paideuma* 7 (Winter 1978): 552–58.

Sorrentino, Gilbert. "The Poetry of Louis Zukofsky; The Handles Are Missing." *Village Voice*, June 7, 1976, 77.

Taggart, John. "Intending a Solid Object: A Study of Objectivist Poetics." Ph.D. diss., Syracuse University, 1975.

———. "Zukofsky's 'Mantis.' " *Paideuma* 7 (Winter 1978): 507–22.

Terrel, C. F., ed. *Louis Zukofsky: Man and Poet.* Orono: University of Maine Press, 1979.

Tomlinson, Charles. "Objectivists: Zukofsky and Oppen, a Memoir." *Paideuma* 7 (Winter 1978): 429–45.

Williams, William Carlos. "An Extraordinary Sensitivity." *Poetry* 60 (September 1942): 338–40.

———. "Louis Zukofsky." *Agenda* 2 (December 1964): 1–4.

———. "A New Line Is a New Measure." *New Quarterly of Poetry* 2 (Winter 1947–1948): 8–16.

———. "Review of an 'Objectivist' Anthology." *Symposium* 4 (January 1933): 114–16.

Yanella, Phillip R. "On Louis Zukofsky." *Journal of Modern Literature* 4 (September 1974): 74–87.
Zukofksy, Celia. *A Bibliography of Louis Zukofsky.* Los Angeles: Black Sparrow Press, 1969.
———. "Year by Year Bibliography of Louis Zukofsky." *Paideuma* 7 (Winter 1978): 603–10.

Appendix

A complete entry on each of the following poets and dramatists can be found in *Jewish American Women Writers: A Bio-Bibliographical and Critical Sourcebook*, ed. Ann R. Shapiro (Westport, CT: Greenwood Press, 1994).

Shirley Kaufman (1923–   ) Ed. B.A., UCLA; M.A. in Creative Writing, San Francisco State University. M. Bernard Kaufman, three daughters; Hillel M. Daleski. Teaches creative writing to Israelis in English. Major Works: *The Floor Keeps Turning* (1970); *Gold Country* (1973); *From One Life to Another* (1979); *Claims* (1984); *Rivers of Salt* (1993).

Irena Klepfisz (1941–   ). B. Warsaw, Poland. Ed. B.A. in Yiddish and English, CCNY; M.A. and Ph.D., University of Chicago. Taught English literature in CUNY. Major Works: *Periods of Stress* (1975); *Keeper of Accounts* (1982); *Different Enclosures* (1985); *A Few Words in the Mother Tongue: Poems Selected and New* (1971–1990).

Maxine Kumin, née Winokur (1925–   ) B. Germantown, Pennsylvania. Ed. B.A. in History and Literature Radcliffe College. M. Victor Kumin, three children. Taught at Tufts University, University of Massachusetts, Columbia, Brandeis, Princeton, and Massachusetts Institute of Technology. Major Works: *Halfway* (1961); *The Nightmare Factory* (1970); *Nurture* (1989); *Looking for Luck* (1992).

Rhoda Lerman, née Sniderman (1936–   ) B. Far Rockaway, New York. Ed. B.A., English University of Miami. M. Robert Lerman, three children. Taught at University of Colorado, Syracuse, Hartwick College, SUNY, Buffalo. Major Works: *Call Me Ishtar* (1973); *The Girl That He Marries* (1976), *Eleanor: A Novel* (1979), *The Book of the Night* (1984), *God's Ear* (1989).

Karen Malpede (1945–   ) B. Wichita Falls, Texas. Ed. B.A. in English, University of Wisconsin; M.A. in Theatre Criticism, Columbia. One daughter. Taught at Smith College, NYU. Major Works: *A Lament for Three Women* (1979); *A Monster Has Stolen the Sun* *and Other Plays* (1987); *Better People. Angels of Power* (1991); *Us. Women on the Verge* (1992).

Robin Morgan (1941–) B. Lake Worth, Florida. Television role of Dagmar in ''I Remember Mama.'' Ed. Columbia, nonmatric. M. Kenneth Pitchford, one son; div. Co-founded WITCH (Women's International Terrorist Conspiracy from Hell). Taught at New College, Sarasota, Florida. Ed. *Ms.* Major Works: *Monster: Poems* (1972); *Lady of the Beasts: Poems* (1976); *Death Benefits: Poems* (1981); *Depth Perception: New Poems and a Masque* (1982); *Upstairs in the Garden: Poems Selected and New: 1968–1988* (1990).

Alicia Ostriker, née Suskind (1937–). B. New York City. Ed. B.A., Brandeis; Ph.D. in English, NYU. M. Joseph Ostriker, three children. Teaches at Rutgers University. Major Works: *A Dream of Springtime: Poems 1970–78* (1979); *A Woman under the Surface: Poems and Prose Poems* (1982); *Stealing the Language: The Emergence of Women's Poetry in America* (1986); *The Imaginary Lover* (1989); *Green Age* (1989); *The Nakedness of the Fathers* (1994).

Linda Pastan, née Olenik. B. New York City. Ed. Radcliffe, B.A. in English; Simmons, Library Science; Brandeis, M.A. in English. M. Ira Pastan, three children. Poet laureate, Maryland. Major Works: *A Perfect Circle of Sun* (1971); *Aspects of Eve* (1975); *The Five Stages of Grief* (1978); *Waiting for My Life* (1981); *PM/AM: New and Selected Poems* (1982); *The Imperfect Paradise* (1988); *Heroes in Disguise* (1991).

Ruth Whitman (1922–). M. Cedric Whitman, two daughters. One son from second marriage. M. Morton Sacks. Ed., B.A., Radcliffe in Greek and English; M.A., Harvard. Taught at Radcliffe, Harvard, Holy Cross, University of Denver and Fulbright, Hebrew University, Jerusalem, and MIT. Major Works: *The Passion of Lizzie Borden: New and Selected Poems* (1973); *Tamsen Donner: A Woman's Journey* (1977); *The Testing of Hannah Senesh* (1986); *Laughing Gas: Poems New and Selected 1963–1990* (1991); *Hatshepsut, Speak to Me* (1992).

Susan Yankowitz (1941–). B. Newark, New Jersey. Ed. B.A., Sarah Lawrence, M.F.A., Yale Drama School, M. Herb Leibowitz, one son. Major Works: *Terminal* in *Three Plays by the Open Theatre* (1972); *The Land of Milk and Funny* (1974); *Alarms. Female Voices* (1988); *Night Sky* (1992).

Selected Bibliography

JEWISH-AMERICAN DRAMA

Abramson, Glenda. *Modern Hebrew Drama*. New York: St. Martin's Press, 1979. (Chapter on Israeli and world Holocaust drama)

Ben Zvi, Linda, ed. *Theater in Israel*. Ann Arbor: University of Michigan Press, 1996.

Catalogue of Plays of Jewish Interest. New York: Jewish Theater Association and National Foundation for Jewish Culture, 1981.

Cohen, Edward, ed. *New Jewish Voices—Plays Produced by the Jewish Repertory Theatre*. Albany: SUNY Press, 1985. (With a list of plays produced by the theatre, 1974–1984)

Cohen, Sarah, B., ed. *Jewish American Women Drama*. Syracuse, NY: Syracuse University Press, 1997.

Coleman, Edward. *Plays of Jewish Interest on the American Stage, 1752–1821*. Vol. 35. New York: Publications of the American Jewish Historical Society, 1939, 227–80.

The Drama Review. Jewish Theater Issue, 24, No. 3 (1980).

Fuchs, Elinor. *Plays of the Holocaust—An International Anthology*. New York; Theater Communications Group, 1987. (With a selected bibliography of plays of the Holocaust)

Glicksberg, Charles. "The Jewish Element in American Drama." *The Chicago Jewish Forum* 10, No. 1 (Fall 1951), 110–15.

Isser, Edward. *Stages of Annihilation: Theatrical Representations of the Holocaust*. Madison, NJ: Fairleigh Dickinson Press, 1997.

Joseph, Herbert, ed. *Modern Israeli Drama*. Madison, NJ: Fairleigh Dickinson Press, 1983.

Landa, Myer Jack. "The Jew and the Drama." *The Jewish Chronicle* (August 27, 1920), 21.

Landis, Joseph. *The Great Jewish Plays*. New York: Avon Books, 1972.

Lifson, David. *The Yiddish Theater in America*. New York: Thomas Yoseloff, 1965.

Mersand, Joseph. *The American Drama Presents the Jew: An Evaluation of the Treatment of Jewish Characters in Contemporary Drama*. New York: New York Public Library, 1939.

———. *Traditions in American Literature: A Study of Jewish Characters and Authors*. 1939; rpt., Port Washington, NY: Kennikat, 1968.

Sandrow, Nahma. *Vagabond Stars: A World History of the Yiddish Theater*. New York: Harper and Row, 1977.

Schiff, Ellen. *From Stereotype to Metaphor: The Jew in Contemporary Drama*. Albany, NY: SUNY Press, 1982. (Full bibliography on the subject of Jews in world drama)

———, ed. *Awake and Singing: Seven Classic Plays from the American Jewish Repertoire*. New York: Penguin Books, 1995. (Excellent introduction to the subject. The footnotes refer to studies and articles on early Jewish-American drama)

———. *Fruitful and Multiplying: Nine Contemporary Plays from the American Jewish Repertoire*. New York: Penguin Books, 1996. (Excellent introduction to the subject. The footnotes refer to studies and articles on early Jewish-American drama)

Skloot, Robert. *The Darkness We Carry: The Drama of the Holocaust*. Madison: University of Wisconsin Press, 1988. (The Notes at the end of the book contain items, including articles related to the Holocaust drama)

———. *The Theater of the Holocaust: Four Plays*. Madison: University of Wisconsin Press, 1982.

Taub, Michael, ed. *Israeli Holocaust Drama*. Syracuse, NY: Syracuse University Press, 1996. (Introduction and bibliography)

———. *Israeli Issue: Modern International Drama*. 1993.

———. *Modern Israeli Drama in Translation*. Portsmouth, NH: Heinemann Press, 1993.

JEWISH-AMERICAN POETRY

Fishman, Charles, ed. *Blood to Remember: American Poets on the Holocaust*. Lubbock: Texas Tech University Press, 1991.

Fried, Lewis, ed. *Handbook of American Jewish Literature*. Westport, CT: Greenwood Press, 1988.

Knopp, Josephine. *Contemporary Jewish Writing*. Urbana: University of Illinois Press, 1975.

Pacernik, Gary. *Memory and Fire: Ten American Jewish Poets*. New York: Peter Lang, 1989.

Rothenberg, Jerome, et al., eds. *A Big Jewish Book*. New York: Anchor Press, 1978.

Schwartz, Howard. *Voices from the Arc—The Modern Jewish Poets*. New York: Avon Books, 1980.

Shapiro, Ann, ed. *Jewish American Women Writers—A Biocritical Sourcebook*. Westport, CT: Greenwood Press, 1990.

Wisse, Ruth. *A Little Love in Big Manhattan—Two Yiddish Poets*. Cambridge, MA: Harvard University Press, 1988.

Translations from Yiddish

Betsky, Sarah Zweig, ed. *Onions and Cucumbers and Plums*. Detroit: Wayne State University Press, 1958.

Harshav, Barbara, and Benjamin Harshav, eds. *American Yiddish Poetry*. Berkeley: University of California Press, 1986.

Howe, Irving, et al., eds., *The Penguin Book of Modern Yiddish Verse*. New York: Penguin Books, 1988.

Whitman, Ruth. *Modern Yiddish Poetry*. Detroit: Wayne State University Press, 1995.

Translations from Hebrew

Bargad, Warren, and Stanley, Cheyet, eds. *Israeli Poetry—A Contemporary Anthology*. Bloomington: Indiana University Press, 1986.

Carmi, T. *The Penguin Book of Hebrew Verse*. New York: Penguin Books, 1981.

General Anthologies

Adcock, Fleur, ed. *Twentieth Century Women Poetry*. London: Faber, 1987.

Allison, Alexander et al., eds. *The Norton Anthology of Poetry*. New York: Norton, 1983.

Evans, David, ed. *New Voices in American Poetry*. Cambridge, MA: Winthrop, 1973.

Hall, Donald, ed. *Contemporary American Poetry*. New York: Penguin Books, 1971.

Hoover, Paul, ed. *Postmodern American Poetry*. New York: Norton, 1994.

Messerli, Douglas, ed. *From the Other Side of the Century—A New American Poetry, 1960–1990*. Los Angeles: Sun and Moon, 1994.

Pack, Robert. *The Breadloaf Anthology of Contemporary American Poetry*. Hanover, NH: University Press of New England, 1985.

Poulin, A., Jr, ed. *Contemporary American Poetry*. Boston: Houghton Mifflin, 1985.

Rothenberg, Jerome, and Pierre Joris, eds. *Poems for the Millennium*. Berkeley: University of California Press, 1996.

Drama Index

Note: **Boldface** numbers refer to dramatists who are featured in the sourcebook.

About Last Night, 118
Across the River and into the Jungle
  (Kopit), 68
Adding Machine, The (Rice), 4
Adventures of Homer McGundy, The
  (Lebow), 105, 107
Aeschylus, 180
After the Fall (Miller), xv, 142, 147–49,
  151
Agamemnon (Aeschylus, Swados), 180
Albee, Edward, 13, 15, 61, 72, 142, 184
Alfred, William, 127
Alfred Trilogy, The (Horovitz), 62, 63
Alice [or Wonderland] in Concert
  (Swados), 180–81
All My Sons (Miller), 4, 73, 141, 143,
  145, 146, 147, 151, 156
All over Town (Schisgal), 167
Allen, Annulla, 127, 130
Allen, Woody, xv, 6, **10–17**, 73, 84
Altered States (Chayefsky), 26
Altman, Robert, 26, 69
American Buffalo (Mamet), 115–16, 118,
  119, 120, 121, 122
American Clock, The (Miller), 142, 156

American Daughter, An (Wasserstein),
  191, 196, 197
American Drama Since World War II
  (Weales), 100
American Dream, The (Albee), 72
Americanization of Emily, The (Chayef-
  sky), 26
Angels in America (Kushner), xv, 8, 79,
  80, 81–85, 86, 87, 88
Anne Frank, 122
Annie Hall (Allen), 84
Annulla: An Autobiography (Mann), 5,
  128, 129, 130, 132
Another Woman (Allen), 15
Ansky, Szymon, 26, 28, 80
Anyone Can Whistle (Sondheim,
  Laurents), 96
Apology, 45
Army Service Present, 96
Arthur, Beatrice, 11
Ashes, 128
Ashley, Elizabeth, 177
As Is (Hoffman), 49
Assignment, The (Kopit), 70
Assignment Home, 96

Asylum: Or, What the Gentlemen Are Up To, Not to Mention the Ladies (Kopit), 69
Atkinson, Brooks, 100
Aubade (Kopit) (originally titled *Through a Labyrinth*), 68
Auerbach, Doris, 75
Austin, Lynn, 91
Author! Author! (Horovitz), 61, 63
Avni, Ran, 7, 111
Awake and Sing! (Odets), 5, 6, 8
Ayckbourn, Alan, 21

"Bachelor Party, The" (Chayefsky), 28
Bachelor Party, The (Chayefsky), 26
Baird, Zoe, 196
Baitz, Jon Robin, xv, 6, **18–24**
Baldwin, Alec, 118, 122
Bamman, Gary, 128
Barking Sharks (Horovitz), 62
Barnes, Clive, 48, 57, 75, 183–84
Barry, Julian, 115
Barth, Belle, 34, 35
Basement, The (Schisgal), 171
Beatty, John Lee, 117
Beckett, Samuel, 61, 68, 72, 114, 117
Bellow, Saul, 34, 36, 42, 114
Belt, The (Sifton), 4
Bent (Sherman), 173, 174–75, 176–77
Bergman, Ingemar, 13, 15
Berle, Milton, 54
Berman, Shelley, 8
Bernstein, Charles, xvii
Bernstein, Leonard, 96
Betsey Brown: A Rhythm and Blues Musical (Shange, Mann), 129, 131, 132
Beveridge, Thomas, 71
"Big Deal, The" (Chayefsky), 28
Bigsby, Christopher, 117
Bishop, Andre, 92
Blake, Josh, 63
Blatt, Kenneth Stuart, 171
Bogart, Humphrey, 12
Bond, James, 12
Bone-the-Fish (Kopit), 70
Book of Job, 183
Boys in the Band (Crowley), 81

Bradish, Gaynor, 68, 74
Brantley, Ben, 139, 189, 197
Brechner, Stanley, 7
Brecht, Bertolt, 26, 74, 80
Bright Room Called Day (Kushner), 80, 85–86, 87, 88
Brighton Beach Memoirs (Simon), 5
Broadway Bound (Simon), 6
Broken Glass (Miller) xvi, 142, 150–51, 156, 188
Bronnenberg, Mark, 79
Brook, Peter, 180
Brown, Arvin, 115
Brown, Jo Giese, 128
Brown, Joe, 106
Bruce, Lenny, 120
Brustein, Robert, 30, 121, 189
Bryden, Bill, 115
Bryne, Barbara, 128
Buck (Ribman), 162, 163, 164
Buffalo Bill and the Indians: Or, Sitting Bull's History Lesson (Kopit), 69
Bullets over Broadway, 45
Burial of Esposito, The (Ribman), 160–61
Bush, George, 86

Cabin, The (Mamet), 113
Caesar, Sid, 10
Caine Mutiny Court Martial, The (Wouk), 5
Camel (Mamet), 114
Canby, Vincent, 24, 133
Candide (Voltaire), 174
Cannibals Just Don't Know Better (Fierstein), 48
Capek, Karel, 75
Captains Courageous (Kipling, Horovitz), 61
Carlsen, James W., 175
Carlson, Susan, 197
Carnal Knowledge (Feiffer), 39
Carroll, Baikida, 129
Casino Royale (Allen), 10
"Catch My Boy on Sunday" (Chayefsky), 28
Catered Affair, The (Chayefsky), 26
Cather, Willa, 114
Cazale, John, 61

Celluloid Closet, The, 45
Central Park West (Allen), 11, 13, 15
Ceremony of Innocence, The (Ribman),
160, 162, 164
Chaikin, Joseph, 69
Chamber Music (Kopit), 69, 71, 72
Chapman, Robert, 68
Chayefsky, Paddy, **25–32**
Cheers, 45
Chekhov, Anton, 18, 72, 117, 119, 177,
180
Cherry Orchard, The (Chekhov), 18, 72,
119, 180
Chinese, The (Schisgal), 170
"Chips Are Down, The" (Horovitz), 61
Chopin, Frederic, 93
Chopin Playoffs, The (Horovitz), 63
Christiansen, Richard, 115–16
Christmas Carol, A (Dickens), 105
Cibula, Nan, 117
Clayburgh, Jill, 61
Clinton, Bill, 196
Closet Madness (Schisgal), 168
Clum, John, 49
Clurman, Harold, 15
Cody, Buffalo Bill, 72–73
Cohan, George M., 189
Cohen, Arthur A., xvii
Cohen, Ed, 111
Cohen, Ron, 133
Cohen, Sarah Blacher, **33–37**
Cohn, Roy, xv, 81, 82–84, 88
Cohn, Ruby, 116
Cold Storage (Ribman), 159, 161–62
Cole, Susan Letzler, 133
Comden, Betty, 96
Comeback, The (Horovitz), 59
Conference of the Birds (Swados), 181
Conquest of Everest, The (Kopit), 69
"Conquest of Television, The" (Kopit),
70
Consequences of Goosing, The (Schisgal),
168
Conversations with My Father (Gardner),
xv, 5, 20, 53, 54, 55, 56, 57
Cool Million, A (West), 93
Corneille, Pierre, 80
Corrente, Michael, 116

Counsellor-at-Law (Rice), 4
*Cowboy, the Indian and the Fervent
Feminist, The* (Schisgal), 168
Cracks (Sherman), 174, 176
Crawling Arnold (Feiffer), 39–40
*Creation of the World and Other Busi-
ness, The* (Miller), 142, 151
Crouch, Paula, 107
Crouse, Lindsay, 118
Crowley, Matt, 81
Crucible, The (Miller), 4, 142, 143, 145–
47, 150, 154, 156
Cryptogram, The (Mamet), 114, 117,
119, 124
Cyparis (Lebow), 102, 105, 107

Daddy's Girls, 45
Danger: Memory: Two Plays (Miller),
142, 156
Dangerous Corner, A (Priestly, Mamet),
118
Daniels, Marc, 111
Daniels, Robert L., 133
Dark Pony (Mamet), 114, 117
"David Mamet: All True Stories"
(Bigsby), 117
Davis, Ossie, 49
Day of the Games (Ribman), 159
*Day the Whores Came Out to Play Ten-
nis, The* (Kopit), 69, 72, 74
*Days and Nights of a French Horn
Player* (Schisgal), 166
Death (Allen), 11, 14
Death Knocks (Allen), 11, 13–14
Death of a Salesman (Miller), xv, 4, 73,
121, 137, 141, 143, 145, 151, 153–54,
156
Deconstructing Harry (Allen), 11
Deeny (Mamet), 117
Delany, A. Elizabeth, 129, 132
Delany, Sarah L., 129, 132
Der gute Mensch von Sezuan (Brecht), 80
Designing Women, 189
Deuce, The (Horovitz), 61
Dickens, Charles, 105
Dietz, Susan, 163
Disappearance of the Jews, The (Mamet),
113, 117, 122, 123

Discovery of America (Kopit), 70
Dispatches: A Rock Musical (Swados),
    181, 184
Do I Hear a Waltz? (Sondheim,
    Laurents), 96
Doll's House, A (Ibsen), 128
Don Juan in Texas (Kopit), 68
Don't Drink the Water (Allen), 11, 12,
    13, 15
Doonesbury (Trudeau, Swados), 184
Dr. Jekyl and Ms. Hyde, 45
Dreiser, Theodore, 114
Drescher, Fran, 163
Dreyfus, Richard, 61
Driving Miss Daisy (Uhry), 186, 187–88,
    189
Duck Variations (Mamet), 114, 115, 120
Ducks and Lovers (Schisgal), 166, 167
Duncan, Isadora, 176
Durang, Christopher, 42
Durrenmatt, Frederick, 72, 75
Duval, Robert, 115
Dybbuk, A (Ansky, Kushner), 80
Dybbuk, The (Ansky), 28, 55, 127

Earplay, 128
eda-Young, Barbara, 63
Eder, Richard, 176
Edge, The (Mamet), 118
Edmund (Mamet), 117, 119, 120–21, 123
Egan, Philip J., 163
Eichelberg, Ethel, 46
8 1/2 (Fellini), 70
Eliot, T. S., 62
Eliot Loves (Feiffer), 39
Empress of Eden, The (Lebow), 102, 106
Enclave, The (Laurents), 97, 98
End of the Day, The (Baitz), 20–22, 23
End of the World (Kopit), 70, 71, 73, 75
Endgame (Beckett), 72
Enemy of the People, An (Ibsen, Miller),
    142, 145
Esslin, Martin, 40, 41–42, 74
Esther: A Vaudeville Megillah (Swados),
    181, 182, 183
Execution of Justice (Mann), 129, 130,
    131, 132, 133

Face, The (Laurents), 96, 97
Fair Country, A (Baitz), 18, 23
Fales, Nancy, 60
Falsettoland (Finn), 92
Falsettos (Finn, Lapine), 92, 93
Family Business (Goldberg), 6
Fanny Kelly (Mann), 128
Feiffer, Jules, **38–43**
Feiffer's People (Feiffer), 39
Feingold, Michael, 139
Fellini, Federico, 15, 70
Fenelon, Fania, 4, 150
Ferber, Edna, 8
"Few Kind Words from Newark, A"
    (Chayefsky), 25
Fiddler on the Roof, 49
Fields, Totie, 34, 35–36
Fierstein, Harvey, xv, 7, **44–52**, 96
Fifth Season, The (Regan), 5
Fighting over Beverley (Horovitz), 60, 62
Film Society, The (Baitz), 18–19
Final War of Olly Winter, The (Ribman),
    159, 160
Fingernails Blue as Flowers (Ribman),
    161
Finn, William, 92
Fiorello!, 127
First Is Supper (Berman), 8
Flannery, James, 107
Flatulist, The (Schisgal), 170
Flight to the West (Rice), 4
Floating Lightbulb, The (Allen), 6, 11,
    13, 15
Flowering Peach, The (Odets), 6
Flynn, Kimberly, 79, 80
Focus (Miller), 142, 143, 144–45, 147
Foley, James, 122
Foreman, Richard, 70
Forever Game, The (Gardner), 54
Forget Him (Fierstein), 46, 47, 48
Fornes, Maria Irene, 120
Fosca (Tarchetti), 93
Found a Peanut (Margulies), 137
Four of Us, The: The Story of a Family
    (Swados), 181, 184
Fox, Michael J., 93
Frank, Ann, 138
Frankel, Gene, 69

Franken, Rose, 8
Frankl, Victor, 49
Franz, Dennis, 116
Freedman, Morris, 74
Freeman, Gerald, 69
Freeman, Morgan, 163, 186
Freud on Broadway (Sievers), 100
Frieder, Sol, 63
Friedman, Bruce Jay, 73
Fruitful and Multiplying (Schiff), 7
Fugue in a Nursery (Fierstein), 44

Garbo Talks, 45
Gardner, Herb, xv, 5, 20, **53–58**
Geis, Deborah, 120
Gelber, Jack, 69
Gemini (Kopit), 68
Genesis: A Living Conversation (Moyer), 181, 184
Gentlemen's Agreement, 100
Gere, Richard, 175
Getting Even (Allen), 11
Ghost Sonata (Strindberg, Swados), 180
Ghosts (Ibsen), 70
Gideon (Chayefsky), 26, 27, 29, 30
Gill, Brendan, 121
Ginsberg, Allen, xv, xvi, xvii
Girgus, Sam, 15
Glass Menagerie, The (Williams), 13, 128
Glengarry Glen Ross (Mamet), 114, 116, 117, 118, 119, 120, 121–22, 123
God (Allen), 11, 14
Goethe, Johann von, 80
Goldberg, Dick, 6
Goldberg Street (Mamet), xvi, 113, 117, 122, 123
Golden Door, The, 114
Gone with the Wind, 188
Good Help Is Hard to Find (Kopit), 70
Good Person of Setzuan, The (Brecht, Kushner), 80
Goodbye People, The (Gardner), 5, 53, 54–55, 56, 57
Gray, Frances, 48–49
Gray, Simon, 20, 21
Great White Hope, The (Sackler), 5
Green, Adolph, 96

Green, William, 49
Greensboro (A Requiem) (Mann), 129, 130–31, 133
Grey, Joel, 163
Grosbard, Ulu, 15, 115
Gross, Gregory, 49
Grown Ups (Feiffer), 39, 41, 42
Guare, John, 120
Gussow, Mel, 41, 48, 106, 133, 184, 189
Gypsy (Sondheim, Laurents), 96, 100

Hackett, Buddy, 10
Haggadah, The: A Passover Cantata (Swados), 181, 182
Hair!, 181, 184
Hallelujah, Baby! (Laurents), 96, 98
Hallmark Hall of Fame, 189
Hamlet (Shakespeare), 72
"Hands of a Stranger" (Kopit), 70
Hannah and Her Sisters (Allen), 15
Hansberry, Lorraine, 5
Harelik, Mark, 5
Harris, Ed, 122
Harry, Noon and Night (Ribman), 159–60, 163
Harvest, The, 45
Haunted Host, The (Patrick), 45
Haut Gout (Havis), 5
Having Our Say (Mann), 129, 132, 133
Havis, Allan, 5
He and She, 128
Heavenly Theatre, The (Kushner), 80
Hedda Gabler (Ibsen), 128
Heidi Chronicles, The (Wasserstein), 191, 194–95, 196, 197
Hellman, Lillian, 8, 24, 26
Hemingway, Ernest, 68
Henning, Joel, 75
Henry Lumper (Horovitz), 62
Henry, William A., lll, 88
Hepburn, Katherine, 96
Herman, Jerry, 96
Hero, The (Kopit), 69
Herr, Michael, 181, 184
Hill, Anita, 122
Hinden, Michael, 119
Hirsch, Foster, 15–16
Hirsch, Judd, 54

Hoffman, Dustin, 116, 163
Hoffman, William, 49
Hold Me (Feiffer), 39
Holden, Stephen, 41, 184
"Holiday Song" (Chayefsky), 26, 27, 29
Hollywood Playhouse, 96
Home of the Brave (Laurents), 96, 97–98, 100
Homecoming, The (Pinter), 61, 114
Homer, Winslow, 62
Homicide (Mamet), 113, 118
Homonucleus of Cordoba (Lebow), 106
Honest-to-God Schnozzola, The- (Horovitz), 60
Hoofman, Aaron, 5
Hopkins, Anthony, 118
Hopper, Edward, 62
Horovitz, Israel, xv, **59–67**
Hospital, The (Chayefsky), 26, 30
House of Games (Mamet), 118, 122
How I Crossed the Street for the First Time All by Myself (Gardner), 54
How We Reached an Impasse on Nuclear Energy (Schisgal), 168, 169
Hudgins, Christopher, 120
Huffman, Felicity, 117, 118
Hunt, Linda, 129
Hurst, Fannie, 8

I Can't Help It (Lebow), 102
Ibsen, Henrik, 26, 70, 142, 145
Iceman Cometh, The (O'Neill), 141
Illusion (Corneille, Kushner), 80
I'm Not Rappaport (Gardner), xv, 53, 54, 56, 57
I'm with Ya, Duke (Gardner), 54
Immigrant, The (Harelik), 5
Impromptu (Lapine, Kernochan), 93
"In a Child's Name" (Kopit), 70
In the Shadow of Love: A Teen AIDS Story, 45
Incident at Vichy (Miller), 142, 143, 144, 149–50, 151
Independence Day, 45
Indian Wants the Bronx, The (Horovitz), 60
Indians (Kopit), 69, 71, 72–73, 74
International Stud, The (Fierstein), 44

Into the Woods (Sondheim, Lapine), 92
Invitation to a March (Laurents), 100
Ionesco, Eugene, 61
Isn't It Romantic? (Wasserstein), xvi, 6, 191, 192–94, 195
Israel Horovitz Trilogy, An (Horovitz) (Also known as: *The Sault Ste. Marie Trilogy*), 60, 63
Isser, E. R., 107, 132
It's Called the Sugar Plum (Horovitz), 59, 60
Ivey, Judith, 6

J. B. (MacLeish), 29
Jacobi, Martin, 6
Jans, Alaric, 114
Jay, Ricky, 117, 118
Jerusalem (Swados), 181, 182
"Jingle Bells" 131
Job (Swados), 181, 182
Johnston, J. J., 115, 117
Jolly (Mamet), 117
Jonah (Swados), 181, 182
Joseph Dintentfass (Mamet), 118
Journey of the Fifth Horse (Ribman), 159, 160, 162
Jumping-Off Place, The (Weales), 163, 171
Jung, Karl, 91

Kaiser, Georg, 75
Kalem, T., 15
Kane, Leslie, 65
Kanin, Garson, 25
Katz, Johnathan, 118
Kauffmann, Stanley, 48
Kaufman, George S., 5, 15
Kazan, Alfred, 6
Keaton, Diane, 61
Keepers, The (Lebow), 102, 105
Keil, Robert, 127
Kernochan, Sarah, 93
Kerr, Walter, 48, 177
Kiefer, Daniel, 88
King, Alan, 15
Kissel, Howard, 49
Kissinger, Henry, 42
Klaic, Dragan, 75

Klein, Alvin, 74
Kleist, Heinrich von, 117
Koch, Ed, 83
Koch, Joanne, 34, 36
Koch, Kenneth, xvi, xvii
Kolin, Philip C., 132
Konigsberg, Allen Stewart (Woody
    Allen), 10
Kopit, Arthur, xv, **68–78**
Kramer, Larry, 49
Kramer, Richard E., 132
Kull the Conqueror, 45
Kushner, Tony, xv, xvi, 8, **79–89**

La Cage aux Folles (Fierstein), 45, 47,
    48, 49, 96
La Celestina (Rojas), 80
*La Fin de la Baleine: An Opera for the
    Apocalypse* (Kushner), 80
La Fleuve Rouge (Laville, Mamet), 119
Ladies Locker Room, The (Cohen), 34–35
LaGuardia, Fiorello, 127
Lahr, John, 41, 75, 87
Lahti, Christine, 22
Lakeboat (Mamet), 114, 117, 119–20
Lamont, Rosette C., 163–64
Langham, Michael, 128
Lapine, James, 6, **90–94**
Last Night of Ballyhoo, The (Uhry), xvi,
    186, 188, 189
Last Yankee, The (Miller), 142, 156
Latent Heterosexual, The (Chayefsky),
    26, 27, 29, 30
Laurents, Arthur, **95–101**
Laville, Pierre, 119
Lawrence, Wally, 68
Lax, Eric, 10, 15
Leader (Horovitz), 60
Lebow, Barbara, xv, 8, **102–8**, 132
Legs Diamond (Fierstein), 49
Lemmon, Jack, 122
Leroux, Gaston, 70
Lessing, Norman, **109–12**
Letters to Iris (Horovitz), 61
Levinson, Barry, 118
Lewis, Allen, 74
Life in the Theatre, A (Mamet), 117, 120
Life with Mikey (Lapine), 93

L'Illusion (Corneille, Kushner), 80
Line (Horovitz), 60, 61
Listening Out Loud (Swados), 184
Litko (Mamet), 114
Little, Cleavon, 54
Little Joe Monaghan (Lebow), 102, 103–
    4, 105, 106
Little Johnny Jones (Cohan, Uhry), 186,
    188
Little Murders (Feiffer), 40
Lloyd, Christopher, 177
Loesser, Frank, 186
Loman Family Picnic, The (Margulies), 6,
    137, 139
Loss of Memory (Laurents), 97, 99
*Louisiana Territory; or, Lewis and Clark—
    Lost and Found* (Kopit), 69
Loving, 45
Lubow, Arthur, 87
Luck, Pluck, and Virtue (Lapine), 93
Luftmensch, The (Mamet), 113, 122, 123
Lunden, Jeffrey, 70
Lupone, Patti, 117
Luv (Schisgal), 166, 167

Mackinac (Mamet), 115
MacLeish, Archibald, 26, 29
Macy, William H., 114, 115, 117, 119
Madden, John, 70
Madhouse in Goa, A (Sherman), 176, 177
Maggio, Michael, 70
Make-Believe Town (Mamet), 113
*Making a Scene: The Contemporary
    Drama of Jewish-American Women*
    (Cohen), 34
Malamud, Bernard, 42, 142
Mamet, David, xv, xvi, 65, 70, 74, 75,
    113–26, 132
Man and His Symbols (Jung), 91
Man Behind the Gun, The, 96
Man Who Had All the Luck, The (Miller),
    141
Manhattan (Allen), 13
Mann, Emily, xv, 5, **127–35**
Mantegna, Joe, 117, 118
March of the Falsettos (Finn), 92
Margulies, Donald, xv, 6, 8, **136–40**
Marranos (Mamet), 115

Martin, Steve, 118
"Marty" (Chayefsky), 27
Marty (Chayefsky), 26, 30
Marx Brothers, 177
Mason, Jackie, 15
McCarthy, Joseph, 79, 82
McCullers, Carson, 184
McDonald, R. David, 127
McKellen, Ian, 177
Meadow, Lynn, 69
Medea (Euripides, Swados), 180, 181
Meisner, Sanford, 114
Memory of Two Mondays, A (Miller), 59,
    142
Menachem Mendel (Sholem Aleichem),
    123
Merman, Ethel, 44
Merritt, Michael, 117
Messiah (Sherman), 173–74, 175–76, 177
Meyer, Kate Beaird, 132
Meyer, Marlena, 60
Mhil'daiim (Kopit), 69
Miami Vice, 45
Middle of the Night (Chayefsky), 26, 27,
    28
Milk, Harvey, 129, 131
Millennium Approaches (Kushner), 81,
    83, 84, 85
Miller, Arthur, xv, xvi, 4, 24, 26, 27, 28,
    73, 133, 137, **141–58**, 184, 188
Misfits, The (Miller), 142
Mistral, Gabriela, 182
Model Apartment, The (Margulies), xvi,
    8, 136, 137, 138, 139
Molly Picon's Return Engagement (Sarah
    Cohen), 34
Molodowsky, Kadia, 182
"Monte Sant' Angelo" (Miller), 154–55
Moscone, George, 129, 131
Mosher, Gregory, 115, 117, 119, 120,
    122
Mostel, Zero, 46
"Mother, The" (Chayefsky), 28
Moyers, Bill, 181, 184
Mr. Peters' Connections (Miller), 142
Mrs. Doubtfire, 45
Muhammed, Elijah, 127

Murder She Wrote, 45
My Good Name (Laurents), 97, 99

*Naked: One Couple's Journey through
    Infertility* (Mann), 128
Nelson, Richard, 132
Nemerov, Howard, xvi, xvii
Network (Chayefsky), 26, 30
Newman, Paul, 119
Nick and Nora (Laurents), 99
Nightclub Cantata (Swados), 181, 183–84
Nightingale, Benedict, 75
Night Witch (Lebow and Wittow), 103
Nine (Kopit), 70
No One Will Be Immune (Mamet), 118
No T.O. for Love (Chayefsky), 25
No Villain (Miller), 142
Normal Heart, The (Kramer), 49
Norman, Marsha, 61
North Shore Fish (Horovitz), 60, 62
Novick, Julius, 74
Nussbaum, Mike, 117

Objectivists, xvi–xvii
Odets, Clifford, xv, 4, 5, 6, 8, 26, 27, 28,
    29, 30, 132
Oedipus, 128
*Oh Dad, Poor Dad, Momma's Hung You
    in the Closet and I'm Feelin' So Sad*
    (Kopit), 68–69, 71–72, 73, 74
O'Hara, Frank, 184
Old Neighborhood (Mamet), 117, 124
"Old System, The" (Bellow, Cohen), 35
Old Wine in a New Bottle (Schisgal), 170
Oleanna (Mamet), 117, 118, 120, 122
Oliver, Edith, 41, 49, 57, 75
"On Paul Ickovic's Photographs"
    (Mamet), 116
On the Runway of Life (Kopit), 68
On Tidy Endings (Fierstein), 45, 47
O'Neill, Eugene, 5, 26, 60, 61, 141, 142
Ozick, Cynthia, 34, 42, 123

Pacino, Al, 61, 115, 122
Paint Your Wagon (Chayefsky), 26
Papp, Joseph, 180, 182
Park Your Car in Harvard Yard (Horo-
    vitz), 60

Parnell, Peter, 60
Parr, Jack, 10
Passing By (Sherman), 174
Passing through from Exotic Places (Ribman), 161
Passover (Mamet), 113
Passion of Josef D., The (Chayefsky), 26, 27, 29–30
Passione d'Amore, 93
Passion (Sondheim, Lapine), 93
Patrick, Robert, 45
Payofski's Discovery (Horovitz), 61
Perestroika (Kushner), 80, 83, 84, 85
Perlman, Arthur, 70
Peter Pan, 111
Peters, Bernadette, 177
Phantom of the Opera, The (Leroux, Kopit), 70, 74
Photograph (Stein, Lapine), 91
Picon, Molly, 34, 36
Pidgeon, Rebecca, 118
Piece of the Action, A (Gardner), 54
Pinter, Harold, 61, 114, 122
Pirandello, Luigi, 75
"Plain Brown Wrapper, A" (Mamet), 113
Plath, Sylvia, 183–84
Play It Again, Sam (Allen), 11, 12, 15
Playing for Time (Miller), 4, 142, 150
Poison Tree, The, 161
Politically Incorrect, 45
Popkins (Schisgal), 169
Pork (Warhol), 44
Posnock, Ross, 88
Postman, The (Schisgal), 166
Postman Always Rings Twice, The (Mamet), 118
Pouf Positive (Patrick), 45
Prairie du Chien (Mamet), 117
Price, The (Miller), 4, 142, 143, 151–53, 156
Priestly, J. B., 118
Primary English Class, The (Horovitz), 59, 60
Prince, Harold, 70
"Printer's Measure" (Chayefsky), 27
"Promontory Point Revisited" (Kopit), 70
Pugliesi, Frank, 60

Pushcart Peddlers, The (Schisgal), 169

Quannapowitt Quartet, The (Horovitz), 62
Questioning of Nick, The (Kopit), 68, 71, 73

Rabbi and the Toyota Dealer, The (Schisgal), 170
Rabe, David, 120
"Rake, The" (Mamet), 114
Randy Newman's Faust (Mamet), 118
Rap Master Ronnie (Trudeau, Swados), 184
Rats (Horovitz), 60
Reagan, Ronald, 82, 86
Real Thing, The (Stoppard), 75
Redgrave, Vanessa, 26
Regan, Sylvia, 5, 8
"Reluctant Citizen, The" (Chayefsky), 27
Reunion (Mamet), 114, 119, 128
Reverberations (Schisgal), 171
Ribman, Ronald, **159–65**
Riccio, Thomas, 70
Rice, Elmer, xv, 4
Rich, Frank, 41, 57, 75, 87, 177
Richard II (Shakespeare), 59
Richards, David, 75, 197
Richardson, Tony, 70, 127
Ride Down Mr. Morgan, The (Miller), 142
Rifkin, Ron, 22
Road to Nirvana (Kopit), 70, 73, 74, 75
Robards, Jason, 53, 60
Robber Bridegroom, The (Uhry), 186–87, 188
Robbins, Jerome, 69, 96
Robinson, Edward G., 26
Rodgers, Richard, 96
Roehm, Ernst, 174
Rojas, Fernando de, 80
Roosevelt, Franklin Delano, 63, 64
Rose Tattoo, The (Williams), 72
Rosen by Any Other Name, A (Horovitz), 63, 64
Rosenberg, Ethel, 83

Rosenbergs, The, 81,
Rosenfeld, Seth Svi, 60
Rosten, Leo, 123
Roth, Philip, 42, 73
Roudané, Matthew, 119
Rug Merchants of Chaos, The (Ribman), 162–63
Runaways (Swados), 180, 181, 182, 184
Russia, Poland (Mamet), 113

Sackler, Howard, 5
Safe Sex (Fierstein), 46, 47, 48, 49
Sagal, Peter, 62, 65
Salesman in Beijing (Miller), 142
Sand, George, 93
Savran, David, 132–33
Schacter, Steven, 114
Schiff, Ellen, 132, 182
Schisgal, Murray, **166–72**
Schlemiel the First (Singer, Cohen), 34
Schloff, Aaron, 189
Schrecks (Schigal), 166
Schroeder, Patricia R., 133
Schvey, Henry, 120
Secrets of the Rich (Kopit), 69
Seeger, Pete, 180
Serban, Andrei, 180
Serlin, Bruce, 60
Sesame Street, 45
Seurat, George, 92
Seventh Seal, The (Bergman), 13
74 Georgia Avenue (Schisgal), 169–70
Sexaholics (Schisgal), 169
Sexual Perversity in Chicago (Mamet), 114, 115, 118, 119
Shange, Ntozake, 129
Shapiro, David, xvii
Shapiro, Harvey, xvii
Shawl, The (Mamet), 117, 118, 120
Shayna Maidel, A (Lebow), xvi, 8, 102, 103, 104, 105, 106–7, 132
Shepard, Sam, 49, 65
Shepherd, Richard F., 111
Sherbert, Linda, 107
Sherman, Johnathan Marc, 60
Sherman, Martin, **173–79**
Shewey, Don, 48
Sholem Aleichem, 123, 152

Side Effects (Allen), 11
Sievers, David, 100
Sifton, Paul, 4
Sight Unseen (Margulies), 136, 137, 138–39
Silverstein, Shel, 118
Simon, John, 48, 49, 57, 75, 121, 133, 184, 189, 194
Simon, Neil, 5, 6, 49, 53, 73
Simple Kind of Love, A (Schisgal), 166
Simpsons, The, 45
Sing to Me Through Open Windows (Kopit), 68, 69, 71, 74
Singer, Isaac Beshevis, 34, 36
Sisters Rosensweig, The (Wasserstein), xvi, 191, 195–96, 197
Sitcom (Barry), 115
Situation Normal (Miller), 142
Skelton, Red, 45–46
Skloot, Robert, 63, 65, 176–77
Skulnik, Menasha, 5
Slavs! (Kushner), 80, 85, 86–87, 88
Smith, Anna Deavere, 129
Smith, Melanie, 132
Smits, Jimmy, 163
Solitary Thing, A (Sherman), 173
Solomon, Alisa, 184
Some Freaks (Mamet), 113
Son Who Hunted Tigers, The (Ribman), 161
Sondheim, Stephen, 91, 92, 93, 96
Song of Songs (Swados), 182, 183
Sophie & Totie & Belle (Cohen), 33, 34, 36
Sophie Tucker Red Hot Yiddish Mama (Cohen), 34
Southern, Hugh, 49
Spanish Prisoner, The (Mamet), 118
Spared (Horovitz), 61
Speed-the-Plow (Mamet), 75, 113–14, 116, 117, 118, 120, 122, 124
Spewack, Bella, 8
Spinella, Stephen, 80
Spookhouse (Fierstein), 47–48, 49
Squirrels (Mamet), 120
Stardust Memories (Allen), 15
"Starstruck" (Kopit), 70
Stein, Gertrude, 91

Steinberg, Sex, and the Saint (Horovitz), 59
Stella (Goethe, Kushner), 80
Still Life (Mann), 128, 131, 132, 133
Stoppard, Tom, 20, 75
Strawberry Statement, The (Horovitz), 61
Streep, Meryl, 177
Street Scene (Rice), 4
Strong-Man's Weak Child (Horovitz), 61,
  64
Strong-Men (Horovitz), 61
Styne, Julie, 96
Substance of Fire, The (Baitz), xvi, 6, 18,
  19–20, 22
Suddenly, Last Summer (Williams), 72
Summer Romance (Schisgal), 168
Summertime, 96
Sunday in the Park with George
  (Sondheim, Lapine), 92
Sunstroke (Ribman), 161
Superman, 68
Swados, Elizabeth, **180–85**
Swados, Harvey, 180
Sweet Table at the Richelieu (Ribman),
  162
"Swellegant Elegance," 45

Table Settings (Lapine), 6, 91, 92
Take the Money and Run (Allen), 10
Tamahori, Lee, 118
Tandy, Jessica, 186
Tarchetti, I. U., 93
Taubman, Howard, 57
Tenth Man, The (Chayefsky), 26, 27, 28–
  29, 30
*There Are No Sacher Tortes in Our Soci-
  ety!* (Schisgal), 167
They Shall Not Die (Wexley), 4
They Too Arise (Miller), 4, 142, 143–44,
  146–47, 150
Thieves (Gardner), 54, 57
Thin Man, The, 96
Things Change (Mamet, Silverstein), 118
Things Went Badly in Westphalia (Sher-
  man), 174
36 (Lessing), 109–111
This Is Not Going to Be Pretty (Fier-
  stein), 45
Thomas, Clarence, 122

Thousand Clowns, A (Gardner), 53–54,
  55–56, 57
Three Hotels (Baitz), 18, 22–23
Three Sisters (Chekhov), 119
Tiger, The (Schisgal), 166, 167
Time of the Cuckoo (Laurents), 96
Timebends (Miller), 4, 142
Times of Harvey Milk, The, 45
Tiny Tim Is Dead (Lebow), 102, 103,
  105, 106
To Dwell in a Place of Strangers (Kopit),
  68
Today, I Am a Fountain Pen (Horovitz),
  63
Tomei, Marisa, 87
Tootsie (Schisgal), 166, 168
Torch Song Trilogy (Fierstein), 44–45, 46–
  47, 48
Torgov, Morley, 63
Trains (Lebow), 103, 105
Trudeau, Gary, 184
Tucker, Sophie, 34, 35
Turgenev, Ivan, 160
Turning Point, The (Laurents), 96
Twelve Dreams (Lapine), 91
Twilight: Los Angeles, 1992 (A. D.
  Smith), 129
Tynan, Kenneth, 30, 49
Typists, The (Schisgal), 166–67

Uhry, Alfred, xv, xvi, **186–90**
Ullmann, Liv, 70
Uncle Vanya (Chekhov), 119
Uncommon Women and Others (Wasser-
  stein), 191–92
Unexpected Tenderness (Horovitz), 62–
  63, 63–65
Untouchables, The (Mamet), 118

Value of Names, 128
Vanya on 42nd Street (Mamet), 119
Veblen, Thorsten, 114
Verdict, The (Mamet), 118, 119
Vetere, Peter, 60
Vidal, Gore, 30
View from the Bridge, A (Miller), 142,
  146
"Vint" (Chekhov), 119

Visit, The (Durrenmatt), 72
Voltaire, 174

Wag the Dog (Mamet), 118
Waiting for Lefty (Odets), 4
Wakefield Plays, The (Horovitz), 59, 60, 62
Waldman, Bob, 186
Walsh, J. T., 115, 117
Warhol, Andy, 44
Wasserstein, Wendy, xv, xvi, 6, **191–98**
Way We Were, The (Laurents), 97, 98–99
Weales, Gerald, 15, 74, 75, 99–100, 163, 170–71
Weekend Near Madison, A, 128
Weisel, Elie, 181, 182
Welcome Stranger (Hoofman), 5
Wellwarth, George, 71, 74, 75
We're No Angels (Mamet), 118
Wernblad, Annette, 15
West, Nathanael, 93
West Side Story (Bernstein, Laurents), 96, 98, 100
Wetzeson, Ross, 65
Wexley, John, 4
What Happened to Thorne's House? (Kopit), 69
What's New, Pussycat? (Allen), 10, 11
What's Up, Tiger Lily? (Allen), 10
What's Wrong with this Picture? (Margulies), 137–38, 139
When She Danced (Sherman), 176, 177
White, Dan, 129, 131
White House Murder Case, The (Feiffer), 39, 41

Who Is Harry Kellerman and Why Is He Saying Those Terrible Things about Me? (Gardner), 54
Who's Afraid of Virginia Woolf? (Albee), 13
Widows and Children First! (Fierstein), 7, 44–45
Widow's Blind Date, The (Horovitz), 60, 61, 63, 64
Williams, Barry B., 65
Williams, Tennessee, 5, 11, 13, 72, 142, 156, 184
Wilson, August, 5
Wilson, Edwin, 75, 175
Wing-Davy, Mark, 129
Wings (Kopit), 70, 71, 73, 75
Without Feathers (Allen), 11
Wittow, Frank, 102
Woods, The (Mamet), 117
Woolf, Leonard, 192
Wouk, Herman, 5
Wyman, David, xvi

Yeston, Maury, 70
You Can't Take It with You (Kaufmann), 15
You Never Know What's Coming Next (Kopit), 68
You Strike a Woman, You Strike a Rock: The Story of Winnie Mandela (Mann), 128

Zeifman, Hersh, 122
Zimmer (Margulies), 137
Ziskin, Victor, 71
Zuckerman, Stephen, 63

Poetry Index

Note: **Boldface** numbers refer to poets who are featured in the sourcebook.

A (Zukofsky), 598, 599
"Abishag" (Glück), 270
"Abomunist Manifesto" (Kaufman), 255
"About This Course" (D. Shapiro), 545
Abrams, Sam, 438
Accidental Center (Heller), 291, 292, 295
Adam's Soul (H. Schwartz), 523
Adams, Leonie, 268
"Adler" (Stern), 584, 585
Adler, Jacob, 584, 585
Adler, Mortimer, 487
Adorno, Theodor, 202, 236, 496
Adult Bookstore (K. Shapiro), 557
Adventures of the Letter I (Simpson), 563, 565, 566, 569
Aeneid (Virgil, Mandelbaum), 383, 384, 387, 590
"After a Lost Original" (D. Shapiro), 546
After a Lost Original (D. Shapiro), 542, 543, 544, 546, 547
"After Joyce" (Kostelanetz), 339
After the Digging (A. Shapiro), 536, 539–40
"Afterword to My Father, An" (Bell), 209

"Again for Hephaistos, the Last Time" (Howard), 308
"Against Gravity" (Bloch), 222
Against Our Vanishing (Grossman), 279, 283, 285
"Ah Sun Flower" (Blake), 254
Ahad ha-Am, 324
Ahearn, John, 387
Airplane Dreams (Ginsberg), 260
Akhmatova, Anna, 350
Akiba, 511
"Akiba" (Rukeyser), 511
"Al and Beth" (Simpson), 568
Albers, Joseph, 587
Albritton, Rogers, 212
Aldan, Daisy, 366
"All Hallows" (Glück), 272
All My Yesterdays Were Steps (Teitelboim, Kramer), 346
All of Us Here (Feldman), 235, 238
Allen, Donald, 331, 433, 562
Allen, Woody, 258
Alone with America (Howard), 202, 309, 591
Also Sprach Zarathustra (Nietzsche), 276
Altamira (Sklarew), 577

Alter, Robert, 223–24, 399, 400, 471
Altieri, Charles, 238, 440
"America" (Ginsberg), 251, 257, 258, 262
"America" (Ignatow), 317
"America! America!" (Schwartz), 517
America a Prophecy (Rothenberg, Quasha), 492, 494
"American Jewish Clock, The" (Heller), 293, 294
"American Poetry" (Simpson), 566, 568
American Poetry Since 1945 (Stepanchev), 568
Amichai, Yehuda, 206, 220–21, 383, 396, 522
Amulet (Rakosi), 457
Andersen, Hans Christian, 525
Anderson, Margaret, 450
Andrade, Carlos Drummond de, 587
Andre Spire and His Poetry (Burnshaw), 226
Andrews, Bruce, 212, 213
"Angel Poem" (Stern), 583
Angels in America: A Gay Fantasia on National Themes (Part One) (Kushner), 352
Angkor Wat (Ginsberg), 263
"Anniversary" (Bloch), 222
"Anti Semitism" (Oppenheimer), 439
Antin, David, 256, 259, 491, 494, 497
Antiquities of the Jews (Josephus), 466
Antonioni, Michaelangelo, 503
Apocalyptic Messianism and Contemporary Jewish-American Poetry (Gitenstein), 469, 497, 522
Apollinaire, Guillaume, 502
"Appointment Card, The" (Ignatow), 317
Aquinas, Thomas, 386
Ararat (Glück), 271
Arber, Edward, 466
Arbus, Diane, 411
Archbishop Romero, 363
Arendt, Hannah, 480
Arguelles, Ivan, 388
Ariadne's Thread: A Collection of Contemporary Women's Journals (Lifshin), 375

Ariosto, Ludovico, 333
Aristophanes, 332
Arrowsmith, William, 569
Art of Love, The (Koch), 331
Art of Poetry, The (Koch), 332
Artifice of Absorption (Bernstein), 213, 215
Arrivistes, The (Simpson), 561, 564
"Around the Fish: After Paul Klee" (Moss), 402
"As Flowers Are" (Kunitz), 352
"Ash and the Oak, The" (Simpson), 564
Ashbery, John, 216, 330, 331, 333, 542, 543
"Assimilation" (Feldman), 236–37
At Fifty (Oppenheimer), 434, 437
At the End of the Open Road (Simpson), 562, 565, 566, 569
"At the Fire Fountain" (Moss), 404
"At the Jewish New Year" (Rich), 478
"At the Turkish Bath" (Fein), 231
At the Turkish Bath (Fein), 230, 231
Atlas, James, 516, 519
Atlas of the Difficult World, An (Rich), 480
Audubon, John James, 276
Auden, W. H., 235, 290, 302, 308, 353, 403, 413, 417, 480, 557
Auster, Paul, 304, 469
"Autumn Leaves" (Ignatow), 313
"Avant-Garde Propellants of the Machine Made of Words" (Heller), 295

Baal Shem Tov, 325, 495
Ba-alei Chayim, Tzar, 322
Bacon, Francis, 276
Bailey, William, 590
Balakian, Peter, 585
Baraka, Imamu Amiri, 489, 490
Barber, David, 540
"Bar-Mitzvah Poem for My Son Adam" (Schwerner), 530
Barnes, Djuna, 469
Barthes, Roland, 471
Bartlett, Lee, 529
"Baruch" (Simpson), 570
"Basement, The" (A. Shapiro), 538–39
Basho, 398, 599

Bataille, George, 594

Bat-David, Dvorah, 485

"Battle, The" (Simpson), 564

Battle Report (H. Shapiro), 550, 551

Baudelaire, Charles, 307

Bawer, Bruce, 516, 518

"Beaded Pear, The" (Simpson), 568

Beast in View (Rukeyser), 512

"Beasts, The"(Rakosi), 453–54, 458

Beautiful Contradictions, The (Tarn), 595

"Because I am a Woman" (Sklarew), 576–77

Beckett, Tom, 216

Bedient, Calvin, 238, 272

"Before You" (Rakosi), 452

"Behaving Like a Jew" (Stern), 582

Bell, Marvin, **209–11**

Bellow, Saul, 563, 570

Benjamin, Walter, 277, 294, 303, 387, 397

Bentley, Gerald Eades, 487

Berger, Charles, 592

Bergman, Ingemar, 392

Berlin Lost, A (Kostelanetz), 338

Bernstein, Charles, **212–19**, 471

Berrigan, Ted, 330

Berryman, John, 317, 370, 489

Bersenbrugge, Mei-Mei, 502

Bertholf, Robert, 440, 441

Best Hours of the Night, The (Simpson), 567, 570

Between (Rothenberg), 496

"Between Assassinations" (A. Shapiro), 539

"Beyond Power: A Sequence" (Rosenthal), 489

Bhagavad Gita, The, 398

"Bialystock Stanzas" (Heller), 292–93

Biblical Song of Songs, The (Bloch, Bloch), 223

Bibliography of Modern Prosody, A (K. Shapiro), 556

Bidart, Frank, 443

Biespeil, David, 272

Big Jewish Book, A: Poems and Other Visions of the Jews from Tribal Times to the Present (Rothenberg, Lenowitz), 492, 494

"Bird, The" (Simpson), 565

Bishop, Elizabeth, 309, 403, 587, 589

"Black Day" (Rakosi), 455

Black Riders, Contemporary Poetry Meets Modern Theory, 216

Blackburn, Paul, 496

"Blackness of Jews, The" (Fishman), 247

Blake, William, 251, 254, 257, 268, 282, 322, 398, 445, 481, 494, 542, 595

Blanchot, Maurice, 469

Blaser, Robin, 212

Blasing, Mutlu Konuk, 463

Blast (Lewis), 460

Blau, Milton, 346

"Blessed, The" (Stern), 583

Blessing over Ashes, A (H. Schwartz), 523

Bloch, Ariel, 220, 223

Bloch, Chana, **220–25**

Blood, Bread, and Poetry (Rich), 476, 477, 479, 480

"Blood Red Nail Polish Madonna" (Lifshin), 377

Blood to Remember (Fishman), 246, 249

Bloom, Harold, 231, 234, 304, 309, 408, 464, 483, 532, 591, 592

Blue Swallows, The (Nemerov), 412

Blue Tattoo (Lifshin), 376

Blues of the Sky: Interpreted from the Original Book of Psalms (Rosenberg), 484

Bly, Robert, 313, 316, 562, 569, 570

"boat, the" (Schwerner), 530–31

Bogan, James, 519

Bogan, Louise, 519

Bogen, Don, 271–72

Bonds, Diane, 272

"Book of Father Dust, The" (Grossman), 283

Book of Hours, The (Rilke, Mitchell), 396

Book of J., The (Bloom, Rosenberg), 483, 484

Book of Job, The (Mitchell trans.), 396, 397, 599

Book of Pictures, The (Rilke, Mitchell), 396

Book of Psalms, 398
"Book of the Dead, The" (Rukeyser), 509
"Boom!" (Nemerov), 413
Bosworth, Patricia, 411
Bourgeois Poet, The (K. Shapiro), 556
Bowen, Elizabeth, 403
Boyarin, Daniel, 259
Boychuk, Bohden, 502
Boyle, Kay, 542
Bradley, George, 591
Bradstreet, Anne, 481
Braun, Richard E., 344
Bread Without Sugar (Stern), 579, 580
"Breaking Open" (Rukeyser), 508
Breaking Open (Rukeyser), 510
Bregman, Marc, 525
Breslin, Paul, 570
Breton, Andre, 594
Bright Nails Scattered on the Ground, The (Grossman), 284
"Brise Marine" (Mallarmé), 387
Brodsky, Joseph, 202
"Broich's Boat" (Fishman), 247
"Broken Objects, Discarded Landscape" (D. Shapiro), 546
Brooks, Cleanth, 488
Bromwich, David, 285, 309–310
Brown, Ashley, 408
Brown, John, 509
Browning, Robert, 308, 309
Bruce, Lenny, 251, 333
Buber, Martin, 364, 493, 497, 595
"Buddha in Glory" (Rilke, Mitchell), 396
"Building of the Skyscraper, The" (Oppen), 425
Buried City (Moss), 402, 408
Burning Bush, The (Kramer), 345, 346
Burning Mystery of Anna in 1951, The (Koch), 332
Burnshaw, Stanley, **226–28**
Burroughs, Joan, 261
Burroughs, William, 252, 253, 260, 261
"Burrow, The" (Kafka), 588
"Business" (Ignatow), 317
"Busy Man Speaks, The" (Bly), 316

By Contraries (Rudman), 502, 503, 504, 505
"By No Means Native" (Rich), 478
By the Waters of Manhattan (Reznikoff), 461
By the Well of Living and Seeing, New and Selected Poems 1918–1973 (Reznikoff), 462
Byron, Lord, 203, 288, 332, 333
"Bystander at the Massacre, The" (Feldman), 235

"Cabin, The" (Simpson), 568
"Cacti" (Oppenheimer), 437
"Cain" (Nemerov), 414
"Call, The" (Feldman), 236, 237
Called Home (Kessler), 320
Calvino, Italo, 523
"Cape Hatteras: 1939" (Fishman), 248
Caplan, Brina, 524
Captive Soul of the Messiah, The (H. Schwartz), 523
"Carentan O Carentan" 564, 569
"Carl Rakosi in the 'Objectivist' Epoch" (Crozier), 458
Carlyle, Thomas, 308
Carmi, T., 206, 227
Carr, Lucien, 252
Carruth, Hayden, 264, 438, 440
"Car Trouble" (Simpson), 568
"Carved Nakedness, The" (Layton), 358
"Casket Closed" (Rudman), 503
Cassady, Neal, 252, 253, 254, 260, 261
"Cathedral of Pearls" (Levertov), 366
Cather, Willa, 445
Catullus (Zukofsky), 599
Cavafy, Constantine, 445
Cavell, Stanley, 212
Caviare at the Funeral (Simpson), 563, 566, 568, 570
Celan, Paul, 204, 494, 497
Celebration for Stanley Kunitz on His 80th Birthday, A, 353
"Cento Virgilianus" (Strand), 590
Century of Yiddish Poetry, A (Kramer), 346
"Chad Gadya, One Little Goat" (Kessler), 321

Chagall, Marc, 258

Change of World, A (Rich), 477, 478, 480

"Channuka Madonna" (Lifshin), 377

Charkow, Natalie, 303

Charles, Ray, 256

Chaucer, Geoffrey, 203

Chekhov, Anton, 403, 566, 570

Chelmaxioms: The Maxims, Axioms, Maxioms of Chelm (Mandelbaum), 384, 388

Chess, Richard, 582–83, 585

Chief Modern Poets of England and America (Rosenthal, Nelson, Sanders), 488

Chi-Ha, Kim, 508, 510

"Childe Harold's Pilgrimage" (Klein), 325

Chilton, Harrison R., 469

Christenson, Paul, 498, 533

"Christmas Morning" (Nemerov), 413

"Christmas Story, The" (A. Shapiro), 537

"CIA Dope Calypso" (Ginsberg), 261

Ciardi, John, 353

"Circus, The" (Koch), 332

"City Elegies" (Pinsky), 445

"City Ethic" (H. Shapiro), 550–51

Clarel (Melville), 519

Cliff, Michelle, 478

Coates, Joseph, 387

Cohen, Arthur A., 542

Cohen, Leonard, 328, 359

"Cohen on the Telephone" (Hollander), 302

Cohen-Cheminet, Genevieve, 471

Coherent Splendor, A (Blasing), 463

Collected Early Poems (Rich), 478

Collected Poems (Nemerov), 412, 414, 415, 416

Collected Poems (Rakosi), 453, 454, 455–56, 457, 458

Collected Poems of George Oppen (Oppen), 422, 423, 424, 425, 427, 429

Collected Poems of Irving Layton, The (Layton), 356

Collected Poems of Muriel Rukeyser (Rukeyser), 508, 511

Collected Prose (Olson), 494

Collected Prose (Rakosi), 448, 457, 458

Collier, Michael, 552

Colum, Mary, 519

"Coming of Light, The" (Strand), 589

Commedia (Dante, Mandelbaum), 384, 385

"Commentary Text Commentary Text Commentary Text" (D. Shapiro), 543

"Committee Room, The" (Rukeyser), 511

Commodity of Dreams, A (Nemerov), 412

"Communion" (Ignatow), 317

"Compassionate People, A" (Reznikoff), 464–65, 466, 467

Complete Poems, The (Reznikoff), 462

Congregation: Contemporary Writers Read the Jewish Bible (Rosenberg), 484

"Consolation" (Ignatow), 313

Contemporary American Poetry (Poulin), 566

Content's Dream: Essays 1975–1984 (Bernstein), 213

Continuous Life, The (Strand), 590, 591, 592

"Contra Naturam" (Howard), 308

Controlling Interests, 213

"The Converts" (Bloch), 221–22

Convictions Net of Branches: Essays on the Objectivist Poets and Poetry (Heller), 291, 292

Cooper, Jane, 513

Corbett, William, 440

"Cordova" (Levertov), 365

Corn, Alfred, 591

Corso, Gregory (Gregorio Nunzio), 253

"Cosmopolitan Greetings" (Ginsberg), 262

Cosmopolitan Greetings (Ginsberg), 261

"Cote de Neiges Cemetery" (Layton), 356

Counting Myself Lucky: Selected Poems, 1963–1992 (Field), 242

Courtesy, The (A. Shapiro), 536, 537, 538, 539

"Courts at Lawton Street, The" (A. Shapiro), 539

Covenant (A. Shapiro), 536, 538, 539, 540
Cox, C .B., 569, 570
Crackling of Thorns, A (Hollander), 302
Crane, Hart, 281, 445
Crane, R. S., 487
Creation, The (Mitchell), 398
Creeley, Robert, 216, 331, 332, 355, 358, 432
"Cripples, The" (Klein), 326
Cross, Tom Peete, 487
Crozier, Andrew, 453, 457
"Cruise" (Rukeyser), 510

Dachy, Marc, 339
"daddy, can you staple these two stars together to make an airplane" (Schwerner), 529
Damages, The (Howard), 308
Dance of Leah, The (Fein), 229, 230
Dance of the Intellect, The, 216
Dancer, The (Oppenheimer), 432
"Dancing, The" (Stern), 583
"Dancing Party, The" (Rudman), 504
Daniels, Kate, 508, 513
Dante, 205, 384, 385, 386, 396, 444, 446, 529, 591
Dark City (Bernstein), 213
Dark Fields of the Republic (Rich), 480, 481
Dark Harbor: A Poem (Strand), 590, 591, 592
Darker (Strand), 587, 588–89, 591
Daughters of Troy (Euripides, Rudman, Slavitt, Washburn), 502
Davenport, Guy, 597, 598, 599, 600
"David Ignatow: Prophet of Darkness and Nothingness" (Pacernick), 317, 318
Davidowicz, Lucy, 583
Davie, Donald, 289
Davies, Alan, 216
"Day of Atonement" (Reznikoff), 467
"Day without Night" (Glück), 270
"Days and Nights" (Koch), 332
Days and Nights (Koch), 332
Day's Portion, A (H. Shapiro), 550, 552

"Dead Will Not Praise You, The" (D. Shapiro), 542
"Dear Miss Monroe" (Oppenheimer), 438
"Death Mazurka, The" (Fishman), 248
Death Mazurka, The (Fishman), 245, 246, 247
"Death of Moishe Lazarovitch" (Layton), 356
"Declaration" (Rakosi), 455
"Dedication" (Feldman), 236
Deleuze, Gilles, 544
Dembo, L. S., 469
Derrick, Neil, 241, 242
Derrida, Jacques, 544
Descending Figure (Glück), 269, 272
"Desdichada" (Rukeyser), 510
Deutsch, Babette, 568
Deutscher, Isaac, 258
"Devil's Trill Sonata, The" (D. Shapiro), 545
Dharma Bums (Kerouac), 566
Diamond Cutters and Other Poems, The (Rich), 478
Diamond Tree, The (H. Schwartz), 525
Dickey, James, 569
Dickinson, Emily, 212, 481
Dirda, Michael, 290
"Disasters" (Oppen), 427–28
"Discovery of America, A" (Simpson), 564
Discrete Series (Oppen), 420, 421, 422, 423, 424, 426, 428
Diverse Voices (Rudman), 502, 503
Divine Comedy (Dante, Mandelbaum), 387
Diving into the Wreck (Rich), 477, 479
"Do the Meditation Rock" (Ginsberg), 261
Dobyns, Stephen, 300
"Dog Life" (Strand), 590
Dolin, Sharon, 456
Donne, John, 352, 595
Donohue, Dennis, 238
Door in the Hive, A (Levertov), 363
Door Standing Open, The (Mezey), 393
Dorn, Edward, 318
Dos Passos, John, 331

Double Image, The (Levertov), 363, 364

Drach, Ivan, 350

"Dream" (Ignatow), 317

Dream Assembly, The (H. Schwartz, Schachter, Shalomi), 525

Dream of a Common Language, The (Rich), 479

Dream of Governors, A (Simpson), 565, 569

"Dress Department"(Kramer), 345

Dress of Fire, A (Ravikovitch, Bloch), 221, 223

Droles de Journal (Rakosi), 458

Dropping Ashes on Buddha (Mitchell), 396, 398

Dryden, John, 387, 396

"Drying Out" (Oppenheimer), 431, 432

Duchamp, Marcel, 497

Dudek, Louis, 355, 358

Duffy, William, 562

Duino Elegies (Rilke, Mitchell), 396

Duncan, Robert, 331, 440, 496, 594

Dunn, Douglas, 570

DuPlessis, Rachel Blau, 533

"During the Eichmann Trial" (Levertov), 363, 364

Dutiful Son, The (Oppenheimer), 432, 435

Dylan, Bob, 258

"Dysraphism" (Bernstein), 216

Eagleton, Terry, 569

Early and Late Testament (Bradshaw), 227

"Early in the Morning" (Simpson), 564

Earnshaw, Doris, 363

"Earth Hard: David Ignatow's Poetry" (Mills), 317–18

Earthly Measures (Hirsch), 298, 299, 300

Eberhart, Richard, 519

Ecce Kosti, Published Encomia, 1967–1995 (Kostelanetz), 339

Economou, George, 497

Ehrenpreis, Irving, 591

Eichmann, Adolph, 367

Eidus, Janice, 379

Eight Nights of Hanukah, The (Kostelanetz), 338

"1881: Whitman's Impact on American Jewish Poetry" (Kramer), 345

Ein Verlorenes Berlinin, 338

"El Salvador: Requiem and Invocation" (Levertov), 363

"Elegy for a Dead Soldier" (K. Shapiro), 556

"Elegy for My Father" (Moss), 407

"Elegy for My Father" (Strand), 589

"Elegy for My Sister" (Moss), 406

Elijah's Violin (H. Schwartz), 524–25

Eliot, T. S., 281, 352, 365, 366, 386, 412, 413, 417, 451, 452, 460, 464, 489, 516, 518, 542

Elliott, George P., 289

Emmanuel, Lynn, 285

"Emotions of Normal People" (Bernstein), 213

End of Beauty, The (Graham), 276

End of Intelligent Writing, The (Kostelanetz), 336, 337

"Endor" (Nemerov), 414

Engels, Frederick, 346

English in Virginia, April, 1607, The, 466

English Prosody and Modern Poetry (K. Shapiro), 556

Enlightened Heart, The (Mitchell), 397, 398

Enlightened Mind, The (Mitchell), 397

Ere-Voice (Rakosi), 457

Ernst, Jimmy, 565

Erosion (Graham), 276

Escape into You, The (Bell), 209

Eshelman, Clayton, 494, 496

Eskimo Songs and Stories (Field), 242

"Essay on Psychiatrists" (Pinsky), 444

Ether Dome, The (Grossman), 279, 281

Euripides, 502

"Europe and America" (Ignatow), 315–16

"Eve" (Nemerov), 413

Evening Train (Levertov), 366

Ex Cranium, Night (Rakosi), 458

Exiled in the Word (Rothenberg, Lenowitz), 492, 531

"Exodus, Joshua at Sechem" (Rezni-koff), 468
Explanation of America, An (Pinsky), 444–45
Exploring Poetry (Rosenthal, Smith), 488
"Expulsion, The" (Stern), 579, 581
"Extermination of the Jews, The" (Bell), 209
Eye, The (H. Shapiro), 549
Ezrahi, Sidra DeKoven, 471

Facing the Tree (Ignatow), 316
Fact of a Doorframe, The: Poems Selected and News 1950–1984
Fall of America, The: Poems of These States (Ginsberg), 260, 261, 263, 264
"Falling Asleep with Your Children" (Fishman), 248
"Family, The" (Bloch), 222
"Family Portrait" (Layton), 356
"Fanatics" (A. Shapiro), 539
Fancy's Sketch Book (Moise), 202
Fast, Howard, 346
"Father and Son" (Feldman), 238
"Father and Son" (Kunitz), 350, 353
Father Coughlin, 369
"Father Guzmann" (Stern), 580
Federigo, or the Power of Love (Nemerov), 412
Feeley, Paul Terrence, 416
Fein, Richard J., **229–32**
Feldman, Irving, 202, **233–39**, 516
Fellow Feelings (Howard), 308
Ferlinghetti, Lawrence, 255
Fiedler, Leslie, 337
Field, Edward, **240–44**
Fifth Book of the Maccabees, The (Rezni-koff), 466
"Fifth Finding" (Mandelbaum), 384
"Fighting in Europe, The" (Simpson), 564
Figured Wheel, The (Pinsky), 444, 445
"Figures of Thought" (Nemerov), 415
Figures of Thought (Nemerov), 412
Final Reckoning (Layton), 358
Finding Them Lost (Moss), 404, 407
"Fingerprints"(Bloch), 222
Finnegans Wake (Joyce), 388

Firewalkers, The (Fishman), 247–48, 249
"First American Poetry Disc" (Lifshin), 378
First Blues (Ginsberg), 260, 261
"First Day, The" (Nemerov), 414, 415
Firstborn (Glück), 269–70
Fishman, Charles, **245–50**, 299, 346
"Fission" (Graham), 276
Fitzgerald, Robert, 590
Five New Poets (Sklarew), 576
Flamm, Matthew, 552
Flaubert, Gustave, 565
Flint, R. W., 417
"Flood" (Feldman), 238
Flowers of Evil (Baudelaire, Howard), 307
"Foggy Lane, The" (Simpson), 567
"For Benjamin Moloise, Hanged in Pretoria Prison" (Kramer), 345
For My Brother Jesus (Layton), 358
For My Neighbors in Hell (Layton), 358
For the Sleepwalkers (Hirsch), 298, 300
"For Uncle Nat" (Heller), 294
"For Years Her Parents Never Said a Word About It" (Lifshin), 278
Forché, Carolyn, 249
Ford, Whitey, 448
Foster, Edward, 296
Four Books of the Maccabees, 466
Four Poems to Spring (Oppenheimer), 432
"Four Sad Poems on the Delaware" (Stern), 583
Four Who Entered Paradise, The (H. Schwartz), 523
Franciosi, Robert, 470
Francis of Assisi, 398
Frank, Jacob, 494
Freedman, Steven, 264
"Freight" (Lifshin), 378
Freilicher, Jane, 330
"Fresh Air: Social Constructions of Reality at Coney Island" (Feldman), 236
Freud, Sigmund, 411, 588, 590
"Friday Night Quartet" (D. Shapiro), 545
Friend, Robert, 241

From the Backyard of the Diaspora (Sklarew), 576, 577
"From the Childhood of Jesus" (Pinsky), 445
"From the Imagined Life of Ruvn-Yankev Troonk" (Fein), 231
Frost, Robert, 333, 460, 557
Frye, Northrop, 358
Funsten, Kenneth, 378
Full Heart, A (Field), 242
"Funny, We Don't Look Jewish" (Oppenheimer), 439
Furtwangler, Wilhelm, 323

Gabriel's Palace: Jewish Mystical Tales (H. Schwartz), 524, 525
Gall, Sally M., 488
Galles, Arie, 496
Garber, Frederick, 497
Gates, The (Rukeyser), 508, 510
Gates of Wrath, The: Rhymed Poems 1948–1951 (Ginsberg), 252, 260
Gates to the New City: A Treasury of Modern Jewish Tales (H. Schwartz), 524
Gathering the Sparks (H. Schwartz), 522
Gaudier-Brzeska, Henri, 460
Gazer's Spirit, The: Poems Speaking to Silent Works of Art (Hollander), 301
Gelpi, Albert, 463, 481
Gematria (Rothenberg), 496
Genesis (Mitchell trans.), 396, 397, 399
Genesis: Selections from Book II (D. Schwartz), 517
Genesis I (D. Schwartz), 516, 519
Gentle Weight Lifter, The (Ignatow), 313
Geography of Poets, A (Field), 242
George, Laurie, 272
"Getting It Right: Joel Oppenheimer's Poetry" (Michael Joyce), 441
"Ghost" (Simpson), 563
"Ghost Worm Monster, The" (Bloch), 222
Giacometti, Alberto, 302
Gilbert, Jack, 353, 580
Gingerich, William, 534
Ginsberg, Allen, **251–66**, 288, 301, 303, 307, 322, 331, 333, 489, 565, 599

Ginsberg, Louis, 251–52, 258, 261
Ginsberg, Naomi, 256, 261
Gioia, Dana, 404
Gitenstein, Barbara, 469, 497, 522, 524
Glatstein, Jacob (Yankev Glatshteyn), 201, 230
Glück, Louise, **267–74**, 353
Gnomes and Other Occasions (Nemerov), 412
Gnostic Gospels, The (Pagels), 484
Godard, Jean-Luc, 503
"God's Cigar" (Kessler), 322, 323
Gogol, Nikolai, 445
"Going Back" (Simpson), 563
Going To and Fro and Walking Up and Down (Reznikoff), 461
"Going to the World of the Dead" (Ginsberg), 261
Goldbarth, Albert, 231
Golden Trumpet, The (Kramer), 346
"Good Angel, The" (Ignatow), 314
Good News of Death (Simpson), 564, 569
Goodman, Paul, 519
Gospel according to Jesus, The (Mitchell trans.), 396, 397
"Gothic Landscape" (Layton), 356
Gottlieb, Robert, 307
Gould, Jean, 363, 364, 367
Gracq, Julien, 307
Graham, Jorie, **275–78**, 547
Grand Concourse (Kessler), 320, 323
Gray, Yohma, 571
Great American Desert, The (Oppenheimer), 433
"Green Shepherd, The" (Simpson), 565
Greenberg, Eliezer, 479
Greenwald, Ted, 212
Griaule, Marcel, 594
Grooms, Red, 331
Grosholz, Emily
Grossman, Allen, 202, **279–87**, 375, 588
"Grossman's Lament" (Stern), 285
Grumman, Bob, 339
Guattari, Felix, 544
Guenther, Charles, 526
Guest, Barbara, 330, 333
Guide to the Ruins (Nemerov), 412, 417

Guilory, Daniel L., 300
Guimond, James, 295
Gunn, Thom, 407
Gurdjieff, 240
Guthrie, Ramon, 489

H. D. (Hilda Doolittle), 255, 481
Hagely, Richard, 580
Halliday, Mark, 285
Hall, Donald, 562, 569
Hall, John, 457
Halpern, Moshe-Leib, 201, 303
Hamilton, Ian, 569
Hampl, Patricia, 300
Hannibal, 567
Happy Hour (A. Shapiro), 536, 537, 540
Hard Hours, The (Hecht), 288, 289
Hardy, Thomas, 489
"Harold" (Ignatow), 315
Harrison, Jim, 457
Harte, Bret, 202
Harvard Anthology of Contemporary American Poetry (Vendler), 469
"Harvey Shapiro—An Appreciation" (Ray), 551
Hass, Robert, 353, 396, 443
Hatlen, Burton, 428, 470
Hath Not a Jew (Klein), 325
Hayden, Hyram, 562
Heaney, Seamus, 532, 569
Heap, Jane, 450
"Heavy Bear Who Goes with Me, The" (D. Schwartz), 516
Hecht, Anthony, **288–90**, 303, 405, 569
Heidegger, Martin, 388, 429
Heifetz-Tussman, Malka, 201
Heine, Heinrich, 204, 344, 346
Hejduk, John, 543
Hejinian, Lyn, 215
Heller, Michael, **291–97**, 317, 429, 458
Helmling, Steven, 598, 599
Herbert, George, 220, 221, 223
Here and Now (Layton), 355
"Heroes, The" (Simpson), 564
Hildegard of Bingen, 398
Hill, Geoffrey, 236, 279, 532
Hindus, Milton, 469
Hirsch, Edward, 272, **298–300**, 585

Hirschman, Jack, 491
"His Life" (H. Shapiro), 550
"His Present Discontents: A Sequence" (Rosenthal), 489
"Historic Pun" (Oppen), 426
"History" (Graham), 276
"History of My Heart" (Oppenheimer), 445
Hitleriad, The (Klein), 325, 326
Hoffman, Daniel, 569
Hofmannsthal, Hugo von, 299
Hogg, James, 562
Hollander, Anne, 303, 307
Hollander, John, 236, 238, **301–5**, 307, 404, 588
Holmes, John Clellon, 252, 576
Holocaust (Reznikoff), 462, 463, 465, 466
Homecoming Game, The (Nemerov), 412
Homer, 384, 387, 445
Horace, 445
"Hot Dog" (Stern), 583
"House" (D. Shapiro), 546
House (Blown Apart), 543, 544, 546
House on Marshland, The (Glück), 269, 272
"Houses" (Oppenheimer), 437–38, 440
"How I Became a Writer" (H. Schwartz), 522
"How I Painted Certain of My Pictures" (Bernstein), 213
"How to Live on Long Island" (Simpson), 567
Howard, Richard, 202, 238, 301, **306–11**, 333, 404, 408, 570, 591
Howe, Irving, 479, 517
"Howl" (Ginsberg), 251, 255, 263, 264, 565
Howl and Other Poems (Ginsberg), 252, 255, 256, 263, 264
Hughes, Langston, 346
Hughes, Ted, 594
"Hum Bom" (Ginsberg), 260, 261
Humboldt's Gift (Bellow), 563
Huncke, Herbert, 253
Hutchins, Robert Maynard, 487
Hybrids of Plants and of Ghosts (Graham), 276

"I Can't Stop It" (Ignatow), 312
I Never Told Anybody: Teaching Poetry Writing in a Nursing Home (Koch), 332
"I Write Out of an Uncreated Identity" (H. Shapiro), 549
"Ice House in Summer, The" (Nemerov), 414–15
"Ice-Storm, The" (Pinsky), 446
"Idea, The" (Strand), 590
"If It All Went Up in Smoke" (Oppen), 428
(if personal) (Schwerner), 529
Ignatow, David, **312–19**, 440, 551, 552
Illuminations (Benjamin), 277
"Illustrious Ancestors" (Levertov), 365
"Image, The" (Ignatow), 314
Image and the Law, The (Nemerov), 412, 417
"Image of the Engine" (Oppen), 424
Imaged Words and Worded Images (Kostelanetz), 337
Images from the Holocaust (Fishman), 245
Imperial Messages: One Hundred Modern Parables (H. Schwartz), 523–24
"Impossible to Tell" (Pinsky), 446
Improved Binoculars, The (Layton), 358
"In a Dark Time, on His Grandfather" (Heller), 293
In Defense of Ignorance (K. Shapiro), 556
"In Dreams Begin Responsibilities" (D. Schwartz), 516–17, 518
In Dreams Begin Responsibilities (D. Schwartz), 515, 516, 517
"In Germany" (D. Shapiro), 546
In Love with the Gratuitous: Rereading Armand Schwerner (Paul), 533
In Memoriam: 1933 (Reznikoff), 461, 465
"In My Observatory Withdrawn" (Grossman), 284
"In Praise of the Diaspora" (Klein), 325
In Praise of the Impure: Poetry and the Ethical Imagination (A. Shapiro), 533
In Search of the Primitive (Paul), 497
"In the Beginning" (Bloch), 221

In the Builded Place (Heller), 291, 293, 295–96
"In the Garden" (Bloch), 221
"In the Kingdom of Pleasure" (A. Shapiro), 538
"In the Land of the Body" (Bloch), 222
"In the Mid-East" (Hirsch), 299
"In the Midwest" (Hirsch), 299
"In the Naked Bed, in Plato's Cave" (D. Schwartz), 516
"In the Neighboring Cell" (Rudman), 503
In the Neighboring Cell (Rudman), 502
In the Room We Share (Simpson), 565, 566
"In the Suburbs" (Simpson), 567
In Time: Poems 1962–1968 (Oppenheimer), 433, 436, 438
Indigo and Other Poems (Kramer), 346
Inferno (Dante, Mandelbaum), 385
Inferno (Dante, Schwerner), 529
"Influence of Kinship Patterns upon Perception of an Ambiguous Stimulus, The" (Bernstein), 213
Inside the Onion (Nemerov), 412
Intellectual Things (Kunitz), 350, 353
"Interview with Michael Heller, An," 429
Interviews and Encounters with Stanley Kunitz (Kunitz), 351
"Inventory of Destructions, An" (Grossman), 281
Islets/Irritations, 213
"Isolation of Modern Poetry, The" (D. Schwartz), 516
"Israel in the Park" (Tarn), 595
"Iviefdea" (Kostelanetz), 339

Jabés, Edmund, 428, 532
Jacob, Max, 332
"Jacob's Ladder, The" (Levertov), 364–65
Jacob's Ladder, The (Levertov), 364, 365
James, Henry, 303
James, William, 303, 304
January (D. Shapiro), 542
Jarrell, Randall, 317, 417, 489, 561, 568

"Jasper Johns and David Shapiro: An Analogy" (S. P. Miller), 547

Jefferson, Thomas, 397

"Jerome" (Mitchell), 398–99

Jerome Rothenberg: A Descriptive Bibliography (Polkinhorn), 498

Jerusalem the Golden (Reznikoff), 461, 463

Jewish War, The (Josephus), 466

Jews of the United States, The, 344

Jimenez, Juan Ramon, 562

"Job" (Mitchell), 399

Job Speaks: Interpreted from the Original Hebrew Book of Job (Rosenberg), 484

Joel Oppenheimer: An Introduction (Thibodeaux), 440

"John the Baptist" (Simpson), 566

Johns, Jasper, 544, 547

Jong, Erica, 558

Joris, Pierre, 492, 493, 494

"Joseph's Pockets" (Stern), 579, 583

Josephus, Flavius, 466

"Journals/Divagations" (Schwerner), 532

Journeyman (Mandelbaum), 383

Joyce, James, 326, 386, 460, 491, 503

Joyce, Michael, 438, 441

Just Friends/Friends and Lovers: Poems 1959–1962 (Oppenheimer), 437

Justice, Donald, 407, 591

"Kaddish" (Ginsberg), 256–57, 261, 263

Kaddish (Kostelanetz), 338

Kaddish and Other Poems (Ginsberg), 256, 263, 304

"Kafka" (Mitchell), 399

Kafka, Franz, 205, 333, 523, 588, 590, 595

Kafka's Ear (Fein), 231

"Käthe Kollwitz" (Rukeyser), 510–11

Kaufman, Bob, 255

Keats, John, 249

"Keeping Things Whole" (Strand), 588, 589

"Keine Lazarovitch, 1870–1959" (Layton), 356

Kelly, Robert, 491, 492, 494, 562

Kennedy, John F., 276

Kenner, Hugh, 358, 489, 533, 598

"Kenneth Koch: A Tragedy" (Rivers, O'Hara), 330

Kermode, Frank, 484

Kerouac, Jack, 252, 253, 255, 259, 260, 261, 542, 566

Kertesz, Louise, 513

Kessler, Jascha, 551

Kessler, Milton, **320–23**

Keyes, Claire, 481

"Khurbn" (Rothenberg), 496

Khurbn (Rothenberg), 493, 496

"Killer Poet" (Strand), 590

Kind of Order, A Kind of Folly, A: Essays and Conversations (Kunitz), 351

King My Father's Wreck, The (Simpson), 563

Kinnell, Galway, 353

Kinsella, Thomas, 231

Kinzie, Mary, 277–78, 417

Kirsch, Robert, 524

Klee, Paul, 416

Klein, Abraham Moses, **324–29**, 355, 358, 359

Klepfisz, Irena, 259, 480

Knowledge (Heller), 291, 292

Knox, Bernard, 387

Ko, or a Season on Earth (Koch), 330, 333

Koch, Kenneth, **330–34**, 353, 502, 542

Koethe, John, 546, 547

Kostelanetz, Richard Cory, **335–42**

Koufax, Sandy, 445

"Kral Majales" (Ginsberg), 260

Kramer, Aaron, **343–48**

Kreisel, Henry, 328

Kremer, S. L., 249

Krounfeld, Chana, 223

Kunitz, Stanley, 268, **349–54**, 502, 554, 558

Kushner, Tony, 352

La Fontaine, Jean de, 288

La Terra Promessa (Ungaretti, Mandelbaum), 383

"Lair" (Pinsky), 444

"Lamentations" (Glück), 270

Landrey, David, 441

"Language of New York, The" (Oppen), 426

Lao-tzu, 395, 397, 398
Last Happy Occasion, The (A. Shapiro), 536, 539
Late Hour, The (Strand), 589, 590, 591
Lateness (D. Shapiro), 543, 545
Lautreamont, 332
Lavigne, Robert, 255
Lawrence, D. H., 460
Lay of the Love and Death of Cornet Christoph Rilke, The (Rilke, Mitchell), 396
Layton, Irving, 328, **355–61**
Lazarus, Emma, 202, 204–6, 345, 469
Lazer, Hank, 216, 498
Leaflets (Rich), 479
"Leak in History, A" (Rich), 480
Leaning South (Lifshin), 378
Leaving Another Kingdom (Stern), 579, 580, 581, 583, 584, 585
Leaving the Door Open (Ignatow), 314
"Leg, The" (K. Shapiro), 556
"Legend" (Glück), 270
Lehman, David, 304
Leithauser, Brad, 289, 290
Lenowitz, Harris, 492, 531
Leopardi, Giacomo, 388
"Letter to the Front" (Rukeyser), 512
Letters of Delmore Schwartz, The (D. Schwartz), 518, 519, 554
Letters to a Young Poet (Rilke-Mitchell), 396
Levenson, Christopher, 358
Levertov, Denise, 249, 318, **362–68**, 508
Levi, Jan Heller, 513
Levi, Paul, 594
"Leviathan" (Oppen), 424
Levin, Gabriel, 522
Levinas, Emmanuel, 282, 284
Levine, Philip, 202, 303, **369–74**
Lévi-Strauss, Claude, 594
Lewis, Wyndham, 460
Lewisohn, Ludwig, 327
Leyeles, A., 201
Leyvik, H., 201
Lichtenstein, Roy, 331
Lieberman, Laurence, 407
Life and Letters (Feldman), 238

Life of Poetry, The (Rukeyser), 507, 509, 511, 513
Life Studies (Lowell), 229, 489
Lifshin, Lyn, **375–81**
Light Holds, The (H. Shapiro), 551
Lightfall, The (Schwerner), 529
Lightworks: Interpreted from the Original Hebrew Book of Isaiah (Rosenberg), 484
Like a Hill (Oppenheimer), 433
Like Most Revelations (Howard), 309
Lilith's Cave: Jewish Tales of the Super-natural (H. Schwartz), 524, 525
Lindop, Grevel, 569
Lining Up (Howard), 308
"Link" (Simpson), 568
Lionhearted, a Story about the Jews in Medieval England, The (Reznikoff), 461
Lips Unsealed (Lifshin), 375
Lithuania: New and Selected Poems (Sklarew), 577
"Lives of the Toll Takers, The" (Bernstein), 213
Living Root (Heller), 294
"Lobster, The" (Rakosi), 453
Locke, Duane, 569
Logan, William, 277
Lolita (Nabokov), 276
"Long Island Springs" (Moss), 402, 406
Longenbach, James, 309
Longfellow, Henry Wadsworth, 205
"Lookout: Mont Royal" (Klein), 326
Lorca, Federico Garcia, 491, 494, 562
Lorde, Audre, 477
Lost Book of Paradise, The (Rosenberg), 484, 485
"Lost Language, The" (Feldman), 236, 237
"Lost Poem, A" (Levertov), 365
"Lot's Wife" (Nemerov), 414
L'Ouverture, Toussaint, 309
Love and War, Art and God (K. Shapiro), 558
"Love Bit, The" (Oppenheimer), 436
Love Bit and Other Poems, The (Oppenheimer), 433
Lovemaker, The (Mezey), 390

"Lover, The" (Oppenheimer), 436
Lowell, Robert, 229, 263, 271, 309, 317,
  332, 353, 483, 489, 562
Lowry, Malcolm, 503
Lu Chi, 599
Lucky Life (Stern), 580, 583
Luxemburg, Rosa, 480
"Luzzato" (Reznikoff), 463–64
"Lycidas" (Milton), 326
Lynch, Michael, 308, 309
"Lynchings of Jesus, The" (Rukeyser),
  509, 511
Lyotard, Jean-François, 544

Ma Rainey, 255
Macdonald, Dwight, 518
Maclean, Norman, 487
MacLeish, Archibald, 412
MacLow, Jackson, 216, 494
"Mad Potter, The" (Hollander), 303
Madoff, Steven, 289
"Madonna of the Magnificat" (Layton),
  356
"Madonna Who Shifts for Herself" (Lif-
  shin), 377
"Magic Curtain, The" (Kunitz), 351
Mahler, Gustave, 595
Making of Americans, The (Stein), 212
Malamud, Bernard, 321
Mallarmé, Stephen, 385, 387, 547, 599
Man Holding an Acoustic Panel, A (D.
  Shapiro), 543, 545
"Man Who Married Magdalene, The"
  (Simpson), 566
Mandel, Eli, 328
Mandelbaum, Allen, **382–89**
Mandelstam, Osip, 576
"Manipulator, The" (Bell), 209
"Manufacturing" (A. Shapiro), 537
*Marginalization of Poetry: Language and
  Literary History*, 216
Margritte, 581
"Margritte Dancing" (Stern), 581
Mariani, Paul, 388
Marilyn Lives! (Oppenheimer), 434
Maritain, Jacques, 424
Markish, Peretz, 531

Martin, Wendy, 481
Martz, Louis L., 303
Marx, Karl, 346
"Mary Snorak the Cook, Skermo the
  Gardener, and Jack the Parts Man Pro-
  vide Dinner for a Wandering Stranger"
  (Grossman), 284
"Master of the Name, The"(Tarn), 595
Materialism (Graham), 276–77
Materials, The (Oppen), 424
Matisse, Henri, 299
Matthews, Harry, 331
Mayer, Bernadette, 330
Mayes, Frances, 222, 223
Maynard, John Arthur, 253
Mayne, Seymour, 328
McCaffery, Steve, 497
McClatchy, J. D., 304, 540
McGann, Jerome, 214, 215, 216, 547
McGrath, Thomas, 346
Meadowlands (Glück), 271
Meaning a Life: An Autobiography (Mary
  Oppen), 423
*Measured Response, A: Poets Respond to
  Viet Nam and Desert Storm* (Fishman),
  245
"Mediterranean" (Rukeyser), 510
Melodramatist, The (Nemerov), 412
Melville, Herman, 519
Memorial"(Pinsky), 444
"Mending Sump" (Koch), 333
Mercian Hymns (Hill), 532
Merrill, James, 303
"Merritt Parkway" (Levertov), 364
Mersmann, James F., 366–67
Merwin, W. S., 309, 353, 488, 569
Messerli, Douglas, 463
Metamorphoses (Ovid, Mandelbaum),
  383, 387
Meyer, Gerard Previn, 568
Meyers, Burt, 392
Mezey, Robert, 299, **390–94**
"Mezuzah" (A. Shapiro), 538
Mezzrow, Mezz, 256
"Miami Beach" (Moss), 402
Mickiewicz, Adam, 231
Middleton, Christopher, 594

Millennium Hotel, The (Rudman), 501, 502, 503, 504, 505
Miller, Arthur, 323
Miller, L., 345
Miller, Nolan, 587
Miller, Stephen Paul, 542, 547
Millions of Strange Shadows (Hecht), 289
Mills, Ralph, Jr., 317, 393
Milosz, Czeslaw, 236, 443
Milton, John, 206, 326, 542
Mind Breaths (Ginsberg), 260, 261
"Mind's Own Place, The" (Oppen), 423
"Minestrone Madonna" (Lifshin), 377
"Minor Role, A" (Levertov), 365
Mirages: Travel Notes in the Promised Land (Burnshaw), 227
Miriam's Tambourine (H. Schwartz), 525
Mirrors and Windows (Nemerov), 412, 417
Misgivings (Howard), 308
Miss Right (Oppenheimer), 433
Mitchell, Stephen, 221, **395–401**
Mixed Company (A. Shapiro), 536, 537, 539
Modern Hebrew Poem Itself, The (Burnshaw), 227
"Modern Lives" (Simpson), 564
Modern Poets, The: A Critical Introduction (Rosenthal), 488
Modern Poetic Sequence, The: The Genius of Modern Poetry (Rosenthal, Gall), 488
Modernists, 214
Moise, Penina, 202, 469
Moliere, 203
Molodowsky, Kadia, 479
Monaghan, Pat, 300
Monroe, Harriet, 450, 451, 460
Monroe, Marilyn, 376
Montague, John, 489
"Montreal" (Klein), 326
"Monument, The" (Bishop), 589
Monument, The (Strand), 589, 590, 591
"Moonrise in Ancient Sumer: Armand Schwerner's *The Tablets*" (Van Spanckeren), 533
Moore, Marianne, 353, 453, 460
Moore, Richard, 388

Moran, Ronald, 569
"More Life" (Strand), 590
"Morning at Dachau, A" (Fishman), 247
Morris, William, 215
Morrison, Julia, 577
Mortal Companions (Fishman), 246–47, 248
Moser, Barry, 383
"Moses" (Nemerov), 414
Moss, Howard, **402–10**
Moss, Stanley, 353
Mottram, Eric, 495, 497
"Mountain, The" (Klein), 326
mountain, fire, thornbush (H. Shapiro), 550
Moyers, Bill, 582
Mr. and Mrs. Baby (Strand), 590, 591
"Mud Dancing" (A. Shapiro), 539
Muir, Edwin, 489
Murao, Shigeyoshi, 255
Muriel Rukeyser: Out of Silence (Daniels), 508, 513
Muriel Rukeyser Reader, A (Levi), 513
Murray, G. E., 570
"Mustache Drawn on Captain Patterson, A" (Rakosi), 457
"My Father in the Night Commanding No" (Simpson), 566
"My Father's Funeral" (K. Shapiro), 557
My Friend, My Father (Burnshaw), 227
"My Life by Somebody Else" (Strand), 589
My Sister Life (Pasternak, Rudman, Boychuk), 502
"My Wife's Grandfather, Dead" (Oppenheimer), 439
Mystery in the Garden, The (Rudman), 502
"Myth of the Blaze (1972–1975)" (Oppen), 427

Nachman of Bratslav, 523
names, dates, places (Oppenheimer), 434, 437
Names and Local Habitations (Oppenheimer), 440
Names of the Lost (Levine), 371
Namjoshi, Suniti, 358

Nash, Ogden, 353
National Cold Storage Company (H. Shapiro), 551
"Near Perigord" (Pound), 280
"Nebuchadnezzar, Solus" (Nemerov), 414
"Necessities of Life" (Rich), 478
Nelson, John Herbert, 488
Nemerov, Howard, 405, **411–19**
Neruda, Pablo, 316, 562, 595
Neusner, Jacob, 399–400
New American Poetry, The: 1945–1960 (Allen), 331, 433, 562
New and Selected Essays (Nemerov), 412
New and Selected Poems (Nemerov), 412
New and Selected Poems (K. Shapiro), 558
"New Colossus, The" (Lazarus), 204
New Geography of Poets, A (Field), 242
New Literary History, 216
New Lyrics for the Bride of God (Tarn), 595
New Modern Poetry, The: An Anthology of American and British Poetry Since World War II (Rosenthal), 488
New Poems (Rilke, Mitchell), 396
New Poetries and Some Old, The (Kostelanetz), 338
New Poets, The (Rosenthal), 263
New Poets of England and America, The (Simpson, Hall, Pack), 562
New Selected Poems (Moss), 406, 407
New Selected Poems (1970–1985), (Rothenberg), 493
New Spaces: Poems 1975–1983 (Oppenheimer), 437
New Young German Poets (Rothenberg), 492
Next Room of the Dream (Nemerov), 412
Next Year in Jerusalem (H. Schwartz), 525
Next-to-Last Things (Kunitz), 351, 353
Nichol, bp, 497
Nietzsche, Frederick, 276, 323, 358, 589
Night and Fog, 376
Night Before Christmas, The (Nemerov), 413
"Night Game, The" (Pinsky), 445

Night Parade, The (Hirsch), 298, 300
Nijinsky, Vaslav, 308
Nims, John Frederick, 488
"1948: Jews" (Rich), 471
1933 (Levine), 371, 372
"No One Else" (Koch), 333
No Traveller (Howard), 308
"Noli Me Tangere" (Bloch), 222
"Non Returnable Bottle Madonna" (Lifshin), 377
North of Jamaica (Simpson), 561, 562, 565, 570
Not Made of Glass (Lifshin), 378
Not This Pig (Levine), 370
"Note on the 'Objectivists,' A" (Rakosi), 451
Notebooks of Malte Laurids Brigge, The (Rilke, Mitchell), 396
Notes from the Castle (Moss), 405, 407, 408
Notes from the River (Stern), 581
"Notes toward a Politics of Location" (Rich), 479–80
Novum Organum (Bacon), 276
Nowhere Steps, The (Rudman), 502

"O Western Wind" (Oppen), 425
"O What Can Ail Thee, Knight at Arms?" (Simpson), 566
Oak in the Acorn, The (Nemerov), 412
Oates, Joyce Carol, 353
"Objectivists" Anthology, An (Oppen, Zukofsky), 420
O'Brien, Geoffrey, 498
Odysseus, 271
Odyssey, The, 271, 384, 387
"Of Commerce and Society" (Feldman), 236
"Of Being Numerous" (Oppen), 425–26
Of Being Numerous (Oppen), 420, 425–26, 428
"Of Hours" (Oppen), 427
"Of the Great House" (Grossman), 281, 283
Office, The (Field), 242
O'Flaherty, Patrick, 358
O'Hara, Frank, 330, 331, 332, 333, 552
"Old Cracked Tune, An" (Kunitz), 351

"Old Darn House, The" (Kunitz), 351
Old Horsefly, The (K. Shapiro), 558
"Old Poet's Tale, The" (Rakosi), 458
Old Savage/Young City (Tarn), 595
Olsen, Tillie, 256
Olson, Charles, 318, 331, 440, 494, 497, 594
"On a Text: Jonah IV, xi" (Nemerov), 414
"On American Literature and the Younger Generation of American Jews" (D. Schwartz), 516
"On an Occasion of National Mourning" (Nemerov), 413
"On Description" (Graham), 277
"On Freedom's Side: The Songs and Poems of Aaron Kramer" (Kramer), 344
On Freedom's Side (Kramer), 344
On Lies, Secrets, and Silence (Rich), 479
On Occasion (Oppenheimer), 433, 437, 439
"On Seeing the Statues of Ezekial and Jeremiah in the Church of Notre Dame" (Layton), 356
On the Edge (Levin), 370
"On the Eve of the Warsaw Uprising" (A. Shapiro), 537
"On the Giving of the Tallis" (Oppenheimer), 439–40
On the Giving of the Tallis (Oppenheimer), 434
"On the Neglect of Poetry in the United States" (Simpson), 566
"On the Proposed Partition of Czechoslovakia" (Rakosi), 455
One and the Many, The (Ignatow), 316
"One Train" (Koch), 332
One Train (Koch), 332, 333
"One Train May Hide Another" (Koch), 332
"Open Closed Open" (Amichai), 223
Oppen, George, 292, **420–30**, 451, 461, 469, 471, 496, 530
Oppen, Mary, 420, 421, 461
Oppenheimer, J. Robert, 349
Oppenheimer, Joel, **431–42**
Opposing Shore, The (Gracq, Howard), 307

Orlovsky, Peter, 253, 255, 260
"Orphaen Lost" (Rakosi), 452
"Orpheus" (Mitchell), 399
"Orpheus, Eurydice, Hermes" (Rilke, Mitchell), 396
Orr, Gregory, 502
O'Sheel, Shaemas, 346
Ostriker, Alicia, 234–35, 264, 272
Ouaknin, Marc-Alain, 462
"Our Angels" (H. Schwartz), 522–23
Our Life in Poetry (Rosenthal), 488
"Out of the Pulver and the Polished Lens" (Klein), 325
"Outrage Is Annointed Levity" (Feldman) 236
Ovid, 387, 581
Owens, Rochelle, 492
Ozick, Cynthia, 248, 469, 523, 525–26, 577

Pacernick, Gary, 317, 318
"Pacific Ideas—A Letter to Walt Whitman" (Simpson), 566
Pack, Robert, 562
Page-Turner, The (D. Shapiro), 543, 545, 547
Pagis, Dan, 206, 236, 395, 398
Pagles, Ellen, 484
Paglia, Camille, 323
"Painter Dreaming in the Scholar's House, The" (Nemerov), 415–416
Palach, Jan, 545
Pan's Eyes (Oppenheimer), 434
"Parable, A" (Glück), 270
Parables and Portraits (Mitchell), 398
Paradise Poems (Stern), 581
Paradiso (Dante, Mandelbaum), 385, 386
"Part of a Journey" (Mezey), 391
Pascal, Blaise, 387
"Passing Through" (Kunitz), 351
Passing Through: The Later Poems (Kunitz), 351, 352, 353
Passport to the War, A (Kunitz), 350, 353
Past Keeps Changing, The (Bloch), 221, 222, 223
Pasternak, Boris, 502
Patai, Raphael, 595

Paul, Sherman, 497, 533
Paz, Octavio, 594
Peale, Rembrandt, 397
People Live Here (Simpson), 564, 567, 570
Perelman, Bob, 214, 215, 216
"Perfect Poem, The" (Mandelbaum), 385
"Perfect Son" (A. Shapiro), 538
"Perfect Woman Reads a Page of Kant, The" (Mandelbaum), 385
"Periodontics" (Simpson), 567
Perloff, Marjorie, 216, 366, 428
Person Place and Thing (K. Shapiro), 557
"Personal Manifesto" (Rothenberg), 493
Peterson, Jeffrey, 458
Pettingell, Phoebe, 300, 408
"Pharoah" (H. Shapiro), 550
Phelps, Donald, 440
Philoctetes (Sophocles, Schwerner), 533
Philosopher's Window, The (Grossman), 281, 285
Philosophical Investigations (Wittgenstein), 212
"Piano Player Explains Himself, The" (Grossman), 284
Picasso, Pablo, 581
Pinsker, Sanford, 580, 581, 585–86
Pinsky, Robert, **443–47**, 540
Pitches, Arena, Fields, Turfs (Kostelanetz), 337–38
Planet News (Ginsberg), 260, 263
Plath, Sylvia, 263, 271, 489
Plato, 207, 276
"Please Master" (Ginsberg), 260
Pleasures of Peace, The (Koch), 331
Plumly, Stanley, 570
Podhoretz, Norman, 337
"Poem" (Rukeyser), 510
"Poem about People" (Pinsky), 444
"Poem as Mask, The" (Rukeyser), 511
"Poem at the Bathroom Door, by Adam" (Schwerner), 529–30
"Poem Beginning 'The' " (Zukofsky), 598, 599
"Poem 56" (Ignatow), 314
"Poem Out of Childhood" (Rukeyser), 509, 512

Poems (Ignatow), 315, 317
Poems (Klein), 325
Poems by Abraham Reisen (Reisen, Kramer), 345
Poems for Nathan and Saul (Bell), 209
Poems for the Game of Silence (Rothenberg), 493
Poems for the Millenium: The University of California Book of Modern and Postmodern Poetry (Rothenberg, Joris), 493, 494
Poems from Deal (D. Shapiro), 543, 546
Poems from the Floating World (Rothenberg), 492
Poems 1923–1941 (Rakosi), 452, 453, 457
Poems of a Jew (K. Shapiro), 489, 556, 557
Poems of Stanley Kunitz, 1928–1958, The (Kunitz), 353
Poems of the United Nations, 344
"Poet Gets Hair Cut, Retains Strength" (Oppenheimer), 439
Poet in the World, The (Levertov), 367
Poetic Justice, 213
Poetic License, Radical Artifice, 216
Poetic Vision of Muriel Rukeyser, The (Kertesz), 513
Poetics, A, 213, 215
Poetry, The Ecology of the Soul: Talks and Selected Poems (Oppenheimer), 434, 441
Poetry and Fiction (Nemerov), 412, 417
Poetry and the Common Life (Rosenthal), 488, 490
"Poetry as Confession" (Rosenthal), 489
Poetry in English: An Anthology (Rosenthal), 488
Poetry Wreck, The: Selected Essays 1950–1970 (K. Shapiro), 556
Poet's Art, The (Rosenthal), 488
Poets for Africa (Fishman), 245
Poirier, Richard, 304
"Poland of Death" (Grossman), 283, 285
Poland/1931 (Rothenberg), 492, 495
Pole Vaulter, The (Layton), 358
Politics and Form in Postmodern Poetry (Blasing), 463

Politics of Form: Poetry and Public Policy, The (Bernstein), 215
"Politics of Translation, The" (Bloch), 223
Polkinhorn, Harry, 498
Pollitt, Katha, 238
"Poor Jew, A" (Bell), 209
Pope, Alexander, 288
"Populist" (Oppen), 428
Portrait of the Artist as a Young Man (Joyce), 326, 460
"Portrait of the Poet as Landscape" (Klein), 326
Portraits from Memory (Kostelanetz), 337
Potency Clinic, The (Field), 242
Poulin, A., Jr., 566
Pound, Ezra, 215, 280, 281, 292, 336, 358, 386, 390, 412, 420, 423, 427, 428, 440, 450, 460, 469, 488, 494, 495, 516, 597
"Power: A Sequence" (Rosenthal), 489
Power, Kevin, 497
Powers of Thirteen (Hollander), 302
PPPPPP: Selected Writings of Kurt Schwitters (Rothenberg, Joris), 493
Pre-Faces and Other Writings (Rothenberg), 493, 494, 497
"Present State of Poetry, The" (D. Schwartz), 516
"Previous Tenant, The" (Simpson), 567
Primer of Ezra Pound, A (Rosenthal), 488, 489-90
Primitive (Oppen), 427
"Principle of Fit, The" (Antin), 256
"Pripet Marshes, The" (Feldman), 234
Pripet Marshes, The (Feldman), 236
Probable Volume of Dreams, A (Bell), 209
"Prodigal Son, The" (Mitchell), 399
Proofs and Theories (Glück), 269, 271
Proust, Marcel, 253, 308, 403
Provoked in Venice (Rudman), 502
Prunty, Wyatt, 417
Purdy, A. W., 358
Purgatorio (Dante, Mandelbaum), 385, 386

Quantities (Howard), 308
Quasha, George, 492
Quasimodo, Salvatore, 383
"Quiet Desperation" (Simpson), 567

"Rabbi's Dream, A" (Tarn), 595
Rabelais, François, 388
"Radical Departures" (Moss), 404
Raffel, Burton, 599
Rahv, Philip, 337, 502
Rakosi, Carl, 440, **448-59**, 469
Randall, Margaret, 432
Randall Jarrell (Rosenthal), 488
Rankin, Rush, 272
Ratner, Rochelle, 522
Rauschenberg, Robert, 432
Ravikovitch, Dahlia, 221, 223, 480
Ray, David, 550, 551
"Reading the Headlines" (Ignatow), 316
"Readings of History"(Rich), 478
Realm of Unknowing (Rudman), 502
Reasons for Moving (Strand), 587, 588, 591
"Reception and Influence of American Poetry in France, 1918-1950, The" (Koch), 330
Red Coal, The (Stern), 579, 580, 585
Red Robins, The (Koch), 331
Reflections on Espionage (Hollander), 302, 304
Reflexions on Poetry and Poetics (Nemerov), 412, 417
Refusers, The (Burnshaw), 226, 227
Region of Unlikeness (Graham), 276
Reimagining the Bible: The Storytelling of the Rabbis (H. Schwartz), 525
Reisen, Abraham, 344, 345
"Reluctant Bodhisattva, A" (Mitchell), 399
"Remains, The" (Strand), 589
Rembrandt, 397
"Remembering Carl Rakosi: A Conjectural Reconstruction of 'The Beasts' " (Crozier), 458
Reports of My Death (K. Shapiro), 555
Repositionings: Reading of Contemporary Poetry, Photography and Performance Art (Garber), 497-98

Republics of Reality (Bernstein), 215

"Requiem for a Friend" (Rilke, Mitchell), 396

"Rescue the Dead" (Ignatow), 316–17

Rescue the Dead (Ignatow), 316

Residue of Song (Bell), 210

"Retreating Light" (Glück), 270

Reverdy, 502

Revolution of the World (Rothenberg), 492

Rexroth, Kenneth, 488, 497, 542, 595

Reznikoff, Charles, 292, 425, 451, **460–75**, 551, 552, 567

"Reznikoff's Nearness" (Bernstein), 213

Rhyme's Reason (Hollander), 302

Rhythms (Reznikoff), 461

Rich, Adrienne, 352, **476–82**, 511, 599

Ricoeur, Paul, 463

Rider (Rudman), 501, 502, 503, 504

"Rider Held Back, The" (Simpson), 565

"Right Now" (Kessler), 322

"Rightful One, The" (Ignatow), 314

Rilke, Rainer Maria, 204, 276, 299, 344, 395, 396, 398

Rimbaud, Arthur, 299

Rinpoche, Chögyam Trungpa, 261, 262

"Rite of Passage" (Oppenheimer), 439

"Rites and Ceremonies" (Hecht), 289

"River Road" (Kunitz), 351

Rivers, Larry, 330, 331

Riverside Drive (Simpson), 561

Road Came Once, A (Kessler), 320

Rockefeller, J. D., 257

Rocking Chair and Other Poems, The (Klein), 326

Rodin, August, 308

Roethke, Theodore, 350, 489

Romans, Marialuisa de, 383

Ronch, Isaac E., 345

Rose, Where Did You Get That Red: Teaching Great Poetry to Children (Koch), 331

Rosenberg, David, **483–86**

Rosenberg, Ethel, 480

Rosenberg, Liz, 272

Rosenbergs, 257, 258

Rosenfeld, Morris, 344, 345

Rosenthal, M. L., 231, 235, 238, 263, **487–90**, 571

Rossini, Giacomo, 308

Rossman, Steven R., 523

Roth, Cecil, 207

Roth, Henry, 595

Rothenberg, Jerome, **491–500**, 529, 531, 562

Rough Trades (Bernstein), 213, 215

"Route" (Oppen), 426

Rubin, Louis, 417

Rudman, Mark, 223, **501–6**

Rudolf, Anthony, 524, 570

Ruin Revived, The (Rudman), 502

Rukeyser, Muriel, 363, **507–14**, 554, 558, 580

Rules of Sleep (Moss), 402, 408

"Runner, The" (Simpson), 564, 569

Running to Paradise: Yeats's Poetic Art (Rosenthal), 489

Ryan, Michael, 353

Sabbath Lion, The (H. Schwartz), 525

Sabina, Maria, 494

Sacco and Venzetti, 509

"Sacred Objects" (Simpson), 570

"Sadness and Happiness" (Pinsky), 444

Sadness and Happiness (Pinsky), 444

"Safe Methods of Business" (Bernstein), 215

Sahn, Seung, 395, 398

Sailing into the Unknown: Yeats, Pound, and Eliot (Rosenthal), 488–89

Sailing Too Far (Kessler), 320

"Salmon and Red Wine" (Reznikoff), 466

Salt Garden, The (Nemerov), 412, 417

"Salutations to Fernando Pessoa" (Ginsberg), 262

"Same Moon above Us, The" (Stern), 581

Samuel, Maurice, 327

Sanders, Gerald DeWitt, 488

"Sands of Paran, The" (Grossman), 280

"Santa Claus" (Nemerov), 413

"Saratoga" (Moss), 405

"Saturnalia" (Glück), 269

Savantasse of Montparnasse, The (Mandelbaum), 386–87, 388
"Say Pardon" (Ignatow), 317
Say Pardon (Ignatow), 314
"Scene of a Summer Morning" (Feldman), 236, 237
Schachter-Shalomi, Zalman, 525
Schapiro, Meyer, 542
Schapiro, Nancy, 522
Schechner, Mark, 258
Schiller, Frederick, 344
Schjeldahl, Peter, 378
Schlemmer, Oscar, 581
Scholem, Gershon, 294, 505, 525, 595
Schreiber, Maeera, 264
Schultz, Bruno, 588, 590
Schuyler, James, 309, 330, 331, 333
Schwab, Joseph J., 487
Schwartz, Chaim, 345
Schwartz, Delmore, 330, **515–20**, 554, 558, 563
Schwartz, Howard, **521–27**
Schwartz, I. J., 345
Schweizer, Harold, 238
Schwerner, Armand, 492, **528–35**
Science of Goodbyes, The (Sklarew), 576
Scorsese, Martin, 275
Scott, Dred, 309
"Screaming Poem" (Oppenheimer), 437
"Sea of Grass" (Simpson), 565
Seamless Web, The: Language—Thinking, Creature—Knowledge (Burnshaw), 227
Searching for the Ox (Simpson), 563, 566, 570
Seascape: Needles Eye (Oppen), 427
"Seasons, The" (D. Shapiro), 542, 546
Seaweed (Schwerner), 529
Second Scroll, The (Klein), 326–27
Secrets of the Tribe, The (Bloch), 221, 222–23
"Seedings" (Rothenberg), 496
Seedings (Rothenberg), 496
"Seeing Leni Riefenstahl's *Triumph of the Will*" (Rothenberg), 495
Segal, George, 235
Selected Poems (Levine), 372
Selected Poems (Moss), 402

Selected Poems (Rakosi), 457
Selected Poems (Simpson), 564, 567
Selected Poems (Strand), 588, 589, 590, 591
Selected Poems and Three Plays of William Butler Yeats (Rosenthal), 488
Selected Poems 1928–1958 (Kunitz), 352, 353
Selected Poetry of Rainer Maria Rilke (Mitchell), 396
Selected Poetry of Yehuda Amichai (Amichai, Bloch, Mitchell), 221
Selerie, Gavin, 497
"Self-Interview" (Rudman), 503
"Self-Portrait as the Gesture Between Them" (Graham), 276
"Semite" (Oppen), 427
Seneca Journal, A (Rothenberg), 495, 496
"Seneca Journal 6" (Rothenberg), 496
"Sensitive Knife, The" (Stern), 583
Sentences (Nemerov), 412
"Sentences My Father Used" (Bernstein), 215
Separate Way (Reznikoff), 461, 462
"Serenade" (Kramer), 344
"Services" (Rakosi), 456
Sexton, Anne, 263, 271, 489, 513
Shaker House Poems (Lifshin), 377
Shakespeare, William, 203, 268, 332, 398, 445, 503, 504, 542, 561, 597
Shaking the Pumpkin (Rothenberg), 492, 494
Shapiro, Alan, **536–41**
Shapiro, David, 330, **542–48**
Shapiro, Harvey, **549–53**
Shapiro, Karl (Jay), 489, 516, **554–59**
She: A Sequence of Poems (Rosenthal), 489
Sheehan, Donald, 309
"Shekhina" (Tarn), 595
Shelley, Percy Bysshe, 281
Shenandoah (D. Schwartz), 515, 516, 517, 518, 519
Sherry, James, 216
"Shimon Bar Yochai" (Tarn), 595
Shoa, 376
Sholem Aleichem, 231, 258
Shoptaw, John, 215, 216

"Shorelines" (Moss), 402
Shover, Joseph Bov, 345
Sidney, Philip, 282
Sighted Singer, The (Grossman), 280, 285
Signorelli, Luca, 276
Signs of the Lost Tribe (H. Schwartz), 522
"Silence, The" (Mezey), 392
"Silent Generation, The" (Simpson), 565
Silliman, Ron, 213, 216
Silver, Rabbi Hillel, 307
Simic, James, 522
Simon, Linda, 470
"Simon, the Barber" (A. Shapiro), 537–38, 540
Simple Truth, The (Levine), 371, 372
Simpson, Louis, **560–74**
Singer, Isaac Bashevis, 337, 491, 570
"Sirventes on a Sad Occurrence" (Oppenheimer), 436, 439
Sirventes on a Sad Occurrence (Oppenheimer), 433
Sitta, Carlo Alberto, 338–39
Sitting Bull, 497
"Six-Pointed Star" (Fishman), 247
Skelton, Robin, 358–59
Sklarew, Myra, **575–78**
Slavitt, David, 502
Sleeping with One Eye Open (Strand), 588, 591
"Sleeping with Women" (Koch), 332
Sleep-Walking Beneath the Stars (H. Schwartz), 522
"Small Moment" (Nemerov), 414
Smart, Christopher, 322, 589
Smith, Dave, 408, 570
Smith, Leverett T., 440
Snodgrass, W. D., 263
Snyder, Gary, 260
Snapshots of a Daughter-in-Law (Rich), 478
"So It Happens" (Feldman), 236, 237
"Soap" (Stern), 583–84, 585
Solomon, Barbara Probst, 484
Solomon, Carl, 252
"Song of Degrees, A" (Nemerov), 414
Sonnets to Orpheus, The (Rilke, Mitchell), 396

Soper, Brian, 489
Sophist, The (Bernstein), 213, 215
Sorrentino, Gilbert, 599
"Sorrows of American-Jewish Poetry, The" (Bloom), 309, 532
"Sound and Sense of the Sleight-of-Hand Man, The" (Lehman), 304
"sounds of the river Narajana" (Schwerner), 531
Sounds of the River Narajana and the Tablets I–XXIV (Schwerner), 530
"Sources" (Rich), 478, 480
Spanos, William, 497
"Special Report on the Holocaust" (Fishman), 247
Spector, Robert, 272
"Spectrum Elegy" (Fishman), 247
"Speech at Soli, The" (Oppen), 427
Speed of Darkness, The (Rukeyser), 508, 510, 511
Spelling the Word: George Herbert and the Bible (Bloch), 221, 223
Spencer, Theodore, 519
Spenser, Edmund, 206
Spicehandler, Ezra, 227
Spiegelman, Willard, 417
Spinoza, Baruch, 397
"Spinoza" (Mitchell), 399
Spire, Andre, 226
Spiritus I (Rakosi), 458
"Split at the Root: An Essay on Jewish Identity" (Rich), 476
"Squeal" (Simpson), 565
St. John, David, 210
Stafford, William, 569
Stand Up, Friend, with Me (Field), 241–42
"Standard" (Moss), 405
Stars in My Eyes (Field), 242
Stars Which We See, Stars Which We Do Not See (Bell), 210
"Stasis and Dynamis: Two Modes of the Literary Imagination (Crashaw, Hopkins, Joyce and T. S. Eliot)" (Mandelbaum), 382
"Statement for the Times" (Ignatow), 317

Stein, Gertrude, 212, 214, 259, 339, 491, 494, 497
Steiner, George, 594
"Stein's Identity" (Bernstein), 213
Stepanchev, Stephen, 568
Stern, Gerald, 248, 285, 303, **579–86**
Stevens, Wallace, 235, 285, 330, 332, 397, 417, 451, 452, 460, 481, 544, 589, 591
Stitt, Peter, 299, 408, 570
Stokowski, Leopold, 542
Stone, Ruth, 323
Stories, Fables, and Other Diversions (Nemerov), 412
"Story about Chicken Soup, A" (Simpson), 565
"Story of Our Lives, The" (Strand), 589
Story of Our Lives, The (Strand), 589, 591
Straight Hearts' Delight and Honorable Courtship, 255
Strand, Mark, 202, 502, **587–93**
Strauss, Richard, 299
Stroffolino, Chris, 547
Stryk, Lucien, 295
"Summa Lyrica" (Grossman), 280, 284
Summa Theologica (Aquinas), 386
Summer Knowledge (D. Schwartz), 515
Summoning of Stones, A (Hecht), 289
"Sunday at the State Hospital" (Ignatow), 317
"Sunflower Sutra" (Ginsberg), 254
"Survival: Infantry" (Oppen), 424
Sutherland, John, 355
"Swimmer, The" (Layton), 355
Swimmer in the Air, A (Moss), 407
"Sylvia" (Stern), 579
Symposium (Plato, Xenophon), 207
Syrkin, Marie, 461

Tablet V (Schwerner), 533
Tablets, The (Schwerner), 532, 533
"Take Me Out to the Ballgame" (Pinsky), 445
Tales of the Hasidim: The Later Masters (Buber), 364
Tall Story (Nemerov), 412
Tangled Vines (Lifshin), 375

Tao Te Ching (Mitchell trans.), 396, 397
"Tao-Chi" (Mitchell), 399
Tarn, Nathaniel, **594–96**
Tate, Allen, 515–16, 519
"Tattered Kaddish" (Rich), 480
Taylor, Charles, 469
Taylor, John, 238
Taylor, Robert, 485
Teardrop Millionaire, The (M. Rosenfeld, Kramer), 345
Technicians of the Sacred (Rothenberg), 492, 494
Tedlock, Dennis, 497
Teitelboim, Dora, 344
"Tell Me a Riddle" (Olsen), 256
Terrible Threshold: Selected Poems, 1940–1970 (Kunitz), 351
Tesserae (Levertov), 365
Testimony: A Recitative, the United States, 1865–1915 (Reznikoff), 461, 462, 463, 466, 471
Testimony: Contemporary Writers Make the Holocaust Personal (Rosenberg, 484
"Testing-Tree, The" (Kunitz), 351–52
Testing-Tree, The (Kunitz), 351, 353
Thackeray, William M., 308
That Dada Strain (Rothenberg), 493
Theory of Flight (Rukeyser), 508, 509
"There Are Such Springlike Nights" (Molodowsky, Rich), 479
"There Were Screams through Double Doors" (Lifshin), 378
There You Are (Simpson), 568
"They Feed They Lion" (Levine), 371
They Feed They Lion (Levine), 370
Thiers, Adolphe, 471
This Garland, Danger (Kunitz), 352
This in Which (Oppen), 425
This World (H. Shapiro), 551
Thomas, Dylan, 375
"Three Compositions on Philosophy and Literature" (Bernstein), 212
"Three Oppen Letters with a Note" (Oppen), 421, 423–24
"Three Skies" (Stern), 583
"Three Tears" (Stern), 583
"Through the Binoculars" (Heller), 295

"Through the Eye of a Needle" (Mitch-ell), 399
Tillinghast, Richard, 570
Time's Power (Rich), 480
"To an Idea" (D. Shapiro), 544
To an Idea (D. Shapiro), 543, 544, 545, 547
"To Aunt Rose" (Ginsberg), 257
To Be Alive (Field), 242
"To Ford Madox Ford in Heaven" (Wil-liams), 489
"To Levine on the Day of Atonement" (Mezey), 391, 393
"To Marina" (Koch), 332
To Move into the House (Fein), 230, 231
"To Persecuted Foreigners" (Moise), 203
"To the Babylonians" (Nemerov), 414
"To the Six Million" (Feldman), 236
"To the Western World" (Simpson), 566
"To William Carlos Williams in Heaven" (Rosenthal), 489
"Tom Jefferson" (Levine), 371
"Touch Me" (Kunitz), 352
Toy Fair, The (Moss), 403, 407
Tractatus (Wittgenstein), 277
Travels of the Itinerant Freda Aharon, The (Sklarew), 577
Treasury of Jewish Poetry, A, 344
Treasury of Yiddish Poetry, A (Green-berg, Howe), 479
Tremblay, Bill, 296
"Trial, The" (Rukeyser), 509
Trial of a Poet (K. Shapiro), 556
Tribe of John: John Ashbery and Con-temporary Poetry, The (Shoptaw), 216
Trible, Phyllis, 399
"Tributes to Henry Ford" (Kostelanetz), 337
Trilling, Lionel, 301
"Tristia" (Mandelstam), 576
Triumph of Achilles, The (Glück), 270
Turner, Nat, 509
Turning Wind, A (Rukeyser), 508
"Twentieth Century Unlimited" (Rothen-berg), 496
"Twilight Under Pine Ridge" (Mezey), 391
"Two Trees" (Stern), 581

Two-Part Inventions (Howard), 308, 309
"Tunnel, The" (Strand), 588
Types of Shape (Hollander), 302
"Typology of the Parabolist" (Heller), 317
Tzara, Tristan, 494

Unamuno, 589
Ulysses (Joyce), 460
"Uncle Speaks in the Drawing Room, The" (Rich), 478
"Uncreation, The" (Pinsky), 445
Understanding Poetry (Brooks, Warren), 488
"Undertaking, The," (Glück), 270
"Unearthly Voices" (Hirsch), 299
Ungaretti, Giuseppe, 383
Untermeyer, Louis, 346
Untitled Subjects (Howard), 308
Upanishads, The, 398
U.S. 1 (Rukeyser), 509
Uses of Adversity, The (Oppenheimer), 434

Vallejo, César, 562
Van Doren, Mark, 301, 346, 562, 565
Van Spanckeren, Kathryn, 533
"Variations on a Theme by William Car-los Williams" (Koch), 333
Variety Photoplays (Field), 242
Vendler, Helen, 263, 272, 277, 408, 469
Venetian Vespers (Hecht), 289
Venus de Milo, 204
"Vermeer" (Mitchell), 399
Vessels (H. Schwartz), 522
Vienna Blood (Rothenberg), 493, 495
"View from Pisgah, The" (Nemerov), 414
"View of the Terrace, A" (Rich), 478
Vigil (Shapiro), 536
Village (Field), 242
Villon, François, 569
"Violent Collaborations"(Ginsberg), 261
Virgil, 383, 384, 590
"Visions of Daniel" (Pinsky), 445
"Visiting Yeats's Tower" (Rosenthal), 489
Visual Language (Kostelanetz), 338

"Voice" (D. Shapiro), 546
Voices within the Ark: The Modern Jewish Poets (H. Schwartz), 524
"Volhynia Province" (Simpson), 564
Vosnesensky, Andrei, 350, 567

Waddington, Miriam, 328
Wagner, Richard, 323
"Waiting in the Service Station" (Simpson), 568
Wakoski, Diane, 367, 492
Walk with Tom Jefferson, A (Levine), 371, 372
Walker, Alice, 477
Waller, Fats, 445
Walpole, Horace, 308
"Walter Benjamin: A Lost Poem" (D. Shapiro), 546
"Wandering Jew, The" (Mezey), 393
Want Bone, The (Pinsky), 444, 445
"War against the Jews, The" (Stern), 583, 585
War Stories (Nemerov), 412
Warhol, Andy, 331
Warren, Robert Penn, 488, 557, 591
Washburn, Katherine, 502, 551
Waste Land, The (Eliot), 460, 542
"Waterwall Blues" (Moss), 402
Watson, Craig, 216
Watten, Barrett, 216
"We Came Naked" (Ignatow), 315, 316
"We Have a Print of Marc Chagall's Picture of a Green-Faced Jew" (Reznikoff), 464
Weil, Simone, 282
Weinberger, Eliot, 463, 595
Weinper, Z., 345
Weldon, Fay, 563
Weldon, Ron, 563
"Wellfleet Whale, The" (Kunitz), 351
Wershba, Joseph, 346
Wesker, Arnold, 594
Western Approaches, The (Nemerov), 412
Wharton, Edith, 308
"What Ari Says When He's Five" (Schwerner), 529
"What Can Yiddish Mean to an American Poet?" (Fein), 230

What Is Found There (Rich), 476, 477, 478, 480
"What Is the Sabbath?" (Stern), 582
"What One Remembers" (Levertov), 365
"What Work Is" (Levine), 371
What Work Is (Levine), 372
"When We Dead Awaken: Writing As Revision" (Rich), 479
"White" (Strand), 589
White, Edmund, 408
White, J. P., 238
"White Night" (Molodowsky-Rich), 479
"White Shroud" (Ginsberg), 261
White Shroud (Ginsberg), 261
White Sun Black Sun (Rothenberg), 492, 493, 495
White-Haired Lover (K. Shapiro), 557
Whitemore, Reed, 346, 417
Whitman, Walt, 229, 251, 259, 260, 308, 316, 321, 322, 344, 345, 346, 358, 489, 509, 566, 585, 589, 595
"Why I Meditate" (Ginsberg), 262
Why Is the House Dissolving? (Lifshin), 377
"Wichita Vortex Sutra" (Ginsberg), 260, 261
Wiesel, Elie, 317
Wilbur, Richard, 405
Wild Gratitude (Hirsch), 298
Wild Iris, The (Glück), 269, 270
Wild Patience Has Taken Me This Far, A (Rich), 479
Wilder, Thornton, 487
Will to Change, The (Rich), 479
William Carlos Williams Reader, The (Rosenthal), 488
Williams, C. K., 585
Williams, Oscar, 519
Williams, William Carlos, 259, 260, 292, 317, 358, 372, 412, 420, 432, 438, 453, 457, 460, 461, 469, 489, 497, 551
Williamson, Alan, 295, 570
Wilson, Edmund, 336
Window, The: New and Selected Poems (Ravikovitch, Bloch, Bloch), 223
Winter Come, a Summer Gone, A: Poems 1946–1960 (Moss), 407
"Winter Morning" (Glück), 270

"Winter Night: Mont Royal" (Klein), 326

Wishes, Lies, and Dreams (Koch), 331

Wisse, Ruth, 231

Wittgenstein, Ludwig, 212, 276, 277, 544

Wojahn, David, 571

Woman on the Bridge over the Chicago River, The (Grossman), 285

Woman Poems, The (Oppenheimer), 433, 436, 437

Women of Trachis (Pound), 533

Wonder Child and Other Jewish Fairy Tales, The (H. Schwartz), 525

Wood, Michael, 304

Woodlawn North (Kessler), 320

Woolf, Virginia, 503

Wooten, Anna, 272

Wordworks (Kostelanetz), 339

work, the joy and the triumph of the will, the (Schwerner), 534

"Working Late" (Simpson), 566

Works and Days (Feldman), 236

World Is a Wedding, The (D. Schwartz), 517

Wound and the Weather, The (Moss), 402, 403

Wright, James, 352, 522, 562, 569

"Write the Power" (Perelman), 216

Wrong Season, The (Oppenheimer), 433

Wyatt, Thomas, 375

Wykes-Joyce, 489

Xenophon, 207

"Yahrzeit" (A. Shapiro), 538, 539

Yeats, W. B., 268, 281, 282, 285, 330, 398, 489, 505

Yerbugh, Rhoda, 272

"Yiddish" (Fein), 230, 231

"Yiddish Lessons in Brighton Beach" (Fein), 231

"Yiddish Poet Yankev Glatshteyn Visits Me in the Coffee Shop, The" (Fein), 230

"Yiddishe Kopf" (Ginsberg), 262

Yohai, Simon bar, 494

"Yom Kippur" (Rich), 480

Yoseloff, Thomas, 344, 346

Younger Son, The (K. Shapiro), 555

Your Native Land, Your Life (Rich), 476, 477, 478, 479, 480

Zangwill, Israel, 365

"Zen Master" (Mitchell), 399

"Zero" (Kessler), 322

Zevi, Sabbatai, 494

Zorn, John, 214

Zucker, David, 458

Zukofsky, Louis, 292, 420, 421, 440, 450, 451, 452, 457, 461, 469, 530, 567, 594, **597–603**

Zukofsky, Paul, 598

About the Editors and Contributors

DROR ABEND-DAVID writes poetry and creative criticism and has a special interest in Yiddish poetry in New York during the 1920s and 1930s.

KARLA ALWES is Professor of English at the State University of New York, College at Cortland. She is the author of *Imagination Transformed: The Evolution of the Female in Keats' Poetry* and articles on women in literature. She was chair of the Multicultural and Genders Studies Council at Cortland for four years.

NEIL ARDITI's work has appeared in *Raritan* on Shelley's "Adonais."

WILLIAM JAMES AUSTIN is Assistant Professor of English at the State University of New York in Farmingdale. An accomplished musician, he has written music and lyrics for Lou Rawls, Hammer, and other rock and jazz notables. His poetry has been published in *The Boston Literary Review*, and *Timbuktu*, among others, and in the art magazine *Appearances*. *Underworld 1 and 2*, a book of his poetry, was published in 1994, and his critical analysis of deconstructionism was published in 1996.

MERLE BACHMAN's interests include Yiddish poetry, ethnicity, and modernism. She is an accomplished poet and has published widely in journals favoring experimental and cross-genre approaches to writing, such as *Talisman: A Journal of Contemporary Poetry and Poetics, First Intensity*, and *ABACUS*. Bachman is a student of Yiddish language and culture and is dedicated to the recovery and recognition of American-Yiddish literature.

JOSHUA SAUL BECKMAN specializes in the poetry of Allen Ginsberg and Charles Reznikoff. He has been affiliated with the School of Humanities and the Arts at Hampshire College and recently received a fellowship at the Montalus Center for the Arts in Saratoga Springs, New York.

KAREN BENDER lives and writes in New York City.

JOSHUA BERG is a graduate student at the University of Ohio.

CHARLES S. BERGER is Professor of English at the University of Utah. He has written articles on modern and contemporary forms of American literature and is author of *Forms of Farewell: The Late Poetry of Wallace Stevens*.

THEODORE BLANCHARD has done a translation of Xenophanes in the *World Treasury of Poetry* (1997), and an excerpt from his novel was published in the summer 1997 issue of *Pequod*.

RACHEL FELDHAY BRENNER is Associate Professor of Hebrew Literature at the University of Wisconsin-Madison. She is the author of *Assimilation and Assertion: The Response to the Holocaust in Mordecai Richler's Writing* (1989) and *A. M. Klein: The Father of Canadian Jewish Literature* (1990).

DAVID CAPLAN, in addition to his scholarly publications, has published his poetry in the *New England Review* and *Seneca Review*.

CATHARINE GABRIEL CAREY's reviews have appeared in the *English Journal* and the *Virginia English Bulletin*, and she has presented papers at the Modern Language Association (MLA) and Four C's conferences.

MICHAEL CASTRO is a St. Louis-based poet who has published five books of poems, most recently *(US)* (1991). Castro is also the author of *Interpreting the Indian: Twentieth Century Poets and the Native American*, a study of Native American influences on modern poetry (1991), the founding editor of *River Styx Magazine*, and the host of the *Poetry Beat* radio program. He teaches at Lindenwood College in St. Louis.

RICHARD CHESS is Associate Professor in the Language and Literature Department at the University of North Carolina in Asheville. He is the Director for the Center of Jewish Studies at the university and is author of a book of poems, *Tekiah* (1995).

MIRIAM MARTY CLARK is Associate Professor and Director of the Great Books program at Auburn University. She has published essays on a number of twentieth-century poets and fiction writers, including Howard Nemerov, A. R. Ammons, Virginia Woolf, Alice Munro, Ann Beattie, Grace Paley, William Trevor, and Raymond Carver.

GENEVIEVE COHEN-CHEMINET is Maître de Conférences in Paris IV–Sorbonne.

MARIA DAMON is the author of *The Dark End of the Street: Margins in*

American Vanguard Poetry (1993) and a member of the National Writers' Union. She is Associate Professor of English at the University of Minnesota.

NORMAN J. FEDDER—a widely produced playwright on Jewish themes—is Distinguished Professor and Director of Graduate Studies in the Theatre Program of Kansas State University.

THOMAS FINK is Professor of English at La Guardia (CUNY). He has published *The Poetry of David Shapiro* (1993) and a book of his own poetry, *Surprise Visit* (1993), and is coeditor of *Literature around the Globe* (1994). His work has been published in *Contemporary Literature, American Poetry Review*, and *Modern Poetry Studies.*

NORMAN FINKELSTEIN is the author of a book of poetry, *Restless Messengers* (1992), and two books of criticism, *The Utopian Moment in Contemporary American Poetry* (2d ed., 1993) and *The Ritual of New Creation: Jewish Tradition and Contemporary Literature* (1992). He is Professor of English and Department Chair at Xavier University, Cincinnati.

HUGH FOX teaches in the Department of American Thought and Language at Michigan State University. Among his many publications is *Lifshin: A Critical Study* (1985).

ROBERT S. FRIEDMAN has lived in New York City and is particularly interested in the work of Harvey Shapiro.

BARRY FRUCHTER is an Assistant Professor of English at Nassau Community College. He recently presented a paper on contemporary critiques of *Mein Kampf* at the 1997 NEMLA in Philadelphia. He has an article on the agenda and threat of the Far Right in the Fall 1997 issue of *Socialist Review.*

BEN FURNISH has taught at the University of Missouri-Columbia and Avila College. He has work forthcoming in *Novels into Film* and the *Encyclopedia of Soviet Culture.*

JONATHAN GILL has written and lectured on Louis-Ferdinand Céline, George and Ira Gershwin, Langston Hughes, Ezra Pound, and Walt Whitman.

LYMAN GILMORE taught literature and psychology for thirty years before writing *Don't Touch The Poet: The Life and Times of Joel Oppenheimer.* He and Joel were friends and colleagues at New England College the last six years of Joel's life.

LOSS PEQUEÑO GLAZIER, poet, is a Director, Electronic Poetry Center (http://wings.buffalo.edu/epc) and Webmaster, University Libraries, State University of New York at Buffalo. Publications include *Leaving Loss Glazier* (1997), *The Parts* (1995), *Small Press: An Annotated Guide* (1992), *The Fishtail* (1997), and *Tenoshhteetlán* (to be published). A variety of works are available on his author home page (http://wings.buffalo.edu/epc/authors/glazier). Present recent projects include sound files, greps, program-based poetry, and visual, kinetic, and hypertextual works.

WILLIAM HARMON is James Gordon Hanes Professor of English at the University of North Carolina, Chapel Hill. He is the author of five books of poetry and the editor of the fifth through seventh editions of the *Handbook to Literature* and of two poetry anthologies.

JOHN HOLLANDER is Sterling Professor of Literature at Yale University. Among his many books are criticism: *The Untuning of the Sky* (1961) and *Rhymes Reason* (1981); poetry: *Jiggery-Pokery* (with Anthony Hecht) (1966) *Tesserae and Other Poems* (1993), and *Tales Told of the Fathers* (1975); and many volumes he has edited, among which are *Modern Poetry: Essays in Criticism* (1968) and *The Gazer's Spirit: Poems Speaking to Silent Works of Art* (1995).

CAREN IRR is Assistant Professor at Penn State University, where she teaches English and American Studies. She is the author of *The Suburb of Dissent: Cultural Politics in the United States and Canada during the 1930's*.

EDWARD ISSER is Assistant Professor of Theatre at Holy Cross University. Formerly a professional actor who appeared in numerous shows on- and off-Broadway, he has contributed articles to *Modern Drama* and *Bernard Shaw Annual*. His book *Stage of Annihilation: Theatrical Representation of the Holocaust* was published in 1997.

PIERRE JORIS's most recent books include *Winnetou Old* (poems), *Breathturn* by Paul Celan (translation), and, with Jerome Rothenberg, *Poems for the Millennium: The University of California Book of Modern and Postmodern Poetry*, volume 1 of a global anthology of twentieth-century avant-garde writings. Joris teaches in the Department of English at SUNY–Albany.

DANIEL KANE teaches writing at New York University in the College of Arts and Sciences. He has published poetry in *Denver Quarterly, Exquisite Corpse*, and *Mudfish*.

LESLIE KANE is Professor of English at Westfield State College in Massachusetts. She is the author of *The Language of Silence: On the Unspoken and the Unspeakable in Modern Drama* and editor of *David Mamet: A Casebook, Israel Horovitz: A Collection of Critical Essays*, and *Glengarry Glen Ross: Text and Performance*. Her essays, reviews, and interviews on Pinter, Mamet, Shepard, Miller, and Horovitz have appeared in *The Pinter Review, American Drama, American Theatre, Theatre Journal*, and *The Yearbook on English Studies*, as well as collected essays. President of the David Mamet Society, editor of the *David Mamet Review*, and a Fulbright Scholar, Kane is completing *Weasels and Wisemen*, a study of Jewish tropes in the work of David Mamet.

BURT KIMMELMAN is Assistant Professor of English at New Jersey Institute of Technology and the author of several books, including *The "Winter Mind": William Bronk and the American Tradition* (forthcoming), *The Poetics of Authorship in the Later Middle Ages: The Emergence of the Modern Literary Persona* (1996), and a collection of poems, *Musaics* (1992). He is also Senior Editor of *Poetry New York: A Journal of Poetry and Translation.*

BLOSSOM STEINBERG KIRSCHENBAUM is Researcher at Brown University's Department of Comparative Literature. She has translated the works of Giuliana Morandini, Paola Drigo, and Marina Mizzau as well as other short fiction from Italian, Yiddish, and Slovak works.

BETTE H. KIRSCHSTEIN is an Assistant Professor of Literature and Communications at Pace University in Pleasantville, New York. She has contributed several entries to the forthcoming *Encyclopedia of British Women Writers.*

DENNIS A. KLEIN is Professor of Spanish in the Department of Modern Languages at the University of South Dakota in Vermillion. He has widely published on the subjects of Hispanic and British drama. Professor Klein is the author of three books on Peter Shaffer and of *Blood Wedding, Yerma, and The House of Bernarda Alba: García Lorca's Tragic Trilogy.* He served as the contributing editor to *García Lorca: An Annotated Primary Bibliography* and *García Lorca: A Selective Annotated Bibliography of Criticism* and contributed to *Peter Shaffer: A Casebook* and *Israel Horovitz: A Collection of Critical Essays.* Professor Klein is head Hispanic bibliographer of the Modern Language Association's International Bibliography.

JOSEPH LEASE is the author of two books of poetry, most recently, *Human Rights.* His poems have been published widely in *Grand Street, Colorado Review,* the *Paris Review,* and elsewhere. He is poetry editor of the *Boston Book Review.*

JENNIFER LEWIN is interested in relationships between dreams in Renaissance epic and lyric poetry and theories of the imagination in oneirocriticism. Other interests include American philosophy, poetic theory, contemporary poetry, and the history of British drama.

HERBERT LIEBMAN is an NEA-Award winning playwright and a widely published short story writer who is Associate Professor of English at the College of Staten Island (CUNY). His full-length critical work *The Dramatic Art of David Storey: The Journey of a Playwright* was published in 1996.

ELIZABETH LLOYD-KIMBREL is Projects Manager and writer for Monadnock Media, Inc. She has published on a variety of subjects such as Chaucer in *Mediaevistik* and Marya Zaturenska in *American National Biography.*

DARRELL B. LOCKHART is a Lecturer in Spanish at the University of Arizona. He is the editor of *Jewish Latin American Writers: A Dictionary* (1996) and the author of *Latin American Jewish Literature* (1997).

STEPHEN MONTE is currently translating the poetry of Victor Hugo.

RICHARD MOODY is a specialist in modern drama.

ANDREA MOST received the 1996–1997 Wasserman Fellowship to pursue her research on Jews in American theatre at the American Jewish Historical Society. She worked as a film and theatre producer in Boston and New York with such companies as the Wooster Group.

BENJAMIN NELSON is Professor of English and Comparative Literature at Fairleigh Dickinson University, Teaneck, New Jersey. He is the author of *Tennessee Williams: The Man and His Work* and *Arthur Miller: Portrait of a Playwright*. He lectures and writes on theatre, film, and Jewish-American literature.

MICHAEL C. O'NEILL is Director of Theater at Lafayette College and an Adjunct Associate Professor at New York University. He has directed college and professional theatre in the United States and abroad. His writings about the theatre and his dramatic criticism have appeared in numerous essay collections, as well as in *Theatre Journal, Renascence, The Eugene O'Neill Review, The Polish Journal*, and the *New York Times*.

HARRIET L. PARMET, Professor Emerita in the Department of Modern Foreign Languages and Literature at Lehigh University, has taught Hebrew there since 1976. She specializes in modern Israeli literature in translation and has coauthored a study of feminist religious views on reproductive technologies and a major article on Haviva Reik, a heroine of the Holocaust. Instrumental as a founder in Lehigh's Jewish Studies Program, she has published in *Midstream, Feminist Teacher, Journal for Feminist Studies in Religion*, and *Studies in American Jewish Literature*.

TAMRA PLOTNICK is a graduate student at the City University of New York.

LINDA RODRIGUEZ is Assistant Director of the Women's Center at the University of Missouri–Kansas City. Her book of poetry, *Skin Hunger*, was published in 1994. She has also written and published fiction and nonfiction and is currently finishing her second novel. Her nonfiction book, *Facing the Blank Page: Taking the Fear Out of Writing*, was published in 1998.

MARK RUDMAN, a distinguished poet, is Assistant Director and Adjunct Professor, the Graduate Writing Program, New York University. He has been editor in chief of *Pequod*, a journal of contemporary literature and literary criticism, since 1984 and has, among his many awards and honors, been a recipient of the National Book Critics Circle Award in Poetry in 1995 for his collection of poems, *Rider*.

OREN SAFDIE is Artistic Director of the West End Dramatists in New York.

ELLEN SCHIFF is Professor Emerita from North Adams State College in Massachusetts. She is the author of *The Jew in Contemporary Drama* (1982) and two anthologies of Jewish-American drama: *Awake and Singing* (1995) and *Fruitful and Multiplying* (1996).

ADAM SCHONBRUNN has a Ph.D. in English from Penn State University and lives in Safid, Israel.

STEVEN SCHREINER is an Associate Professor of English at the University of Missouri–St. Louis. His poems have appeared in *Poetry, Prairie Schooner, Missouri Review*, and other journals. He is the author of *Too Soon to Leave* (poems, 1997).

CHRIS SEMANSKY's poetry, stories, reviews, and essays have appeared in hundreds of journals and magazines, including *Cimarron Review, College English, American Letters and Commentary, Mississippi Review*, and *Postmodern Culture*. His book of poems, *Death, But at a Good Price*, received the Nicholas Roerich Prize for 1991. He has taught at a number of universities and colleges in the States.

JOEL SHATZKY is Professor of English at the State University of New York, College at Cortland. He has published widely in the field of Jewish studies in such journals as *Studies in Jewish American Literature, Jewish Frontier*, and *Jewish Currents*. He has edited a book, *Theresienstadt: Hitler's Gift to the Jews* by Norbert Troller, translated by Susan Cernyak-Spatz (1991), and has coedited, with Michael Taub, *Contemporary Jewish-American Fiction: A Bio-Bibliographical and Critical Sourcebook* (1997).

KENNETH SHERWOOD cofounded the Electronic Poetry Center at the State University of New York, Buffalo.

STEVE SHOEMAKER is currently a visiting Assistant Professor at Wake Forest University. He received his Ph.D. from the University of Virginia in 1997; his dissertation, which he is currently revising for book publication, is a study of the "Objectivist" movement. His essay on Louis Zukofsky has been published in *Upper Limit Music: The Writing of Louis Zukofsky* (University of Alabama Press, 1997).

DAVID R. SLAVITT has taught, lectured, and given poetry readings at Yale, Harvard, Bennington, Hollins College, the University of Texas, the Folger Library, and the Library of Congress. He has also been a visiting lecturer and professor at the University of Maryland, Drexel, Temple, Columbia, Rutgers/Camden campus, Princeton, and the University of Pennsylvania, where he presently teaches. A prolific author, he has translated the classics, written novels under his own name and pseudonyms, and produced a number of books of poems. Among his latest books are *Sixty-One Psalms of David* and *Epic and*

Epigram: Two Elizabethan Entertainments. His translation of *A Crown for the King of Solomon Ibn Gabrol* was published in 1997.

ERIC STERLING is an Assistant Professor of English at Auburn University in Montgomery, Alabama. He has published articles on Jewish authors such as Arthur Miller, Nelly Sachs, and Shimon Wincelberg as well as essays on Rolf Hochhuth's play *The Deputy.* Currently, he is writing a book on Holocaust literature.

DIANE STEVENSON teaches creative writing at Hunter College (CUNY). She is a poet who lives in the Bronx and has recently completed a detective novel, *Car Thief.*

MICHAEL TAUB has been Associate Professor in the Department of Judaic Studies at the State University of New York at Binghamton and Visiting Professor at Vassar College. He is the author of many works on Jewish studies and a translator of Israeli drama into English. He is editor of *Modern Israeli Drama in Translation* (1996) and *Israeli Holocaust Drama* and is coeditor with Joel Shatzky of *Contemporary Jewish-American Fiction: A Bio-Bibliographical and Critical Sourcebook* (1997).

DANIEL TOBIN has published poems in many literary journals, among them *Poetry, The Nation, The Paris Review, The Tampa Review* and *Doubletake.* His essays and reviews have appeared in *The Yeats/Eliot Review, Literature and Belief, Complexities of Motion: The Longer Poems of A. R. Ammons,* and elsewhere. In 1995 his poetry won "The Discovery"/*The Nation* Award. In 1996 he was awarded a creative writing fellowship from the National Endowment for the Arts. He is currently an Associate Professor of English at Carthage College.

MICHELE S. WARE is a Visiting Assistant Professor of American Literature at Wake Forest University. She has published and presented essays on Muriel Rukeyser, American women's political poetry, Edith Wharton, and the American short story.

HENRY WEINFIELD is a poet, translator, and critic who teaches at the University of Notre Dame. He is the author of three collections of poetry, a translation of and commentary on the *Collected Poems* of Stéphane Mallarmé, and a critical study of Gray's "Elegy."

SHEVA ZUCKER, born in Winnipeg, Canada, holds a Ph.D. in comparative literature from the Graduate Center of the City University of New York. She teaches Yiddish language and Jewish literature at Duke University and has taught at Columbia University, as well as universities in Israel, Russia, and Moldova. Zucker is the author of the textbook *Yiddish: An Introduction to the Language, Literature & Culture.* She writes and translates mostly on topics related to Women in Yiddish Literature.

ISBN 0-313-29461-5

90000>

EAN

9 780313 294617

HARDCOVER BAR CODE